Christology in the Making

JAMES D. G. DUNN

Christology in the Making

A New Testament Inquiry into the Origins of the Doctrine of the Incarnation

SECOND EDITION

SCM PRESS LTD

334 00215 X

First published 1980
by SCM Press Ltd
26–30 Tottenham Road, London N1 4BZ
Second edition 1989

Phototypeset by Input Typesetting Ltd
and printed in Great Britain by
The Camelot Press Ltd
Southampton

To
Catriona, David
and Fiona

CONTENTS

Preface   ix

Foreword to Second Edition   xi

Abbreviations   xl

  I   INTRODUCTION   1
    §1 The origin of the doctrine of the incarnation as an
        issue   1

 II   THE SON OF GOD   12
    §2 Introduction   12
    §3 The first-century 'context of meaning'   13
    §4 Jesus' sense of sonship   22
    §5 Jesus' divine sonship in the earliest Christian
        writings   33
    §6 Jesus' divine sonship in the post-Pauline writings of
        the New Testament   46
    §7 Conclusions   60

III   THE SON OF MAN   65
    §8 Introduction   65
    §9 Who is this 'son of man'? – the Jewish answer   67
   §10 Who is this 'son of man'? – the Christian answer   82
   §11 Conclusions   95

 IV THE LAST ADAM   98
   §12 Introduction   98
   §13 Adam and the plight of man   101
   §14 Adam and Christ   107

§15 Pre-existent Man?   113
§16 Conclusions   125

V   SPIRIT OR ANGEL?   129
§17 Introduction   129
§18 Spirit of God in pre-Christian Judaism   132
§19 Spirit of Christ   136
§20 The angel of the Lord   149
§21 Conclusions   159

VI   THE WISDOM OF GOD   163
§22 Introduction   163
§23 Wisdom in pre-Christian Judaism   168
§24 Christ as Wisdom in Paul   176
§25 Christ as Wisdom in the post-Pauline writings of
        the New Testament   196
§26 Conclusions   209

VII THE WORD OF GOD   213
§27 Introduction   213
§28 Logos in pre-Christian thought   215
§29 The word of God in first-century Christian thought   230
§30 The Word incarnate   239
§31 Conclusions   248

VIII CONCLUSION   251
§32 Summary   251
§33 And so . . .   258

Notes   269

Bibliography   354

Indexes   404

PREFACE

What follows is intended as a preliminary to a larger inquiry into the beginnings of Christianity – an attempt to clarify as far as possible the historical actuality of Christianity in its first and most formative period during which the documents later declared canonical were written.

Some movements have no dominant figure in the beginning; but Christianity began with Jesus. And it was *the meaning of Jesus*, of what he had said and done, together with what the first Christians understood him to be and to have been, to be doing and to have done, which was the most significant factor in the new sect's own developing self-understanding and developing sense of distinctiveness over against the other religions, sects and philosophies of the time. Hence the need to focus particular attention on this area of Christianity's beginnings.

'Christology' of course is a narrowing of the complete wholeness of 'the Christ-event' – a reduction to mere words of the much more than verbal impact of the historical figure and the risen Lord – and any insights here will have to be complemented (and if need be corrected) by the questionings and findings which emerge from viewing other aspects of Christianity's beginnings from different perspectives. It should also be stressed that what follows is not intended as a comprehensive study of all aspects of NT christology. The quest for Jesus' own self-understanding is not made a central endeavour, nor an investigation of the relation between 'the historical Jesus and the Christ of faith'. No attempt is made to deal with the resurrection of Jesus as such, to analyse the significance of several important christological titles, or to discuss the question of Christ's second appearing. The object in the following pages is simply and solely to inquire into the origin or origins of the doctrine of the incarnation – a limited, but as will soon become apparent, a large enough task for one study.

The material has been worked over several times. In particular ch. VI has known four different recensions, and ch. III suffered the fate of the potter's vessel described in Jer. 18.4. An invaluable part of the process has been feedback during and after several lectures and seminars at which

I tried out various chapters and sections. Ch. VI (in its earliest form) was read as a paper to our postgraduate seminar here at Nottingham, at the Oxford Congress on Biblical Studies in April 1978, and in a second recension at the University of Hull later the same year. All six chapters formed the basis and background of a series of lectures for a course at St George's College, Jerusalem, in March–April 1979, and four of the six likewise served for the Vacation Term for Biblical Study at Oxford in July–August of the same year. A summary treatment to elucidate the main conclusions was offered in seminars at Tantur, the Ecumenical Institute for Advanced Theological Studies, situated appropriately midway between Jerusalem and Bethlehem (April 1979), at the Institute for the Study of Christian Origins in Tübingen (May 1979), and at the Universities of Glasgow, Stirling and Lancaster (November 1979).

My thanks are also due to those who read over an earlier draft for their perceptive and helpful comments – Professor C. F. D. Moule (Cambridge) and Dr D. R. Catchpole (Lancaster), and particularly Professors G. B. Caird (Oxford) and G. N. Stanton (London) and R. Morgan (Oxford). I am grateful too to those who allowed me to see books and articles at manuscript and proof stage – Professor Caird, my colleague at Nottingham Dr P. M. Casey, Professor P. Stuhlmacher (Tübingen), Dr A. J. M. Wedderburn (St Andrews), Dr N. T. Wright (Cambridge) and John Bowden of SCM Press. Our own weekly postgraduate NT seminar has concentrated on christology during the first half of 1980 and helped sharpen a number of points. Finally I should like to record my gratitude to the British Academy who helped finance my trip to Palestine, though research there concentrated on my larger Beginnings of Christianity project, and the Deutscher Akademischer Austauschdienst who enabled me to spend a month in Tübingen consulting literature not readily available in this country.

The kindness and interest shown by many, particularly Père Benoit and Professor Murphy-O'Connor of the École Biblique, Jerusalem, by Ted Todd Dean of St George's College, Jerusalem, by Professors Bartchy, Hengel and Stuhlmacher in Tübingen, by Professor Haacker in Wuppertal, and by Professor Macquarrie and Dr Vermes in Oxford, prompt many happy memories as I come to the end of a project which has filled most of my research time for the past three years. Above all, what can I say of the patience and support of my dear wife Meta while 'the book' once more dominated the dining room table for weeks on end (what indeed?), not to mention that of our three pride-and-joys (groans deleted) to whom 'the book' is dedicated.

University of Nottingham   James D. G. Dunn
June 1980

FOREWORD TO SECOND EDITION

The need for a further printing provides a welcome opportunity to add a fresh Foreword. The opportunity is welcome for several reasons. Not least because it enables me to underline a feature of my writing which perhaps should have been given a clearer expression before this. That is, that I regard any writing (and lecturing) which I do as part of an ongoing dialogue. While striving to put my thoughts and insights in as finished a form as possible I have never presumed I was giving the final word on a subject. Writing helps me to clarify my own thinking; but my hope is also to help clarify the particular issues and considerations most relevant to these issues for others. Naturally I seek to find answers to my questions and offer up my own conclusions. But not in any attempt to bully readers into agreement: more with the objective of provoking them to respond, to join in the dialogue, in the hope that out of the continuing and larger dialogue a clearer and fuller picture will emerge – for myself as well as for others engaged in the dialogue. *Christology* was itself part of a dialogue on the subject of earliest christology and the doctrine of the incarnation in particular, and certainly provoked a number of responses in reviews, articles and subsequent monographs. But a dialogue which ends with a single statement and various replies is no dialogue. And with eight years now passed and the first wave (or should I say ripple?) of interest now subsided it is probably just about the right time to attempt to carry forward the dialogue a stage further.

I am glad to make the attempt for three further reasons. First, it is clear from a number of these responses that the objectives and methodology of *Christology* have been often ignored or misunderstood. This suggests that a brief restatement of these objectives and methods is desirable and might help promote a fuller understanding and a better dialogue than we have so far achieved. Second, as part of the ongoing dialogue, I naturally wish to respond to my critics – to point out where they have, in my view at least, misperceived my intentions, disregarded key factors which ought to be determinative in the exegesis of important NT passages, or shown too little awareness of the historical context out of which such texts came. There are also, of course, weaknesses in my own presentation, which have come to light as a result of the dialogue, as I had hoped, and which I am happy to acknowledge. And third, my own understanding of the meaning and significance of the NT data has not, of course, remained static since 1980. The dialogue has helped clarify and crystallize fuller insights into the beginnings of christology, particularly in the area of Johannine christology, and into the continuing considerable importance of what happened in that period for subsequent theology and for Christianity's knowledge and understanding of God.

I

The starting point of *Christology in the Making* was the unassailable observation that the NT documents cover an intense period of innovation and/or development in what we now call 'christology'. Before Jesus, 'christology' either did not exist, or existed, properly speaking, only in different forms of 'messianic expectation'. At the end of that period an advanced and far-reaching christology is already in place, which does not hesitate to speak of Jesus as 'God'. Before Jesus appeared on the scene we can speak of a wide range of speculation within early Jewish thought about God and particularly about his means of interacting and communicating with his creation and his people. At the end of that period there is a clearly articulated Christian view that much or most of that speculation has come to focus in Jesus Christ in a complete and final way.

In other words, the NT covers a period of development and itself constitutes in some measure that development. There is presumably no dispute here. The task I set myself, then, was simply to trace out, as best as possible, the course of that development, without assuming that it was a regular or even development,[1] and without predetermining whether it was an organic development (tree from seed) or an evolutionary development (mutation of species). And the dialogue which has ensued has been most fruitful when it has been clearly perceived that the issue under discussion is about *how quickly* that development proceeded, not about *whether* it happened. I had and have no doubts that 'christology' developed very fast indeed, under the massive stimulus of the Christ event (his ministry seen in the light of his death and resurrection). My question was, and is, whether it developed quite so quickly as, for example, Hengel has argued in his influential and otherwise wholly excellent little study on *The Son of God*.[2]

In particular, with the debate about *The Myth of God Incarnate*[3] still very much alive (1978–79), it seemed both wise and desirable to focus this analysis on the emergence of the Christian doctrine of incarnation. Here too some kind of development had to be assumed. Whether or not we can properly speak of a concept of 'incarnation' already in the thought world of the time, Greco-Roman or Jewish, and if so, in what sense, was obviously one of the questions which required scrutiny. In *Christology* I attempt to avoid prejudging the issue by declining to define the concept of 'incarnation' too closely at the start: the word itself indicates with sufficient clarity the area under investigation – some form of 'enfleshment' or embodiment – and any narrower definition might have put 'off limits' potentially fruitful lines of inquiry.[4] But even so, some form of development must be presupposed – at the very least from a non-Christian (or not yet Christian) concept of 'incarnation' to a specifically Christian one, if not from more diverse envisagings of divine embodiment and revelation to the specifically Christian concept of God incarnate in definitive and final form in Christ.

Here again the issue as it was envisaged at the time of writing and as it has come to sharper focus in the ensuing dialogue is the speed of development. There was no question in my mind that the doctrine of incarnation comes to clear expression within the NT – certainly at least in a sense which clearly foreshadows the further growth or evolution to the full blown doctrine of the historic Christian credal statements. On almost any reckoning, John 1.14 ranks as a classic formulation of the Christian belief in Jesus as incarnate God. Assuming then, as most do, that John's Gospel is one of the latest documents in the NT, the question was whether John 1.14 is best understood simply as a variation on an already well formed conception of incarnation or as itself a decisive step forward in the organic growth or evolution of the Christian doctrine. Not whether, but how quickly the (or a) Christian doctrine of incarnation comes to expression within the period and range of Christian teaching spanned by the NT documents – that was the question.

Given that (on the basis of John 1.14) we can speak of a 'NT docrine of incarnation' and therefore of canonical authority for the doctrine, the question as posed might seem to smack too much of idle academic curiosity. Does it matter whether Jesus believed himself to be 'the incarnate Son of God'? Does it matter whether Paul, and other NT writers, mark an earlier stage in the development towards the full-blown Christian doctrine, or even stages in diverse developments and trajectories? Others might answer in the negative: it does not matter. For myself it does. It matters what Jesus thought about himself. For if we can uncover something at least of that self-understanding, and if it differs markedly from subsequent Christian doctrine of Christ, then we have discovered a serious self-contradiction at the heart of the Christian doctrine of incarnation itself. For we then have to admit that the doctrine of God submitting himself to the full rigours of historical existence is not after all accessible to historical inquiry. This has been a fundamental issue at the heart of christology in fact from the beginning but most pressingly over the past two hundred years. It will not go away. It matters too whether Paul had a doctrine of incarnation. For the Pauline letters are the only NT writings which belong indubitably to the first generation of Christianity. And the later we have to postpone the emergence of the Christian doctrine of incarnation the more real becomes the possibility that the doctrine is the product not of organic growth ('development' as from seed to plant), but of grafting a different growth on to the earlier (non-incarnation) stock, or of transmutation into a different species (by 'hellenization', philosophization, or whatever). Besides which, it should matter to Christian theology what Paul, the first great Christian theologian and most influential of all Christian theologians, thought and taught on the subject. Apart from anything else, if there is a clear continuity between the earlier and the later christological formulations, a right understanding of Paul may well help us to a right understanding of the later texts. So I make no apologies for posing the question of how and how quickly the Christian doctrine of the incarnation emerged and developed in the first two or three generations of Christianity.

So much for the chief objective of *Christology in the Making*. As to the *method* of pursuing this objective, that can be most simply focused in two phrases – 'historical context of meaning' and 'conceptuality in transition'. I had hoped that the first of these two in particular would have been clear in *Christology* itself.[5] But evidently not, and it became necessary to spell them out with greater explicitness in 'In Defence of a Methodology'.[6] Here it must suffice to repeat the central consideration in each case, which, to be sure, follows as a more or less immediate corollary from what has just been said above.

By 'historical context of meaning' I have in mind the task of trying to hear the words of the text as the writer of these words intended those for whom he wrote to hear them. That I continue to regard as the primary exegetical (though by no means the only hermeneutical) task confronting the NT scholar. Our only real hope of achieving that goal is by setting the text as fully as possible into the historical context within which it was written – both the broader context of the cultural, social, linguistic etc. conditioning factors of the time, and the narrower context of the immediate circumstances of writer and readers which must have determined in greater or less degree the choice of themes and formulation of the writing. In all this the text *by* itself cannot provide sufficient check on what we hear it saying; for there are so many allusions and taken-for-granteds which depend on the fact that the document is a *historical* document (a document of a particular time and place in history), which would be wholly apparent to writer and reader of the time, and on which much of its meaning depends, but which are now hidden from us by our remoteness from that historical context. The text *does* provide the check; but it is only the text set *within its historical context* which can do so adequately.

If then it is legitimate, as it surely is, to distinguish, for example, what Jesus said about himself from what subsequent believers said about him, or between what Paul intended to say and what later Christian theology made of his words, it is important and necessary for the exegete to undertake that difficult task of getting behind subsequent interpretation and later context to the original intention behind these words within their original context. Apart from anything else, the very fact that these words were preserved and cherished is indication enough that their original impact was significant and substantial. It cannot be unimportant for Christian theology to uncover as far as possible that original 'word of God' encounter which provided the decisive impulse towards their being reckoned in due course as holy scripture.[7]

The character of historical process and the implication of 'development' is that meaning changes, and that language even while remaining the same gathers to itself new meaning. Here the problem of relativity is as serious for historical study as it is for scientific study. We the observers do not occupy a fixed point from which to observe other fixed points in time and space. We are caught within the flux of history, as were those to whom we look back. To abstract the NT documents from history is not to exempt them from the problem of relativity; it simply makes them historical vagrants and mercenaries, vulnerable to anyone who takes them over. But to set them within their original historical contexts underlines and brings to focus the problem of relativity for the exegete. At least we can get some sort of 'fix' on the problem. For we can take cognisance of the relative character of our own (twentieth-century) context; and by study of the first-century period we can gain some overall impression of the social, cultural, intellectual flux from within which the NT writings emerged, and which they bring to expression in their own terms. In other words, the problem of historical relativity is itself relative to the nature of the subject matter under investigation and the amount of information available to us relating to both the subject matter and its historical context.

All this I try to encapsulate in the phrase 'conceptuality in transition'. I use 'conceptuality' for the obvious reason already noted that words change in meaning even when the words themselves remain unchanged. The task of historical exegesis requires a recognition that important concepts will often be in transition. They may be on their way to becoming something else, something slightly but perhaps significantly different in the meaning they are heard to express. This will be all the more likely in the case of documents (e.g. Paul's letters) which were recognized to have more than merely occasional significance from the first, and especially where they deal with a subject (christology) of particular and growing significance for the movement (Christianity) within which these documents first emerged. For not all concepts are in transition to the same degree; conceptuality in transition is also a relative phenomenon. It is this fact which gives us some hope both of recognizing the more volatile concepts and of gaining at least a relative 'fix' on them through correlating them with the less volatile concepts. In short, the task of tracing out the development of the Christian doctrine of the incarnation may not be quite so difficult as at first appeared.

If then we bring together the task of historical exegesis, the problem of historical relativity, and the fact of christology developing in or into a concept of incarnation, it becomes an inescapable part of that task to try to get inside the process of development. Here the important work is 'inside'. To trace the course(s) of developing christology from *outside* is comparatively easy, especially when we allow ourselves to see the end from the beginning and read the intermediate stages in the light of that end. But genuinely to locate oneself *within* the process, and genuinely to take seriously the fact of conceptuality in transition, is to limit oneself to the possibilities available at the time of writing, to take a stand within the inevitably limited horizon of writer and readers, who did not and could not know how the words written were going to be taken and understood in subsequent years and decades. This is *not* to say that subsequent understanding of a text should be debarred from contributing to a historical exegesis of that text. As a general rule one may assume a continuity between earlier and later understandings within a community which cherished the text. In which case the understanding which evolved must be able to illuminate the understanding from which it evolved. But it does mean that subsequent understanding should not be used as a grid to predetermine the scope of exegesis, to limit or elaborate what the text within its original context was intended or heard to say simply by reference to the subsequent understanding. Evaluation of the legitimacy of subsequent interpretation is in large part the responsibility of the subsequent generation, but partly also depends on the meaning of the text intended by the person whose text it primarily is, the one who wrote it – always allowing for the fact that contexts of meaning change and words and concepts evolve, and such evaluation has to take all that into account. If scripture is to have a continuing critical (canonical) role, that depends in part at least on allowing the meaning intended by Paul etc, and heard by those for whom they wrote to exercise a critical function in relation to the use subsequently made of what they wrote.[8]

This must suffice as a restatement of the objectives and methodology of *Christology*. I wish I could feel confident that any further dialogue about *Christology* or the issues it deals with would take account of these stated objectives and methodology. But experience so far has not been very encouraging. Nevertheless, may the dialogue continue.

II

In attempting to take the dialogue further it becomes necessary to respond to those who have offered criticism of *Christology in the Making*. This is both a welcome and an unwelcome task: welcome because it allows me to clarify my position on disputed points, to set the record straight where appropriate, to restate the most pertinent concerns in controverted passages, and to acknowledge fresh indebtedness on issues which required more analysis than they received in *Christology*; unwelcome because it means having to express some sharpness of disagreement and counter-criticism in a public forum with several whom I count as good friends and with whom I would much rather have out such points of dispute in private, at least in the first instance.[9]

I have in mind, first of all, those alluded to earlier – those who have failed, in my view, to take account of the methodological points elaborated above. For instance, several critics and exegetes seem to have thought that a straightforward appeal to the 'obvious' or 'plain meaning' of the text was sufficient response to my discussion of such passages as Col. 1.15–20.[10] But 'obvious' to whom? 'Plain' in what context? Obvious to *us*, who look back to the text with the much developed hindsight of nearly two millennia. But the question is surely whether that understanding of the text was equally as obvious to *the original author and readers*, equally obvious when the text is set into the context within which it was framed. Where we are attempting to locate an original insight or statement within a process of developing conceptuality, that is surely a necessary and important question for historical exegesis.

For example, the talk of God sending his Son in Gal. 4.4 and Rom.8.3. Anyone reading these texts in the light of the similar sounding and prominent Johannine formula would naturally understand Paul (or the formulation he draws on) to imply a sending from heaven.[11] But given (1) that John's formulation may well belong to his more developed (and later) christology, (2) that talk of God sending could be used equally for the commissioning of a prophet as of the sending of an angelic being from heaven,[12] and (3) that the thrust of the passage is directed to Jesus' mission of redemptive death, I still find myself asking whether the formula would have been intended or initially heard to carry with it the inevitable implication of the pre-existence of the Son. Even the emphasis in both passages on the Son's humanity (to use later teminology) may not be sufficient to clinch the point (sent his Son as a man),[13] for the force of the intermediate phrases in both instances is to point up the significance of the Son's *death* not the mode of his being sent. So Gal.4.4 may quite properly be paraphrased: God sent his Son, a typical human being,[14] a Jew, that he might redeem Jews, and that we (human beings) might become sons (note the a b b a structure). And the point of the equivalent phrase in Rom. 8.3 ('in the likeness of sinful flesh and as a sacrifice for sin') is not to emphasize the Son's humanity so much as to emphasize the degree of his identification with *sinful* humanity, so that his death might function as a sin-offering and effective condemnation of *sin*.

Another example is I Cor. 15.44–49. It is clear that several of my critics simply take it for granted that 'the man from heaven' (15.47) must and can only be understood in terms of Christ's pre-existence.[15] This, I must confess, I find astonishing. For the whole thrust of the argument in context is focused on the resurrection and is built on a sequence of parallel contrasts – physical/ spiritual, earthly/heavenly, first man/second man – where it is clear enough that the second half of each contrast refers to the resurrection state. This includes the description of the second man as 'from heaven', for it is precisely his heavenly image which provides the pattern for the resurrection state of others (15.49). Paul has already made this clear earlier in the same chapter: Christ in his resurrection is the 'firstfruits of those who have fallen asleep'; *as risen* he is the archetype of resurrected humanity (15.20–23). And in the immediate context he has been at some pains (for whatever reason) to insist that the spiritual does *not* precede the psychical (15.46). Hence in relation to (first) Adam, Christ is *last* Adam (15.45). It would throw his argument into complete confusion if he was understood to mean that 'the *second* man from heaven' was actually the pre-existent one, and therefore actually first, *before* Adam. In the other key texts I am more hesitant, with more open questions than firm answers. But here I must say there does not seem to be much room for dispute. And if commentators can read such a clearly eschatological/resurrection text as a reference to Christ's pre-existence it simply underlines the danger we run in this most sensitive of subjects of reading the text with the presuppositions of subsequently developed dogmas and of failing to let the context (in this case the context of the argument itself) determine our exegesis.

The dialogue has probably been more fierce over the christological hymns, Phil. 2.6–11 and Col.1.15–20, than anywhere else. It is clear from comment and conversation that some regard the questions I pose and suggestions I make in relation to these texts as insubstantial and wholly implausible, if not absurd, if not perverse.[16] I am mildly surprised at this and wonder if the weight of my questions and tentativeness of my suggestions have been adequately appreciated. (For those who think the meaning 'obvious', alternative suggestions may be tiresome and irritating and deserve to be dismissed as quickly as possible.) But perhaps I can try once more and focus on the heart of the exegetical issues as I see them.

In the case of Phil. 2.6–11 it still seems to me that of all the contexts or paradigms of thought within which the text may be read in the endeavour of historical exegesis (Son of God, Servant, Wisdom, Gnostic Redeemer myth), the one which provides the most coherent and most complete (the claim is relative) reading is Adam christology.

v.6a   – in the form of God (cf. Gen. 1.27);[17]

v.6b   – tempted to grasp equality with God (cf. Gen. 3.5);[18]

v.7   – enslavement to corruption and sin – humanity as it now is (cf. Gen. 2.19, 22–24; Ps 8.5a; Wisd 2.23; Rom. 8.3; Gal. 4.4; Heb. 2.7a, 9a);[19]

v. 8   – submission to death (cf. Wisd. 2.24; Rom. 5.12–21; 7.7–11: I Cor. 15.21–22);

vv.9–11 – exalted and glorified (cf. Ps 8.5b–6; I Cor. 15.27, 45; Heb. 2.7b–8, 9b).[20]

Others may 'fit' better at individual points; but I still await a demonstration of another paradigm which 'fits' so well over all. Nor do I think it enough to attempt a rebuttal by showing how poorly the paradigm actually fits the case of Jesus.[21] As I tried to make clear in *Christology*[22] the Philippians hymn is an attempt to read the life and work of Christ through the grid of Adam theology; the points of stress within the hymn are there simply because the 'fit' is not exact or precise (though still closer than other suggested paradigms). It is the Adamic *significance* of Christ which the hymn brings out, of his life and death and exaltation (as in Rom. 5, I Cor. 15 and Heb. 2), not necessarily a chronological parallel phase by phase. This is why it still seems to me an open question as to whether the hymn contains any thought of pre-existence, *other than the pre-existence involved in the paradigm* – that is, the metahistorical character of the Adam myth. The point of the hymn is the epochal significance of the Christ-event, as determinative for humankind as the 'event' of Adam's creation and fall, with the question of pre-existence rather more an irrelevance and distraction than a help to interpretation.[23] It is because Christ by his life, death and resurrection has so completely reversed the catastrophe of Adam, has done so by the acceptance of death by choice rather than as punishment, and has thus completed the role of dominion over all things originally intended for Adam, that the paradigm is so inviting, and so 'fitting' in the first place.

With Col. 1.15–20 the issues of 'context of meaning' and 'conceptuality in transition' become most acute. Hopefully, for the purposes of continuing the dialogue, it can be accepted that the language used of Christ in this hymn is determined by the application of Wisdom categories to him, or by the identification of Christ with Wisdom if you like. This claim was documented in sufficient detail in *Christology*[24] and is not the issue in dispute. The issues are twofold: what was the understanding of Wisdom within Judaism prior to this use of it in reference to Christ? and what is the significance of its use in reference to Christ?[25]

On the first I remain persuaded that the Wisdom figure in pre-Christian Jewish writing functions within the context of Jewish monotheism and would be understood by the great bulk of Jews as poetical description of divine immanence, of God's self-revelation and interaction with his creation and his people; it was a way of speaking of divine agency rather than of a divine agent distinct from God in ontological terms. I do not want to become embroiled in debate on this particular issue here, since it would become too involved, and since the case set out in *Christology* I regard as still sound.[26] Let it suffice to say that this is at least a plausible context of meaning for the Colossian hymn; that is to say, it is at least quite likely that in reading Col. 1.15–20 Paul and his readers had in mind the understanding of Wisdom as a vivid personification of God's immanence.

But if that *was* the context of meaning then how would the hymn have been understood? *Not* as an identification of Jesus with a divine being or agent independent or of distinct from God. But more likely in parallel to the way ben Sira and Baruch identified Wisdom with the Torah (Sir. 24.23; Bar. 4.1) – that is, as a way of expressing the divine significance of Jesus, that the Creator God had revealed himself and his divine wisdom in and through Jesus as nowhere else. But this is where the difficulty of locating the text within a developing 'conceptuality in transition' becomes so difficult. With Col. 1.15–20 are we still at the beginning of the transition from poetic personification to Jesus understood as 'God', or are we already some way into the transition? Some think the answer obvious: it is Christ, Jesus Messiah, to whom is attributed a role in creation. But is that so clear? Or is this basically a further example of the vigorous poetic imagery of Wisdom applied to Jesus? The fact that the language could be used of Jesus without any perceived threat to monotheism is surely significant here (cf. I Cor. 8.6).[27] As also the fact that the same hymn goes on to speak of 'God in all his fulness choosing to dwell in Christ' and of his pre-eminence being the consequence of his resurrection (Col. 1.18–19).[28]

I hope I am not being perverse or unnecessarily awkward. But it does still seem to me that there are legitimate questions here. I do not advocate my suggested exegesis as though that is necessarily the correct one, even as historical exegesis. But it surely cannot be simply dismissed or ruled out of order by anyone who recognizes the relevance and importance of the 'context of meaning' and 'conceptuality in transition' issues and who allows the possibility that Jewish understanding of Wisdom had not yet moved beyond the character of poetic personification.

Probably the most striking example of failure to take account of historical context of meaning is the assumption made by several critics that the exaltation of Jesus would have been understood to carry with it the clear implication of Christ's divine status and pre-existence.[29] Such an assumption seems to ignore completely the fact that in the Judaism of the time several historical figures were being spoken of in terms of exaltation and of exercising functions hitherto attributed to God alone without similar implications being drawn – for example, Enoch, Elijah, Abel, Moses, and possibly Melchizedek. The issue is more complex, as we shall see later. All I ask here is whether it is so clear as some evidently think that talk of Jesus' exaltation and sharing in God's judgment would *ipso facto* carry with it thought of Christ's divinity and pre-existence. After all, Jewish writings towards the end of the first century could still speak of Ezra and Baruch being taken up from earth to heaven without any such implications crossing the horizon (IV Ezra 14.9; II Bar. 13.3; etc.). And the (final?) saying of Q could envisage the twelve participating in final judgment, where it would be ridiculous to read in any idea of them thereby being understood as divine (Matt. 19.28/ Luke 22.30; cf. I Cor. 6.2). So too the argument that Jesus is divine because he forgave sins or pronounced them forgiven (Mark 2.5–10) must reckon with similar authority being exercised by his disciples (according to John 20.23).[30] Even in the case of the exalted Jesus' dispensing the Spirit (Acts 2.33), it has to be recalled that this function of Christ is understood by Luke as fulfilment of the Baptist's expectation of an unknown (but apparently not divine)[31] coming one (Acts 1.5; Luke 3.16).[32]

More recently a critic boldly asserts that the term 'Son of God' and the concept of 'pre-existence' belong together in the NT ('the two cannot be separated').[33] As a description of Johannine christology this is a wholly legitimate summary, but as a general description of 'NT christology' it begs far too many questions and ignores the range of meaning and application for language of divine sonship in Jewish as well as the wider thought forms of the times.[34] Still more striking is the claim: 'The idea of apotheosis was acceptable to pagans of the centuries before and after Christ, but to one who has lived in the light of the OT can it be anything but a nonsense?'[35] This has point only if we take 'apotheosis' in a strict sense. But the plain fact is that there were not a few Jews at the time of Jesus to whom the concept of apotheosis, or at least, transformation into heavenly being was by no means a nonsense. We need not depend on the disreputable case of Herod Agrippa (Acts 12.22). Enoch and Elijah had both been taken to heaven according to OT tradition (Gen. 5.24; II Kings 2.11), and speculation regarding Enoch gave a major emphasis to the idea of such a transformation (Jub. 4.22–3; I Enoch 12–16; II Enoch 22.8). Similarly with regard to Adam in the Testament of Abraham 11, not to mention Isaiah in the (probably Christian) Ascension of Isaiah (particularly 9.30). In II Macc. 15.13 Jeremiah appears in a vision as one distinguished by his grey hair and authority, and of marvellous majesty and authority'. And according to Josephus there was speculation as to whether Moses had been taken or had returned to 'the deity' (*Antiquities* 3.96f.; 4.326).[36] This is the historical context within which emerged the particular claims of christology (arising out of the resurrection of Christ). To disregard that context so completely leaves any argument which does so without exegetical credibility and undermines any Christian apologetic using such an argument.

If some have failed to grasp the method used in *Christology in the Making* and what it means for exegesis, others seem to have misunderstood its objective. In one case[37] the brief review description fits quite well a principal emphasis of my earlier *Unity and Diversity in the New Testament*.[38] But it bears little resemblance to *Christology*. So much so that I am still not sure which of the two volumes the reviewer intended to describe.[39]

Much more serious and damaging have been the double critique of Carl Holladay, first in his *JBL* review, and then in a follow-up article in *NovTest*.[40] I have already replied in some detail[41] and will have to refer those interested in a more detailed response to that article with its regrettably necessary somewhat forthright counter critique. Here I will confine myself to one of Holladay's main points which has been echoed more recently by Hurtado.[42] The charge is (in Hurtado's terms) that I arbitrarily and incorrectly ignored the pagan religious traditions of the Greco-Roman period, a charge to which I am vulnerable particularly because I dated the emergence of the Christian doctrine of the incarnation late in the first century CE, when there would have been several decades during which Christian thinking in this area could have been directly influenced by pagan cults and myths.

Were the point simply that I had not provided anything like a thorough investigation of what we may call here simply 'pagan parallels', it is, of course, wholly accurate. But that was *not* my objective. Nor was I attempting some grandiose overview of how divine–human interaction was conceived in the world of antiquity.[43] However desirable such an overview, it is not in my competency to provide it. My concern in *Christology* was, and is, much more limited: to trace the emergence of the Christian idea of incarnation *from inside* (not the emergence of the concept of 'incarnation' *per se*); to follow the course of development (whether organic or evolutionary), as best as possible, whereby the concept of Christ's incarnation came to conscious expression in Christian thought.[44] As a student of the New Testament, not unnaturally, it was primarily an exegetical task I set myself – the task of exegeting the most important NT passages on the subject.

That involved no 'bias against pagan traditions'[45] – another charge I found puzzling and misdirected.[46] On the contrary, ch. 2 draws on such traditions to demonstrate how broadly consistent within Greco-Roman as well as Jewish circles was the context of meaning of the key concept 'son of God'. And I find it difficult to understand how Holladay could accuse me of radically divorcing early Christianity from its environment,[47] when the discussion of (probably) the most important chapters, 6 and 7, is very much about a Hellenistic–Jewish *sophia* and *logos* speculation which demonstrated to what considerable degree Hellenistic Judaism was part of and indebted to the broader Hellenistic thought world. At this point I really did begin to wonder whether Holladay had some other book in mind, since the book he was criticizing seemed to bear so little resemblance to what I wrote, or whether he had read much beyond ch. 2![48]

'Context of meaning', of course, does not imply that every religious attitude, practice and form wherever expressed in the ancient world may have had equal influence on earliest Christianity. It hardly needs arguing that there will have been a more immediate context of meaning within the much broader context of meaning. In the case of Christianity that more immediate context is certainly Judaism, including Hellenistic Judaism. This is quickly and fully borne out by each of the lines of inquiry pursued in the following chapters. I do not mind confessing that it was principally because the emergence of the Christian doctrine of incarnation, as expressed in the NT texts, found such ready and such complete explanation within that context (however the exegetical issues of texts like Col. 1.15–20 are resolved) that it seemed unnecessary and superfluous (not least given the length of the book) to look further.[49] In such study as I made of the broader context I found no cause even to suspect that there might have been any other or more direct influence.[50] Nor have I had my attention drawn, by Holladay or Hurtado, to any other more direct influence from 'pagan cults and myths' (that is, other than through Hellenistic Judaism). I am certainly open to persuasion on the subject and would willingly discuss potentially significant texts like Justin, *Apol* 1.20–22. But so far no one has tried to persuade me – by documented evidence at least.

A major problem about having to complete a manuscript and go to press is that new items of major relevance come to hand in the period between the completion of the manuscript and its publication. Reviewers, if they so choose, can then indulge in some point scoring by observing that the later volume has not taken note of the earlier publication. Thankfully I did not suffer too much on that account. Alternatively there are books which appear after one's own but which propose alternative theses or marshall other material of such relevance to one's own discussion that one cannot but regret having been unable to take fuller account of them before letting one's own manuscript go. But such is the nature of dialogue by article and book, and the possibility of continuing the dialogue here at least enables me to make some amends in at least two cases.

I have in mind first S. Kim's, *The Origin of Paul's Gospel*.[51] Kim's thesis provides a welcome reassertion of the importance of Paul's conversion, or shall we say simply, Damascus road experience, as a central and formative influence on Paul's theology. The only trouble is that he 'goes over the top'. For he not only maintains that central features of Paul's christology and soteriology were derived from the Damascus road event, but he is even prepared to argue that they were formed to a considerable extent in that event itself. Where this bears on the discussion of my *Christology* is in the considerable amount Kim builds on the 'image' language of II Cor. 4.4. Paul not only recognized Christ to be 'the image of the invisible God', but also as 'the em-bodi-ment (*sic*) of the divine glory'; and the experience must immediately have led Paul to Dan. 7.13, because he too had seen a heavenly figure 'like a son of man' just as Daniel did.[52] But the logic is not entirely sound. Others saw visions of glorious figures (angels, Enoch, Adam, etc.) without the corollary of divinity being drawn, as we have already noted. And his treatment of Dan. 7.13 takes no account of the considerations which proved decisive for me in ch. 3 of *Christology*.[53] Even with the 'image' language itself (II Cor. 4.4), it is by no means so clear that the thought is of (divine) Wisdom rather than of (human) Adam, given that the context has in view a growing Christian conformity to that image (II Cor. 3.18), which seems to tie in much more closely to the Adam christology of Rom. 8.29 and I Cor. 15.45–9. Kim in fact seems to be in some danger of amalgamating a number of different motifs into another of those twentieth-century constructs (like the Gnostic Redeemer myth, or the 'divine man') so beloved of scholars looking for a source for earliest Christian theology. Without for a moment denying that the Damascus road encounter was a formative factor of the first significance in shaping Paul's theology, or that there is a very complex interrelation between the different motifs just mentioned, I remain unpersuaded by Kim's attempt to concertina such major developments in first-century christology into that single event.[54]

My principal regret with regard to *Christology* is that I had been unable to take proper account of the work of Christopher Rowland. I should have been alive to his Cambridge PhD thesis (1974)[55], as Kim was, but his 1979 and 1980 articles[56] only reached me when the manuscript was complete and at proof stage (in pre-word-processor days that meant a text incapable of significant revision), and the major publication which emerged from his thesis did not appear till 1982.[57] This meant that I also failed to give enough attention to an important strand in Jewish apocalyptic and merkabah mysticism in which visions of a glorious archangel are prominent.[58] The point is that the christological issue can no longer be posed simply in terms of whether Christ was thought of as an angel.[59] Nor is it simply a question of whether the exalted Jesus was seen in angelomorphic terms, as is clearly the case in the vision of Rev. 1.13–16. The importance of Rowland's work has been to raise the question as to whether there was already in pre-Christian Judaism some kind of bifurcation in the conception of God. In particular, the similarity in description between Ezek. 1.26 (God) on the one hand, and Ezek. 8.2 and Dan. 10.5–6 (a glorious angel) on the other, suggests as one possibility a readiness on the part of at least some to envisage a merging, or transfer of divine attributes between God and a grand-vizier angel, or a 'splitting in the way in which divine functions are described'.[60]

All this would make excellent sense as the context of meaning of Rev. 1.13–14, with its merging of features from the Ezekiel 1 and Daniel 10 visions as well as from both figures of the Dan. 7.9–14 vision ('one like a son of man', *and* ancient of days – hair like pure white wool).[61]

As should be already clear I have found this whole line of investigation very fruitful, and it has continued to influence my own further studies in the area of earliest christology as I shall indicate in the next section. A full discussion of Rowland's and Fossum's work is beyond the scope of this new Foreword, but a few brief comments are probably in order. Three main questions arise. (1) How significant is it that the clearest evidence of influence from this strand of Jewish conceptuality comes in Revelation – itself one of the latest of the NT writings? Does it indicate a very early stage in developing christology, or another expression of the very vigorous movement of thought in this area which seems to have characterized both Jewish and Christian understanding of divine self-revelation particularly in the decades following the disaster of AD 70?[62] (2) How much of the similarity of language used of glorious figures who appear in apocalyptic and mystical visions is due to the fact that there was, perhaps inevitably, a limited stock of imagery available for such descriptions? In other words, may it not be that the similarity of language betokens nothing more than a common dependence on a limited number of traditional formulae or hallowed phrases used in the literary description of such visions, 'a cliche-like description of a heavenly being'?[63] To what extent in these descriptions was there a deep reflection on the being of God, rather than conformity to a genre pattern? I do not pretend to know the answers to these questions, but I do think they have to be asked, and if necessary left open.[64] The last question raises another line of questioning. (3) Does the language used in these visions, or the appearance of an angel 'in whom God's name dwells' really signify a bifurcation in God within the conceptuality of pre-Christian Judaism?[65] Can we, should we, recognize some sort of diversification within the divine unity, a kind of 'binitarianism' already in Jewish thought before christology as such emerged? Alternatively expressed, is Rev. 1.13–14 simply a further expression of the sort of thing that had been happening for some time in Jewish apocalyptic and mysticism, or does it mark some new stage or departure or quantum leap, in that this language was now being used of one who had lived on earth within living memory? The question is similar to that which has to be posed with regard particularly to the figure of Wisdom in pre-Christian Judaism. And I suspect the answer is the same: that for Jews sensitive of the need to maintain their monotheism within a polytheistic world, such language was not perceived as a threat to their fundamental confession that 'The Lord our God is one Lord' (Deut. 6.4).[66] It is to Hurtado's credit that he has seen and discussed the issue so much in these terms, and I find myself very much in sympathy with his main conclusions.[67]

We will have to return to the subject below. But perhaps we may conclude here by simply noting that the angelomorphic description of the exalted Christ, which is certainly a feature of Revelation, and which certainly came to powerful lasting expression in the Byzantine Pantocrator, does not seem otherwise to have provided the highroad for developing christological thought in the intervening period.

III

Since the first edition of *Christology* my understanding of the beginnings of christology has itself developed and become further clarified – not least as a consequence of having had to interact with the critical responses discussed above. The value of dialogue is in part that it forces dialogue partners to sharpen their insights, to reformulate points which have miscarried or been misunderstood, and to tackle issues which they had previously left fuzzy. But in part also that it requires revision of previously inadequate formulations, and opens the mind to fresh insights and to alternative or complementary or fuller perspectives. This I regard as the value and necessity of the collegial enterprise of scholarship and, if it does not sound too pretentious, of the common search for truth. In the present case I can briefly indicate three developments in my own understanding of 'Christology in the Making' which should now be incorporated into *Christology in the Making* to provide a more complete and up-to-date expression of my views.

It soon became clear to me that I had given too little attention to John's Gospel. I had been too easily content to conclude that with John 1.14 the idea of incarnation had been clearly expressed, so that after a careful study of that verse in context there was little need for a fuller investigation of John's Gospel. The decisive step had been taken, and as a NT investigation the study of the emergence of the doctrine of incarnation was more or less complete. The question is certainly raised as to how the Fourth Evangelist held together the Wisdom/Logos christology of the Prologue and the Son of God christology of the rest of the Gospel,[68] but left hanging. That is obviously unsatisfactory, and the lingering dissatisfaction on this point, compounded with the sharpened perspective provided by Gruenwald and Rowland, pointed the way forward.[69]

Part of the context of meaning of the Fourth Gospel is provided by the visionary and speculative concerns of Jewish apocalypse and mysticism. At this period there was considerable interest in the possibility of gaining heavenly knowledge through visions and ascents to heaven. Such ascents are attributed to Enoch, Moses, Abraham, Adam, Levi, Baruch and Isaiah.[70] And the practice of merkabah mysticism, particularly the desire to experience for oneself a mystical ascent to or revelation of the throne of God, is too well attested for the first-century period to be ignored.[71] A similar concern is reflected in the Fourth Gospel: both in the repeated inquiry as to Jesus' origin – the Evangelist's answer, of course, is 'from heaven' (see particularly 6.41–42; 7.27–29, 42, 52; 8.23; 9.29; 19.9); and in the distinctively Johannine emphasis on Jesus as the revealer of heavenly knowledge, both as the Son of Man who has come down from heaven (3.12–13; 6.61–2) and the Son of God sent from heaven (1.17–18, 49–51; 3.10–13, 32; 7.16–18; etc.). John's objective at this point is clearly to focus such yearnings on Jesus: he alone has seen God and can thus make him known (1.18); the true Israelite will recognize that the Son of Man is the only link between heaven and earth (1.47–51); 'no one has ascended into heaven but he who descended from heaven, the Son of Man' (3.13); 'he who comes from heaven is above all and bears witness to what he has seen and heard' (3.31–2); no one has seen the Father except he who is from God; he has seen the Father' (6.45–6); etc. Here the language of divine agency[72] is centred on Christ in an exclusive way as a major point of Christian polemic, apologetic or evangelism.

What also becomes clear is that John is using this complex of motifs in order to present Jesus as the self-revelation of God. The exclusiveness of the claim made for Christ's revelatory significance means that he also transcends such other claimants to heavenly knowledge and divine agency by the uniqueness of his relationship with the Father and by the closeness of continuity between the Father and the Son. He and the Father are one (10.30). To see him is to see the Father (12.45; 14.9). He embodies the glory of God (1.14; 12.41). He utters the divine 'I am' (particularly 8.28, 58; 13.19). The Son's obedience to the Father is not so much a way of expressing his subordination to God, as though that was already an issue; it is more a way of expressing the authority and validity of the Son's revelation of the Father, the continuity between the Father and the Son (5.17; 10.28–9; 14.10).[73]

But this is simply to elaborate in other terms what the Prologue says by means of its Wisdom/Logos language: as the incarnate Logos Jesus is the self-expression of God. God's own 'self-exegesis' to his human creatures (1.18); as the Son of God he reveals the Father. In other words the question left hanging at the end of the brief study of John's Gospel in *Christology* about the relation between the Wisdom/Logos christology of the Prologue and the Son of God christology elsewhere in the Gospel can be resolved. *Not* by concluding that they are two divergent and incompatible christologies, but by recognizing that in the Fourth Evangelist's hands they are mutually complementary. Behind the Son language of John is not a concern to distinguish Jesus from God, by subordination or however. It is not a concern with relationship between the Father and the Son in that sense. The concern is rather to make clear that the Son is the authentic, the only authentic representation of God to man. He is God's wisdom/self-revelation incarnate. 'The Fourth Evangelist really did intend his Gospel to be read through the window of the prologue'.[74] To avoid confusion, therefore, it would be better to speak of the Johannine Christ as the incarnation of *God*, as God making himself known in human flesh, not as the incarnation of the Son of God (which seems to be saying something other).[75]

It also becomes clear from John's Gospel, to a degree I had not appreciated when I wrote *Christology*, that the main issue at that period was monotheism. Was Christianity a monotheistic faith from the beginning?[76] The question arises precisely because the development of christology was part of (a) broader movement(s) of thought within the Judaism of the first century and early second-century period. As we can now see, such reflection about translated patriarchs, glorious angels, and heavenly wisdom was bound, sooner or later, to put severe strain on Jewish monotheism, on the fundamental Jewish belief in the oneness of God. But when did that strain become apparent, and when did it become severe? I still see no evidence from the period prior to the end of the first century that Jews in general, including Christian Jews, perceived it as a threat to their monotheistic faith; and I am delighted to find Hurtado in agreement.[77] Patriarchs were glorified, not deified; the glorious angel forbade worship or joined in the worship; Wisdom was domesticated as Israel's Torah. Similarly in Paul: Jesus is Lord, but God is still his God ('the God and Father of our Lord Jesus Christ'); his super-exaltation is 'to the glory of God the Father' (Phil. 2.11); he can be confessed as mediator in creation in the same breath as the confession that God is one (I Cor. 8.6); he is divine Wisdom, first-born from the dead, indwelt by God – all in one hymn (Col. 1.15–20).[78] All this makes me question whether it is historically justified to speak of a binitarianism or bifurcation in the conception of God in Jewish thought in the period prior to the end of the first century AD. Here again the 'conceptuality in transition' point needs to be taken with all seriousness. We may say where certain trends were leading – or, to be more accurate, where certain trends in the event led. That tells us nothing of the self-understanding involved at the different stages within these trends. And the crucial point for us is that at no time prior to the end of the first century, so far as we can tell, was there any sense of mutual incompatibility or self-contradiction within the Jewish and earliest Christian understanding of God and of the various forms of divine agency.

It is equally clear, however, that such strains were becoming apparent at the end of the first century. IV Ezra 8.20–1 seems to be directed against claims to be able to see God and describe God's throne; the rabbinic polemic against angelology probably goes back to our period; there are explicit cautionary notes concerning the chariot chapter in the Mishnah; and the apostasy of Elisha ben Abuyah in recognizing a second divine power in heaven, thus denying the unity of God, is remembered as a notorious episode from this period in rabbinic tradition.[79] Here too, however, the most striking attestation comes in the Fourth Gospel. For it is precisely the Johannine claim that Jesus, as the incarnate self-revelation of God, can himself be called 'God' which evidently proved unacceptable to 'the Jews' of John's time (John 5.18; 10.33).[80]

It would appear then that the period between the Jewish revolts (AD 70–132) saw an escalation or intensification in Jewish (including Jewish-Christian) reflection on knowledge of God and divine agency – including talk of glorious angels bearing the divine name, the quest for heavenly ascent and vision of the divine throne, further speculation about the man-like figure in Daniel 7,[81] and the developing Christian devotion to Jesus and reflection on the divine significance of Jesus.[82] The rabbis in the post-70 decades began to see this exploration of the limits of acceptable monotheism as no longer acceptable, as increasingly a threat to the unity of God. And this seems to have been a major factor in their successful attempt to define Judaism much more tightly and to draw a much tighter boundary round Judaism thus redefined. What needs to be remembered here, however, is that what was thereby excluded or put under heavy suspicion was not simply emerging Christianity but also these other strains of apocalyptic and mystical Judaism. The Christian assessment of Jesus by John belongs within a broader spectrum of Judaism, where such exploration of ways of conceptualizing God's self-revelation was acceptable and not perceived as a threat to God's oneness. But it also belongs to that transition of conceptuality and understanding where the strongest voices within Judaism were beginning to see such theological and spiritual innovation as just such a threat.

At the same time it has to be made clear that the Fourth Evangelist himself would not have shared that view. He evidently continued to believe, as those before him, that such reflection was consistent with Jewish monotheism. Even such talk applied to one who had been alive just sixty or seventy years ago need not be seen as a threat to God's unity. If this thesis is correct it brings to focus several points of considerable importance. A make-or-break issue between emerging rabbinic Judaism and emergent Christianity was the significance attributed to Jesus, in particular the conviction on the part of the rabbis that Christian claims for Jesus were now becoming too much of a threat to the primary Jewish confession that God is one. Within the post-70 context of broader Jewish speculation the exclusive claims made particularly by the Fourth Evangelist and his circle were seen as too adventurous or too irresponsible to be tolerated; it had to become a choice between living as a Jew and affirming such claims for Christ. John himself, however, saw the claims he expressed as simply a focusing of these other speculations on Jesus and as no more a threat to monotheism than they had been previously. His christology was still essentially an elaboration of Wisdom christology – Christ as the embodiment (incarnation) of God's self-revelation.[83]

If there is anything in this then it has important corollaries for our understanding of the continuing development of christology in the period following John, and indeed for our understanding of the classic doctrines of God and Christ. The first great christological battle of the Christian period was not over docetism (Ignatius) or modalism (Tertullian); it was over monotheism. The issue was whether in applying such earlier speculation about divine revelation to Christ, and thus developing it further, Christianity had moved beyond the bounds of acceptable diversity within Jewish monotheism – whether, in a word, Christianity was still after all a monotheistic faith. As we have just noted, the dominant Jewish view was that Christianity had lost this struggle; it had succumbed to an unacceptable view of God; it was no longer monotheistic; it believed that there were two divine powers in heaven; it was (together with other Jewish sub-groups) now a Jewish heresy. But in Christian eyes the battle which the Fourth Gospel represents was a victory for monotheism – for monotheism redefined, but monotheism nonetheless. Christ was the incarnate Logos, a self-manifestation of God, the one God insofar as he could make himself known in human flesh – not the incarnation of a divine power other than God. Christianity was still monotheistic; the only difference was the belief that this God had manifested himself in and as human flesh; this Jesus now provided a definitive 'window' into the one God; he was (and is) 'God' as the self-manifestation of God, not as one somehow other than God.

It is of crucial importance to Christianity that this issue was the first major christological dispute to be resolved, that Christianity, at least as represented by John, faced up to this challenge to its self-understanding and resolved it within a monotheistic framework. The claim, of course, is still disputed by both Jews and Islam, for whom Christianity is irretrievably polytheistic, or at least bitheistic or tritheistic – believing in two or three Gods. But in the face of the temptation to abandon monotheism and the charges that it had done so, Christianity continued to maintain that its belief in Christ amounted only to an accommodation within earlier monotheistic faith, or, more precisely, a fuller appreciation of monotheism in the light of God's self-revelation in Christ. This battle over monotheism has been largely lost sight of in studies of the early christological debates, partly because it falls awkwardly into the gap between the NT and the patristic era, and partly because it was regarded as having been already won and settled by the subsequent apologists.[84] That presumably is why the first internal debates which capture the attention in the second and third centuries are those which take for granted the deity of Christ (docetism and modalism), and why Logos christology is the highroad of developing Christian orthodoxy.

The importance of this issue (Christianity as monotheistic) having been faced and won is, not least, that it enables us the better to understand the later developments in christological dogma. For it was only at Nicea that the hitherto dominant Logos-christology gave way to the dominance of Son of God language. With Logos-christology the emphasis is essentially the same as that in John's Gospel – on the *continuity* between the Father and the Son, since the Son is the Word, the self-expression of God. With that emphasis having become established beyond peradventure, that is, christology as an expression of Christian monotheism, the debate could move on to the tricky question of the *relationship* between the Father and the Son. But this is a shift of emphasis, not any kind of abandoning of the monotheistic position already so firmly established. The point can often be lost sight of (like the earlier debate about monotheism) and attention be focused too quickly on the awkwardness and, to our eyes, artificiality of the Nicene and subsequent credal formulations. And an emphasis on Christ as the Son, independent of that earlier Logos-christology, can easily become in effect an expression of the very bitheism or tritheism of which Judaism and Islam accuse Christianity. It is of crucial importance for a right appreciation of Christian orthodoxy, therefore, to bear in mind that Father/Son Trinitarian language has to be read and understood *within the context of Christian monotheism*. If the credal Son of God language is not understood as an expression of Logos-christology it is misunderstood.[85]

A final point of importance is the bearing of all this back on the interpretation of the same key NT christological texts which provided the focus of *Christology in the Making* and which have been so much at the centre of the continuing dialogue. What the dialogue soon brought home to me with increasing strength is the serious danger to Christian monotheism unperceived by several at least of my critics. The importance of setting these texts within the historical context of meaning and of recognizing conceptuality in transition is indicated by the correlative recognition that these developments in earliest christology took place within and as an expression of Jewish-Christian monotheism. In contrast, the too quick resort to the 'obvious' or 'plain' meaning actually becomes in some cases a resort to a form of bitheism or tritheism. So, for example, the assumption that the Logos of John 1.1 can be substituted by 'Christ',[86] or the argument that Col. 1.15 would have been intended by Paul as a description of Christ, that is, of Jesus Messiah.[87] In contrast, classic orthodoxy is that Jesus Christ is he whom the Word of God *became* in the incarnation. The mistake, or so it seems to me, is the equivalent of treating 'person' in the Trinitarian formula ('one substance, three persons') as 'person' in the sense that we now understand 'person', or, more to the point, in the way that Jesus of

Nazareth was a person. If the pre-existent Word of God, the Son of God, is a person in that sense, then Christianity is unavoidably tritheistic.[88] And if we take texts like Col. 1.15ff. as straightforward descriptions of the Jesus who came from Nazareth we are committed to an interpretation of that text which has broken clearly and irrevocably from monotheism. Likewise if we assume that the Father/Son language of John's Gospel has in view more the relationship between the Father and the Son (of Nicene and post-Nicene concern) than the continuity of Logos christology (of pre-Nicene concern) we lose sight of the primary monotheistic control which prevents such language slipping into polytheism.

Not for the first time, then, I find that a careful exegesis of scripture, which takes the text with full seriousness in its historical context, and which has seemed to some an abandoning of cherished orthodoxies, is actually more faithful to scripture, and in this case to Trinitarian orthodoxy, than some of those who have levelled such criticisms. The ironic fact is that disregard for questions of context of meaning and conceptuality in transition has in some cases resulted in the defence or affirmation of a christology at odds with that of the later creeds. What has been understood as a defence of orthodoxy against the apparent reductionism of *Christology in the Making*, has become, irony of ironies, a statement which subsequently should have been regarded as heresy.

Well now, that should be enough for the moment to provoke another round of dialogue – if anyone bothers to read this. Let's hope so, for I still do not regard this as in any sense a final word on the subject and am quite confident that I have still much to learn in this whole area. The first round of debate has been personally highly profitable in instructing, correcting and enlarging my own theological thinking. I look forward to the next round with keen anticipation.

NOTES

1. Some reviewers have criticized me for an over confident scheme of development based on inevitably uncertain dating of documents. I should make it clear therefore that for the most part I take as my working hypothesis consensus dating for the relevant documents; the only significant dispute would be over the Similitudes of Enoch, though even here my tentative suggestion of a late first century AD date is one which commands wide support – see e.g. Hurtado (below n. 26), pp. 149 n. 8 and 150 n. 17. See below n. 40 and my response (n. 41); also below n. 81.

2. M. Hengel, *The Son of God: the Origin of Christology and the History of Jewish-Hellenistic Religion*, SCM Press 1974. It was a particular pleasure that C. F. D. Moule took the point so well in his *JTS* 33, 1982, pp. 258–63 review (p. 261).

3. J. Hick (ed.), *The Myth of God Incarnate*, SCM Press 1977.

4. One of the criticisms levelled at *Christology* was this failure to define the key term. I have attempted to a more careful delineation in the article 'Incarnation', forthcoming in the *Anchor Bible Dictionary*.

5. See Index, 'Context of meaning'.

6. 'In Defence of a Methodology', *ExpT* 95, 1983–84, pp. 295–9. In other discussions, including *New Testament Theology in Dialogue*, ed. with J. Mackey, SPCK 1988, p. 16, and *The Living Word*, SCM Press 1988, pp. 11–12, I have put the same point in terms of the 'limited horizons' of the biblical writer (as of anyone writing within history). See also below n. 49.

7. See further my *Living Word* (above n. 6).

8. See further my 'Levels of Canonical Authority', *HBT* 4, 1982, pp. 13–60, reprinted in *Living Word* (above n. 6), pp. 141–92.

9. Regrettably the dialogue has been almost exclusively an English language dialogue.

10. See e.g. J. F. Balchin, 'Paul, Wisdom and Christ', *Christ the Lord. Studies in Christology presented to D. Guthrie*, IVP 1982, pp. 204–19 (here particularly p. 215): D. Hagner in *Reformed Journal* 32, 1982, pp. 19–20; A. T. Hanson, *The Image of the Invisible God*, SCM Press 1982, especially ch. 3; L. Morris, 'The Emergence of the Doctrine of the Incarnation', *Themelios* 8/1, 1982, 15–19, though in much more measured tone (here p. 19); Moule (above n. 2), p. 260.

11. Cf. e.g. Hanson (above n. 10) pp. 59–62; I. H. Marshall, 'Incarnational Christology in the New Testament', *Christ the Lord* (above n. 10), pp. 7–8; C. E. B. Cranfield, 'Some Comments on Professor J. D. G. Dunn's *Christology in the Making* with Special Reference to the Evidence of the Epistle to the Romans', *The Glory of Christ in the New Testament. Studies in Christology in Memory of G. B. Caird*, ed. L. D. Hurst and N. T. Wright, Clarendon, 1987, p. 271.

12. See below, *Christology*, pp. 38–9. Contrast R. T. France, 'The Worship of Jesus: A Neglected Factor in Christological Debate?' *Christ the Lord* (above n. 10), p. 34 – 'The idea of Jesus' "being sent" . . . inevitably implies his pre-existence'; similarly R. P. Martin, 'Some Reflections on New Testament Hymns', in the same volume, p. 48.

13. See above n. 11.

14. See again below, *Christology*, p. 40.

15. Hanson (above n. 10), pp. 63–4, 80; R. P. Martin, *The Spirit and the Congregation. Studies in 1 Corinthians 12–15*, Eerdmans, 1984, pp. 153–4.

16. Several have characterized the exegesis offered as 'minimizing' or 'minimalist' or 'reductionist' – e.g. T. Weinandy in *Theological Studies*, June 1981, p. 295, Hagner (above n. 10) p. 19, C. Stead in *Religious Studies* 18, 1982, p. 96, L. Sabourin in *Religious Studies Bulletin* 3, 1983, p. 113, and R. G. Hamerton-Kelly in *Virginia Seminary Journal*, December 1983, pp. 29–30. 'The height of implausibility . . . a crude adoptionism' – Hanson (above n. 10) pp. 74–5. B. Demarest thinks that 'exegetical and theological fidelity have been sacrificed on the altar of scholarly novelty' (*Journal of the Evangelical Theological Society* 25, 1982, p. 108). Contrast the sympathetic reviews by H. Wansbrough in *The Tablet*, 7 March 1981, and D. Senior in *CBQ* 44, 1982, pp. 320–2, and more qualified criticism of D. M. Smith on the same point, in *Interpretation* 37, 1982, p. 293.

17. The case for recognizing the synonymity of *eikon* and *morphe* is conveniently summarized by Kim (below n. 51), pp. 200ff.

18. A reference to Gen. 3.5 still seems to me to shed most light on this disputed phrase. In the recent most thorough discussion of the debate by N. T. Wright, '*harpagmos* and the Meaning of Philippians 2.5–11', *JTS* 37, 1986, pp. 321–52, no real consideration is given to the factors which weighed most heavily with me (below, *Christology*, pp. 116 and 311 n. 73). Cf. Wanamaker (below n. 21), pp. 187–8.

19. Despite Marshall (above n. 11), p. 6, v. 7 seems to make sufficient sense as an elaboration of the contrast of Adam's fallen state – including the recapitulative, 'And being found in form as man' (see further below, *Christology*, 117–8).

20. The interweaving of Ps 8 and Ps 110.1 is a feature of Adam christology as we find it in Paul; see below, *Christology*, pp. 108ff. I thus find surprising the judgment of L. J. Kreitzer, *Jesus and God in Paul's Eschatology*, JSNTSupp 19, JSOT, 1987, pp. 224f. n. 72, that vv 9–11 'breaks the mould of any Adamic motif'. Contrast Fossum (below n. 60), pp. 293–7 (particularly p. 296). Kreitzer has, however, taken the 'context of meaning' point (p. 247 n. 104).

21. As in the most thorough recent attempt to refute the Adam christology exegesis, by C. A. Wanamaker, 'Philippians 2.6–11: Son of God or Adamic Christology?', *NTS* 33, 1987, pp. 179–93; here pp. 182–3. In such a brief response I must, regrettably, confine myself to the specific point at which Wanamaker has criticized my *Christology*. Wanamaker's suggestion (p. 192 n. 14) that I have changed my mind on the subject of Adam christology fails to appreciate that *Christology*, at this point deals with the full sweep of Adam christology, including the stage prior to Christ's exaltation in which his Adamic role is one of identification with fallen Adam ('sinful flesh'; Rom. 8.3 and Gal. 4.4), prior to his role as 'last (= resurrected) Adam' (I Cor. 15.45). Likewise L. D. Hurst. 'Re-enter the Pre-existent Christ in Philippians 2.5–11'. *NTS* 32, 1986, pp. 449–57, has not really taken my point that the language including the aorists is drawn from the Adam story and gains its force by relation to (and contrast with) that story. If the language has point as a *contrast* to the Adam tale, it does not require a precise one-to-one reference to Christ's life or elements therein. More general characteristics can then be gathered into language whose form is determined primarily by the Adam reference, Christ's story told in the 'shape' of Adam's in order to show how the damage was undone.

22. *Christology*, 119–20.

23. It might be pointed out that a Jesus who makes an Adamic choice is more of a model for Christian behaviour (Phil. 2.1–13) than a pre-existent Christ; but that would be to broaden the discussion beyond what is appropriate here. I suspect the same is true of II Cor. 8.9. R. P. Martin, *2 Corinthians*, WBC 40, Word 1986, p. 263, rejects my line of inquiry cursorily but does not engage with the considerations which still seem to me to carry some weight; here I may simply refer to my 'Methodology' (n. 6) p. 299.

24. *Christology*, pp. 165–6, 189–93.

25. Since there seems to have been some confusion on the point, may I simply note: I do not question that the Colossian hymn speaks of the pre-existence of Christ; my question is what that means; my answer, that it is the pre-existence of Wisdom which is attributed to Christ.

26. *Christology*, pp. 168–76. I am encouraged by support on this point from L. W. Hurtado, *One God, One Lord. Early Christian Devotion and Ancient Jewish Monotheism*, SCM Press and Fortress 1988, ch. 2, particularly pp. 46–8. Hurtado criti-

cizes particularly Fossum (below n. 60) at this point, but his reference to Fossum is incorrect. Equal criticism can, however, be levelled at A. J. Hultgren, *Christ and His Benefits. Christology and Redemption in the New Testament*, Fortress 1987, p. 7, who fails to appreciate the richness and vigour of the poetical imagery used by the Jewish wisdom writers. Nor am I sure what R. H. Fuller, 'The Theology of Jesus or Christology? An Evaluation of the Recent Discussion', *Semeia* 30, 1984, pp. 105–16, means by his distinction of Wisdom as 'an aspect within the very being of God' (p. 109). I agree, of course, that the Wisdom language invites resolution in terms of some kind of distinction in God, but that it was *perceived* to do so, experienced as a possible embarrassment for monotheism, is something which only emerged later – partly, I would suggest, as a result of using the language of a historical person, Jesus.

27. Balchin (above n. 10) follows the logic of 'the plain meaning' by arguing that 'The dangerous implications would have been obvious to Paul's monotheistic countrymen' (p. 215). He has no evidence for the assertion. On the contrary, it is the lack of such evidence and the fact that language like Col. 1.15ff. could be used of Christ without any sense of threat to Jewish monotheism at that stage, which continues to reinforce my serious doubts that 'the plain meaning' is the meaning first intended and understood. Similarly with D. Brown, *The Divine Trinity*, Duckworth 1985, who criticizes me for ignoring 'the possibility that Paul may have attributed pre-existence to Christ without realising all its implications' (p. 157). But implications as perceived by whom and when? Implications are as relative as the language and concepts used.

28. These latter points have not been addressed by critics who have assumed my questions and suggestions could be answered simply by reference to the first half of the hymn. See also my *Dialogue* (above n. 6), pp. 54–64. Similar points could be made with reference to Heb. 1.3–4; but my exegesis of that passage has not drawn much fire, and see now L. D. Hurst, 'The Christology of Hebrews 1 and 2', *The Glory of Christ* (see above n. 11), pp. 151–64.

29. In my 'Methodology' (above n. 6), p. 296 I refer particularly to several contributors to the Guthrie Festschrift (above n. 10). See also Cranfield (above n. 11), p. 274.

30. For the wilder arguments of R. Gruenler, *New Approaches to Jesus and the Gospels*, Baker 1982, which do not warrant the title 'exegesis', I must be content simply to refer to my response in 'Methodology' (above n. 6), p. 297. Equally implausible is the argument of P. B. Payne, 'Jesus' Implicit Claim to Deity in his Parables', *Trinity Journal* 2, 1981, 3–23, that because Jesus in his parables used imagery which in the OT refers to God he meant it to refer to himself and therefore thought of himself in some sense as God – a double non-sequitur. However since it is not, properly speaking, part of the dialogue with *Christology*, I will simply refer to my brief comments on it in 'Incarnation' (above n. 4).

31. 'The thong of whose sandals I am not worthy to untie' (Luke 3.16) presumably indicates a difference in status of degree rather than of kind; to deny, as though thinkable, what would be regarded as unthinkable (the comparability of status of a human being and a divine figure) would be a mark of impiety, not of humility.

32. *Pace* M. M. B. Turner, 'The Spirit of Christ and Christology', *Christ the Lord* (above n. 10), pp. 168–90 (particularly pp. 182–3).

33. K. Runia, *The Present-day Christological Debate*, IVP 1984, p. 93.

34. See e.g. below, *Christology*, ch. 1.

35. Cranfield, 'Comments' (above n. 11), p. 275.

36. See further Hurtado (above n. 26), pp. 56–63.

37. G. L. Bray, 'Recent Trends in Christology', *Themelios* 12.2, 1987, pp. 52–56 (here p. 53).

38. *Unity and Diversity in the New Testament*, SCM Press 1977.

39. L. E. Keck, 'Toward the Renewal of New Testament Christology', *NTS* 32, 1986, 362–77, warns that 'inquiring who first spoke of Christ's pre-existence is no substitute for trying to understand what doing so entails' (p. 374). I should not assume, however, that this is aimed at my *Christology*, since one of my concerns throughout is precisely 'to understand what' use of pre-existence language for Christ 'entails'.

40. *JBL* 101, 1982; 'New Testament Christology: A Consideration of Dunn's *Christology in the Making*', *NovT* 25, 1983, pp. 257–78, reprinted in *Christology and Exegesis: New Approaches*, ed. R. Jewett, *Semeia* 30, 1984, pp. 65–82 (I cite the title as given in the *Semeia* volume). The contribution by A. Segal in the same volume, 'Pre-existence and Incarnation: A Response to Dunn and Holladay', pp. 83–95, presupposes Holladay's critique, is also weakened by a less than adequate appreciation of the scope and objective of *Christology* (pp. 83–5), and fails to appreciate the nuances of a 'conceptuality in transition' ('Dunn wants to place everything of importance to christology in Jesus' self-consciousness' – p. 89).

41. 'Some Clarifications on Issues of Method: A Reply to Holladay and Segal', *Semeia* 30, 1984, pp. 97–104 (full title in n. 40).

42. *One God* (see above n. 26), p. 6.

43. 'It makes no concerted effort at systematic investigation of comparable notions in the world of late antiquity' (Holladay, p. 78).

44. I can see now that my italicization of the final sentence of §3.5 (p. 22) may have been misleading on this point; and for this I apologize. The aim of §3 should have been clear, however (it is repeated in the next sentence). The summary of §32.1 (pp. 251–3) would probably reinforce the misunderstanding, but is intended, of course, as a summary of the study actually carried out. Readers should therefore note that the first of the agenda questions asked below on pp. 5–6 is more circumscribed that at first appears by the fact that I regard the primary context for earliest Christianity as Judaism, including Hellenistic Judaism. See also my article 'Incarnation' (above n. 4).

45. Holladay (above n. 40), p. 76.

46. Perhaps I should repeat that my occasional reference to 'popular superstition' was not intended as a Christian 'put-down' (a similar criticism is made by F. M. Young in *Theology* 84, 1981, p. 304), but as an echo of a common attitude among intellectuals in the Greco-Roman world. Cf. for example G. W. Bowersock, 'Greek Intellectuals and the Imperial Cult in the Second Century A.D.', *Le culte des souverains dans l'Empire Romain*, Genève (1973), pp. 179–206: 'As far as can be told, in the age from Augustus to Constantine, no person in the Roman empire addressed a prayer to a monarch, alive or dead' (p. 180); 'Domitian's claim to be *deus* was a genuine outrage' (p. 199). Note also below, *Christology*, pp. 251–2.

47. Holladay (above n. 40), p. 76.

48. According to his *JBL* review (above n. 40), 'Non-NT texts from Jewish and Greco-Roman backgrounds are treated, but only indirectly' (pp. 610–1). I

accept the reference to Greco-Roman texts as fair comment. For the rest, words fail me!

49. In my response to Holladay (above n. 41, pp. 100–3) I expressed the point in terms of the 'limited horizons' of the first Christian writers in contrast to the unlimited overview possible to us of later generations. The point is well taken by P. R. Keifert, 'Interpretive Paradigms: A Proposal Concerning New Testament Christology', *Semeia* 30, 1984, pp. 203–14 (here pp. 206–7). See also above n. 6.

50. The preliminary survey summarized in pp. 19–22 provided little encouragement to look in another direction. Of course I took fully into account the main hypothesis of the past two or three generations – viz. the Gnostic Redeemer myth (see index).

51. *The Origin of Paul's Gospel*, WUNT 2.4, Mohr-Siebeck 1981.

52. Kim (above n. 51), pp. 226, 227, 251.

53. Of course Kim did not have *Christology* to hand either. But it is somewhat surprising that in his later monograph, *'The "Son of Man" ' as the Son of God*, WUNT 30, Mohr-Siebeck 1983, he pays no attention whatsoever to *Christology*, or, much more important, to the discussion by M. Casey, *The Son of Man: The Interpretation and Influence of Daniel 7*, SPCK 1980.

54. See further my critique of Kim in ' "A Light to the Gentiles": the Significance of the Damascus Road Christophany for Paul', *The Glory of Christ* (see above n. 11) pp. 251–66.

55. *The Influence of the First Chapter of Ezekiel on Jewish and Early Christian Literature.*

56. See below, *Christology*, Bibliography, p. 392.

57. *The Open Heaven. A Study of Apocalyptic in Judaism and Early Christianity*, SPCK 1982.

58. I. Gruenwald, *Apocalyptic and Merkabah Mysticism*, AGAJU XIV, Brill 1980, also reached me too late; as also R. Bauckham, 'The Worship of Jesus in Apocalyptic Christianity', *NTS* 27, 1980–81, pp. 322–41.

59. Hurtado (above n. 26), p. 73 justifiably criticizes me on this score.

60. Rowland, *Heaven* (above n. 57), pp. 94–113 (here p. 96). See also J. E. Fossum, *The Name of God and the Angel of the Lord*, WUNT 36, Mohr-Siebeck 1985.

61. The feature is consistent with others in Revelation – particularly the fact that the Lamb shares the throne (7.17; 22.1) and that both the Lord God and the soon coming Christ call themselves 'Alpha and Omega' (1.8; 22.13).

62. See again below, section III. Fossum (above n. 60) assembles the material for his discussion from such a broad canvas of time and context that it is very difficult to draw him into a dialogue on development and on conceptuality in transition.

63. W. Zimmerli, *Ezekiel 1*, Hermeneia, Fortress 1979, p. 236, cited by Hurtado (above n. 26), p. 76.

64. Cf. Bauckham (above n. 58): 'the glory of all angels to some extent resembles the glory of their Maker' (p. 327).

65. E.g. in Apoc. Ab. the angel Jaoel, 'a power by virtue of the ineffable name that dwells in me' (10.9) and described in the same sort of powerful imagery (11.2), is also noted as worshipping God (17.2, 6ff.).

66. Rowland argues the parallel with Jewish Wisdom speculation the other way: 'What we have here is the beginning of a hypostatic development similar to that connected with divine attributes like God's word and wisdom' (*Heaven*, above n. 57, p. 100). But I suspect that Jewish monotheists would have found

the talk of 'hypostatic development' meaningless and denied what it attempts to affirm.

67. Hurtado (above n. 26) ch. 4, with critique of Rowland and Fossum on pp. 85–90.

68. See below, *Christology*, pp. 244–5.

69. What follows is a summary of the main line of argument in my 'Let John be John; A Gospel for its Time', *Das Evangelium und die Evangelien*, hrsg. P. Stuhlmacher, WUNT 28, Mohr-Siebeck 1983, pp. 309–39.

70. Details in Dunn, 'John' (above n. 69), p. 323.

71. Details in Dunn, 'John' (above n. 69), pp. 323–4.

72. See particularly J. A. Buhner, *Der Gesandte und sein Weg im 4. Evangelium*. Mohr-Siebeck 1977.

73. Cf. particularly M. L. Appold, *The Oneness Motif in the Fourth Gospel*, WUNT 1, Mohr-Siebeck 1976.

74. Dunn, 'John' (above n. 69), p. 334. P. Schoonenberg uses this as a spring-board for further theological reflection, in his Bellarmine Lecture. 'A sapiental reading of John's Prologue: some reflections on views of Reginald Fuller and James Dunn', *Theology Digest*, 33, 1986, 403–21.

75. For Matthew I may refer to an important thesis in its final stages by one of my postgraduates, David Kupp, on Matthew's christology as a christology of divine presence (particularly Matt. 1.23; 18.20; 28.20).

76. Hence the title of the article which was my first attempt to reorder the findings of *Christology* as a way of answering this question – 'Was Christianity a Monotheistic Faith from the Beginning?', *SJT* 35, 1982, pp. 303–36. The import-ance of the issue came home to me particularly in my debate with M. Wiles in *Theology* 85, 1982, pp. 92–8, 324–32, 360–1.

77. This, indeed, is one of Hurtado's main theses (above n. 26). In distinction from my *Christology* he limits his discussion to 'the very first few years of Christ-ianity, when it was thoroughly dominated by Jews and functioned as a sect of ancient Judaism' (p. 6). That is a description which actually takes us more or less up to the end of the first century, at least so far as the NT documents themselves are concerned. So far as I can see, it was only when monotheism was perceived to have become an issue that the final split between Christianity and *rabbinic* Judaism became inevitable and unavoidable.

78. Contrast again Balchin (above n. 27).

79. Details in Dunn, 'John' (above n. 69), pp. 324–5.

80. I am not really persuaded by Hurtado's argument that the Christian mutation of the ancient understanding of divine agency had a 'binitarian shape' more or less from the first (above n. 26, pp. 99–114). For all that there was praise, invocation, acclamation of the exalted Christ from very early on, it is less clear that we can speak of *worship* of Christ as such prior to, significantly, the Fourth Gospel (John 20.28) and Revelation (Rev. 5.8, 11–14; etc.). The earlier devotional practices were evidently not yet seen as a qualification, or threat to monotheism; that presumably means that they were still understood by Christian and other Jews as within the bounds of what was acceptable – a transmutation under way, to be sure, but whether already deserving the description 'binitarian' is another question. That apart, I naturally welcome Hurtado's emphasis on the importance and theology-generative character of the earliest Christians' religious experience

(pp. 114–24, particularly p. 121), conducive as it is to the main theme of my *Jesus and the Spirit*, SCM Press 1975.

81. I include here not only IV Ezra 13, but also John's Gospel and Revelation, and probably I Enoch 37–72; the degree to which the Son of Man speculation of the Similitudes of Enoch 'fits' within the other Son of Man speculation which we know belongs to that period strongly suggests that I Enoch 37–72 should likewise be dated to this period – that is, post 70 (see above n. 1).

82. Is it significant that at about the same time the emperor Domitian caused outrage by claiming to be *deus* rather than *divus* (see Bowersock, above n. 46, pp. 198–9)?

83. Against Wiles then (above n. 76, p. 95) I want to emphasize, more than I do in *Christology*, the continuity between the Fourth Evangelist's christology and both what preceded John – here I am closer to J. A. T. Robinson, 'Dunn on John', *Theology* 85, 1982, pp. 332–8 – and the 'orthodox' christology which built on John. But see also M. Wiles, 'Person or Personification? A Patristic Debate about Logos', *The Glory of Christ* (above n. 11), pp. 281–9.

84. I have in view the internal debates within Christian self-understanding. The Jewish-Christian option of Jesus as prophet or adoptionism was regarded (no longer) as a viable option for Christian faith and treated as a heresy. That is, options which might have made possible the continued unity of Jew and Christian were dismissed in mutual recrimination and in charge and counter-charge of heresy.

85. The point is developed in the debate with Wiles (above n. 76), pp. 327–9.

86. *The Living Bible* translation.

87. Marshall (above n. 11), pp. 9, 13, does not hesitate to speak of Christ as a 'pre-existent Being', or as 'a personal agent of creation alongside the Father' (*Trinity Journal* 2, 1981, p. 245).

88. This point was brought home to me by G. W. H. Lampe, *God as Spirit*, Clarendon 1977, pp. 135–6. In the same connection Schoonenberg (above n. 74) refers to K. Rahner, *The Trinity*, Herder 1970, pp. 105–15.

ABBREVIATIONS

AB	The Anchor Bible, Doubleday
AHGFFB	*Apostolic History and the Gospel: Biblical and Historical Essays presented to F. F. Bruce*, ed. W. W. Gasque and R. P. Martin, Paternoster 1970
Arndt & Gingrich	W. F. Arndt and F. W. Gingrich, *A Greek-English Lexicon of the New Testament*, ET Chicago 1957
ATE	*Apocalypses et Theologie de l'Esperance*, Congres de Toulouse (1975), ed. L. Monloubou, Paris 1977
AWJEC	*Aspects of Wisdom in Judaism and Early Christianity*, ed. R. L. Wilken, Notre Dame 1975
Beginnings	F. J. Foakes-Jackson and K. Lake, *The Beginnings of Christianity Part I: The Acts of the Apostles*, Macmillan Vol. I, 1920; Vols. IV and V, 1933
BJRL	*Bulletin of the John Rylands Library*, Manchester
Black	Black's New Testament Commentaries, A. & C. Black
Blass-Debrunner-Funk	F. Blass and A. Debrunner, *A Greek Grammar of the New Testament and Other Early Christian Literature*, ET and ed. R. W. Funk, Cambridge University Press 1961
BNTE	*The Background of the New Testament and its Eschatology: Studies in Honour of C. H. Dodd*, ed. W. D. Davies and D. Daube, Cambridge University Press 1954

Bousset-Gressmann	W. Bousset and H. Gressmann, *Die Religion des Judentums im späthellenistischen Zeitalter*, HNT 21, ⁴1966
BR	*Biblical Research*
BZ	*Biblische Zeitschrift*
CBQ	*Catholic Biblical Quarterly*
CHIJK	*Christian History and Interpretation: Studies presented to John Knox*, ed. W. R. Farmer, C. F. D. Moule and R. R. Niebuhr, Cambridge University Press 1967
CIMCT	*Current Issues in Biblical and Patristic Interpretation: Studies in Honour of M. C. Tenney*, ed. G. F. Hawthorne, Eerdmans 1975
CINTI	*Current Issues in New Testament Interpretation: Essays in Honour of O. A. Piper*, ed. W. Klassen and G. F. Snyder, SCM Press 1962
CJMS	*Christianity, Judaism and Other Greco-Roman Cults: Studies for Morton Smith*, 3 vols., ed. J. Neusner, Leiden 1975
Clarendon	New Clarendon Bible, Oxford University Press
CNT	Commentaire du Nouveau Testament, Neuchatel et Paris
CSNT	*Christ and Spirit in the New Testament: Studies in Honour of C. F. D. Moule*, ed. B. Lindars and S. S. Smalley, Cambridge University Press 1973
EB	Etudes Biblique, Paris
ed.	editor/edited by
EKK	Evangelisch-Katholischer Kommentar zum Neuen Testament, Zürich and Neukirchen
EncJud	*Encyclopaedia Judaica*, Jerusalem
ENTT	E. Käsemann, *Essays on New Testament Themes*, ET SCM Press 1964
EQ	*Evangelical Quarterly*
ET	English translation
ETL	*Ephemerides Theologicae Lovanienses*
EvTh	*Evangelische Theologie*
ExpT	*Expository Times*
FRPRB	*The Future of our Religious Past: Essays in Honour of R. Bultmann*, ed. J. M. Robinson, SCM Press 1971
GMEH	*Gott und Mensch: Gesammelte Aufsätze von Ernst Haenchen*, Tübingen 1965

Hennecke, *Apocrypha*	E. Hennecke, *New Testament Apocrypha*, ed. W. Schneemelcher, ET ed. R. McL. Wilson, SCM Press Vol. I, 1973; Vol. II, 1974
Herder	Herders Theologischer Kommentar zum Neuen Testament, Freiburg Basel Wien
Hermeneia	Hermeneia Commentaries, Fortress Press, Philadelphia
HNT	Handbuch zum Neuen Testament, Tübingen
HTR	*Harvard Theological Review*
HUCA	*Hebrew Union College Annual*
ICC	The International Critical Commentary, T. & T. Clark
IDB	*The Interpreter's Dictionary of the Bible*, 4 vols., Abingdon 1962
IDBS	*IDB* Supplementary Volume 1976
JAAR	*Journal of the American Academy of Religion*
JB	The Jerusalem Bible
JBL	*Journal of Biblical Literature*
JCHTHC	*Jesus Christus in Historie und Theologie: Neutestamentliche Festschrift für H. Conzelmann*, hrsg. G. Strecker, Tübingen 1975
JGCWDD	*Jews, Greeks and Christians: Religious Cultures in Late Antiquity. Essays in Honour of W. D. Davies*, ed. R. Hamerton-Kelly and R. Scroggs, Leiden 1976
JJS	*Journal of Jewish Studies*
JMAV	*Jesus und der Menschensohn. Für Anton Vögtle*, hrsg. R. Pesch and R. Schnackenburg, Freiburg 1975
JQR	*Jewish Quarterly Review*
JSJ	*Journal for the Study of Judaism*
JSNT	*Journal for the Study of the New Testament*
JSS	*Journal of Semitic Studies*
JThC	*Journal for Theology and Church*
JTS	*Journal of Theological Studies*
KAHS	*Das Kirche des Anfangs: Für H. Schürmann*, hrsg. R. Schnackenburg, J. Ernst und J. Wanke, Freiburg 1978
KEK	Kritisch-exegetischer Kommentar über das Neue Testament, Göttingen
KuD	*Kerygma und Dogma*
Lampe	G. W. H. Lampe (ed.), *A Patristic Greek Lexicon*, Oxford University Press 1961

Liddell & Scott	H. G. Liddell and R. Scott, *A Greek-English Lexicon*, revised H. S. Jones, Oxford University Press 1940, with Supp., 1968
LXX	Septuagint
Moffatt	The Moffatt New Testament Commentary, Hodder and Stoughton
Moulton & Milligan	J. H. Moulton and G. Milligan, *The Vocabulary of the Greek Testament*, Hodder and Stoughton 1930
MT	Massoretic text
NCB	New Century Bible, Oliphants
NDNTS	*New Dimensions in New Testament Study*, ed. R. N. Longenecker and M. C. Tenney, Zondervan 1974
NEB	New English Bible
NIDNTT	*The New International Dictionary of New Testament Theology*, 3 vols., Paternoster 1975–78
NIV	New International Version
NovT	*Novum Testamentum*
NTCEHB	*Neues Testament und christliche Existenz. Festschrift für H. Braun*, hrsg. H. D. Betz und L. Schottroff, Tübingen 1973
NTD	Das Neue Testament Deutsch, Göttingen
NTETWM	*New Testament Essays: Studies in Memory of T. W. Manson*, ed. A. J. B. Higgins, Manchester 1959
NTGOC	*Neues Testament und Geschichte: Historisches Geschehen und Deutung im Neuen Testament*, O. Cullmann Festschrift, hrsg. H. Baltensweiler und B. Reicke, Zürich and Tübingen 1972
NTKRS	*Neues Testament und Kirche: Für R. Schnackenburg*, ed. J. Gnilka, Freiburg 1974
NTQT	E. Käsemann, *New Testament Questions of Today*, ET SCM Press 1969
NTS	*New Testament Studies*
OTS	*Oudtestamentische Studiën*
par.	parallel
RAERG	*Religions in Antiquity: Essays in Memory of E. R. Goodenough*, ed. J. Neusner, Leiden 1968
RB	*Revue Biblique*
RGG	*Die Religion in Geschichte und Gegenwart*, ³1957ff.
RHLLM	*Reconciliation and Hope: New Testament Essays on Atonement and Eschatology*, L. L. Morris

	Festschrift, ed. R. J. Banks, Paternoster 1974
RHPR	*Revue d'Histoire et de Philosophie religieuses*
RJAGJJ	*Der Ruf Jesu und die Antwort der Gemeinde*, Festschrift für J. Jeremias, hrsg. E. Lohse, Göttingen 1970
RQ	*Revue de Qumran*
RSR	*Recherches de Science religieuse*
RSV	Revised Standard Version
SBL	Society of Biblical Literature
SBS	Stuttgarter Bibel-Studien
Schürer, *History*	E. Schürer, *The History of the Jewish People in the Age of Jesus Christ*, revised ed. G. Vermes, F. Miller and M. Black, T. & T. Clark Vol. I, 1973; Vol. II, 1979
SE	*Studia Evangelica*
SJT	*Scottish Journal of Theology*
SLAPS	*Studies in Luke Acts*, P. Schubert Festschrift, ed. L. E. Keck and J. L. Martyn, Abingdon 1966
SNT	Supplement to *Novum Testamentum*
SNTS	Studiorum Novi Testamenti Societas
SP	*Studia Patristica*
SPCIC	*Studiorum Paulinorum Congressus Internationalis Catholicus 1961*, Rome 1963
StTh	*Studia Theologica*
Strack-Billerbeck	H. L. Strack and P. Billerbeck, *Kommentar zum Neuen Testament aus Talmud und Midrasch*, München 1926–28
Supp.	Supplement
TDNT	*Theological Dictionary of the New Testament*, 10 vols., Eerdmans 1964–76, ET *Theologisches Wörterbuch zum Neuen Testament*, hrsg. G. Kittel und G. Friedrich, 9 vols., Stuttgart 1933–73
TDOT	*Theological Dictionary of the Old Testament*, Eerdmans 1974f., ET *Theologisches Wörterbuch zum Alten Testament*, hrsg. G. J. Botterweck und H. Ringgren, Stuttgart 1970f.
THNT	Theologischer Handkommentar zum Neuen Testament, Berlin
ThQ	*Theologische Quartalschrift*
TLZ	*Theologische Literaturzeitung*
TR	*Theologische Rundschau*
TS	*Theological Studies*

TTZ	*Trierer Theologische Zeitschrift*
TZ	*Theologische Zeitschrift*
UDNTT	*Unity and Diversity in New Testament Theology: Essays in Honour of G. E. Ladd*, ed. R. A. Guelich, Eerdmans 1978
VC	*Vigiliae Christianae*
VT	*Vetus Testamentum*
VuF	*Verkündigung und Forschung*
ZAW	*Zeitschrift für die alttestamentliche Wissenschaft*
ZKG	*Zeitschrift für Kirchengeschichte*
ZKT	*Zeitschrift für Katholische Theologie*
ZNW	*Zeitschrift für die neutestamentliche Wissenschaft*
ZTK	*Zeitschrift für Theologie und Kirche*

Abbreviations for biblical and other ancient texts should be sufficiently obvious and require no explanation here (though if in doubt see the Indexes); but I attach a list of abbreviations used for the writings of *Philo* (listed alphabetically) since they are cited in brief form, may be less familiar and abbreviations are less standardized:

Abr.	*De Abrahamo*
Agr.	*De Agricultura*
Cher.	*De Cherubim*
Conf.	*De Confusione Linguarum*
Cong.	*De Congressu quaerendae Eruditionis gratia*
Decal.	*De Decalogo*
Det.	*Quod Deterius Potiori Insidiari Soleat*
Ebr.	*De Ebrietate*
Fuga	*De Fuga et Inventione*
Gig.	*De Gigantibus*
Heres	*Quis Rerum Divinarum Heres sit*
Immut.	*Quod Deus Immutabilis sit*
Jos.	*De Josepho*
Leg.All.	*Legum Allegoriae*
Legat.	*De Legatione ad Gaium*
Migr.	*De Migratione Abrahami*
Mos.	*De Vita Mosis*
Mut.	*De Mutatione Nominum*
Opif.	*De Opificio Mundi*
Plant.	*De Plantatione*
Post.	*De Posteritate Caini*
Praem.	*De Praemiis et Poenis*
Prob.	*Quod Omnis Probus Liber sit*

Qu.Ex.	*Quaestiones et Solutiones in Exodum*
Qu.Gen.	*Quaestiones et Solutiones in Genesin*
Sac.	*De Sacrificiis Abelis et Caini*
Sobr.	*De Sobrietate*
Som.	*De Somniis*
Spec.Leg.	*De Specialibus Legibus*
Virt.	*De Virtutibus*
Vit.Cont.	*De Vita Contemplativa*

When a number of Philo references are cited together they are usually set out following the order of the Loeb edition of Philo's works (see Index).

I

INTRODUCTION

§1. THE ORIGIN OF THE DOCTRINE OF THE INCARNATION AS AN ISSUE

> I do not think it can be reasonably gainsayed that Christianity has meant historically, faith in the person of Jesus Christ, considered as very God incarnate, so much so that if this faith were gone, Christianity in its characteristic features would be gone also.[1]

Few indeed would dispute Gore's claim, made in the first of his 1891 Bampton Lectures, that historically speaking Christian faith has been faith in the incarnation, the conviction that Jesus of Nazareth was the Son of God incarnate. We need only think of the controversies of the early centuries which shaped the classic credal statements of Christianity – controversies basically as to whether it was possible for the divine truly to become one with humanity without ceasing to be divine, creeds all striving to express the central claim that true God became true man in Jesus Christ. We need only recall the famous assertions which proved decisive then and which still echo down the centuries with telling power – particularly the striking epigrams of Athanasius: 'He became man that we might become divine' (αὐτὸς ἐνηνθρώπησεν ἵνα ἡμεῖς θεοποιηθῶμεν – De Inc. 54);[2] and Gregory of Nazianzus: 'What has not been assumed cannot be restored (τὸ ἀπρόσληπτον ἀθεράπευτον); it is what is united with God that is saved' (Ep. 101.7);[3] or the later thesis of Anselm in Cur Deus Homo? –

> If, therefore, as is certain, it is needful that that heavenly state be perfected from among men, and this cannot be unless the above-mentioned satisfaction (for sin) be made, which no one *can* make except God, and no one *ought* to make except man, it is necessary that one who is God-man should make it (II.6).

In the present century we need only refer to the massive importance of the incarnation in Karl Barth's *Church Dogmatics* – for example, his thesis at the head of §57:

> The subject-matter, origin and content of the message received and proclaimed by the Christian community is at its heart the free act of the faithfulness of God in which he takes the lost cause of man, who has denied him as Creator and in so doing ruined himself as creature, and makes it his own in Jesus Christ, carrying it through to its goal and in that way maintaining and manifesting his own glory in the world;[4]

or the influential restatements offered over the past thirty years by Karl Rahner[5] – for example:

> What do we Christians mean when we profess our faith in the incarnation of the Word of God? That is what we must try to say in ever new ways. It is the whole task of Christology, which will never be completed.[6]

> The Saviour is himself a historical moment in God's saving action exercised on the world. He is a moment of the history of God's communication of himself to the world – in the sense that he is a part of the history of the cosmos itself ... It must also be underlined in this connection that the statement of God's *Incarnation* – of his becoming *material* – is the most basic statement of christology.[7]

At the same time we cannot ignore the fact that since the Enlightenment the traditional doctrine of the incarnation has come under increasing pressure to explain and justify itself. In the nineteenth century the challenge of scientific rationalism to any dogma claiming an authority which rested solely on revelation inevitably resulted in various redefinitions rather more amenable to the spirit of the times – in particular, incarnation as Jesus' unique God-consciousness (Schleiermacher), incarnation as the supreme idea of God-manhood actualized in one individual, Jesus (Hegelians), incarnation as the self-limitation by the Son of his divine mode of existence (Kenoticists).[8]

In the twentieth century however the sharpest questioning has been directed not so much to the doctrine itself as to its *origin*, with historical exegesis providing the challenge rather than philosophical speculation. A. Harnack had already defined the development of dogma as the progressive hellenization of the gospel, as the transplanting of the gospel of Jesus 'into Greek modes of thought', a process which goes back to Paul himself.[9] The History of Religions school which pioneered the investigation of Christian origins within the context of the religious thought and practice of the wider Hellenistic world, raised the more provocative question of whether the whole idea of God become man had in fact simply been taken over from surrounding religious syncretism, an already well developed myth of a divine figure descending to earth to redeem the elect (the so-called 'Gnostic redeemer myth') borrowed by the early Christians and applied to the risen Jesus. With Harnack's formulation, the dogma of the incarnation could be said to have originated simply as a translation equivalent as the gospel of Jesus was re-expressed in the wider and different categories of Greek philosophy. But if the dogma originated as a foreign import into Christianity of an already established Gnostic myth the issue becomes more serious: *did the doctrine of the incarnation begin as an alien intrusion into Christianity?* In the last thirty years or so the question as thus posed has been answered with an increasingly confident No! (see below ch. IV). But the question has not been silenced: new evidence in the form of the Nag Hammadi codices[10] and more sophisticated or more carefully qualified revisions of the Gnostic redeemer myth hypothesis[11] have kept the issue alive.

That the doctrine of the incarnation and its origins is a crucial issue in all this has not always been clear. The issue has been obscured partly by the fact that much of the better known NT christological discussion has focused on 'the titles of majesty' (Hoheitstitel) ascribed to Jesus in the NT,[12] and partly by the fact that much of the debate stimulated by the History of Religions school has consisted of articles and monographs on specific NT passages (particularly the christological hymns).[13] It would also be true to say that in the post-World War II period the main thrust of inquiries into christological origins has been in a different direction – attempts to push forward a new quest of the historical Jesus,[14] or to trace the continuity between the message of Jesus and the post-Easter christology of the earliest churches.[15] The veritable flood of studies on the resurrection of Jesus in the 1950s and 1960s[16] is sufficient indication that scholarly and popular interest was focused more on the issue of Christ's *post*-existence' than on the issue of his *pre*-existence'.[17]

In the past few years however there has been a revival of interest, particularly within English speaking NT scholarship, in the question of the incarnation as such and particularly in the origins of the doctrine – a revival of interest signalled by the studies of J. Knox, *The Humanity and Divinity of Christ* (1967), G. B. Caird, 'The Development of the Doctrine of Christ in the New Testament', *Christ for us Today*, ed. N. Pittenger (1968), pp. 66–80, F. B. Craddock, *The Pre-existence of Christ in the New Testament* (1968), the symposium, *Christ, Faith and History: Cambridge Studies in Christology*, ed. S. W. Sykes and J. P. Clayton (1972), R. G. Hamerton-Kelly, *Pre-existence, Wisdom and the Son of Man* (1973), J.A.T. Robinson, *The Human Face of God* (1973), M. Wiles, *The Remaking of Christian Doctrine* (1974), particularly ch. 3, A. T. Hanson, *Grace and Truth: a Study in the Doctrine of the Incarnation* (1975), G. W. H. Lampe, *God as Spirit: the Bampton Lectures 1976* (1977), the well-publicized symposium entitled *The Myth of God Incarnate*, ed. J. Hick (1977), including contributions on the NT from M. Goulder and F. Young, which provoked several responses, particularly the sequel, *Incarnation and Myth: the Debate Continued*, ed. M. Goulder (1979), in which C.F.D. Moule and G.N. Stanton join in the NT debate, the fuller contribution of D. Cupitt, *The Debate about Christ* (1979), and J.P. Mackey, *Jesus: the Man and the Myth* (1979), particularly ch. 6.[18]

All of these focus attention on the doctrine of the incarnation and particularly its origin with differing degrees of intensity and from different angles. Consider, for example, the following quotations.

> The assertion of pre-existence was at first an assertion only about the context or background of Jesus' human existence, not about its nature or intrinsic character ... Paul undoubtedly affirmed the pre-existence of Christ and, in whatever precise terms he pictured it, it was a transcendent, a heavenly state, far removed in kind from our earthly human existence ... In the Fourth Gospel it (the manhood of Jesus) has been so transformed by the divinity surrounding it on all sides, as it were, as no longer to be manhood in any ordinary sense ... We can have the humanity without the pre-existence and we can have the pre-existence without the humanity. There is absolutely no way of having both.[19]

> Incarnation, in its full and proper sense, is not something directly presented in scripture. It is a construction built on the variegated evidence to be found there.

> Talk of his (Jesus') pre-existence ought probably in most, perhaps in all, cases to be understood, on the analogy of the pre-existence of the Torah, to indicate the eternal divine purpose being achieved through him, rather than pre-existence of a fully personal kind.[20]

> God indwelt and motivated the human spirit of Jesus in such a way that in him, uniquely, the relationship for which man is intended by his Creator was fully realized ... the same God, the Spirit who was in Jesus ... A union of personal deity with human personality can only be a perfected form of inspiration ... incarnation, unless understood in inspirational terms is inadequate ... In Jesus the incarnate presence of God evoked a full and constant response of the human spirit ... When Jesus is identified with the pre-existent Son, belief in a true incarnation of God in Jesus is weakened.[21]

> Jesus, the man of universal destiny.

> Paul appropriated the idea of Jesus' incarnation in the course of dialectic with the Samaritan missionaries in Corinth and Ephesus between 50 and 55 ... the incarnational speculations introduced into the church by Simon Magus and his fellow-Samaritans ...[22]

> In the New Testament Jesus was the embodiment of all God's promises brought to fruition ... such a characterization represents New Testament christology better than the idea of incarnation ... It is eschatology, not incarnation, which makes Christ final in the New Testament ... Christ is final for Paul, not as God incarnate, but as last Adam.[23]

God's Son is not a second coequal person alongside God the Father, but simply Man 'filled' with God, united with God.[24]

Alternatively we may consider the following.

What we have seen in these New Testament materials (on the pre-existence of Christ) is the adapting of what was adopted from the culture.[25]

The Hellenistic Church gave prominence to the pre-existence of Christ . . . by identifying Christ with Wisdom, but in so doing . . . they were simply giving their own form to an impulse which was expressed in the Palestinian traditions by means of apocalyptic categories, and which derives ultimately from Jesus' own use of the title 'Son of Man'.[26]

Some of the 'highest' christology in the New Testament is already present, by implication at least, in the earliest datable documents of the New Testament . . . Jesus is recognized as transcending the bounds of humanity.[27]

When New Testament 'incarnational' christology is examined carefully with the tools of historical criticism, it frequently runs *against* first-century Jewish and Hellenistic religious currents. Available categories are used, but *always* with qualification.[28]

In one way or another then all these studies raise searching questions about the origin of the doctrine of the incarnation. Unfortunately none of them has been able to investigate the questions raised in sufficient detail; not surprisingly since in most cases we are dealing with brief essays forming part of a symposium, or individual chapters in wider studies, or more popular lecture formats where detailed analysis is inappropriate or with more restricted investigations which do not cover the whole range of material or do so only from a more limited perspective.[29] However provocative and stimulating their insights and claims none provides that thorough analysis of NT texts against their contemporary background without which these insights and claims cannot properly be evaluated.

There seems therefore to be a need for such a study – a sufficiently detailed investigation of the NT materials in their historical contexts in the light of the questions raised by the recent debate, as indeed also of those questions which still remain in force from the earlier debates concerning the Gnostic redeemer myth hypothesis.[30] The questions can be posed thus: *How did the doctrine of the incarnation originate?* Was it original to Christianity, a unique claim unparalleled in the religious beliefs of the time and indebted only to Christian revelation for its central assertion? or an idea, a concept taken over from earliest Christianity's Hellenistic environment? or some kind of syncretistic amalgam of many diverse aspirations of the religious spirit of the time for redemption from corruption and sin? *How and when did it first come to expression* – as a new and unheard of development in christology made by second- or third-generation Christians? or an explicit unfolding of something implicit in Christian faith in Jesus from the first, perhaps even Jesus' own claim for himself? *What precisely was it that was being expressed in these initial statements which now speak to us so clearly of incarnation?* What meaning would the original authors of these statements have intended their readers to hear? How would the first readers have understood them? In particular, since 'pre-existence' has been so much to the fore in the recent discussion, *What does it mean to speak of 'the pre-existence of Christ' in the NT?* – that the NT writers thought of Jesus himself as having existed in heaven before his life on earth, or of Jesus as the embodiment/incarnation of a heavenly being other than God, or of Jesus as God himself come to earth? or do such distinctions fail to appreciate the sophistication of their thought, or at least its difference from our own? Finally we might ask, Do the NT writings throw any light on the value or otherwise of using the word '*myth*' to describe the doctrine, whether in its beginnings or in its subsequent formulation?

These are the questions which motivate the present investigation. My interest in them began during my research for *Unity and Diversity in the New Testament* (1977), when I came to an increasing recognition of the centrality in first-century Christianity of a particular faith in Christ – that the 'unifying element' in earliest Christianity was

> the unity between the historical Jesus and the exalted Christ, that is to say, the conviction that the wandering charismatic preacher from Nazareth had ministered, died and been raised from the dead to bring God and man finally together, the recognition that the divine power through which they now worshipped and were encountered and accepted by God was one and the same person, Jesus, the man, the Christ, the Son of God, the Lord, the life-giving Spirit . . . Christianity begins from and finally depends on the conviction that in Jesus we still have a paradigm for man's relation to God and man's relation to man, that in Jesus' life, death and life out of death we see the clearest and fullest embodiment of divine grace, of creative wisdom and power, that ever achieved historical actuality, that the Christian is accepted by God and enabled to love God and his neighbour by that same grace which we now recognize to have the character of that same Jesus.[31]

In that book I could offer only a brief treatment of our present subject,[32] and already had in mind the need for a more extended study. Initially this was conceived as only one or two essays, on Christ and Wisdom and Christ and Adam. But the publication of *The Myth of God Incarnate* and the controversy it aroused soon led me to the conclusion that a much fuller and more careful investigation of the whole area was called for.

The range of material to be covered is fairly clear and can readily be grouped under different headings. We can scarcely avoid analysing the Son of God and Logos/Word language, the two most important categories in the classic patristic formulations. Hamerton-Kelly's monograph (above p. 3) reminds us that 'Son of Man' cannot be ignored. Several of the contributors to the current debate clearly think that Jesus as 'the Man intended by God' is the key to the whole (see the quotations on pp. 4f.), so that New Man or Last Adam offers another heading. Lampe in particular points to the relation between Jesus and the Spirit of God, or God as Spirit, as a further area (above p. 4). And most previous investigations in this area have suggested that Wisdom christology is the strongest antecedent to a full blown incarnation christology.[33]

We start with '*the Son of God*'. 'Son of God' language was always prominent in early Christian talk of Jesus and before long (fourth century) established itself as the central and decisive christological title. In addition, as we shall see, it offers a better hope than the other prominent post-Easter ascriptions of providing some sort of link and continuity with Jesus' own self-understanding. So our initial question is, What did the first Christians (and Jesus himself?) mean when they spoke of Jesus as God's son, or Son of God, or the Son of the Father? Did this description or title always imply the idea of incarnation – that Jesus was the incarnation of a heavenly (pre-existent) Son of God? – or did the thought of incarnation only enter into or grow out of the title after it had been used of Jesus for some time? (ch. II). From Son of God we turn to *Son of Man*. Not only do the two phrases go naturally together (Son of God and son of man), but the 'one like a son of man' in Dan. 7.13 seems to provide us with just such a heavenly figure, and in I Enoch the Son of Man seems to be clearly pre-existent. Since Jesus was obviously identified *as* the Son of Man, and with reference to Dan. 7.13 in earliest Christian tradition, can we not conclude straightforwardly that Jesus was identified *with* a heavenly individual who therefore (by implication) had descended from heaven and become incarnate in or as Jesus? (ch. III). The discussion of Son of Man leads naturally to a discussion of *Adam* (since both 'son of man' and *adam* in Hebrew idiom and language mean 'man'). Here we have the most plausible evidence that the Gnostic redeemer myth was rooted in part at least in a fairly widespread pre-Christian speculation concerning the first Man. Should the association between Adam and Christ within the NT be interpreted accordingly (Christ as the Heavenly or Prototype Man come to earth)? or should we interpret the Adam christology present in the NT differently? (ch. IV).

From descriptions or titles which might refer to heavenly beings we turn to heavenly beings as such. Angels were often conceived as intermediaries in Jewish thought at the time of Jesus. And since '*angel*' was a very broad category, might it be the case that the doctrine of the incarnation began as an assessment of the risen Christ in such angelic categories? More plausible candidates present themselves in what appear to be divine intermediary figures who in Jewish thought were less easily distinguishable from God himself. The *Spirit of God* – Jesus was understood by the NT writers as a man inspired by the Spirit. But where does the language of 'inspiration' become less appropriate and language of 'incarnation' become more appropriate? (ch. V). The *Wisdom of God* – that Jesus was very early on described in terms drawn from pre-Christian speculation concerning divine Wisdom is the nearest thing we have to a major consensus in this whole area. What was the significance of this Wisdom language when used of Jesus? Should we not simply say that Christ was identified as pre-existent Wisdom? Or more boldly that Christ was understood to be the incarnation of heavenly Wisdom come to earth? (ch. VI). The *Word of God* – next to 'Son of God' the divine 'Logos' is the most prominent title in the patristic discussions which shaped the classic statements on the Trinity and the incarnation. The concept *logos* (word) was also prominent from the earliest days of Christian writing. But how soon can we speak of a Logos-christology? Is the most important single NT statement in this whole investigation ('the Word became flesh' – John 1.14) a new departure taken by the prologue to John's Gospel, or simply an epigrammatic crystallization of what was already firmly rooted in the pre-Johannine literature and thought? (ch. VII). With the Logos incarnate who already in the Fourth Gospel is the Son of the Father we have come full circle and conclusions can be drawn (ch. VIII).

I should explain at once that this division of the material is somewhat arbitrary – necessarily so, because inevitably so: any analysis of complex thought or profound claim from a perspective nineteen centuries removed in time and culture is bound to be arbitrary in some degree. But the alternative methods of proceeding, such as examining our available evidence (Christian, pre-Christian and non-Christian) in chronological order or in some geographical sequence, would have resulted in equally arbitrary ordering of the evidence and almost certainly have produced a much more ungainly and confusing discussion. I am also aware that my proposed division of the material involves the serious danger of compartmentalizing the discussion overmuch – the danger, for example, of drawing conclusions regarding the Son of God and Son of Man language without taking into account the subsequent discussion of Wisdom – the danger, in other words, of forgetting that these different formulations would not have been independent of each other in much of the theologizing of the time, but would simply have been different facets of more complex and interlocking ways of assessing the significance of Jesus.[34] Mindful of this danger I have tried to let the different chapters interact with each other even when it meant assuming the conclusions of later paragraphs in the earlier, and in the final overview in chapter VIII we will be able to step back and see more clearly the overall pattern formed by the interweaving of the different threads already examined in individual detail. .

Three more preliminary remarks are probably called for. First, I have not attempted to define 'incarnation' at the outset. This neglect is deliberate. There is considerable risk that any such definition would pre-set the terms and categories of the investigation and prevent the NT authors speaking to us in their own terms. He who defines too closely what he is looking for at the start of a NT study in most cases will find it soon enough, but usually in his wake will be left elements which were ignored because they were not quite what he was looking for, and material and meaning will often have been squeezed out of shape in order to fit the categories prescribed at the outset. This danger has not always been successfully avoided in the recent investigations of 'pre-existence' in the NT. Or again, terms whose current technical meaning owes most to later developments and clarifications can be too readily superimposed upon the first-century material and hinder rather than help us in trying to understand the meaning intended by these writings. This danger, of *confusing* rather than *clarifying* the historical analysis, is present in a too ready use of terms like 'incarnation', 'myth', 'hypostasis' and 'adoptionist' in exegeting the NT. My concern has been all the time, so far as it is possible, *to let the NT writers speak for themselves, to understand their words as they would have intended, to hear them as their first readers would have heard them*, and thus to let their own understanding(s) of Christ emerge, and in particular their own concept(s) of 'incarnation' take its (their) own shape. If we are serious in our quest for the origins of the doctrine of the incarnation we must let the NT evidence speak in its own terms and dictate its own patterns. My description of our subject matter as 'an inquiry into the origins of the doctrine of the incarnation' is to be understood therefore as indicating the *area* of our inquiry, not as positing any particular definition of incarnation or presupposing any particular statement of 'the doctrine of the incarnation'.[35]

Secondly, what follows is a fairly restricted inquiry with limited aims. It is not a philosophical essay on the concept of incarnation as such. I am well aware of at least some of the wider issues which have been involved more or less from the beginning (not only since the Enlightenment or in the present century). But I could not hope to tackle them in sufficient depth or with sufficient rigour. The problem of how it is possible to think of God or the Son of God become man cannot be discussed independently of the problems of how to think of God, how to conceive of personality, how to conceptualize the relation between spirit and matter, between 'time' and 'eternity'. Nor is what follows intended as an exercise in dogmatic theology, although I may say that my respect for the patristic formulations and creeds has grown as my research proceeded. In neither of these areas have I sufficient expertise to handle the issues involved. The following study is simply *a historical investigation into how and in what terms the doctrine of the incarnation first came to expression*, an endeavour to understand in its original context the language which initially enshrined the doctrine of the incarnation or out of which the doctrine grew. By this I mean that the following investigation is primarily a NT study. Other literature both earlier and later will of course be extensively used. To understand the language of the NT in its original intention naturally involves asking where that language came from, what its background was, how it was being understood in the wider usage of that time – not, I should perhaps add, because the wider usage will necessarily determine its meaning in the NT, but because without awareness of the historical context of usage we will be unable to enter into the thought world of the time and so be unable to grasp the nuances of the NT usage, to hear what the first readers were intended to hear. Nevertheless, whatever light we may or may not shed on other Christian and non-Christian writings the primary aim will always be to elucidate the meaning of the relevant material within the NT itself.

It follows, thirdly, that the reader should not engage with *Christology in the Making* in the hope of finding either a defence of or an attack on any specific view of the incarnation. To answer the questions outlined on pp. 5f. above will not necessarily clarify the classic credal statements on the incarnation and will almost certainly not resolve the wider issues mentioned in the preceding paragraph. I do not pretend that answering these questions will necessarily make the doctrine of the incarnation any more or any less believable, any more or any less thinkable for twentieth-century man. But to know and grasp what it was that the first two or three generations of Christians believed concerning Jesus in its own terms and in the context of their own times cannot be unimportant and may shed much light on the why and how of the doctrine which has been so central in Christianity. And for those who like myself find the definition of Christianity more clearly provided by the NT than by the creeds of Catholic Christendom the answers to these questions will have a critical bearing on faith itself. But all should bear in mind that truly to hear the NT writers speaking in their own terms requires that the listener be open to the possibility that some of his preconceived ideas will be challenged and have to be rejected even when others are confirmed.

Finally I should perhaps say that I am all too conscious of the daunting nature even of the limited task I have set myself, and of my own inadequacy when confronted with the multiplicity and diversity of the evidence involved, not to mention the voluminous secondary literature. I have occasionally wondered whether it would be wiser to hold the material back and to reassess it again after a gap of several years. But the current debate shows how necessary it is for someone to work through the evidence in detail, and I am sufficiently confident that my conclusions have relevance and significance which goes beyond the current debate. So I decided to let the material go forward, warts and all. I cannot hope to have provided a final or definitive treatment, simply a contribution to the study of Christian beginnings, an attempt to shed a little more light on an area where weighty assertions and far-reaching claims are too often too casually made. I certainly cannot hope to have avoided errors in judgment and misplaced emphases (no doubt kindly readers will draw my attention to them in due course), but perhaps some of the material collected here, or the perspective presented here, or individual exegetical findings and conclusions will help prevent more serious errors and emphases more wildly misplaced.

II

THE SON OF GOD

§2. INTRODUCTION

> We believe . . . in one Lord Jesus Christ, the Son of God, begotten from the
> Father, only begotten, that is, from the substance of the Father, God from
> God, light from light, true God from true God, begotten not made, of one
> substance with the Father, through whom all things came into being, things
> in heaven and things on earth, who because of us men and because of our
> salvation became incarnate, becoming man . . . .[1]

None of the other titles or ways of assessing Christ which we will be
examining has had both the historical depth and lasting power of 'Son
of God'. Insofar as any titles can be said to have been part of Jesus' own
teaching 'Son of Man' probably has the stronger claim than 'Son of God'.
But whatever high significance 'Son of Man' had in apocalyptic contexts
in the first-century Christian texts, for second century Christian writers
it had come to denote simply Christ's human sonship in contrast to his
divine sonship (see below p. 65). And in the controversies of the third,
fourth and fifth centuries it was the understanding of Christ as Son of
God which provided the absolutely crucial category in defining the nature
of Christ's pre-existent deity, with 'Son' replacing 'Logos' as the more
suitable language in formulating the relationships of the divine persons
within the Godhead (see also below pp. 213f.), and the definition of
'sonship' growing steadily more precise – not merely 'son of God', but
God's only Son (μονογενής), a term rescued from the Gnostics by Irenaeus;[2] 'begotten not made', one of the central thrusts made at Nicaea
against Arius; 'begotten before all ages', an assertion of the eternal generation of the Son which became a regular feature of the post-Nicene
creeds. These credal formulations have stamped a clear and lasting
impression on Christian thought of subsequent generations up to and
including the present day. So much so that it is generally taken for

granted, axiomatic, part of the basic definition of what Christianity is, that to confess Jesus as 'the Son of God' is to confess his deity, and very easily assumed that to say 'Jesus is the Son of God' means and always has meant that Jesus is the pre-existent, second person of the Trinity, who 'for us men and our salvation became incarnate'.

The title 'Son of God' is therefore of inescapable importance for our study. An inquiry into the origins of the doctrine of the incarnation can hardly ignore it. And the questions which have to be asked are fairly obvious: Did the Son of God language when used of Jesus always have this connotation of denoting deity, of signifying pre-existent divinity? If so, why was it applied by the earliest Christians to Jesus? – what was it about Jesus that caused the first disciples to call him 'Son of God'? If not, how soon did the Son of God confession come to bear this significance, and why? – was the new significance already implicit in the earlier confession, simply an unfolding of what always had been true of Christ, or was it a new departure, a claim made about Jesus which his first disciples would have been unwilling or not yet ready to affirm?

Our task is clear. We will look first at the wider use of the term 'son of God' at the time of Jesus and the first Christians. This will enable us to answer the crucial question: *What would those who first used this language about Jesus expect their hearers and readers to understand by the phrase?* This does not of course exclude the possibility that the first Christians (or Jesus himself) intended to fill the phrase with new or distinctive meaning. But it will help to make us aware of the hearers' and readers' 'context of meaning', and so enable us the better to detect the occasions when a speaker or writer intended to adapt or transform the phrase in a particular way to make a distinctive claim for Jesus. With this in mind we will go on to look more closely at the question of whether Jesus spoke or thought of himself as the Son of God, and then at the NT passages in which the language of sonship is used of Jesus, as far as possible in chronological order.

§3. THE FIRST-CENTURY 'CONTEXT OF MEANING'

§3.1   What would it have meant to their hearers when the first Christians called Jesus 'son of God'? All the time in a study like this we must endeavour to attune our listening to hear with the ears of the first Christians' contemporaries. We must attempt the exceedingly difficult task of shutting out the voices of early Fathers, Councils and dogmaticians down the centuries, in case they drown the earlier voices, in case the earlier voices were saying something different, in case they intended their words to speak with different force to their hearers. Equally we must beware of assuming that patterns and parallels which have become suggestive or apparent to us from the vantage point of twentieth-century History of Religions research were visible or intentional within the first century itself. Where language and ideas are in a process of development we who can see the end result of the process should beware of reading that resultant meaning into the earlier stages of the development. What may be 'obvious' to the twentieth-century scholar who can gather together material from all sides and periods of the ancient world may have been by no means obvious or intended by the NT writer whose perspective was limited by the range of conceptualizations open to him within his own particular (and limited) historical context.

Consequently we must ask, what did the phrase 'son of God' mean at the time it was first used of Jesus? How broad or how precise was the idea of divine sonship in the first half of the first century AD? In particular, did the phrase 'Son of God' carry the same significance in the first century as it does in the later creeds? Our problem here is illustrated by the otherwise unimportant issue of whether we should capitalize the noun 'son' in reference to Jesus from the beginning. Such questions we can hope to answer only by listening to the way(s) in which the language of divine sonship was used at the time of the first Christians. Only then will we have any idea what those listening to Paul and the others would have understood by the phrase 'son of God'. Only then will we have any hope of determining whether Paul and the others intended to assume an already widely familiar meaning or whether they intended to invest the phrase with new significance. We will look first at the range of meanings embraced by 'son of God', and then note briefly the ranges of application of the words 'divine' and 'god', since concepts of divinity and divine sonship clearly do and in the past did overlap to a considerable extent.

§3.2 *Son of God* was a phrase widely used in the ancient world. The meaning of the phrase in Jewish and Greek writings has been surveyed several times in recent years, so nothing more than a summary at this point is necessary.[3]

Those familiar with the wider circles of Hellenistic culture would know that (1) some of the legendary *heroes* of Greek myth were called sons of God – in particular, Dionysus and Heracles were sons of Zeus by mortal mothers.[4] (2) *Oriental rulers*, especially Egyptian, were called sons of God. In particular, the Ptolemies in Egypt laid claim to the title 'son of Helios' from the fourth century BC onwards,[5] and at the time of Jesus 'son of god' (υἱὸς θεοῦ) was already widely used in reference to Augustus.[6] (3) *Famous philosophers* also, like Pythagoras and Plato, were sometimes spoken of as having been begotten by a god (Apollo).[7] (4) And in Stoic philosophy

Zeus, the supreme being, was thought of as father of *all men* (since all shared in divine reason),[8] as we are reminded by the quotation from the Greek philosopher Aratus (third century BC) in Paul's speech at Athens – 'For we are indeed his offspring' (Acts 17.28).[9]

Even those whose cultural horizons were more limited to the literature and traditions of Judaism would be aware that 'son of God' could be used in several ways:[10] (5) *angels or heavenly beings* – 'the sons of God' being members of the heavenly council under Yahweh the supreme God (Gen. 6.2,4; Deut. 32.8; Job 1.6–12; 2.1–6; 38.7; Ps. 29.1; 89.6; Dan. 3.25); (6) regularly of *Israel or Israelites* – 'Israel is my first-born son' (Ex. 4.22; Jer. 31.9; Hos. 11.1; see also e.g. Deut. 14.1; Isa. 43.6; Hos. 1.10); (7) *the king*, so called only a handful of times in the OT – II Sam. 7.14 (taken up in I Chron. 17.13; 22.10; 28.6), Ps. 2.7 and 89.26f.[11]

In intertestamental Judaism these uses of 'son of God' were developed. (8) In I Enoch angels are called 'sons of heaven' and 'sons of the God of heaven' (13.8; 106.5; also 69.4–5; 71.1).[12] (9) Philo in his unique blend of Stoic and Jewish thought calls God 'the supreme Father of gods and men' (*Spec. Leg.* II.165; *Opif.* 84) and frequently speaks of God as Father in relation to *creation* (e.g. *Heres* 236; *Spec. Leg.* III.189), not hesitating to call both the cosmos God's Son (*Immut.* 31f.; *Spec. Leg.* I.96) and the Logos 'God's first-born' (*Conf.* 146; *Som.* I.215).[13] (10) Not only is Israel as a whole called 'son of God' (Wisd. 9.7; 18.13; Jub. 1.24f.; Ps. Sol. 17.30), but *individual Israelites*, specifically the righteous man (Wisd. 2.13,16,18; 5.5; Sir. 4.10; 51.10; Ps.Sol. 13.8), the Maccabean martyrs ('children of heaven' – II Macc. 7.34), or those who do what is good and pleasing to nature (*Conf.* 145–7; *Spec. Leg.* I.318). In the Hellenistic Jewish romance Joseph and Asenath (late first century AD? perhaps earlier), Joseph is called 'the son of God' by the Egyptian Asenath (and other non-Jews) because of his great beauty (6.2–6; 13.10; 21.3).[14] (11) In particular, attention has recently been drawn to two Jewish *charismatics* remembered in rabbinic literature – one Honi, the 'circle-drawer' (first century BC), who according to tradition prayed to God 'like a son of the house' and had the reputation of enjoying a relationship of intimate sonship with God which ensured the success of his petitions (Taan. 3.8);[15] the other Hanina ben Dosa, from the generation following Jesus, whom a heavenly voice was said to have addressed as 'my son' (bTaan. 24b).[16] (12) Finally, the Dead Sea Scrolls have thrown up three interesting fragments: one speaks of the time 'when (God?) will have begotten the *Messiah* among them' (1QSa 2.11f.);[17] in the second, the hoped for Davidic Messiah is described specifically in the language of divine sonship using II Sam. 7.11–14 ('he shall be my son') and possibly associating it with Ps. 2.7 (4QFlor. 1.10-*fin.*);[18] the other says of one who apparently is to be a mighty king (Messiah?) – 'He shall be hailed (as) the Son of God, and they shall call him Son of the most High (4QpsDan Aª; cf. Test. Levi 4.2).[19]

The degree of similarity between the use of 'son of God' within Jewish writings and its use in the wider Hellenistic world is noticeable. In particular, it was obviously a widespread belief or convention that the king was a son of God either as descended from God or as representing God to his people. So too both inside and outside Judaism human beings could be called 'sons of God' either as somehow sharing the divine mind or as being specially favoured by God or pleasing to God. We shall delay further comment till we have cast our net more widely.

§3.3 Insofar as 'son of God' contains some affirmation of divinity or of relation to deity it obviously overlaps with two other words of similar connotation – the adjective *'divine'* and the noun *'god'*. Does their use in application to men shed any light on the complementary term 'son of God'?

(a) For nearly half a century the concept of the *'divine man'* has attracted important sections of NT scholarship,[20] with the focus in the most recent phase falling principally on the link between divinity and miracle working – the 'divine man' as one who speaks and acts with overwhelming power and thus demonstrates his divinity. The discussion however has been something of a wild goose chase since there is no clear or single concept of a 'divine man' in our period, as more recent and more careful analyses have shown.[21] In broad terms 'divine' evidently meant something or someone related in some way to God or the gods; and where the heavenly was thought to be in continued interaction with the earthly its application to human beings covered the full range of this interaction. Thus heroes were frequently called 'divine' in Homer,[22] and from Augustus onwards 'divine' became a fixed term in the imperial cult, 'the divine Caesar'.[23] At the other end of the spectrum it could mean simply 'pious', 'godly'.[24] In between it was regularly used in the sense of 'extraordinary, outstanding' (of men specially favoured or gifted by God or the gods or heaven) or 'inspired' (as a prophet).[25] For example, Josephus's most regular use of the adjective seems to fall within this middle range of meaning (*Bell.* IV.625; *Ant.* II.232; III.180; VIII.34,187,234,243; X.35,241; XVIII.64).[26] Since 'divine' is not used in the NT of Jesus (or anyone else) we need not pursue our inquiry here any further. The point to be noted is simply that when the adjective 'divine' was used of individuals at the time of Jesus and the first Christians its range of application was somewhat similar to that of 'son of God'.

(b) It will occasion little surprise when we realize that *'god'* also was used with a similar range of application to particular men. Once again we find that heroes were sometimes called 'god';[27] and that 'god' was a regular title of emperors and kings from Hellenistic times onwards[28] – we may think, for example, of Antiochus Epiphanes (= God made manifest).[29] Similarly, as with 'divine', 'god' was quite often used of famous or important individuals – again philosophers in particular;[30] for example, Empedocles says, 'I go about among you an immortal god, no more mortal',[31] and in Philostratus Apollonius defends himself against the emperor Domitian on the count of being called a god by arguing that 'every man who is considered good is honoured with the title of "god" ' (*Apollonius of Tyana* VIII.4). Rather more striking is the fact that the king or judges in Israel seem on one or two occasions to be called 'gods' even within the OT itself (Ps. 45.6; 82.6; cf. Ex. 21.6; 22.8; Isa. 9.6f.) – a significant factor when we recall how these Psalm passages are used in reference to Jesus in Heb. 1.8 and John 10.34f. respectively.[32] More striking still is the degree to which despite its monotheism Judaism in the first century AD and thereafter could accommodate talk of some of its great figures of the past in terms approaching deity. In particular, III Enoch has been cited:[33] in III Enoch 3–16 Enoch is taken up to heaven and becomes Metatron, the Prince of the Presence, even being called 'the lesser Yahweh' (12.5 – with reference to Ex. 23.21, 'For my name is in him');[34] but the date of the book is uncertain and is probably later than our period;[35] and although the heresy of calling Metatron a second 'divine power in heaven' is traced back to Elisha ben Abuya (*c.* 110–135), it may reflect Christian influence of one sort or another (see below pp. 80f.).[36] The passages which do come from the first century AD or earlier relate chiefly to Moses. Josephus twice reports the possibility of speculation that Moses had been taken or had returned to the deity (τὸ θεῖον) (*Ant.* III.96f.; IV.326; cf. Philo, *Mos.* II.288). Philo expounds Ex. 4.16 and 7.1 in several places and does not scruple to say such things of Moses as 'He (God) appointed him as god' (*Sac.* 9), or of one as 'no longer man but God' (*Prob.* 43; see also *Som.* II.189; *Mos.* I.158; *Qu.Ex.* II.29).[37] And in the 'Moses Romance' of Artapanus (first or second century BC) Moses is said to have been deemed worthy to be honoured like a god and to have been named Hermes by the Egyptian priests (*Frag.* 3.6, in Eusebius, *Praep.Ev.* IX.27).[38]

§3.4   In the light of all this evidence what can we say about the context of meaning for the earliest Christian description of Jesus as 'son of God'? Several points call for comment by way of clarification.

(*a*) *The language of divine sonship and divinity was in widespread and varied use in the ancient world and would have been familiar to the contemporaries of Jesus, Paul and John in a wide range of applications.* When used in reference to individual human beings it could denote anything from a righteous or pious man, one who lived in close accord with the divine, to a heavenly

or semi-heavenly being, including on the way particularly kings and
rulers and especially wise or gifted or inspired men. We should not ignore
the fact that all three terms examined above ('son of God', 'divine', 'god')
had a similar breadth of reference. Our own modern speech is familiar
with the wide and sometimes casual application of a description like
'godly' or 'divine' ('he was absolutely divine'). But centuries of Christianity have made us hesitate to be quite so free in our use of 'son of God'
or 'god' when speaking of other men. What we must try to reckon with
is the fact that the contemporaries of the first Christians were not so
inhibited. *In the first century AD 'son of God' and 'god' were used much more
widely in reference to particular individuals than is the case today.*

(*b*) Granted this breadth of usage and a certain casualness in the
freedom with which this language was used, we should not assume that
all those who heard the first Christians speak of Jesus as 'son of God'
would necessarily hear or understand the same thing. We know from
Acts 14.11–13 and 28.6 how simple was the faith of many ordinary folk,
how ready they were to accept the stories of ancient heroes as factual
events, how readily they saw in an extraordinary event proof of another
man's deity.[39] But we know too that the more sophisticated, then as now,
thought little of such talk of deity, and could pour scorn on it as idle
speculation when they chose (note particularly Seneca's *Pumpkinification
of Claudius*, AD 54, and Lucian's *de morte Peregrini* 39–40).[40] *Talk of divine
sonship and divinity could be taken quite literally by some, and by others as a
sophisticated metaphor or an idle tale unworthy of respect.* Luke tells us how Paul
reacted to the superstition of the simple folk of Lystra (Acts 14.14–18),
and shows us a Paul who was familiar with the wider ranges of philosophical thought on the same subject (Acts 17.28f.). But we must always
remember to ask how sophisticated were the readers of his letters.

(*c*) If the distinction between simple and sophisticated hearers is potentially important, so too is the distinction between Jew and Gentile.
There is no question of a clear cut difference between 'Judaism' and
'Hellenism' in their respective talk of divine sonship and divinity. On the
contrary Jewish sources have shown almost as wide a range of usage as
non-Jewish. But it would be unfair to the evidence if we did not draw
attention to the fact that *Jewish writings tend to be more scrupulous and less free
in their attribution of divine sonship and divinity to men.* (1) In the OT itself
only the handful of texts referred to above (§3.2 (7)) clearly speak of an
individual as 'son of God' (the king), and on each occasion it is probable
that the language denotes legal legitimation rather than adoption, with
any suggestion of physical sonship deliberately excluded.[41] As for the
righteous man or the charismatic being a 'son of God' there is no suggestion in any of the texts in question of an individual man being thereby
somehow divinized. (2) Philo's language is the boldest, but he does

exercise a noticeable restraint in his description of individuals as 'sons of God' or 'divine', only rarely using either of historical persons.[42] Similarly we must notice that despite some extravagant language with regard to Moses, he is elsewhere quite clear that Ex. 4.16 and 7.1 ascribe deity to Moses only in a relative sense, of Moses in relation to Aaron and Pharaoh, of a wise man in relation to a foolish man, of mind in relation to mouth or soul (*Leg.All.* I.40; *Det.* 161f.; *Migr.* 84; *Mut.* 128), and the overall impression is that he deliberately refrained from interpreting the two Exodus passages literally.[43] Likewise it is significant that Artapanus and Josephus report talk of Moses' deification as a speculation or opinion held by *others* – as a speculation *ruled out* by Moses (Josephus, *Ant.* IV.326), as an opinion held by *Egyptian priests (Frag.* 3.6).[44] The point to be underlined is that *Jewish apologists in and before the first century AD could use extravagant language attributing deity in some sense to particular individuals and yet not intend it to be taken literally and without wishing to diminish the distinction between God and man.* It is only in the probably later text of III Enoch that this distinction becomes really threatened.

§3.5   Perhaps the most striking of all is the surprising absence within the range of materials surveyed above of the idea of a son of God or divine individual who descends from heaven to earth to redeem men such as might explain the rise of similar (sounding) language about Jesus particularly in the Fourth Gospel. We certainly have examples of men being exalted to divine status.[45] In respect to Jewish traditions the nearest equivalent belief not unnaturally focused on great figures of the past whose end was obscure – Moses and Elijah, Jeremiah, Enoch and Melchizedek.[46] But as we saw above, the Jewish authors who report such ideas about Moses are careful to distance themselves from them (p. 19 above). Similarly Elijah is never deified in Jewish or Christian thinking.[47] Jeremiah appears in II Macc. 15.13f. as a figure of heavenly majesty, but this is out of character with the normal Jewish interest in Jeremiah in our period.[48] Enoch is described as one transformed into angel-like form (Asc. Isa. 9.9; cf. Jub. 4.23; I Enoch 71.11; II Enoch 22.8), and is identified as the Son of Man in the Similitudes of Enoch (I Enoch 71.14; see below III n.64) and as Metatron in III Enoch, identifications which evidently gave rise to the heresy of the 'two powers' in rabbinic eyes (see above p. 17 and below pp. 80f.) – but in each case issues of dating make the material problematic for us to use (see above p. 17 and below pp. 77f.). And the appearance of Melchizedek in the Dead Sea Scrolls (11Q Melch.), in the role it would seem of captain of the heavenly hosts, possibly implies belief that Melchizedek had been exalted to angelic status, one of the archangels in heaven (cf. the role of Michael in 1QM 9.15f.; 17.6) (though see also below pp. 20f. and 152f.). But none of these provide us with a possible background to Christian belief in Jesus as Son of God come down from heaven. What other evidence is there?

We have examples of gods appearing in the guise of men, as in the legend of Baucis and Philemon (Ovid, *Metam.* VIII.626–721);[49] but again these hardly provide a precedent for us. Here too we can mention instances where men were taken for gods – Moses (above p. 17), Herod Agrippa (Acts 12.20–3; Josephus, *Ant.* XIX.343–50), Paul and Barnabas (Acts 14.8–18) – but at a level of popular superstition which Jews and Christians would not and did not approve (as the same passages make clear).[50] We have examples of men who are said by some to be offspring of a union between some god and a mortal woman (Dionysus, Heracles, Alexander the Great);[51] but this was foreign to Jewish thought and Jewish writers seem to have avoided the conception completely (including Philo, the Jewish writer most open on many points to Greek thought).[52] We have the idea of the king/pharaoh as the offspring of a god or indeed as the manifestation of a god on earth (above pp. 14f., 17); but this was probably merely conventional language (as indeed the similar Jewish talk may imply – above p. 18), and when it was taken too seriously by a king the Jewish reaction was strong (Dan. 11.36; cf. II Thess. 2.3–12). We even have talk which sounds like incarnation – in Plutarch Romulus speaks of 'the gods from whom I came' (Plutarch, *Lives: Romulus* 28.2), and Augustus is represented by Virgil as Apollo come to earth (*Eclogues* IV.6–10) and by Horace as Mercury descended in the guise of a man (*Odes* I.2.41–52);[53] but how seriously this sort of language was taken by the ancient world may be judged by Celsus's comment – 'O Jews and Christians, no god or son of god either came or will come down (to earth)' (Origen, *cont.Cels.* V.2).[54]

We come nearer the mark with Jewish angelology. As we shall see in chapter V, Jewish tradition was long familiar with the idea of angels appearing on earth, and in the literature of the period we have examples of archangels being sent to earth (e.g. Tob. 3.16f.; Joseph and Asenath 14–17; Test. Job. 2–5; Test. Abr. 7.3–17); but these are usually 'short-term visitors', messengers sent for a particular purpose,[55] and the narrators usually make it clear that they cannot be thought of as divine beings who have become human beings.[56] If 11QMelch. was thinking of the Melchizedek of Gen. 14 as an angel descended it was probably because the Genesis narrative invited the understanding of Melchizedek as such a short-term visitor (cf. Heb. 7.3 – but see further below pp. 152f.).[57] The suggestion that already the writer to the Hebrews thought of Melchizedek as 'a divine being in human form'[58] ('without mother' and 'without father' implying a superhuman origin) expresses the optimism of the earlier History of Religions School that it was possible to trace the origins of the Gnostic redeemer myth back to a pre-Christian

date (but see below ch. IV). These adjectives are better explained however by reference to the typically rabbinic exegetical principle (what is
not in the text, is not),[59] or, as we shall see, by recognizing some influence
from Philo or Philonic thought on Melchizedek as an embodiment or
allegorical expression of the Logos (see below pp. 53f.).[60] The only exception at this point seems to be the so-called Prayer of Joseph, which
speaks of an archangel (Israel) who became (incarnate as) the patriarch
Jacob; but this fragment is preserved only in Origen[61] and presupposes
a more developed ranking among the archangels[62] than we find elsewhere
in the first century AD (cf. and contrast the earlier formulations in Jub.
2.2; I Enoch 20; 61.10; and the relatively undeveloped angelology of the
Revelation of John), so that a date before the second century AD becomes
difficult to maintain. Of the other 'immortals' mentioned above (p. 19)
who could be conceived as descending (again) to earth from their exalted
role in heaven, only Elijah and Enoch come into question (particularly
I Enoch 90.31; Apoc. Elijah 3.90–9), though here again the interpretation
of the material and its possible influence at a sufficiently early stage to
affect our inquiry is very debatable.[63] We shall have to consider this
whole range of material and its bearing on our subject more fully below
(pp. 92–5 and 152–4).

There is also the possibility that the earliest of the Gnostic redeemers,
Simon and Menander, provide a sufficiently early parallel.[64] But though
the individuals are from the first century it is much less certain that the
teaching which saw any of them as heavenly redeemers descended to
earth goes back so far.[65] The strongest evidence of such a first-century
belief concerning Simon is the striking phrase in Acts 8.10, according to
which Simon was hailed by the Samaritans as 'the power of God which
is called Great'. Behind Luke's description probably lies a claim by Simon
himself, 'I am the Great Power' (Μεγάλη Δύναμις) – a claim presumably
to be the highest god (cf. Mark 14.62).[66] However it by no means necessarily follows that pre-existence is implied by this phrase:[67] it may be,
alternatively, that Simon laid claim to be possessed by the Great Power
at moments of high inspiration or in order to work magic (if he was
indeed a magician – cf. Acts 8.11),[68] or indeed that he had been apoth-
eosed into the Great Power at some point in his career (see above n.45;
cf. Acts 12.22; Suetonius, *Twelve Caesars* IV.22 – Gaius Caligula). The
wider question of the Gnostic redeemer myth we will return to in chapter
IV.

There remain the strongest candidates and the claims that Jewish
writers had already embraced the thought of a pre-existent Messiah or
Son of Man, or of pre-existent divine intermediaries between God and
man, particularly Spirit, Wisdom and Word, any of whose missions to
earth might conceivably have implied or given rise to the idea of incar-

nation. In every case the discussion of these possibilities is too complex to be summarized here and final conclusions must await the findings of subsequent chapters. In the meantime, having cleared the ground somewhat in preparation for the main investigation we can at least draw the provisional conclusion that *there is little or no good evidence from the period prior to Christianity's beginnings that the Ancient Near East seriously entertained the idea of a god or son of god descending from heaven to become a human being in order to bring men salvation, except perhaps at the level of popular pagan superstition.*[69]

§3.6   *Conclusion.* Our aim has been to discover as far as possible the context of meaning within which earliest Christian talk of Jesus as God's son would have been understood by those who first heard it. Our study of the terms 'son of God', 'divine' and 'god' when used of men, has shown how broad was the overlap, or how extensive the interaction between the realms of God and men in the thought of the time. None of these terms in themselves indicate where the individual so described stands within that interaction. They all denote one who is related to God (the divine) in some way – that is quite clear. But whether the relationship is of an individual who lived in close accord with God (specially favoured by God, specially pleasing to God), or of something much more (embodying deity in some way), that is not clear. *Certainly 'son of God' as applied to Jesus would not necessarily have carried in and of itself the connotation of deity.* So too the degree of caution observed by those from within the Jewish tradition, including those most influenced by the wider categories of Hellenistic philosophy, and the lack of pre-Christian parallels which might have provided a source for the Christian doctrine of incarnation (heavenly redeemers descending to earth), should make us equally cautious about offering hasty hypotheses concerning Hellenistic influence on the first (Jewish) Christians. With this fuller awareness of the context of meaning in mind we can now turn to examine the particular application of the language of divine sonship to Jesus.

§4. JESUS' SENSE OF SONSHIP

§4.1   Did Jesus speak or think of himself as God's Son? Can we even hope to answer this question? And if the answer both times is Yes, what significance would it have? – son of God in what sense? – as a heavenly being who had taken earthly form? as the Davidic Messiah? as a 'righteous man'? as a charismatic teacher or healer? or what?

The whole issue of Jesus' self-consciousness and its significance is one which has remained at the forefront of NT christological study more or less throughout the past two centuries. This long running debate gives us a fair idea of the problems involved in any modern attempt to speak of Jesus' self-consciousness or sense of sonship in particular. So it is worth pausing briefly to remind ourselves of the course of the debate and how it has highlighted the problems. The debate itself can roughly be categorized as falling into three or four broad and overlapping phases. During the *first* phase we may say that the issue was posed primarily in terms of *Jesus' consciousness of divinity*, with the classical two natures doctrine of Christ's person providing the starting point for the debate. The problem had always been how to conceive of the two natures coexisting in one person. But when in the nineteenth century it was reformulated in terms of Jesus' self-consciousness the problem became all the sharper: could a single personality combine a truly human consciousness with a consciousness of pre-existent divinity? Two classic treatments from this period offered alternative answers. F. D. E. Schleiermacher felt that the answer must be negative and proceeded to offer a more subtle restatement in terms of Jesus' consciousness of God operative in him.[70] H. P. Liddon however found no difficulty in reaffirming the classic position in terms of Jesus' consciousness, stating boldly, for example, that in John 8.58 'He unveils a consciousness of Eternal Being'.[71]

The striking feature about these treatments is that both expositions were dependent on the Fourth Gospel to a critical degree,[72] and where Liddon's position continues to be maintained, in conservative circles or popular apologetics, the same dependence on the Fourth Gospel is still evident.[73] But the heirs of Schleiermacher could not follow his path. Already before his *Life of Jesus* was published (the lectures were delivered in 1832) the Fourth Gospel was becoming more and more suspect as a straightforward historical source for discovering Jesus' self-consciousness, and with the growing recognition of its theological character,[74] attempts to rediscover Jesus' own self-estimate had to shut themselves up more and more to the first three Gospels. This move away from the Fourth Gospel as a source for determining Jesus' self-consciousness marks the beginning of the *second* phase, during which the characteristic focus of discussion became *Jesus' messianic consciousness*. Some denied that Jesus had any consciousness of messiahship, but the great bulk of Liberal Protestant scholarship in the latter decades of the nineteenth century and early decades of the twentieth affirmed Jesus' messianic consciousness with confidence.[75] During this phase the typical questions were whether the development of Jesus' self-consciousness could now be traced – with the most significant moments usually identified as his baptism, the reaction consequent upon the failure of his initial hope ('the Galilean spring time'), and Peter's confession at Caesarea Philippi – and whether Jesus regarded himself as Messiah or rather as Messiah designate.

As undue reliance on the historicity of the Fourth Gospel marks the first phase, so the assumption that Markan priority implies the reliability of Markan chronology marks the second. So too it has been the increasing abandonment of that assumption, consequent upon the work of W. Wrede and the early form critics, which has marked the emergence of the *third* phase. Characteristic of this phase has been a growing recognition of the fragmentariness of our source material,[76] and of the difficulty if not impossibility of uncovering a historical individual's self-consciousness – how can we at 2,000 years remove in time and culture put ourselves in the shoes of, enter into the mind of one from whom we have nothing direct and most of whose sayings are uncertain as to original context and form?[77] Consequently there has been an extensive retreat from the idea that Jesus entertained an explicit christology, and a widespread feeling that even if we could talk of 'consciousness of divinity' or 'messianic consciousness' we could never hope to uncover it by historical-critical methods.[78] At best, where the quest of the historical Jesus has not continued to be seen as a wild goose chase, scholarly inquiry has tended to focus on the possibility of discerning an *implicit christology* in the words and deeds of Jesus,[79] or, in one formulation of the issue, on the possibility of speaking of Jesus' self-*understanding* rather than self-consciousness.[80]

We should perhaps distinguish a *fourth* phase emerging most clearly in the past few years and marked by something of a swing back of the pendulum and an attempt by some scholars to reclaim older positions. Thus, for example, whereas the Bultmann circle has largely dominated the post World War II discussion in this area, we now find P. Stuhlmacher, pupil and successor of E. Käsemann at Tübingen, readily affirming the authenticity of such crucial logia as Mark 10.45 and 14.62 as words of the historical Jesus and (in retreat from an earlier conclusion) maintaining the historicity of Matt. 11.2–6/Luke 7.18–23.[81] Outside the Bultmann circle the continued advocacy of J. Jeremias has succeeded in bringing back the question of sonship to the centre of the debate:[82] his demonstration that addressing God as *abba* (Father) was a characteristic and distinctive feature of Jesus' prayer-life has been widely accepted even though with qualifications in many instances.[83] Already in 1958 V. Taylor was building on Jeremias's early work in his NT christology, with chapter headings including 'The Divine Consciousness of Jesus' and 'The Emergence of the Divine Consciousness of Jesus'.[84] At the same time increasing attempts have been made to recall the testimony of the Fourth Gospel to the discussion; its value as a historical source has been reasserted,[85] its discourses have been brought forward again as yielding authentic utterances of the historical Jesus,[86] and the recent attempts to argue for its composition within the first generation of Christianity (pre-AD 70)[87] will doubtless provide some encouragement in this direction.

The discussions of preceding decades thus set our agenda. We must clarify, first, whether we today can hope to know or say anything about Jesus' self-consciousness; second, whether the evidence of the Synoptic Gospels will allow us to draw any firm conclusions about Jesus' consciousness of sonship in particular; and third, whether we can after all draw in the evidence of John's Gospel at this point.

§4.2   Can the historian hope to penetrate into the self-consciousness (or self-understanding) of a historical individual? The answer must be in the affirmative, otherwise history would be nothing more than a dreary catalogue of dates and documentation. It is because the historian experiences his study as a real encounter with vital personalities that his task is so exciting. He can inquire after motivation and intention, after the meaningfulness of words, acts and events for the individuals involved at the time, and, if he has adequate source material, a critical eye and a sensitive ear, can hope for positive answers. He can never be certain that he is right, but he would not be worthy of his profession if he did not expect to provide a plausible and convincing character study of his chosen subjects.

In many instances there will be particular utterances or comments of particular individuals which will provide as it were a key which unlocks the mystery of the historical personality, a clue to his or her character, a window into his or her soul. I think for example of such revealing comments made by Louis XIV, the epitome of the absolute monarch. In his *Memoirs* (ET 1806) he writes:

> In my heart I prefer fame above all else, even life itself . . . In exercising a totally divine function here on earth, we must appear incapable of turmoils which could debase it.

The modern historian reading such a statement quite legitimately concludes: 'In genuine faith Louis viewed himself as God's representative on earth and considered all disobedience and rebellion to be sinful'.[88] Equally revealing is Churchill's description of the night in May 1940, following his invitation by the king to form a Government:

> As I went to bed at about 3 a.m. I was conscious of a profound sense of relief. At last I had the authority to give directions over the whole scene. I felt as if I were walking with destiny, and that all my past life had been but a preparation for this hour and for this trial.[89]

Now, of course, both examples are taken from the personal writings of the individual concerned, and in the case of Jesus we have nothing like that, only sayings passed down to us at best second or third hand. The point which does emerge however is that *statements of historical personalities can so embody their feelings and a consciousness (or conviction) as to their own significance, even if only at a particular point in their lives, that we today can know* *something of their feelings and sense something of that consciousness through these* *same statements.* So the question we must ask is whether we have any such statements or utterances attributed to Jesus which go back to him. In my judgment the answer is almost certainly Yes. For example, there are those sayings of Jesus which express what Bultmann himself called 'the immediacy of eschatological consciousness' (Matt. 11.5f./Luke 7.22f.; Matt. 13.16f./Luke 10.23f.; Matt. 12.41f./Luke 11.31f.; Luke 12.54–6),[90] and in subsequent chapters we shall meet more which embody a con- sciousness of eschatological power (e.g. Matt. 12.28/Luke 11.20) and authority ('Amen', 'But I say . . .').[91] The question which confronts us in the present chapter is whether we have any of Jesus' actual words which embody a 'sense of sonship', or even a consciousness of *divine* sonship. A not inconsiderable problem of course is how we might expect to recognize such a consciousness of divine sonship, of being divine, should we be confronted with a saying which expresses it. That is hardly a problem we could hope to resolve in the abstract, if at all. It is however a question which we must bear in mind as we turn to examine actual sayings of Jesus.

§4.3   Will the evidence of the Synoptic Gospels allow us to draw any firm conclusions about Jesus' consciousness of sonship, about Jesus' un- derstanding of his relationship with God? I have examined this question in detail in an earlier study[92] and here need do little more than summarize my earlier findings and carry forward the discussion on the basis of these earlier detailed arguments.

(*a*) First, as Jeremias has shown, *abba* (Father) was a characteristic feature of Jesus' prayers. This mannerism is attested in all five strata of the Gospel tradition, it is a consistent feature of his recorded prayers and of his teaching on prayer, and in the only two references to an *abba*-prayer in the literature of the earliest Christians (Rom. 8.15f.; Gal. 4.6) it is referred back to the Spirit of the Son, the Spirit who gives believers a share in his sonship.[93] It is excessively difficult therefore to avoid the conclusion that *it was a characteristic of Jesus' approach to God in prayer that* *he addressed God as 'abba'* and that *the earliest Christians retained an awareness* *of this fact in their own use of 'abba'.*[94]

(*b*) Second, Jesus' habit of addressing God as 'abba' distinguished Jesus in some degree from his contemporaries.[95] Here the argument is more difficult and has come under attack. The problem is that Jeremias has overstated his case when he claims that 'we do not have a single example of God being addressed as "Abba" in Judaism'.[96] For one thing we have some of the evidence cited above (pp. 15f.) which at least suggests that 'the righteous man' in Wisdom circles thought of himself as God's son (Wisd. 2.13,16) and addressed God as 'Father' with a degree of intimacy which in Aramaic could well have been expressed by 'Abba' (Wisd. 14.3; Sir. 23.1,4; 51.10; III Macc. 6.3,8). So too with the Jewish charismatics mentioned above (p. 15). Vermes in fact maintains that 'whereas the customary style of post-biblical prayer is "Lord of the universe", one of the distinguishing features of ancient Hasidic piety is its habit of alluding to God precisely as "Father" '.[97] And for another, we cannot exclude the possibility that Jesus' use of *abba* reflects a much wider prayer habit of which we no longer have knowledge since it was a 'domestic piety' and found no written expression (since it needed none). It may indeed be, as M. Smith maintains, that '*abba* comes from lower class Palestinian piety. Since we have almost no other evidence for such piety – the rabbis and Qumranites were learned cliques – Jesus' usage cannot safely be supposed unique.'[98]

Nevertheless, despite Jeremias's overstatement, it is still possible to argue that Jesus stands out from his contemporaries at this point. (1) The use of *abba* as an address to God was in some degree unusual, because of its note of family intimacy. We may contrast here the prayers which all pious Jews probably said every day or every week (what became the Kaddish, the Eighteen Benedictions, and possibly other Morning and Evening Prayers).[99] We are not entirely lacking in knowledge of the prayers used regularly by Jesus' contemporaries both inside and outside the synagogue. And on the evidence we have Jesus' *abba*-prayer does strike a distinctive note. In particular it is worth observing that 'the Lord's prayer' is in effect an adaptation of one of these prayers (the Kaddish), presumably an adaptation for his disciples' private devotions of a prayer widely used in Galilee and/or Judea at that time, and an adaptation which begins precisely by introducing the intimate word *abba* (Luke 11.2). (2) Again, on the evidence we have there is nothing elsewhere approaching the regularity and consistency with which Jesus used *abba* in his prayers. For example, Sir. 23.1,4 is a much more elaborate form of address, and both in Josephus and the Mishnah Honi the circle-drawer's prayer begins with the more formal 'King of the universe' or 'Lord of the world' (*Ant.* XIV.24; Taan. 3.8; though cf. Matt. 11.25/Luke 10.21). (3) The clear implication of Rom. 8.15f. and Gal. 4.6f. is that Paul regarded the *abba* prayer as something distinctive to those who had received the eschatological Spirit. Had it been in common usage within any other large group or class within Palestine or Judaism Paul could hardly have thought of it in this way, as a distinguishing mark of those who shared the Spirit of Jesus' sonship, of an inheritance shared with Christ. In short, *the evidence points consistently and clearly to the conclusion that Jesus' regular use of 'abba' in addressing God distinguished Jesus in a significant degree from his contemporaries.* The claims made for the distinctiveness of

Jesus' *abba*-prayer are much more firmly rooted in contemporary documentation than any of the alternative views.[100]

(*c*) Granted then that Jesus' use of *abba* was both characteristic and
distinctive, how *significant* is this for our inquiry? Here the matter becomes
much more imponderable. Some things however we can say with a fair
amount of confidence. For one thing, we know *abba* primarily as a word
belonging to the family and expressive often of intimate family relationship – hence presumably its unfitness for the solemnity of prayer in the
view of almost all Jesus' contemporaries.[101] So we are justified in concluding that Jesus' use of it was not merely a formal convention, but
expressed *a sense of sonship*, indeed, on the basis particularly of Mark
14.36, of intimate sonship. For another, when we consider how Jesus
taught his own disciples to address God in the same way (particularly
Luke 11.2), the probability emerges with considerable strength that Jesus
saw his disciples' sonship as somehow *dependent* on his own.[102] Add in
here the testimony of Mark 12.6 and Luke 22.29f., both of which have a
fair claim to be part of Jesus' original teaching,[103] and we may conclude
that Jesus sensed an *eschatological uniqueness* in his relationship with God
– as the one whose ministry was the climax to God's purposes for Israel
(Mark 12.2–6), a ministry through which God was already bringing
about a new covenant intimacy for some at least (cf. I Cor. 11.25 and
Mark 14.24 with Jer. 31.31–4, and Matt. 7.7–11 par. and Luke 11.2 with
Hos. 1.10f.) – as the son who had the unique role of bringing others to
share in the kingdom to which he had already been appointed (Luke
22.29f.).[104]

But can we go further? Can we speak of a consciousness on the part of
Jesus of *divine* sonship, of consciousness of a sonship not merely eschatologically unique but also '*proto*logically' unique ('begotten before all
ages'), of consciousness of a sonship *qualitatively* distinct from that of his
disciples? Here unfortunately the ice becomes progressively thinner, and
the danger becomes critical of (dogmatic) theology outrunning exegesis
– especially since passages like Matt. 5.48, 17.25f., Mark 3.34f. and Luke
20.36 warn us against overstressing Jesus' consciousness of a distinction
between his own sonship and that of his disciples. In fact only three
Synoptic passages offer much hope of sustaining such bolder claims –
Mark 12.6, Mark 13.32 and Matt. 11.27/Luke 10.22.[105] In the first case
however the distinction between 'servants' and '(beloved) son' in Mark
12.2–6 provides no sure foundation since the contrast can be fully explained as part of the dramatic climax of the parable.[106] As for the other
two sayings, it is precisely in Jesus' reference to himself as 'the Son' that
most scholars detect evidence of earliest Christians adding to or shaping
an original saying of less christological weight.[107] And if indeed Mark
13.32 does go back in its entirety to Jesus himself, yet it would go beyond

the evidence to conclude that it implies a consciousness of 'superhuman existence' on the part of Jesus; it is more likely that Jesus was looking forward with apocalyptic assurance to his future glory in the presence of God (cf. Luke 12.8f. 'angels of God', with Matt. 10.32f. 'my Father').[108] So too with Matt. 11.27, especially if original in some form like that argued for by Jeremias,[109] we may well have a saying which confirms our earlier conclusion – that Jesus' sense of sonship was one of intimacy in the councils of God and of eschatological significance, unique in the degree and finality of the revelation and authority accorded to him (as compared with prophetic consciousness – Amos 3.7);[110] but more than that we cannot say with any confidence (see further below pp. 199f.). Schweitzer's claim that Matt. 11.27 'may be spoken from the consciousness of pre-existence'[111] is never more than a possibility, neither finally excluded nor positively indicated by careful exegesis.[112] This is the frustrating character of our evidence. Just when our questioning reaches the 'crunch' issue (Was Jesus conscious of being the divine Son of God?) we find that it is unable to give a clear historical answer.[113]

§4.4   Is this then the point at which *the Fourth Evangelist* comes to our aid? Can the testimony of the Fourth Gospel be called in to give that clearer answer? Certainly John's answer seems clear enough. A regular feature of Jesus' discourses in the Fourth Gospel is precisely his talk of God as his Father and of himself as God's Son – he calls God 'Father' more than 100 times and himself 'Son' 22 or 23 times. For the first time we find one of the key words of the later creeds used of Jesus – μονογενής (only-begotten) – not only in the prologue but in one of Jesus' discourses (John 1.14, 18; 3.16, 18). Linked with the Father-Son theme is the regularly expressed conviction of his own *pre-existence* – of a prior existence in heaven with the Father (6.62; 8.38; 10.36; 17.5), of his descent from heaven (3.13; 6.33, 38, 41f., 50f., 58), of his coming from God (3.31; 8.42; (13.3); 16.27f.; 17.8) into the world (3.19; 9.39; 10.36; 12.46; 16.28; 18.37). The climax is probably reached in the most powerful of the 'I am' sayings, where Jesus' claim to pre-existence achieves its most absolute expression – 'Before Abraham was, I am' (8.58).

So a clear enough picture emerges. But can we assume that John's intention was to give these various expressions as utterances of the historical Jesus? Can we assume that the Fourth Evangelist's concern at this point was to paint a portrait of Jesus as he actually was, to record, like a faithful stenographer, what he actually said? The reassertion of the Fourth Gospel as a historical source and the renewed realization that its tradition has firm historical roots at least at several places gives some encouragement on this score. Unfortunately, however, it is precisely at the point which concerns us that the case is weakest, precisely here that the indications are strongest that John is presenting us with developed rather than original tradition. Consider the following points.

(a) Dodd's careful comparison of Johannine and Synoptic traditions has indeed brought to our attention several sayings and sequences of sayings which most probably stem from Synoptic or Synoptic-like tradition. But he has also highlighted still more clearly how distinctive are the Johannine discourses which make use of these sayings – 'constructed on a characteristic pattern which has no parallel in the Synoptic Gospels'.[114] No one can dispute the vast differences between the discourse style in the Fourth Gospel and Jesus' teaching recorded in the Synoptics. The point is that the style is *so consistent* in John (whether in Galilee or Judea, to crowd or individual, to peasants or Pharisee, to disciples or hostile 'Jews') and *so consistently different* from the Synoptics that it can hardly be other than a Johannine literary product, developing and shaping the tradition according to a pattern largely imposed on it. The best explanation still remains that the Johannine discourses are meditations or sermons on individual sayings or episodes from Jesus' life, but elaborated in the language and theology of subsequent Christian reflection.[115]

(b) In particular, this is clearly true of the whole Father-Son tradition in John. Jeremias has noted the following statistics for the use of 'Father' for God in the words of Jesus – Mark 3, Q 4, special Luke 4, special Matthew 31, John 100 – and draws the inevitable conclusion: 'There was a growing tendency to introduce the title "Father" for God into the sayings of Jesus.' Even more striking are the statistics for the phrase 'the Father' – Mark 1, Q 1, special Luke 2, special Matthew 1, John 73.[116] On this evidence it is scarcely possible to dispute that here we see straightforward evidence of a burgeoning tradition, of a manner of speaking about Jesus and his relation with God which became very popular in the last decades of the first century.[117] The closest parallel in all this is Matt. 11.27 par. So once again we can detect the probable *root* from which John developed his whole motif, but once again the comparative isolation of Matt. 11.27 within the Synoptic tradition underscores the extent to which John has *developed* the motif. In other words, in Matt. 11.27 we have what clearly became a growth point of tradition, not the developed tradition itself, an element within the very early Jesus-tradition which showed potential for exploitation as a christological motif, but which in itself is scarcely capable of bearing the christological significance of the developed tradition.[118]

(c) Much the same has to be said about the sayings which assert Jesus' pre-existence. The point again is the complete lack of real parallel in the earlier tradition: no other Gospel speaks of Jesus coming down from heaven and the like; the clearer the implication of pre-existence in any saying, the more distinctive its Johannine character. Again it is possible to see a Synoptic-type root for the weighty 'I am' sayings – Mark 6.50, 13.6, 14.62; but again the indications are clear and strong that the weightier Johannine sayings are a *development* from the earlier tradition at best tangential to the earlier tradition. For the Markan 'I am' sayings are simply affirmative utterances ('It's me', 'I am he', 'Yes'), as Matthew clearly indicates (Matt. 24.5; 26.64). But John has probably seen a potential link with the 'I am' of Isa. 43.10 and exploited it accordingly (especially John 8.24, 28, 58; 13.19). It is surely scarcely credible that a saying like John 8.58, or the other 'I am' sayings ('the bread of life', 'the light of the world', etc.), were part of the earliest Jesus-tradition, and yet nothing approaching them appears in the Synoptic Gospels. Why should they be so completely neglected if part of the authentic sayings of Jesus, and why should only John preserve them? The most obvious explanation once again is that in a relatively insignificant element of the earlier tradition John has found the inspiration to fashion an invaluable formula for expressing Christianity's claims about Christ.[119]

(*d*) The argument that the Fourth Gospel was written prior to AD 70 does not affect the above considerations,[120] so I will confine myself to three comments only. First, it is an unsound premise that second genera-tion Christianity must have been as affected by the fall of Jerusalem and the destruction of the temple as Judaism was. The Stephen traditions (Acts 6–7) are evidence enough of how quickly the temple became un-important for Hellenistic Jewish Christianity.[121] Second, the relationship between Christianity and Judaism reflected in the Fourth Gospel is most clearly that of the 80s and 90s when the breach between synagogue and church, between Jesus' 'disciples' and 'the Jews', had become final (see especially John 9.22; 12.42). No earlier period provides such a recogniz-able or plausible historical life setting for the Fourth Gospel (cf. *Dial.* 16, 47).[122] Third, as most commentators agree, I John contests a docetic-like christology whose closest parallels are the earliest forms of Gnosticism proper which probably emerged round about the turn of the first century AD (cf. I John 4.2f.; 5.6 with Ignatius, *Magn.* 1.2; *Smyrn.* 1–3; 5.2).[123] Since the Fourth Gospel seems to have more or less the same situation in view (cf. John 1.14 with I John 4.2 and John 19.34 with I John 5.6) it is most probably to be dated to the same period – late first century AD.[124]

The upshot of all this is that, despite the renewal of interest in the Fourth Gospel as a historical source for the ministry of Jesus, *it would be verging on the irresponsible to use the Johannine testimony on Jesus' divine sonship in our attempt to uncover the self-consciousness of Jesus himself.* For all the indications of the Johannine tradition having historical roots, at the point which affects us the indications are even stronger than the original trad-ition has been considerably worked over and developed. The Johannine christology of conscious pre-existent sonship, of self-conscious divinity, belongs most clearly to the *developed* tradition and not to the original. Rather than assume that the Fourth Evangelist intended to record the very words of Jesus, the implication is that John's Gospel is the Evangelist's meditation on Jesus' ministry and its significance for his own day, intended as a portrait rather than a photograph, as a statement of conviction concerning Jesus' unique role and its importance as seen with the benefit of hindsight and faith (cf. e.g. 2.22; 12.16; 20.9), rather than a historical documentary.[125] Consequently, in looking for the origin of a christology of sonship in the sayings and life of Jesus we are forced back upon the Synoptic material reviewed above (§4.3).

§4.5 *Conclusion.* (1) We need not despair of getting back to Jesus' understanding of his role and mission. There are various sayings and speech mannerisms which can be traced back to Jesus with confidence and which uncover for us something of his self-consciousness. (2) In particular, our evidence is such that we are able to say, again with confidence, that Jesus understood and expressed his relationship to God in terms of *sonship*. Indeed we may say further that his consciousness was of an *intimacy* of sonship which, as embodied in his regular and characteristic address in prayer, 'Abba', still lacks any real parallel among his contemporaries. To that extent Jesus' sense of sonship was something *distinctive*. (3) Still more, there is sufficiently good testimony that Jesus taught his disciples to regard themselves as God's sons in the same intimate way, but also that he regarded their sonship as somehow *dependent* on his own, that he thought of their sonship as somehow derivative from his. Added to this is the probability that he saw his sonship in part at least as an *eschatological* commissioning, God's final attempt to recall the vineyard Israel to its rightful ownership, God's viceroy in disposing membership of his kingdom. In which case we can speak of Jesus' consciousness or conviction that his sonship was something *unique*. (4) Beyond that we run out of firm evidence. The evidence does not prevent us from speculating beyond it – that his consciousness *was* of divine sonship, of a qualitative distinctiveness, of a metaphysical otherness – but neither does it encourage such speculation. Alternatively, it still remains open to us to say, Of course Jesus was much more than he ever knew himself to be during his earthly life. But *if we are to submit our speculations to the text and build our theology only with the bricks provided by careful exegesis we cannot say with any confidence that Jesus knew himself to be divine, the pre-existent Son of God.*[126] (5) Nevertheless the christology of a sonship distinctive in its sense of intimacy and unique in its consciousness of eschatological significance and of the dependency of others on it, that can only be called *a high christology* – higher certainly than a christology of a righteous man or a charismatic exorcist, higher perhaps even than that of a Davidic Messiah – though, if so, how much higher we cannot say. This is of crucial importance for all subsequent christology, for without these elements of distinctiveness and uniqueness all the developments in christology subsequent to Easter, not to mention the developments of subsequent centuries, would be in danger of losing touch with Jesus as he actually was. To these developments we now turn.

§5. JESUS' DIVINE SONSHIP IN THE EARLIEST CHRISTIAN WRITINGS

How was Jesus' sonship understood and spoken of among the first Christians? The most obvious way of answering this question is to examine the NT passages which speak of Jesus' sonship as far as possible in chronological order. In concentrating on a series of individual texts we will have to guard against a twofold danger – on the one hand of reading particular texts in the light of others, of letting other (and later) texts influence our interpretation on sensitive issues – on the other of reading particular texts too much in isolation from other elements in the christological thought of the time, of building too large a conclusion on too narrow a base. In both cases there is a real danger of jumping too quickly to a conclusion, of imposing a pattern on our material. Here as elsewhere we must let the evidence speak for itself, all the while trying to hear with the ears of the original listeners/readers, all the while trying to enter into what the original speaker/writer would have expected his listeners/readers to understand by his words. In this section we look at the statements of first generation Christianity – that is, roughly speaking, so far as our documents are concerned, the pre-Pauline and Pauline formulations.

§5.1 *Jesus as Son of God in earliest Christianity.* It is not always possible to penetrate back to the earliest post-Easter stage of particular traditions or motifs – our earliest documents in the NT (the letters of Paul) did not begin to appear till nearly twenty years after Jesus' death and resurrection. But in the present instance we are in the fortunate position of having some passages which by widespread consent do take us back to a pre-Pauline and probably very early stage of Christian speech and reflection about Jesus as God's Son. I refer particularly to the (probably) pre-Pauline formula used by Paul in Rom. 1.3f. and to what appears to have been the earliest apologetic use of Ps. 2.7 by the first Christians.

(a) *Rom. 1.3f.* Paul in introducing himself to the Christians in Rome immediately speaks of 'the gospel concerning his (God's) Son, who was descended from David according to the flesh and designated Son of God in power according to the Spirit of holiness by his resurrection from the dead, Jesus Christ our Lord' (RSV). It is generally agreed that the opening and closing phrases ('concerning his Son' and 'Jesus Christ our Lord') are Pauline additions, and most think that 'in power' has to be regarded in the same way, though I am less certain of this.[127] This would leave the unadorned formula as –

came from the seed of David	in terms of the flesh,
designated Son of God (in power)	in terms of the Spirit of holiness
as from the resurrection of the dead (cf. II Tim. 2.8).[128]	

The crucial factor in our attempt to reach back to the original sense of this pre-Pauline formula is the meaning of the second clause. Ὁρισθέντος ('designated' RSV) has sometimes been rendered 'declared, shown to be'.[129] But the contemporary evidence does not really support such a rendering and it is hard to escape C. E. B. Cranfield's firm conclusion:

> There is little doubt that we should decide for the meaning 'appoint', 'constitute', 'install'. . . . It can be used very frequently with the meaning 'fix', 'determine', 'appoint'; and this is the sense it has in all its other occurrences in the NT. No clear example, either earlier than, or contemporary with the NT, of its use in the sense 'declare' or 'show to be' has been adduced.[130]

So, 'appointed Son of God . . .' is the most obvious sense, though it is possible to argue for the sense 'determined' or 'decreed' (cf. Luke 22.22; Acts 2.23; 17.31), perhaps with an allusion to Ps. 2.7 ('I will tell of the decree of the Lord: He said to me, "You are my son, today I have begotten you" ').[131]

The other key phrase in our present inquiry is the last – 'as from the resurrection of the dead' (ἐξ ἀναστάσεως νεκρῶν).[132] The ἐξ must mean either 'from the time of' or 'on the grounds of'.[133] And the ἀναστάσεως νεκρῶν almost certainly refers to the eschatological resurrection of the dead ('the general resurrection') rather than to Jesus' own resurrection *from* the dead as such. The latter is obviously in mind too, but the phrase seems to encapsulate the primitive Christian view that in Jesus' resurrection the resurrection of the dead had begun, Jesus' resurrection being as it were the first sheaf (ἀπαρχή) of the eschatological harvest of the resurrection.[134]

When we put these two sets of findings together we gain a fairly clear exegesis. There are two main possibilities. (1) If 'in power' is a later (Pauline) addition to the original formula, then the original formula asserts that *Jesus' divine sonship stemmed from his resurrection*, whether simply as from that event by pre-determined decree, or as an appointment made at or consequent upon 'the resurrection of the dead'. (2) If 'in power' was part of the pre-Pauline formula then we have the similar but qualified assertion that Jesus' divine sonship·*in power* stemmed from his resurrection. Implicit within this latter formulation could be the recognition that in at least one strand of messianic expectation the Son of David was also thought of as Son of God (above pp. 15f.); in other words, while we must take seriously the formula's antithesis between the Son of David and Son of God, it is a formal antithesis and should not be pressed too far. Here we should also bear in mind that sayings referring to Jesus as God's 'son' during his ministry in Palestine would probably be in circulation among the churches already (Mark 12.6; Matt. 11.27/Luke 10.22 – Q; and perhaps Mark 13.32), as also the tradition of Jesus' *abba*-prayer (Rom. 8.15; Gal. 4.6).

What is clear, on either alternative, is that *the resurrection of Jesus was regarded as of central significance in determining his divine sonship*,[135] either as his installation to a status and prerogatives not enjoyed before, or as a major enhancement of a sonship already enjoyed. What is also clear is that *there is no thought of a pre-existent sonship here*.[136] Even if we may legitimately detect the suggestion of an 'eternal decree', there can be no doubt so far as the formula is concerned that what was decreed only came about at 'the resurrection of the dead'. Whether the idea of pre-existence enters with Paul's introductory addition ('concerning his Son') is a question to which we must return (below n. 173). Finally we must note that once again sonship is seen in *eschatological* terms: *the divine sonship of which the original formula speaks is a sonship which begins from the resurrection*; something of tremendous significance for Jesus (the subject of the divine decree or appointment), something of eschatological import (the beginning of the resurrection of the dead), took place in the resurrection of Jesus and it is characterized in terms of Jesus' divine sonship.

(*b*) *Ps. 2.7*, 'You are my son, today I have begotten you', is one of the more important proof texts used in earliest Christian apologetic (Mark 1.11; Luke 3.22D; Acts 13.33; Heb. 1.5; 5.5).[137] Though it remains uncertain whether it was accorded messianic significance at Qumran (see above p. 15), it was part of a psalm which lent itself to messianic interpretation in terms of a Davidic king (v. 2 – 'the Lord's anointed'; v. 6 – 'I have set my king on Zion, my holy hill'). So its application to Jesus is hardly surprising and the psalm was probably taken up as soon as the first Christians began to examine their (Jewish) scriptures for prophecies of Jesus the messiah/anointed one.

There is a wide measure of agreement that the earliest (traceable) Christian use of Ps. 2.7 was probably in reference to Jesus' resurrection along the lines of Acts 13.33.[138] For one thing the resurrection of Jesus appears to have been the central affirmation of the earliest Christians, as not only the sermons in Acts but also the pre-Pauline formulae testify (Acts 2.24–32; 4.1–2, 33; 10.40f.; 13.30–7; 17.18, 30f.; Rom 1.3f.; 4.24f.; 8.34; 10.9; I Cor. 15.3–11; I Thess. 1.10; II Tim. 2.8).[139] So the reference of an obvious messianic proof text to Jesus' resurrection was wholly to be

expected. For another, the particular significance attributed to the resurrection by referring Ps. 2.7 to it is wholly of a piece with the christological emphasis elsewhere in the Acts sermons (particularly Acts 2.36
– 'God has made him both Lord and Christ', that is, by raising him from
the dead). It is not impossible that this is a theological theme developed
by Luke,[140] but much more likely that it is one of several primitive
christological emphases which Luke has faithfully preserved and reproduced.[141] And for another, the use of Ps. 2.7 in Hebrews also reflects an
association with Jesus' exaltation, with Ps. 2.7 being taken as an allusion
to Jesus' appointment to high-priestly status consequent upon his suffering (1.3–5; 5.5–10; 7.28; see below §6.4). From this we may justifiably
deduce that the association between Ps. 2.7 and Jesus' resurrection/ex-
altation was a basic and primitive characteristic of early Christian
apologetic.

If then Acts 13.33 does preserve the earliest Christian use of Ps. 2.7 we
must note what that means. Acts 13.33 –

> We bring you the good news that what God promised to the fathers, this he
> has fulfilled to us their children by raising Jesus; as also it is written in the
> second psalm,
>> 'You are my Son,
>> today I have begotten you'.

Here clearly the resurrection of Jesus is spoken of as a fulfilment of the
divine promise to Israel, a promise expressed in Ps. 2.7. The significant
feature of this verse is that it uses the language of 'begetting' and specifies
a particular birth-day, a day on which someone (the king, the Messiah)
becomes God's son. According to Acts 13.33 and earliest Christian apologetic, that day was the resurrection of Jesus. In other words, *primitive
Christian preaching seems to have regarded Jesus' resurrection as the day of his
appointment to divine sonship, as the event by which he became God's son.*[142]

On the basis of Rom. 1.3f. and Acts 13.33 we may conclude therefore
that the first Christians thought of Jesus' divine sonship principally as a
role and status he had entered upon, been appointed to at his resurrection.[143] Whether they thought of him as already God's son during his
earthly ministry we cannot say. But even if they did recall his 'abba-
relationship' with God while on earth, *they nevertheless regarded Jesus' resurrection as introducing him into a relationship with God decisively new, eschatologically distinct, perhaps we should even say qualitatively different from what he had
enjoyed before* (before and after birth was the imagery used).

§5.2 *Jesus as Son of God in Paul.* We turn next to Paul as the one whose
writings are probably the earliest in the NT (the divine sonship of Jesus
has apparently no particular significance for Q). Paul speaks of Jesus as

God's Son 17 times. This small figure may indicate that thought of Jesus' sonship was relatively unimportant for Paul (he uses 'Lord' of Jesus nearly 230 times), although word counts are an uncertain basis on which to build such a conclusion. In several instances it may simply be a way of referring to Jesus without making a specific point about sonship, thus indicating that the title or status attributed to Jesus was already established and familiar to his readers. On the other hand, when we look at the particular instances more closely we see that Jesus' sonship is linked with a number of themes and apparently not by accident.

(a) It occurs in an *eschatological* context in one of the earliest occurrences – I Thess. 1.10: '. . . to wait for his Son from heaven, whom he raised from the dead, Jesus who delivers us from the wrath to come.' We may note that the earlier link between Jesus' sonship and his resurrection is here further attested – all the more significant if I Thess. 1.9f. contains an echo or summary of the early Hellenistic Jewish Christian preaching to Gentiles, as seems probable (cf. II Cor. 1.19).[144] The thought of Jesus as the Son to come from heaven is unusual, particularly for Paul, but is a natural extension of an understanding of Jesus' sonship in eschatological terms. Very much in line with this is the way Paul speaks of Jesus as Son in I Cor. 15.24–8, as the one who reigns in his kingdom (so Col. 1.13) until the final climax 'when he hands over the kingdom to God the Father' and is himself subject to God 'in order that God might be all in all'. Here a comparison with Luke 22.29 is obviously in order.

(b) Paul also speaks of Jesus as Son in contexts where the thought is of the exalted Christ's relationship with those who believe in him. God's act in revealing his Son in Paul was the decisive factor in commissioning (and converting) Paul (Gal. 1.16; cf. Rom. 1.9). Here we might compare the *revelatory* character of Jesus' sonship in Matt. 11.27/Luke 10.22. Paul talks also of fellowship with God's Son (I Cor. 1.9), of a faith in God's Son which enables him to live in intimate communion with Christ (Gal. 2.20), of a knowledge of the Son of God which is a growing up to the measure of Christ's fullness (Eph. 4.13). What this might mean is more clearly spelt out in Paul's talk of Christians *sharing in Christ's sonship*. Those who experience the Spirit of sonship, the Spirit of God's Son crying 'Abba! Father!', are thereby assured that they are children of God, heirs of God and joint heirs with Christ (Rom. 8.15–17; Gal. 4.6f.). And, more explicitly, believers are 'predestined to be conformed to the image of God's Son', in order that (by his resurrection) he might be the eldest of a new large family of God (Rom. 8.29). The link between Spirit and sonship we will have to return to in chapter V, and the thought of Jesus as first born of a new family we will investigate further in chapter IV. In the meantime the implied link between Jesus' sonship and resurrection ('firstborn', that is, from the dead – cf. Col. 1.18; Rev. 1.5) should be

noted, as also the reappearance of another theme linked with Jesus'
sonship in the Jesus-tradition – Jesus' sonship as a relation with God in
which others can share (above p. 28).

(c) A more distinctively Pauline association is that between Jesus as
God's Son and his *death* on the cross: Rom. 5.10 – 'reconciled to God by
the death of his Son'; Rom. 8.32 – 'He who did not spare his own Son
but gave him up for us all'; Gal. 2.20 – 'the Son of God, who loved me
and gave himself for me'.[145] It is possible that God's act of giving up his
Son was thought of in terms of a coming into the world and not simply
as a handing over to death.[146] But elsewhere Paul always uses the word
'hand over' (παραδίδωμι) of Jesus with specific reference to his death
(Rom. 4.25; Gal. 2.20; Eph. 5.2, 25; cf. II Cor. 4.11) and the 'for us'
(ὑπὲρ ἡμῶν) puts a specific reference to Christ's passion almost beyond
question (Rom. 5.6–8; 14.15; I Cor. 1.13; 11.24; 15.3; etc.).[147] Nevertheless
it is significant that Paul speaks of Jesus as God's Son prior to his
resurrection and exaltation, and the addition of 'concerning his Son' to
the earlier formula which emphasized resurrection-sonship (Rom. 1.3f.
– see above pp. 33f.) removes any doubt that Paul thought of the earthly
Jesus as God's Son prior to his becoming 'Son of God in power'.

(d) There remain the two passages where Paul speaks of Jesus as *'sent'*:
Gal. 4.4 – 'When the time had fully come, God sent forth his Son, born
of woman, born under the law, . . .'; Rom. 8.3 – God 'sending his Son in
the likeness of sinful flesh and for sin condemned sin in the flesh'. Here
it is widely agreed that the thought of pre-existence has been introduced
or assumed by Paul.[148] Yet this is in fact less certain than we from our
later perspective might think. Galatians 4.4 in particular is all too easily
read as though Paul actually wrote something like, 'God sent forth (from
heaven) his Son (by means of his being) born of (a) woman, (by means
of his being) born under the law'. It may be natural *for us* to read in the
sense of the bracketed words. The question we must examine is whether
it was as natural for Paul's readers to do so. To achieve an answer we
must examine the text and its meaning with some care.

§5.3 *The meaning of Gal. 4.4.* The following considerations will help us
to sketch in the context of meaning for our exegesis of Gal. 4.4.

(a) The verb translated *'sent'* (ἐξαποστέλλω) would have been familiar
to Paul's readers in the general sense of 'sending away' or 'sending on
their way' messengers and the like. But biblical Greek uses it quite
frequently of *God* sending forth, and this is obviously the background for
Paul's language here. God 'sends forth' agents to do his will, including
the plagues of Egypt and the judgments prophesied by Amos (e.g. Ex.
9.14; Ps. 105.28; Amos 1.4, 7, 10, etc.). In particular there are two broad
groups that he 'sends forth': a *heavenly being* (about 10 times in the LXX),

including angel (Gen. 24.40; Ps. 151.4 LXX; in NT Acts 12.11), spirit/ Spirit (Judg. 9.23; Zech. 7.12; in NT cf. Luke 24.49), and wisdom (Wisd. 9.10); and a *human messenger* (about 14 or 16 times), including Moses (Ex. 3.12(A); Ps. 105.26; Mic. 6.4), Gideon (Judg. 6.14), and most often the prophets (Judg. 6.8; II Chron. 36.15; Jer. 1.7; 7.25; Ezek. 2.3; 3.5f.; Micah 6.4; Obad. 1; Hag. 1.12; Mal. 3.1; in NT of Paul's own commissioning in Acts 22.21).[149] It is evident from this that ἐξαποστέλλειν when used of God does not tell us anything about the origin or point of departure of the one sent; it underlines the heavenly origin of his *commissioning* but not of the one commissioned. So far as its use in Gal. 4.4 is concerned therefore all we can say is that Paul's readers would most probably think simply of one sent by divine commission.[150]

(*b*) Would the fact that it was '*his Son*' who was sent not resolve the ambiguity of the verb? Here we must reckon with the unusualness of the formulation so far as the original readers' biblical context was concerned. On the one hand prophets are 'sent' by God but are never called God's 'sons'. On the other the wise man in Jewish literature is called God's son (above p. 15) but is never 'sent' by God.[151] What of 'heavenly beings'? Angels are called 'sons of God' (above p. 15) but not individually, only as a collective entity (except Dan. 3.25, but there is nothing to suggest an association of thought between Dan. 3.25 and Gal. 4.4).

A much more plausible allusion would be to Wisd. 9.10, where the writer calls for Wisdom to be sent forth (ἐξαπόστειλον) 'from the holy heavens', and where seven verses later the giving of wisdom is set in parallel to the sending of the holy Spirit 'from on high'. Galatians 4.4, 6 set in a not dissimilar parallel God's sending forth first of his Son and then of the Spirit of his Son – a formulation which could well have been prompted by Wisd. 9, with the implication that the Son was to be identified in the reader's mind with *Wisdom*.[152] But Wisdom is always a female figure (σοφία) and is never called God's 'son' in pre-Pauline literature.[153] So an identification of God's son in Gal. 4.4 as heavenly Wisdom would be not altogether a natural step for Paul's readers to take. Paul himself does make an explicit identification of Christ as the 'wisdom of God' in the (probably) later letter I Cor. 1.24, 30, but that may be the first time he made the equation (below pp. 177–9), and his subsequent implicit Christ = Wisdom allusions are set in and dependent on their cosmic contexts (Christ's relation to creation – I Cor. 8.6; Col. 1.15–17).[154] Moreover, there is no clear indication anywhere in Paul that he ever identified Christ (pre-existent or otherwise) with the Logos (Word) of God (*à la* Philo – see below pp. 230f.). Consequently the argument that a Wisdom (or Logos) allusion was intended in Gal. 4.4 is plausible and attractive but not wholly persuasive.

A still more plausible background to Gal. 4.4 is not the broader Hellenistic-Jewish context, but the more specific Christian tradition that Jesus both thought of himself as God's son (see above §4.3) and spoke of himself as 'sent' by God (Mark 9.37 pars.; 12.6 pars.; Matt. 15.24; Luke 4.18; 10.16).[155] In particular we should note Mark 12.6 – in the parable of the dishonest tenants Jesus would have been identified precisely as the son whom the father sent (ἀπέστειλεν) last of all. Here we have the father sending his son in what can fairly be called an eschatological act – Mark 12.6; last of all, 'in the end' NEB (ἔσχατον) – just as in Gal. 4.4 God sends his son 'at the fullness of time'. Moreover, at the same point in the parable (Mark 12.6f.) we have a close conjunction of the ideas of sonship and inheritance – again just as in Gal. 4.4–7. *There is no more immediate parallel to Gal. 4.4 or more obvious allusion intended than that provided by Jesus' own manner of speaking about himself and by his parable of the dishonest tenants.*[156] In which case we cannot safely assume that Paul intended here an allusion to Christ as pre-existent Son or Wisdom of God. Paul and his readers in writing and reading these words may well have thought only of the man Jesus whose ministry in Palestine was of divine commissioning and whose uniquely intimate relation with God was proved (and enhanced) by his resurrection, despite his rejection by the stewards of Israel's heritage.

(c) Do the following phrases shed any more light on our question – 'born of woman, born under the law'? Γενόμενον (born) refers to Jesus as one who had been born, not necessarily to his birth as such.[157] The more specific word for the event of giving birth is γεννάω (e.g. Matt. 1.16; 19.12; John 3.5–8; Gal. 4.23), whereas there is a less specific time reference in γίνομαι (to become, come to be) which often makes it difficult to distinguish it from the verb 'to be' (εἶναι)[158] and which allows the participle γενόμενος to be used regularly with a noun in the sense 'former' ('who had been').[159] Moreover, 'born of woman' was a familiar phrase in Jewish ears to denote simply 'man' (Job 14.1; 15.14; 25.4; IQS 11.20f.; IQH 13.14; 18.12f., 16; Matt. 11.11) – man is by definition 'one who is/has been born of woman'. So the reference is simply to Jesus' ordinary humanness, not to his birth.

Why then does Paul introduce this phrase if not to emphasize the true humanity of a heavenly being? If the natural implication of Paul's language was that he was referring to the man Jesus, whose ministry in Palestine was sufficiently well known to his readers, why bother to say that he was a man? Here is a consideration of some weight whose import can be clarified only by seeing the passage as a whole. Only then will we see the relation of each clause to the others and its function within the whole. The movement of thought is best illustrated by setting out the passage as follows:

A   ὅτε δε ἦλθεν τὸ πλήρωμα τοῦ χρόνου
B   ἐξαπέστειλεν ὁ Θεὸς τὸν υἱὸν αὑτοῦ,
C   γενόμενον ἐκ γυναικός,
D   γενόμενον ὑπὸ νόμον,
E   ἵνα τοὺς ὑπὸ νόμον ἐξαγοράσῃ,
F   ἵνα τὴν υἱοθεσίαν ἀπολάβωμεν.

A   When the fullness of time had come
B   God sent forth his Son,
C   born of woman,
D   born under the law,
E   in order that he might redeem those under the law,
F   in order that we might receive adoption (as sons).

Two points call for comment. First, it is fairly obvious that a double contrast is intended: most clearly between lines D and E – 'born under the law to redeem those under the law'; but also between lines C and F – '(his Son) born of woman . . . that we might receive adoption (as sons)'. Here the larger context is important for our understanding of 4.4f. Paul has been talking towards the end of chapter 3 and into chapter 4 of the offspring of Abraham (the Jews) as children, minors, and as slaves, in bondage to the law. So in v. 4 Paul's intention seems to be to present one who also knew what it means to be a child, a minor, to be under the law, but whose divine commissioning aimed to free the offspring of Abraham from their bondage and inferior status (as children who are no better than slaves – v.1). We have in fact here what M. D. Hooker has called 'interchange in Christ'[160] – Jesus was sent as one who experienced the condition of man in all its inferiority and bondage in order that man might be delivered from that condition and given a share in Christ's sonship (through the gift of the Spirit of the Son – v.6), no longer a slave but a son (v.7). Indeed we are in touch at this point with an important strand of Paul's christology which we will examine in detail below – his Adam christology (ch. IV). Jesus was sent as man (born of woman, not of a woman), that is, his divine commissioning was as one who shared the lot of (fallen) Adam (= man), in order that man might share in his risen humanity, as last Adam (cf. Rom. 8.29 and see further below pp. 111–13).

Second, the chief thrust of Gal. 4.4f. is clearly *soteriological* rather than christological[161] – God sent his Son in order to redeem. . . . This observation obviously strengthens the conclusion reached immediately above, that the phrase 'born of woman' is chosen to express a primarily soteriological point – 'born of woman' as describing a *state* prior to the decisive act of redemption (as also 'born under the law') rather than a particular *event* in the life of Christ. For the redemptive act is clearly not Jesus' birth;[162] Jesus' being or having been born of woman, born under the law is rather the prior condition which makes possible the act of redemption

('. . . in order that he might redeem'). In other words Gal. 4.4f. really belongs with the preceding and distinctively Pauline group of Son-passages (§5.2c) and is actually directed more to Jesus' *death* as Son than to the event of his birth.[163] Thus it becomes still clearer that *Paul has no intention here of arguing a particular christological position or claim, incarnation or otherwise.*

(*d*) In view of all this is it still possible to conclude that a christology of incarnation is presupposed or intended? – we must speak in terms of 'incarnation', not merely of a concept of pre-existence, since the talk is not just of God's Son being sent by God, but of God's Son, born of a woman, sent by God. Is then thought of Jesus' birth as the incarnation of a pre-existent Son of God implied here? Would Paul's readers have drawn such an inference? Could Paul have expected his readers to recognize such an implication? Here we must reckon with the striking fact observed above (§3.5) that there seems to have been *little real precedent for such an idea of incarnation,*[164] very little which might have prompted such an inference or invited such an implication. Indeed we would be hard pressed to find any real parallel in this period for language which speaks both of a divine sending and of a divine begetting *in the same breath,* since in fact these are *alternative* ways of saying the same thing, of describing the divine origin of the individual in question or of his commission.[165] So far as we can tell, such language only appears in Christian writings of the second century subsequent to the ideas of virginal conception in Matthew and Luke and the sending of the pre-existent Logos in John and as the *harmonization* of them (Ignatius, *Eph.* 7.2; Aristides, *Apology* 15.1; and especially Justin, *Apol.* I.21.1; 32.10–14; 63.15f.; *Dial.* 45.4; 84.2; 85.2; 127.4).[166] It follows that if Paul intended to imply what we now call the doctrine of the incarnation in Gal 4.4 he would have been taking *a radically new step,* something his readers could hardly have expected to come from a Jew.[167] And if he did intend to take that step we would have expected his earliest recorded intimation of it to be a much more explicit and careful exposition (cf. the care he takes to expound his understanding of who the seed of Abraham really are – Gal. 3).

It is however possible to argue that the similar statements in Rom. 8.3 and John 3.17, I John 4.9, 10, 14 are indications of a more widely used and earlier formula,[168] are indications, in other words, of a fair amount of explicit teaching on Christ's pre-existence and incarnation in Paul's churches to which Gal. 4.4 alludes. Unfortunately the argument here too is less persuasive than at first appears. (1) The only regular feature in all these statements is the phrase 'God sent his Son', and (a point of no great significance) the verbs used in Rom. 8.3 and Gal. 4.4 are different – Rom. 8.3 (πέμπειν), Gal. 4.4 (ἐξαποστέλλειν).[169] (2) Our present discussion is not much assisted, for while the later (Johannine) references in the context of the Fourth Gospel are clearly incarnational ('sent into the world' – though note John 17.18), the earlier (Pauline) references are just as clearly ambiguous (see below on Rom. 8.3), and an interpretation without thought of pre-existence is just as likely. So evidence of a doctrine of incarnation framed in terms of 'God sending' and prior to Paul's letters is not in fact available to us. (3) The Johannine passages have a distinctively Johannine character – 'world' is one of the Johannine circle's favourite words (over 100 times), and the affirmation that 'God sent me' has become a stereotyped formula on the lips of the Johannine Christ (17 times with ἀποστέλλειν, never ἐξαποστέλλειν, and 24 times with πέμπειν). This strongly suggests that once again we have here another example of a Johannine development and expansion of a much slighter element in the Jesus-tradition (see above pp. 30f.) – an element which had no incarnational overtones, and which when taken up by Paul remained at best ambiguous, but which probably the Johannine circle itself developed in an explicitly incarnational direction (see below §6.5). (4) Had Paul indeed taught a doctrine of incarnation (the pre-existence of the Son of God, the man Christ Jesus) in his mission it would inevitably have been open to misunderstanding and abuse – the sort of misunderstanding and abuse which followed his teaching on the resurrection and Lordship of Christ at Corinth (see particularly I Cor. 1–4; 15; II Cor. 10–13) – so that a greater clarification and fuller exposition of it would almost certainly have appeared elsewhere in his writings. It does not seem a very sound basis for an exegesis of Gal. 4.4 to argue both that Paul had already taught an explicit doctrine of incarnation, and also that such a novel teaching caused scarcely a ripple in the often troubled waters of the Pauline mission. In short, *it would appear unwise to base exegesis of Gal. 4.4 on the assumption that Paul's readers would have at once recognized an allusion to a specific and already well established Christian teaching on Jesus as the* incarnate *Son of God.*

One further and rather surprising consideration seems to emerge from all this. Since what certainly became the Christian idea of incarnation would probably have sounded strange to Paul's hearers (and to Paul?), perhaps Christian keenness to find an incarnation interpretation here has pushed exegesis in the wrong direction. Perhaps indeed 'born of woman', insofar as it has christological significance, is to be understood as a *denial* of a simplistic view of Jesus as a divine being come to earth. The one sent as God's Son was one 'born of woman', (simply) a man, not a divine being metamorphosed into or appearing as a human being. Alternatively, in view of the Galatians' hankering after the law (given 'through angels' – Gal. 3.19), perhaps the christological thrust is simply that 'God sent forth (directly, not by an angel) his Son (not some heavenly being, but one) born of woman, born under the law . . .'. Such a complexity of thought is unlikely, but the fact that an argument can be pushed as far in this direction as in the opposite direction (towards a doctrine of incarnation) is a further warning that Paul and his readers would have understood the language of Gal. 4.4 in a very different context from our own.

It has become steadily clearer therefore that Gal. 4.4 cannot be taken, as it so often is, as making a straightforward assertion or embodying an obvious presupposition that Jesus was the incarnation of a pre-existent divine being, the Son of God in that sense. That such was Paul's view is still possible and is certainly not ruled out by Gal. 4.4. But Gal. 4.4 hardly affords anything like clear or firm evidence in favour of such a hypothesis. On the contrary Gal. 4.4 can be understood quite adequately and comprehensively as a version of the familiar Pauline association between Jesus' sonship and his redemptive death (above p. 38) – Jesus as the Son of God sent by God as one born of woman born under the law to redeem (by his death) those likewise under the law and bring those likewise born of woman to share in the relation of sonship which he had himself enjoyed during his ministry and now could 'dispense' to others as the first born of the eschatological family of God. In short, *we cannot safely conclude from Gal. 4.4 that Paul believed in or was already teaching a doctrine of incarnation.*

§5.4   As for *Rom. 8.3* we need say little more, since the same considerations apply with little modification – 'God, by sending (πέμψας) his own Son in the (precise) likeness of sinful flesh and as a sacrifice for sin, condemned sin in the flesh, in order that the just requirement of the law might be fulfilled in us . . .'.[170] (1) It is marginally more likely that the verb used (πέμπειν) would suggest to Paul's readers the sending of a divine being from heaven, since in the LXX it is used only four times with God as the subject, all in the book of Wisdom and including the sending of Wisdom and of the Spirit in 9.10 and 9.17 (the other references are 12.25 and 16.20).[171] On the other hand πέμπειν is clearly more or less synonymous with (ἐξ)αποστέλλειν – as Wisd. 9.10 and the Johannine parallel to Mark 9.37 and Luke 10.16 suggest (John 13.20). In particular, we might note that Luke uses πέμπειν both in speaking of Elijah's divine commissioning (Luke 4.26) and in the parable of the dishonest tenants for the father's sending of his son (Luke 20.13). It may also be significant that just as Rom. 8.3 speaks of God sending 'his own Son', so the Markan and Lukan versions of the parable of the dishonest tenants speak of the father sending his 'beloved Son', and that the thought of others participating in the son's inheritance is central in both contexts (Mark 12.7–9 pars.; Rom. 8.14–17). So here too the Synoptic traditions, particularly the parable of the dishonest tenants, probably provides a closer parallel to and explanation of Paul's language in Rom. 8.3 than the sending of Wisdom.

(2) The phrase 'in the (precise) likeness of sinful flesh' probably has the same function in Rom. 8.3f. as the phrase 'born of woman, born under the law' had in Gal. 4.4f. For the thrust of Paul's thought is as clearly soteriological in Rom. 8.3f. as it is in Gal. 4.4f. In other words, 'in the precise likeness of sinful flesh' describes the character of Jesus' sonship prior to his 'sacrifice for sin', which meant that his 'sacrifice for sin' achieved a condemnation of sin in the flesh, in order that. . . . Here once again we seem to be dealing with an expression of Paul's Adam christology rather than a specific or implicit christology of incarnation – the one who is God's own Son (prior to his death as well as after his resurrection) is one whose divine commissioning did not lift him above human sin and suffering, but rather brought about the condemnation of sin in the flesh through his death as a man of 'sinful flesh' and as a 'sacrifice for sin' (see below pp. 111f.). Not incarnation seems to be in view here, for that would probably have required a much more careful statement than the ambiguous language Rom. 8.3 uses, but an affirmation of the complete oneness of Christ with sinful man making his death effective for the condemnation of sin by the destruction of its power base (the flesh).[172] In short, Rom. 8.3 like Gal. 4.4 probably belongs together with the other passages where Paul associates Jesus' sonship with his death, rather than in a separate category. But like Rom. 1.3f. it affirms divine sonship of his whole life and not just in connection with the climax of his death and resurrection.[173]

Finally with regard to Paul's christology as expressed in Romans, does the very real possibility that *Rom. 9.5* refers to Christ as God ($\theta\epsilon\acute{o}\varsigma$) help us here? Regretfully no: the punctuation intended by Paul and the meaning of the doxology is too uncertain for us to place any great weight on it. The argument on punctuation certainly favours a reference to Christ as 'god'.[174] But Paul's style is notably irregular and a doxology to Christ as god at this stage would be even more unusual within the context of Paul's thought than an unexpected twist in grammatical construction.[175] Even if Paul does bless Christ as 'god' here, the meaning of 'god' remains uncertain, particularly in view of our earlier discussion (above pp. 16f.). Is it a title of exaltation, like 'Son of God' in the then parallel Rom. 1.3f.? – a status and honour ('god over all') accorded to Christ at his resurrection, like 'Lord' (cf. Acts 10.36; I Cor. 15.24–6; Phil. 2.9–11) which however Paul uses to distinguish the exalted Christ from God?[176] Or is there a deliberate echo of Ps. 45.2 and 6, where the king is addressed as god?[177] Or is it another way of saying 'God was in Christ . . .' (II Cor. 5.19)?[178] Whatever the correct rendering of the text it is by no means clear that Paul thinks of Christ here as pre-existent god.

§5.5 *To sum up.* The earliest post-Easter talk of Jesus as God's Son was in distinctively eschatological terms. Whether these very first Christians thought of Jesus prior to his resurrection in terms of sonship we cannot tell. But *the language of the earliest post-Easter confession of Jesus' sonship and the earliest apologetic use of Ps. 2.7 certainly seem to have placed the decisive moment of 'becoming' quite clearly on the resurrection of Jesus.*[179] Paul is familiar with this understanding of Christ's divine sonship and refers to Jesus as God's Son in similarly distinctive eschatological contexts, in terms both of Christ's relation to God and of Christ's relation to those who have believed in him. In addition his understanding of Jesus' sonship included Jesus' life, and particularly his death, and not least the character of his life ('born of woman . . .', 'in likeness of sinful flesh . . .') which gave his death its particular quality of being 'for us'. It is possible that in the two passages where he speaks of God sending his Son (Rom. 8.3 and Gal. 4.4) he means to imply that the Son of God was pre-existent and had become incarnate as Jesus; but it is as likely, indeed probably more likely, that Paul's meaning did not stretch so far, and that at these points he and his readers thought simply of Jesus as the one commissioned by God as one who shared wholly in man's frailty, bondage and sin, and whose death achieved God's liberating and transforming purpose for man.

§6. JESUS' DIVINE SONSHIP IN THE POST-PAULINE WRITINGS OF THE NEW TESTAMENT

As we move from the first into the second generation of Christianity, talk of Jesus as Son of God assumes greater importance for several NT authors, though by no means for all (totally absent from the Pastorals, James and I Peter). So far as our subject is concerned there is less controversy over the significance of individual texts, so that we can proceed at a rather faster pace. We look first at the Synoptic Gospels, Mark, Matthew and then Luke-Acts, followed by Hebrews and finally John's Gospel and letters, as being among the latest of the NT documents. Whether or not Matthew, Luke and Hebrews are in correct chronological order does not affect our discussion.

§6.1 *Mark.* The importance of the Son of God confession for Mark is indicated by its prominence in his Gospel, not in terms of frequency but in its occurrence at key points. Whether or not the title occurs in the first sentence (the textual evidence is indecisive), it can still fairly be claimed that the whole Gospel is suspended between the heavenly intimation of 1.11 and the centurion's confession in 15.39. The initial testimony of the voice from heaven is confirmed somewhat paradoxically by those of the demoniacs (3.11; 5.7). Subsequently the turning point (in the Gospel) of Peter's confession of Jesus as the Christ at Caesarea Philippi (8.29) is complemented by the further confirmation of the heavenly voice on the mount of transfiguration (9.7). Finally in the climax of the trial before the Sanhedrin, when the High Priest puts the crucial question to him, 'Are you the Christ, the Son of the Blessed?' (14.61), Jesus' answer seems to add his own confession to the rest, '(You say that) I am', confirming to the readers the clear implications of 12.6 and 13.32.

It is fairly clear that there is no thought of pre-existence in all this.[180] 'Son of God' (if original) in 1.1, is like 'Jesus Christ', simply a designation of the central figure in the ensuing narrative. Likewise thought of pre-existence attaches no more to the 'beloved son' of 12.6 than it does to the servants sent before him (see above n. 106). Mark 13.32 implies an intimacy of the Son with the Father like that or even superior to that of the angels; but again pre-existence is not integral to the thought (cf. Amos 3.7). And 14.61f. has a purely messianic connotation (see above p. 15). Similarly the confessions of 3.11, 5.7 and 15.39 would seem to imply recognition simply of one specially commissioned or favoured by God (see above pp. 15f.) without necessarily evoking the idea of a divine being sent from heaven.

More interesting is 1.11, where we have the striking feature of Ps. 2.7 being cited in reference to the descent of the Spirit on Jesus at Jordan.[181] Here an OT passage which played a key role in primitive Christian apologetic concerning the resurrection of Jesus (§5.1(b) above) is used of an earlier event in Jesus' life. Whether Mark intended it or not, his treatment at this point left his account open to the interpretation that Jesus first *became* Son of God at the beginning of his ministry, by endowment with the Spirit and divine ratification, and Mark evidently took no pains to rule out such an interpretation.[182]

The most plausible indication that, despite 1.10f., Mark believed Jesus to be the heavenly Son of God become incarnate, comes in 9.2–8, the account of Jesus' transfiguration.[183] The indications, however, if anything point in another direction – that Mark saw the episode as foreshadowing Jesus' resurrection and exaltation. (1) He has framed the episode with reference to Christ's resurrection and parousia (8.38; 9.9) – a literary device which is unlikely to be accidental and is probably intended to highlight the significance of the intervening passage.[184] (2) Talk of Jesus' transformation (μεταμορφώθη) and of the overshadowing cloud (v. 7) recalls both the 'glorification' of Moses in his mountain top encounter with God (Ex. 34. 29 – δεδόξασται LXX), and the divine presence in the cloud overshadowing the wilderness tabernacle (Ex. 40.35) – allusions which may exhaust most of the significance of these details for Mark. (3) The 'dazzling white' garments are typically those of heavenly beings (cf. e.g. Dan. 7.9; Matt. 28.3; Acts 1.10), but this sort of imagery is regularly used in apocalyptic also for the resurrection body or to denote the glorification of the saints (e.g. Dan. 12.3; I Enoch 91.38; 108.11f.; I Cor. 15.51–3; Phil. 3.21; Rev. 3.4f.; II Bar. 51.3, 5, 10).[185] So there is certainly nothing like a clear allusion to pre-existent glory here, and probably no implication of incarnation at all.[186]

If anything, Mark's chief concern in his Son of God christology seems to be to emphasize the link between Jesus' sonship and his death. This is clearly so in the climax of 15.39: 'Only in the moment when Jesus dies with a loud cry does the first man, a Gentile, confess that he was the Son of God.'[187] So too it is in the context of his most anguished suffering that his most explicit prayer of intimate sonship is preserved (14.33–6), just as it is in the context of his trial that he for the first and only time assents to the designation 'Son of the Blessed' (14.61f.). Likewise in the parable of the dishonest tenants it is precisely because he is the son that the tenants put him to death.[188] Moreover, if there is anything in the thesis that Mark was seeking to correct an inadequate christology which centred on Jesus as a miracle worker and perhaps used the title 'Son of God' merely in that sense,[189] then it is significant that Mark corrected it by emphasizing the close relation between Jesus' sonship and his suffering and death rather than by presenting a more careful or explicit doctrine of incarnation. Finally, it may just be possible that the use of 'beloved' in 1.11 and 9.7 was intended to recall the offering up of Isaac (Gen. 22.2, 12, 16), for the *Aqedah* (the binding of Isaac) certainly played a significant role in subsequent Jewish and Christian theology and may already have been a subject of meditation at the time Mark wrote his Gospel.[190] In which case the theme of Jesus as the suffering Son of God would run through the whole Gospel. Be that as it may, it is sufficiently clear that *Mark's chief emphasis is on the Son of God as one whose anointing with the Spirit was with a view to his suffering and dying, as one who is to be recognized as Son of God precisely in his death and not simply in his subsequent resurrection and exaltation.*

§6.2 *Matthew* reproduces nearly all of Mark's Son (of God) references, though with a number of discreet modifications in some instances; three more come from Q material and another six are unique to Matthew, due in at least some cases to Matthean redaction of earlier material. On the basis of this evidence it can be argued that Son of God is the most important christological affirmation for Matthew.[191] This is certainly indicated by his redactional additions of the title in 14.33 and 16.16, where 'You are the Son of God' is set forth as the appropriate confessional response for the disciples of Jesus (cf. 26.63's modification of Mark 14.61).

And it is probably confirmed by the considerable expansion of talk of God as Father in the sayings of Jesus which we noted above (p. 30).

One of the most striking features of Matthew's Son of God christology is his clear identification of Jesus with Israel (Matt. 2.15; 4.3, 6)[192] – Jesus is the one who fulfils the destiny of God's son Israel. Here, as we shall see in a moment, Matthew is trying to teach us that Jesus' descent from David is only part of the truth about Jesus ('son of David' in reference to Jesus comes most frequently on the lips of those outside the immediate circle of Jesus' disciples – 9.27; 12.23; 15.22; 20.30f.; 21.9, 15; cf. 22.45; elsewhere only in 1.1 and 1.20). We should note also the way Matthew strengthens Mark's association between Jesus' divine sonship and his death by inserting extra material at 27.40 (echoing the temptation of 4.3, 6 – 'If you are the Son of God . . .') and 27.43, by strengthening the allusion to Jesus' death in 21.39 through his modification of Mark, and probably by implying thought of the suffering righteous man in his expanded account of Jesus' baptism (3.15).[193]

At two points Matthew perhaps comes closer to attributing pre-existence to Jesus as Son of God than any Christian writer before him. As we shall see below, by appending 11.28–30 to the Q passage (11.25–7/Luke 10.21f.), he identifies Jesus as Wisdom, and though thought of pre-existence is not present in this context it is but a step away, since Wisdom was already familiarly thought of as pre-existent (see below pp. 200f., 205). And in Matt. 28.19, the title Son is used with Father and Holy Spirit in a triadic formulation which foreshadows, in at least some degree, the later trinitarian understanding of God; though here too it should be noted that the idea of pre-existence is absent (we are still far from talk of the eternal being of God in its threefold inner relationships), and the authority Jesus claims and expresses in his commission is that of the risen one (28.18; as also in 18.20 and 28.20).

How does the virgin birth, or more precisely, the virginal conception of Jesus fit into all this? – probably the single most striking feature of Matthew's christology (1.18–25). One of the oddest features in these verses is the *absence* of Son of God terminology; in the birth narratives Jesus is called 'son (of God)' by implication only at 2.15, where the flight to Egypt is taken as a step towards his fulfilment of Hos. 11.1. It could be argued from this that Matthew wished to confine his understanding of Jesus as Son of God to Jesus in his mission – as fulfilling Israel's destiny and as from his anointing at Jordan (2.15; 3.17; 4.3, 6 – the only Son of God references in the first seven chapters). But closer analysis of Matt. 1–2 makes it quite clear, as R. E. Brown's masterly study shows, that Matthew's intention in chapter 1 is to give an account of *the divine origin of Jesus* – not merely son of David, but also Son of God; descended from David sure enough (1.1–17), but more important, conceived by the power of the Holy Spirit (1.18–20).[194] We have already noted (above p. 42) that this was an unheard of step to take, for, as Justin Martyr rightly insisted long ago (*Apol.* I.33), it claimed for Jesus a unique conception – the offspring of a human mother, but through an act of God's creative power, *not* through sexual intercourse with a divine being.[195] The point which bears upon our study is that Matthew presumably understands this as Jesus' *origin*, as the *begetting* (= becoming) of Jesus to be God's Son (1.16, 20). As Brown notes, there is in Matthew 'no suggestion of an incarnation whereby a figure who was previously with God takes on flesh'.[196] The thought of pre-existence is not present at all in this context.[197] In fact, a christology of pre-existence (as we shall see) and a christology of divine conception are best understood as two *different* developments from the earlier emphases on the resurrection as the decisive moment in Jesus' divine sonship and on Jesus' death 'for us' as the characteristic mark of Jesus' sonship. And as we mentioned above (p. 42) it is only in the second century that the two christologies are harmonized and merged.[198]

In short, where the earliest post-Easter formulation seems to have understood Jesus' divine sonship in terms of his resurrection, where Paul thought of Jesus' sonship in terms of his death and of his relations as the risen one with God and with those who believed in him, and where Mark thought of Jesus' sonship as from his anointing with the Spirit at Jordan and in terms particularly of his suffering and death, *Matthew has extended the understanding of Jesus' divine sonship by dating it from his conception and attributing that to the (creative) power of the Spirit* and by depicting Jesus' sonship in terms of his mission which fulfilled the destiny of God's son Israel.

§6.3   We need not linger long over *Luke-Acts* since teaching about Jesus' sonship is not a characteristic or important aspect of Luke's writings. The nine references in the body of his Gospel are all drawn from the earlier tradition in Mark and Q with no modifications of any significance for our study, though we might just note that 9.31 (Moses and Elijah spoke with Jesus about 'his exodus') strengthens the forward looking emphasis of the transfiguration narratives, and that in 10.22 the Matthean equation of Jesus with Wisdom has not yet been made (see below p. 206). Similarly the two references in Acts to the preaching of Paul are probably drawn from traditions of early Christian proclamation (Acts 9.20; 13.33).[199]

In his birth narrative however Luke is more explicit than Matthew in his assertion of Jesus' divine sonship from birth (1.32, 35; note also 2.49). Here again it is sufficiently clear that a virginal conception by divine power without the participation of any man is in view (1.34).[200] But here too it is sufficiently clear that it is a begetting, a becoming which is in view, the coming into existence of one who will be called, and will in fact be the Son of God, not the transition of a pre-existent being to become the soul of a human baby or the metamorphosis of a divine being into a human foetus. Luke does state a little more fully, and with powerful imagery, the means by which this divine begetting would take place – by the Holy Spirit coming upon Mary, and the power of the most High overshadowing her (1.35). The latter verb (ἐπισκιάσει) may well contain an allusion to the divine presence which overshadowed the tabernacle in the wilderness (Ex. 40.35), but the thought is not that of a divine presence (or being) *becoming* or being embodied in Jesus; in this phrase Luke's intention is clearly to describe the creative process of begetting, not that which was begotten.[201] Similarly in Acts there is no sign of any christology of pre-existence.[202]

The recurrence in Luke 1 of the sequence and balance in christological affirmation – son of David, son of God (1.32f., 35) – suggests that behind both Matthew's and Luke's very different birth narratives lies an earlier affirmation to that effect. But it also suggests that this earlier affirmation is in turn a *development* of the still earlier, more antithetically structured juxtaposition of Davidic and divine sonship such as is preserved by Paul in Rom. 1.3f. When this development took place we cannot now tell. But the most obvious implication is that just as Paul complemented the earlier formula by asserting Jesus' divine sonship of his earthly life and specially his death, and just as Mark did the same by suggesting that the moment of Jesus' divine begetting was at the very beginning of his ministry rather than at his resurrection, so the tradition of a conception by the power of the Spirit complemented (or corrected) the earlier tradition by asserting the moment of Jesus' divine begetting as his conception – he was the Son of God from the first, there was never a time in his life when he was not Son of God. Luke in particular seems to be familiar with the earlier belief (Acts 13.33) and possibly also the Markan variation – for what is arguably the original form of Luke 3.22 attributes the full sentence from Ps. 2.7 to the heavenly voice at Jordan ('You are my son, today I have begotten you'),[203] and Luke's placing of his genealogy (3.23–38 – '. . . the son of Adam, the son of God') *after* the account of Jesus' anointing and acclamation at Jordan may reflect an earlier belief that *that* was the moment of Jesus' begetting.[204] If this is the case, however, the fact that Luke retains these earlier emphases suggests that he saw no contradiction between them. Both Paul (in Rom. 1.3f.) and Luke here supplement earlier formulations concerning Jesus as Son of God without thereby denying the significance of the resurrection for Jesus' divine sonship.

§6.4 There is no doubt about the importance of Jesus' divine sonship for the author of the letter to the *Hebrews*. He talks of it regularly, particularly through the first seven chapters, and 4.14 implies that 'Jesus is the Son of God' was a basic confession common to the author and his readers.[205] But when we go on to inquire after his understanding of Christ's sonship we are confronted with a sharp division of opinion. On one evaluation of the evidence the author of Hebrews sees Christ as a heavenly being throughout, his earthly life being 'nothing but an interlude in a larger, heavenly life', 'only an episode in a higher existence'[206] a christology which John Knox in more careful terms describes as a 'close approximation to a pure kenoticism'.[207] On the other, for the author of Hebrews Christ is essentially 'son by appointment', 'appointed heir to the whole universe' (1.2) 'not in virtue of some precosmic divine existence, but as the pioneer of man's salvation . . .'; 'the author of Hebrews has no place in his thinking for pre-existence as an ontological concept. His essentially human Jesus attains to perfection, to pre-eminence, and even to eternity'.[208]

The reason for this divergence of opinion is plain. For Hebrews describes Christ as God's Son in language which seems to denote pre-existence more clearly than anything we have met so far: particularly 1.2 – 'in these last days God has spoken to us by a Son, whom he appointed heir of all things, through whom also he created the world . . .'; and 7.3 – Melchizedek 'is without father or mother or genealogy, and has neither beginning nor end of life, but resembling the Son of God he continues a priest for ever' (see also 10.5). At the same time, there is more 'adoptionist' language in Hebrews than in any other NT document – that is, language which speaks of Jesus as becoming, or being begotten or being appointed to his status as the decisive intermediary between God and man during his life or in consequence of his death and resurrection: note in particular, 1.4 – by his passion and exaltation he *became* superior to angels and has inherited a title superior to that of the angels; and 1.5, 5.5–10 – by his exaltation he was begotten as God's Son and by virtue of his passion appointed God's high priest.[209]

What is the explanation of this odd juxtaposition of seemingly contradictory themes? How can the writer speak of Jesus both as a 'Son . . . through whom God created the world' and as a son appointed by virtue of his passion and begotten by means of his exaltation? I suspect the answer lies in part at least in the other rather odd juxtaposition which characterizes his writing, the unique synthesis of Platonic and Hebraic world views, or more precisely Platonic cosmology and Judaeo-Christian eschatology, which his letter achieves.[210] This comes to clearest expression in the section which forms the climax of his argument, 8.1–10.18. On the one hand he develops God's instruction to Moses ('See that you make everything according to the pattern which was shown you on the mountain' – Ex. 25.40) along the lines of Platonic dualism, contrasting the heavenly realm of ideas/ideals and the earthly world of imperfect shadows/copies (particularly 8.5; 9.1, 23f.; 10.1). But at the same time he merges it with the Judaeo-Christian dualism which sets in contrast old age and new age, old covenant and new covenant (8.6–13; 9.8–12, 15, 26; 10.1, 9, 16). The first covenant with its priesthood, tabernacle and sacrifices was not only the old order which has been superseded by the new, it was also the imperfect shadow of the heavenly temple, of the one real priest and the sacrifice by which he opened the way into the very presence of God (9.11–14, 24–6; 10.19–22; and earlier 4.14–16; 7.24–6). Now we know where the author of Hebrews has derived the eschatological presentation from – this is a consistently strong motif throughout earliest Christianity. But it is also clear enough that his use of Platonic cosmology is derived from the sort of Hellenistic Judaism which we see also reflected in Philo (particularly *Leg. All.* III.100–3).[211]

How does this help with our understanding of the author of Hebrew's christology? The answer suggests itself that *the awkward tensions in his presentation of Christ are the result of his merging these two world views* – that the mediator of the new covenant on the one scheme is the eschatological Christ, the highpriest who is chosen from among men (5.1), the Son who is made perfect through suffering (2.10; 5.9), and on the other scheme is the heavenly reality beside whose priestly and sacrificial ministry all other and earlier priesthood and sacrifice is imperfect and inadequate (7; cf. the explicit but undeveloped assertion of Col. 2.17). This would help to explain the puzzling features of the passages which concern us most in the present study. 1.2–4 – on the one hand, we have one whose divine sonship is introduced as the eschatological contrast to the prophets, one whom God appointed ('in the last days'?) heir of all things – the eschatological sonship with which we are already familiar; on the other, one through whom God created the world, one who is the radiance of his glory and who bears the stamp of his nature – the language of Hellenistic Jewish writing about divine wisdom and similar to what Philo says about the Logos (see below pp. 166, 207). 3.2–6 – on the one hand, we have one who has been appointed to his task, as Moses was, and who has shown the faithfulness of a son where Moses was but a servant; on the other, one who in the awkward verses 3–4 seems to be thought of both as the son of the builder (God) and as the builder himself, probably reflecting the same kind of ambivalence we find in Philo's talk of the Logos (see above p. 15 and below §28.3).[212] 5.6, 7.3, 15–17 – on the one hand, we have the Son of God who is simply the typological and eschatological fulfilment of Melchizedek whose priesthood, by means of exegeting the silence of scripture (see above p. 21), could be described as eternal – Jesus meets the specifications since his resurrection demonstrated 'the power of an indestructible life' (7.16); on the other, the uncertainty as to whether the Son's priesthood is the antitype (Melchizedek's priest-hood resembles that of the Son) or whether Melchizedek's is the antitype (the Son is appointed to the order of Melchizedek), suggesting perhaps that the author of Hebrews sees them *both* as an embodiment of the heavenly ideal, again reflecting Philo's identification of Melchizedek with the Logos (*Leg. All.* III.82)[213] – bearing in mind that elsewhere Philo calls the Logos both God's Son (above p. 15) and highpriest (*Gig.* 52; *Migr.* 102; cf. *Heres* 201; in *Fuga* 108–9 the high priest is called 'divine logos . . . whose father is God').[214] 10.5–10 may also gain some illumi-nation here – on the one hand, an emphasis on Christ as the one who had been appointed with a view to his dying ('you have prepared a body for me . . . through the offering of the body of Jesus Christ once for all'); on the other, the words of Ps. 40.6–8 ascribed to him 'at his coming into the world' (εἰσερχόμενος εἰς τὸν κόσμον – cf. Heb. 1.6), which presum-ably must denote an utterance from the perspective of heaven (or the pre-existent soul? – cf. Wisd. 8.19f.) prior to existence on earth.[215]

If there is anything in all this it suggests that *the element of Hebrews' christology which we think of as ascribing pre-existence to the Son of God has to be set within the context of his indebtedness to Platonic idealism and interpreted with cross-reference to the way in which Philo treats the Logos.* We have yet to examine Philo's teaching on the Logos (ch. VII), as also the significance of the Wisdom allusion in Heb. 1.2–4 (ch. VI), not to mention his use of Ps. 8.4–6 in Heb. 2.6–9 (ch. IV); but the indications thus far are that the language of pre-existence in Hebrews is at least to some degree a reflection of the author's use of Platonic cosmology. That is to say, what we may have to accept is that the author of Hebrews ultimately has in mind an *ideal* pre-existence, the existence of an idea in the mind of God, his divine intention for the last days; for if Philo's treatment of the Logos is any guide such conceptualization of the Son could be very elastic, and include everything from pure idealism (within a strict monotheism) to language which at any rate seems to envisage a divine being independent of God (as in 1.2 and 10.5).

This tentative suggestion will have to await the fuller exploration of later chapters, but for the moment we should note two considerations which arise from our immediate concern in this chapter and which may strengthen its appeal. The first is a feature which marks off the author of Hebrews from other NT writers who make much of Jesus' divine sonship. For unlike them he seems to avoid speaking of God as the Father of the Son (only in the quotation from II Sam. 7.14 in Heb. 1.5), even though he thinks of God as Father of believers and of spirits (12.5–9). Is this because he did not think of the relation between God and the (pre-existent) Son as a personal relationship, but rather of the Son as a manifestation of God's radiance, as the expression of his creative power and purpose (1.2f.), and so of Jesus as the embodiment of that same power and purpose in revelation and redemption (1.2; 3.6)?[216] Such a thesis would certainly help explain the curiously impersonal tone of the 'son' references in these two verses.

The second is the observation that the bulk of the references to Jesus as Son in Hebrews revolve round what we may call the Melchizedek motif of the priest-king (7.2f.). All three OT quotations in 1.5, 8 referred to the king (Ps. 2.7; II Sam. 7.14; Ps. 45.6f.);[217] and five of the remaining Son-references all speak of him as high priest (4.14; 5.5, 8–10; 7.3, 28). This suggests that Melchizedek plays an even more important role in the author's thinking than at first appears. This is wholly plausible since we know that the mysterious figure of Melchizedek attracted rather diverse speculation in first-century Judaism, in particular both at Qumran and in Philo – 11QMelch. apparently using the name for an angelic being (see below pp. 152f.), and Philo treating the Gen. 14 character as an embodiment of the Logos (*Leg. All.* III.82). As we have seen Hebrews seems closer to Philo at this point (above p. 54),[218] so if the Melchizedek motif is more fundamental to Hebrews, then perhaps too the influence of Alexandrian-type philosophy is more pervasive in Hebrews than at first appears.

Our conclusions on Hebrews can only be tentative at this stage. But what appears thus far is that Hebrews shows us yet another way in which second generation Christianity elaborated or supplemented the earlier language of eschatological sonship. The author has by no means abandoned the earlier language and the understanding of Jesus' sonship which it expressed: he preserves the use of Ps. 2.7 to denote a begetting to sonship and an appointing to highpriesthood at exaltation (1.4f.; 5.5–9; 7.28); he reflects a continuing close association between Jesus' divine sonship and his death (5.8; 6.6; 10.29); and his distinction between prophets and son and heir and between servant and son (1.1f.; 3.5) may be a further echo of Jesus' own distinction in Mark 12.2–6. But his own understanding of Jesus' divine sonship has moved beyond these earlier formulations.[219] Not that he thinks in terms of an anointing to sonship earlier in Jesus' life (cf. 1.9) as in Mark. Nor that he thinks of Jesus' birth as such as an incarnation (such is probably not in view in 7.3 and 10.5).[220] *The special contribution of Hebrews is that it seems to be the first of the NT writings to have embraced the specific thought of a pre-existent divine sonship.* At the same time we must not overstate the significance of what the writer to the Hebrews has done. For in the evidence we have reviewed the concept of pre-existence is a far from clearly formulated thought and seems to have emerged more as a corollary to the author's Platonic idealism than as a firm christological perception. *It would certainly go beyond our evidence to conclude that the author has attained to the understanding of God's Son as having had a real personal pre-existence.* In short, a concept of pre-existent sonship, yes; but the pre-existence perhaps more of an idea and purpose in the mind of God than of a personal divine being.

§6.5 *John.* No other documents in the NT regard the Son of God confession so highly as the Johannine writings. It is the Gospel's stated aim to maintain or bring its readers to faith in Jesus as the Son of God (20.31), and confession-like utterances to that effect occur quite frequently throughout the Gospel (1.34, 49; 3.18, 36; 9.35 (?); 11.27; 19.7). If anything the emphasis is even stronger in the first letter of John – 'Whoever confesses that Jesus is the Son of God, God abides in him, and he in God' (4.15); 'Who is he that overcomes the world but he who believes that Jesus is the Son of God?' (5.5; see also 2.22f.; 3.23; 5.10, 13). By way of confirmation we need simply recall the very striking expansion of the Father-Son motif which we saw to be a characteristic of the Fourth Gospel (above p. 30).[221]

At various points the Johannines echo the emphases which characterized the earlier treatments of Jesus' divine sonship, but in each case the earlier understanding is transposed on to a higher plane and the whole motif transfused with a conviction of the Son's pre-existence.

(*a*) Typically Johannine is talk of the Son as *sent* by the Father – the Johannine Jesus speaks regularly of God as 'him who sent me' (4.34; 5.24, 30, 37; 6.38f., 44; etc.). The formulation is obviously dependent on and a considerable elaboration of the earlier tradition (above pp. 40, 42f., 44). But where in the Synoptics the language probably denotes a sense of divine commissioning (quite probably also in Gal. 4.4 and Rom. 8.3 – above §§5.3, 4), here the thought is explicitly of the Son as having been '*sent* (from heaven) *into the world*' (John 3.17; 10.36; 17.18; I John 4.9). This is of a piece with the other distinctively Johannine talk of Jesus as the one who descended from heaven, the Son of Man who will ascend 'where he was before' (particularly John 3.13; 6.33, 38, 62);[222] though we might note in passing that the two motifs (the Son sent by the Father, the Son of Man descending and ascending) are not fully integrated in the Johannine presentation – the Son never 'descends' and the Son of Man is never 'sent' – suggesting perhaps that behind the Fourth Gospel lie two independent developments of earlier Synoptic motifs which John is only in process of harmonizing.[223]

(*b*) The Synoptic tradition presents Jesus as the one who enjoyed a sense of sonship in his prayers to God (above §4.3). But in the Fourth Gospel Jesus is presented as fully conscious of enjoying a relation of sonship to God *prior* to his existence on earth – of having *pre-existed* as the divine Son of God from eternity – e.g., 'I have come down from heaven, not to do my own will, but the will of him who sent me' (6.38); 'I am from above . . . I am not of this world' (8.23); 'I speak of what I have seen with my Father' (8.38); 'I proceeded and came forth from God' (8.42); 'Before Abraham was, I am' (8.58); Jesus claims to be 'him whom the Father consecrated and sent into the world' (10.36); 'I came from the Father and have come into the world; again, I am leaving the world and going to the Father' (16.28).

(c) In the Synoptics Jesus' *abba*-prayer betokened a sense of intimacy in his relation with God (above pp. 27f.). In the Fourth Gospel we are confronted with explicit claims to *a oneness with the Father* which far transcends this, even though a proper sense of the Son's subordination to the Father is retained: e.g. 'Whatever the Father does the Son does likewise' (5.19); the divine prerogatives of Creator and Judge have been granted to the Son (5.21f., 25f.; 6.40; 8.16; cf. I John 5.11f.); the Son is worthy of the same honour as the Father (5.23); 'I and the Father are one' (10.30); 'If you had known me you would have known my Father also' (14.7); 'the Father who dwells in me does his works' (14.10). And once again it is an intimacy which is grounded in Jesus' pre-existence – 'Father, glorify me in your own presence with the glory which I had with you before the world was made' (17.5), 'the glory which you have given me because you loved me before the foundation of the world' (17.24).[224]

(d) The Johannine writers maintain the earlier link between Jesus' divine sonship and his death – 'God sent his Son to be the expiation for our sins' (I John 4.10; see also John 3.16f.; I John 1.7; and the whole motif of the glorification of the Son which includes his glorification on the cross – cf. John 1.14; 17.1).[225] But there is now *no thought of Jesus' status as Son being dependent on or even influenced by his resurrection.* Whatever it means for Jesus that he is the Word become flesh it involves no diminution in his status or consciousness as Son. And whatever it means for Jesus that he is glorified and lifted up on the cross, in resurrection and ascension, it involves no enhancement or alteration in his status as Son.[226] Not unjustly C. H. Dodd concludes his study of the title in the Fourth Gospel:

> The relation of Father and Son is an eternal relation, not attained in time, nor ceasing with this life, or with the history of this world. The human career of Jesus is, as it were, a projection of an eternal relation . . . upon the field of time.[227]

(e) There is still a sense that the Son's relationship with the Father is something that can be shared by his disciples. They too can be said to be 'sent into the world' (17.18; 20.21); they too can abide in the Father and he in them (14.23; 17.21; I John 2.24; 4.15; 5.20).[228] But here too *a clear qualitative distinction* is present in the Johannine writings as nowhere else: for one thing Jesus is the 'only begotten', the 'unique' Son of God (μονογενής – John 1.14, 18 – 'only begotten god'; 3.16, 18; I John 4.9); and for another the Johannines maintain a consistent distinction between Jesus the 'Son' (υἱός) and believers who are exclusively 'children of God' (John 1.12; 11.52; I John 3.1f., 10; 5.2). Unlike other NT writers John cannot think of Jesus as elder brother, first-born in the eschatological family (as in Rom. 8.14–17, 29 – see above pp. 37f.; Heb. 2.10–12 – see below pp. 110f.); his sonship is of a wholly different order (though cf. John 14.3).

(f) Finally, on the association between the titles 'Son of God' and 'God' (cf. 5.18). The argument of John 10.31–8 may certainly be said to reflect the older link between divine sonship and divinity and the ambivalence in their application to kings in ancient Israel (see above pp. 15, 17). But the argument of that passage is of the 'how much more' variety – if the law calls kings or judges 'gods' (Ps. 82.6), how much more is the one 'whom the Father consecrated and sent into the world' worthy of the title? And elsewhere in the Johannine writings there is no question of the title being used in a reduced sense. Not only the pre-existent Logos is god (1.1 – see below p. 241), but also the incarnate Son (1.18), as well as the risen ascended Christ (20.28). I John rounds off its exhortation with these words: 'We know that the Son of God has come and has given us understanding, to know him who is true; and we are in him who is true, in his Son Jesus Christ. This is the true God and eternal life' (I John 5.20).[229]

To sum up, it is quite clear that *in the Johannine writings the divine sonship of Jesus is grounded in his pre-existence*; whatever their context of meaning the readers could scarcely mistake this. The Johannine circle have an understanding of Jesus' divine sonship which is without real parallel in the rest of the NT, of a sonship which even on earth was an unclouded and uninterrupted enjoyment of a relationship with the Father which was his before the world began and which would continue to be his after his return to the Father. The nearest parallel within the NT writings is in the letter to the Hebrews, but that was a somewhat bloodless concept of pre-existence – the Johannine understanding is of a much more personal relationship. This does not necessarily mean of course that with one bound we have reached the language and thought forms of the later creeds. We have not yet reached the concept of an ontological union between Father and Son, of a oneness of essence and substance. In John divine sonship is still conceived in terms of relationship to the Father, a relationship of love (John 3.35; 5.20; 10.17; 17.23–6) – questions of ontology and essence have not yet entered upon the scene.[230] Nor, we must note, is there any thought of virgin birth or virginal conception here. Of incarnation, yes; but it is a becoming flesh of one who was already Son; there is no room for the idea of a divine begetting at a point in time.[231]

In short, *for the first time in earliest Christianity we encounter in the Johannine writings the understanding of Jesus' divine sonship in terms of the personal pre-existence of a divine being who was sent into the world and whose ascension was simply the continuation of an intimate relationship with the Father which neither incarnation nor crucifixion interrupted or disturbed.* Any closer analysis of what 'personal pre-existence of a divine being' meant for the Fourth Evangelist must await our examination of his Logos concept (see below §30.1).

§6.6   In the extant writings of second-generation Christianity we are confronted with quite *a striking diversity of presentations and understandings of Jesus' sonship*. *Mark* seems to see Jesus' sonship in terms of his mission, particularly his suffering and dying, and begins his Gospel with Jesus' anointing for mission at Jordan, with the implication not excluded that as his mission began at that point, so his begetting as Son by the anointing of the Spirit took place then too (Mark 1.11 with its allusion to Ps. 2.7). *Matthew* thinks of Jesus' sonship in terms of a mission that fulfilled the destiny of Israel, and dates Jesus' divine sonship from his conception by the power of the Spirit. *Luke* retains the earlier use of Ps. 2.7 in reference to the resurrection as the moment of his divine begetting, but like Matthew he also presents Jesus' conception by the power of the Spirit as the moment in time when the Son of God came into existence. *Hebrews* tries to accomplish a sophisticated harmonization between Platonic world view and Jewish eschatology, and to retain an understanding of Jesus more suited to the latter – Jesus as one taken from among men and appointed highpriest and Son by virtue of his suffering, death and the power of his indestructible life – while beginning to formulate an understanding of Jesus more suited to the former – Jesus as the embodiment of God's creative and revelatory power. *John* abandons any idea of a divine sonship given or enhanced by resurrection and presents Jesus throughout his Gospel as conscious of his divine pre-existence as Son of God in heaven with the Father prior to his being sent into the world.

We must of course beware of drawing out inferences and conclusions that are unwarranted by the evidence; but it is significant that four out of the five writers we have examined above regard belief in Jesus as Son of God as something central and crucial. So it seems fair to assume that what they say about Jesus' divine sonship is deliberate and chosen with some care to express that belief, to explain their understanding of Jesus' sonship. In which case we cannot afford to minimize the degree of divergence between these different presentations of Jesus' divine sonship; nor may we seek a harmonization of them which discounts or ignores their particular emphases. It may be possible to argue that Mark did not intend to date Jesus' sonship from his anointing at Jordan, and thus achieve a harmonization with the birth narratives of Matthew and Luke

– although it has to be said that any of his readers who recognized the allusion to Ps. 2.7 in Mark 1.11 would most probably understand Mark 1.10f. as Jesus' 'begetting' or appointment as Son. And Hebrews does attempt to hold together a christology of pre-existence with a christology of eschatological sonship, though the attempt is dependent on his success in merging two divergent world views, and even then does not altogether come off.[232] But it is less easy to see how Matthew's and Luke's accounts of the conception of one who would be called Son of God can be harmonized with John's idea of the incarnation of a divine being who always was Son of God from before the foundation of the world. There is certainly no hint of any desire or attempt to harmonize or synthesize them within the NT writings themselves; the earliest attempts along these lines are not until the second century (above p. 42).[233] In all probability we should simply accept that *these are all different attempts to express the character and significance of Jesus' relationship with God*, different pieces of separate jigsaws. Beyond that we begin to run the danger of playing off one NT writer against another or of distorting the distinctive message of each.

§7. CONCLUSIONS

We have drawn conclusions at each step in our discussion and need not repeat them here. All that is necessary is to draw them together and point up their significance.

§7.1 When we compare our opening statements of the Nicene Creed with the picture which has emerged from the NT it is clear that there has been *a considerable development over that period in early Christian belief in and understanding of Jesus as the Son of God*. With Jesus we found it was possible, indeed necessary to speak of his sense of sonship; but we also found that exegesis did not encourage or enable us to speculate beyond that, and that there was no real evidence in the earliest Jesus-tradition of what could fairly be called a consciousness of divinity, a consciousness of a sonship rooted in pre-existent relationship with God. It is significant that the Synoptics written down in the second generation of Christianity preserve this more inchoate sense of sonship in Jesus' prayer and speech even when their own presentation is often more elaborate. In the earliest recoverable post-Easter proclamation and apologetic concerning Jesus' sonship the most striking feature was the way in which Jesus' sonship was spoken of as beginning with and from his resurrection – an understandable emphasis given the mood of exhilaration which the resurrection of Jesus must have brought to the first disciples, but one which was preserved in the writings of the next 50 or 60 years even when their own emphases were different. Paul and Mark seem to agree that Jesus' divine sonship was a feature of his whole ministry but particularly characterized by his suffering and death. Here again we find an emphasis which is maintained in the writings that followed, including Hebrews and John. In Matthew and Luke Jesus' divine sonship is traced back specifically to his birth or conception: Jesus was Son of David by his line of descent, but more important he was Son of God because his conception was an act of creative power by the Holy Spirit. In Hebrews a concept of pre-existence begins to attach itself to thought of Jesus' divine sonship for the first time (so far as we can tell), though it seems to be a rather sophisticated concept dependent in large measure on the writer's attempt to wed Jewish eschatology to Platonic idealism – in other words, the pre-existence more of an idea in the mind of God than of a person. Only in the Fourth Gospel does the understanding of a personal pre-existence fully emerge, of Jesus as the divine Son of God before the world began sent into the world by the Father – and that not as an isolated peak of speculation but as a principal theme of the Gospel repeated again and again in a kaleidescope of variant formulations.

It would be easy to argue on the basis of this evidence that there was a straight line of development from earliest post-Easter confessions down through the Fourth Gospel and beyond, in which the beginning of Jesus' divine sonship was pushed steadily back from resurrection, to anointing at Jordan, to conception and birth, to the beginning of time. But any attempt to draw such a straight line of development would certainly be unwise, if only because we cannot be sufficiently certain of dates of documents or of interrelationships of the communities, individuals, traditions and ideas which lie behind them. Yet, that being said, it is still a very striking fact that when we set out the NT traditions and documents on the best chronological scale available to us a clear development in first-century christology can be traced: where in the beginning the dominant (and only) conception was of an *eschatological* sonship, already enjoyed by Jesus during his ministry but greatly enhanced by his resurrection, at the end of the first century a clear concept of *pre-existent* divine sonship has emerged, to become the dominant (and often the only) emphasis in subsequent centuries.

§7.2 *We should not underestimate the differences between these various understandings of Jesus' divine sonship.* Careful exegesis requires that we give due weight to divergences in earliest Christian thought as well as the convergences. The desire to find and maintain a single Christian orthodoxy always tempts the Christian to harmonize and synthesize where possible. But on what basis here? – that behind these divergent statements there was nevertheless a unified conception? – that Paul and Mark and Matthew and Hebrews are only temporary and tentative fumblings after the something richer and fuller which John finally grasped? That might be argued, quite properly, on the ground of some dogmatic premise, but not in terms of exegesis. The one real attempt within the NT to hold together the christology of eschatological sonship and the christology of pre-existent sonship (Hebrews) does not wholly come off and leaves the two strands only loosely interwoven. There is no attempt to harmonize the ideas of virginal conception and incarnation within the NT itself (not before Ignatius at the earliest). And when John opens the floodgates of his christology of pre-existent sonship it sweeps all before it and leaves no room at all for the earlier stress on Jesus' sonship as an eschatological status and power that opens the way for others to share in. The fact is that these are different and cannot be wholly harmonized without losing something from each. *The NT contains a diversity of christologies of Jesus' divine sonship and to merge them into one common theme is to run the risk of destroying the distinctive emphases of each.*

§7.3   At the same time *we should not overestimate the significance of these differences.* The danger of calling the early post-Easter Son of God passages 'adoptionist' is that 'Adoptionism' is the technical term for that later view which *denied* Christ's pre-existent deity – he was *only* a man adopted by God as Son at his Jordan baptism. But the earliest use of Ps. 2.7 in reference to the resurrection of Jesus can hardly be designated a *denial* that Christ was already God's Son before his resurrection. Nor can we say that Mark was intent to *deny* Jesus' divine sonship prior to the Spirit's descent and the heavenly voice at Jordan. Nor indeed that the birth narratives were deliberately setting their face against the idea of a pre-existent divine sonship. We may justly draw attention to the particular emphases of the respective NT writers (§7.2), but we should not make the mistake of assuming they were seeking thereby to mark off their views from each other, in opposition to each other. All they may be saying, each in his own way, is that our message about Jesus, our story of Jesus, wherever and whenever it begins, is a message, a story about the Son of God. And Luke, as we noted (p. 51), was quite happy to include assertions which seemed to set the decisive christological moment of divine sonship at three different points in Jesus' life (conception and birth, Jordan, resurrection – cf. Rom. 1.3f.; Heb. 1.2–5). In other words, he saw no difficulty in affirming *several* christologically decisive moments in Jesus' life and ministry. All that the evidence permits us to say is simply that at the earlier stage these other ways of speaking of Christ as God's Son were not (yet) in view, that *in the earliest NT formulations the idea of a pre-existent divine sonship of Jesus does not yet seem to have crossed the threshold of thought, is neither affirmed nor denied,* and that of the statements formulated some can be seen from a later perspective to accommodate the thought of pre-existence and incarnation while others sit only awkwardly with it.

§7.4   It follows also that if we do think in terms of a developing Son of God christology (§7.1) we should not assume that it was a development from a *low* christology to a high christology. Although orthodox Christianity followed the high road mapped out by the Fourth Evangelist in elaborating his christology of divine sonship, we should not ignore the fact that *the earlier presentations of Jesus' divine sonship embody just as high a christology in their own terms as the later.*[234] The earlier understanding of Jesus' eschatological sonship, of a uniquely intimate relationship with God which stemmed from the resurrection, of a relationship which was the beginning of a whole new family of God, that is an insight which recognizes and confesses a significance for Jesus and for man's salvation which cannot easily be surpassed. Moreover, since we can also recognize that Jesus himself sensed something of this sonship, an intimate sonship, a sonship he could share, an eschatological sonship, we can trace this high christology back to Jesus and root it in the ministry and teaching of the historical Jesus in a way that is not possible for the later christology of pre-existent sonship.[235] That is a gain of incalculable importance for a faith which claims to be thoroughly historical.

§7.5   Another point should be given brief mention, in the light of the survey in §3. It is often assumed that the thought of Christ's pre-existence emerged as a natural and inevitable corollary to belief in Christ's exaltation – for example, as Knox puts it: 'reflection on the resurrection and on the post-resurrection status of Christ led directly and immediately to the affirmation of his pre-existence.'[236] But §3 has made it clear that in the thought of the ancient world the translation, ascension, apotheosis or deification of an individual by no means entailed the individual's pre-existence. When the Fourth Evangelist has Jesus affirm that 'no one has ascended into heaven but he who descended from heaven' (John 3.13), this would have been by no means obvious to his readers. Jewish readers familiar with speculation regarding Moses, Elijah and Enoch would be more inclined to reverse the clauses of the proposition. And those familiar with the wider religious thought of the time would have examples enough to contest it. *We cannot therefore assume that in the context of first-century thought the development traced out above (§7.1) was simply the outworking of the inherent logic of the initial belief in Christ's resurrection and exaltation.* Before reaching such a conclusion we must check what other influences and insights may have played their part.

§7.6   On a more positive note we should underscore *the importance of the*

Son of God title which has emerged throughout this earliest period of christology. Whatever the point in salvation-history to which these first-century Christians related the manifestation or beginning or enhancement of Christ's relation with God, *it is the title Son of God which regularly and repeatedly bears the primary weight of the claim made.* Whether the thought focuses on Jesus' resurrection and parousia, or on his anointing at Jordan, or on his birth, or embraces the whole of time, it is the language of divine sonship which appears again and again, sometimes without rival. The belief in Jesus as God's Son had the power to absorb and express all these different emphases, showing that ultimately they are not incompatable even if in the original contexts not wholly complementary. The emergence of 'Són of God' as the dominant title for Christ in the fourth century was well justified by its importance in earliest christology.

§7.7 At the same time, when we narrow our focus to the particular question with which this investigation is concerned, we have to repeat that *in the earliest period of Christianity 'Son of God' was not an obvious vehicle of a christology of incarnation or pre-existence.* The christology of a pre-existent Son of God becoming man only began to emerge in the last decades of the first century, and only appears in a clear form within the NT in its latest writings. Certainly such a christology cannot be traced back to Jesus himself with any degree of conviction, and when we pay proper attention to the first-century context of meaning it is less likely that we can find such a christology in Paul or Mark or Luke or Matthew, not to mention those writings which make nothing of Jesus' sonship. In other words, we have not yet discovered any pre-Christian or indeed primitive Christian talk of a Son of God descending to earth which could explain the appearance of such talk in the Fourth Gospel. To put it another way, *the understanding of Jesus as Son of God apparently did not provide the starting point for a christology of pre-existence or incarnation.* Any implication to the contrary which may be overheard in earlier formulations (particularly Gal. 4.4 and Rom. 8.3) is audible only because it is perceived as an echo of clearer affirmations elsewhere (Paul's Wisdom christology). In short, the origins of the doctrine of the incarnation do not seem to lie in the assertion of Christ as Son of God. For the beginnings of a christology of incarnation we must look elsewhere.

III

THE SON OF MAN

§8. INTRODUCTION

Anyone who began his investigation of incarnational christology in the second century AD would hardly think that the title 'Son of Man' had any relevance to the inquiry. For from the second century onwards it almost always denoted simply Christ's humanity in *contrast* to his divinity – not merely son of man, but also Son of God. Thus already in Ignatius, *Eph.* 20.2, more polemically in Barn. 12.10 ('Jesus, not a son of man, but the Son of God') and again in Irenaeus, e.g. *adv.haer.* III.16.7, 17.1 (see also Justin, *Dial.* 76.1; 100; *Odes Sol.* 36.3).[1] The canonical Gospels however show clearly enough that as a title of Christ in the first century it had a much fuller significance than that. What precisely that significance was and what the original sense of the phrase was in the sayings of Jesus is still hotly disputed, as any student of NT issues can hardly fail to be aware. The issues involved were already 'grey-haired' twenty years ago, yet since then the debate has increased in intensity,[2] and still the studies pour forth and the arguments stir scholarly passions.[3] With the passing of time the issues have become more and more complex, with arguments about philology,[4] *religionsgeschichtlich* background,[5] and tradition-historical criticism of particular passages[6] all interwoven and possible options multiplying. Fortunately for us however we should be able to skirt much of the fiercest controversy and focus on a narrower area where the issues though still complex are a little more manageable.

The issues in question are posed for us by a statement of Hamerton-Kelly, his conclusion after a fairly close study of the evidence: 'When Jesus used the self-designation "Son of Man" he and his hearers understood it to imply his pre-existence.'[7] Within this simple assertion are contained several important and highly contentious claims: that Jesus used the phrase 'son of man' more or less as a title; that he used it as a self-designation; that he used it with deliberate allusion to the vision of Dan. 7; that thus used it implied his own pre-existence; and that these implications would be recognized by his hearers.[8] If these claims are justified then we need look no further for the answer to our basic question: the doctrine of the incarnation is a logical development from and inevitable re-expression of Jesus' own claims concerning himself. It is true that .in the tangled debate over Jesus and the Son of Man very few scholars would feel able to follow Hamerton-Kelly all the way, and several find the evidence points in a different direction altogether.[9] Yet the fact that Hamerton-Kelly can reach this conclusion thrusts the Son of Man title to the forefront of our inquiry. If it is indeed possible that this title implied Jesus' pre-existence, that Jesus was thereby identified with a pre-existent figure who had descended from heaven, that Jesus himself intended such an identification, then we can hardly pass by on the other side and let the Son of Man controversy take its own course.

There are however two factors which enable us to cut across much of the debate and at least initially to avoid the most fiercely contested issue (the significance of the phrase for Jesus' own self-consciousness and claims about himself). The first is that *the Son of Man sayings as they now stand in the Gospels clearly refer to Jesus as the Son of Man*. Whatever the tradition-history behind the Son of Man sayings in the Synoptic Gospels and in John, the form in which they are committed to writing makes it obvious that at that stage 'the Son of Man' was a title and at that stage Jesus was identified as 'the Son of Man'. This is self-evident, not only in those Jesus-sayings where one version has 'I' and another 'the Son of Man' (Matt. 5.11/Luke 6.22; Matt. 10.32/Luke 12.8; Mark 8.27/Matt. 16.13), and not only in specific sayings like Mark 8.31 and Luke 22.48, but throughout the Gospels. We need not pause to establish the point more fully since no one would dispute it. The short-circuited question for us thus becomes: Granted that Jesus was identified as the Son of Man when the Gospel traditions were crystallized (no later than the 60s for Mark), was this understood and intended as an assertion of Jesus' pre-existence, as an assertion that one designated 'the Son of Man' had descended from heaven and had appeared or become incarnate among them as the man Jesus of Nazareth?

The second factor is that *the Son of Man tradition as we now have it contains clear allusions to the vision of Daniel 7*. Whatever the tradition-history behind the Son of Man sayings, as they now stand the intention is clearly to identify Jesus as the 'son of man' mentioned in Dan. 7.13f.:

> I saw in the night visions,
> and behoïd, with the clouds of heaven there came one like a son of man,
>   and he came to the Ancient of Days and was presented before him.
> And to him was given dominion and glory and kingdom,

that all peoples, nations and languages should serve him;
his dominion is an everlasting dominion, which shall not pass away,
and his kingdom one that shall not be destroyed.

The influence of this passage is clearest in Mark 13.26 pars. and 14.62 pars. Mark 13.26 – 'And then they will see the Son of Man coming in clouds (Matt. 24.30 adds 'of heaven') with great power and glory'; Mark 14.62 – 'you will see the Son of Man sitting at the right hand of power and coming with the clouds of heaven'. But there are also allusions of greater or less probability in another Mark passage (Mark 8.38), in four Q passages (Matt. 19.28/(Luke 22.30); Matt. 24.27/Luke 17.24; Matt. 24.37/Luke 17.26; Matt. 24.44/Luke 12.40), and in other sayings of Jesus attested only in either Matthew or Luke (Matt. 10.23; 13.41; 16.28; 24.39; 25.31; Luke 12.8; 17.22,30; 18.8; 21.36).[10] So the influence of Dan. 7.13f. on the Son of Man traditions in their present form is clear enough, a conclusion which again no one would really dispute. The question for us can be more sharply defined, therefore: granted that Jesus was identified as the 'son of man' in Dan. 7.13f. by the time of Q and Mark at the latest, was this understood and intended as an assertion of Jesus' pre-existence, as an assertion that the heavenly figure of Daniel's vision had taken flesh as Jesus of Nazareth? Only if we reach an affirmative answer to this question need we go on to inquire when these implications and connotations entered or were read into the pre-Synoptic Son of Man traditions and whether they reflect the mind and self-assertion of Jesus himself.

The issue before us, though only part of the whole debate and to that extent simpler to handle, is still complex. What was the significance intended by the 'son of man' figure in Dan. 7.13f. – a divine individual or an apocalyptic symbol? And whatever the original meaning of Dan. 7's vision, did Jewish thought pick up the imagery in the period prior to the Synoptic tradition and envisage the Son of Man as a pre-existent heavenly individual? And whatever the *religionsgeschichtlich* background to the Gospel traditions do the Son of Man sayings themselves not in fact identify Jesus as a pre-existent heavenly being? These are the questions we must attempt to answer in this chapter.

§9. WHO IS THIS 'SON OF MAN'? – THE JEWISH ANSWER

Was 'the Son of Man' a recognized title for a heavenly redeemer figure in pre-Christian Judaism? How was Daniel's vision understood by the contemporaries of Jesus and the first Christians?

§9.1 *Dan. 7.13f.* Since so much hinges on the interpretation of Daniel's vision this is where we must start. In its present form the vision of 'one like a son of man' is the climax to a much more extended vision or sequence of visions. First Daniel sees 'four great beasts' coming up out of the sea: 'the first was like a lion and had eagle's wings'; the second 'like a bear'; the third 'like a leopard, with four wings of a bird on its back'; the fourth 'terrible and dreadful and exceedingly strong' which grew a little horn with 'eyes like the eyes of a man, and a mouth speaking great things'. Then follows the vision of thrones (note the plural) and the Ancient of Days taking his seat in judgment. The beast is slain, and the dominion (*šolṭān*) of the other beasts is taken away. One like a son of man (*kᵉḇar *nāš*) comes with the clouds of heaven before the Ancient of Days

> and to him was given dominion (*šolṭān*) and glory and kingdom (*malᵉḵû*),
> that all peoples, nations, languages should serve him (*yipᵉlᵉḥûn*),
> his dominion (*šolṭān*) is an everlasting dominion (*šolṭān 'olam*)
> which shall not pass away
> and his kingdom (*malᵉḵû*) one that shall not be destroyed (Dan. 7.14).

In the interpretation that follows the 'one like a son of man' is not mentioned again. But we are told:

> These four great beasts are four kings who shall arise out of the earth. But the saints of the Most High shall receive the kingdom (*malᵉḵû*) and possess the kingdom for ever ('*olam*), for ever and ever (7.17f.).

The vision of the fourth beast is recalled and we are given the further information that the little horn

> made war with the saints, and prevailed over them until the Ancient of Days came and judgment was given for the saints of the Most High, and the time came when the saints received the kingdom (*malᵉḵû*) (7.21f.).

This fuller version of the vision of the fourth beast is then interpreted in more detail, climaxing in the judgment scene when the beasts' dominion is taken away

> to be consumed and destroyed to the end.
> And the kingdom and the dominion and the greatness of the kingdom under the whole heaven shall be given to the people of the saints of the Most High; their kingdom shall be an everlasting kingdom (*malᵉḵût 'olam*)
> and all dominions shall serve (*yipᵉlᵉḥûn*) and obey them (7.26f.).

Two points seem clearly to emerge. First, the 'one like a son of man' is *identical* with 'the saints of the Most High'. Indeed the author seems to take some pains to bring this out: no less than three times he states that what the vision described as the triumph of the 'son of man' is in fact the triumph of 'the saints of the Most High' (7.17f., 21f., 26f.). We may note particularly how closely the wording of 7.14 matches that of 7.17f., 26f.,

and how vision and interpretation seem to be intermingled in 7.17f. and
21f., with 'the saints of the Most High' taking the place of the 'son of
man' over against the beasts. Second, the 'one like a son of man' is one
of five figures in a vision set over against four other visionary figures.
They are depicted like beasts ('*like* a lion', '*like* a bear', '*like* a leopard').[11]
The fifth is depicted '*like* a man' – 'son of man' as is well known simply
denoting a human being (cf. e.g. Ps. 8.4).[12] The conclusion seems clear
enough: *the man-like figure represents the people of Israel*, just as the beast-like
figures represent the enemies of Israel – not surprisingly a very prejudiced
presentation on Israel's behalf.[13]

This interpretation of the 'one like a son of man' would seem to give
a wholly satisfactory exposition of Dan. 7 requiring nothing to be added
to make complete sense of the text.[14] Despite this many have insisted on
arguing that the 'one like a son of man' is more than a symbolical
representative of the saints. Indeed some NT scholars assume with scarcely a second thought that ' "the one like a son of man" must originally
have been an individual heavenly figure'.[15] That is, they assume there
was already within the horizon of Jewish thought some heavenly individual with whom Daniel and his readers would naturally link the man-like
figure of Daniel's vision – even though there is nothing in the vision or
interpretation itself which calls for this fuller interpretation. Who might
such an individual be? The chief candidates put forward in the discussions
of this century are the Messiah, the original man (Adam), Wisdom or an
angel.[16]

(*a*) Was the man-like figure simply a way of representing the *Messiah*,
a new way of expressing the still vital hope of a Davidic king?[17] It is
certainly true that Dan. 7 itself interprets the four beasts as 'four kings'
(7.17), but this was not unnatural where 'king' was a widely recognized
metonymy for 'kingdom' (cf. e.g. 2.44; 8.21f.). And the more striking fact
is that in the interpretation of the 'one like a son of man' *no* king is
mentioned. If the king-messiah had been in view he would hardly have
been omitted in the following verses. Moreover, in the subsequent chapters where a leader of the saints is mentioned he is an archangel, Michael,
'your prince' (10.21; 12.1) not the Messiah. Presumably for the author,
writing at or near the height of the hostility to Syrian overlordship, the
saints of the Most High owned no king but Yahweh.[18] Outside Daniel
the evidence most frequently cited in favour of this view is from the
Similitudes of Enoch (I Enoch 37–71). But as we shall see below (§9.2),
the dating of the Similitudes makes it very questionable whether they can
provide any evidence of the thought behind Daniel; any line of influence
is clearly from Dan. 7 to the Similitudes. The still later Jewish/rabbinic
identification of the Danielic 'son of man' with the Messiah (including

Trypho, according to Justin, *Dial.* 32.1)[19] was probably provoked as much by the Christian interpretation as by the Similitudes.

A rather more plausible line of influence may be drawn from Ps. 80.17 (= 80.18 MT = 79.18 LXX):

> Let your hand be upon the man of your right hand,
>   the son of man whom you made strong for yourself.

As it now stands in the MT and LXX the verse is clearly parallel to v.15 and refers to Israel. But something odd has happened to the text (in the LXX v.15b/16b is identical with v.17b/18b) and v.15b is very probably not original (it also disrupts the metre). In which case the similarity with Ps. 89.21 and Ps. 110.1 suggests that the original reference was to the king.[20] Yet even so there is little or no indication that it was interpreted messianically in either Jewish or Christian texts of our period,[21] far less that it promoted 'son of man' to the status of a messianic title.[22] More to the immediate point, there is no indication that Ps. 80.17 in any way influenced Dan. 7.13f. We should not forget that 'son of man' in Ps. 80.17 is simply a poetic variant for 'man' (as in Ps. 8.4) and was not intended as a title. Given the currency of the Semitic idiom there is no particular reason why in the pre-Christian period 'one like a son of man' should have been linked to Ps. 80.17 and interpreted by it.

Another line of approach is to argue that a concept of the pre-existence of the Messiah was already current within Judaism, and that the apocalyptic figure of Dan. 7.13f. would naturally evoke that concept. The chief evidence cited here is the LXX translation of Ps. 110.3 and Micah 5.2.[23] Ps. 110.2f. –

> The Lord sends forth from Zion your mighty sceptre.
>   Rule in the midst of your foes!
>   . . .
> From the womb of the morning the dew of your youth will come to you.

The LXX translates the last line, 'From the womb before the morning star I brought you forth' (πρὸ ἑωσφόρου ἐξεγέννησά σε).
Micah 5.2 (5.1 Heb.) –

> But you, O Bethlehem Ephrathah,
> who are little to be among the clans of Judah,
> from you shall come forth for me
> one who is to be a ruler in Israel,
> whose origin is from of old, from ancient days.

The LXX translates the last line, 'and his goings forth are from the beginning from days of old' (καὶ ἔξοδοι αὐτοῦ ἀπ᾽ ἀρχῆς ἐξ ἡμερῶν αἰῶνος). In both cases the LXX translation is rather surprising, though both could be justified as free renderings of the Hebrew. In neither

instance does the Hebrew (as we have it) suggest the idea of pre-existence.[24] An influence from Wisdom imagery is arguable (particularly Sir.
24.9 – πρὸ τοῦ αἰῶνος ἀπ᾽ ἀρχῆς ἔκτισέ με), but examined individually
the verbal connections do not appear very strong.[25] If these were indeed
the LXX readings in the pre-Christian period then the most striking
feature is that they seem to have made no impact whatsoever on the
thought of the time. Although Ps. 110.1 and 110.4 were important proof
texts in earliest Christian apologetic (see also below pp. 108f.) Ps. 110.3
is never explicitly cited in the NT period. It was not until Justin took it
up in the middle of the second century AD (*Dial.* 63.3; 76.7) that it began
to be used as a prophecy of Christ's pre-existence.[26] Similarly with Micah
5.2, though often cited by the ante-Nicene fathers, the citation only rarely
extends to the last line, and then without any implication of pre-existence
being drawn from it. This would certainly be a most odd feature if these
LXX renderings were already understood as speaking of the Messiah's
pre-existence. The silence of the first century AD points rather in the
other direction: viz. that such an interpretation only became current after
the pre-existence of Christ was already taken for granted.

Other pieces of evidence sometimes cited[27] are the possible allusions to
the pre-existence of Moses in Ass.Mos. 1.14 and the rabbinic belief in
seven things 'created before the world was created', including the name
of the Messiah (bPes. 54a; bNed. 39b; Targ.Ps.Jon. Zech. 4.7).[28] The
Samaritans certainly seem to have embraced a belief in Moses' pre-
existence,[29] though the beginning of that belief can hardly be dated with
any confidence when the Samaritan documents are so late.[30] The Assumption of Moses,[31] usually dated to the first thirty years of the first
century AD, has been suggested as the earliest expression of such a belief[32]
– Ass.Mos. 1.14: 'He designed and devised me, and he prepared me
before the foundation of the world that I should be the mediator of his
covenant' (Excogitavit et invenit me, qui ab initio orbis terrarum prae-
paratus sum, ut sim arbiter testamenti illius). But the text is a matter of
some dispute,[33] and even as it stands it seems hardly more than a strong
statement of the predetermined choice of one who had a particularly
prominent place in the fulfilment of God's purposes (cf. Jer. 1.5; Gal.
1.15; Eph. 1.4 – see further below §29.2).[34] An allusion to Wisd. 7.22 in
Ass. Mos. 11.15f. is also possible,[35] but to speak of Moses being thereby
represented as an 'incarnation of Wisdom' is too bold.[36] Similarly with
the relevant rabbinic texts, even if the traditions could be dated as early
as the first century AD which is unlikely, and which at any rate can hardly
be assumed. The fact that 'repentance' is one of the seven pre-existent
things must mean simply that the items on the list were *predetermined* by
God to fulfil their function in the outworking of his purpose for his
creation and his people.[37]

The most obvious conclusion therefore is that *there was no conception of a pre-existent Messiah current in pre-Christian Judaism prior to the Similitudes of Enoch.*[38] We should also bear in mind the opinion ascribed to Trypho the Jew in the middle of the second century: Trypho dismisses the idea that Christ pre-existed and asserts, 'We all expect that Christ will be a man (born) of men' (*Dial.* 49.1). This conclusion of course does not exclude the possibility that the man-like figure of Dan. 7 was understood by some as the Messiah. We should not underestimate Jewish hermeneutical readiness to read as much into a text as possible.[39] But equal facility could be shown in excluding possible interpretations, as we see in the case of Isa. 53.[40] And where the hope of a Davidic Messiah was still strong in pre-Christian Judaism (as in Ps. Sol. 17; 4QFlor. 1.10–13; cf. Luke 1.32f.,69)[41] it is not altogether obvious why a man-like figure in heaven symbolizing the saints of the Most High should be identified with him. In short, *we lack any sort of firm evidence that the 'one like a son of man' in Dan. 7 was understood within pre-Christian Judaism as the Messiah*, pre-existent or otherwise.

(*b*) The History of Religions school developed the view that the Danielic 'son of man' has to be understood against the background of a pervasive near eastern speculation concerning *the original man.*[42] Subsequent scholarship has been more impressed by the differences between the Danielic figure and such Iranian, Babylonian, Egyptian and Gnostic parallels as might be adduced.[43] It is true of course that a contrast between beast-like figures arising out of the sea and a man-like figure would be likely to evoke the creation stories, where Adam (= man) is given dominion over the other living creatures (Gen. 1.26f.; 2.19f.), and, more important, the myth of the sea dragon representing primeval chaos. But this latter had already been domesticated within Israelite thought (Job 9.8,13; 26.12; Ps. 74.12–14; 89.9f.; Isa. 51.9), and not least as a way of depicting the final conflict between Israel and her enemies (Isa. 27.1; Jer. 51.34–7; Ezek. 29.3f.)[44] – precisely the same climactic clash between Israel and the encircling world powers which is represented in Dan. 7 and in a not dissimilar way. In other words, the vision of Dan. 7 can fairly be described as an apocalyptic elaboration of Israel's earlier use of the dragon myth. The point is however that in these earlier versions only Yahweh, the beasts and Yahweh's people are involved – no thought of primal man enters in. In Dan. 7 precisely the same three sets of characters appear – the Ancient of Days, the beasts and the 'son of man'. That is to say, Dan. 7's own interpretation of the human figure as 'the saints of the Most High' is wholly of a piece with the earlier thought. The result is the same if we attempt to press the comparison between Adam and the (son of) man of Daniel's vision. For though Jewish thought wrestled much with the Genesis accounts,[45] it did not really reckon with Adam as an eschatological individual.[46] More important is Adam's role as the father of Israel[47] and the claim that creation was for the sake of Israel.[48] Such influence as there was from the account of Adam's dominion over the beasts therefore would be likely to reinforce the already strong impression that the Danielic 'man' is a symbolic representation of Israel. In short, *the use made of creation myths in the vision of Dan. 7 gives no support to the view that the 'one like a son of man' would have been understood as an individual*, Adam, primal man or whoever.

Of the various attempts to set Dan. 7.13f. against a more syncretistic background the most plausible is the thesis that behind the 'son of man' imagery lies a divine figure now degraded but originally depicting another god enthroned by the most high god, the symbolic depiction perhaps of a new (younger) god beginning to take over from the aged god (the ancient of days).[49] But there is no hint of this in Dan. 7; apart from anything else Daniel would hardly have wanted his readers to think of 'one like a son of man' as taking over or usurping Yahweh's role! Moreover, where the pre-history of particular elements within Daniel's vision is so obscure, primary weight in searching for the contemporary understanding of Dan. 7 (second and first century BC) must be given to the meaning which Daniel (the principal or final editor) himself clearly intended – and that, as we have seen, involves the straightforward identification of the 'son of man' with 'the saints of the Most High'. Even someone aware of the background of the imagery used would be unlikely to infer from that alone that the 'one like a son of man' must be understood as a particular individual.[50]

(c) A particular form of the *religionsgeschichtliche* interpretation which deserves special mention finds the source of the 'son of man' imagery within Jewish tradition in the concept of pre-existent *Wisdom*.[51] In fact however there are no clear points of contact between the *eschatological* role of the man-like figure in Dan. 7 and the characteristically primordial role of Wisdom in the wisdom literature (Prov. 8.22–31; Sir. 24.9; Wisd. 7.22; see further below ch. VI).[52] If the Similitudes of Enoch (I Enoch 37–71) are appealed to,[53] we must simply note that in the Similitudes Wisdom is *not* identified with the Son of Man. The talk of personified Wisdom in ch. 42 is independent of the Son of Man material (first mentioned in 46.2). And in the latter the influence of Isa. 11.2 is more prominent (particularly 49.1–3; 51.3; cf. 48.10; 52.4; 62.2) – that is, wisdom is something the Son of Man is given (cf. Ps.Sol. 17.37) – though 48.7 does speak of 'the wisdom of the Lord of Spirits revealing the Son of Man to the holy and righteous'. But *in no instance is there any reason to think that the Son of Man would have been seen as a more elaborate personification of Wisdom*,[54] quite apart from the fact that little conviction can attach to any attempt to find in the Similitudes of Enoch the background for Daniel.[55]

(d) An alternative suggestion is that the man-like figure in Dan. 7 is an angel: we may compare particularly the description of Gabriel in 8.15f. and 10.18 as 'one having the appearance of a man' (kᵉmar'ēh gāber/'ādām) (note also 12.1 – Michael 'the great prince who has charge of your people').[56] But apart from the fact that the formula is different ('one like a son of man'; 'one having the appearance of a man'), the imagery of angelic *leadership* and intervention on behalf of Israel by two different angels (10.13,20f.) is different from the symbolic *identification* of the human figure with the saints of the Most High. Nor is it by any means obvious that the editor who put Daniel together in its present form intended either to equate the saints with angels[57] or the human figure with a particular angel.[58] The clouds of heaven with which the visionary (son of) man comes before the Ancient of Days denote his (Israel's anticipated) exaltation, not his origin (cf. IV Ezra 13.3). Moreover, the fact that I Enoch shows no awareness of any such identification is significant here (cf. I Enoch 40; 54.6; 68.2–4; 71), since with so little evidence of a Son of Man speculation within Jewish literature particular hypotheses about pre-Christian interpretation of the Danielic 'son of man' which cannot draw support from I Enoch are all the more vulnerable. Likewise it is presumably significant that the Qumran sect, who *do* give a considerable place to angelic leadership (see below pp. 151–3) and who evidently valued the book of Daniel, seem to have made nothing of Dan. 7.13f. (see below p. 77). Consequently the thesis that the man-like figure of Daniel's vision was taken as a particular angel rather than as an appropriate apocalyptic symbol for the elect is hardly compelling.[59]

To *sum up*. The assertion that behind Daniel's vision of 'one like a son of man' stands a particular individual has proved groundless. *There are no good reasons for the hypothesis that Daniel or his readers would have understood the human figure of his vision as a particular individual.* This means also that the suggestion that the Danielic 'son of man' would be conceived as pre-existent[60] falls to the ground. It by no means follows that a figure in an apocalyptic vision is pre-existent simply because he appears before God in heaven. Apocalyptic is full of vivid and often bizarre imagery express-ing the visionary's hopes for Israel (Dan. 2.31–45; I Enoch 83–90; IV Ezra 11–12), and the specific thought of pre-existence only becomes a feature of apocalyptic at a later stage.[61] In Dan. 7 the whole thrust of the vision is forward to the eschaton – the judgment scene with the man-like figure clearly representing the final vindication and triumph of the saints over their enemies. Nothing in Dan. 7 encourages let alone requires the reader to go beyond that interpretation, and even where a background can be traced with some plausibility within the syncretistic thought of the Ancient Near East, it is a background already so well assimilated to Jewish monotheism and nationalism as to be wholly submerged into the nationalistic interpretation of the vision which Dan. 7 gives. In short, *for Daniel the '(son of) man' is simply the appropriate symbol for Israel in contrast to Israel's savage enemies.* Of this figure's individual existence or pre-existence there is no suggestion.

§9.2   The next evidence which calls for consideration is *I Enoch 37–71* (usually designated the Similitudes or Parables of Enoch), since these chapters have regularly been taken as the strongest evidence for the existence of a pre-Christian Jewish belief in a pre-existent divine individual called 'the Son of Man'. It is certainly clear enough that the Son of Man is a heavenly *individual* in the Similitudes, and that the author identifies him as the Elect or Chosen One, and indeed as his Anointed One (Messiah).[62] We may note, for example, 46.3f. (the Chosen One having been spoken of just before in 45.3–4)[63] –

> [3]And he (angel) answered me and said to me: 'This (the figure in Daniel's vision) is the Son of Man who has righteousness, and with whom righteousness dwells; he will reveal all the treasures of that which is secret, for the Lord of Spirits has *chosen* him, and through uprightness his lot has surpassed all before the Lord of Spirits for ever. [4]And this Son of Man whom you have seen will rouse the kings and the powerful from their resting-places, and the strong from their thrones, and will loose the reins of the strong, and will break the teeth of the sinners . . .' (this judgmental role is elaborated in the following chapters – 49.2–4; 52.6–9; 55.4; 61.8f.).

Likewise in the two references to the Anointed One (48.10; 52.4) there can be little doubt that the Chosen One, the Son of Man is intended. Moreover, it would almost certainly seem to be the case that in the Similitudes the Son of Man is thought of as *pre-existent*.[64] Note particularly 48.2–6 and 62.6–7 –

> [2]And at that hour that Son of Man was named in the presence of the Lord of Spirits, and his name (was named) before the Head of Days. [3]Even before the sun and the constellations were created, before the stars of heaven were made, his name was named before the Lord of Spirits. . . . [6]And because of this he was chosen and hidden before him before the world was created, and for ever.

> [6]And the mighty kings, and all those who possess the earth, will praise and bless and exalt him who rules everything which is hidden. [7]For from the beginning the Son of Man was hidden, and the most High kept him in the presence of his power, and revealed him (only) to the chosen.

If then the Similitudes speak of the Son of Man as a pre-existent heavenly individual does this indicate an already established Son of Man tradition in the period prior to the Similitudes? We have seen no suggestion of such in Dan. 7 itself; but what of the period between Daniel and the Similitudes? Do the Similitudes provide evidence of a *pre-Christian* Jewish belief in the Son of Man? To answer this question two issues must be clarified: (a) whether the Son of Man passages in the Similitudes give any indication of a pre-Similitudes Son of Man tradition; and (b) the date of the Similitudes.

(a) The most striking feature of the Son of Man passages in the Similitudes at this point is their dependence on Daniel's vision (Dan. 7.9,13). This becomes immediately evident when we consider the care with which the 'Son of Man' is introduced in 46.1–2:[65]

> [1]And there I saw one who had a head of days, and his head (was) white like wool (Dan. 7.9); and with him (there was) another, whose face had the appearance of a man (Dan. 7.13), and his face (was) full of grace, like one of the holy angels. [2]And I asked one of the holy angels who went with me, and showed me all the secrets, about that Son of Man, who he was, and whence he was, (and) why he went with the Head of Days.

Just as significant is the fact that the subsequent references are regularly to *that* Son of Man, in each case referring back to that first usage.[66] Clearly then the 'Son of Man' as a phrase is drawn immediately and directly from the vision of Dan. 7.9–14.[67] Moreover the way in which the author of the Similitudes takes up the phrase strongly suggests that he is introducing a new interpretation of Dan. 7.13f., using the heavenly son of man figure of Daniel's vision as a way of filling out his picture of the Chosen One and transforming the descriptive phrase thereby into something more like a title than it was before (that Son of Man of Daniel's vision).[68] To put the same point another way, one can hardly argue from the usage of the Similitudes itself that the Son of Man was an already well-known figure, or that the author was equating two established and hitherto distinct heavenly beings – the Chosen One (the Messiah) and the Son of Man.[69] Whatever other passages may or may not have influenced his presentation of the Son of Man's role as judge,[70] there is no hint that in his identification of the Chosen One as the human figure of Daniel's vision he was indebted to any predecessor. *At this point the author of the Similitudes depends not only directly but also exclusively on Dan. 7 and the interpretation appears to be a new one introduced by himself.*[71]

How it is that he came to think of this Son of Man as pre-existent is not clear: an equation of the Son of Man with Wisdom is hardly suggested by the Similitudes, as we saw above (p. 73), and since in the end he identifies the Son of Man with Enoch himself (71.14) Dan. 7.13f. would have been likely to suggest something more like apotheosis or exaltation rather than pre-existence.[72] This is a question to which we shall have to return later when we may find that our fuller investigation has some light to shed on the matter (see below §10.3).

(b) If the Similitudes of Enoch is the first Jewish writing to make something of the human figure of Dan. 7.13 and the first evidence we have in non-Christian literature of the (son of) man of Daniel's vision being interpreted as a heavenly individual, it becomes of central importance to ascertain the date of the Similitudes. Are they pre-Christian? Do they launch a concept of the Son of Man as a pre-existent divine being which might have influenced the Synoptic tradition?

The first vital piece of evidence is the testimony of the Dead Sea Scrolls. It has long been realized that the version of I Enoch preserved in Ethiopic is an edited compilation of older material, probably interdependent to some degree but written over quite a lengthy period – the initial parts of an Enoch cycle that includes II (Slavonic) Enoch and the (probably) much later III (Hebrew) Enoch.[73] The Qumran finds have clarified the picture and confirm that I (Ethiopic) Enoch consists of several distinct Books of Enoch.[74] The significant factor however is that while Cave 4 at Qumran has provided fragments of *every* other section of I Enoch,[75] *not one fragment of the Similitudes has appeared.* This in itself need not imply a post-AD 70 date for the Similitudes, since no trace of the Assumption of Moses has been found either, and the Assumption is usually dated early in the first century AD (though see above n.32). We do not know, in other words, when the Qumran library stopped taking in new manuscripts and what their principles of selection were.[76] But the Enoch corpus was clearly popular at Qumran, and the Similitudes are evidently inspired by and intended to be an addition to that corpus. Moreover the book of Daniel was just as popular,[77] and there is some evidence that the Covenanters were themselves influenced by Daniel's vision (Dan. 7.9f.),[78] even though no allusion to 7.13f. itself has been found. In other words, the interests of the Qumran sect and of the author of the Similitudes seem to overlap to a considerable extent. So there is a certain unlikelihood that the sect would have been ignorant of or have rejected or ignored the Similitudes had they been produced prior to the 60s of the first century AD. Overall then the absence of I Enoch 37–71 from the Dead Sea Scrolls may well tip the balance of probability against a pre-AD 70 date for these chapters.[79] The evidence however is too slender to permit a firm judgment on the point: 56.7 may well imply that Jerusalem was not yet destroyed, though the reference to the Parthians and Medes in 56.5 could refer either to the conflict of 40–38 BC or conceivably to Trajan's campaign against the Parthians in AD 113–17.[80] What we can say with greater firmness is that any hypothesis which *depends* on a BC or early AD dating for the Similitudes may well be building castles in the air.[81]

The second important piece of evidence is that any influence from the Similitudes on the Gospel traditions of the Son of Man cannot be traced back earlier than Matthew and John with any probability. The passages in Matthew where it is most plausible to see some dependence on the Similitudes are Matt. 19.28 and 25.31f.:[82] 19.28 – 'when the Son of Man sits upon his throne of glory' (in judgment); 25.31f. – 'then will he (the Son of Man) sit on his throne of glory' (in judgment). We may compare I Enoch 45.3 – 'On that day the Chosen One will sit on the throne of glory' (in judgment) – similarly 55.4; 61.8; 62.5 ('that Son of a Woman' (?)); 69.27 ('that Son of Man'). That the Son of Man has a decisive role in the final judgment when he comes in glory is clear enough in the pre-Matthean tradition (e.g. Mark 8.38; 13.26f.), and also that he sits at the right hand of God (Mark 14.62),[83] but nowhere else does the Gospel tradition speak of the Son of Man exercising judgment while sitting on his throne of glory. So some link between the Similitudes and Matthew is quite possible.[84] Similarly the thought and language of John 5.27 is closer to I Enoch 69.27 than anything in the Synoptic tradition:[85]

> John 5.27 – the Father has given him (the Son) authority to execute judgment, because he is the Son of Man;

> I Enoch 69.27 – the whole judgment was given to the Son of Man.

The point is however that any link or parallel is to be found *only in the Matthean and Johannine redaction*; if we look for earlier influence we can find no firm handhold in the pre-Matthean strata.[86] At best therefore, of the four Evangelists only Matthew and John may be adjudged to know the Similitudes, and Matthew is usually dated to the 80s of the first century and John to the 90s. Once again then we find ourselves pushed towards a date subsequent to Q and Mark, and most probably, subsequent to AD 70. Nor can we ignore the possibility that the influence runs the other way, with the author of I Enoch 37–71 borrowing motifs from the Jewish Christian style of referring to the exalted Christ's role as judge and using them to elaborate his own new (shall we say counter) thesis that the Danielic son of man was none other than Enoch; for Enoch was certainly a focus of escalating speculation in some Jewish circles from about the turn of the first century AD, if the rest of the Enoch cycle is anything to go by (see further below pp. 80f. and §10.3).

In short, *there is nothing in I Enoch 37–71 to suggest that there was a pre-Christian Jewish tradition concerning the Son of Man as a heavenly individual* (whether redeemer or judge), nothing to suggest that the early Christian Son of Man tradition knew or was influenced by the Similitudes, and what other evidence there is points towards a post-AD 70 date at the earliest for the Similitudes themselves. The immediate corollary of particular importance for our inquiry is that so far as I Enoch is concerned *the concept of the Son of Man as a pre-existent heavenly individual cannot be traced back within Jewish (non-Christian) circles to a pre-70 date.* What then of the other non-Christian Jewish evidence?

§9.3   What other evidence is there which might shed light on Jewish understanding or use of Daniel's vision of 'one like a son of man' in the first century AD? Only *IV Ezra* and possible indications of *early rabbinic speculation* and controversy are likely to be of sufficient relevance.[87]

(*a*) Whatever the disagreements over the date of the Similitudes of Enoch there is almost universal agreement regarding the date of IV Ezra – post AD 70, during the last decades of the first century AD. Nevertheless it is quite possible that it reflects earlier Jewish tradition, so we cannot ignore it. The key passage is ch. 13 (following RSV of II Esdras) –

> ¹After seven days, I dreamed a dream in the night; ²and behold, a wind arose from the sea and stirred up all the waves. ³And I looked, and behold, this wind made something like the figure of a man (or, one like the resemblance of a man) come up out of the heart of the sea. And I looked, and behold, that man flew with the clouds of heaven; and wherever he turned his face to look, everything under his gaze trembled . . .

It is even clearer than in the Similitudes that 'this man' is to be identified as *the Messiah* –

> ³² . . . then my Son will be revealed, whom you saw as a man coming up from the sea;

> ⁵¹I said, . . . 'Why did I see the man coming up from the heart of the sea?' ⁵²He said to me, 'Just as no one can explore or know what is in the depths of the sea, so no one on earth can see my Son or those who are with him, except in the time of his day' (cf. 7.28f. – 'my Son, the Messiah').

That some sort of concept of *pre-existence* is involved is also implied, though it is even more debatable than with the Similitudes whether it is the pre-existence of the person, or the predetermined purpose of God, or even the eschatological manifestation of an exalted individual (Enoch, Moses, Elijah?) which is in view[88] –

> 7.28 – 'My Son, the Messiah, shall be revealed with those who are with him . . .'

> 12.32 – 'This is the Messiah whom the Most High has kept until the end of days, who will arise from the posterity of David . . .'

> 13.25f. – 'As for your seeing a man coming up from the heart of the sea, ²⁶this is he whom the Most High has been keeping for many ages . . .'

> 14.9 – 'You shall be taken up from among men, and henceforth you shall live with my Son and with those who are like you, until the times are ended' (cf. 6.26).

At the same time it is sufficiently clear that the use of 'man' as a messianic reference is derived simply from the Dan. 7 vision – reworked to be sure (with an element from Dan. 2 drawn in at v.6), but with the allusion to Dan. 7.13 hardly disputable – 'one like the resemblance of a man', who 'came up out of the sea' (like the beasts in Dan. 7.3) and who 'flew with the clouds of heaven' (IV Ezra 13.3); and the initial setting of the two visions are almost identical (IV Ezra 13.2 = Dan. 7.2).[89] Subsequent references to the 'man' are all back to this initial figure – 'the man who came up out of the sea' (v.5); 'After this I saw the same man ...' (v.12); 'As for your seeing a man come up from the heart of the sea ...' (v.25); and see vv. 32 and 51f. cited above. The intention therefore is clearly to identify the Messiah with the man-like figure of Daniel's vision. And the identification is made as a way of explaining the vision, both the original vision of Daniel (by implication) and the reworked version of IV Ezra. In other words, there is no indication whatsoever in IV Ezra that this was an already established interpretation of Dan. 7, *no indication whatsoever either that Dan. 7 was already interpreted messianically or that 'the Man' was an established title for God's anointed redeemer.*

In particular, there are no grounds at all for seeing in IV Ezra 13 proof that 'Son of Man' was an already recognized title for the Messiah in Jewish circles prior to IV Ezra.[90] To be sure, we cannot be finally certain that in the (probably) semitic original 'son of man' did not stand behind 'man' of the various versions known to us, for, of course, in semitic idiom 'son of man' does mean 'man'. But since translations of other 'son of man' references (both Jewish and Christian writings) have made a habit of retaining the semitic idiom it is more likely that the rendering of Daniel's 'son of man' by 'man' was the work of the original author. If so, the probability is further strengthened that 'Son of Man' did not function as a title in pre-Christian Jewish messianic expectation.[91] All that we can say with any assurance is that IV Ezra provides another, and it would appear quite independent example,[92] of the way in which Daniel's vision stimulated fresh hope of final vindication and victory even after the catastrophe of AD 70. That the seer interpreted Dan. 7.13 as a reference to the Anointed One and used language of pre-existence to describe him is certainly striking, but there is nothing in IV Ezra itself to suggest that a concept of a pre-existent heavenly redeemer (Messiah, Son of Man, or whoever) had been attained within (non-Christian) Judaism prior to AD 70.

(*b*) The rabbinic evidence of most interest to us is that concerning the origin of the two powers heresy. A. F. Segal's investigation on this point has thrown up two important findings. The first is that the earliest form of the heresy was not dualistic (= Gnostic – two opposing powers), rather more ditheistic (in the rabbis' eyes) or 'binitarian' (that is, probably Christian). The second is that Dan. 7.9f. seems to have played a part in the evolution of the heresy.[93] The implication is that at some stage within Jewish circles there were those who identified the human figure of Dan.

7.13 as a second god. Or, to put the point more carefully, the implication is that in some Jewish circles speculation focused on the 'son of man' in Daniel's vision, identifying the figure not simply as a particular individual (an exalted, translated human being, or whatever), and not simply as a pre-existent heavenly being (archangel, or whatever), but as a divine being who shared in the glory and authority that is (in rabbinic orthodoxy) God's alone. Difficult as it is to date the beginning of the two powers heresy, an important fact is that it is attributed first to Elisha ben Abuya (c. 110–135), a contemporary of Akiba.[94] This fits well with what we have already found and suggests the following picture: that in the period between the two Jewish revolts (70–132) messianic hope, apocalyptic fervency and/or merkabah mysticism intermingled in a speculation stimulated by and in part at least centred upon Dan. 7.13, and that in one case at least the rabbis judged the speculation to have got out of hand.[95] How much of that speculation was due to influence from or reaction against Christian belief in Jesus as the Son of Man is a question we will have to return to. For the moment we need only draw two conclusions: first, we have a third strand of evidence which points to *the end of the first century and beginning of the second century AD as a period of somewhat intense and escalating speculation regarding the 'son of man' of Daniel's vision* as a heavenly or divine and (in some sense) pre-existent individual; and second, so far as we can tell, it was not until the latter half of this period that the rabbis came to the conclusion that this speculation was a threat to their monotheism.[96]

§9.4   To sum up our findings from Jewish (non-Christian) sources. Well might the Fourth Evangelist represent the Jerusalem crowd as asking, 'Who is this son of man?' (John 12.34), for our evidence is that without the carefully constructed allusion to Dan. 7.13 and its equally careful interpretation such as we have found in the Similitudes of Enoch and IV Ezra the phrase would have had no clear reference for a Jew in the period before AD 70. That is to say, we have thus far found *no evidence of a Son of Man concept in pre-Christian Judaism*, nor any evidence that prior to the Similitudes of Enoch and IV Ezra Jewish faith had articulated a belief in a pre-existent heavenly redeemer/Messiah.[97] What we do have is a confluence of indications that in the aftermath of AD 70, when in some Jewish circles faith found expression of hope once again in apocalyptic (IV Ezra, II Baruch, Sibylline Oracles IV and Apocalypse of Abraham) Daniel's vision not surprisingly proved a source of inspiration to at least one and probably two writers (Similitudes of Enoch, IV Ezra).[98] In Daniel's vision of a man-like figure coming in clouds to the Ancient of Days and representing the final triumph of the saints they found a cryptic (but typically apocalyptic) reference to the Anointed One, God's escha-

tological redeemer whose coming in judgment was certain. To express
this assurance the language of pre-existence was used – the Son of Man
hidden (in God's purpose?) from the beginning. In at least one case in
the speculation which this heavenly figure provoked, he was accorded
such a glorious and divine status that the rabbis perceived a threat to
their monotheism and withdrew to the safer interpretation of the 'one like
a son of man' as a symbol for the Messiah or the saints. The extent to
which, if at all, Christian understanding of Jesus as the Son of Man
played any part in all this may become apparent after our next section.

§10. WHO IS THIS 'SON OF MAN'? – THE CHRISTIAN ANSWER

We have already drawn preliminary conclusions about the Jewish answer
to our question, Who is this 'son of man'? But of course our survey of
relevant Jewish evidence is incomplete, since much of our earliest Christian writings can quite properly be classified as Jewish as well, or perhaps
more precisely Jewish-Christian. Do they shed any further or different
light on the subject? There is no question that in the Gospels as they
now stand the Son of Man is a title, and for a particular individual –
Jesus. Nor is it possible to dispute the influence of Dan. 7 on a significant
proportion of the Synoptic Son of Man references (see above pp. 66f. and
n. 10). So we can press at once into the central area of our inquiry, and
in such a way fortunately that we do not need to reach decisions on the
other contentious issues in the ongoing Son of Man debate. The inquiry
can be divided simply into two main questions: Is there any indication
that the identification of Jesus as the Son of Man in the NT writings was
based on a prior concept of the Son of Man as a heavenly individual
already current in Judaism? And, whatever the answer to the first question, Did this early Christian identification of Jesus as the Son of Man
carry any implication that this Son of Man had enjoyed a heavenly pre-
existence?

§10.1 We ask first then, Is there any evidence from the NT writings
themselves of an already established Son of Man concept lying behind
the NT's identification of Jesus as the Son of Man?, any evidence in the
NT that Jesus was identified with a particular individual whose existence
in heaven had already, previously been deduced from Dan. 7.13? The
most plausible indication of such an already established belief lies in the
oddly sounding third person character of the Son of Man references, not
least, indeed especially those which allude to Dan. 7.13. When one reads
the sayings cited above in n. 10, it would not be unnatural to conclude

that the speaker (Jesus) is alluding to someone else – 'Then they will see the Son of Man coming in clouds with great power and glory' (Mark 13.26); 'I am (the Christ); and you will see the Son of Man sitting at the right hand of power, and coming with the clouds of heaven' (Mark 14.62); etc. Of course, not all these particular Son of Man references can be traced back very far into the tradition – most obviously Matt. 16.28 (cf. Mark 9.1). Fortunately for us however we do not need to engage in a detailed tradition-historical inquiry into each saying, for the issue confronting us does not depend on the outcome of such inquiries. Whatever the origin of this 'third person characteristic' in the sayings alluding to Dan. 7.13 it still poses the same question to us: Does it denote a distinction between the speaker and the one designated the Son of Man? We can proceed therefore simply by looking at the various possibilities in turn.

Whatever the course of development charted by historical critical analysis of the Son of Man sayings it is bound to end up with one or other of the following conclusions.

(a) This third person characteristic which seems to differentiate Jesus from the Son of Man is a post-Easter formulation, as are all the Son of Man sayings.[99] However, no one wishes to suggest that the earliest churches did actually distinguish the exalted Christ from some other heavenly Son of Man. So in this case we are confronted with a somewhat odd hypothesis: that the post-Easter interpretation of Jesus' resurrection, exaltation and/or hoped for parousia drew on Dan. 7.13 with the intention of identifying Jesus as the 'son of man' of Daniel's vision, but in such a way that the identification is not entirely explicit.

(b) Alternatively, the first Christians took up a speech mannerism of Jesus himself whereby he referred to himself or his mission cryptically under the phrase 'son of man', meaning 'man' or 'I as a man'.[100] In this case the third person characteristic goes back to Jesus himself. But the first Christians, looking for scriptures to explain what they believed had happened to Jesus (death and resurrection), hit upon the almost identical phrase in Dan. 7.13 and used it to express their faith in Jesus' exaltation and/or coming again, while preserving the particular third person characteristic of Jesus' speech in their own formulations (whether expressed under prophetic inspiration or in midrashic exegesis of Dan. 7 or of the Jesus-tradition itself).

In either of these first two instances ((a) and (b)) our question is answered: the link between Jesus and the man-like figure in Dan. 7 was first forged by the post-Easter church(es) as they sought scriptural proof for their belief concerning Jesus, with Dan. 7.13 for some reason either giving rise to or giving scriptural backing for the hope that Jesus would soon 'come on the clouds of heaven'. In both cases the interpretation of Dan. 7.13 as referring to Jesus was an innovative exegesis which we owe to some unknown individual or community in earliest Christianity and provides no evidence of an earlier Son of Man concept based on Dan. 7. In both cases the identification of the human figure in Daniel's vision as a particular individual was a step first taken within Christianity under the stimulus of the first Easter. In both cases Daniel's 'son of man' became a title (the Son of Man) for the first time, so far as we can tell, when earliest Christianity interpreted the phrase as a reference to or description of the exalted Christ.

(c) A third possibility is that one or more of the Dan. 7.13 references using this third person characteristic be found to go back to Jesus himself, leading to the conclusion that *Jesus* identified the 'son of man' in Daniel's vision as the heavenly being who would vindicate his mission and message at the end (particularly Luke 12.8f.)[101] – perhaps an angel (cf. Job 16.19; 33.23; see below pp. 151–3) or even Enoch (cf. again Jub. 4.22f.; I Enoch 12–16). Considered in itself this offers quite a plausible interpretation of our evidence, especially if the interpretation of Dan. 7.13 is credited to Jesus himself, since with such an influential figure it would be surprising if some innovative exegesis did not go back to him.[102] However, as an interpretation of the origin of the link between the Gospel Son of Man sayings and Daniel's vision it does run counter to the rest of our evidence to such an extent that its plausibility is seriously undermined.

(1) If the suggestion is that Jesus owed his confidence in a heavenly Son of Man vindicator to an already current interpretation of Dan. 7.13, then we should recall that we have found no clear evidence of such an interpretation of Dan. 7.13 prior to AD 70 elsewhere in the literature of the period. The Jewish (non-Christian) documents which do offer such an interpretation (Sim. En. and IV Ezra) seem to be introducing it as a new interpretation, and neither can with any confidence be dated early enough to have influenced Jesus. To build a counter thesis on the third person characteristic of the Son of Man sayings in the Gospels is bold but not entirely convincing.

(2) If alternatively it was Jesus himself who originated this interpretation of Dan. 7.13, it is almost as strange that it has left no trace in non-Christian Jewish tradition, since at no point in Sim. En. and IV Ezra can a convincing argument be sustained that these authors were conscious of an earlier interpretation of Dan. 7.13, let alone one they might have favoured. Yet if the early Christian identification of the Danielic son of man with Jesus could be countered by reference to Jesus' own belief that that son of man was someone else, we might have expected some hint of it in non-Christian Jewish writing of the period, especially that which interpreted Daniel's son of man in a not dissimilar way.[103]

(3) In either case the even more striking fact is that we have no other trace of Jesus' own interpretation in the subsequent Christian traditions.

But if Jesus spoke so clearly of the Son of Man as a heavenly A. N. Other whose eschatological role would be so decisive, and it was the earliest Christians who identified Jesus with this Son of Man, we would have expected some hint of this in the preservation or echo of this initial identification. But nowhere do the first Christians say of Jesus in their preaching or apologetic, 'He is that Son of Man'.[104] Yet we know that the identification of Jesus with other eschatological figures was canvassed and queried (Mark 6.15 pars.; 8.28 pars.; Matt. 11.3 par.; see further below §10.3), and we have clear credal or evangelistic affirmations identifying Jesus as the Messiah, the prophet like Moses, the Son of God (e.g. Mark 8.29; Acts 3.22f.; 9.20) – just as we have in I Enoch 71.14 precisely the sort of identification that presupposes a recognized Son of Man concept ('You are the Son of Man . . .') which we do *not* find in the Christian tradition. It is difficult therefore to avoid the conclusion that first-century Christian tradition, early or late, shows no knowledge of a heavenly Son of Man with whom the risen Jesus could be identified. Moreover, the total silence of the tradition concerning such an identification strongly suggests that no such identification was ever made, especially when we contrast that silence with the clear evidence that the first Christians were eager to equate Jesus with other figures that featured in Jewish eschatological hope.

(4) Not least in importance is the fact that we have absolutely no other evidence in the sayings of Jesus that Jesus himself ever looked for some other eschatological redeemer to follow him (cf. the references in n. 10 above), or some heavenly advocate whose role would be decisive in the final judgment (cf. Luke 12.8f.). The Jesus-tradition is consistent through and through in affirming the eschatological finality of Jesus' own mission (see e.g. Matt. 11.5f./Luke 7.22f.; Matt. 13.16f./Luke 10.23f.; Matt. 12.41f./Luke 11.31f.; Luke 12.54–6),[105] and there is no other suggestion that Jesus' own role in the final judgment might be dependent on some other heavenly individual (contrast Matt. 19.28/Luke 22.29). The awkward facts for this whole hypothesis are: that it is built solely upon a small handful of Son of Man sayings; that in the end it depends entirely upon the at best apparent distinction between Jesus and the Son of Man (which derives from the third person characteristic of all the sayings); and that its sole justification is an interpretation of these sayings which so far as we can now tell was never embraced or affirmed at any point within the earliest Christian tradition.[106]

In short, *to build a thesis of a Son of Man concept already current in the first half of the first century AD prior to the identification of Jesus as the Danielic son of man, is to build castles in the air*, for it depends entirely on the existence of an interpretation of certain sayings which in any case is at best tentative for the postulated original form of these sayings, and which *ex hypothesi* was abandoned before it had become established and before it could leave any trace anywhere else within let alone beyond the earliest Christian circles – what some might call a hermeneutical quark!

(d) A fourth possibility is for the tradition-historical inquiry to conclude that one or more of the Dan. 7.13 allusions originated with Jesus, but as a *self-reference*. That is, Jesus himself first alluded to Daniel's vision as a way of expressing his confidence in God's ratification of his mission – Daniel's prophetic vision of one like a son of man coming with the clouds would find fulfilment in his own still future vindication.[107] Alternatively he saw in the Danielic son of man who symbolized the saints of the Most High in their triumph after suffering an expressive symbol for his whole ministry, his present role and anticipated suffering as well as his future vindication.[108]

Certainly the striking fact that in the Gospels the phrase (the son of man/Son of Man) occurs only and always in the sayings of Jesus[109] points firmly to the conclusion that its use in the Christian tradition originated with Jesus himself. Moreover the consistency of the third person characteristic, the unvarying use of the definite article in the phrase (*the* son of man), also suggests that we are here confronted with a speech mannerism of a particular individual. It may be pushing the evidence too far to draw the further deduction that this very characteristic contains an allusion to Dan. 7.13 – *that* son of man of Daniel's vision.[110] If Jesus was responsible for introducing a new individualizing interpretation of Dan. 7.13 we would have expected some evidence of an initial exegetical identification, such as we noted in I Enoch 46.1f. and IV Ezra 13.1f. On the other hand, in the Jesus-tradition we have only a limited amount of explicit exegesis which can be traced back to Jesus himself with any confidence (particularly Mark 12.26f. pars.; but note also Matt. 11.10/ Luke 7.27; Mark 7.6f. par.; 12.36f. pars.) – a fact which could signify either that some of Jesus' exegesis has been lost (overshadowed by the light of the fuller exegesis which the resurrection permitted), or, more likely, that Jesus' style of exegesis was often allusive (cf. the clearly implied allusions to Isa. 61.1f. in Luke 6.20bf./Matt. 5.3–6 and Matt. 11.2–6/Luke 7.18–23).[111]

Alternatively the conclusion to be drawn from tradition-historical inquiry may be that the initial use of the phrase ('the son of man') was without reference to Dan. 7.13 (cf. (b) above), but that the only grounds for denying one or more of the Dan. 7.13 allusions to Jesus as well is the different significance of the phrase (on the one hand = man, or I as a man; on the other, with reference to Dan. 7.13). In this case a plausible hypothesis would be something as follows.[112] Jesus, already using the phrase 'the son of man' as a way of speaking of his own mission and/or himself, sooner or later came to the conclusion that his ministry was bound to end in arrest and/or death.[113] But if it is hardly likely that Jesus did not foresee what was liable to happen to him, it is equally unlikely that he saw his anticipated death as a disaster to be avoided. On the contrary, the greater likelihood is that he looked with confidence beyond such a death to God's vindication of his cause (cf. Wisd. 5.1–5).[114] Somewhere within this train of thinking it is entirely plausible that his speech mannerism (the son of man) should have triggered off the recognition that Dan. 7.13 is a reference to that vindication. The apparent distinction between Jesus and the Son of Man in a saying like Luke 12.8f. would then simply be the effect of Jesus' own adaptation of his regular speech usage to incorporate an allusion to Dan. 7.13. Indeed we may well wonder whether anyone familiar with the characteristic Hebraic idiom of referring to the same entity in two complementary lines by different phrases[115] would ever have found the third person usage in Luke 12.8f. as odd as (some) modern commentators do, or ever have thought it referred to someone other than Jesus.

In either case then we have an interpretation of the Danielic son of man which goes back ultimately to Jesus. It has left no mark on the non-Christian Jewish tradition, but that may simply reflect the fact that earliest Christian evangelism and apologetic seems to have made little use of a Son of Man christology on its own account, and it is possible that somewhere behind the two power heresy later condemned by ortho-dox rabbinic Judaism is to be detected the influence of such a christology (see above pp. 80f. and n. 93). But it has left a sufficiently clear mark on the Jesus-tradition itself and outside the Gospels at least in Acts 7.56.

All things considered then, and depending on the results of tradition-critical study of the individual Son of Man sayings, the most likely conclusions are twofold. First, *the earliest traceable interpretation of Dan. 7.13 as a particular individual goes back to earliest Christianity or to Jesus himself.* As non-Christian Jewish literature has given insufficient evidence of a pre-Christian concept of the Son of Man, so too we have found no real evidence of such a pre-Christian use of Dan. 7.13 in the Christian liter-ature. Second, *this interpretation of Dan. 7.13 probably initially emerged as a way of expressing either Jesus' own hope of vindication or the first Christians' belief that Jesus had been vindicated after death and would soon 'come with the clouds of heaven'.* In other words, there probably never was a time when 'the Son of Man' was understood by Jesus or the first Christians as someone other than Jesus himself (if Jesus did so his belief has made no more lasting or greater impact than the possible ambiguity of Luke 12.8f.). In short, *it was most probably in the interpretation of Dan. 7.13 as a reference to Jesus that an individualizing exegesis of Dan. 7.13 first emerged.* What then was the signifi-cance of that identification and how does it bear on our inquiry?

§10.2 'In using this self-designation ('Son of Man'), Jesus implied his own pre-existence.'[116] Leaving aside the question of whether such an implication can be traced back to Jesus himself, Hamerton-Kelly's assertion nevertheless poses the issue for us: Do the Son of Man sayings in the Gospels imply the Son of Man's pre-existence? Would that inference have been drawn from them at any stage of their tradition-history in first-century Christianity? And when we look beyond the Gospels can we find any other evidence within the NT which throws light on this issue?

(a) *The Son of Man in the Gospels.* When we put our question to the Gospel material one point emerges at once, particularly in an inquiry which has focused on the Son of Man sayings which show some allusion to Dan. 7.13: viz., that all these sayings refer to the *future* state and role of the Son of Man. In not one instance where Jesus is portrayed as the Danielic son of man is there any perceptible implication that Jesus is thereby understood as a pre-existent being hidden in heaven prior to his (initial) manifestation on earth. There is of course a conception of what Hamerton-Kelly calls 'apocalyptic pre-existence'[117] – the idea that the one who is to come from heaven existed in heaven *prior* to that coming – but in the passages in question the thought is obviously of Christ's coming *again* subsequent to his exaltation, not of his first coming, so that no thought of pre-existence prior to Jesus' earthly ministry and no pre-cursor of a doctrine of incarnation is involved in any way. Hamerton-Kelly also suggests that 'the pre-existence of Jesus is implied' in the idea that Jesus fulfilled scripture – 'that ideal pre-existence of the Messiah', that is in the plan of God.[118] But the thought does not go beyond the idea that the inspired prophet can see into the future or is privy to God's plans for the future, and though it is quite possible that the concept of a real pre-existence first emerged as a deduction from or elaboration of the concept of ideal pre-existence there is no hint that such a development already lies behind any of the passages mentioned (cf. e.g. Mark 12.35–7; Matt. 1.2–17; see further below §29.2).

More weighty is the conclusion that in Q Jesus is understood as the eschatological envoy of Wisdom (see also below pp. 198ff.). But it is difficult to see how a concept of this envoy's pre-existence emerges from Q; if the idea of the Son of Man's humility is indeed involved in Matt. 11.19/Luke 7.34f., Matt. 8.20/Luke 9.58 and Matt. 12.32/Luke 12.10,[119] it is by way of contrast with the Son of Man's *future* (not pre-existent) glory – quite possibly with some allusion to the humility-vindication contrast in the case of the saints of the Most High in Dan. 7.21–7 or of the righteous man in Wisd. 5.1–5 (see above n. 114). Similarly with the more significant passages in Mark adduced by Hamerton-Kelly. The Son of Man's authority to forgive sins '*on earth*' (Mark 2.10) would almost certainly be understood as an anticipation of his future role in eschatological judgment (Mark 8.38; 13.26f.; 14.62), not as a reflection of his previous authority in heaven.[120] Nor can it safely be maintained that Mark's account of the transfiguration (Mark 9.2–8) 'makes explicit the view of Jesus as a pre-existent heavenly being',[121] since, as we have already seen, the transfiguration is presented in Mark as a foreshadowing of Christ's resurrection and exaltation (above pp. 47f.). More plausible is the suggestion that 'in Mark 10.45 the phrase "the Son of Man *came*" implies pre-existence', a coming from heaven.[122] But we have already seen (above pp. 39f.) that such formulae can equally well be used of a prophet, and when used in self-reference the claim would be of a divine *commission* not of a divine origin – as when Josephus says to Vespasian, 'I come to you as a messenger of greater destinies' (*Bell.* III.400), or Jeremiah and Obadiah proclaim 'a messenger has been sent (out) among the nations' (Jer. 49.14 LXX 30.8; Obad. 1).[123] Finally, so far as the Synoptic evidence is concerned, we need comment only briefly on Hamerton-Kelly's conclusion, drawn from possible links between Matthew and the Similitudes of Enoch, that 'pre-existence before creation is probably implied by . . . (the) identification of Jesus with . . . the Enochian Son of Man in Matthew'.[124] For once again such points of contact as there are between Matthew and the Similitudes focus attention on the eschatological role of the Son of Man in the final judgment, and while Matthew may possibly have been aware of the pre-existence attributed to the Son of Man in the Similitudes (if he did in fact know the Similitudes – see above pp. 77f.), there is nothing to show that he intended a similar implication to be read into his own use of the Christian Son of Man tradition. It is difficult therefore to avoid Tödt's conclusion 'that *there is not a single Son of Man saying within the Synoptic tradition which links up with the concept of pre-existence from apocalyptic literature*'.[125]

It is only when we look beyond the Synoptic Gospels that we find the pre-existence of the Son of Man clearly envisaged in sayings attributed to Jesus. This is manifestly the case in at least two Son of Man sayings found only in the Fourth Gospel: John 3.13 – 'No one has ascended into heaven but he who descended from heaven, the Son of Man'; 6.62 – 'What if you were to see the Son of Man ascending where he was before?'; and perhaps also 1.51 – 'Truly, truly, I say to you, you will see heaven opened, and the angels of God ascending and descending upon the Son of Man.' But once again, as with the Johannine Son of God christology (above §§4.4 and 6.5), we are confronted with the problem that the Johannine sayings are so very different from those in the Synoptics. In particular, any influence of Dan. 7.13 is hardly, if at all, to be seen (most likely 5.27; cf. 17.2);[126] and if 1.51 can be traced back to pre-Johannine tradition it is most likely as a reference to Christ's resurrection or parousia (cf. Mark 14.62 pars.; Matt. 16.27f. pars.) which has been 'de-

eschatologized' and only thereby given any overtone of pre-existence it
may possibly contain.[127] Moreover, in the two clear pre-existence sayings
(3.13; 6.62) the terminology is so thoroughly Johannine that it is difficult
to discern a pre-Johannine form behind them, and almost certainly not
a form which presupposed the Son of Man's pre-existence: the decisive
feature is the descending/ascending motif which is distinctive of the
Fourth Gospel and which cannot be linked with the Son of Man language
prior to the Fourth Gospel (cf. John 6.33, 38, 41f., 50f., 58; 20.17).[128] In
other words, it is well nigh impossible to escape the conclusion that *the
pre-existence element in the Johannine Son of Man sayings is a distinctively Johannine
redaction or development of the Christian Son of Man tradition*.[129]

But how is it that the thought of the pre-existence of the Son of Man
(as indeed of the Son of God) has become such a striking and distinctive
feature of the Fourth Gospel? Has there been some intermediate stage
between the Synoptic tradition and the Fourth Gospel such as will explain
this new departure in John? We saw how the understanding of Jesus as
the Son of God seems to have expanded steadily backwards as the first
century proceeded. Did anything similar happen with the Son of Man
language? It is possible, of course, that the talk of the Son of Man's
descent (from heaven) and ascent (where he was before) is simply a
reflection of the Fourth Evangelist's strong incarnational christology so
evident elsewhere in the Gospel. Here too an influence (direct or indirect)
from some speculation regarding the first man (Primal Man myth) has
become a less popular explanation in recent years, and most favour a
more immediate influence from 'Wisdom speculation'.[130] But is there any
evidence of a more direct link through a Son of Man christology prior to
John? Is there any evidence, in other words, that elsewhere in first-
century Christianity Jesus was already spoken of as the pre-existent Son
of Man?

(*b*) *A Son of Man christology outside the Gospels?* As is well-known there is
only one passage outside the Gospels where Jesus is explicitly designated
'the Son of Man' – the words attributed to Stephen at the end of his
speech: 'Behold, I see the heavens opened, and the Son of Man standing
at the right hand of God.'[131] Here it is clearly the exalted Christ who is
in view, and the scene reflects a similar emphasis to that in Luke 12.8f.
– the Son of Man's eschatological role in vindicating those who suffer
rough justice on earth. Attempts have been made to find a Son of Man
christology behind the christological use of Ps. 8 in I Cor. 15.27 and Heb.
2.6–8 – 'What is man that you are mindful of him, and the son of man
that you care for him?' (Ps. 8.4); in particular to argue that the 'son of
man' reference in Ps. 8.4 made possible the application of Ps. 8.6 to
Christ ('You have given him dominion over the works of your hands').[132]
But as we shall see below, Ps. 8.6 is drawn in primarily to supplement

Ps. 110.1 in Christian apologetic and preaching, and the christological motif in evidence in both Heb. 2 and I Cor. 15 is best described as Adam christology (see below pp. 108–11). In fact *nowhere* in Paul is there any hint or mention of the Son of Man,[133] and in Heb. 2.6 (quoting Ps. 8.4) the author appears to be unaware either of the eschatological significance of the phrase ('the son of man') in apocalyptic tradition or of its christological usage in the tradition of Jesus' words.[134]

Much more striking and hopeful are Rev. 1.13 and 14.14, the only other direct allusions to Dan. 7.13 in the NT outside the Synoptic Gospels (together with Rev. 1.7): Rev. 1.13 – 'I saw seven golden lampstands, and in the midst of the lampstands one like a son of man . . .'; Rev. 14.14 – 'Then I looked, and lo, a white cloud, and seated on the cloud one like a son of man . . .'. In both cases there is no doubt that Christ is the one thus identified with Daniel's 'son of man'. Two features deserve comment. First, although it is clearly the exalted Christ who is in view and his role as eschatological judge (1.16, 18; 2–3; 14.14–20), the figure in the vision is somehow *merged with God*: the description of the 'one like a son of man' in 1.13 continues, '. . . his head and his hair were white as white wool, white as snow' – a description drawn from Daniel's description of the Ancient of Days (Dan. 7.9)![135] and the same figure goes on to identify himself as 'the first and the last' (Rev. 1.17), a title more or less synonymous with the Lord God's claim, 'I am the Alpha and the Omega' (1.8), as 22.13 makes plain. Second, the phrase used, 'son of man', is *not a title* (not 'the Son of Man'), but simply a direct allusion to the human figure of Daniel's vision ('one like a son of man'). Indeed at this point Revelation is more like the Similitudes of Enoch and IV Ezra than anything else, for like these other apocalyptists the seer seems to be taking a fresh inspiration from Dan. 7.13 without any visible debt to or awareness of an earlier use made of the vision (whether in Christian or non-Christian tradition).[136]

Here then *in Revelation we have the exalted Christ recognized as the Danielic 'son of man' and in a context in which there is also attributed to him the status of Creator or at least some part in the beginnings of all things*, being designated 'the first' as well as 'the last'. Unfortunately we can no more use this evidence to illuminate the pre-Johannine Son of Man christology than we can use the Similitudes of Enoch or IV Ezra to illuminate the pre-Christian understanding of Dan. 7, for Revelation is as late as or later than the Fourth Gospel, and the usages are widely divorced from each other – a title owing little or nothing to Dan. 7 in the one case, an interpretative use of Daniel's phrase in the other. Rather the importance of Revelation's evidence lies in another direction: for here we have Dan. 7.13 used yet again as a description of a heavenly individual's role in judgment (Messiah/Christ) in apocalyptic speculation of the late first century AD, an interpretation moreover which may well reflect that wider apocalyptic speculation rather than any particular teaching on Jesus as 'the Son of Man', and an interpretation indeed which may well have seemed to pose some threat to Jewish monotheism. In other words, *Revelation may reflect not so much specifically Christian theologizing about Christ as the Son of Man, but a lively apocalyptic or mystical speculation in Jewish-Christian* (or Jewish and Christian) *circles which drew its inspiration in part at least from the vision in Dan. 7 and which gave rise to what the rabbis subsequently condemned as the heresy of saying there are two divine powers in heaven.*

§10.3 *Once more, Enoch.* Before closing the door quite so firmly on the possibility that the Revelation of John does reflect an earlier christology we should however pause to examine one further possibility: that behind this late first-century apocalyptic speculation regarding the Danielic 'son of man' involving Enoch on the one hand and Christ on the other, lies an earlier speculation regarding Enoch's role as an actor in the eschatological drama. It is after all quite plausible that some speculation should have focused on one or both of the only two figures in Jewish history who had been translated to heaven without death (Enoch and Elijah) and who thus could be envisaged as hidden or reserved in heaven until they could intervene once again at God's command in the affairs of earth. And in fact we have a most fascinating scatter of evidence which links Enoch and Elijah and which does seem to envisage their having an eschatological role on earth: I refer to I Enoch 90.31, the Apocalypse of Elijah, the possibility that Enoch is 'one of the ancient prophets' linked with Elijah in Luke 9.8, 19, and the possibility that it is Enoch and Elijah who are the 'two witnesses' in Rev. 11.3 (an interpretation which had very strong patristic support).[137] Could it be then that Enoch and/or Elijah were already seen as heavenly redeemers in Jewish and/or Christian thought in the first century AD, and that this belief lies behind the flowering of apocalyptic speculation regarding the Danielic son of man in the last decades of that century?[138] Could it be indeed that John the Baptist in heralding a fire-dispensing 'Coming One' (Matt. 3.7–12/Luke 3.7–9, 16f.) had in mind Elijah (or Enoch) coming *from heaven* in final judgment?[139]

It is exceedingly difficult to trace the growth of this particular tradition, and even more so to assess its influence on earliest Christian thought. In its most influential earlier form only Elijah was in view, as the forerunner of the end (Mal. 3.1–3; 4.5; Sir. 48.10f.; Mark 6.15 par.; 8.28 pars.; 9.11f. par.; John 1.21; see also *Sib. Or.* II.187–9; Justin, *Dial.* 49).[140] And initially the hope was probably not so much of Elijah himself coming down from heaven as of an eschatological prophet anointed with 'the spirit and power of Elijah' (Luke 1.17). This was certainly the understanding involved when John the Baptist was identified with Elijah within earliest

Christianity (Mark 9.11–13/Matt. 17.10–13; Matt. 11.10/Luke 7.27; Mark 1.2; Matt. 11.14; Luke 1.16f., 76) – there is never any suggestion that John the Baptist had descended from heaven. And the association between Elijah and Moses in the transfiguration scene (Mark 9 pars.) and most probably intended in Rev. 11.3f. (see below p. 94) suggests that the thought is more of a messianic prophet ('a prophet like Moses' – see below §19.1) than of a heavenly visitant or incarnation.[141] At what period this understanding of the Elijah tradition was enlarged to include the thought of Elijah himself as having been hidden away by God with a view to a later reappearance we can no longer say; but perhaps a pointer is given by the *Biblical Antiquities* of pseudo-Philo who identifies Elijah with Phinehas (Num. 25), preserved in secret by God until his ministry as Elijah, then lifted up to heaven and reserved there 'until I remember the world. And then will I bring you and you shall taste what is death' (48.1). Pseudo-Philo is probably to be dated to about AD 100.[142] We may note also that it is about this time that IV Ezra 14.9 (cited above p. 79) gives expression to the similar idea of Ezra being 'taken up from among men' to live in heaven 'until the times are ended'. About this time too II Baruch gives voice to a similar idea concerning Baruch as one who did not die but was taken from this earth to be 'preserved until the consummation of the times' (13.3; 25.1; 43.2; 46.7; 48.30; 76.3).[143] In addition, we might justifiably compare from within Christian tradition, Rev. 12.5, where the new born Messiah is 'caught up to God and to his throne'. In other words, once again we may have to look to the post-AD 70 decades as a turbulent period of reassessment for Jewish faith which threw up several new ideas and formulations of eschatological hope.

The texts linking Enoch with Elijah do not seem to shed much fuller light. (1) It is certainly true that Elijah is associated with Enoch in I Enoch 90.31 (cf. 89.52), and that the two are envisaged as being brought down (from heaven) at the time of the final judgment.[144] But the significance intended is unclear. Elijah (the ram) seems to be one of the heavenly conductors of the visionary rather than one who is an actor in the vision with the seer; and Enoch himself seems to function only as visionary spectator (ending up asleep in the middle of the transformed saints! – 90.39). So possibly the movement in 90.31 would have been understood simply as a visionary scene-changing, along the lines of, for example, Ezek. 3.12–15 and I Enoch 17–36. (2) The Apocalypse of Elijah probably takes up this passage from I Enoch, when in talking of the judgment of the shepherds of the flock (cf. I Enoch 90.22, 25), it continues: 'Thereupon down come Elijah and Enoch and lay aside the flesh of the world and take on their spiritual flesh and will pursue the Son of Unrighteousness, and will put him to death' (*Apoc. Elijah* 24.11–15).[145] But the dating of the Apocalypse is notoriously difficult: in its present form it is a Christian document from the third or fourth century, and though several scholars would recognize an earlier Jewish document behind it, which has been dated to the first century BC,[146] the passage just quoted uses a concept of 'spiritual flesh' and a form of the anti-christ expectation which already probably reflects Christian influence.[147] Consequently the Apocalypse of Elijah is a rather shakey platform on which to build any conclusions regarding a pre-AD 70 Enoch speculation which might have influenced earliest christology.[148] (3) Luke 9.8, 19 has two noticeable differences from the parallel tradition in Mark 6.15. Mark reports the different popular rumours regarding Jesus as 'It is Elijah' and 'It is a prophet like one of the prophets'. In Luke the rumours are 'that Elijah has appeared' and 'that one of the ancient prophets has arisen'. In other words, the tradition which seems to make plausible some identification of Jesus with Enoch ('he is one of the ancient prophets') also expresses the identification in terms of resurrection or human vocation (cf. Acts 3.22; 7.37) rather than in terms of an appearing or coming (down) from heaven.[149] (4) As for Rev. 11.3f. itself, commentators are generally agreed that the author intends to refer to Elijah and Moses (note particularly vv. 5f.),[150] and there is certainly no discernible link between 11.3f. and the identification of Daniel's 'son of man' as the exalted Christ in 1.13 and 14.14. In view of this, the patristic interpretation of the two witnesses as Elijah and Enoch probably reflects the fact that Enoch became the focus of considerable speculation in Jewish apocalyptic and mystical circles in the second century AD rather than an earlier Enoch speculation which John the seer was turning to his own account.

We must conclude therefore that *there is in the period prior to the end of the first century AD no clear or firm evidence of a belief in the coming of Elijah or Enoch as a coming of the translated prophet or patriarch himself from heaven.* I Enoch 90.31 was perhaps interpreted in that way, but if so the interpretation has left no clear trace in first-century Jewish and Jewish-Christian speculation, apart from the uncertainly dated Apocalypse of Elijah. It is certainly possible that at an early stage Jesus was reckoned to be fulfilling the role of the expected Elijah (or of the eschatological prophet like Elijah – cf. Mark 6.15 par.; 8.28 pars.), just as he certainly was hailed as the one who fulfilled the hope of a prophet like Moses (see below §19.1), though if so, the Christian identification of the Baptist as Elijah soon swamped that. But in our sources we have nothing to show that Jesus was ever identified with Enoch.[151] All this makes it *very doubtful whether Jewish speculation regarding Enoch and Elijah in heaven ever influenced earliest christology or provided a stimulus towards an assessment of Jesus as one who had been reserved (or hidden) in heaven prior to his mission on or coming to earth*[152] – very doubtful too whether Jewish speculation regarding Enoch and Elijah had developed sufficiently prior to AD 70 to be able to provide such a stimulus or to explain the Johannine presentation of Jesus as the Son of Man who had ascended whence he first descended. Such indications as there are point more to the decades following AD 70 as the period when such Jewish (and Jewish-Christian) speculation regarding Elijah and Enoch (and others) began to blossom.

§10.4   More or less the same answer has to be given to the whole question of the pre-existence of the Son of Man as such. *A Christian understanding of Jesus as the pre-existent Son of Man cannot be dated prior to the same late stage in the first century.* In the Synoptics it is always a question of the Son of Man's eschatological role in judgment or his humility prior to exaltation which is in view, never of a pre-existent role or status. So too in the only other reference to Jesus as 'the Son of Man' outside the Gospels (Acts 7.56). Elsewhere the identification of Jesus as the Son of Man or Danielic 'son of man' seems to have made no impact or left no trace other than on the Johannine writings. In one case (the Fourth Gospel) we see what appears to be a distinctively Johannine elaboration of the Jesus' Son of Man sayings to embrace the dimension of pre-existence. In the other (Revelation) we see what appears to be a use made of Dan. 7.13 which has more in common with other late first-century apocalyptic handling of Daniel's vision than with the tradition of Jesus' sayings. But in both cases we are most probably dealing with late first-century AD documents which at this point reflect an understanding of Jesus already reached earlier and in terms other than those provided by Daniel's vision.

§11. CONCLUSIONS

§11.1   *On the basis of the evidence available to us it is not possible to speak with any confidence of a pre-Christian Son of Man concept.* There is no indication whatsoever that the 'one like a son of man' in Dan. 7.13 was intended to represent a particular individual or would have been interpreted as such in the pre-Christian period. In the Similitudes of Enoch and IV Ezra Daniel's manlike figure is indeed identified with a particular individual, the Messiah, but in each case the interpretation is offered as though it was a new insight, and in neither case can a strong enough argument be sustained to enable us to use them as evidence of Jewish belief prior to AD 70. In Christian sources themselves there is no evidence (apart from the ambiguity of Luke 12.8f.) that Jesus looked for the Son of Man as a heavenly being, or that Jesus was identified with a heavenly figure whose existence and role had previously been deduced from Dan. 7.13f. There is some evidence of a pre-Christian belief that at the end Enoch and/or

Elijah would reappear from heaven (whither they had been translated without death), but no evidence that such a belief influenced earliest christology or interacted with the messianic interpretation of Dan. 7.13 prior to the Similitudes.

§11.2   *The earliest datable interpretation of Daniel's 'son of man' as a particular individual is the Christian identification of 'the son of man' with Jesus,* whether first made by the post-Easter communities or by Jesus himself – the vision of Daniel being seen as a description of the exalted and vindicated Christ 'coming with clouds' in final triumph and judgment. For some reason this particular belief regarding Jesus did not make much lasting impact on Christian thinking beyond the tradition of Jesus' sayings. Nor does it seem to have influenced non-Christian use of Dan. 7. The reason is probably the same in both instances – the teaching about Jesus as the Son of Man was an esoteric teaching confined to those circles which were devoted to passing on and meditating upon the sayings of Jesus.

§11.3   *The thought of the Son of Man as a pre-existent heavenly figure does not seem to have emerged in Jewish or Christian circles before the last decades of the first century AD.* Initially in Christian circles Daniel's vision was interpreted eschatologically, the Son of Man as a figure of final judgment. But as the first century drew towards its close there was a remarkable growth of interest in the Dan. 7 figure, and specifically in the Son of Man (or Man) as a pre-existent heavenly being. Despite their similarities these diverse interpretations of Dan. 7 do not seem to be dependent on each other. These two facts suggest that in the aftermath of the disastrous first Jewish revolt several circles within Jewish and Christian apocalypticism and mysticism turned to examine afresh a writing which, after all, had been designed to encourage the faithful when confronted with similar opposition (and which probably played its part in encouraging the subsequent revolts in 115 and 132). In the Christian circles that produced Revelation the 'one like a son of man' was identified afresh with the exalted Christ, and the assertion that he was 'the first' confirmed belief that he was also 'the last', his final triumph sure. In one at least of the Jewish circles the focus was on Enoch and in one case at any rate the resulting elaboration of Daniel's vision soon came to be seen as a threat to Jewish monotheism. Whereas with the Fourth Evangelist the elaboration of the Son of Man sayings tradition to embrace the dimension of pre-existence was accompanied by a reinterpretation of earlier Christian eschatology and in consequence a slackening of interest in Dan. 7.

§11.4   The upshot is that if we are to find the origin of incarnational christology within this complex of Jewish-Christian theologizing we are pushed towards a date in the period AD 70–100, the period when belief in the Son of Man as a pre-existent heavenly being seems to have crystallized in two or three or four different writings all about the same time. Why there was this comparatively sudden (or so it would appear) upsurge of speculation concerning a heavenly Messiah is not clear to us. Its most direct roots could possibly be in a belief that in heaven there were two immortals, eminent servants of God who had never died and who therefore could still participate in affairs on earth as men. But the evidence for such a belief within Judaism prior to AD 70 is again exceedingly thin; and even if it did exist it has left no discernible mark on Christian tradition – Jesus is nowhere clearly identified with Elijah and certainly nowhere identified with Enoch. Whence then did the concept of the Son of Man's pre-existence emerge? To find the answer we must cast our net in another direction.

IV

THE LAST ADAM

§12. INTRODUCTION

One of the most influential attempts in this century to explain the origin of the doctrine of the incarnation is the so-called Gnostic redeemer myth. In the generation following the 1914–18 war in Europe the chief exponent of this hypothesis was R. Bultmann. Bultmann sums up the 'basic idea' of the myth which remains 'constant' amid the variations:

> The demonic powers get into their clutches a person who originates in the light-world either because he is led astray by his own foolishness or because he is overcome in battle. The individual selves of the 'pneumatics' are none other than the parts or splinters of that light-person. Hence, in their totality they constitute that person – who is frequently called Primal Man – and for whose total redemption they must be released and 'gathered together'. . . . Redemption comes from the heavenly world. Once more a light-person sent by the highest god, indeed the son and 'image' of the most high, comes down from the light-world bringing gnosis. He 'wakes' the sparks of light who have sunk into sleep or drunkenness and 'reminds' them of their heavenly home. . . . And going ahead he prepares the way for them, the way which he, the redeemer himself, must also take to be redeemed. For here on earth he does not appear in divine form, but appears disguised in the garment of earthly beings so as not to be recognized by the demons. In so appearing, he takes upon himself the toil and misery of earthly existence and has to endure contempt and persecution until he takes his leave and is elevated to the world of light.[1]

Bultmann believed that the substance of this myth was already current in the first century AD and that early christology was indebted to this concept of 'a cosmic figure, the pre-existent divine being, Son of the Father, who came down from heaven and assumed human form'. In particular it was as the Gnostic redeemer that Christ is praised in the pre-Pauline hymn quoted in Phil. 2.6–11. The myth is also alluded to in II Cor. 8.9 and 'provides the terminology for the christology of John'.[2]

If Bultmann is correct in this hypothesis then we certainly have an important influence on early Christian thought which would go a long way towards explaining the language and ideas behind the Christian doctrine of the incarnation. However, since the publication of Bultmann's *Theology* it has become increasingly evident that his formulation of the myth is an abstraction from later sources. There is nothing of any substance to indicate that a gnostic redeemer myth was already current at the time of Paul. On the contrary all the indications are that it was a *post*-Christian (second-century) development using Christian beliefs about Jesus as one of its building blocks[3] – so that when, for example, the Naasene hymn has Jesus asking the Father to 'send' him that he might 'descend' to the earth (Hippolytus, *Ref.* V.10), this is best explained as language drawn from the NT tradition rather than as a contributory factor to it (see above §§3.5, 5.3 and 6.5 and below VII n. 14). More recent attempts to defend Bultmann's thesis on the basis of the Nag Hammadi documents, particularly *The Apocalypse of Adam* and *The Paraphrase of Shem* are hardly more convincing.[4] These are typical of second-century Gnostic (particularly Sethian) writings with their multiplicity of aeons and angels or powers (cf. Epiphanius, *Pan.* 39.1–3; Hippolytus, *Ref.* V. 19.1–22.1); there are fairly clear allusions to Christian teaching about Jesus in the former (*Apoc. Ad.* V.77–9); and the polemic against (Christian) baptism in the latter probably alludes to the Christian account of Jesus' baptism and anointing by the Spirit at Jordan (*Par. Shem* VII.31–32 – including a reference to the tradition about fire kindling in the Jordan when Jesus went down to the water, a tradition found elsewhere only in Justin, *Dial.* 88.3).[5] The argument that absence of more explicit allusions to Christianity points to a pre-Christian origin is an odd one. Since various strange sects today make only passing or garbled reference to Christian teaching, it would hardly be surprising if the same was true in the second century. After all at that period Christianity was still only one (rather variegated) element in the much larger melting pot of religious-philosophical speculation in the eastern Mediterranean, so it would hardly constitute an indispensable component in every flight of religious fancy then or later (as some of the other Nag Hammadi tractates in Codex VI also indicate).

One component part of the developed myth is the contrast centring on Adam. This could take the form of a straight antithesis between Adam who fell and the (pre-existent) Christ who reversed and rectified Adam's failure (*Gosp. Phil.* II.71.16–21 = logion 83; cf. Irenaeus' theory of recapitulation –, *adv. haer.* particularly III.21.10; 22.4). But more often the contrast was between a heavenly Adam and the earthly Adam (*Gosp.*

Phil. II.58.17–22 = logion 28), with the heavenly man thought of as an angel (= Light Adam – *Origin World* II.108.19–22) or as an aeon (= first Man etc. – *Eugnostos* III.8.27–30; *Sophia* III.104.6–9; see also Irenaeus, *adv. haer.* I.29.3; I.30.1f.), and Adam understood as made 'according to the likeness of the first, perfect Man' (*Apoc. John* II.15.9–13). It is in these terms that we find the idea of the heavenly Man, the heavenly counterpart of Adam, who is also the redeemer (*Sophia* III.100.16–101.15; Hippolytus, *Ref.* V.6.4–7).

The point is that when we pose the hypothesis of a pre-Christian speculation concerning a heavenly redeemer in terms of a heavenly man/earthly man antithesis it begins to look more plausible. For while there is no clear talk in pre-Christian sources of a redeemer being sent from heaven, we do have *some indications that speculation on the heavenly man/earthly man contrast was already current at the time of Paul.* For one thing Philo exegetes the two creation narratives in Gen. 1-2 by using a somewhat similar distinction: 'There are two types of men; the one a heavenly man, the other an earthly. The heavenly man, being made after the image of God, is altogether without part or lot in corruptible and terrestrial substance; but the other was compacted out of . . . "clay" ' (*Leg. All.* I.31; see also *Opif.* 134; *Leg. All.* I.53f; *Qu. Gen.* I.4); moreover, in one treatise he seems to identify the heavenly man with the Logos (*Conf.* 41,62f., 146f.). And for another, Paul himself seems to be aware of some such distinction – 'the *first* man is of the earth, the *second* man is from heaven' (I Cor. 15.45–7) – his *denial* that the spiritual (= heavenly) man *precedes* the earthly in his own interpretation of Gen. 2.7 being possibly directed against something like Philo's heavenly man/earthly man interpretation of Gen. 1.26f. and 2.7,[6] perhaps indeed against precisely the sort of teaching which we find in developed form in the Nag Hammadi tractate *On the Origin of the World* ('the first Adam of the light is spiritual . . . the second Adam is soul-endowed . . . the third Adam is earthy . . .' II.117.28–31).

All this indicates that a closer look at the Adam/Christ parallel in the NT is necessary and may well repay closer attention. Was earliest Christian thought about Christ and Adam, Paul in particular, dependent or parasitic upon speculations and formulations about a pre-existent heavenly Man? Did Paul in contrasting Christ with Adam inevitably think of Christ as a pre-existent power or angel or other heavenly being? The question hitherto has been debated principally in terms of the Gnostic, Manichean, Mandaean and now Nag Hammadi documents, their dates and sources; and results so far as they affect the NT background have never been more than inconclusive. However, not enough care has been taken to ask whether there is a coherent and consistent understanding of the Christ/Adam contrast in the NT documents themselves and if so what influences lie behind it. It is this aspect of the whole issue which is most relevant to us and which we will examine in the present chapter.

§13. ADAM AND THE PLIGHT OF MAN

Adam plays a larger role in Paul's theology than is usually realized – and even when that role is taken into account it is often misunderstood. Adam is a key figure in Paul's attempt to express his understanding both of Christ and of man. Since soteriology and christology are closely connected in Paul's theology it is necessary to trace the extent of the Adam motif in Paul if we are to appreciate the force of his Adam christology.

§13.1. *Paul's understanding of man as he now is is heavily influenced by the narratives about Adam in Gen. 1–3* and especially the account of Adam's 'fall' in Gen. 3. Man is fallen Adam. This is particularly clear in Paul's most systematic statement of his theology – the letter to the church at Rome.

(a) *Rom. 1.18–25.* This whole passage has been influenced by the narratives of the creation and fall to a significant degree.[7] Paul is speaking in general terms of 'men who by their wickedness suppress the truth' (1.18). But in the following verses we could readily replace the generalized plural 'they' by the singular 'Adam' and the passage would read like a summary description of Gen. 1–3. This is not surprising: since *'ādām* (Hebrew) means 'man', what can be said of Adam can be said of men in general, what is true of men in general is true of Adam. Moreover, Jewish wrestling with the problems of evil and death was already indebted to Gen. 3,[8] and Paul closely shares the wider Jewish concern on these points, though his answer is very different.[9] So if Paul was looking for language to describe the plight of sinful man it was only natural that he should turn to the account of man as he was intended to be and as he became.

Thus lying behind vv.19ff. is almost certainly the picture story of Gen. 2 – Adam as man enjoying knowledge of God plainly revealed to him (1.19, 21), as crown of God's creation enjoying the full benefits of God's power manifested in creation (1.20), enjoying the truth of God as yet unclouded by sin (1.25). But, as Gen. 3 goes on to relate, Adam did not honour God as God or accept his role with gratitude (1.21), he did not acknowledge God (1.28); instead he believed the serpent's distortion of God's command, exchanged the truth of God for a lie (1.25 – Gen. 3.4f.: 'You will not die. For God knows that when you eat of it your eyes will be opened, and you will be like God, knowing good and evil'). That is to say, he rebelled against his dependence on God for knowledge, against his subordinate status of creature before Creator. In consequence he became not more like God, but less than the man he was, futile and confused (1.21), not more like the Creator, but less than the creature he had been made (1.25). Claiming to be wise, he became a fool (1.22). Thinking to be like God he rejected his dependence on God, and became not *in*dependent but dependent on things – he exchanged the glory of the immortal God for images resembling mortal man or birds or animals or reptiles (1.23).

It is, of course, unnecessary to argue that Gen. 1–3 is the only OT passage Paul had in mind when he wrote Rom. 1.18–23. In particular it is clear that v. 23 draws on the language of Ps. 106.20 and perhaps also Jer. 2.11 (see also Deut. 4.15–18).[10] But Ps. 106.19f. speaks specifically of the making and worship of the golden calf at Sinai (cf. Deut. 4.15), and in Jewish tradition the idolatry of the golden calf was frequently associated with the fall of Adam, the two being seen as the archetypal sins threatening man and Israel.[11] So too the movement of thought in Rom. 1.24–8, where the emphasis falls on sins of sexual perversion, probably owes more to Gen. 6.1–4 than to speculation about sexual overtones in the account of the fall. But here too we must recognize that Gen. 6.1–4 was part of the same complex of texts by reference to which Jewish theology attempted to account for the origin of sin (Jub. 5.1–10; I Enoch 6–11; 64f.; 86; Test. Reub. 5; II Enoch 18.4f.; II Bar. 56.10).[12] In most cases we are dealing with complementary and related ideas (as Rom. 1 demonstrates), within which Adam and Gen. 3 played an important role. In the case of Rom. 1 itself, Adam and the fall narrative is probably the most important element. This conclusion is strengthened by the fact that Gen. 3 lies behind several other passages in Romans, and so provides a thematic element running through the first half of the letter.

(*b*) *Rom. 3.23* – 'All have sinned and lack the glory of God.' The verb ὑστεροῦνται (lack) can be taken in two ways: either they lack the glory of God in the sense that they have *forfeited* what they once had; or they lack the glory of God in the sense that they *fail to reach* the eschatological glory in which only the righteous will share. The latter was the more favoured view in the earlier part of the century;[13] but there has been a growing consensus among recent commentators that the primary allusion is to the glory once enjoyed by Adam.[14] In fact, both ideas were probably already current in Jewish theology in the first century AD, and both the thought and the language were probably familiar to Paul before he wrote Rom. 3.23.[15] So it is quite probable that he intended the verb to be ambiguous, to contain both meanings. Indeed it is quite likely that *both* senses were prompted by the Gen. 3 narrative. Man, Adam, by virtue of his creation in the image of God was given a share in the glory of God, the visible splendour of God's power as Creator. But by his sin he forfeited that glory. Not only so, but his exclusion from the garden shut him out from the tree of life, cut him off from the eternal life that God had intended him to enjoy (Gen. 3.22–4 – 'lest he put forth his hand and take also of the tree of life, and eat, and live for ever'). In short, Rom. 3.23 is best read as summing up concisely Paul's analysis of man in terms of Gen. 3: man's plight was that he had attempted to escape his creature-liness and to snatch at divinity, and thereby had forfeited the glory he already enjoyed and failed to attain the fuller glory God had intended for him. And if the influence of Gen. 3 is not quite as strong, even so an allusion to Adam is almost certain.

(c) *Rom. 5.12–19* we need not discuss – the allusion to Adam as the one through whom sin and death entered the world is specific, and the treatment of the Adam/Christ parallel and contrast is thoroughly Jewish in character.[16] Whether or not Paul expounds here a doctrine of original sin is irrelevant to our present study. It is enough that Paul is clearly thinking in terms of Gen. 3 ('the transgression of Adam', 'the wrongdoing of that one', 'one who sinned', 'death reigned through that one', 'the disobedience of the one man'), and that he uses the story of Adam's fall to explain the plight of all men ('sin', 'death', 'condemnation', 'sinners'). As Christ is the representative head of all who believe unto righteousness (cf. 8.29), so Adam is the representative head of all who sin unto death. We will have to return to this parallel between Adam and Christ later on (see below pp. 111, 127).

(d) *Rom. 7.7–11.* There is widespread agreement among commentators that there is at least some allusion to Gen. 2–3 here, and the probability is very strong that the whole passage is considerably influenced by the Adam narrative, is indeed largely modelled on the account of Adam's fall. As E. Käsemann points out: 'There is nothing in our verses which does not fit Adam, and everything only fits Adam.'[17] This is not im-mediately clear in v. 7 which speaks of knowledge of sin coming through the law and instances covetousness with reference to the tenth com-mandment. But the rabbinic view that Adam received the (several) com-mandments of the law in the single command not to eat from the tree of the knowledge of good and evil may well go back to Paul's time.[18] And the belief that covetousness or lust was the root of all sin was certainly well established among Paul's contemporaries (cf. Philo, *Decal.* 142, 150, 153; *Opif.* 152; James 1.15). In Apoc. Mos. 19.3 in fact 'lust' is described as 'the root and beginning of every sin' and is directly equated with Eve's disobedience in the garden.

With Rom. 7.8 the influence of Gen. 3 becomes more noticeable and we have what is almost a description of the tactics of the serpent (per-sonified as 'sin').

Sin – the serpent – was in the Garden even before man, but had no opportunity of attacking man until the command 'Thou shalt not eat of it' (Gen. 2.17) had been given. It was precisely by means of this command, the prototype of all law and religion, that the serpent tempted man.[19]

Romans 7.9f. can be fully explicated only by reference to Adam. Only if he was thinking of Adam could Paul properly say that he was alive once apart from the law, and that the coming of the commandment brought sin to life and resulted in death for him. For a life 'apart from law', and a 'coming' of law which resulted in sin and death, was true of Adam in a way that it would not be true of anyone born after or under the law.[20] The commandment intended to regulate and prosper his life ('You may freely eat of every tree of the garden, but of the tree of knowledge of good and evil you shall not eat' – Gen. 2.17), became the means of his death ('in the day that you eat of it you shall die' – Gen. 2.17). Finally with Rom. 7.11, 'for sin, finding opportunity in the commandment, deceived (ἐξηπάτησεν) me and by it killed me', we have a fairly explicit echo of the woman's complaint in Gen. 3.13 – 'The serpent deceived (ἠπάτησεν) me and I ate.'[21] It twisted the instruction of the Creator given for man's good and made it sound like the legislation of a dictator fearful of losing his special status and prerogatives. Thus deceived, man clutched at a godlike life and grasped only death.

Since the influence of Gen. 2–3 is so clear we can understand more fully why Paul puts the passage in first person singular terms ('I') – not because he is referring to himself alone, or to some particular individual, Adam or otherwise, but because he is referring to *adam* = man, the typical human 'I', himself included, of course.[22] For Paul here, Adam in Gen. 2–3 is everyman.[23] We should not turn the equation into an allegory, and attempt to identify a period in Paul's or the Jew's or everyman's life when he was 'alive once apart from the law'.[24] That would be to misunderstand Paul. The description is of everyman to be sure, but the formulation of it is determined almost wholly by the narrative in Gen. 2–3.[25] It is possible for him so to describe the plight of the typical 'I' in terms of Gen. 2–3 only because he thinks of Adam as man, of man as fallen Adam.

(e) Lastly, *Rom. 8.19–22* – 'the creation was subjected to futility (ματαιότητι)'. Here we need simply note that Paul shares what became the regular rabbinic view, that creation was caught up in Adam's fall – a natural conclusion to be drawn from the curse of Gen. 3.17f. ('cursed is the ground because of you').[26] There is probably a deliberate harking back to the description of Adam's/man's fallenness in Rom. 1. Like Adam, creation became futile, empty, ineffective[27] (1.21 – ματαιόομαι; 8.20 – ματαιότης), like Adam in bondage to corruption and decay (1.23 – φθαρτός; 8.21 – φθορά). This is the plight of Adam, of man and his world (cf. I Cor. 15.42–50).

To sum up then, there can be no doubt that the figure of Adam plays an important role in Paul's theology. *In his most careful analysis of the plight of man he draws repeatedly on the account of Adam and his fall in Gen. 2–3.*

§13.2 *Salvation as the reversal of Adam's fall.* In the preceding section we have examined the influence of the creation and fall narratives on Paul's understanding of man. Now we must draw attention to the influence of the same narratives on his understanding of salvation. This will bring us closer to our own particular concern, since Christ as the effecter of that salvation is thereby caught up in the same Adam motif.

(*a*) Paul describes man's salvation in many ways, using many metaphors. In particular he understands *salvation as the fashioning or reshaping of the believer into the image of God.*

In the priestly account of creation man is made in the image of God, or perhaps, more precisely, in the image of the gods/angels who made up the heavenly council – God (*ᵉlōhîm*) speaks to his heavenly council(?), 'Let us make man in our image, according to our likeness' (Gen. 1.26). The motif of man made in the divine image does not play a large part in Jewish thought – it seems to have been taken more or less for granted (Gen. 1.26f.; 5.1; 9.6; Sir. 17.3; Wisd. 2.23; Test. Naph. 2.5; Apoc. Mos. 10.3; 12.1; 33.5; 35.2; Life Adam 14.1f.; 37.3; IV Ezra 8.44; II Enoch 65.2; Philo see above p. 100).[28] More striking is the fact that there is little or no thought of the divine image being effaced or obscured in Adam as a consequence of his fall (cf. Gen. 5.1–3; 9.6; James 3.9).[29] On the other hand the belief that the faithful would become like the angels (I Enoch 104; Mark 12.24f.; II Bar. 51.10, 12; cf. 1QS 11.7f.; 1QH 3.22; 11.12f.) probably owes something to the belief that Adam/man was 'created exactly like the angels' (I Enoch 69.11), 'a second angel' (II Enoch 30.11; cf. Gen. 1.26). And we should also note the vision in I Enoch 85–90 in which Adam is depicted as a white bull (85.3) and in which eschatological salvation is depicted as the transformation of all the beasts and birds into white bulls (90.37f.).[30]

Paul's ideas on the image of God seem to have been developed against this Jewish background. I Cor. 11.7 ('man is the image and glory of God') raises the question as to whether Paul too thought that man still retained the divine image. But this is untypical of his thought elsewhere.[31] The dominant motif in Paul is that man is rather the image of *fallen* Adam, shares his corruptibility (I Cor. 15.49),[32] and that salvation consists in the believer being *transformed* into the image of God (II Cor. 3.18), consists in a progressive *renewal* in knowledge according to the image of the Creator (Col. 3.10; Eph. 4.24). So there is something of an Adam soteriology here – salvation as a restoration of man to that image in which Adam had been created.

(b) The same theme emerges, but with greater clarity, when we examine Paul's use of the word 'glory'. Paul understands *salvation as the restoration of the believer to the glory* which man now lacks as a result of his/ Adam's sin (Rom. 3.23). Here again he shares a view widely held among his Jewish contemporaries. There may have been no real idea that Adam forfeited the image of God by his fall, but there was certainly a firm conviction that he had forfeited the glory of God (see above n. 15). Moreover, the hope of participating in eschatological glory (above n. 15) would naturally be understood by some at least as a reversal of Adam's loss. Thus in *Gen. Rab.* 12.6 and *Num. Rab.* 13.12 glory (or lustre) is one of six things taken from Adam which would be restored in the world to come (see also *Gen. Rab.* 11.2; 21.5; *Deut. Rab.* 11.3).[33] And already at Qumran the glory anticipated by the faithful covenanters is spoken of as 'all the glory of *adam*/Adam' (IQS 4.23; CD 3.20; IQH 17.15).[34] So when Paul speaks of salvation as a 'sharing the glory of God' (Rom. 5.2; cf. 8.18, 21), as a being transformed into God's image 'from one degree of glory to another' (II Cor. 3.18; cf. 4.17), or as a being called 'into God's own kingdom and glory' (I Thess. 2.12), there can be little doubt that he was thinking of salvation as an attaining that glory which Adam forfeited and all men now lack by virtue of sin (Rom. 3.23).

(c) At this point we begin the transition to christology. For bound up with this understanding of salvation and integral to it is Paul's conviction that *Jesus is the indispensable model or pattern for this process*. Salvation for Paul is essentially a matter of being conformed to the pattern which is Christ. We see this most clearly in Paul's use of the same two terms which constitute his Adam soteriology – 'image' and 'glory'. For it is not Adam, unfallen Adam, who is the image into which believers must be transformed, but *Christ*: it is God's purpose to conform believers 'to the image of his Son' (Rom. 8.29); 'as we have borne the image of the man of dust, we shall also bear (φορέσομεν)[35] the image of the man of heaven' (I Cor. 15.49); it is Christ who is 'the image of God' (II Cor. 4.4; Col. 1.15; cf. 3.10). So too the glory in which believers share is the glory of Christ (II Cor. 4.4, 6;[36] Phil. 3.21; II Thess. 2.14); to be glorified for Paul is to be glorified *with* Christ (Rom. 8.17; Col. 3.4).[37]

It is at this point too, of course, that Paul's theology diverges from the formulations of his Jewish contemporaries. Up to this point his assertions would have gained a ready acceptance from many if not all of his fellow Jews – the idea of all men as somehow caught up in Adam's fall, of man as fallen Adam, and the idea of salvation as a renewal of God's image in Adam and a restoration of God's glory forfeited by Adam. But in Paul's theology Adam is pushed aside at this point, and Christ alone fills the stage. Adam becomes merely the type of fallen man, and another Adam appears as alone the final man to whom believers must be conformed.[38]

But it is Christ playing an Adamic role – it is Christ playing the role in reversing the fall equivalent to the role that Adam played in the fall; as the plight of man can be described as a sharing in the fallenness of Adam, so the hope of the believer can be described as that of sharing in the glory of Christ. 'For as by a man came death, by a man has come also the resurrection of the dead. For as in Adam all die, so also in Christ shall all be made alive' (I Cor. 15.21f.).

It is this Adam christology which we must now subject to closer analysis.

§14. ADAM AND CHRIST

Thus far we have been able to demonstrate the extent to which the creation and fall narratives inform Paul's understanding of man and of salvation. The Adam motif is a substantial strand in the warp and woof of Paul's theology, and even when not explicit its influence spreads out widely and throws a considerable light on his understanding of the Christian gospel.[39] Paul's Adam christology is an extension of this motif and wholly consistent with it, and we may hope that an examination of it will illuminate his wider christology in a similar way.

§14.1   The first point which calls for comment is that *when Paul uses Adam language explicitly of Christ he is referring primarily to Christ risen and exalted.* As Adam stands for fallen man, so Christ stands for man risen from the dead. Adam denotes life that leads to death; Christ denotes life from the dead (I Cor. 15.21f.). So more clearly later on in the same chapter, I Cor. 15.45: Christ, the last Adam, is the risen Christ.[40] Paul here makes a careful contrast between Adam and Christ. He takes the text from Gen. 2.7, 'the man became a living soul', and adds two words to heighten the antithesis – 'The *first* man *Adam* became a living soul' (I Cor. 15.45). That is to say, Adam represents all men, every man, man with the breath of life in him, man as distinct from the beasts. Whereas 'the last Adam became life-giving Spirit' – that is, at his resurrection and exaltation when he became the 'source' of the Holy Spirit to all who believe (though see below pp. 143–7 for a more careful statement). The contrast is between old creation and new, between two levels of life – the life of this earth and this world, man the living soul, and the life of the world to come, the life beyond death. Or to be more precise, the contrast is between the two men who represent these two creations – 'the man of dust' who returns to the dust from which he was made, whose image all men bear, and 'the man of heaven', that is, not Christ thought of as pre-existent, but the risen Christ into whose image believers will be transformed when he returns from heaven (15.47–9).[41] Or to be still more precise, the contrast is between man the *recipient* of the breath of life which constitutes him a living being, and Christ the *giver* of the life of the age to come, the life of the Spirit – a role which became Christ's only with resurrection and exaltation (see below §19.2). As the first Adam came into existence (ἐγένετο) at creation, the beginning of the old age, so the last Adam (as such) came into existence at resurrection, the beginning of the age to come. The same point is implicit elsewhere in Paul – particularly Rom. 8.29, where Christ's Adamic role as eldest brother in a new family of men begins with his birth from the dead (cf. Col. 1.18),[42] and Phil. 3.21, where a share in the lost Adamic glory is finally attained by transformation of our lowly body to be like Christ's resurrection body.[43] In short, as I have noted elsewhere (see n. 40), *Christ's role as second man, as last Adam, does not begin either in some pre-existent state, or at incarnation, but at his resurrection.* For Paul, the resurrection marks the beginning of the representative humanity of the last Adam.[44]

§14.2 Up to this point in Paul's Adam christology we have seen only complete discontinuity between Adam and Christ. The last Adam begins where the first Adam ended. The first Adam ends in death, the last Adam begins from resurrection. It is the *exalted Christ* who bears the image and glory that Adam lost; it is to the image and glory of the exalted Christ that believers will be conformed. But is there not some continuity between Adam and Christ? What of the earthly Jesus, the Jesus who also died? Does the Adam christology say anything about this Jesus?

In attempting to answer this question we arrive at one of the most fascinating transition points or points of development in earliest christology. I refer to *the christological use of Ps. 8.* Psalm 8 seems to have been first brought into christological reflection by being attached to the more important Ps. 110. There is no doubt that Ps. 110.1 provided the earliest Christians with one of their most important proof texts –

> The Lord says to my lord: 'Sit at my right hand,
> till I make your enemies your footstool'.

It was a passage alluded to again and again in earliest Christian apologetic and in proclamation of the resurrection of Jesus (Mark 12.36 pars.; 14.62 pars.; Acts 2.34f.; Rom. 8.34; I Cor. 15.25; Eph. 1.20; Col. 3.1; Heb. 1.3, 13; 8.1; 10.12f.; 12.2; I Peter 3.22).[45] What is significant for us is the way in which again and again Ps. 8.6 was drawn in to supplement the latter half of Ps. 110.1 –

> Ps. 8.6b – 'You have put all things under his feet'
> (πάντα ὑπέταξας ὑποκάτω τῶν ποδῶν αὐτοῦ).[46]

This has happened most clearly in I Cor. 15.25–7, Eph. 1.20–2 and Heb.

1.13–2.8, but it is also evident in Mark 12.36 = Matt. 22.44 (ὑποκάτω
τῶν ποδῶν σου) and I Peter 3.22 – 'who is at the right hand of God
. . . with angels, authorities and powers subject (ὑποταγέντων) to him'.
Here then we have a text (Ps. 8.6) which almost always appears in
association with Ps. 110, but also an association which is reflected across
a wide spectrum of NT writings. It is unlikely that they all derived it
from Paul independently. And anyway Paul uses it in a way that suggests
the association was already established before he took it up. So what we
have in Ps. 8.6 is a text which was adopted by earliest Christian apologetic
to fill out Ps. 110.1's description of Christ's exalted authority as Lord –
a development which happened at a very early stage and left its imprint
on earliest Christian apologetic throughout the first decades of
Christianity.[47]

The point for us is that *Ps. 8.6 provided a ready vehicle for Adam christology.*
A description of Christ's Lordship (by association with Ps. 110.1), it was
also a description of God's purpose and intention for *adam*/man –

> Ps. 8.5f. – You crowned him with glory and honour . . .
>   You put all things under his feet.

The most effective use of Ps. 8.5f. as an expression of Adam christology
is Heb. 2.8f. The writer notes that if Ps. 8 is a statement of God's purpose
for men then it has not in fact been fulfilled – 'we do not yet see all things
put under him. Instead what we do see is Jesus . . . crowned with glory
and honour because of the suffering of death . . .'. In other words, it is
Jesus who fulfils God's original intention for man – Jesus exalted after
death. The risen Jesus is crowned with the glory that Adam failed to
reach by virtue of his sin. The same christology is reflected in the two
Pauline passages already mentioned, I Cor. 15.27 and Eph. 1.22 – God
'has put all things under his feet (πάντα ὑπέταξεν ὑπὸ τοὺς πόδας αὐτοῦ)'
– both clearly referring to the risen Christ, and both asserting that what
the Psalmist affirmed to be God's plan for man has been fulfilled in the
risen Christ. Notice here too that the climax of his rule over all things is
Christ's own submission to God – the very antithesis of Adam's sin (I
Cor. 15.24–8).

Finally we should note Phil. 3.21. This is the only allusion to Ps. 8.6
which is independent of Ps. 110.1[48] – 'Christ who will change our lowly
body to be like his glorious body, by the power which enables him even
to subject all things to himself (ὑποτάξαι αὐτῷ τὰ πάντα).' The thought
here is very like that of I Cor. 15.45–9. The glory which Christ received
on exaltation was not for himself alone. By virtue of his exaltation Christ
not only became a glorious body, received the glory that Adam lacks
(Rom. 3.23), but also he received that power over all things which was
intended for man/Adam in the beginning (Ps. 8.6) and which now enables

him to transform believers into his image (Phil. 3.21). In other words, the last Adam is that life-giving Spirit whose power will be most manifest in the transformation of our mortal bodies into spiritual bodies like that of Christ (Rom. 8.10f.; I Cor. 15.45–9; Phil. 3.21). The independence from Ps. 110.1 of the Phil. 3.21 allusion to Ps. 8.6, and its coherence with these other typically Pauline themes, strongly suggest that Phil. 3.21 is Paul's own formulation and that the Adam christology it expresses is one that was of considerable importance for Paul.

§14.3 But now comes the transition. For Ps. 8.6 cannot be referred to Christ without some regard to the preceding verses – 8.4f. If 8.6 is a statement of God's intention for man, then 8.4–6 is simply a fuller state-ment of that intention – God's programme for the man he created:

> 4 What is man that you are mindful of him,
>   and the son of man that you care for him?
> 5 You made him a little less than the angels,
>   and crowned him with glory and honour;
> 6 And you set him over the work of your hands,
>   having put all things in subjection under his feet.

If the last three lines are to be referred to the exalted Christ (a christ-ological exegesis already well established before Paul used it in his letters), then it is a plausible exegesis to take the preceding line as a reference to Christ *before* his exaltation – 'you made him a little lower than the angels'. This in fact is the way Heb. 2.6–9 interprets the passage. The author first quotes Ps. 8.4–6 (8.5–7 LXX)[49] – God's programme for man. But then (as we have already seen) in v. 8b he points out that the programme has broken down – 'However we do not yet see all things put in subjection to him'; God's intention for man has not yet been fulfilled in everyman. What we do see is one man in whom the programme has been fulfilled: 'we see Jesus who for a little while was made lower than the angels, crowned with glory and honour because of the suffering of death, so that by the grace of God he might taste death for every one.' Not only the latter part of the programme has been fulfilled in Jesus (Ps. 8.5b–6), but the earlier part too (Ps. 8.5a). The divine programme for man which broke down with Adam has been run through again in Jesus – this time successfully. *It was by playing out the role of Adam that Christ became last Adam*: Adam led man to death and not glory; but Jesus by his life, suffering and death became the pioneer opening up the way through death for those who follow him (Heb. 2.9). By his complete oneness with men in their subjection to death and the devil he was able to share the death that all men die and so to conquer it. This total solidarity with men 'in every respect' (κατὰ πάντα) was indispensable if his glory beyond death was to be something man could share too (Heb. 2.10–18). In short, Christ could not become last Adam, progenitor of a new manhood beyond death, if he had not first been Adam, one with the manhood which the first Adam begot.

Psalm 8.4–6 thus provided scope for a larger Adam christology – an Adam christology which embraced both earthly as well as the exalted Jesus. This development (in christological use of Ps. 8, backwards from v.6 to v.5a) probably predates Paul's letters too,[50] since it seems to be reflected in I Cor. 15 and to provide the backcloth for Rom. 5.12–19.[51] In I Cor. 15 it is likely that there is an underlying connection of thought between vv.20, 27 and 45–9, to the effect that Christ too first bore 'the image of the man of dust' before he became 'the man from heaven' (v.49), that he too was a 'living soul' before he became 'life-giving Spirit' (v.45). For only he who died as men die could become 'the first fruits of those who have fallen asleep' (v.20), which is another way of saying, only he who fulfilled the divine programme for man by being inferior to the angels (Ps. 8.5a) in the suffering of death could also bring that programme to its completion by having 'all things put in subjection to him' (v.27) at his resurrection.[52]

The same point comes to expression in Rom. 5.12–19, with its repeated and forceful contrast between Adam and Christ. Adam and Christ are alike (Adam the type of Christ – v.14) in that in both cases the action of one man had fateful consequences for those who followed. Both also died, but here the similarity ends. For where Adam's death was the conse-quence of his trespass, his disobedience, Christ's death *was* his act of righteousness, his act of obedience. The implication is that Christ will-ingly accepted the consequences of Adam's sin, that Christ's death was a freely chosen embracing of Adam's death. By freely following out the consequences of Adam's disobedience (i.e. death), Jesus burst through the cul-de-sac of death into life. He went all the way with the first Adam to the end of Adam in death. But beyond death he re-emerged as a new Adam whose hallmark is life from the dead. By sinking to the depths with man in death, the depths of his present plight, he was able to catch up man in resurrection, to make it possible for God's original intention for man to be fulfilled at the last. The point can be expressed thus:

> Adam's disobedience ———> death
> Christ obedience to death ———> life.

To fill out the picture of Paul's Adam christology which is clearly emerging we need only refer briefly to Rom. 8.3 and the earlier passages Gal. 4.4 and II Cor. 5.21 (cf. Eph. 2.14f.). Romans 8.3 – 'God sending his own Son[53] in the precise likeness of sinful flesh (ἐν ὁμοιώματι σαρκὸς ἁμαρτίας) and as a sacrifice for sin (περὶ ἁμαρτίας) condemned sin in the flesh . . .'. It is generally agreed that 'flesh' in Paul is not something evil in itself, but denotes man in his weakness and corruptibility.[54] 'Sinful flesh' means therefore not sin-committing flesh, but flesh under the dominion of sin (cf. 6.6; 7.14) – that is, man in his fallenness, man dominated by his merely human appetites and desires and in bondage to death (cf. 7.5). So whatever ὁμοίωμα means exactly,[55] the phrase 'precise likeness of sinful flesh' must denote Jesus in his oneness with sinful man, in his complete identity with fallen Adam.[56] Likewise there is widespread agreement that περὶ ἁμαρτίας alludes to the sin offering in the OT,[57] so that again we most probably have a reference to Jesus' death. We have here therefore a form of Adam christology merged with an understanding of Jesus' death in sacrificial terms. And once again it is specified that the way in which Jesus resolved the plight of sinful man was by or through his death – and again (8.4) it is indicated that his death made it possible for the Spirit to shape man according to God's intention (expressed in the law). In short, what we have here is an Adam christology in which the latter half is tacit (the risen Christ, the last Adam), and in which the emphasis falls on the first half, the oneness of Christ with the first Adam, fallen man.

Similarly in the earlier passages, Gal. 4.4 and II Cor. 5.21. As we saw above (§5.3), Gal. 4.4 presents Jesus as the Son of God, 'born of woman, born under the law', sent 'to redeem those under the law' to achieve for them a share in his sonship through the Spirit (4.6f.). The implication which follows from the structure of the passage (see above p. 41) is that we have a variation in the same Adam christology-soteriology: Jesus wholly shared man's frailty and bondage to the law, shared, that is, man's condition as a child of Eve,[58] a descendant of fallen Adam, in order that through his death fallen man might come to share his liberation from the law and sin (cf. Rom. 6.5–11), might come to share the Spirit of his sonship. We may paraphrase Paul's underlying thought at this point as follows: Adam was the son of God (cf. Luke 3.38) whose sonship was distorted if not destroyed by the fall; Israel was the son of God whose sonship was something inferior, no better than slavery (Gal. 4.1); but Jesus is the son of God who shared that distorted and inferior sonship to the full and to death and by his resurrection made it possible for others to share the full sonship of his risen life. So too II Cor. 5.21, but using again the language of sacrifice and sin offering – 'For our sake God made him to be sin who knew no sin, so that in him we might become the righteousness of God'. Jesus, the sinless one, became wholly one with the sinner/Adam, so that those who become one with the risen Christ, the last Adam ('in him'), might share in the righteousness of God, that is, fulfil the intention of God in creating man in the first place.[59]

In each case therefore the idea is of Jesus as sharing the fallenness of sinful man, of Adam, so that his death might become a means to creating a new man, a new humanity.[60] In other words, *before he became last Adam*

Jesus shared wholly the lot of the first Adam. The christology lying behind all this is that the resolution to the plight of man is provided not as it were by scrapping the previous model and starting afresh with a new humanity wholly independent of the old, but precisely by Christ following through Adam's plight to the end (death) and thus becoming a new Adam in resurrection beyond death. The way in which Jesus becomes last Adam is by following the path taken by the first Adam. Christ starts his saving work by being one with Adam in his fallenness, before he becomes what Adam should have been. He follows in Adam's footsteps and at the point where Adam comes to an end in death he takes over and becomes what Adam did not become, and no longer could become. He becomes one with man in his falling shortness in order that through death and resurrection he might lift man to God's glory. He becomes one with man in his sinfulness in order that by the power of his life-giving Spirit he might remould man in God's righteousness. He becomes what Adam fell to by his disobedience in order that Adam might become what Christ was exalted to by his obedience.

§15. PRE-EXISTENT MAN?

We now come to what is the key question for the present study. We have traced the Pauline (and pre-Pauline) Adam christology backwards from a christology focusing only on the risen Christ ('image' and 'glory'), through the transition afforded by Ps. 8, to a christology of Christ the one man who fulfilled God's purpose for man – a christology embracing the earthly as well as the exalted Christ. Can we trace this Adam christology still further backwards to embrace an earlier stage of pre-existence? Can we detect in Paul not just a two-stage Adam christology (Adam = earthly Jesus; last Adam = exalted Jesus) but a three-stage Adam christology (pre-existent Man, Adam, last Adam)? Is there already in Paul an expression or anticipation of the second-century Gnostic myth of the Primal Man who also acts as redeemer? Attempts to trace some connection through the Son of Man christology have carried little conviction (see above pp. 72f., §10 and below n. 86). But I Cor. 15.45–7 may possibly show the influence of some earlier heavenly man/earthly man formulation (see above p. 100). And it is arguable that the two texts referred to by Bultmann at the beginning of this chapter (Phil. 2.6–11; II Cor. 8.9) also evince such influence or provide some proof that a decisive step towards the Primal Man myth had already been taken.[61] These are the texts which must now be examined. We start with Phil. 2.6–11 since it is the longest passage and offers greater possibility of clarifying the thought than the allusive I Cor. 15.45–7 and much briefer II Cor. 8.9.

§15.1 *Phil. 2.6–11* certainly seems on the face of it to be a straightforward statement contrasting Christ's pre-existent glory and post-crucifixion exaltation with his earthly humiliation. The movement of thought is sometimes likened to a parabola – the curve of divine self-humbling from heaven to earth reaching its lowest point in death, the death of the cross, and then sweeping heavenwards again in Christ's exaltation to divine lordship over all. However, this straightforward interpretation has to assume that Christ's pre-existence was already taken for granted – an assumption we cannot yet make on the basis of our findings thus far. And its immediate appeal in terms of exegesis depends to a surprising extent on the interpretation of two verbs – ὑπάρχων ('being' – v.6a) as referring to a timeless pre-existence (but see below n. 67), and γενόμενος (v. 7b) as referring to Christ's birth (e.g. RSV – 'being born in the likeness of men'), which is more plausible but which again becomes less obvious on closer examination (see below p. 116 and n. 76). In fact, as J. Murphy-O'Connor has recently maintained, not without cause, the common belief that Phil. 2.6–11 starts by speaking of Christ's pre-existent state and status and then of his incarnation is, in almost every case, a presupposition rather than a conclusion, a presupposition which again and again proves decisive in determining how disputed terms within the Philippian hymn should be understood.[62]

How then should the hymn be understood – in what appears (to us) the most obvious way, or in some other way? The key question here is, once again, the background against which the hymn has to be set, the context of thought to which the author was indebted, which the first readers would presuppose, and on which consequently a faithful exegesis of the hymn must depend to a decisive degree. What precisely that context was continues to be one of the more contentious issues in modern NT scholarship,[63] and to debate the various options phrase by phrase would make for a lengthy, complex and confusing discussion. However, a conclusion on this issue has grown steadily clearer and stronger for me over the past few years, and the most obvious course, and clearest exposition, will be simply to explain the exegetical reasons why that conclusion has become so persuasive.

In brief, the most informative and probable background in my judgment is the one we have been sketching in throughout this chapter – that of the Adam christology which was widely current in the Christianity of the 40s and 50s. It seems to me that Phil. 2.6–11 is best understood as an expression of Adam christology, one of the fullest expressions that we still possess.[64] We have already seen how *widespread* was this Adam christology in the period before Paul wrote his letters – a fact not usually appreciated by those who offer alternative exegeses of the hymn. Moreover it can readily be seen that the outline of thought in the Philippian hymn fully matches the two-stage christology evident elsewhere in first generation Christianity (see above §14) – free acceptance of man's lot followed out to death, and exaltation to the status of Lord over all, echoing the regular primitive association of Ps. 110.1 with Ps. 8.6. It is the way in which this Adam christology comes to expression in Phil. 2.6–11 which I must now attempt to demonstrate in more detail.

(a) Whatever the precise division of vv. 6–7 into lines and strophes,[65] the structure of vv. 6–7 seems to indicate a basic movement of thought running from v. 6a to v. 7c:

> [6]who being in the form of God
> did not count equality with God something to be grasped,
> [7]but emptied himself,
> taking the form of a slave,
> becoming in the likeness of men.

Verse 7d, 'and being found in form as man' (= v. 8a – ETs), provides the bridge to the next movement: for it clearly picks up the last clause of the first movement, the end result of the first stage of Christ's odyssey, and by means of the passive construction makes it the basis for the next movement of thought, the next stage – Christ's death.[66]

If we concentrate on vv. 6a–7c initially, it quickly becomes evident that its development is determined by a double contrast: first between 'form of God' and 'form of a slave', the former in which he was (ἐν μορφῇ Θεοῦ ὑπάρχων), the latter which he accepted (μορφὴν δούλου λαβών);[67] and second between 'equality with God' and 'in likeness of men',[68] the former which he did not consider a prize to be grasped (οὐχ ἁρπαγμὸν ἡγήσατο τὸ εἶναι ἴσα Θεοῦ), the latter which he became (ἐν ὁμοιώματι ἀνθρώπων γενόμενος). The best way to understand this double contrast is as an allusion to Gen. 1–3, an allusion once again, to the creation and fall of man. In the first contrast, μορφή Θεοῦ probably refers to Adam having been made in the image (εἰκών) of God and with a share of the glory (δόξα) of God: for it has long been recognized that μορφή (form) and εἰκών (image) are near synonyms and that in Hebrew thought the visible 'form of God' *is* his glory.[69] Μορφὴ δούλου probably refers therefore to what Adam became as a result of his fall: he lost his share in God's glory and became a slave[70] – that is, either to corruption (the parallel with Rom. 8.18–21 is close),[71] or to the elemental spirits (cf. Gal. 4.3).[72]

In the second contrast 'equality with God' probably alludes to Adam's temptation (Gen. 3.5 – '. . . you will be like God/the gods . . .'),[73] and therefore 'likeness of men' probably by way of contrast denotes the kind of man that Adam became and so the kind of man that all men now are.[74] Here again we may observe a close parallel in an earlier Pauline expression of Adam theology – Rom. 1.23: 'they changed the glory of the immortal God for the likeness (ὁμοιώματι) of the image of mortal man. . . .' (see above p. 102). Or in the equivalent contrast of Rom. 7.7–11, he who was alive with the life given him by God coveted more and found only death. As these parallels indicate we are here in the contrast familar to Greek thought between God/the gods as possessing incorruption, immortality,[75] and man as corruptible, subject to death. As Adam was made in the divine image and 'for incorruption' (ἐπ' ἀφθαρσίᾳ) (Wisd. 2.23), so the contrast to that is the state in which man now lives out his present life, in slavery to death and corruption (Wisd. 2.24; Rom. 8.21). That is to say, his fall was a receiving (λαβών) the form of a slave, of man's continuing bondage, and a becoming (γενόμενος)[76] in the likeness of men, of corruptible dying mankind.[77]

The problem of how the author intended the two contrasts to be related to each other has a long history: in particular, what can the distinction between 'form of God' and 'equality with God' amount to? and is 'equality with God' something that was not possessed and so grasped at, or something already possessed and so grasped retentively (the ambiguity of ἁρπαγμός).[78] Moreover, what did he lose of that which he had previously possessed? What did he become that was different from what he was when he made his choice? It is quite likely however that here too the Adam allusion both explains the presence of the ambiguity and resolves the puzzle. For the same problems were in effect presented to the interpreter of Gen. 1–3: how should one relate the creation account in Gen. 1 to the account in Gen. 2?[79] and what did Adam seek to grasp and what did he lose? Adam was already in the image of God (Gen. 1.26f.) and was created 'for immortality' (Wisd. 2.23 – he could have eaten freely of the tree of life and so lived for ever, Gen. 3.22). But he chose to grasp at the opportunity to be (completely) like God (knowing good and evil for himself – Gen. 3.5, 22). Snatching at the opportunity to enhance the status he already had, he both lost the degree of equality with God which he already enjoyed and was corrupted by that which he coveted (cf. Rom. 1.21–3; 7.9–11). Not content with being like God, what God had intended, he became like men, what men now are. The contrast in other words is between what *Adam* was and what he became, and it is this Adam language which is used of Christ. It is quite probable therefore that the author of the Philippian hymn was conscious of this ambiguity in the Adam narrative and intended to reflect it in his own formulation.[80]

If then so much of the language and ideas of vv. 6–7c is drawn from Gen. 1–3 and the Adam theology so widespread elsewhere in earliest

Christianity and contemporary Judaism, we can understand how and why it is that the writer of the Philippian hymn used it of Christ. For *Phil. 2.6–7c is of a piece with the Adam christology we have already observed in other passages within the NT.* What we have here is in fact very similar to Heb. 2.6–9 and is understood as a fuller description of what was involved in the divine programme for man being run through again with Jesus. Christ faced the same archetypal choice that confronted Adam, but chose *not* as Adam had chosen (to grasp equality with God). *Instead* he chose to empty himself of Adam's glory and to embrace Adam's lot, the fate which Adam had suffered by way of punishment. That is, in the words of the hymn, 'he made himself powerless' (ἐκένωσεν),[81] freely accepting the lot and portion of man's slavery (to corruption and the powers) – μορφὴ δούλου, the antithesis of μορφὴ Θεοῦ; he freely chose to share the very lot and fate of all men – ὁμοίωμα ἀνθρώπων, the antithesis of τὸ εἶναι ἴσα Θεοῦ – mankind's mortality and corruptibility, the antithesis of God's immortality and incorruption. What is expressed in one phrase in Rom. 8.3, 'sent in the very likeness (ὁμοιώματι) of sinful flesh', is expressed in two phrases in Phil. 2.7, 'taking the form of a slave, becoming in the very likeness (ὁμοιώματι) of men'.

(*b*) In the last two sections of the hymn (vv. 7d–8 and 9–11) the Adam christology covers the ground with which we have now become familiar – Christ as Adam, subject to death, and as Last Adam, exalted as Lord over all. As in Heb. 2.6–8, the programme is run through again and the divine intention for man expressed in Ps. 8.6 becomes at last fulfilled in the one who became Lord.

> And being found in form as man,
> [8]he humbled himself
> becoming obedient to death . . .
> [9]Wherefore God has exalted him to the heights
> and bestowed on him the name which is over every name,
> [10]that at the name of Jesus every knee should bow . . .
> [11]and every tongue should confess that Jesus Christ is Lord.[82]

Verse 7d is particularly revealing. As the wording indicates, 'and being found in form as man (σχήματι ὡς ἄνθρωπος)', it resumes where the first movement of thought had reached. Indeed, we may say it recapitulates the thought of the whole section, with the influence of the Adam narratives still strong. Μορφὴ δούλου, ὁμοίωμα ἀνθρώπων and σχῆμα ὡς ἄνθρωπος are all more or less synonymous,[83] all variant ways of describing the character of fallen Adam, all drawn from Adam theology. In particular, as in Phil. 3.21 verbal forms of σχῆμα and μορφή describe the transformation of the believing man to share the glory of the last Adam, so in Phil. 2.7b, d σχῆμα and μορφή describe the reality of man lacking the glory in which and for which Adam was created.[84] Moreover, the ὡς ἄνθρωπος may be a direct echo of the LXX wording of the serpent's temptation, 'You shall be as God' (Gen. 3.5 – ὡς θεοί) – thinking to be as God, he proved himself to be (εὑρεθείς)[85] but man; claiming to be wise, he became a fool (Rom. 1.22). Here of course the language is used to describe the human character of Christ, but precisely of *Christ evaluated theologically as Adam*: his life proved him to be in form as man. Notice, *not* 'as *a* man', but *as man* – that is, as representative man, as one with fallen man, as Adam.[86]

With the Adamic character of Jesus' earthly life thus re-emphasized, the hymn follows out the pattern, Adam who dies, last Adam who emerges the other side of death as Lord. 'As man he humbled himself and became obedient unto death (even death on a cross)' (Phil. 2.8). This may simply be spelling out the full implication of v. 7a–b – 'he emptied himself taking the form of a slave' – for it is just possible that ἑαυτὸν ἐκένωσεν is a direct rendering of the Hebrew of Isa. 53.12 ('he emptied out his life to death'),[87] and crucifixion was widely thought of in the Roman world as 'the slaves' punishment'.[88] Alternatively, Phil. 2.8 may be carrying the thought forward beyond that of the first section: he chose freely to embrace not only Adam's degradation as a slave (to corruption and the powers), as a mere man, as (fallen) man, but also his death. Either way we need simply note that the theme of Christ's 'obedience' in the NT always occurs in reference to his suffering and death, and probably always contains an allusion to Adam's act of *dis*obedience which brought death into the world (so clearly in Rom. 5.19, and probably also in Heb. 5.8).[89] In either case therefore the hymn states of Jesus what the other expressions of Adam christology (particularly Rom. 5; 8.3 and Heb. 2.9–18) also state of Jesus, that *he freely chose to embrace the death that Adam experienced as punishment*.

Finally with Phil. 2.9–11 we enter the last section of the hymn, and the 'last Adam' stage of the christology, when the last Adam by his 'superexaltation' (ὑπερύψωσεν) attains a far higher glory than the first Adam lost. It is rather striking that *these verses contain in more elaborate form precisely the two affirmations about Christ that the earliest form of Adam christology made*: the use of Ps. 110.1 to assert the claim that the Lord God has installed Christ at his right hand and given him also the title Lord (no higher status and title was possible); and the conjoined use of Ps. 8.6 to claim that God has put all things under his feet. Certainly the use of the strongly monotheistic passage (Isa. 45.23) adds a new dimension to the christological claim, but apart from that the assertion of universal homage before Christ (Phil. 2.10) is simply the obverse of the assertion of the universal sovereignty of Christ (Ps. 8.6).[90] Thus we can see that the motifs of Adam christology run through the complete Philippian hymn, from beginning to end. It is presumably precisely because it is such a description of Christ as Adam and last Adam (and not simply a description of Christ's abasement and exaltation in itself) that Paul can use the hymn to strengthen his ethical exhortation to his converts at Philippi.

In short, I may hope that my initial claim has been well enough established: that Phil. 2.6–11 is an expression of Adam christology. Throughout the Philippian hymn, particularly in the first half, the figure of Adam lurks in the background – just as he does elsewhere in Paul's use of the words 'image' and 'glory' in his soteriology, and in I Cor. 15 (see above pp. 105f. and 109, 111), not to mention Heb. 2. Throughout the Philippian hymn there is the same sort of implicit contrast between Adam and Christ which we noted regularly above (§14). *The Christ of Phil. 2.6–11 therefore is the man who undid Adam's wrong*: confronted with the same choice, he rejected Adam's sin, but nevertheless freely followed Adam's course as fallen man to the bitter end of death; wherefore God bestowed on him the status not simply that Adam lost, but the status which Adam was intended to come to, God's final prototype, the last Adam.

(c) If our conclusion is sound, that Phil. 2.6–11 is through and through an expression of Adam christology, then the question of whether it also speaks of Christ's *pre-existence* becomes clearer. The point to be grasped is that the question cannot be answered without reference to the Adam christology which forms the backbone of the hymn. Since the thought is dominated by the Adam/Christ parallel and contrast, the individual expressions must be understood within that context. The terms used in the hymn do not have an independent value; *their sense is determined by their role within the Adam christology*, by their function in describing Adam or more generally God's purpose for man.

This means that the initial stage of Christ's odyssey is depicted as equivalent to Adam's status and choice in the garden. Now Adam was certainly not thought of as pre-existent – though perhaps strictly speaking as pre-historical, or, being the first man on the earth, as transhistorical/ typical.[91] So no implication that Christ was pre-existent may be intended. If Christ walks in Adam's footsteps then Christ need be no more pre-existent than Adam. Nor indeed is there any implication that Christ was contemporaneous with Adam, acting in a similarly transhistorical situation. In point of fact, in earliest Christian Adam theology Christ always presupposes Adam, Christ's odyssey presupposes the plight of Adam, of Adam's offspring. As I Cor. 15.45ff. insists, the temporal order is clear: Adam first, Christ second – Christ is *last* Adam, *Adam precedes Christ*. Adam was not a copy of a pre-existent Christ, but 'a type of *him who was to come*' (Rom. 5.14; see further below pp. 126f.). It would seem therefore that the point of the parallel between Adam and Christ is not dependent on any particular time scale – pre-existence, pre-history or whatever. *The point focuses rather on the* choice *confronting Adam and Christ.* The Philippian hymn does not intend to affirm that Jesus was as historical or as prehistorical as Adam, but that the *choice* confronting Christ was as *archetypal* and determinative for mankind as was Adam's; whether the choice was made by the pre-existent Christ or the historical Jesus is immaterial to the Philippian hymn.

Here then we can see the point of Murphy-O'Connor's initial criticism and the danger for good exegesis of assuming too quickly that the phrases 'being in the form of God' and 'becoming in the likeness of men', necessarily imply a thought of pre-existence. For the language throughout, and not least at these points, is wholly determined by the creation narratives and by the contrast between what Adam grasped at and what he in consequence became. It was Adam who was 'in the form of God', Adam who 'became what men now are' (in contrast to what God had intended for them). The language was used *not* because it is first and foremost appropriate to *Christ*, but because it is appropriate to *Adam*, drawn from the account of Adam's creation and fall. *It was used of Christ therefore to bring out the Adamic character of Christ's life, death and resurrection.* So archetypal was Jesus' work in its effect that it can be described in language appropriate to archetypal man and as a reversal of the archetypal sin. The point being made here is parallel to that made above concerning Rom. 7.7–11 (p. 104). As when reading Rom. 7.7–11 we are not to think of some specific time in the life of Paul or the Jew when he was 'alive once apart from the law', so when reading Phil. 2.6–11 we should not try to identify a specific time in Christ's existence when he was in the form of God and before he became like men. As Rom. 7.7–11 is just a way of describing the character and plight of all men now, so *Phil. 2.6–11 is simply a way of describing the character of Christ's ministry and sacrifice.* In both cases the language used is determined wholly by the Adam stories and is most probably not intended as metaphysical assertions about individuals in the first century AD.

But what meaning can the opening lines have as a description of Christ unless they are a description of a pre-existent choice to become incarnate? Even if the parallel between Adam and Christ focuses on the *choice* confronting both rather than on temporal relationship or metaphysical states, how can we say of the earthly Jesus that he was confronted with such a choice? In what sense, or when was the *earthly* Jesus confronted with a choice as archetypal as Adam's – in childhood, at Jordan, in the wilderness, at Caesarea Philippi? To press this question is probably once again to misunderstand what the hymn is trying to do. It does not seek to narrate a particular event or temptation as such, but simply describes in Adam language *the character of Christ's whole life* – just as Rom. 7.7–11 describes the plight of everyman. Quite possibly the author assumed

Christ's sinlessness and was in effect trading on its corollary – viz. that he who did not sin need not have died (cf. Rom. 5.12c) (that is, he need not have become a slave to corruption like the rest of men). The fact that he did die, however, implies that he did make the archetypal choice, or that his whole life constituted his willing acceptance of the sinner's lot (cf. II Cor. 5.21).[92] In other words, Phil. 2.6–8 is probably intended to affirm that Christ's earthly life was an embodiment of grace from beginning to end, of giving away in contrast to the selfish grasping of Adam's sin,[93] that every choice of any consequence made by Christ was the antithesis of Adam's, that every stage of Christ's life and ministry had the character of a fallen lot freely embraced. As the temptation tradition in the Gospels depicts the conflict character of Jesus' whole ministry in terms of Israel typology in language drawn from Deut. 6–8 (Matt. 4.1–11/Luke 4.1–12),[94] so Phil. 2.6–11 depicts its character in terms of Adam typology in language drawn from Gen. 1–3.

§15.2   The other Pauline passage which could be understood to speak of the self-giving of Christ as the heavenly Man is II Cor. 8.9 – 'You know the grace of our Lord Jesus (Christ), that though he was rich, yet for your sake (δι' ὑμᾶς) he became poor, so that (ἵνα) by his poverty you might become rich.' To elucidate this verse commentators regularly point out the close parallel with Phil. 2.6ff., and conclude that it speaks of the pre-existent Christ ('being rich') choosing to become incarnate ('became poor'). But once again we should be wary of assuming that the context of thought was an already established christology of incarnation.[95] Would it have been so obvious to Paul's readers that he was speaking of the incarnation or of Christ's descent from heaven?

(a) When Paul elsewhere speaks of '*grace*' (= 'gracious gift', or 'gracious act') in connection with what Christ has done he was always thinking of his death and resurrection (see especially Rom. 5.15,21; Gal. 2.20f.; Eph. 1.6f.). Nowhere else does he talk of Christ's 'gracious act' as his becoming man.

(b) The salvation effecting act in earliest Christianity is always the death and resurrection of Christ. We should notice in particular the equivalent ὑπέρ ... ἵνα ('for the sake of ... in order that') formulation in II Cor. 5.21, Gal. 3.13f., I Peter 3.18, and the close parallels in Rom. 4.25, 8.3f., Gal. 4.4,[96] Heb. 2.14 and I Peter 2.24 (cf. Rom. 15.3; Heb. 12.2). These are the closest parallels to the διὰ ... ἵνα formulation of II Cor. 8.9.

(c) We should not assume that the contrast is between spiritual wealth (pre-existence) and *spiritual* poverty (incarnation).[97] The regular contrast then current was between spiritual wealth and *material* poverty (Tobit 4.21; II Cor. 6.10; James 2.5; Rev. 2.9; cf. I Cor. 1.5; 4.8; II Cor. 9.11), and this would have been a not unexpected sense in the context of II Cor. 8.

A reference to Jesus' own material poverty freely embraced cannot be dismissed out of hand therefore; we cannot exclude the possibility that sayings like Mark 10.28–30 and Matt. 8.20/Luke 9.58 lie behind the thought expressed in II Cor. 8.9 (note in the immediate context 8.2). But the parallels referred to above make it more likely that the allusion is to Jesus' death – the richness of his communion with God (expressed in his *abba* prayer and his full confidence in God – Matt. 6.25–33) set in sharp contrast with the poverty of his desolation on the cross ('My God, my God, why have you forsaken me?' – Mark 15.34).[98] The imagery of riches/poverty would naturally be suggested to Paul in the context of his appeal to the Corinthians that they join in 'the gracious act' of his collection for the poor in Jerusalem (II Cor. 8–9) – as appropriate an imagery in this context as the sacrificial imagery earlier in the letter (sinless/sin – II Cor. 5.21),[99] and a not inappropriate association (poverty and crucifixion) in the context of the times where crucifixion was such a degrading and humiliating punishment ('Riches buy off judgment, and the poor are condemned to the cross').[100]

Alternatively we may simply have here a variation on the Adam christology which has been the subject of this chapter – Jesus' 'being rich' (πλούσιος ὤν) as the equivalent of his 'being in the form of God' (ἐν μορφῇ Θεοῦ ὑπάρχων), and his 'becoming poor' (ἐπτώχευσεν) as the equivalent of his 'emptying himself' (ἑαυτὸν ἐκένωσεν).[101] Adam's enjoyment of God's fellowship could readily be characterized as a 'being rich', just as his fall resulted in his 'becoming poor'. The rabbis certainly speculated about the contrast between Adam's created state and his state after his sin, and characterized his fall as a loss and deprivation of what he had previously enjoyed (particularly his glory, his immortality and his height).[102] So in the language of Adam christology Jesus could be characterized as one who freely embraced the lot of fallen Adam, including above all his death, not as a punishment for any sin of his own but as a 'gracious act' – in this instance the particular imagery (riches/poverty) being prompted by the context. This would seem to make better sense of II Cor. 8.9 within the larger context of Paul's theology than an incarnation interpretation. It would be untypically manichean for Paul if the rich/poor contrast was intended as a contrast between divinity and humanity (cf. Gosp. Thos. 2,30). Paul would not think of *creatureliness* as poverty over against the riches of deity. But he could readily think of Adam's *fallenness* as poverty over against the riches of his fellowship with God, just as the reverse antithesis, becoming rich (despite our poverty), presumably denotes a coming into fellowship with God (cf. Rom. 11.12; I Cor. 1.5; 4.8; II Cor. 6.10; 9.11; and the not so very different profit and loss imagery in Phil. 3.7f.). Though he could have enjoyed the riches of an uninterrupted communion with God, Jesus freely chose to embrace the poverty of Adam's distance from God, in his ministry as a whole, but particularly in his death, in order that we might enter into the full inheritance intended for Adam in the first place.[103]

§15.3   We have shown thus far how readily Phil. 2.6–11 (and II Cor. 8.9) can be interpreted within the context of the Adam christology of earliest Christianity and against the background of first-century Jewish thought concerning Adam. Should we look any further? In particular, does the implication of Paul's argument in I Cor. 15.45–7 (see above p. 100) throw any more light on the subject? The implication, that is, that some at Corinth thought of the earthly, soulish (Adam) as appearing later than the heavenly, spiritual (Man?)? Could Paul in Phil. 2.6–11 after all be taking up a speculation about such a heavenly man which was already developing towards the Primal Man and heavenly Redeemer of the later Gnostic systems? It is certainly true that Phil. 2.6–11 was used in the second-century Gnostic elaborations of the basic myth – in Valentinianism (Clem.Alex., *Exc.Theod.* 35.1; 43.4), by the Sethians (Hippolytus, *Ref.* V.19.21) and elsewhere (*Acts of Thomas* 27; see also Hippolytus, *Ref.* V.7.11; 8.22). So clearly Phil. 2.6–11 was compatible in some degree with Gnostic thought. And Bultmann's thesis that Phil. 2.6–11 already presupposes a developed form of the Gnostic myth (see above pp. 98f.) has not lacked support in the subsequent debate.[104] But any line of influence between Phil. 2.6–11 and Gnostic thought most probably runs the other way; that is to say, the (later) Gnostic statements almost certainly depend on Phil. 2.6–11 itself rather than on any (hypothetical) Gnostic formulation lying behind the Philippian hymn. Moreover, other points of contact between Phil. 2.6–11 and the Gnostic redeemer myth are best explained by the fact that both share the same background (the early Jewish speculation about Adam and the early Adam christology outlined above), whereas the differences between the two are if anything more impressive than the similarities.[105]

What then of Philo's antithesis between the heavenly man (of Gen. 1.26f.) and the earthly man of Gen. 2.7 (above p. 100)? And what about the implications of I Cor. 15.45–7? Do these not indicate the beginnings of a heavenly man redeemer figure speculation which might have influenced Paul or the Philippian hymn? The answer is probably a straightforward No. When we set Philo's exegesis of Gen. 1–2 within the wider context of his thought it becomes quite clear that he does not think of the heavenly man as a person, let alone as a divine redeemer. Philo's distinction between heavenly man and earthly man derives basically from the Platonic distinction between the heavenly world of ideas and the earthly world of inferior copies. Philo's 'heavenly man' is the heavenly counterpart of earthly man, 'a bloodless idea', a 'passive prototype and model' which has neither cosmological nor soteriological function.[106] Philo's own description both makes this quite clear and also shows how far his thought is from that of Paul in I Cor. 15.44f.: 'He that was after the (divine) image was an idea or type or seal, *an object of thought* (only), *incorporeal* (νοητός, ἀσώματος) . . .' (*Opif.* 134). As he emphatically states earlier in the same work, the world of ideas does not exist in some place, that is, it does not have a real existence other than as thought in the mind of the thinker (*Opif.* 17–19; see further below §28.3). In short, this, the only clearly pre-Christian material of relevance, cannot be counted as support for the hypothesis of a pre-Christian Gnostic Primal Man myth and does not suggest any thought of a pre-existent divine person who might become incarnate. On the contrary it shows how speculation about the relation of heaven to earth and about the first man might range widely *without* provoking or implying the thought of a real pre-existence in relation to Adam.

Nor can we argue on the basis of I Cor. 15.45–7 that Paul or his readers would naturally or inevitably have moved this Philonic-type speculation in the direction of postulating Adam's or the second Adam's pre-existence. Quite the contrary, for Paul makes it abundantly clear that Christ is *second*. Christ is not prior to Adam, either temporally or logically – he comes *after* Adam, he is the *last* Adam.[107] Here in fact Paul deliberately and decisively distances himself from any potentially gnostic concept of redemption, for where the logic of Gnosis is that the redeemer *must* be first,[108] Paul's logic is quite different. Where Philo derived his exegesis from a Platonic model applied to Gen. 1–2, and the Gnostics derived their exegesis from a more extensive cosmological dualism similarly used, Paul derived his exegesis *from the resurrection of Christ*. Paul's use of Adam speculation was oriented not according to mythicizing preoccupation with the world's beginnings, but according to the eschatologically new that had happened in Jesus' resurrection, and the world's ending which that foreshadowed; and his Adam christology focused not on some original man who had descended from heaven but on the second man whom he expected to return from heaven shortly, whose image as the resurrected one Christians would share (vv.47–9 – see also above n.41).[109]

If then Paul sets his face so firmly against any gnosticizing use of Gen. 1–2 in I Corinthians it is hardly likely that the same Paul would use language in II Cor. 8.9 and Phil. 2 which might be understood by his contemporaries as an abandonment of that whole eschatological perspective. In other words, had there been any real danger of these passages being interpreted of a pre-existent heavenly man it is doubtful whether Paul would have used them without a good deal more qualification. All of which makes it very unlikely that a Primal Man myth had developed far enough to provide either background or context for any of Paul's writings.[110]

§15.4 So far as we can tell therefore, the context of thought on which Paul was drawing and which would illumine his words for his readers did not yet include the thought of a pre-existent original Man who descended from heaven as redeemer of men. All that our evidence shows us is (1) a Platonic distinction between heavenly man (an idea) and earthly man (Adam) in Philo; (2) a more widespread attempt to use the Adam narratives to explain man's plight and hope of salvation in apocalyptic, rabbinic and not least earliest Christian writers – not linked with the (apocalyptic) Son of Man (see above III n. 134, IV n. 86)[111] and not yet tied in to speculation about Wisdom; [112] (3) the emergence of a fully fledged and more integrated primal Man myth in second-century Gnostic texts – to which Christian belief in Christ as last Adam, exalted as Lord made a decisive contribution (see above n.3), including the Philippian hymn itself (above p. 123). If then II Cor. 8.9 and Phil. 2.6–11 had been penned in the middle of the second century there would be little dispute that the writer was thinking of Christ as a pre-existent divine being – the context of thought, including particularly the myth of the Primal Man-redeemer, would make that clear. But these passages were written in the middle of the first century, and the most obvious and only really clear context of thought to inform their meaning is the Adam theology and christology widespread in earliest Christianity. In short, *Adam christology provides not only a plausible context of thought for Phil. 2.6–11 (and II Cor. 8.9) but also the most plausible context of thought.* Alternative explanations in terms of a Gnostic or proto-Gnostic Primal Man speculation are not only unnecessary but also unconvincing.

§16. CONCLUSIONS

§16.1 Our task has once again been the crucial but difficult one of trying to attune our twentieth-century ears to the concepts and overtones of the 50s and 60s of the first century AD in the eastern Mediterranean. What was the context of thought within which Paul would have written and his readers have understood passages like Phil. 2.6–11 and II Cor. 8.9? Unless we can read these texts with a sympathetic sensitivity to the presuppositions of the first readers to guide us we will not enter into the meaning which Paul intended. In this chapter I have attempted to demonstrate how important and widespread was Adam theology in earliest Christianity – as a way of understanding and expressing the plight of man, the salvation offered by the gospel, and above all the role of Christ in making that salvation possible. I have also attempted to demonstrate how plausible is the interpretation of Rom. 8.3, Gal. 4.4, Phil. 2.6–11 and perhaps also II Cor. 8.9 in terms of that Adam christology. That is to say, I have shown *how natural it would have been for Paul's readers to interpret these passages in the light of, with the aid of, and as an expression of this Adam theology* familiar more or less throughout earliest Christianity, or at least throughout earliest Hellenistic Jewish Christianity.

I do not believe it is possible to demonstrate a more plausible context of thought for the time at which Paul wrote. First-century readers of Phil. 2.6–11 no doubt knew talk of heavenly beings who descended to earth for some purpose, but the idea of a heavenly being becoming man in order to die would be strange to them (see above §3.5). Evidence of a Son of Man speculation in such terms prior to the synthesis offered by the Fourth Gospel is totally lacking, and there are no points of contact between beliefs regarding Enoch/Elijah and the Adam theology which certainly lies behind Phil. 2 in one degree or another (see further above ch. III). And in the present chapter we have uncovered no real evidence that the concept of a heavenly archetype of Adam had developed beyond that of a Platonic idea by the time of Paul – no real evidence, in other words, of an already established belief in a heavenly first man who became the redeemer of Adam's offspring. The Adam christology which we *have* uncovered was itself probably one of the chief tributaries which flowed (or was diverted) into the Gnostic redeemer myth. We have yet to examine the thesis of a widespread Wisdom myth and cannot exclude the possibility that if a concept of pre-existence was already attached to Christ (through identification with Wisdom) it would have been read into Phil. 2.6 as well. But the indications thus far are that Wisdom speculation and Adam theologizing had not yet been brought into interaction (see above n.87). The Adam christology of the NT documents is consistent and coherent within itself and does not require the presupposition of any proto-Gnostic redeemer myth to explain its origin or meaning. In short, Phil. 2.6–11 etc. may well, unwittingly, have provided a stimulus towards the Gnostic redeemer myth, but these texts cannot be reckoned an expression of or reaction to it.

§16.2 The main emphasis in Adam christology, for Paul at least, is *eschatological*. Christ as last Adam is *eschatological* man. His role as last Adam begins with and stems from his resurrection, not from pre-existence, or even from his earthly ministry (see above pp. 107f.). E. Schweizer objects to 'the strict limitation of the "last Adam" to the Risen One', since 'the "man" of Rom. 5.15–19 is in contrast to that of I Cor. 15.22, the earthly Jesus'.[113] But Schweizer here fails to appreciate the full scope of the Adam christology. Strictly speaking what Paul says about the 'last Adam' in I. Cor. 15.45 cannot be directly equated with what he says about the 'man' in Rom. 5. In terms of I Cor. 15, the role of Christ as archetypal man begins only from the resurrection (15.45). Until believers have come to bear the image of the heavenly man, the risen Christ, they bear the image of the man of dust (15.46–9). The archetype of the first Adam stamps all men with death and until death; the archetype of the last Adam is the image and the power of resurrection from the dead (15.21f.). In terms of the Ps. 8 christology, Christ only completes the divine purpose for man with his resurrection; only then is he crowned with glory and honour. Prior to that Christ was, like Adam, 'lower than the angels' (Heb. 2.6–9). In other words, up to and including his death Christ himself was patterned according to the archetype of the first Adam, 'born of woman' (Gal. 4.4), 'in the (precise) likeness of sinful flesh' (Rom. 8.3); only with the resurrection did Christ become himself archetype of a new man, eschatological man, last Adam.

Thus in Rom. 5.15–19 Paul is talking not about the 'last Adam' as such, but about the earthly Jesus patterned according to the archetype of Adam (Rom. 5.14), about the man who 'recapitulated' Adam's fate (as an act of obedience rather than a consequence of sin), who repeated but reversed the drama which brought about man's fallenness (so also Phil. 2.6–11). That is to say, he is talking about Jesus as the one who shattered the mould of Adam's archetype, who broke through Adam's death to resurrection beyond, to a new humanity beyond (cf. Eph. 2.14f.). It is in this sense that Paul can speak of Jesus' death as a kind of pattern (as in Phil. 3.10),[114] as a pattern, that is, for the way through Adam's fate to resurrection beyond. But the new humanity is life from the other side of death, shaped by power from the other side of death (the life-giving Spirit). Paul does not usually speak of the believer being patterned according to the image of the earthly Jesus, his ministry, his teaching.[115] And he thinks in terms of the believer sharing in Christ's death only because Christ has lived through Adam's fate to resurrection life beyond; so that only those who share in the death of Adam as experienced by Christ will share also in the resurrection life of Christ, that is, only those who follow out the pattern of Adam to death with Christ will be stamped with the pattern of Christ's resurrected humanity, only those who follow the footsteps of the pioneer will be crowned like him with honour and glory and thus fulfill God's original purpose for man.[116]

§16.3 All this raises the question whether the pre-existence-incarnation interpretation of these key passages in Paul and Hebrews is properly grounded in exegesis of these passages. Has that interpretation properly understood the character and thrust of earliest Christianity's Adam christology? It is quite true that once the context of the original Adam theology faded from the immediate perspective the language which derived from that theology lent itself to a pre-existence-incarnation interpretation, particularly in the case of Phil. 2.6–11. Indeed, even when the Adam allusion remained in the forefront of the interpretation the development of Gnostic speculation about the Primal Man, the pre-existent divine redeemer, inevitably encouraged a pre-existence-incarnation interpretation. But from what we have seen of the Adam christology in Paul and elsewhere in the earliest decades of Christianity, that interpretation goes beyond the meaning and intention of the original Philippian hymn and its use by Paul. It may even be that the pre-existence-incarnation interpretation of Phil. 2.6–11 etc. owes more to the later Gnostic redeemer myth than it does to Phil. 2.6–11 properly understood as an expression of first generation Adam christology – one way of outbidding and countering the appeal of the Gnostic systems.

How much truth is contained in the last comment is hard to discern. What we can say with more confidence is that the reading of these passages with the presupposition of a pre-existent heavenly redeemer resulted in a critical shift in Adam christology – a shift from a christology of death and resurrection to a christology of incarnation – and not only in christology, but also in the concept of redemption which goes with it. For an inevitable corollary was that incarnation became steadily more central as the decisive christological moment which determined the character of the redeemer figure – now seen as the divine being who united humanity with his deity, rather than as one who conquered where Adam failed, who died and rose again where Adam ended only in death. Likewise incarnation became steadily more central as the decisive act of redemption – a tendency already evident in Irenaeus who can speak of Christ 'attaching man to God by his own incarnation' (*adv. haer.* V.1.1) – so that later theology had to look for meaning in Christ's death more as the paying of a ransom to the devil than as the ending of the first Adam that last Adam might come to be. To explore this further would take us too far from our present task (the beginnings of christology); but it is certainly arguable that all these subsequent developments are the consequence in part at least of losing sight of the original meaning and intention of the Adam christology, that is, as one of the earliest attempts to spell out the sense of eschatological newness, of participating in a new humanity which was God's original intention for man but which now could be enjoyed only through sharing in the life from death of the risen Christ, the last Adam.

V

SPIRIT OR ANGEL?

§17. INTRODUCTION

> That with emphasis on God's transcendence he becomes increasingly more elevated has, as is well known, in late Judaism led to the development of the belief in a series of intermediaries, who stand between God and the world and, so to say, mediate his action to the world. First and foremost among these intermediary beings are the hypostases (Wisdom, the Shekinah, the Word) and angels, of which Judaism knows a number each with his particular individuality.

With these words of H. Ringgren[1] we are introduced to what increasingly has come to be recognized as the most fruitful area of investigation in any inquiry into the origins of the Christian doctrine of the incarnation. One of the major features of late pre-Christian and non-Christian Judaism is the tremendous development of language which can readily be understood as denoting *intermediate beings* between God and man. In Hellenistic Judaism the most striking of these 'intermediate beings' were *Wisdom* and *Logos* (Word) – we need for the moment merely mention Wisdom's apparently independent role in creation, for example, in Wisd. 8.4–6 (see further below ch. VI), and the dominant role of the Logos in Philo (e.g. *Leg.All.* II.86; *Agr.* 51; see further below ch. VII). In Palestinian Judaism, particularly the apocalyptic writings, *angels* were accorded a much more extensive and significant role than hitherto as intermediaries between heaven and earth, including that of intercessors on man's behalf (Tobit 12.15; I Enoch 9.3; 15.2; 89.76; 99.3; Test. Levi 3.5; 5.6f.; Test.Dan 6.2; IQH 6.13).[2] And in rabbinic Judaism it can be argued that there was a clear tendency to hypostatize the *name* of God (Yoma 3.8; 4.2; 6.2;[3] and strikingly also in the Similitudes of I Enoch – 39.7, 9, 13; 41.2, 6; 43.4; 45.2f.; 46.6–8; 47.2; 48.7,10; etc.),[4] and the *glory* of God (the Shekinah – e.g. Sanh. 6.5; Aboth 3.2; Targ.Onkelos on Ex. 33.14f.; 34.6,9).[5] Here we might mention also the *Memra* of Yahweh which is regularly named in place of Yahweh in the Targums,[6] and the way in which in rabbinic Judaism the *Torah* came to be regarded almost as a divine being independent of God.[7] Not least the same line of argument could lead to the conclusion that the *Spirit* of God was hypostatized in pre-Christian Judaism, being treated as a (semi-)independent divine agent, whether through identification with Wisdom, as in the Wisdom of Solomon (1.4f., 7; 9.17), or in connection with the Spirit's role in creation (Judith 16.14; II Bar. 21.4).[8]

The point of course is this: if pre-Christian Judaism was already thinking in terms of divine hypostases and intermediaries then to that extent Judaism's monotheism was already being diluted or at least modified, to that extent precedents were being evolved for a Christian doctrine of Jesus as divine mediator, and to that extent room was being made for a Christian doctrine of incarnation, that is of a Jesus Christ who was the incarnation of one of these 'intermediary beings'. The situation however is not so straightforward as at first appears. For in fact there has been a strong resistance for some time from rabbinic specialists to the line of interpretation presented above; those most familiar with rabbinic Judaism have consistently and firmly denied that rabbinic Judaism ever made room for intermediate beings between God and man. It is true that the 'name', the 'glory', the 'memra' serve in some degree to protect the holy transcendence and wholly otherness of God: in the Targums the grosser anthropomorphisms of Genesis in particular are avoided by speaking instead of the Memra of Yahweh; and the holiness of the divine name can similarly be protected by speaking instead of the 'name' or the 'glory'. Such language does indeed provide something of a 'buffer' for divine transcendence; but we should not conclude from this that the rabbis thought of God as remote and distant from men.[9] On the contrary these so-called 'intermediary beings' are better understood as ways of asserting God's *nearness*, his involvement with the world, his concern for his people. *These words provided expressions of God's immanence without compromising his transcendence.* In particular, the name, the glory, the memra are simply circumlocutions for 'God', a more reverent way of speaking about God acting in relation to men, and may by no means be regarded as personal divine beings distinct from God.[10] That the rabbis were themselves aware of the ambiguities involved in this procedure and strongly resisted any interpretation which might threaten monotheism is indicated by a saying of rabbi Eliezer (late first century AD):

> He who translates a verse (from the Bible) literally is a liar. He who adds to it commits a blasphemy. For instance, if he translated: 'And they saw the God of Israel' (Ex. 24.10), he spoke an untruth; for the Holy One . . . sees, but is not seen. But if he translated: 'And they saw the glory of the Shekinah of the

God of Israel' he commits blasphemy; for he makes three, viz. Glory, Shekinah and God.[11]

But this may not resolve the issue for us. For it is an issue which spills out beyond the confines of rabbinic Judaism. As scholars have increasingly recognized over the past twenty to thirty years, pre-rabbinic Judaism was a much more varied and diverse phenomenon than the more rigid categories of Mishnah and Talmud would allow. We must ask therefore whether the same sort of language when used within the broader forms of first-century AD Hellenistic Judaism (both inside and outside Palestine) was used with the same circumspection. May it not be the case that the monotheism of Hellenistic Judaism was indeed modified by talk of Wisdom, Word and Spirit, not to mention angels?[12] May we not in fact have to reckon with a rather more syncretistic Judaism than the normative Judaism which the rabbis developed – a Judaism, that is to say, where the language of 'intermediary beings' did in fact partly derive from and partly stimulate belief in personal divine beings distinct from and in some degree independent of God?

So our question re-emerges: *did pre-Christian Judaism provide language for the earliest Christians which, when they applied it to Jesus, became the language of pre-existence and incarnation?* And not just language: *did pre-Christian Judaism provide earliest Christianity with a conceptualization of divine hypostases or intermediaries between God and man which led the earliest Christians inevitably to identify Jesus with one (or more) of these divine beings?* The most important debate here centres round the language of Wisdom and Logos (Word) and we will have to devote complete chapters to each of these (chs. VI and VII). First however we will deal with the other two major alternatives – the Spirit and angels. In all this area of course we are not dealing with clearly defined and distinct entities. They all overlap to one degree or other and provide alternative ways of speaking about divine interaction with the human and earthly. But Wisdom and Logos became dominant categories in Hellenistic Judaism and so require separate study as the best examples of Hellenistic Judaism's attempt to wrestle with the problems of speaking at all about God's interaction with the world. Spirit and angels are less important for our purposes here. But we cannot ignore them, and they are most conveniently treated together since they too overlap to some extent (I Enoch 15.4,7; Jub. 1.25; 2.2; 15.32; 1QH 1.11; 13.8; 1QM 10.12; 13.10; Acts 8.26, 29, 39; 23.9; Heb. 1.7,14; Asc. Isa. 9.36, 39f.; 10.4; 11.33 – 'the angel of the Holy Spirit'; and see below pp. 152 and 156f.).[13]

So we must ask: Was the Spirit already thought of as a semi-independent hypostasis at the time of Jesus? Did pre-Christian Jewish angelology provide an opening for some Christians to identify Jesus with an angel?

Such questions become all the sharper for us as soon as we recognize *how strong was the tendency in early Christianity to think of Jesus in Spirit or angel terms*. Paul for one seems to have identified (the risen) Christ with the Spirit ('the last Adam became life-giving Spirit' – I Cor. 15.45), and it is possible to argue that Paul elsewhere equated 'Christ Jesus' with 'the angel of God' (Gal. 4.14 – assuming an allusion to a Galatian belief in angels; cf. Gal. 1.8; 3.19f.).[14] Moreover, as we shall see, it is arguable that with the Johannine Paraclete we have a two-way link between the Spirit of truth and an angelic mediator (Michael) on the one hand, and between the Holy Spirit and Christ (the first Paraclete) on the other (see below pp. 147f. and 156f.). Most striking of all, we know that several Christian writers in the patristic period (second to fourth centuries) actually spoke of the incarnation in terms of the *Spirit* becoming flesh (Hermas, *Sim.* V.6.5; IX.1.1; Tertullian, *Prax.* 26; Cyprian, *idol.* 11; Hilary *Trin.* 2.26).[15] So too Jewish Christians of the second and third centuries specifically affirmed that Christ was an angel or archangel (Tertullian, *carn.Chr.* 14.5; Epiphanius, *Pan.* 30.16.4; Clem. *Recog.* II.42; *Hom.* XVIII.4).[16] As for more 'orthodox' second-century Christian writers, Hermas seems to have been influenced by this understanding of Christ as the chief archangel (*Vis.* V.1; *Sim.* VII.5; IX.6.1),[17] and Justin makes a great play of the OT theophanies in his proof of the pre-existence of Christ, including those where the one who appears is identified as 'the angel of the Lord' (e.g. *Dial.* 56.4,10; 58.3; 59.1; 61.1; 128.1).[18]

Our task in this chapter thus becomes clear. We must inquire – To what extent were these subsequent equations between Christ and Spirit, Christ and angel, rooted in a pre-Christian hypostatization of Spirit or a pre-Christian exaltation of angelic mediation between God and men? To what extent was this language of second and subsequent centuries rooted in the earliest christology of the first century? In other words, does pre-Christian understanding of Spirit and angels give any clue to the why and how of the origins of the doctrine of the incarnation? And if the first Christians did make any sort of equation between Christ and Spirit, or between Christ and an angel (including 'the angel of the Lord'), did this imply or carry with it the thought of Christ as pre-existent?

§18. SPIRIT OF GOD IN PRE-CHRISTIAN JUDAISM

The continuity of thought between Hebraic and Christian understanding of the Spirit is generally recognized.[19] For the background to earliest Christian conceptualization of the relation between Jesus and the Spirit of God therefore we must concentrate on pre-Christian Judaism.

§18.1 *Spirit in OT literature*. There can be little doubt that from the earliest stages of pre-Christian Judaism 'spirit' (*rûaḥ*) denoted *power* – the aweful, mysterious force of the wind (*rûaḥ*), of the breath (*rûaḥ*) of life, of ecstatic inspiration (induced by divine *rûaḥ*).[20] This basic connotation of 'Spirit' has been regularly recognized since H. Gunkel's famous monograph on the operations of the Holy Spirit.[21] In particular, 'Spirit of God' denotes *effective divine power* (as most clearly seen in the last of the three meanings just outlined). In other words, on this understanding, *Spirit of God is in no sense distinct from God*, but is simply the power of God, *God himself acting powerfully in nature and upon men*. It is true that at this early stage there can be talk of a spirit sent by God, as though it was a distinct entity, but in the key instances (Judg. 9.23; I Sam. 16.14–16; I Kings 22.19–23) this language is clearly an attempt to resolve the problem of evil ('an evil spirit', 'a lying spirit') within the framework of monotheism ('God sent', 'a spirit of the Lord for evil', 'the Lord has put'). When however the talk is of the Spirit of God the understanding is not merely of a power *from* God, but of the power *of* God, of God himself putting forth efficacious energy. This comes out most clearly at several points. Thus, for example, in I Samuel Saul's state can be equally well described as '*the Spirit of the Lord* departed from Saul' (16.14) and as '*the Lord* had departed from Saul' (18.12). The wind at the crossing of the Red Sea can be called poetically the blast (*rûaḥ*) of God's nostrils (Ex. 15.8; II Sam. 22.16), a vigorous metaphor taken up by other writers (Job 4.9; Ps. 18.15; Isa. 30.27f.; 40.7; Wisd. 11.20). 'The Spirit of God' is synonymous with 'the breath of the Almighty' (Job 33.4; 34.14; Ps. 33.6). In Isa. 31.3 the power of *rûaḥ* is taken as the distinguishing characteristic of God just as the weakness of flesh is the characteristic of men. And in Isa. 30.1 and 40.13 'my Spirit' and 'the Spirit of the Lord' simply denote the divine 'I'. Particularly in Ezekiel 'the Spirit' is synonymous with 'the hand of the Lord' (Ezek. 3.14; 8.1–3; 37.1). Finally we may note Ps. 139.7 where 'your Spirit' is set in synonymous parallelism with 'your presence'. Clearly then for these writers 'Spirit of God' is simply a way of speaking of God accomplishing his purpose in his world and through men; 'Spirit of God' means God in effective relationship with (and within) his creation. To experience the Spirit of God is to experience God as Spirit.[22]

§18.2 But what about *the intertestamental period*? Does the same hold true there? Or does 'the Spirit of God' come to denote something more like a separate divine entity distinct from God? As we have seen (above n. 8) it is indeed possible to argue that 'Spirit of God' came to be represented more as a distinct hypostasis in the later strata of the OT and in post-biblical Judaism. Apart from the references already cited (p. 130) we could refer to such passages as Ps. 104.30 ('When you send forth your

Spirit they are created'), Ps. 143.10 ('Let your good Spirit lead me on a level path!'), Isa. 63.10 ('But they rebelled and grieved his Holy Spirit'), and to the rabbinic habit of quoting scripture with the words, 'The Holy Spirit says'.[23] But I have to confess that I see little difference between such usages and those of earlier periods. Psalm 104.30 and Judith 16.14 are simply elaborations of the traditional view that all life is the creative breath of God. In Isa. 63.9–14 God's 'Holy Spirit', 'the Spirit of the Lord', are simply variations on the divine 'I', along with 'the angel of his presence' and 'his glorious arm'.

With the Wisdom of Solomon the issue becomes more complex. Here the issue really depends on the author's understanding of Wisdom, and the question of whether he regards Spirit ($\pi\nu\epsilon\tilde{\nu}\mu\alpha$) as a hypostasis is drawn in principally because $\pi\nu\epsilon\tilde{\nu}\mu\alpha$ provides him with a basic definition of Wisdom (Wisd. 1.6; 7.22; cf. 9.17) (see further below ch. VI). Otherwise in Wisd. 1.7 we have a thought which goes no further than that of Ps. 139.7 – 'the Spirit of the Lord' simply denoting God's cosmic power and presence.[24] In Philo, for all the complexity of his thought, the understanding of the Spirit is fairly straightforward. It is drawn principally from Gen. 2.7: $\pi\nu\epsilon\tilde{\nu}\mu\alpha$ is the divine breath which forms the soul (*Leg. All.*I.32f.; III.161; *Plant.* 18), or more precisely, the rational part of the soul (*Heres* 55–7; *Qu.Gen.*II.59). He can speak of 'the mediant spirit' ($\tau\grave{o}$ $\mu\acute{\epsilon}\sigma\sigma\nu$ $\pi\nu\epsilon\tilde{\nu}\mu\alpha$ – *Leg. All.*I. 37), but only in the sense of the divine breath breathed out on man. That we are far from any concept of an intermediary being is shown most clearly by *Spec. Leg.*IV.123 – 'Clearly what was then breathed was ethereal spirit or something, if such there be, better than ethereal spirit, even an effulgence of the blessed, thrice blessed nature of the godhead'.[25] Not surprisingly then in his treatment of prophecy Philo can attribute it equally to the 'divine Spirit breathed from on high' (*Virt.* 217), to the state of divine possession ($\check{\epsilon}\nu\theta\epsilon\sigma$, $\theta\epsilon\sigma\phi\acute{o}\rho\eta\tau\sigma$ – *Heres* 249, 258, 264; *Mos.* II.246), or simply to 'God, who makes full use of their (the prophets') organs of speech to set forth what he wills' (*Spec.Leg.* I.65).[26] Josephus too seems to identify God's Spirit with God himself since he can speak synonymously both of God's Spirit dwelling in the temple and of God himself dwelling in the temple (e.g. *Ant.* VIII.102, 106, 114 – Solomon prays, 'I entreat you also to send some portion of your Spirit to dwell in the temple, that you may seem to us to be on earth as well').[27] As for the rabbinic formula ('The Holy Spirit says'), is this any more than what we might call a *literary hypostatization*? – that is, a habit of language which by use and wont develops what is only an apparent distinction between Yahweh and one of these words and phrases used earlier to describe his activity towards men (here particularly in inspiring scripture).[28] Have we in all these cases any more than a personification, a literary (or verbal) device to speak of God's action without becoming involved every time in a more complicated description of how the transcendent God can intervene on earth? – in other words, simply a useful shorthand device ('Spirit of God', 'glory of God', etc.) which can both express the character of God's immanence in a particular instance and safeguard his transcendence at the same time without more ado.

In point of fact, in the period which most concerns us (Judaism just before the emergence of Christianity), the role attributed to the Spirit seems to have been greatly *diminished*. The cosmic speculation which gave such prominence to Wisdom and Logos hardly touched Spirit.[29] In Hellenistic Wisdom literature the Spirit is given hardly any prominence. In talk of the divine-human relationship Wisdom is the wholly dominant figure, with 'spirit' as we have seen not much more than a way of defining Wisdom (Wisd. 1.6f.; 7.22–5; 9.17), and with even prophecy attributed to Wisdom rather than to the Spirit (Wisd. 7.27; Sir. 24.33). Philo still thinks of the Spirit as the Spirit of prophecy ('the prophetic Spirit' – e.g. *Fuga* 186; *Mos.* I.277),[30] but while in his treatment of creation the divine Spirit has a place (see above p. 134), the dominant category is clearly the divine Logos (see below §28.3).[31] As for the apocalyptic writings, talk of the Spirit is simply an echo of the earlier (OT) language, but this has been largely swamped (particularly in the Testaments and I Enoch) by the growth of interest in the human spirit, and particularly in angelic or demonic spirits: in apocalyptic literature overall references to the human spirit outweigh those to the Spirit of God by nearly 3:1, and references to angelic and demonic spirits outweigh the latter by 6:1 (in striking contrast to both OT and NT).[32] In rabbinic writings the Spirit is preeminently the Spirit of prophecy.[33] But this is a role which belongs almost entirely to the past: with the rabbis the belief becomes very strong that Haggai, Zechariah and Malachi were the last of the prophets and that thereafter the Spirit had been withdrawn (see particularly Tos.Sotah 13.2; earlier expressions in Ps. 74.9; Zech. 13.2–6; I Macc. 4.46; 9.27; Josephus *cont.Ap.* I.41; II Bar. 85.1–3)[34] – though, of course, they also echo the earlier prophetic hope that in the end-time the Spirit would be poured out.[35] Still more striking is the way in which the Spirit to all intents and purposes is subordinated to the Torah: the Spirit inspired the Torah, and the Torah is the voice of the Spirit ('the Holy Spirit says'), but that also means that the Spirit does not speak apart from the Torah. Similarly in Targum and Talmud the Shekinah becomes the dominant way of speaking about the divine presence.[36] The only real exceptions to all this within pre-Christian Palestinian Judaism were the Qumran covenanters; only in the Dead Sea Scrolls does 'Spirit' come back into prominence as a force in present experience (especially IQS 3.13–4.26). But here, as Ringgren readily admits, there is no idea of the Spirit as a hypostasis; 'the holy spirit is . . . simply a manifestation of God's saving activity'[37] (cf. e.g. IQS 2.3 with 4.2–4, and IQH 1.21 with 12.11f.).

Why was it that the Spirit faded in prominence so dramatically in pre-Christian Judaism? Perhaps it was because in Palestinian Judaism particularly 'Spirit' had become too closely identified with a particular experience of divine immanence (inspiration to prophesy) and very few (if any) were prepared to lay claim in their own right to such experience. Perhaps in Hellenistic Judaism there was too much danger of the Spirit of Jewish theology becoming identified with the much more materialistic spirit of Greek, particularly Stoic thought (see above n. 19) – certainly there was some danger of the Wisdom of Solomon's and even Philo's talk of the Spirit being so misunderstood. Whatever the reason, the fact remains that most pre-Christian Jewish writers preferred other concepts and phrases rather than 'Spirit' when they attempted to put into words their own experience or understanding of divine immanence, of God's relation with his creation.

§18.3   To sum up, *there is little or nothing in pre-Christian Judaism to prepare for the sort of identification between Jesus and the Spirit which Paul and John seem to have envisaged, and nothing to provoke the idea of an incarnation of the Spirit in or as a man.* The idea of God's Spirit as a power and presence (i.e. God's) which can be experienced in this world – that thought is well established.[38] The idea of this divine power inspiring, transforming a man, and the hope for such experiences again in the coming age – that too. But *of the Spirit as an entity in any sense independent of God, of Spirit as a divine hypostasis, there is nothing.* For the explanation of developments within Christianity at this point we will have to look to the inner dynamic of Christianity itself.

§19. SPIRIT OF CHRIST

How then do the NT writers conceive of the relationship between Jesus and the Spirit? If it is the case that in pre-Christian Judaism the (Holy) Spirit is simply one way of describing God's self-manifestation (in power) – and a manner of speaking which at the beginning of the Christian era was less popular than in earlier times – how would that have influenced Jesus in his own self-understanding in relation to the Spirit, and how would it have influenced the first Christians' attempt to express their understanding of the relation between Jesus and the Spirit? As we shall see, on this point there is a remarkable consistency of opinion throughout the NT documents, and our consideration of the relevant material can be more schematic than is usually appropriate.

§19.1 *Jesus the man of the Spirit.* What was the relation between Jesus of Nazareth and the Spirit of God? How was it understood?

(*a*) As always Jesus' own answer to this question would be of considerable importance to us. And we can in fact make a fair guess at *Jesus' own answer*; here too we can say something with confidence about Jesus' self-understanding (always bearing in mind the broader considerations mentioned above – §4.2). For, as I have shown elsewhere,[39] there are good grounds for tracing back to Jesus himself several statements, all of which are best understood as giving expression to a *consciousness of inspiration,* a sense of divine commissioning behind his preaching and of divine power in his ministry of healing. We may note particularly Matt. 12.28/Luke 11.20 – 'Since it is by the Spirit (or finger) of God that I cast out demons, then has come upon you the kingdom of God' – where the order of the words draws the hearers' attention to the Spirit (finger) of God as the source of the power which made his act (or word) of exorcism so effective. This was evidently Jesus' own explanation for his success as a healer – and it is in terms of an empowering by the Spirit (or agency) of God. Similarly there is clear enough evidence that Jesus thought of himself as one in whom Isa. 61.1f. was being fulfilled: the Spirit of the Lord was upon him, because the Lord had anointed him to bring good tidings to the poor . . . (note particularly Luke 6.20f./Matt. 5.3–6; Matt. 11.5/Luke 7.22). The character and effectiveness of his preaching with regard to 'the poor' Jesus evidently attributed to the Spirit of God upon him and working through him, to the commissioning and empowering of God himself. Also relevant here is the fact that Jesus seems to have thought of himself as a *prophet,* or at least as standing within the prophetic tradition (note particularly Mark 6.4 pars.; Luke 13.33). Hence too his willingness to speak of himself as one 'sent' by God (note particularly Matt. 10.40/Luke 10.16; Matt. 15.24; and see above p. 40).[40] Jesus evidently saw no difficulty in describing himself in straightforwardly prophetic terms, a prophet being by definition one who is inspired by the Spirit.[41]

These passages have still more to tell us, for according to the same evidence it was not simply as a prophet that Jesus saw himself. Rather the clear implication is that he saw his role as unique: his was the role of eschatological prophet (Isa. 61.1), of the coming one, the anointed one of prophetic hope (Matt. 11.3–6/Luke 7.20–3);[42] only through his Spirit-empowered ministry was the eschatological rule of God realized (Matt. 12.28/Luke 11.20; 'something greater than Jonah' – Matt. 12.41/Luke 11.32).[43] Yet nevertheless his concept of his ministry, and so far as we can tell his understanding of himself, did not break clear of prophetic language (even if his favourite self-designation was 'the son of man' – see above §10.1), and his understanding of his relationship with the Spirit was consistent with and to a considerable extent contained within the category of prophet.[44] Not only so, but his concept of the Spirit of God seems to have been wholly in line with what we have found to be the consistent Jewish understanding – 'Spirit of God' as a way of explaining an experience of inspiration and effective power as coming directly from God himself. Hence the inconsequential nature of the disagreement between Matthew and Luke as to whether Jesus spoke of 'Spirit of God' or 'finger of God' (Matt. 12.28/Luke 11.20): it comes to the same thing anyway; both phrases attribute the exorcisms to God's own power – that is why the exorcisms can be understood as manifestation of the final rule and victory of God over evil.[45] Hence too the equivalence between the phrases 'the Spirit of the Lord is upon me' and 'the Lord has anointed me' (Isa. 61.1). In short, *Jesus seems to have understood the relation between himself and the Spirit in terms primarily of inspiration and empowering*, that is, as the power of God himself filling him and coming to manifestation through him.

(*b*) The same emphasis is also a feature of *the earliest preaching* of the Jerusalem community. We may note particularly the speeches attributed to Peter and Stephen in Acts 3 and 7, where Deut. 18.15, 18 is explicitly quoted: the promise of Moses – 'God will raise up for you a prophet from your brethren as he raised me up' (Acts 3.22; 7.37). In each case the message is clear enough: Jesus is the one in whom this prophecy has been fulfilled; he is the prophet like Moses, the one whose intimacy of relationship with God and whose fullness of inspiration by God would mark the climax of God's purpose for Israel, just as the same feature had marked out Moses in the heyday of the exodus and the giving of the law at Sinai. That Luke has drawn this equation from primitive Christian apologetic is widely agreed.[46] Here we should also mention Acts 10.38, where Peter reminds Cornelius 'how God anointed Jesus of Nazareth with the Holy Spirit and with power; how he went about doing good and healing all that were oppressed by the devil, for God was with him'. That this too is an ancient evangelistic formulation is made probable by the primitiveness of the title used for Jesus ('Jesus, him from Nazareth') and the indications that behind the passage lie primitive exegetical traditions using particularly Ps. 107.20 but also Isa. 61.1.[47] The point is once again that Jesus was presented as a man inspired by God, as one whose secret of success was the outworking of divine power through him, or, which is the same thing, whose secret of success was that 'God was with him'. Likewise we may note the way in which Jesus' death from earliest Christian times was also presented as in continuity with the death of the prophets (Mark 12.1–9; Luke 13.33; Acts 7.52; I Thess. 2.15f.).[48]

Paul does not help us much here, since he says so little about the pre-Easter Jesus, though it is certainly plausible that in Rom. 1.3f. the 'according to the flesh/according to the Spirit' antithesis reflects for Paul its more usual connotation of the eschatological tension in which the believer is caught (Rom. 8.4f.; Gal. 4.29; cf. Rom. 2.28; 8.6; Gal. 3.3; 5.16f.; 6.8; Phil. 3.3f.). That is to say, it is possible that Paul meant that Jesus' installation as Son of God (in power) 'according to the Spirit' was in part at least the consequence of his having lived 'according to the Spirit'.[49] It is certainly true that for Paul *believers'* hope of sharing in the resurrection, of a spiritual body (body of the Spirit), was at least to some extent dependent on their living according to the Spirit now (Rom. 8.6, 11, 13, 23; Gal. 6.8); and Paul did regard Jesus' resurrection as the archetype of believers' resurrection (Rom. 8.11; I Cor. 15.20–3). So he could have intended his readers to understand that Jesus' pre-resurrection life was similarly archetypal – that Jesus, as sharing Adam's lot, nevertheless showed Adam the way to last Adam-(resurrection)-humanity in the Spirit, by himself living according to the Spirit.[50] Be that as it may, it is certainly true that at this first generation stage of Christian apologetic, Jesus was presented in prophetic terms; *the first Christians also (including Paul?) understood the relation between the earthly Jesus and the Spirit in terms of inspiration and empowering.*

(c) When we turn to *the Gospels' presentation* of Jesus the picture is remarkably the same. In the Gospels Jesus is consistently portrayed as one whose ministry was empowered by the Spirit – that is, as one whose effectiveness is to be explained in large part by a unique measure of divine power which he experienced himself and the impact of which others experienced through his words and deeds.[51] His ministry only began after the Spirit descended upon him (or into him) at Jordan – all strata of the Gospels agree on this, including John, and probably Q (Mark 1.10; Matt. 3.16; Luke 3.22; John 1.32f.).[52] All three Synoptics also agree that this heavenly annunciation and anointing was immediately followed by a period of testing, into which Jesus was driven by the Spirit which had come upon him (Mark 1.12; Matt. 4.1; Luke 4.1) – again evidently understood as a necessary preliminary to his ministry. So too agreement on all four levels of the Synoptic tradition is firm that one of the characteristic features of Jesus' ministry (exorcisms) was a clear manifestation of the power of the Spirit, clear evidence of the eschatological rule of God, so that any refusal to recognize this constituted an unforgiveable blasphemy (Matt. 12.28/(Luke 11.20); Mark 3.29/Matt. 12.31f./Luke 12.10). Again most commentators agree that in the words of the heavenly voice on the mount of transfiguration there is a deliberate allusion to Deut. 18.15 ('Hear him' – ἀκούετε αὐτοῦ – Mark 9.7 pars.). In other words all three Synoptists maintain the earlier equation of Jesus with the prophet like Moses.[53]

Beyond this the evidence becomes more diverse. Matthew and particularly Luke go out of their way to emphasize that the whole of Jesus' ministry, all his healing and preaching, was in the power of the Spirit in fulfilment of Jewish prophecy (Matt. 12.18; Luke 4.18; see also Luke 4.14; 10.21). And the same two authors, as we have seen, emphasize that not only his ministry but his very life itself was brought about by the same divine power (above pp. 49f., 50f.); that is to say, not just his ministry, but his whole life was a manifestation of the power of God (Matt. 1.18, 20; Luke 1.35). In addition we need simply note: that Mark does not hesitate to use a very forceful word (ἐκβάλλω – drive out, expel) in describing the Spirit's compulsion under which Jesus went into the desert to be tempted (Mark 1.12) – very much a picture of the prophet compelled by a power he cannot gainsay (Matthew and Luke both soften the picture by altering the verb – Matt. 4.1; Luke 4.1);[54] that Luke has some fondness for describing Jesus as a 'prophet' (Luke 7.16, 39; 13.33; 24.19);[55] and that Matthew and Luke both develop the elements of Moses typology in their presentation of Jesus – Matthew, for example, by his clearly implied parallel between the 'slaughter of the innocents' in Matt. 2.16–18 and Ex. 1.22, and by his gathering of Jesus' teaching into five blocks (5–7; 9.36–10.42; 13.1–52; 17.22–18.35; 23–25),[56] and Luke by presenting Moses and Elijah as speaking with Jesus on the mount of transfiguration about his 'exodus' (Luke 9.31),[57] and by his allusions to Deuteronomy in his 'travel narrative'.[58] Overall then we have a motif which runs through each of the first three Gospels and which comes to prominence at key points in the Synoptic account of Jesus' life and ministry (birth, beginning of ministry, explanation of the most striking features of his ministry, transfiguration). So here too there can be little doubt that *the Evangelists also understood the relation between Jesus and the Spirit in terms primarily of one inspired and empowered, a prophet like Moses.*

Here then is a fact of some importance for our study – the extent to which the Evangelists were prepared to retain the category of prophet in their description of Jesus, to retain the picture of Jesus as a man inspired by the Spirit. This was not simply the original self-effacing language of Jesus himself, or the first fumbling attempts of the earliest preachers and apologists. This was still the language being used when Christianity was already about fifty years old. Even as late as the Synoptists the earthly Jesus is presented in prophetic terms, as one who was inspired by the Spirit of God. Of course for the Evangelists Jesus was never just another prophet (cf. Matt. 12.41f. par.; 13.16f. par.; Luke 16.16 par.);[59] much more was he Messiah, the anointed of the Lord, the one who fulfilled the role of the Servant of Yahweh, the uniquely commissioned agent of God's purpose at the end of the age (see again Mark 8.28f.; Matt. 12.18; Luke 4.18).[60] But this was a role which nevertheless they were able and content to describe in prophetic terms. It is true that the language is beginning to prove less satisfactory as we draw near to the end of the century. Where Mark and Matthew show that Jesus' promise to his disciples of inspiration in times of trial was in terms of divinely given inspiration (Mark 13.11; Matt. 10.19),[61] Luke presents it (in one version) as a promise Jesus himself will fulfil ('*I* will give you a mouth and wisdom . . .' – Luke 21.15) – Jesus presented as looking forward to the time when he will be the inspirer rather than the inspired.[62]

More noticeable are the developments in John: there is still an echo of the 'prophet like Moses' language (John 7.52(?);[63] 12.47f. – Deut. 18.18f.; cf. John 14.10; 17.8; 18.37),[64] but 'prophet' as a title has been almost completely relegated to the status of one of the less than satisfactory opinions of the fickle crowd, only a stage on the way to faith (see particularly John 4.19; 6.14; 7.40; 8.52f.; 9.17);[65] like Mark, John describes Jesus' spirit in very human terms (Mark 2.8; 8.12; John 11.33; 13.21 – language avoided by Matthew and Luke), but where Matthew and Luke describe Jesus' death in terms of his (human) spirit (Matt. 27.50; Luke 23.46) John uses a deliberately ambiguous phrase ('he handed over the Spirit' – John 19.30) which foreshadows the giving of the Spirit in 20.22 and seems thus already to equate Jesus' spirit with the Holy Spirit.[66] Evidently then the Fourth Evangelist is moving beyond the more limiting confines of a prophet christology – hardly surprising in view of his very high Son of God christology (see above §6.5). What is surprising, however, is that despite this he retains so much of the prophet language, and especially that he still retains the description of Jesus as one endowed with the Spirit at Jordan (John 1.32f.; 3.34). Even though he sees Jesus as the incarnation of the eternal Logos 'full of grace and truth' (John 1.14), he is unable to dispense with the earlier picture of Jesus as a man inspired by the Spirit.[67]

(*d*) We have then an important finding for our study: *Jesus is presented consistently as a man of the Spirit during his life and ministry*; not as one who could freely dispense the Spirit (even in John 'the Spirit was not yet' until Jesus was glorified in death, resurrection and ascension – John 7.39); nor as one who was an embodiment, or incarnation of the Spirit (Luke 1.35 cannot be interpreted in this way – see above p. 51 – even if the option of so understanding Jesus presented itself to Luke, which is unlikely, it is evident that he rejected it).[68] From Jesus himself to the Fourth Evangelist at the end of the first century Jesus is understood as a prophet – more than a prophet to be sure, but so far as the relation between Jesus and the Spirit is concerned the category of prophet consistently provides the most suitable language and understanding – *Jesus of Nazareth a man inspired and enabled by the power of God* to fulfil his eschatological role.

§19.2 *The life-giving Spirit, the Lord of the Spirit.* If the testimony of the

NT writers on the relation between earthly Jesus and Spirit of God is clear enough, what of their testimony on the relation between exalted Christ and Spirit of God? If the earthly Jesus was man of the Spirit, what of the risen Christ? At first the answer seems clear also: he who on earth was a man inspired by the Spirit by his resurrection became the one who dispenses the Spirit. This at least seems to be the message of Luke-Acts and John, the only NT writings which give us anything approaching a before-and-after-Easter comparison on this point. In Luke-Acts Jesus' relation to the Spirit (like his divine sonship – see above pp. 51, 62) seems to fall into three stages: first, when his (human) life was the creation of the Spirit (Luke 1.35); second, when he was anointed with the Spirit and became the uniquely empowered man of the Spirit (Luke 3.22 – perhaps even 'begotten' to a new level of sonship, 3.22D; 4.18; Acts 10.38) – this stage continued *after* his resurrection until his ascension (Acts 1.2); and third, when on his exaltation to God's right hand it was given to him to pour out the Spirit on others (Acts 2.33).[69] So too in the Fourth Gospel the glorified Jesus is presented as the one from whom the Spirit will come, the one will will send the Paraclete, the one who bestows the Spirit (John 7.39; 15.26; 19.30; 20.22; cf. 4.10, 14). Here we might also note the Baptist's prediction of one to come who would baptize in Spirit and fire (Matt. 3.11/Luke 3.16; Mark 1.8; John 1.33): all the Evangelists are agreed that this prediction was not fulfilled by Jesus before his death,[70] and Luke and John are quite explicit that its fulfilment marked the beginning of Jesus' ministry as the glorified and exalted one (Luke 24.49; Acts 1.5, 8; 2.33; 11.16; John 7.39; 20.22). This should not be taken to indicate that in Luke and John's view the exalted Christ has completely taken over the role of God as the one who gives the Spirit: for in Acts 1.5 and 11.16 the promise of the Spirit is put in the 'divine passive' ('you will be baptized with the Holy Spirit') and in 15.8 the gift of the Spirit is explicitly attributed to God – indeed even in 2.33 the exalted Jesus is simply the intermediary in the bestowal of the Spirit ('having received from the Father the promise of the Holy Spirit, he has poured out this . . .'); and John is equally happy to say that it is the Father who will send the Spirit (John 14.17, 26; even 15.26 where Jesus says, 'I will send the Paraclete to you from the Father'). Nevertheless their testimony is clear: *by virtue of his resurrection and exaltation Jesus the man of the Spirit became Lord of the Spirit*; the one whose ministry was uniquely empowered by the (eschatological) Spirit became by his resurrection the one who bestowed the Spirit on others; or more precisely, by his resurrection he began to share in God's prerogative as the giver of the Spirit.

How far back does this understanding of the relation between exalted Christ and the Spirit go? The evidence so far considered does not provide a clear answer: we cannot be certain whether Acts 2.33 is drawn from early tradition;[71] it is probable that the Baptist's prediction was cherished by the first Christians as having been fulfilled by Pentecost and subsequent outpourings of the Spirit, but whether they thought of Jesus as the baptizer in Spirit is put in doubt by the 'divine passive' form of Acts 1.5 and 11.16; and the Johannine passages are too much fashioned in terms of Johannine theology to permit any clear conclusion that these particular formulations stem from the earliest churches. What then of Paul? – the only one whose testimony takes us back with certainty to the first generation stage of early Christianity. Four observations on Paul's theology at this point seem to be called for.

(a) At first sight a consistency of testimony seems again to emerge; for the feature of Paul's pneumatology which most readily catches the eye of the commentator is Paul's readiness to describe the Spirit as 'the Spirit of Christ', 'the Spirit of God's Son', 'the Spirit of Jesus Christ' (Rom. 8.9; Gal. 4.6; Phil. 1.19). But in fact Paul never actually attributes the Spirit to Christ as the one who bestows the Spirit on others.[72] Whereas he regularly calls the Spirit 'the Spirit of God' (Rom. 8.9, 11, 14; I Cor. 2.11, 14; 3.16; 6.11; 7.40; 12.3; II Cor. 3.3, 17f.; Eph. 3.16; 4.30; Phil. 3.3), and in addition regularly describes *God* as the one who gives the Spirit (I Cor. 2.12; II Cor. 1.21f.; 5.5; Gal. 3.5; 4.6; Eph. 1.17; I Thess. 4.8; cf. the 'divine passives' of Rom. 5.5; I Cor. 12.13 – 'baptized in Spirit' again not attributed to Christ, as in Acts 1.5 and 11.16; Eph. 1.13; cf. also II Tim. 1.7; Titus 3.5f.). In Paul Christ is Lord, but never explicitly in relation to the Spirit. Thus, *where Luke and John seem happy to attribute the gift of the Spirit equally to God and to the exalted Christ, Paul thinks only to attribute it to God.*[73]

Here we might mention also Paul's midrash on Ex. 34.29–35 in II Cor. 3.7–18. In the course of interpreting the significance of that story in typological or allegorical fashion, he identifies the *shining* of Moses' face as the (fading) glory of the old dispensation (vv. 7–11), the *veil* Moses put over his face as that which still hides the temporary character of the old covenant from the Jews (vv. 12–15), and the *Lord* to whom Moses turned and before whom he removed the veil as the Spirit (vv. 16–18). Verse 17, 'Now the Lord is the Spirit' has frequently been taken as Paul identifying the exalted Christ with the Spirit.[74] But in fact the clause is intended as the interpretative key to unlock the meaning of Ex. 34.34 cited in 3.16. As NEB rightly translates – 'However, as Scripture says of Moses, "whenever he turns to the Lord the veil is removed". Now the Lord of whom this passage speaks is the Spirit' (3.16f.). And this interpretative equation between Yahweh (of the OT text) and the Spirit (of his readers' present experience) he continues into v. 18 – 'And because for us there is no veil over the face, we all reflect as in a mirror the splendour of the Lord; thus we are transfigured into his likeness, from splendour to splendour; such is the influence of the Lord who is Spirit' (NEB).[75] The point for us is the identification Paul thus makes between Yahweh and the Spirit, where it would appear that 'Lord' = 'Spirit' = 'Spirit of the Lord' (vv. 17f.). For Paul the Spirit experienced by the first Christians is to be identified with that presence of Yahweh which Moses experienced 'whenever he went in before the Lord to speak with him' (Ex. 34.34) – the Spirit is the presence of Yahweh. Here then Paul clearly stands within the mainstream of Jewish thought about the Spirit: *for Paul as much as for the earlier Jewish writers the Spirit is the dynamic power of God himself reaching out to and having its effect on men.*

(*b*) On the other hand Paul is clear enough that some sort of transformation in the relation between Jesus and the Spirit took place at Jesus' resurrection, as his use of the older formula in Rom. 1.3f. ('appointed Son of God in power according to the Spirit of holiness as from the resurrection of the dead') and the very phrase 'Spirit of Christ' indicate. This is also suggested by a certain coyness in his talk of Jesus' resurrection. Paul firmly believed both that Christ's resurrection was the archetype of every Christian's resurrection (I Cor. 15.20, 44–9) and that the Christian's resurrection would be effected by the power of the Spirit (Rom. 8.11). But he seems to shy away from the logical corollary – that *Christ's* resurrection was also effected by the power of the Spirit.[76] We may note particularly Rom. 1.3f. – 'appointed Son of God in power according to the Spirit of holiness as from the resurrection of the dead' – where 'Spirit' and 'resurrection' both qualify 'Son of God' but no attempt is made to relate them to each other; Rom. 6.4, where the context seems to cry out for some reference to the Spirit, but Paul seems deliberately to avoid it – 'that as Christ was raised from the dead through the *glory* of the Father, so also we should walk in *newness of life*'; Rom. 8.11 – 'If the Spirit of him who raised Jesus from the dead dwells in you, he who raised Christ Jesus from the dead will also give life to your mortal bodies through his Spirit that dwells in you' – where it would have been much easier to say simply, 'If the Spirit that dwells in you gave life to Jesus he will also give life to you'; I Cor. 6.14 – 'God raised the Lord (means not specified) and will also raise us up through his power (means specified)'; II Cor. 13.4 – 'He was crucified in weakness, but lives (not was raised) by the power of God'. Paul is happy to speak of Christians' resurrection body as a spiritual body, a body of Spirit (σῶμα πνευματικόν – I Cor. 15.44, 46), a body vivified by the Spirit (Rom. 8.11); but he never quite brings himself to say that of Christ's resurrection. He uses near synonyms ('glory of the Father', 'power of God' – Rom. 6.4; II Cor. 13.4), but never the more specific 'God raised Jesus by/through the Spirit'. In short, *if Paul hesitates to present the exalted Christ as Lord of the Spirit, he also hesitates to present Jesus' risen life as a creation of the Spirit.*[77]

(c) The relation between Christ and Spirit becomes clearer when we realize that Paul regards Jesus as now in some sense *the definition of the Spirit*; it is the Jesus-character of his and his converts' experiences of the Spirit which marks them out as authentic.[78] I Cor. 12.3 – the experience of inspiration is authenticated as an experience of the Holy Spirit when the Lordship of Jesus is affirmed thereby. Romans 8.14–17 – the hallmark of a life 'led by the Spirit of God' is the experience of sonship, an experience which reproduces Jesus' own relationship with God ('Abba, Father'), so that the believer becomes thereby a 'fellow-heir with Christ' (see also above pp. 26f.). II Cor. 3.18 – the Spirit of God may be recognized as that power which transforms the believer into the image of God as mirrored in the face of Jesus Christ (4.4, 6; cf. Rom. 8.29; I Cor. 15.49). I Cor. 12 and Eph. 4.1–16 – if the Spirit is the Spirit of the body of Christ, then the action of the Spirit may be known as that power which enables the members of the body to function (charismatically) in harmony and thus to grow together towards the full stature of Christ (cf. Gal. 6.1f.; Rom. 15.5). In all these instances Paul seems to think of the Spirit as in some sense determined by Christ – not in the sense that Christ himself has taken control of the Spirit (see (a) above), but in the sense rather that the Spirit has been shaped and characterized by its relationship to Jesus, both the earthly Jesus (particularly Rom. 8.15f.) and the exalted Christ (particularly Rom. 8.29; I Cor. 15.49). That power in which he lived as Son then (Rom. 8.15f.) and now (Rom. 1.4 – but see above (b)) is the power of the Spirit; precisely that power and only that power may be recognized by Christians as the Spirit of God.

(d) The relation between exalted Christ and the Spirit can be expressed even as an equation: I Cor. 15.45 – 'the last Adam became the life-giving Spirit'. 'The last Adam' is obviously Christ (see above pp. 107f.). But it is equally obvious that 'the life-giving Spirit' (πνεῦμα ζωοποιοῦν) is the Spirit of God; the parallel with II Cor. 3.6 ('the Spirit gives life' – ζωοποιεῖ), not to mention John 6.63 ('it is the Spirit that gives life' – τὸ δε πνεῦμα ἐστιν τὸ ζωοποιοῦν), probably puts this beyond dispute.[79] Here too we may recall the familiar observation that in Rom. 8.9–11 'Spirit of God dwells in you', 'you have the Spirit of Christ', and 'Christ is in you' are all more or less synonymous formulations; just as in I Cor. 12.4–6 'the same Spirit', 'the same God' and 'the same Lord' are all equivalent expressions to describe the source of the diverse charismata.[80] Again in I Cor. 6.17 Paul likens the relationship between Christ and believer to the physical union of sexual intercourse: 'he who is united to a prostitute is one body (σῶμα) . . . but he who is united to the Lord is one Spirit (πνεῦμα)'; as σῶμα is the medium of union between two human beings, so πνεῦμα is the medium of union between the exalted Christ and the Christian, where probably Paul is thinking of both the

Spirit of Christ and the human spirit (cf. Rom. 8.16). These passages make it abundantly clear that for Paul *no distinction can be detected in the believer's experience between exalted Christ and Spirit of God.* The experience of new life and of charismatic endowment can be referred equally to God, the Spirit and the exalted Christ; the experience of intimate union with the exalted Christ is only possible insofar as Christ can be understood and recognized in terms of spiritual power. If Christ is the definition of the Spirit, then the Spirit is the medium for Christ in his relation to men. If the Spirit of God is now to be recognized only by the Jesus-character of the spiritual experience he engenders, then it is also true that for Paul Christ can be experienced now only in and through the Spirit, indeed only *as* the Spirit.[81]

It thus becomes clear that Paul's view of the relation between Christ and the Spirit is a good deal more complex than the sort of formulation with which this section (§19.2) began. If we were to attempt to summarize what can be said with some confidence (bearing in mind our earlier findings in chs. II and IV), it would have to be along the following lines. (1) For Paul it would not be true to say that the exalted Christ was Lord of the Spirit; by his resurrection he did not gain the authority of the one God to dispense the Spirit to men. But neither would it be true to say that his resurrection life was simply a creation of the Spirit: he was the first of a new resurrection humanity, the firstborn (from the dead) of a new family of God (see also above, pp. 37f.); but he was not simply the first man to be raised by the power of the Spirit. (2) 'Spirit of Christ' in one sense means the Spirit who inspired the earthly Jesus, so that the character of his life on earth before God shows us what the character of a life led by the Spirit now should be. But it must also denote the Spirit of the exalted, living Christ, since equally by definition, the Spirit is the Spirit that makes alive; that is to say, the character of the Spirit as the life-giver is equally determined by the character of Christ's resurrection. It is the power of life through, beyond death that the Christian experiences; it is the risen Christ who is the pattern for the new humanity (see also above pp. 107f.). In short, for Paul *the Spirit of Christ means the Spirit of Christ past and present* (3) The exalted Christ and the Spirit of God are one and the same so far as the believer's experience is concerned; when attempting to speak of his experience of grace or power Paul evidently could make no distinction between God (as Spirit), Spirit (of Christ) and Christ. But for Paul that is true only at the level of the believer's experience; when he speaks of the relation between the exalted Christ and God there is nothing of this equivalence between Christ and Spirit (see particularly I Cor. 15.24–8). That is to say, in Paul's understanding *the exalted Christ is not merely synonymous with the Spirit,* has not been wholly absorbed as it were by the Spirit, so that 'exalted Christ' becomes merely a phrase to describe the Spirit (as a phrase like 'in Christ' could suggest). The exalted Christ has for Paul a real existence in relation to God; the equivalence between Spirit and Christ is only a function of the believer's limited perception.[82]

To sum up, it would appear that in Paul's thought the category 'Spirit (of God)' and the category '(exalted) Christ' overlap. Each defines and limits the other – the Spirit defined by Christ and 'limited' to that which accords with the character of the earthly Jesus and exalted Lord, Christ experienced as Spirit and 'limited' to Spirit in his relationship with men. But neither has wholly subsumed the other under it as a subordinate category, neither has wholly absorbed the other so as to leave no remainder – so that all we have to deal with now is the Christ-Spirit. 'Spirit' and 'Christ' are alternative ways of describing God's approach to men now, but more has to be said about each beyond the area of overlap: the Spirit remains primarily the power of God (however much it manifests the character of Christ); Christ has a relation to God where the category of Spirit seems to have no clear place. To put it another way, in Paul's thought the exalted Christ assumes a uniquely intermediate status: before God he appears as firstborn Son, firstborn of a new family of resurrected humanity, first instalment of a new relationship between God and man; before man he appears as life-giving Spirit, not just the first instalment of that new relationship, but as the one who makes that relationship possible for others – not just 'living spirit', but 'life-giving Spirit'. This is about as much as we can say; to venture a more precise formulation at this point would be to press Paul for a precision which he did not attain and which he may well have refused to attempt.

We began this section (§19.2) by observing the straightforward answer which Luke and John seem to give to the question, How was the relation between exalted Christ and the Spirit conceptualized by the NT writers? The answer was that by his resurrection and exaltation Jesus had become Lord of the Spirit. We have gone on to show that in Paul the answer is more complex. This contrast between Paul and the later writers however should not be pressed too hard. In *Acts* we have indeed a distinction between exalted Christ and present Spirit which is hard to dispute – the Spirit active in the mission of the disciples, while Christ is absent in heaven.[83] Yet in the matter of guidance at decisive moments in that mission Luke does not seem particularly clear on the distinction between guidance by the Lord (in a vision – as in 9.10–16; 18.9f., 22.17–21), guidance by an angel (directly(?) or in a vision – 8.26; 10.3–6), and guidance by the Spirit (as in 8.29; 10.19, 16.6), and indeed in one instance speaks of guidance by 'the Spirit of Jesus' (16.7). With *John* too the distinction between the Son as the sender of the Spirit and the Spirit who is sent is not clear either, for he seems to understand the coming of the

Spirit as fulfilling the promise of Christ's return (particularly John 14.15–26) and to envisage the 'other Paraclete' as 'the presence of *Jesus* when Jesus is absent'.[84] So although Luke and John do not permit us to penetrate into their thought on this point even as far as we can with Paul, it is clear enough that they shared something at least of Paul's understanding of *the exalted Christ as both in some sense identical with the Spirit in the believer's experience and as standing before God as Son in his own right as well as for others* (cf. e.g. John 14.1–3; Acts 2.33; I Cor. 15.24–8).

§19.3   How then was the relation between Jesus and the Spirit understood in the beginning of Christianity? We can summarize our findings in §19 as follows. (1) For the NT writers generally *the Spirit is the Spirit of God, the effective power of God himself.* This is obviously true when speaking about Jesus' conception and of his ministry, but it is also true in speaking of the Spirit after Jesus' exaltation. However much the Spirit can be understood as the Spirit of Christ, the Spirit is still primarily the Spirit of God, God himself reaching out to and touching, vitalizing, dynamizing man at the heart of his being. At this point earliest Christian thought is wholly of a piece with its Jewish antecedants.

(2) *This power Jesus of Nazareth experienced in a unique, eschatological measure during his life.* He himself claimed as much, and the Evangelists reinforce his claim. Indeed, according to Matthew and Luke his very conception was effected by this power; so that his anointing at Jordan was a further experience of that power, perhaps we should say an enhancing of the power of God already manifested in his very life, or at least a special equipping for his mission as the decisive figure of God's purpose at the climax of the age (whether expressed in terms of Messiah or eschatological prophet or whatever). Not least of significance in our inquiry is the consistent way Jesus himself, the earliest Christian apologists and the NT writers generally speak of Jesus' relation to the Spirit in prophetic terms – not as an embodiment of the Spirit, or incarnation of the Spirit, but as *a man inspired by the Spirit.*

(3) All are agreed too that *with the resurrection a new phase began in Jesus' relation to the Spirit.* Paul hesitates to present Jesus' resurrection simply as the work of the Spirit, and Luke and John are willing to go further and present the exalted Christ as Lord of the Spirit. The clear implication is that none of them wanted to think of Jesus' risen life as a creation of the Spirit in the way that Matthew and Luke presented Jesus' earthly life as the creation of the Spirit. A *transformation* had taken place in the relationship between Jesus and the Spirit. This also means that Jesus' risen life is different from that of believers who follow him – the last Adam became not just spiritual body, not just living spirit, but life-giving Spirit (I Cor. 15.45). At the same time, for Paul in particular, the exalted Christ

is representative man, last Adam, firstborn of a new family, whose image men will share in the resurrection. He is not merely the Christ, not merely a failed visionary whose heroic spirit still inspires today, but the Christ who fulfilled his vision, who himself is the guarantee and archetype of the new risen humanity – though how the Spirit relates to Christ in terms of his own risen humanity is left obscure. So in some sense that is not clear the life-giving Spirit and exalted Christ *merge* in Paul's thinking, the Spirit can now be thought of as the Spirit of Christ – that is, as that power of God which is to be recognized by the consciousness of oneness with Christ (and in Christ) which it engenders and by the impress of the character of Christ which it begins to bring about in the life of the believer. But in another sense Spirit and Christ remain distinct – it is of a distinct personality that the Spirit confesses 'Jesus is Lord'. The paradox can be stated (but not resolved) thus: *if the exalted Christ is to the believer as life-giving Spirit, he is to God as firstborn Son.* It is presumably in this indeterminate intermediate role of the exalted Christ between man and God as Son and between God and man as Spirit that we find the uncomfortable dynamic which was an important factor in pushing Christian thought in a Trinitarian direction.

§20. THE ANGEL OF THE LORD

Did the first Christians think of Jesus as an angel – whether as an angel incarnate as a man, or as a man exalted to become an angel? If 'angel' is indeed 'one of the names given to Christ up to the fourth century' (Danielou – above n. 17), was it acceptable as a designation of Christ in the first century and if so how widespread was it? To clarify the issues involved here and their implications for our study we must turn again to Christianity's Jewish background, for in its doctrines of angels Christianity again stands in direct line of descent from pre-Christian Judaism.

§20.1   *Angels in the Old Testament.* In the earlier documents of the OT the evidence is of two kinds. First there are the angels who presumably comprise 'the host of heaven' (Gen. 28.12; I Kings 22.19), those whom we have already met under the names 'sons of God', 'holy ones', 'sons of the Most High'.[85] Secondly, within the earliest strata of Jewish writings we also encounter a being described as 'the angel of Yahweh' – who, for example, appears and speaks to Hagar in Gen. 16.7–12 (cf. Gen. 21.17f.) and to Moses in Ex. 3.2. The former ('the host of heaven') are of no real relevance to our particular inquiry. Even if previously they were autonomous gods who in the meantime had been subordinated to Yahweh in Israel's faith,[86] so far as our literature is concerned they certainly have no degree of autonomy or independence from Yahweh. Indeed, they are little more than part of the royal trappings, the courtly retinue whose presence serves to enhance the kingly glory and unique majesty of Yahweh (cf. particularly Ps. 89.5–8; 148.2; Neh. 9.6).[87] Except as forerunners to the angelic intermediaries of the intertestamental period they have little importance for us.

More important is 'the angel of Yahweh', especially in view of Justin's identification of the angel of Yahweh with the pre-existent Christ (above p. 132). Yet to understand the angel of Yahweh as a being somehow independent of Yahweh is basically to *mis*understand what the ancient writers intended. For it is clear enough even from a cursory study of the passages in question that *'the angel of Yahweh' is simply a way of speaking about Yahweh himself.* Thus, after the angel of the Lord has appeared and spoken to Hagar the narrative continues: 'So she called the name of the *Lord* who spoke to her, "You are a God of seeing"; for she said, "Have I really seen God and remained alive after seeing him?" ' (Gen. 16.13). Similarly in the other version of the same tale the angel of God speaks in the first person as God (21.17f.). In Jacob's dream the angel of God says, 'I am the God of Bethel' (31.11–13). In the theophany in the burning bush he who appears to Moses is described both as 'the angel of the Lord' and 'the God of Abraham, Isaac and Jacob' (Ex. 3.2–6). Finally we might note Judg. 2.1, where 'the angel of the Lord' says 'I brought you up from the land of Egypt . . . I will never break my covenant with you . . .'. Clearly in all these cases it is impossible to distinguish between the angel of Yahweh and Yahweh himself; they are obviously one and the same person. And the same is most probably true of other passages where it is a 'man' who appears to Abraham (Gen. 18 – 'the Lord'), to Jacob (32.24–30 – 'I have seen God face to face') and to Joshua (Josh. 5.13–15). Somewhat more ambiguous is the status of the angel who led Israel through the exodus and wilderness wanderings (Ex. 14.19; 23.20, 23; 32.34; 33.2f.; Num. 20.16), but in fact the same equation seems to hold, since the divine presence in the pillar of fire and of cloud is thought of both as 'the angel of God' and as 'the Lord' in Ex. 14.19f., 24. In other words, in these instances too the 'angel' is a way of describing the presence and saving power of Yahweh.[88]

In short, this *angel* talk seems to have been an early, still unsophisticated attempt to speak of God's immanent activity among people and within events on earth without either resorting to straightforward anthropomorphism or abandoning belief in his holy otherness. *Spirit* talk seems in fact to have been an early alternative to this, perhaps even replacing it as the charismatic prophecy and leadership of the judges and early monarchy replaced the earlier leadership of the wilderness and conquest period (perhaps, that is, a leadership attested by vision and dream gave way to a leadership attested by ecstasy). Whatever the historical actuality behind these narratives, both Spirit of God and angel of God are best understood as ways of speaking about God in his active concern for men and approach to men – as also other phrases, like 'the glory of Yahweh', 'the face of God', 'the name of Yahweh' and 'the hand or finger of Yahweh'.[89] In every case the protest of rabbinic scholars against hypothesizing a Judaism which made room for divine intermediaries applies here too, and we may doubt whether any Jewish Christian would have been tempted to anticipate Justin by seeing in any of these Christ in a pre-existent form.

§20.2 *Angels in pre-Christian Judaism.* What then of the intertestamental period? Did the elaboration of a Jewish angelology in the post-exilic period (to which we drew attention above p. 129) make room for a specific divine intermediary who might early on have been identified with Jesus? Here we need not concern ourselves with the lesser ranks who were variously regarded as messengers, or spirits that control the movements of nature (wind, seasons, stars), or guardian angels of the nations, and so on (e.g. Dan. 10.13, 20; Jub. 2.2f.; 15.31f.; I Enoch 75.3; 80.6; 82.10–20; IQH 1.10f.; 11Qtg. Job 29(?); II Enoch 4.1f.).[90] These again are not particularly relevant to our study, except insofar as they testify to a growing readiness to conceptualize individual personal heavenly beings somehow distinct from God but yet agents of the divine will. Also not particularly relevant are the hostile angels and demons, whose leader is variously named as Satan, Semjaza, Azazel, Mastema, Belial/Beliar.[91] More relevant for us are those angels who are depicted as standing in especially close relation to God. These archangels, 'the angels of the presence' (Jub. 1.27, 29; 2.2; etc.; Test. Levi 3.5; Test. Jud. 25.2; IQH 6.13), are specifically named, four being most prominent – Michael, Gabriel, Raphael, Sariel/Uriel/Phanuel[92] (Dan. 8.16; 9.21; 10.13; Tobit 12.15; I Enoch 9.1f.; 20.1–8; 40; IQM 9.15; 4QS1 37–40; IV Ezra 5.20).[93] Even here we probably still have to say with von Rad, 'the angels of Judaistic angelology are always a naive representation of the omnipresent and omniscient Word and will of Yahweh'.[94] On the other hand, the developing concept of personalized divine beings close to God certainly begins to open the way for a monotheism modified in practice, however firm in theory.

The most significant development here is the emergence of *angelic intercessors and intermediaries.* This is already hinted at in Job's appeal to his 'witness in heaven', his 'vindicator' (Job 16.19; 19.25), apparently conceived as a mediating angel (33.23; see also Zech. 1.12). In Tobit too Raphael describes himself as 'one of the seven holy angels who present the prayers of the saints and enter into the presence of the glory of the

Holy One' (Tobit 12.15; see also I Enoch 9.3; 99.3; 104.1). In the
Testament of Levi the archangels are described as those 'who minister
and make propitiation to the Lord for all the sins of ignorance of the
righteous', and we meet 'the angel who intercedes for the nation of Israel
and for all the righteous' (Test. Levi 3.5; 5.6f.; see also Test. Dan. 6.2).[95]
A parallel strand is the developing idea of supreme angels who intervene
on behalf of God's people, interposing themselves between the righteous
and the hostile angels – Michael (Dan. 10.13, 20f.), the angel of the
presence (Jub. 18.9–12 = 'the angel of the Lord' in Gen. 22.11; Jub.
48.9–19; Ass. Mos. 10.2), the Prince of light (IQS 3.20, 24 = the angel
of truth; CD 5.18; IQM 13.10; 17.6 = 'the great angel'). The significance
of this development is that already before Christianity angels had ceased
to be presented merely as spokesmen of Yahweh, agents of the divine
oversight of nature and nations. Supreme angels are envisaged as sufficiently independent of God to act as intercessors on behalf of men before
God, as intermediaries between man and God.

Particularly interesting is the evidence of the extent to which even the
strongly Torah centred community at Qumran could accommodate a
widening range of conceptualizations of the relationships between divine
and human. Here we might note, in addition to the passages cited immediately above, the large measure of overlap between the Prince of light
and the Spirit of truth (IQS 3.20, 24; 4.23f.),[96] foreshadowing in some
degree the language and ideas of the Fourth Gospel (see below p. 156).
Most intriguing of all at this point is the mysterious Melchizedek of
11QMelch. The text is in a fragmentary state and its reconstruction
involves many disputed readings. But the key passage is one of the
clearest (lines 9–11):[97]

> [9]That is the time of the acceptable year of Melchize(d)ek . . . the holy ones of
> El to the rei(gn) of judgment, as it is written [10]concerning him in the hymns
> of David who says; 'Elohim (stan)deth in the congre(gation of God); among
> the Elohim he judgeth' (Ps. 82.1). And concerning him he says: [11]'(Above)
> them return thou on high; El shall judge the nations' (Ps. 7.8) . . .

It seems clear enough that Melchizedek is seen as a heavenly being: the
first 'Elohim' of line 10 most probably refers to him.[98] Since 'elohim' (as
well as 'sons of Elohim') could be understood as referring to angels (above
n. 86), the thought is probably that Melchizedek was an archangel –
perhaps the angel of Ex. 23.20f. ('my name is in him'), since the use of
'elohim' in reference to a single (arch)angel is unexpected. And if
11QMelch. is wholly of a piece with Qumran thought expressed in other
documents the probability becomes quite strong that Melchizedek is
another name for Michael: Melchizedek seems to be the angelic leader
of the holy ones who executes judgment on Belial and his host (lines 13–

14) – a role given to Michael in IQM 13.10–12, 17.5–8 (cf. Dan. 12.1;
Ass. Mos. 10.2; Rev. 12.7–9).[99]

How the community or author understood Melchizedek's relation to
the Melchizedek of Gen. 14 remains unclear. The Gen. 14 narrative could
be interpreted as the brief appearance on earth of an archangel (line 11
seems to be referred to Melchizedek as returning on high; see also above
p. 20).[100] Alternatively the historical Melchizedek was understood to have
become an archangel, and the (descent)/return language refers to his
eschatological role as leader of the saints in the final conflict and his
return to pronounce final judgment in heaven. But such an apotheosis
would be surprising at Qumran and is only paralleled in the (later)
equation of Enoch with the Son of Man in I Enoch 71.14 and with
Metatron in III Enoch 3–16 (see further above pp. 17, 76). A further
possibility which is by no means to be ruled out is that *no* allusion was
intended to the figure of Gen. 14 – after all the reference to Gen. 14 in
IQapGen. 22.14–17 (not to mention Jub. 13.25) gives no hint of any such
Melchizedek speculation, and no reference to Ps. 110.4 has so far been
discovered in the Dead Sea Scrolls. Rather the name Melchizedek (king
of righteousness) could have been formed as a titular description of the
archangel Michael, just as Melchiresha (king of wickedness) seems to
have been formed as a titular description of Belial (4QTeharot[d] 2.2;
4Q'Amram[b] 2.3);[101] Kohenzedek (priest of righteousness) seems to have
been coined in a similar way in bSuk. 52b.[102] In short, like 'Prince of
lights', 'King of righteousness' could simply be one of the titles for the
principal archangel formulated by the Qumran sect in order to heighten
the eschatological antithesis between Michael and Belial, 'the Prince of
light(s)' set against 'the angel of darkness' (IQS 3.20f.; IQM 13.5f., 10–
16), 'king of righteousness' against 'king of wickedness'.

Whatever the intended meaning of 11QMelch., the document clearly
allows the possibility of a more adventurous interpretation. It is not so
surprising then that round about the end of the first century AD there
appeared the Apocalypse of Abraham with an interpreter angel Jaoel, 'a
power in virtue of the effable Name that is dwelling in me' (Apoc. Ab.
10 – referring to Ex. 33.21), reflecting the same strain of mystical speculation which lies behind the figure of Metatron and which led to the two
powers heresy (see above pp. 80f. and n. 94). And somewhere in the
second century (probably – see above. p. 21) we have the Prayer of
Joseph with Jacob presented as 'an angel of God and a ruling spirit',
indeed as 'the archangel of the power of God and supreme commander
among the sons of God' (in rank far above the angel Uriel), who 'had
descended to earth and had tabernacled among men and had been called
by the name Jacob' (see above p. 21 n. 62). However esoteric these
documents, the fact that they could appear within Jewish circles[103] shows

just how much Jewish thought could accommodate - from angels which are merely personfications of God's will coming to effect, through personalized divine beings whose functions are distinct from and over against those of God, to archangels who bear the name of God, to a supreme angel that became incarnate as a historical individual. Once again therefore the question inevitably poses itself to us: where did earliest Christian understanding of Jesus fit into this sort of speculative thought?

§20.3 *Christ and angels.* Did the first Christians think of Jesus as an angel? So far as the *earthly* Jesus is concerned the answer is clearly in the negative. In the Synoptic Gospels Jesus is quite distinct from angels who are represented as guarding him (Matt. 4.6/Luke 4.10), serving him (Mark 1.13/Matt. 4.11) and helping him (Matt. 26.53; Luke 22.43). Particularly noticeable is the fact that at both his birth and resurrection the angel of the Lord (in Luke = Gabriel) is featured in a way that makes it impossible to confuse the two (Jesus and the angel), in a way indeed which suggests that the possibility of equating Jesus with the angel of the Lord had never entered the Evangelists' heads (Matt. 1.20, 24; 2.13, 19; 28.2, 5; Luke 1.11, 19, 26–38; 2.9f.; 24.23; also John 20.12; contrast *Epistula Apostolorum* 14).[104]

What then of the *exalted* Christ? Was there any attempt to identify the risen Jesus with an angel, as having become an angel by virtue of his resurrection? – bearing in mind the saying of Jesus himself that those who rise from the dead 'are like angels in heaven' (Mark 12.25 par.; Luke 20.36 – 'equal to angels'). Here too the answer seems to be a less certain but still fairly emphatic No! In the apocalyptic Son of Man logia angels are mentioned several times, either as the Son of Man's companions or train or court (Mark 8.38 pars.; Luke 12.8f.; Matt. 25.31), or as the Son of Man's messengers of final salvation or of judgment (Mark 13.27 par.; Matt. 13.41), but always with each distinct from the other in status and role (cf. Mark 13.32 par.; John 1.51). In Acts it is true that Luke makes no clear distinction between guidance by the Lord and guidance by an angel (see above p. 147), but that means simply that the present reader can see no rhyme or reason why in one case it is the Lord who guides and in another an angel. It does not mean that Luke himself actually confused the two (contrast 'the Spirit of Jesus' – Acts 16.7), especially since elsewhere there is no suggestion that the 'angel of the Lord' or the 'angel of God' is to be identified with the exalted Christ (5.19; 8.26; 10.3, 7, 22; 11.13; 12.7–11, 23; 27.23), and indeed in 12.11 the 'angel of the Lord' is explicitly interpreted to mean 'the Lord has sent his angel'. Most striking of all is the way in which Christ is regularly exalted *above* the angels, with the angels numbered among the lesser beings who are subject to him and who bow before him in worship (Phil. 2.9–11; Col. 1.16f.;

2.8–10; Heb. 1; I Peter 1.12; 3.22; Rev. 5.11–14). Here again it is worth noting that according to the ancient apologetic use of Ps. 110.1 and Ps. 8.6 (see above §14.2) this is a status Christ first attained by his resurrection and exaltation (Phil. 2.9–11; Heb. 1.3f.; I Peter 3.22). It would appear that as soon as the question arose – Had Jesus been exalted to angelic status and power? – the NT writers responded by asserting that he had been exalted far above that to share the Lordship of God himself over all other created beings in heaven on earth or under the earth.[105] It is certainly the case that such an exalted being could be conceptualized as an angel (see again particularly *The Prayer of Joseph*; and cf. the description of Melchizedek in 11QMelch. and of the Son of Man in the Similitudes of Enoch – I Enoch 46.1; 61.10). But there is no evidence thus far that any NT writer thought of the exalted Jesus in this way, and the writer to the Hebrews refutes the suggestion with vigour – 'To what angel did God every say . . .' (Heb. 1.5).[106]

What of Gal. 4.14 (see above p. 132 and n. 14)? As it stands it could imply some equation between 'angel of God' and 'Christ Jesus', either as an allusion to the Galatians' beliefs, or indeed to Paul's own. Similarly Gal. 1.8 – 'Even if we, or an angel from heaven, should preach to you a gospel contrary to that which we preached to you, let him be accursed.' Here too Paul could be alluding to a high evaluation of angels on the part of the Galatians: Even if one whom you honour most highly as a messenger of God. . . . On the other hand, if Paul knew that the Galatians cherished a specific angel christology, this would be an odd argument to use since their response would presumably be: We attribute our message to no ordinary angel, but to Christ himself. The decisive weight however must be given to Gal. 3.19. For whatever deductions about Paul's or the Galatians' regard for angels may be open to us in 1.8 and 4.14, there can be little doubt that in 3.19 angels denote inferiority: the law 'was ordained by angels through an intermediary. Now an intermediary implies more than one; but God is one'. It is true that the main negative thrust is directed towards the mediatorship of Moses, but it is clear enough that his use of the tradition about the law given by angels serves also to devalue it when placed alongside the promise; that it was ordained through angels is certainly not intended to emphasize the law's grandeur and sublimity, but rather its inferiority (cf. 4.9).[107] In which case it again becomes much less likely that the Galatians had a specific angel christology, for they would have attributed their own high regard for the law to the angel-Christ and Paul's argument in 3.19 would have lost much of its force. Still less likely is it that Paul would have lightly accepted the equation Christ = angel and intended it in 4.14, for the same reason. Paul was not accustomed to making hard debating points and then throwing them casually away. The obvious solution to the problem posed by these three passages is that the Galatians did have a high regard for angelic messengers, but had not thought of Christ as an angel. Paul acknowledges their high angelology (hence 1.8), but regards revelation by means of angels as nevertheless inferior to the promise and the gospel (hence 3.19), so that 4.14 is best understood as an ascending scale (cf. Mark 13.32) not an equation – 'you received me as an angel of God (a divine messenger), as (you would have received) Jesus Christ (himself)'. In short, no angel christology is evident behind the letter to the Galatians, either in the thought of the Galatians or, still less, in the thought of Paul himself.

Our conclusion here seems to be confirmed by what Paul says elsewhere. In II Thess. 1.7 he echoes the apocalyptic language about the Son of Man (here Lord Jesus) descending 'from heaven with his mighty angels' – the royal prince with his own elite troops. In I Cor. 6.3 angels are depicted as subject to the judgment of the saints, inferior even to those who themselves must appear before the judgment seat of Christ (II Cor. 5.10). And in Col. 2.18f. 'worship of angels' is clearly disparaged as something which detracts from the Christians' loyalty to Christ (cf. Rom. 8.38).[108] *In no case can Paul's language plausibly be taken to presume or presuppose an angel-christology*, and the logical implication in each case is that the exalted Christ was conceived as quite distinct from angels (cf. I Tim. 3.16; 5.21) and qualitatively superior in status – Lord of angels, as well as men.

In one other NT passage it has been suggested that Christ and angel have merged in the author's mind – Rev. 10.1. Here the description of the 'mighty angel descending from heaven, wrapped in a cloud, with a rainbow over his head, and his face like the sun, and his legs like pillars of fire' has indeed some similarity to that of the exalted Christ in 1.15f. and 14.14–16.[109] But the similarity in description is probably due to the comparatively limited range of symbolism available to the author when striving to capture the effect of such a vision of a heavenly being of overwhelming power and majesty (cf. Ezek. 8.2; Apoc.Ab. 11; II Enoch 1.5). An equation with Christ need hardly be intended and is much less probable when we recall the distinction John maintains between Christ and angels elsewhere (Rev. 1.1 and 22.16 – angel as Christ's personal messenger; 3.5; 14.10; and contrast 5.11–14 with 19.10 and 22.8f.).[110]

The only other likely direct influence from Jewish angelology on Christian thought at this point is to be found in the Johannine concept of the Paraclete. This possibility is considerably increased when we recognize: (1) that 'Spirit of truth' is a distinctive term common to both the Dead Sea scrolls and the Fourth Gospel (1QS 4.23f.; John 14.17; 15.26),[111] and probably provides some sort of link with the angel of truth on the one hand (IQS 3.20, 24) and certainly with the Paraclete on the other (John

14.16f.; 15.26);[112] and (2) that the Targum on Job translated the angelic 'mediator' of Job 33.23 (also 16.19) by transliterating the Greek word παράκλητος (Paraclete).[113] In other words, *somewhere behind the Johannine characterization of the Spirit as Paraclete probably lies the Jewish concept of angelic mediation.* And while in the Fourth Gospel it is only the Spirit who is so designated, we should recall that in I John 2.1 the word is used to describe 'Jesus Christ the righteous', where the idea of heavenly mediation is very prominent. Even so, it does not necessarily follow that the Johannine church thought of Jesus as an angel – that is hardly likely in view of the high Logos christology of the Johannine prologue (see below §30.1). All it may mean is that the Johannine tradition transferred the idea and role of heavenly mediation from the archangels of late pre-Christian Judaism to the exalted Christ of Christianity. Or more accurately, since the idea of Christ's heavenly mediation was already well established within Christianity (particularly Rom. 8.34),[114] probably we should say simply that the Johannine church took over some of the terminology of contemporary Jewish angelology and transferred it partly to the Spirit and partly to Christ. Whereas the writer to the Hebrews found it necessary to exalt Christ's role as heavenly mediator by distinguishing him clearly from the angels, the Johannine churches simply absorbed some of the language of Jewish angelogy and made it their own without further comment.

Finally we should mention the suggestion that 'the angel of the Lord' in the OT would have been read by some NT writers as a reference to Jesus himself; in other words, that Justin Martyr's identification of the angel of the Lord as the *pre-existent* Christ would have been familiar among first-century Christians, part of a wider belief in the pre-existent Jesus as actually present at certain points in OT history.[115] The suggestion however is at best implausible, not least in view of our findings already in this paragraph (§20.3). For example, the assumption 'that Paul saw in the pillar of cloud the pre-existent Christ' (with reference to Ex. 14.19) can hardly be based on I Cor. 10.2, where 'the cloud' together with 'the sea' make up the watery element of the Israelites' baptism, and where it is Moses who is most obviously understood as the type or equivalent of Christ ('baptized into Moses' – see further below §24.3). There is no thought whatsoever of Christ being in the cloud (or being the cloud) – such an equation complicates and confuses Paul's thought without justification.[116] The complementary assertion is that various OT quotations must have been understood by Paul and the other NT writers as having been spoken by Christ (e.g. Rom. 10.6–8; Heb. 3.7–11),[117] or as having been addressed to Christ present there and then (e.g. Rom. 10.15; James 5.11 referring to Jonah 4.2).[118] It is true of course that some OT texts which speak of 'the Lord' were referred to the exalted Christ (particularly Joel 2.32 in Rom. 10.13, and Isa. 45.23 in Phil. 2.10f.); but it is quite another to argue that in doing this the NT writers thought of Jesus already as 'the Lord' prior to his life on earth and resurrection-exaltation (contrast Phil. 2.9–11), or that this identification was frequently made by them in reading OT texts (especially when again and again the context makes it clear that the NT writer is thinking simply of God – Acts 2.39; 3.22; 4.26; Rom. 4.6–8; 11.2–4, 33f; 15.9–11; I Cor. 3.19f.; II Cor. 6.16f.; Heb. 7.21; 8.8–11; 10.30f.; 12.5–7; James 5.4; I Peter 1.23–5).[119] In all such instances of 'the "real presence" method of interpretation of the OT',[120] the NT writers' use of the OT is wholly explicable in terms of hermeneutic methods currently employed, with the OT passages in question providing either prophecies which could be taken to apply to their own day, or types which could now be seen to foreshadow the reality of Christ and his salvation, or occasionally allegories which could be interpreted christologically.[121] In short, despite its ancient lineage in the patristic period, this particular thesis does not in fact provide us a way into the thought of the NT writers or into their christology. *There is no evidence that any NT writer thought of Jesus as actually present in Israel's past*, either as the angel of the Lord, or as 'the Lord' himself.

§20.4   So far as we can tell then *no NT writer thought of Christ as an angel*, whether as a pre-existent divine being who had appeared in Israel's history as the angel of the Lord, or as an angel or spirit become man, or as a man who by exaltation after death had become an angel. 'The angel of the Lord' in the early Jewish texts is most obviously a way of speaking about Yahweh himself, and when 'the angel of the Lord' reappears in the writings of Luke and Matthew there is no real possibility of confusing him with Jesus. The idea of Jesus as an incarnation of an angel never seems to have entered the head of any NT author. And while there was evidently a high regard for angels, perhaps even angel-worship in some of Paul's churches, there is no clear evidence that any first-century Christian community actually thought of *Christ* as an angel. Any attempt to set the exalted Christ merely on the level of the angels was resisted with great vigour, particularly by Paul in his letter to Colossae and by the writer to the Hebrews. Even with the background of angelic mediation behind the concept of the Spirit as Paraclete on earth and the exalted Christ as Paraclete in heaven: that simply means that the Johannine circle transferred particular terminology used in Jewish angelology to Christ; it does not mean that they only then began to conceive of Christ as a heavenly intercessor or that they therefore considered him to be an angel. In short, the thesis that an angel christology was entertained in some parts of earliest Christianity has little or nothing to sustain it, and the suggestion that any NT author maintained an angel christology runs clearly counter to the evidence.

§21. CONCLUSIONS

We have been able to summarize our findings as we went along, at the end of the last two sections (§§19.3 and 20.4). But some more general comments are called for here.

§21.1 Once again we have seen *the centrality of the resurrection of Jesus in earliest christology*. Only the risen Christ was thought of in terms of the Spirit, in terms of some degree of identity with the Spirit; only as from Easter could the Spirit be understood as the presence of Christ. The possibility of conceptualizing Christ in angel categories or the challenge of an angel christology only occurred with reference to the exalted Christ. There is no thought in any of the passages we have studied of Jesus existing prior to his birth whether as an angel or archangel, a spirit or the Spirit. There is no thought whatsoever of Jesus on earth as the incarnation of angel or archangel, spirit or Spirit. Only with his resurrection did Christ become 'life-giving Spirit'; only as a result of the resurrection can we speak of 'the Spirit of Christ'.

There is one passage which seems to run counter to this conclusion – I Peter 1.10f.: 'the prophets who prophesied of the grace that was to be yours searched and inquired about this salvation; they inquired what person or time was indicated by the Spirit of Christ within them when predicting the sufferings of Christ and the subsequent glory.' However, it is quite possible that the prophets spoken of are Christian prophets:[122] the description of the activity of the prophets ('searched and inquired') would accord well with what we know of prophetic activity in the earliest churches,[123] but not so well with the usual NT picture of the OT prophet; 'the Spirit of Christ' would more likely be understood as a post-Easter reference in view of the way the same phrase and its variations are used elsewhere in the NT (see above pp. 143–6); and the phrase translated 'sufferings of Christ' (τὰ εἰς Χριστὸν παθήματα) is as well, or better translated 'the sufferings for Christ', and so can be understood as 'their (the readers') sufferings' which unite them more closely to Christ[124] and so prepare them for glory – this would certainly accord with the emphasis of the letter on the sufferings of the readers (I Peter 2.19f.; 3.14, 17; 4.15, 19; 5.9f.), and with the typically Pauline idea that suffering with Christ is the way to glory (Rom. 8.17f.; II Cor. 4.10f., 16f.; Phil. 3.10f., 21)[125] which I Peter shares (I Peter 4.13; 5.10). But even if the prophets alluded to are those of the OT, it still does not follow that 'the Spirit of Christ' refers to the Spirit of the pre-existent Christ.[126] Peter may simply mean that the Spirit which forecast the sufferings of Christ thus proved itself to be the Spirit of Christ. That is to say, just as the character of the Christ-event provided a definition of the Spirit (above p. 145) which enabled the first-century believer to distinguish what power and inspiration was to be recognized as of the Spirit, so the character of the Christ-event enabled the first-century believer to recognize what OT prophecies pointed to Christ, were inspired by the Spirit that inspired Christ. It is by no means clear therefore that I Peter 1.10f. disturbs or challenges the conclusions drawn in the preceding paragraph.

In short, what the NT writers say about the relation between Christ and the Spirit accords well with the *eschatological* emphasis which we have found to be characteristic in the earliest Son of God, Son of Man and Adam christologies. *Such identification as there is in the NT between Christ and the Spirit begins with Jesus' resurrection, stems from Jesus' exaltation.*

§21.2 If we can talk properly of a *Spirit-christology* in the NT we are talking of a *two-stage christology*: Jesus the man inspired by the Spirit, the eschatological prophet-like-Moses sent by God, who became by his resurrection the life-giving Spirit, the Lord of the Spirit. It is only the equation of the exalted Christ with the Spirit (in the believer's experience) that disturbs the previously consistent understanding of the Spirit as the Spirit of God, that is as the power of God, as God himself reaching out to men. Prior to Jesus' exaltation the Spirit was not thought of as an independent entity distinct from God – the immanence of God was God as Spirit. This understanding of the Spirit accords entirely with the consistent NT picture of the earthly Jesus, as a man inspired by the Spirit, as one through whom God acted powerfully. Only with Jesus' exaltation does a new factor enter into the previously uncomplicated view of (the immanent) God as Spirit: for now the Spirit is identified more precisely by its relation to Christ; now Christ becomes life-giving Spirit, Lord of Spirit; now the Spirit becomes the presence of Christ, the Spirit of Christ; now Christ (in Christ, with Christ, through Christ) becomes an alternative way of speaking of the immanence of God in human experience; now Christ himself becomes a factor in the total equation, in speaking of and understanding the encounter between God and man.

This disturbance to the earlier concept of God as Spirit has not yet settled down in the NT. What is significant however is that the NT writers make no effort to project Jesus' part in the equation back to the period prior to his resurrection; they seem to see no need (even John) to modify their depiction of Jesus as one anointed and empowered by the Spirit. However much they see the exalted Jesus in terms of the Spirit now and the Spirit in terms of Jesus, it does not seem to affect or modify their picture of the earthly Jesus in terms of prophetic inspiration (only with John is 'prophet' coming to be rejected as an inadequate category of description). *They do not think of Jesus as the incarnation of the Spirit, nor of Jesus as already Spirit prior to his existence on earth* (with the possible exception of I Peter 1.11). They are content to portray Jesus as himself entering the equation as from his resurrection, as himself becoming part of God's encountering man in and through the Spirit by virtue of his exaltation. In this two-stage Spirit-christology we have a clear parallel with the early (pre-Johannine) Son of God christology and with the Adam christology. In each case the pre-resurrection stage *cannot* be expressed in terms of incarnation because only with his resurrection does Jesus become Son of God (in power), last Adam, life-giving Spirit.

§21.3   A Spirit-christology would therefore in the first place be an attempt to understand Jesus of Nazareth in terms of *inspiration* rather than of *incarnation*. It makes the claim that *God himself acted in and through this Jesus*, God as Spirit inspired and empowered him in his words and acts – a christology which arguably gives more weight to the Pauline language of 'God in Christ' than one where Jesus is understood as a distinct pre-existent divine being who came down from heaven to be incarnate through Mary.[127] But in the second place a Spirit-christology has also to be seen as an attempt to understand Christ *as one alive from the dead*, who, on the one hand, still encounters believers through the Spirit and as Spirit, but who also, on the other hand, is not wholly identified with the Spirit. Thus for Paul the Spirit was experienced not only as the Spirit of Christ but also as that Spirit which inspired the confession of Jesus' Lordship. And if anything Luke and John by their willingness to present the exalted Christ as Lord of the Spirit move away from such identification between Christ and Spirit as Paul maintained. In short, the Spirit-christology of the NT writers involves and implies Jesus' post-existence (after death) but does not seem to imply or presuppose Jesus' pre-existence (before birth).[128]

§21.4   Finally we should recall the failure of the NT writers to conceptualize Christ as an angel. In a context of thought where there was a clear tendency to envisage angels as personal heavenly beings independent of God in some degree (intercessors with God, not merely extensions of his will and power), no attempt was made by the earliest Christians to identify Christ with one of these archangels. On the contrary, any suggestion pointing in that direction was ruled out of order. The significance of this will become clearer as we proceed to the subsequent chapters, for as we shall see, angels are the only clear example of late pre-Christian Jewish thought conceptualizing personal heavenly beings with mediatory functions independent of God (in contrast to Shekinah and Spirit, and probably Wisdom and Word – see below chs. VI and VII). *It is precisely this conception of a personal heavenly being functioning as a mediator between man and God and independent of God which the NT writers either ignore or reject as a model for their understanding of Christ* whether on earth or in heaven. This double refusal of the NT writers either to identify Christ as an angel or to understand Jesus of Nazareth as the incarnation of the Spirit shows us just how far first-century christology is from both the speculations of second- and third-century Jewish Christianity and those of some more orthodox patristic theology.

VI

THE WISDOM OF GOD

§22. INTRODUCTION

In an influential article published in 1959 E. Schweizer concluded: 'The idea (Vorstellung) of the pre-existence of Jesus came to Paul through Wisdom speculation.'[1] In a later article he argued that behind the formulation 'God sent his Son, to . . .', common to both Paul and John, 'stands a christology which seeks to grasp Jesus in the categories of the mission of pre-existent Wisdom or Logos'.[2] Subsequently another Swiss contribution, by F. Christ, examining the role of Wisdom (Sophia) christology in the Synoptics, concluded the successive studies of the Synoptic material with the repeated formula:

> Jesus appears . . . as *bearer or speaker of Wisdom*, but much more than that as *Wisdom itself*. As pre-existent Wisdom Jesus Sophia. . . .[3]

The claim that Wisdom christology provides us with the main bridge from the earliest belief in Christ as exalted to the belief that Christ also pre-existed with God prior to his life on earth is a substantial one. So long as the myth of a pre-existent divine (Gnostic) redeemer was thought to provide that bridge the influence of Wisdom terminology at key points in NT christology could be regarded as part and parcel of the larger whole but otherwise of no distinctive significance.[4] Alternatively, where it was taken for granted that belief in Christ's exaltation to Lordship after death would inevitably have carried with it the corollary of his pre-existence for the first Christians, there was no need to look for an explanation of this corollary in a specific Wisdom christology. But when the movement of thought from belief in a 'post-existent' Christ to belief in a 'pre-existent' Christ became less easy to explain (see above pp. 63, 125f.), then the significance of Schweizer's thesis becomes apparent.

The importance of Wisdom terminology at this point is easy to demonstrate. In compiling a list of passages which seem clearly to express a doctrine of Christ's pre-existence few could ignore John 1.1–18, I Cor. 8.5–6, Col. 1.15–17 and Heb. 1.1–3a. Likewise within the Synoptic traditions of Jesus' ministry most would agree that the highest christology is to be found in Matt. 11.27–30. But *all these passages have been influenced to a significant degree by Wisdom terminology*; all express what can properly be called a *Wisdom christology* in one form or other. That is to say, the language of these passages is the language used of the figure of Wisdom in the Wisdom literature of the OT and particularly inter-testamental literature. As we shall see below, in pre-Christian Judaism the figure of divine Wisdom receives considerable prominence, and it is the descriptions of Wisdom which to a very large extent have determined the language of these passages. This point has become familiar within recent scholarship and I need only illustrate it to demonstrate its force.

(*a*) The close parallel between Matt. 11.25–30 and Sir. 51 has long been recognized[5] – particularly the parallel between vv. 28–30 and Sir. 51.23–7.

Matt. 11.28–30 – *Come to me*, all who labour and are heavy laden,
and I will give you rest.
Take my yoke upon you, and learn from me;
for I am gentle and lowly in heart,
and *you will find rest for your souls*.
For my yoke is easy, and my burden is light.

Sir. 51.23–7 – *Draw near to me*, you who are untaught . . .
Put your neck *under the yoke*,
and let your souls receive instruction;
it is to be found close by.
See with your eyes that I have laboured little
and *found for myself much rest*.

(*b*) Similarly the dependence of the Johannine prologue on Jewish talk of Wisdom is well established, the case being forcefully re-expressed in recent years by R. E. Brown.[6] We may note particularly the parallels between John 1.1 and Wisd. 9.9, between John 1.4 and Aristobulus, between John 1.11 and I Enoch 42.2, and between John 1.14 and Sir. 24.8.

John 1.1   – In the beginning was the Word,
and the Word was with God . . .

Wisd. 9.9   – With you is wisdom, who knows your works
and was present when you made the world.[7]

John 1.4   – The life was the light of men.

Aristobulus   – All light comes from her (wisdom) (Eusebius,
Praep. Evang. XIII.12.10).[8]

John 1.11   – He came to his own home, and his own people received
                 him not.

I Enoch 42.2 – Wisdom went forth to make her dwelling among the
                 children of men, and found no dwelling place.

John 1.14   – The Word became flesh and dwelt among us (ἐσκήνωσεν
                 ἐν ἡμῖν).

Sir. 24.8   – The one who created me assigned a place for my
                 tent (σκηνήν). And he said, 'Make your dwelling
                 (κατασκήνωσον) in Jacob'.

(c) In I Cor. 8.6 Paul speaks of Jesus Christ 'through whom are all
things and through whom we exist'. Pre-Christian Judaism was well
accustomed to speaking of Wisdom in just such terms.[9] For example,

Prov. 3.19   – The Lord by wisdom founded the earth;
                 by understanding he established the heavens . . .

Wisd. 8.4–6 – For she (Wisdom) is an initiate in the knowledge of God,
                 and *an associate in his works.*
                 If riches are a desirable possession in life,
                 what is richer than wisdom *who effects all things?*
                 And if understanding is effective,
                 who more than she is *fashioner of what exists?*

Philo. *Det.* 54 – . . . Wisdom, by whose agency the universe was
                 brought to completion (τὴν σοφίαν, δι' ἧς
                 απετελέσθη τὸ πᾶν); similarly *Fuga* 109.

(d) There is nothing precisely parallel to the hymn in Col. 1.15–20,
but the individual ideas have many parallels in pre-Christian wisdom,
not least in Philo.[10] Thus, for example, when we read Col. 1.15, 'He is
the *image* of the invisible God, the *firstborn* of all creation', we must recall
how already Wisdom has been exalted as 'an *image* of God's goodness'
(Wisd. 7.26), as 'the beginning' and '*image*' and 'vision of God' (Philo,
Leg. All. I.43); or again as the first creation or *firstborn* 'in or as the
beginning of his way (or work)' (Prov. 8.22, 25), as 'the *firstborn* mother
of all things' (Philo, *Qu. Gen.* IV.97; cf. *Ebr.* 30f.). And when we read
Col. 1.17,

He is before all things,
    and in him all things hold together,

we must recall how familiar such language was in pre-Christian Hellenistic Judaism. Wisdom is hailed by ben Sira as eternal:

From eternity, in the beginning, he created me,
    and for eternity I shall not cease to exist (Sir. 24.9).[11]

In Prov. 8 Wisdom rejoices in her role in creation:

When he established the heavens, I was there . . .

When he marked out the foundations of the earth,
Then I was beside him, like a master workman (or little child) (8.27–30).[12]

Philo speaks of 'the whole world wrought by divine wisdom' (*Heres* 199). Aristobulus speaks of Wisdom existing 'before heaven and earth' (Eusebius, *Praep. Evang.* VII.14.1; similarly Sir. 1.4). And ben Sira says, 'By his word all things hold together' (43.26; cf. Philo, *Heres* 188; *Fuga* 112; *Qu. Ex.* II.118) – word and wisdom, as we shall see, being more or less interchangeable in this whole tradition.

(e) Finally, in the case of Heb. 1.3f. the parallels with Philo are again striking – what Hebrews says of the Son, Philo says of the Logos.[13] In the writings prior to Philo the clearest parallel is in Wisd. 7.

Heb. 1.3   – He is the radiance (ἀπαύγασμα) of God's glory . . .

Wisd. 7.26   – She is the radiance (ἀπαύγασμα) of eternal light,
                           a spotless mirror of the working of God . . .

Heb. 1.3   – . . . the stamp (χαρακτήρ) of his nature . . .

Philo, *Plant.* 18 – . . . the stamp (χαρακτήρ) is the eternal Word.

Heb. 1.3   – . . . sustaining all things (φέρων τὰ πάντα) by the
                           word of his power.

The nearest parallels to this last line in Philo speak of *God* giving being to what is not and generating all things (τὰ μὴ ὄντα φέρων καὶ τὰ πάντα γεννῶν) (*Heres* 36; also *Mut.* 256), but he also speaks of the Word as the prop which sustains the whole (*Plant.* 8f.; *Som.* I.241).

Several other passages in the NT are held to evince some influence from pre-Christian Jewish Wisdom traditions. In addition to Matt. 11.25–7/Luke 10.21f. and Matt. 11.28–30, the most obvious candidates from the Synoptics are three other passages from Q – Matt. 11.16–19/Luke 7.31–5, Matt. 23.34–6/Luke 11.49–51 and Matt. 23.37–9/Luke 13.34f.[14] In John we might mention the parallels between John 4.14 and Sir. 24.21, between the Bread of Life discourse in John 6 and Prov. 9.5 and again Sir. 24.19–21, and between John 7.34 and Prov. 1.28.[15] In Revelation we may compare Rev. 3.14 with Prov. 8.22 (see below, p. 247).

In Paul further allusions are a matter of some dispute. Schweizer suggests specific Wisdom language in Paul's talk of God 'sending' his Son (cf. Gal. 4.4 and Rom. 8.3 with Wisd. 9.10, 17); but we have already seen reason to doubt this (above pp. 39f.). Behind 'the rulers of this age' (οἱ ἄρχοντες τοῦ αἰῶνος – I Cor. 2.6, 8) some have found an allusion to Bar. 3.9–4.4, particularly 3.16 ('the princes of the nations' – οἱ ἄρχοντες τῶν ἐθνῶν);[16] but most commentators rightly judge that the context favours a reference to supernatural beings thought to control the present world order.[17] On the other hand, most scholars would also agree that I Cor. 10.4 ('the rock was Christ') has been influenced to some degree by the allegorical interpretation of the wilderness rock as Wisdom in Philo, *Leg. All.* II.86, though to what degree remains a more open question to be discussed below (§24.3). Similarly it can plausibly be argued that the association of ideas in II Cor. 3.18 ('we all ... beholding as in a glass the glory of the Lord are being changed into the same image ...') has been prompted by Wisd. 7.26 (Wisdom 'is the radiance, or reflection of eternal light, a spotless mirror of the working of God, and an image of his goodness').[18] And Paul's interpretation of Deut. 30.12f. with reference to Christ in Rom. 10.6f. may well have been influenced by Bar. 3.29f.'s interpretation of the same passage with reference to Wisdom (see further below §24.4).

It is clear therefore that the *tradition of (pre-existent) Wisdom has been influential at many points in NT christology*. In some of the earlier (i.e. Pauline) passages it may be no more than that *language* or *exegesis* has been prompted by specific language or some particular exegesis used in the Wisdom tradition. But in other cases there can be little doubt that the *role* of Wisdom is being attributed to Christ. This is particularly true of the five main passages laid out in more detail on pp. 164–6 where in four out of the five it is by means of a Wisdom christology that a cosmic significance is attributed to Christ. What pre-Christian Judaism said of Wisdom and Philo also of the Logos, Paul and the others say of Jesus. The role that Proverbs, ben Sira, etc. ascribe to Wisdom, these earliest Christians ascribe to Jesus. That is to say, for those who were familiar with this obviously widespread cosmological speculation, the implication was presumably clear: *Jesus was being identified as Wisdom*. Indeed, Paul seems to make the identification explicit in so many words when he proclaims 'Christ the power of God and the wisdom of God' (I Cor. 1.24; also 1.30).[19]

What then did it mean for the first Christians when such Wisdom language was applied to Christ? What was the significance of this identification of Christ as Wisdom? What or who is this 'wisdom' with which/whom Christ is being identified? Does such identification imply an already formulated doctrine of incarnation? In particular, when Paul and the others attribute Wisdom's role in creation to Christ was this intended literally (Jesus himself was there at creation) or do we have some form of poetic hyperbole, which their readers would recognize to be such? – here once again the context of meaning for the first Christians is all important. These questions provide the agenda for the rest of this chapter.

§23. WISDOM IN PRE-CHRISTIAN JUDAISM

What or who was this Wisdom whose descriptions and functions are attributed to Christ in such a broad sweep of NT writings? What or who was this 'wisdom' with which/whom Christ seems to have been identified as early as Paul? To answer this question we must inquire into the meaning of the term 'wisdom' in pre-Christian Judaism, in particular in those passages where it is described as pre-existent and having a role in creation. The key passages here are Job 28, Prov. 8.22–31, Sir. 24, Bar. 3.9–4.4, Wisd. 6.12–11.1, I Enoch 42, and various references to Wisdom in Philo. What or who is Wisdom in all these passages?

Unfortunately the answer is not clear and we find ourselves at this point caught up in a still unresolved debate. The principal options held out to us are as follows: (1) Wisdom is a *divine being*, an independent deity, as in the near parallels in Egyptian and Mesopotamian religions;[20] (2) Wisdom is a *hypostasis* – that is, a 'quasi-personification of certain attributes proper to God, occupying an intermediate position between personalities and abstract beings';[21] (3) Wisdom is nothing more than a *personification* of a divine attribute;[22] (4) Wisdom is the personification of *cosmic order* and is not thought of as divine until a relatively late stage, namely, the Wisdom of Solomon, where however, it remains uncertain whether a conceptually clear definition is achieved.[23] If we are to answer our question, What did it mean that the first Christians identified Christ as Wisdom?, we must attempt to reach some sort of decision as to which of these options is the best interpretation of these OT and intertestamental passages – that is to say, which of these options best represents the meaning that the first Christians would read off from these passages.

When we look more closely at the passages several points become clearer. (*a*) First, if we set out the passages in the most likely chronological order, it becomes evident that there is both a *development* in the talk about Wisdom, and that the development is due in large part to influence (positive and negative) from religious cults and philosophies prevalent in the ancient near East at that time.

> Job 28 – Surely there is a mine for silver,
>   and a place for gold which they refine.
>   . . .
> But where shall wisdom be found?
>   . . .

Here we cannot really speak of a divine attribute, or of a personification; wisdom may be simply 'the order given to the world by God'.[24]

In Prov. 8, Wisdom speaks in the first person – clearly a personification at least. Moreover, the fact that Wisdom is represented as a woman attractive to young men is best explained as due to the influence of the figure of Ishtar-Astarte, the Mesopotamian goddess of love. That is to say, Prov. 1.20–33, 8.1–35, 9.1–6 probably constitutes the author's attempt to counteract the influence of the Astarte cult, by representing Wisdom as much more attractive than the 'strange woman' against whom he warns in chs. 2, 5, 6 and 7.[25]

More attractive to many scholars is the thesis that Prov. 8.22–31, and more clearly Sir. 24, has been greatly influenced by the cult of Isis from Egypt. The chief point of comparison is that Isis proclaims herself as the divine agent who created and sustains the universe, as the teacher who has revealed to men the principles of morality and the laws and arts of civilization – we know of at least one hymn in the first person to this effect which circulated widely throughout the empire of the Ptolemies probably as early as the third century BC.[26]

With the Wisdom of Solomon the divine status of Wisdom and her role in creation comes to clearest expression – Wisdom, the fashioner of all things' (7.22; 8.5f.);

> She reaches mightily from one end of the earth to the other,
>   and she orders all things well (8.1);

> [Wisdom, who] sits besides God's throne (9.4).

Most striking of all is the influence of Stoic thought about cosmic reason, the logos that pervades all creation – most clearly seen in the long description of Wisdom in 7.22ff.:

> intelligent, holy, unique, manifold, subtle, mobile, . . .
> For wisdom is more mobile than any motion;
> because of her pureness she pervades and penetrates all things.
> For she is a breath of the power of God,
>   and a pure emanation of the glory of the Almighty.

Finally, in the case of Philo the influence of both Platonic and Stoic thought is clearly evident (see below pp. 221f.). More disputed is the question of Philo's dependence on the Isis myth. We can see in his quite frequent description of Wisdom as 'mother of all things' (*Leg. All.* II.49; *Det.* 54, 115–17; *Ebr.* 31; *Conf.* 49; *Heres.* 53; *Fuga* 109; *Qu. Gen.* IV. 47) a possible allusion (cf. Apuleius, *Met.* 11.5), and his characterization of Wisdom as 'of many names' (*Leg. All.* I.43) is easy to parallel with Isis 'the myriad-named' (Plutarch, *De Iside* 53; Apuleius, *Met.* 11.5),[27] though whether we should speak of 'dependence' specifically on the Isis myth as such is less clear.[28]

We may conclude then that however deeply rooted in Palestinian soil and Jewish faith was the late Israelite talk of Wisdom,[29] *many of the images and words used to describe her were drawn from wider religious thought and worship*

– the aim being to present the worshippers of Yahweh with as attractive as possible an alternative to the cults and speculations more widely prevalent in their time.

(*b*) Second, we should bear in mind that *language which denoted a hypostasis or independent deity in polytheism would certainly have a different connotation within a monotheistic religion.* Where a polytheistic faith would have little difficulty in counting Wisdom as one more god within the heavenly pantheon, a monotheistic faith could make no such accommodation. However much some Jews might be willing to diffuse their monotheism under the impact of Hellenistic culture, there is no clear evidence that the Wisdom tradition we have been examining ever did so. This is why we cannot simply abstract statements and words out of the contexts of, for example, an Isis hymn on the one hand and ben Sira on the other, and interpret them as equivalents – one of the mistakes too often made by the History of Religions school. *In order to understand what meaning such words and statements had for those who used them, we must interpret them within the context in which they were used.*

Thus when Ringgren examines 'the hypostatization of divine qualities and functions in the ancient near East', the classic study in this field, he concludes that words like *Maat* (truth, righteousness, order and regularity in the cosmos) and *Mēšaru* (righteousness) came to denote independent deities. *Maat*, originally a function of the high god in Egyptian religion becomes 'a self-existent being. And, since the word *maat* is female, it was natural that this being should become a goddess, the daughter of the god'. Similarly with *Mēšaru* in the Babylonian pantheon.[30] But what makes it clear to Ringgren that these are more than merely poetic personifications or abstractions, is that we know of many priests of *Maat*, we know that *Mēšaru* had its own image in the temple and was worshipped there.[31] And this is precisely what is lacking in the Wisdom tradition used by Proverbs, ben Sira, etc. No worship is offered to Wisdom; Wisdom has no priests in Israel. That is to say, *when set within the context of faith in Yahweh there is no clear indication that the Wisdom language of these writings has gone beyond vivid personification.*[32]

So too ben Sira does not make use of or allusion to the hymns of the Isis cult in order to present Wisdom as a figure like Isis in all respects. On the contrary his purpose is quite clearly to identify Wisdom with the *law* – as he says explicitly:

All this is the book of the covenant of the Most High God,
the law which Moses commanded us
as an inheritance for the congregations of Jacob.
It fills men with wisdom, like the Pishon . . . (Sir. 24.23, 25).

Evidently then ben Sira is saying in effect to those attracted by the Isis cult, 'This wisdom, this cosmic order which you see expressed in the figure of Isis and seek for in her cult, we see most clearly, most definitively expressed in the Torah' (similarly with Bar. 3.36–4.4; and cf. Wisd. 6.18).[33]

The same indeed could be said of Philo, although he does not seem to equate Wisdom and Torah explicitly (cf. *Virt.* 62–5), since in fact Wisdom is wholly subordinate to the less personal Logos of Stoic pantheism (and Platonic idealism) in his thought, is indeed not much more than an occasional variant for the Logos when an allusion to the female figure becomes appropriate,[34] and since the Logos itself is clearly to be identified in Philo's mind with the law (explicitly *Migr.* 130)[35] – although of course, Philo's Logos concept is much more complex (see below §28.3). For the Jew of Alexandria as well as the Jew of Palestine the wisdom of God had been most fully and clearly expressed and embodied in the Torah.

It would appear then as though the Jewish wisdom writers do indeed take up some of the more widespread language of Near Eastern religious speculation, and do so *in conscious awareness of its use elsewhere*; but they do *not* draw the same conclusions for worship and practice as the polytheistic religions do. On the contrary they *adapt* this wider speculation to their own faith and make it serve to commend their own faith; to Wisdom understood (and worshipped) as a divine being (one of Isis' many names), they pose *the alternative of Wisdom identified as the law given to Israel by (the one) God.*[36]

(c) Thirdly, we should observe how *fluid* is the concept of Wisdom in the passages we have examined and in the context within which they appear, and how *the Jewish wisdom writers use it alongside affirmations of Jewish monotheism without any sense that the latter is in any way threatened by the former.* In Job 28 wisdom is presented as something inestimably precious, something which is sought as men seek precious stones, something whose location only God knows, something which is found by the man who fears the Lord. In Proverbs the first person poem of chapter 8 is probably for the author of Proverbs simply a more vivid way of saying what he has already said in 2.6 and 3.19:

> For the Lord gives wisdom;
>   from his mouth comes knowledge and understanding (2.6).

> The Lord by wisdom founded the earth;
>   by understanding he established the heavens (3.19).

In ben Sira we may consider the following passages:

> All wisdom comes from the Lord
>   and is with him for ever (1.1).

> To fear the Lord is the beginning of wisdom;

she is created with the faithful in the womb (1.14).

He (the seeker after wisdom) will place his children under her shelter,
    and will camp under her boughs;
he will be sheltered by her from the heat,
    and will dwell in the midst of her glory.
The man who fears the Lord will do this,
    and he who holds to the law will obtain wisdom.
She will come to meet him like a mother,
    and like the wife of his youth she will welcome him (14.26–15.2).

He who devotes himself
to the study of the law of the Most High
will seek out the wisdom of all the ancients,
    and will be concerned with prophecies (39.1).

The Lord has ordained the splendours of his wisdom,
    and he is from everlasting and to everlasting;
Nothing can be added or taken away,
    and he needs no one to be his counsellor (42.21).

Is ben Sira doing any more here than ringing the changes in a sequence
of metaphors designed to encourage study of the Torah as the way to
ensure a life ordered by divine wisdom? Contrast the fact that in at least
two other passages he speaks of creation as God's act without any reference to Wisdom:

The works of the Lord have existed from the beginning of his creation,
    and when he made them, he determined their divisions . . . (16.26).

He who lives for ever created the whole universe;
    the Lord alone will be declared righteous.
To none has he given power to proclaim his works;
    and who can search out his mighty deeds? (18.1, 2, 4).

Quite obviously the man who wrote these lines had *no intention of giving
Wisdom the status of an independent entity*, far less a divine personality side by
side with Yahweh. As he himself says in summary:

Though we speak much we cannot reach the end,
    and the sum of our words is: 'He is the all' (43.27).

For ben Sira then, Wisdom is just a way of speaking about God's ordering
of creation and design for man in the law.[37]
    Similarly with the Wisdom of Solomon, 'Wisdom is a kindly spirit'
(1.6), an attribute of his own words (6.9); wisdom is like a woman (6.12–
16), is defined as 'the most sincere desire for instruction' (6.17), is a
something like gems or radiant like the light (7.8–10, 29), is the mother
of all good things (7.11f.); wisdom is the cosmic order (7.17–21, 8.1), a
spirit pervading all created things (7.22ff.); wisdom is a bride (8.2), an

intimate of God (8.3f.), a teacher of profoundest mysteries (8.8); and so on. But again, lest there be any mistake, the author states clearly:

> God is the guide even of wisdom
> and the corrector of the wise.
> For both we and our words are in his hand,
> as are all understanding and skill in crafts (7.15f.).

> I perceived that I would not possess wisdom unless God gave her to me –
> and it was a mark of insight to know whose gift she was –
> so I appealed to the Lord and besought him,
> and with my whole heart I said:
> 'O God of my fathers and Lord of mercy,
> who hast made all things by thy word,
> and by thy wisdom hast formed man
>   . . .
> give me the wisdom that sits by thy throne
>   . . .
> for even if one is perfect among the sons of men,
> yet without the wisdom that comes from thee
> he will be regarded as nothing' (8.21–9.6).

Once again the position is clear: for all that the author of the Wisdom of Solomon uses the language of Stoicism, he has not the slightest thought of equating wisdom with some pantheistic ultimate reason; and for all the vigour of his imagery, he has not the slightest thought of wisdom as an independent divine being. From start to finish the wisdom of which he speaks is *the wisdom of God* and signifies *God's wise ordering of creation and of those who fear him.*[38]

So too with Philo. Wisdom is pictured as a city and dwelling or a turtle dove (*Leg. All.* III.3; *Heres* 127), is identified with the tent of meeting and the tree of life (*Leg. All.* III.46, 52), or in a favourite metaphor is likened to a fountain (*Leg. All.* II.86f.; *Det.* 117; *Post.* 136–8; *Som.* II.242; *Spec. Leg.* IV.75; *Prob.* 13,117; cf. *Leg. All.* I.64f.). His picture of Wisdom as a mother (particularly Sarah – *Leg. All.* II.82; *Det.* 124; *Cong.* 12f.) should not be abstracted as a separate strand distinct from this consistent allegorizing method, as though the mother imagery proved that Wisdom was a divine personal being or goddess for Philo. It is certainly very unlikely that he intended to evoke the Isis-Osiris myth when he spoke of God as 'the husband of Wisdom' (*Cher.* 49), any more than he expected to be taken literally when he spoke of God impregnating Sarah, Rebekah, Leah and Zipporah (*Cher.* 44–7; see above II n. 52). And though he depicts Wisdom as the mother of the Logos in *Fuga* 108f., he also depicts the Logos as the fountain of Wisdom (*Fuga* 97), which indicates that no specific mythological formulation is in mind but *simply a kaleidescope of imagery none of which may be pressed too hard in isolation from the wider context of his thought.*[39] Further elucidation of that wider context must await the next chapter. But thus far we can say even with Philo there is no real indication that his monotheism is in any way challenged by such talk. On the contrary, he himself affirms that God is 'the fountain of Wisdom . . . the only wise (being)' (*Sac.* 64), that 'the maker of this whole universe was and is God' (*Leg. All.* III.99; see further below pp. 224f.).[40]

In short, if we attempt to give clearer definition to the figure of Wisdom within the monotheism of Israel's religion we seem to be shut up to two alternatives. Either Wisdom is a being clearly subordinate to Yahweh, like the angels, or the heavenly council in Job 1 and 2 (see above pp. 149f.). And yet the functions of Wisdom in creation seem to give her a much greater significance. Or else, and this seems the more plausible, the Wisdom passages are *simply ways of describing Yahweh's wise creation and purpose.*[41] The seemingly attractive third alternative, Wisdom as a divine hypostasis, involves the importation of a concept whose appropriateness here is a consequence of the technical meaning it acquired in the much later Trinitarian controversies of the early church. It has *not* been demonstrated that Hebrew thought was already contemplating such distinctions within its talk of God.[42] On the contrary, for a Jew to say that Wisdom 'effects all things', that Wisdom 'delivered Israel from a nation of oppressors', that 'love of Wisdom is the keeping of her laws' (Wisd. 8.5; 10.15; 6.18), was simply to say in a more picturesque way that God created all things wisely, that God's wise purpose is clearly evident in the exodus from Egypt and most fully expressed in the law he gave through Moses.[43]

(*d*) Finally, we should observe that Wisdom is only one of a number of words which are used in the OT and intertestamental literature as though they denoted divine entities independent of God. For example:

Ps. 85.10f.   – Steadfast love and faithfulness will meet;
                  righteousness and peace will kiss each other.
              Faithfulness will spring up from the ground,
                  and righteousness will look down from the sky.

Ps. 96.6   – Honour and majesty are before him;
                  strength and beauty are in his sanctuary.

Ps. 43.3   – Oh send out your light and your truth;
                  let them lead me,
              let them bring me to your holy hill
                  and to your dwelling!

Ps. 57.3   – God will send forth his steadfast love
                  and his faithfulness.

Job 25.2   – Dominion and fear are with God.[44]

Is this kind of language any different in the end from

Isa. 51.9   – Awake, awake, put on strength,
              O arm of the Lord,

or

Ps. 45.4   – Let your right hand teach you dread deeds!,

or

Wisd. 11.17 – Your all powerful hand,
              which created the world out of formless matter . . .?

Does anyone seriously wish to maintain that the writers of these passages thought of Yahweh's 'arm' and his 'right hand' as independent entities? Again it is possible to see parallels here with what happened in Egyptian religion, where, for example, the 14 *kas* or qualities of the sun god are spoken of as self-existent beings.[45] But, if that was in fact the case, once again we must ask if a parallel from polytheism is a real parallel to what we have read in the texts cited above.

The judgment that in such passages we are more in the realm of Hebraic personification than of Near Eastern 'hypostatization' is further confirmed when we recall that not only divine 'attributes' but also more human characteristics can be personified in precisely the same way. So for example with 'injustice', 'wickedness' and 'sorrow':[46]

Job 11.14 – If iniquity is in your hand, put it far away,
              and let not injustice (LXX – ἀδικία) dwell in your tents.

Ps. 107.42 – The upright see it and are glad;
              and all wickedness (LXX – ἀνομία) stops its mouth.

Isa 35.10 – Sorrow and sighing shall flee away.

All these passages underline our earlier point, that the *primary context* for the disputed Wisdom passages, in the OT and LXX at any rate, is the thought world and literary idiom which comes to expression in such other OT and LXX writings as we have cited above.[47] Only if the passages in question were significantly out of character in relation to that context would we be justified in looking for an alternative primary context. To argue thus is not to deny influence from other contexts (above pp. 169f.); it is rather to question the importance of that influence, to question in particular whether that influence had altered the primary context against which the passages must be interpreted. The thesis here propounded is that the *controlling* context of meaning, even in ben Sira and the Wisdom of Solomon, continues to be the thought world which we have found expressed elsewhere in the OT and LXX, and that such influence as there is from other contexts is *assimilated* to the faith and idioms of Israel's spokesmen. For when we compare the idiom of the disputed passages, on the one hand with the idiom of such other OT and LXX passages as we have instanced above, and on the other with the language of Egyptian and Mesopotamian parallels, does the conclusion not quickly suggest itself that the thought expressed in these disputed passages is closer to the former than to the latter? In which case, unless we are willing to argue that the OT and LXX writers also hypostatized 'righteousness', 'wickedness' and God's 'right hand', we can hardly argue that they hypostatized Wisdom. Consistency demands rather that we interpret all such literary features as personifications.

All in all therefore it seems that we have little ground for dissenting from the views of those most familiar with Jewish thought in its rabbinic expression (above p. 130): viz. that the Hellenistic Judaism of the LXX did not think of Wisdom as a 'hypostasis' or 'intermediary being' any more than did the OT writers and the rabbis. Wisdom, like the name, the glory, the Spirit of Yahweh, was a way of asserting God's nearness, his involvement with his world, his concern for his people. All these words provided expressions of God's *immanence*, his active concern in creation, revelation and redemption, while at the same time protecting his holy transcendence and wholly otherness. We have still to examine Philo more closely, but thus far we can say with confidence that *it is very unlikely that pre-Christian Judaism ever understood Wisdom as a divine being in any sense independent of Yahweh.* The language may be the language of the wider speculation of the time, but within Jewish monotheism and Hebraic literary idiom Wisdom never really becomes more than a *personification* – a personification not so much of a divine attribute (I doubt whether the Hebrews thought much in terms of 'attributes'), a personification rather of a *function* of Yahweh, *a way of speaking about God himself, of expressing God's active involvement with his world and his people without compromising his transcendence.*

§24. CHRIST AS WISDOM IN PAUL

What then is Paul doing when he uses Wisdom language of Christ, when he says of Christ what was said of Wisdom in pre-Christian Judaism, when he seems even to identify Christ with Wisdom? (We start with Paul since his letters are by common consent the earliest Christian writings).[48] The answer is probably best discovered by examining Paul's chief Wisdom passages in chronological order. The passages in question are I Cor. 1–2, I Cor. 8.6, I Cor. 10.4(?), Rom. 10.6–8(?) and Col. 1.15–20.[49]

§24.1   *I Cor. 1.24, 30.* The obvious starting place is I Cor. 1–2. Here we have both the earliest clear link between Christ and wisdom and also the most explicit:

> For Jews demand signs and Greeks seek wisdom, but we preach Christ cru-
> cified, to Jews a stumbling-block, to Greeks folly, but to those who are called,
> both Jews and Greeks, Christ the power and the wisdom of God . . . Christ
> Jesus, who was made wisdom for us from God, righteousness and sanctification
> and redemption (1.22–4, 30).

What is the meaning of this phrase 'Christ the wisdom of God'? Is there in this phrase thought of a pre-existent Wisdom with whom Christ is being identified?

One thing is fairly clear from the context (I Cor. 1.18–2.9) – that Paul here is confronting some opposition in Corinth and is responding to the assertions and language used by his opponents.[50] Indeed we can put the point more strongly: Paul probably takes up wisdom language because it was already being used by the Corinthians. In terms of their under-standing and concept of wisdom, Paul's presentation of his message was unimpressive and its particular content, 'the word of the cross' was foolishness (I Cor. 2.1–5; 1.18–25). Presumably they had their own idea as to what constituted God's method of salvation and saw it as an expression or enactment of divine wisdom – though what precisely they understood by 'wisdom' remains obscure. It evidently gave rise to an elitist spirituality, no doubt based on their superior insight into and knowledge of divine wisdom (I Cor. 2.10–3.4; 8). Moreover, it had cos-mological ramifications: wisdom for the Corinthians had something to do with the 'rulers of this age' (2.6, 8 – see above pp. 166f. and n. 17), and gave them a clearer understanding of the cosmic realities behind this world (hence their confidence with regard to idols – 8.4).[51] However, there is no indication that the Corinthians thought of this wisdom as active in creation, as a personification of divine action (as in the earlier Jewish writings discussed above §23), or as a personal being, an ema-nation from the unknowable God (as in later Gnostic thought).[52] Still less can we conclude that the Corinthians had evolved anything properly to be called a Wisdom christology, in which Christ was identified with a (pre-existent) heavenly being (Wisdom).[53] Paul's polemic in terms of wisdom is directed rather against worldly evaluation of the message of the cross and against over-evaluation of rhetorical skill (1.18–2.5).[54] In-sofar as christology was involved the fault probably lay in an unbalanced emphasis on the exalted glory of Christ ('the Lord of glory'), resulting in a perfectionist soteriology which had no place for the eschatological 'not yet' (2.13–3.1 – 'the spiritual ones'; 4.8; 10.1–12; 15.12).[55] But of a christology of pre-existent wisdom, or of 'Wisdom' as a title used by the Corinthians for Christ we cannot speak.

What then of Paul's response, and of Paul's understanding of divine wisdom? In face of the Greeks seeking for wisdom Paul preached Christ, Christ crucified. In direct antithesis to their understanding of wisdom Paul asserts that *Christ* is God's wisdom – Christ *crucified*. *Divine* wisdom is manifested in the cross and its proclamation. That is to say, Paul here emphatically sets forth Christ crucified as the measure of divine wisdom. The cross is the act of divine wisdom, and demonstrates and defines God's wisdom in a final way for the Christian. To be sure Paul talks of what might be called a 'pre-existent wisdom' (2.7); but it is a wisdom in the sense of 'God's predetermined plan of salvation'.[56] Christ is God's wisdom then, not as a pre-existent being,[57] but as the one who fulfilled God's predetermined plan of salvation, as the one predetermined by God to be the means of man's salvation through his death and resurrection – not just through his resurrection ('the Lord of glory') but through his death (see further below §29.2). In short, in I Cor. 1–2 Christ is the fulfilment or embodiment of God's wise intention 'to bring us to glory' (2.7). Not some act of creation, not even 'the Lord of glory', but Christ crucified is for Paul the determinative embodiment of divine wisdom which rules out of court any alternative definitions or claimants.

We must conclude then: (1) so far as we can tell there is no thought here of wisdom as a pre-existent divine hypostasis or person, either among the Corinthians or in Paul himself. For Paul God's wisdom is essentially God's plan to achieve salvation through the crucifixion of Jesus and through the proclamation of the crucified Christ (I Cor. 1.20–25). (2) At the same time we are not so far from the circle of thought examined above (§23, see also above n. 51). Apart from the idea of a *hidden* wisdom now revealed by God (2.6f.), revealed in the Christ-event not in the law, we may note particularly the linking of the *wisdom* of God with the *power* of God in 1.24. Paul of course is thinking almost entirely here of the Corinthian converts' *experience* of the power of God through the preaching of the cross (1.18; 2.4f.);[58] but he cannot have been unmindful of the fact that 'power' (δύναμις), like 'wisdom' was often used as a way of speaking of God (or of a god).[59] So what Paul probably means is that Jesus is the one in whom the very power that is from God (indeed that *is* God reaching out to men) has been manifested; that Jesus is the one in whom and through whom this divine power of God himself still comes to those who are called. And similarly with wisdom: God's wisdom in its most important expression – as the plan of salvation put into effect by God – is Christ.[60] (3) There is no thought here of Christ as pre-existent. The identification of Christ as God's wisdom was seen to have cosmological implications (2.7f.), but there is here no clear link between God's wisdom and the act of creation, and the idea of pre-existence attaches only to God's plan 'to bring us to glory' (2.7). Indeed 1.30 speaks of Christ

'becoming, being made' (ἐγενήθη) 'wisdom for us from God, righteousness, sanctification and redemption' – that is, as the context indicates, in
and through his death and resurrection – Christ who fulfilled God's plan
of salvation precisely as the crucified and risen one, and thus brought
God's wisdom to expression and thereby can be spoken of as God's
wisdom, the one who precisely by his death and resurrection has become
wisdom for us, the one who realizes God's righteousness, sanctification
and redemption in those who are being saved. (4) A final consideration
is of some importance. The degree to which Paul's description of Christ
here is determined by the situation and language confronting him at
Corinth raises the strong possibility that the initial identification of Christ
as God's wisdom was provoked by the wayward elitism of the Corinthian
'gnostic' faction. There is no evidence that Paul spoke of Christ in wisdom
language before I Corinthians. Perhaps then it was the Corinthians' claim
to wisdom over against Paul and Paul's kerygma which prompted from
him the response: No, *Christ* is the wisdom of God, the crucified Christ
is the embodiment of God's plan of salvation and the measure and fullest
expression of God's continuing wisdom and power.

§24.2   *I Cor. 8.6.* This verse is widely thought to be a quotation by Paul[61]
and so very possibly the earliest statement of belief in the pre-existence
of Christ. To evaluate this claim we must set the verse within its context
in I Cor. 8.

> [4]'Concerning food offered to idols, we know that 'an idol has no real existence',
> and that 'there is no God but one'. [5]For although there may be so-called gods
> whether in heaven or on earth, as indeed there are many gods and many lords;
> [6]but for us there is one God, the Father, from whom all things and we to him,
> and one Lord Jesus Christ, through whom all things and we through him.
> [7]However, not all possess this knowledge . . .

It is obvious that there are indeed pre-Pauline and pre-Christian elements in v. 6. The confession that God is one is clearly Jewish (cf.
particularly Deut. 6.4; James 2.19);[62] the confession that 'Jesus is Lord'
is particularly beloved by Paul but was certainly characteristic of Hellenistic Christianity apart from Paul (Rom. 10.9; I Cor. 12.3; Eph. 4.5; Phil.
2.11);[63] and the use of the prepositions 'from', 'through' and 'to' when
speaking of God and the cosmos ('all things') was widespread in the
ancient world and typically Stoic.[64] But there is no real parallel to Paul's
formulation here (not even I Tim. 2.5), and it seems to me more probable
that Paul himself has put together these earlier and more widespread
elements in response to the situation confronting him at Corinth.

Paul's response to the Corinthians begins from two affirmations made
by the Corinthians, presumably by those who claimed to have
'knowledge' as a way of justifying their conduct in eating meat offered to

idols: 'an idol has no real existence', and 'there is no God but one'.[65] If an idol is 'nothing' (οὐδέν) and 'there is no God but one', then all things were made by him and all that he made for food may be enjoyed by those who worship him (so Paul in 10.26, citing Ps. 24.1 and agreeing with the men of knowledge on this point). Paul accepts these basic assertions of the Corinthians (8.4), and in 8.5–6 he goes on to elaborate them as a statement of 'knowledge' (v. 7), that is, in a way that would commend itself to the Corinthians, but presumably in such a way also as to qualify the conclusions drawn from the two assertions by the knowledgeable ones.

Thus he starts from the common ground of the basic monotheistic faith ('There is one God, the Father');[66] first he adds 'from whom (come) all things', an assertion with which the Corinthians would have been familiar and with which they would no doubt have agreed; but then he also adds 'and we to him' or 'for whom we exist' (RSV). Next he appends to this the basic confession of Hellenistic or Gentile Christianity, 'Jesus Christ is Lord'. But with this he does three striking things. First he asserts that Christ the Lord also is one; thereby he splits the *Shema* (Deut. 6.4), the Jewish confession of monotheism,[67] between God the Father and Christ the Lord in a way that has no earlier parallel.[68] Second he adds 'through whom (came) all things'; thereby he splits the more regular Stoic formulation also between the one God ('from him', 'to him') and the one Lord ('through him'; contrast Rom. 11.36), in a way that is best paralleled in Jewish Wisdom tradition (as we have seen). Third, he again adds a reference to himself and his readers – 'and we (exist) through him' – using the same preposition as in the preceding phrase.

Why has Paul handled these basic assertions of Jewish monotheism and Stoic cosmology in such a free manner? The most obvious answer is that he wishes to stress the unity of creation and salvation, to prevent a split in the Corinthians' thinking between their experience of spiritual power and their attitude to the material world.[69] Hence the insistence in effect that the one Lord (of believers) is not separable from the one God (the creator); the Lord through whom salvation comes is the Lord through whom all things come; salvation for us means that we live *for* the one God from whom all things and *through* the one Lord in the way that all things (come about) through the one Lord. In other words, the spiritual experience of the Corinthians ('we through him') is not to be separated from responsibility to the creator God ('we to him') and is experience of one and the same power which brought all things to be ('all things through him'). The implication of all this for the Corinthians, and one which Paul proceeds to draw out in vv. 7–13, is that the knowing ones must have a sense of responsibility in their handling of created things before God, conscious that their Lord is Lord also of creation, and with due respect for their fellow believers (the rest of 'us').

It does look very much then as though the formulation in I Cor. 8.6 is directed wholly to the situation of the Corinthians – so much so that *it is hard to recognize an earlier formulation behind it*. There are clearly pre-Pauline elements, yet nothing to indicate that they had *already* been united partially or wholly prior to Paul's writing of I Corinthians.

This conclusion still leaves us with something of a puzzle: on the one hand the adaptation of earlier confessional elements does seem rather striking and even controversial; but on the other Paul expresses himself briefly and is content simply to mould these earlier elements into what many understandably have taken to be an already established confession. If his formulation was so controversial would we not expect a much more careful statement by Paul? Or is it possible that what seems to us so controversial was not so in Paul's own thinking? Or was it simply that Paul saw it as a pregnant (epigrammatic) statement of Christian knowledge and wisdom (cf. I Cor. 2.6ff.), 'an utterance of knowledge or of wisdom' (12.8), which was sufficiently self-explanatory as to require application (8.7–13) rather then exposition? Some further considerations drawn from the passage may illuminate both this issue and our wider inquiry.

(*a*) Paul may be drawing what were to him obvious implications from the Lordship of Christ and may intend 8.6b to be a statement about Christ's *present* Lordship. 8.6b is an adaptation, as we have said, of the Hellenistic Christian confession 'Jesus is Lord'. For first-century Christians generally this was a title Jesus received on his exaltation, by virtue of his resurrection (Acts 2.36; Phil. 2.9–11; cf. Rom. 10.9f.; I Cor. 16.22):[70] it was the exalted Lord who had supplanted all other 'lords' and absorbed their significance and rule in regard both to the cosmos and to redemption (8.5–6). Likewise the addition of 'we' to both lines of v. 8 may well indicate that Paul is speaking primarily about the new understanding and the new state of affairs brought about for believers by Christ's Lordship, about the relations between God, Christ, believers and created things that now pertains. What Paul may be saying to the Corinthians then is simply that the whole cosmos ('all things') has to be understood not only as illuminated by some particular Corinthian *gnosis* ('an idol has no real existence' – v. 4), and not only in terms of Jewish monotheism ('there is no God but one'), but also and particularly in the light of the Lordship of Jesus Christ. All things have their focal point in him, in just the same way as 'we' who have acknowledged his Lordship. In other words, we may have to recognize that Paul is not making a statement about the act of creation in the *past*, but rather about creation as believers see it *now* – that just as they have found their *own* true being and meaning through Christ, so faith has enabled them to see that *all things* find their true being and meaning through Christ.[71]

(*d*) Perhaps we should see I Cor. 8.6 as an extension of the thought of I Cor. 1–2. As there he claims that the crucified Christ is the one who fulfils God's plan of salvation, who embodies God's wisdom, so here he extends the thought to assert in effect that God's plan of salvation is continuous with his power in creation. Here the 'folly' to the Gentiles would be that he has united creation and salvation so closely together (breaking down the typical Hellenistic dualism between spirit and matter; cf. 6.12–20). And the 'stumbling block' to the Jews would be that the one Lordship of God (Deut. 6.4) has to be divided with a crucified Christ. If Paul is not thereby abandoning his monotheism (and he seems to recognize no such tension in his affirmation of Jesus' Lordship elsewhere – Rom. 15.6; I Cor. 15.24–8; II Cor. 1.3; 11.31; Eph. 1.3, 17; Col. 1.3; even Phil. 2.11, 'Jesus Christ is Lord to the glory of God the Father'), then presumably he must intend something the same as in I Cor. 1 – *Christ who because he is now Lord now shares in God's rule over creation and believers, and therefore his Lordship is the continuation and fullest expression of God's own creative power.*[72] With this we are close to the third and final consideration.

(*c*) It may be that Paul is more consciously dependent on the wisdom language which he clearly echoes here (see above p. 165), and expects his readers to recognize the allusions (not unnaturally if they made so much of wisdom as I Cor. 1–2 implies). Certainly his splitting of the creative power of God between God the Father and Christ the Lord is precisely what we find in the Wisdom writings of pre-Christian Judaism (cf. above pp. 165f., 171–4). His aim, as we have seen, is to assert that the same divine power is active both in creation and in salvation; he achieves this by describing Christ the Lord in Wisdom language; his meaning then would be that the power of God in creation came so fully to expression in Christ's death and resurrection that it can be said of Christ what was said of Wisdom. That is to say, since presumably for Paul too Wisdom was not a being distinct from God, but was 'the wisdom of God' (I Cor. 1.24), God acting wisely, then *8.6b is not in fact a departure from Jewish monotheism*, but asserts simply that Christ is the action of God, Christ embodies the creative power of God. In other words, *Christ is being identified here not with a pre-existent being but with the creative power and action of God.* And the thought is not of Christ as pre-existent but of the creative act and power of God now embodied in a final and complete way in Christ.[73]

What then seems to us to be the first clear statement of Christ's pre-existence and an important landmark in the development of the doctrine of the incarnation may simply be Paul drawing out the implications of Christ's Lordship in response to the particular problems of the Corinthian

church and using the language of the pre-Christian Jewish wisdom tradition which was particularly apposite for the Corinthian would-be wise.
When we remove I Cor. 8.6 from this context it readily becomes a vehicle
for a christology of pre-existence – that is certainly true. But whether
Paul intended it to be thus understood is certainly more than a little
doubtful.

§24.3 I Cor. 10.1–4.

[1]I want you to know, brethren, that our fathers were all under the cloud and
all passed through the sea, [2]all were baptized into Moses in the cloud and in
the sea, [3]and all ate the same spiritual ($\pi\nu\epsilon\upsilon\mu\alpha\tau\iota\kappa\grave{o}\nu$) food [4]and all drank the
same spiritual drink. For they drank from the spiritual rock which was follow-
ing them; and the rock was Christ.

A reference to Christ as pre-existent is widely accepted here, principally
on the grounds of the parallel in Philo, *Leg. All.* II.86 – 'the flinty rock
is the wisdom of God . . . from which he satisfies the thirsty souls that
love God' (cf. Sir. 15.3).[74] 'Paul identifies Christ with this pre-existent
Wisdom.'[75] 'It was Christ himself who, in the form of a rock and in the
person of wisdom, gave life to the people of God, in the past as in the
present.'[76] I am much less certain however that this is what Paul had in
mind.

It is hardly likely that Paul intended to identify Christ as the wilderness
rock in any literal sense. So 'the rock was Christ' must denote some sort
of allegorical identification: the rock *represents* Christ in some way; as
water from the rock, so spiritual drink from Christ. But is it an allegory
of the realities *then* operative, or something more in the line of a *typological*
allegory of the spiritual realities now experienced by the Corinthians?
The latter seems the more probable, not least because Paul himself
describes the whole affair as τύποι (types) and as happening to the
Israelites τυπικῶς (typologically) in vv. 6 and 11. In vv. 1–2 it is fairly
obvious that the phrase 'baptized into Moses' has been modelled on the
more familiar Pauline formulation, 'baptized into Christ' (Rom. 6.3; I
Cor. 12.13; Gal. 3.27):[77] the passage 'through the sea' and 'under the
cloud' simply provided a typological parallel to the event of becoming a
member of Christ – hence 'baptized into Moses in the cloud and in the
sea' modelled on 'baptized into Christ in the Spirit' (cf. I Cor. 12.13).
The Israelites can be said to have been 'baptized' only as a reflection
backwards into the Exodus narrative of what the Corinthians had experienced; and can be said to have been 'baptized into Moses' only
because Moses served as the typological counterpart of Christ. Similarly
with the latter half of the parallel (vv. 3–4): the manna from heaven and
the water from the rock were simply types of the spiritual sustenance
received by Christians from Christ. In the first half of the midrash it was

unnecessary to identify Moses as the type of Christ – that would have been obvious anyway, and the 'baptized into Moses' rendered a specific identification superfluous. In the latter half however, the type of Christ is less obvious. So to clarify his exegesis Paul simply adds the interpretative note, 'the rock was Christ' – that is, to understand the full message of those wilderness narratives in their application to the situation of the Corinthians (vv. 6, 11) Paul's readers should see the rock then as an equivalent to Christ now.[78] In other words, Paul says to his readers: if you compare yourselves to the Israelites you will see what peril you are in. They experienced the equivalent of what we have experienced: they went through what we can call a baptism; they enjoyed what we can call 'spiritual food' – you only need to equate Moses with Christ (so 'baptized into Moses') and the rock with Christ to see how close the parallel is to your situation – and yet look what happened to them (vv.5, 9f.). 'These things have become types of, or for you' (v. 6); they 'happened to the Israelites typologically, but were written down for our instruction' (v. 11) – so be warned!

Paul then may indeed have been aware of Philo's identification of the rock with wisdom, or at least of Alexandrian Judaism's readiness to interpret the events of the exodus and wilderness wanderings allegorically. But where Philo used the historical narrative as a picture of the more timeless (Platonic) encounter between God and man, Paul used it as a picture of the eschatological realities that now pertain since the coming of Christ. In this typological interpretation it is not actually implied nor does it follow that Paul intended to identify Christ with Wisdom (since the rock = Wisdom, therefore Christ = the rock = Wisdom). Nor does it follow that Christ was thought of as having existed at the time of the wilderness wanderings. All we can safely say is that the allegorical interpretation of Philo (or of Alexandrian Judaism) may well have prompted the more typological interpretation of Paul: as rock = Wisdom in Alexandrian allegory, so rock = Christ in Christian typology.[79] In short, it is not sufficiently probable that I Cor. 10.4 refers to Christ as preexistent for us to make anything of it in our inquiry.

§24.4   Rom. 10.6–10.

[6]The righteousness based on faith speaks thus (Deut. 30.12–14): 'Do not say in your heart, Who will ascend into heaven? (that is, to bring Christ down), [7]or, Who will descend into the abyss?[280] (that is, to bring Christ up from the dead)'. [8]But what does it say? 'The word is near you, on your lips and in your heart' (that is, the word of faith which we preach). [9]For if you confess 'with your lips' Jesus is Lord, and believe 'in your heart' that God raised him from the dead, you will be saved. [10]For man believes with his heart and so is justified, and confesses with his lips and so is saved.

Here again it is quite often assumed that v. 6b is referring to the descent from heaven of the pre-existent Christ, that is, to the incarnation.[81] But here too such considerations as can be marshalled are less than wholly persuasive and the weight of the evidence seems to point in a different direction.

(a) The parallel with Bar. 3.29f. is indeed striking, the point again being that Baruch interprets the same passage (Deut. 30.12f.) with reference to Wisdom.[82]

> Who has gone up into heaven and taken her,
>   and brought her down from the clouds?
> Who has gone over the sea and found her . . .?

What is not clear however is whether we have simply an interpretative use of Deut. 30 prompted by Baruch's, or an actual identification of Christ with Wisdom. The latter depends on the hypothesis that Paul intended his readers to recognize the Baruch allusion and so to make the implied identification; but, as with the similar argument in I Cor. 10.4, the interpretative equation envisaged becomes a little complex – Christ = the 'commandment' of Deut. 30.11 = Wisdom by virtue of Baruch's interpretation. The alternative is that Deut. 30.11–14 offered a piece of rhetoric which attracted different schools within the Judaism of this period – Baruch applying it to Wisdom, Paul to Christ, and the tradition embodied in Targum Neofiti to the Torah.[83]

(b) A second possible consideration is the order of the clauses: the talk of bringing Christ down from heaven precedes the talk of bringing Christ up from the dead. If this is intended as a chronological order, the most obvious interpretation is to take the first (v. 6b) as a reference to the incarnation, since the second (v. 7b) is obviously a reference to the resurrection of Christ. On the other hand there is nothing to indicate whether a chronological order is intended. It is as likely that the order of the clauses has been determined solely by the order of the clauses in Deut. 30.12f. without any particular thought for the chronological relation of the locations within the Christ-event.[84]

(c) A third area of disagreement centres on the logic of Paul's interpretative comment. One possible interpretation is that Paul intended to answer Deuteronomy's rhetorical question with the reply: It is unnecessary; no one needs either to ascend or to descend, because Christ has already descended from heaven (incarnation), Christ has already risen from the dead (resurrection).[85] But this interpretation may be too narrowly restricted to vv. 6f. and neglect the context of the argument in Rom. 10. The point which Paul is trying to make focuses on the contrast between a 'righteousness based on the law' and a 'righteousness based on faith' (vv. 5f.). And to make his point he uses a text which itself is

making a somewhat similar contrast using the spatial imagery of farness
and nearness, the contrast between some far distant commandment (to
find and obey which requires too (?) great exertion from someone) and
the word so near at hand that obedience is straightforward (cf. Philo,
Virt. 183). Each of the schools that take up the passage also focus on the
spatial imagery and adapt it to make their own point. For Baruch it is
impossible for man to find Wisdom (hidden beyond his attainment),[86]
and unnecessary to do so because God who alone knows the way to
Wisdom has already given her to Israel in the law (Bar. 3.29–32, 36–4.4;
cf. Sir. 24.5). For the Targum Neofiti the point is that we do not need
another Moses to ascend to heaven to receive the law or another Jonah
to descend into the depths to bring it up – the law is near. . . . For Paul
the point seems to be that though Christ is distant from those still on
earth (he has ascended to heaven as he had already descended to the
abyss), righteousness is still possible. For righteousness is not something
to be attained by bringing Christ back to earth (nor does it depend on
his bodily presence on earth); righteousness comes rather through believing the word of preaching. Christ may seem far away, inaccessible to
earth-bound men, but the word of faith is near at hand.[87] In short, if the
farness-nearness contrast is as important as it seems, and the order of the
clauses is dependent simply on the order in Deuteronomy, as is quite
likely (see (*b*) above), then it is probable that in v. 6b Paul thinks of
heaven as the place where the ascended, exalted Christ *now* is.

(*d*) If the issue hangs more on parallels within the NT itself, John 3.13
might suggest itself as a possibility which would strengthen the likelihood
of a reference to incarnation in v. 6b (see above pp. 89f.). But the closer
parallel is undoubtedly Eph. 4.9f., which also, perhaps significantly, is a
similar sort of exposition of an OT verse (Ps. 68.18), also with a rather
striking similarity to the equivalent targum to this passage.[88]
Eph. 4.8–10 –

> [8]'Having ascended on high he led a host of captives, he gave gifts to men.' [9]In
> saying, 'He ascended', what does it mean but that he (had) also descended
> into the lower parts of the earth (κατώτερα μέρη τῆς γῆς)? [10]He who descend-
> ed is he who also ascended far above all the heavens (ὑπεράνω πάντων τῶν
> οὐρανῶν), that he might fill all things.

Not least of potential significance is the fact that thought of Christ's
ascension (to heaven) carries with it (again) the implication of a prior
descent to the lower parts of the earth (= 'the abyss' in Rom. 10.7?). To
be sure some commentators think the prior descent was to earth itself
(with 'of the earth' in apposition to 'lower parts') – that is, a reference
to the incarnation.[89] But this must be judged unlikely. (1) κατώτερα
μέρη τῆς γῆς would most naturally be understood as a synonym for

Hades, the place of the dead (cf. Ps. 63.9 LXX 62.10;[90] Tobit 13.2(S); also Ezek. 32.18). (2) A genitive following μέρη (parts) most naturally denotes the whole to which the parts belong – parts *of* the earth, rather than parts *which are* the earth. The argument for a genitive of apposition carries much less conviction.[91] (3) Verse 10 is most obviously framed as an antithesis to v. 9: 'far above all the heavens' corresponding to 'the lower/lowest parts of the earth'.

> If he mounted up above all heavens, the obvious antithesis is that he descended under the earth, not to the earth. This is confirmed by the definition of his purpose: 'in order that he might fill all things'. The 'he descended etc.' and 'he who ascended etc.' denote the outer limits of his journey, and between them lies the all which he fills. But if the one limit is the supreme height of heaven at the right hand of God (1.20), the other will not be earth, but the lowest depths of earth, i.e. the sphere of the underworld, the place of the dead.[92]

(4) What we seem to have here therefore is a variation on the regular association in earliest Christian thought of Christ's death with his resurrection – Christ died and was raised (Rom. 4.25; 8.34; 14.9; I Cor. 15.3–5; II Cor. 5.15; I Thess. 4.14).[93] As the confession of Christ's resurrection carries with it the thought of his (prior) death,[94] so the assertion of his ascension (a formulation determined by the quotation from Ps. 68.18) carries with it the thought of his (prior) descent into the place of the dead.[95]

All this strengthens the probability that a similar movement and balance of thought is intended in Rom. 10.6f.; that is, that thought of Christ's ascension (to heaven) goes hand in hand with thought of his descent into the place of the dead (the abyss).[96] An observation which seems to clinch the point is that the exposition of 'the word' which is 'near' is framed both with a similar movement and balance and with implied reference back to vv. 6f. The word of faith which is near is both the confession (with the lips) of Jesus' Lordship (in heaven) and the belief (in the heart) that God raised him from (the place of) the dead (10.9).

In short, the interpretation of Rom. 10.6f. (or indeed of Eph. 4.9) as a reference to the incarnation is too weakly based to allow us to use these verses as any kind of evidence that a doctrine of the incarnation was already emerging. In our present inquiry it would be wiser to leave Rom. 10.6f. on the sidelines alongside I Cor. 10.4. The most plausible indications of a Wisdom christology in the Pauline letters remain those which ascribe a role to the cosmic Christ in creation. We turn now to the most striking of these.

§24.5 *Col. 1.15–20.* It is widely accepted that this passage is a pre-Pauline hymn interpolated and interpreted to greater or less extent by

Paul.[97] Fortunately for our present purposes it is not necessary to inquire more closely into the original form of the hymn and the extent of the redaction, since the main issues of our inquiry are for the most part unaffected by the disagreements over these questions.[98] Whatever the correct analysis might be, the earlier form seems to have been shaped by wisdom language and to have been taken over by Paul without too much modification of this feature. Most would agree also that the original hymn was constructed in two strophes.[99]

> [15]*He is* the image of the invisible God, *the firstborn* of all creation;
> [16]*For in him* were created all things in heaven and on earth
>   (visible and invisible, whether thrones or dominions
>   or principalities or authorities);
>   *all things* were created *through him* and *to him*.
> [17]He is before all things,
>   and in him all things hold together
> [18]And he is the head of the body (the church).
>
> *He is* the beginning, *the firstborn* from the dead,
>   in order that in all things he might be pre-eminent.
> [19]*For in him* God in all his fullness was pleased to dwell,
> [20]And *through him* to reconcile *all things to him*,
>   making peace (through the blood of his cross) through him,
>   Whether things on earth or things in heaven.

The basic movement of thought also seems clear enough – from Christ's (pre-existent) role in creation (first strophe) to his role in redemption (second strophe), from his relationship with the old creation (protology) to his relationship with the new (eschatology).[100] But whether these first impressions are wholly accurate will depend on what our exegesis of the main clauses and concepts reveals.

(a) *The first strophe (vv. 15–18a).* 'He is the image (εἰκών) of the invisible God (v. 15a). An allusion here to Adam or use of Adam christology as such (as in Phil. 2.6 – see above pp. 114–17) is probably ruled out by v. 16. Much more likely is it that we are once again confronted with wisdom language (see above p. 165). The description of the first clause is very much that of Wisdom; for as we have seen, Wisdom is in fact the immanence of God, the reaching out of the exalted God which the wise man experiences here on earth, that which man may know of God and of God's will.[101] The problem for the pious was precisely the hiddenness of God and the difficulty of knowing his will. The wisdom tradition within Judaism solved the problem by reference to the Torah (see above pp. 170f.). But the Christians solved it by reference to Christ. This raises the possibility that already the thought is of the exalted Christ.[102] For the phrase speaks more of relationship to God than of relationship to creation,[103] and of the relationship that now (or still) pertains ('he *is* . . .'); he

who is thus spoken of represents God, makes God manifest.[104] And while
a Paulinist Christian could agree that God had revealed himself in some
degree through creation (cf. Rom. 1.20), the full revelation had only come
in and through Christ. Only of the Christ crucified and exalted would
Paul say 'he is the image of the invisible God' (II Cor. 4.4).[105]

'The firstborn of all creation' (v. 15b). These three words (πρωτότοκος
πάσης κτίσεως) have been among the most contested in the history of
NT interpretation:[106] was the intention to describe Christ as a *creature*,
the first created being (cf. v. 18b; Rom. 8.29), or to describe Christ's
sovereignty *over* all creation (cf. Ps. 89.27)? It is certainly difficult to give
the phrase a temporal meaning (πρωτο = προ) and at the same time to
avoid the former interpretation;[107] and most modern interpreters, conscious in part at least of the Arian controversy of the patristic church
(Arius was condemned precisely for his championship of the former
interpretation) have opted for the latter – the phrase denoting precedence
in rank rather than priority in time, first over creation rather than first
created being.[108] If this is the correct interpretation then perhaps once
again the thought is primarily of the exalted Christ – 'he, through whom
God already recognizable also in his creation becomes understandable'.[109]
Yet, since the dependence on the wisdom tradition is again so strong here
(above p. 165), we should recall that we have there a similar ambivalence
in the talk of Wisdom, with Wisdom spoken of both as *created* by God
(Prov. 8.22; Sir. 1.4; 24.9) and as the *agency* through which God created
(Prov. 3.19; Wisd. 8.4–6; Philo, *Det.* 54).[110] In which case we may well
have to think ourselves back into the context of thought *prior* to the Arian
controversies and accept that the hymn's and Paul's understanding at
this point shared something of that ambivalence.[111] The important thing
about personified wisdom was that it was a way of speaking of God's
creative activity, of God's creative acts from the beginning of creation.
Whether this means that God's creative power is prior to creation or can
be spoken of as the beginning of creation becomes a question only when
personified wisdom is understood as a personal being in some real sense
independent of God. It is more than a little doubtful whether this question
had ever occurred to Paul or to the hymn writer, presumably because
their thought of personified wisdom was wholly Jewish in character and
the language only became personalized for them when it was the exalted
Christ who was in view.[112]

'For in him were created all things ... (ὅτι ἐν αὐτῷ ἐκτίσθη τὰ
πάντα ...)' (v. 16a). Here it would appear to be quite clear that both
Paul and the pre-Pauline hymn writer are attributing pre-existence to
Christ. The attempt has been made to argue that the thought is of 'the
eschatological new creation' rather than of the old creation spoken of in
Genesis etc.[113] But though indeed the thought of the first strophe most

obviously follows as a corollary from that of the second (rather than the reverse),[114] it is hard to imagine any first-century reader interpreting the first strophe except as a reference to the 'old' creation, particularly in view of the Wisdom and Stoic parallels already adduced (above pp. 165f. and nn. 64, 69).[115] Rather more attractive is the suggestion that the hymnic form has compressed the thought, and that Paul intends the fuller meaning: in him in intention, as the one predetermined by God to be the fullest expression of his wise ordering of the world and its history.[116] This is certainly the way in which the writer to the Hebrews treats the aorist tenses in Ps. 8.5f.: that which the Psalmist referred to the creation of man, Hebrews refers to Christ, since only in Christ is the divine intention for man fulfilled (Heb. 2.6–9 – see above pp. 110f.). So possibly also with Col. 1.16: that which Jewish thought referred to divine wisdom in creation, the Colossian hymn refers to Christ, since only in Christ is the divine intention for creation fulfilled. Yet while this thought is certainly present ('all things were created . . . to him' – εἰς αὐτόν), the hymn also says 'all things were created through him' (δι' αὐτοῦ – both διά and εἰς – v. 16e).

We must rather orient our exegesis of v. 16a more closely round the recognition that once again we are back with wisdom terminology – as perhaps Ps. 104.24 (103.24 LXX) makes most clear (see also above pp. 165f.):[117]

Ps. 104.24 – πάντα ἐν σοφία ἐποίησας;

Col. 1.16 – ἐν αὐτῷ ἐκτίσθη τὰ πάντα.

What does this mean, to say that Christ is the creative power (= wisdom) of God by means of which God made the world?[118] Is the intention of the writer to ascribe pre-existence to Christ as such? Despite its obvious attractiveness that interpretation does not necessarily follow. This may simply be *the writer's way of saying that Christ now reveals the character of the power behind the world*. The Christian thought certainly moves out from the recognition that God's power was most fully and finally (eschatologically) revealed in Christ, particularly in his resurrection.[119] But that power is the same power which God exercised in creating all things – the Christian would certainly not want to deny that. Thus the thought would be that Christ defines what is the wisdom, the creative power of God – he is the fullest and clearest expression of God's wisdom (we could almost say its archetype).[120] If then Christ is what God's power/wisdom came to be recognized as, of Christ it can be said what was said first of wisdom – that 'in him (the divine wisdom now embodied in Christ) were created all things'.[121] In other words the language may be used here to indicate the continuity between God's creative power and Christ without the implication being intended that Christ himself was active in creation.[122]

'He is before all things (πρὸ πάντων) . . .' (v.17). The exegete here has the same problem with πρό as with πρωτότοκος in v. 15b: is it intended in a temporal sense,[123] or is it priority in the sense of superiority in status which is meant,[124] or is a deliberate ambiguity intended? The following clause ('in him all things hold together') if anything supports the first (or third) alternatives and sets us once again wholly in the same Wisdom/Logos context of thought (see above p. 166). In which case again probably we do not have a statement of Christ as pre-existent so much as a statement about the wisdom of God now defined by Christ, now wholly equated with Christ.

'He is the head of the body' (v.18a). Here wisdom parallels are lacking, though the idea of the cosmos as a body was widespread in the ancient world,[125] and Philo can call the Logos 'the head of all things' (*Qu. Ex.*II.117).[126] In the original hymn the thought was basically a variation on what had already been said – 'head' denoting not organic connection or similarity in substance but superiority (as in I Cor. 11.3).[127] But Paul (or already his source) has altered the thought by adding 'the church' as a definition of 'the body'. Why he thus narrowed the thought so dramatically is not clear. But the fact that he did so certainly strengthens the line of exegesis developed above. For one thing the addition of 'the church' indicates that for Paul at any rate the two strophes were not dealing with two clearly distinct subjects (cosmology and soteriology – see above p. 188 and n. 100). And for another he may even have given us a clue to his understanding of the earlier lines – as the body of the cosmos is now defined as the church, so the creative power (= wisdom) of God is now defined as Christ.

(*b*) *The second strophe (vv. 18b–20).* Our inquiry does not necessitate so full a study of the second half of the Colossian hymn, but we must observe some elements which strongly support the exegesis of the first half presented above.

'He is the beginning, the firstborn from the dead . . .' (v. 18b–d). It comes as something of a surprise that at the start of the second strophe we are still caught up in wisdom language (Prov. 8.22; Philo, *Leg. All.* I.43 – cited above p. 165); but that is simply a further reminder that we cannot separate the thought of the two strophes into distinct sections. Here there can be no dispute that it is the exalted Christ who is in view. And here the possible line of interpretation suggested by the first strophe becomes a necessity; for here it becomes clear that Christ can be described in wisdom terminology ('the beginning, the first') precisely because he is the firstborn from the dead. Not only so, but v. 18d makes it still clearer that Christ only gained the status as 'pre-eminent[128] in all things' as a consequence of his resurrection – ' . . . firstborn from the dead in order that he might become in all things pre-eminent' (ἵνα γένηται ἐν πᾶσιν αὐτὸς πρωτεύων). If this last line is an addition by Paul, as several assert,[129] we would have to conclude that Paul is taking the opportunity to underscore the meaning he intends his readers to take out of the first part of the hymn. Either way the line certainly strengthens the impression we have already gleaned from the hymn that when it talks about Christ's primacy in relation to 'all things' we are to think first and foremost of the risen and exalted Christ.

'For in him God in all his fullness was pleased to dwell' (ὅτι ἐν αὐτῷ εὐδόκησεν πᾶν τὸ πλήρωμα κατοικῆσαι – v. 19). The meaning of the word πλήρωμα in the present context has been the subject of almost as much controversy in the history of exegesis as v. 15b.[130] The verb εὐδό-κησεν (was pleased) certainly implies a personal subject,[131] and the parallel of Col. 2.9 indicates that Paul certainly would not think of 'the fullness' as an entity or a being distinct from God (πᾶν τὸ πλήρωμα τῆς θεότητος – 'all the fullness of God's being'). So that in the last analysis πᾶν τὸ πλήρωμα is best taken as a way of speaking about God himself – 'God in all his fullness'.[132] P. Benoit objects that 'in the last resort the divinity of Christ cannot be the effect of a "dwelling" of the divine essence in him, nor the result of the "good pleasure" of God. According to the whole teaching of Paul, Jesus is divine by nature; insofar as he is the Son of God, he does not become divine . . .'.[133] As an alternative interpretation he looks to Stoic thought in which the same word is used to denote the cosmos wholly interpenetrated by the one immanent and material divine principle.[134] In consequence he suggests that the thought is closer to v. 20 than to v. 17b and denotes the uniting of the whole cosmos in Christ by means of his reconciling death and resurrection.[135] This emphasis on Christ's death and resurrection accords well enough with the thought of the second strophe (cf. Eph. 1.10); though the order of clauses following the ὅτι (because) of v. 19 presumably implies that the indwelling of the fullness in Christ preceded Christ's work of reconciliation, which Paul at any rate understood as resulting from the cross – (hence his addition of 'through the blood of his cross'). But the main weakness of the whole argument is that once again it makes exegesis of a first-century text depend on the nuances of subsequent dogmatic formulations which emerged out of the christological controversies of later centuries (here particularly the Nestorian controversy).

What should rather inform our exegesis of this difficult concept is the recognition that somewhat as with v. 15 here too we are caught up in the ambivalence of Hellenistic-Jewish thought concerning the relationship between God and creation – the recognition that to speak of God in interaction with man and creation meant talking sometimes of God acting *directly* upon creation, at others of God acting *through* Wisdom (or Logos, or Spirit, etc.), and at yet others of God immanent within or *throughout* creation (cf. Ps. 139.7; Isa. 6.3; Jer. 23.24; Wisd. 1.7; 7.24; Philo, *Leg. All.* I.44; III.4; *Sac.* 67; *Gig.* 27, 47; *Qu. Gen.* IV.130; and further above pp. 171–4 and below p. 227).[136] In each case the thought was of *God* manifesting *himself* in one way or another to and in and through his creation. It is this tradition of thought in which our hymn writer seems to stand (and Paul too). That is to say, we should probably see here a Hellenistic Jewish Christian writer taking up this kind of thinking and using it to describe Christ, quite probably with conscious dependence on Stoic language.[137]

What then does he say of Christ? The assertion is that Christ (probably the earthly as well as exalted Jesus) is to be understood as the cosmic presence of God: that is to say, the action and manifestation of God which in one sense is inescapable throughout the cosmos has been focused in the man Jesus, or better in the whole 'Christ-event' (his life, death and resurrection); Christ embodied (Col. 2.9 – σωματικῶς, bodily)[138] God's creative energy in as complete a way as it is possible for the cosmos to perceive; which also means that Christ now is to be seen as the definition and norm by which that divine presence and energy can be recognized. The hymn speaks of this indwelling as an act of divine choice, but we should not press this language to insist on a more 'adoptionist' or Nestorian interpretation, any more than we should press the language of the first strophe to insist that the thought is of Christ as pre-existent. The two strophes become quite consistent as soon as we realize that *throughout the hymn we are not talking about God's creative power* per se, *nor of Christ* per se, *but of Christ whom Christians came to recognize as the embodiment and definition of that power* (= wisdom, fullness) – to express which the statements of the first strophe were as appropriate as those of the second.

(*c*) Since we need say no more about the second strophe we can *sum up*. A Christian apologetic (or self-understanding) before the wider circles of Stoic and Hellenistic Jewish thought was bound to attempt some kind of statement regarding the relation of the exalted Lord to creation and to God's power and purpose expressed in creation. Such an attempt was almost bound to use the terminology of the then current philosophical speculation – not least the prepositions 'from', 'in', 'through' and 'for'[139] – just as a Lutheran theologian today attempting to develop a particular view of the Lord's Supper is almost bound to use the prepositional formula 'in, with and under'. In both cases the sequence of prepositions would be used not because the user wished to press every preposition or to give a precision of meaning to every preposition, but because this was the accepted terminology for the subject at hand, and to omit a regularly used preposition could arouse suspicion that the statement was not sufficiently comprehensive. *Is then the Colossian hymn writer trying to say any more than that the creation and Christ must be understood in relation to each other: now that Christ has been raised from the dead the power and purpose in creation cannot be fully understood except in terms of Christ, and so too Christ cannot be fully understood except in terms of that wise activity of God* which has made the world what it is (ἐν), which gives the world its meaning (διά) and which will bring the world to its appointed end (εἰς).

Once again then we have found that what at first reads as a straight-forward assertion of Christ's pre-existent activity in creation becomes on closer analysis an assertion which is rather more profound – not of Christ as such present with God in the beginning, nor of Christ as identified with a pre-existent hypostasis or divine being (Wisdom) beside God, but *of Christ as embodying and expressing (and defining) that power of God which is the manifestation of God in and to his creation.*[140] The claim is not simply that salvation and creation are continuous, one and the same divine energy working in each, but also that the divine energy put forth in creation reaches its completion and goal in Christ, that the divine manifestation in and to creation reaches a wholeness and a fullness of expression in Christ which otherwise is to be found only in the totality of the cosmos. 'He who is the image of the invisible God, . . . he in whom God in all his fullness chose to dwell', shows us what God is like, as in creation so in salvation, more definitively than wonders of cosmos or words of Torah, psalmist, prophet and sage – such is the claim of Col. 1.15–20.

§24.6 *The significance of Paul's wisdom christology.* We have yet to look at the Wisdom christology of the post-Pauline writings. But since the Pauline expressions are so crucial in any attempt to penetrate back to the earliest understanding of the risen Christ as a cosmic power (the 'one Lord'), it is well to pause and attempt to gain as clear a perspective as possible on what Paul's intention and understanding was when he identified Christ as Wisdom. If the considerations marshalled above are at all on the right track, then in the three most important passages examined above (I Cor. 1.24, 30; 8.6; Col. 1.15–20) what we are probably witnessing is the attempt to spell out the significance of the earthly and exalted Christ in terms which Paul's interlocutors were already using, and to do so in such a way as to give these terms exclusive bearing on Christ. In particular, Paul picked up the widespread Wisdom terminology and found it an important tool for asserting the finality of Christ's role in God's purpose for man and creation. But in using Wisdom terminology he inevitably incorporated language and ideas which were appropriate to Wisdom, the personified function of God. It is at least questionable whether in so doing he intended to assert the pre-existence of Christ, or to affirm that Jesus was a divine being personally active in creation. This was simply the language which contemporary speculation and apologetic dictated that he must use if he was to assert the cosmic significance of Christ. If the writers of the OT and intertestamental Wisdom literature would have reacted against a too literal interpretation of their Wisdom material (see above pp. 171, 175f.), then Paul, equally firm in his monotheism (I Cor. 8.6), would likely have reacted in a similar way. In either case, to understand the Wisdom passages as ontological affirmations about 'Christ's eternal being' is most probably to misunderstand them.

Rather, when we set Paul against the background of pre-Christian Jewish talk of divine Wisdom, what he seems to be saying is this. The same divine wisdom which was active in creation we believe to have been active in Jesus; that is, the creator God was himself acting in and through Christ. Not only so, but that divine wisdom is now to be recognized as *wholly identified* with Jesus, so totally embodied in Jesus that the distinctive character of divine wisdom is to be read off not from creation or in terms of speculative knowledge (*gnōsis*), but from the cross (I Cor. 1.18–25); that is, what we actually see in Christ's life, death and resurrection is the very power by which God created and sustains the world (I Cor. 8.6; Col. 1.16f.). That divine concern which shaped the world and established the covenant with Israel, and which had hitherto been seen as expressed most clearly in the Torah, is now to be recognized as most fully and finally manifested in Jesus the crucified and risen one;[141] that is, Christ represents what God is, embodies without remainder the outreaching love of God, reflects as clearly as is possible the character of the one God (Col. 1.15, 19).

Since the point is so important, let me attempt to put it again in a slightly different way. We must grasp the fact that Paul was not seeking to win men to belief in a pre-existent being. He did not have to establish the viability of speaking of pre-existent Wisdom. Such language was widely used, common ground, and was no doubt familiar to most of his readers. Nor was he arguing that Jesus is a *particular* pre-existent being; he was not arguing, for example, that of the wide variety of so-called 'intermediary figures' in the Ancient Near East Jesus must be identified with one and not another. What he was saying is that Wisdom, whatever precisely that term meant for his readers, is now most fully expressed in Jesus – *Jesus is the exhaustive embodiment of divine wisdom; all* the divine fullness dwelt in him. The mistake which many make (unconsciously) is to turn Paul's argument round and make it point in the wrong direction. Because language which seems to envisage pre-existent divine beings is strange to modern ears, it is easy to assume (by an illegitimate transfer of twentieth-century presuppositions to the first century) that this is why the language was used (to promote belief in pre-existent divine intermediaries) and that Paul was attempting to identify Christ with or as such a being. But Paul's talk was of course conditioned by the cultural and cosmological presuppositions of his own day. So he was not arguing *for*

the existence of pre-existent divine beings or for the existence of any
particular divine being. Rather he was arguing *from* the presupposition
of his age that such language is meaningful. Granted that we can speak
meaningfully of the Wisdom of God active in creation, revelation and
salvation, then it is meaningful to identify Jesus as this Wisdom. And the
meaning is, given the understanding of this language within Jewish monotheism, that Jesus is to be seen as the wise activity of God, as the
expression and embodiment of God's wisdom more fully than any previous manifestation of the same wisdom whether in creation or in
covenant.

The same thing was happening of course throughout this earliest period
of Christian thought with the other so-called 'intermediary figures' of
pre-Christian Judaism. Jesus is understood as a manifestation of God's
power (I Cor. 1.24) and righteousness (Rom. 3.21–5; I Cor. 1.30). He is
identified as the image of God and as the embodiment of the glory of
God (II Cor. 3.18; 4.4, 6; see above p. 106). Most striking of all, as the
risen one he is identified with the life-giving Spirit of God (I Cor. 15.45;
see above p. 145), and, later on, in the prologue to John's Gospel, he is
identified with the Logos (Word) of God (John 1.1–18, see below §30.1)
– not surprisingly when we recall that in the literature of pre-Christian
Judaism, Wisdom, Word and Spirit were all near alternatives as ways of
describing the active, immanent power of God (see above §18 and below
pp. 219f., 229f.). The most obvious explanation of all this is that *the first
Christians were ransacking the vocabulary available to them in order that they might
express as fully as possible the significance of Jesus.* They were saying in effect
to Jew and Stoic and to those religious seekers influenced to any degree
by the syncretistic speculation of the time, 'What you understand by
divine Wisdom, the divine image, etc., all these deep and profound
insights into the reality of the cosmos and into relationships between the
divine and human which you express by those concepts, we see and
proclaim to have been most fully expressed and finally realized in Jesus
our Lord'. And if this is the case, then in the final analysis to speak of
Jesus as Wisdom and in the role of divine wisdom is just another way of
saying, 'God was in Christ reconciling the world to himself' (II Cor.
5.19), 'God in all his fullness was pleased to dwell in him' (Col. 1.19).

§25. CHRIST AS WISDOM IN THE POST-PAULINE
WRITINGS OF THE NEW TESTAMENT

Granted then that Paul's chief concern seems to have been to identify the
crucified and exalted Christ with the wisdom by which God created and
sustains the universe, what of the rest of the NT authors? What, in

particular, of the other passages which we cited above in §22 as bearing witness to the importance of Wisdom christology in first-century Christianity? Our simplest procedure is to follow them through in as near chronological order as possible (as in ch. II), though since relative dates and places of origin of the documents in question remain obscure we will look at them independently and not attempt to analyse the interrelationship of the particular formulations.

§25.1 *Matthew.* Like Paul, Matthew seems to identify Jesus as Wisdom. What is particularly important in Matthew's case is that *he achieves this identification by his editing of his source Q.* We can easily demonstrate this by examining the major Wisdom passages in Matthew and comparing them with their Lukan counterpart.

(a) *Luke 7.35/Matt. 11.19.* The text is the conclusion to a brief passage which both have clearly drawn from Q (Luke 7.31–5/Matt. 11.16–19), wherein it formed what is clearly the final element of a collection of sayings relating to John the Baptist (Luke 7.18–35/Matt. 11.2–19). Apart from the last verse the agreement is so close that we can have little doubt as to Q's meaning.[142]

> To what then shall I compare this generation? It is like children sitting in the
> market places and calling to the others –
>   'We piped to you, and you did not dance;
>   we wailed, and you did not mourn.'
> For John came neither eating nor drinking, and they say,
>   'He has a demon'.
> The Son of Man came eating and drinking, and they say,
>   'Behold, a glutton and a drunkard,
>   a friend of taxcollectors and sinners'!

The conclusions of the two versions are however significantly different:

> Luke – 'Yet wisdom is justified by all her children';
> Matthew – 'Yet wisdom is justified by her deeds.'

It is generally agreed that 'children' is more original than 'deeds', and that Matthew has introduced the thought of Wisdom's 'deeds' just as he prefaced the collection of sayings relating John and Jesus by referring to 'the deeds of the Christ' (11.2).[143] But this means that he has identified 'the Christ' as Wisdom – Christ is Wisdom whose deeds John heard about in prison and about which 'this generation' complained.[144] Was Matthew then simply expressing what was already implied in Q? The answer is partly obscured by the question whether 'all' was already in Q or was added by Luke; did Q read '. . . by all her children', or simply, '. . . by her children'? The probability is that 'all', a favourite word of Luke, was indeed inserted by Luke, quite possibly with reference back to

v. 29 ('all the people ... justified God').[145] In this case Wisdom's 'children' would most probably be John and Jesus themselves:[146] the lives and ministries of John and Jesus, despite their different styles (ascetic/ festive), were both expressions of divine Wisdom.[147] If however 'all' did belong to the Q version, then Wisdom's 'children' would hardly be John and Jesus themselves. The meaning would then be that all Wisdom's children are either John and Jesus with their respective disciples,[148] or simply the disciples of John and Jesus. In the latter case it would still not be possible to identify Jesus as Wisdom, however, since in the context John and Jesus are lumped together on the same level – the pericope defends both life-styles as 'the ways of Wisdom'. In which case the meaning of Q would be that both John and Jesus are messengers or *envoys* of Wisdom whose ways they show to their followers.[149] This is most probably the meaning Luke intended (with the allusion to v. 29). Thus, either way, Matthew has gone beyond Q; and an identification of Jesus as Wisdom cannot readily be discerned prior to Matthew.[150] *Where Q at most presented Jesus as the envoy of Wisdom and most probably as the child of Wisdom, Matthew clearly took the step of identifying Jesus as Wisdom herself.*

(*b*) *Matt. 11.25–30/Luke 10.21f.* We have cited Matt. 11.28–30 above (p. 164). However vv. 28–30 are exclusive to Matthew, and the probability, as most recent commentators agree,[151] is that Q contained only Matt. 11.25–7/Luke 10.21f.[152]

> In that hour Jesus said,
> 'I thank you, Father, Lord of heaven and earth,
> that you have hidden these things from the wise and understanding
> and revealed them to babes;
> even so, Father, for such was your gracious will.
> All things have been handed over to me by my Father;
> and no one knows the Son except the Father,
> and no one knows the Father except the Son
> and anyone to whom the Son chooses to reveal him'.

That this can properly be called a Wisdom saying (even apart from Matt. 11.28–30) is now widely accepted.[153] On the question of the relation between Jesus and Wisdom in this saying however opinion has been more divided. Although the attempt to find a consistent Wisdom christology (Christ = Wisdom) in the Q material has met with a firm rebuttal from several scholars,[154] the case is thought by several to be at its strongest in the above saying. In particular the *exclusivity* of the mutual knowledge of the Father and the Son in v. 27 has been highlighted as something that elsewhere is said only of Wisdom – that only God knows Wisdom (Job. 28.1–27; Sir. 1.6, 8; Bar. 3.15–32) and only Wisdom knows God (cf. Prov. 8.12; Wisd. 7.25ff.; 8.3f., 8f.; 9.4, 9, 11).[155]

However, the parallels are not so precise or persuasive as at first appears. (1) The first line of v. 27 ('all things have been handed over to me by my Father') may be as much influenced by apocalyptic thought ('all things' – cf. particularly Dan. 7.14) as by wisdom.[156] (2) In the clearest parallels to v. 27b ('no one knows the Son except the Father'), viz. Job 28, Sir. 1 and Bar. 3, what is hidden to men and known only to God is the *source*, the locus of Wisdom (Job 28.20, 23; Sir. 1.6; Bar. 3.27, 29–31, 36), which, for ben Sira and Baruch at least, is now sited in the Torah (Sir. 24.23; Bar. 3.37–4.1). (3) The Father-Son imagery sits awkwardly with the identification of Jesus as Wisdom, since Wisdom is more naturally spoken of as 'the daughter of God' (as in Philo, *Fuga* 52; *Qu. Gen.* IV.97). (4) The final clause of Matt. 11.27 ('anyone to whom the Son chooses to reveal him') is much less easy to parallel in the Wisdom tradition. The only parallel which F. Christ cites (Wisd. 7.28) is neither very close nor does it express the exclusiveness of the Son's mediation of the knowledge of the Father.[157]

At all these points indeed we may say the closer parallel is to be found in *Israel's claim to election by Yahweh*.[158] (1) In Dan. 7.13f. it is the human figure representing 'the saints of the Most High' who is given dominion over all the nations of the earth. (2) The claim to election, which has of course its own note of exclusivity, is quite often expressed in terms of being 'known' by Yahweh (Gen. 18.19; Ex. 33.12; Num. 16.5 LXX; Jer. 1.5; Hos. 13.5; note particularly Amos 3.2, 'You only have I known of all the families of the earth') and of the chosen ones 'knowing' Yahweh (Ex. 33.13; Ps 9.10; 36.10; Isa. 43.10; Jer. 9.24; Dan. 11.32).[159] (3) The Father-Son imagery is characteristic of Israel's attempt to express its relationship of election with Yahweh (Ex. 4.22; Jer. 31.9; Hos. 11.1; see above p. 15). And one of the closest parallels to Matt. 11.27's talk of a *son knowing* God as *Father* is what is said of the righteous man (within Israel) –

> He claims to have knowledge of God,
> and calls himself a son of the Lord.
>   . . .
> and boasts of having God for his father (Wisd. 2.13, 16; cf. Sir. 4.10; 51.10).[160]

In other words, one of the closest parallels to Matt. 11.27 is from the Wisdom literature indeed, but it speaks of the righteous Israelite, the *disciple* of Wisdom, not of Wisdom herself, as 'the son of God'. (4) A feature of Israel's prophetic message, particularly the Isaianic tradition, is the hope that the knowledge of God given to Israel will become more widespread (Isa. 11.9; 19.21; Hab. 2.14). In Second Isaiah the role of Israel and the Servant in fulfilling this hope is emphasized (Isa. 42.6; 43.10; 49.6) – that is, Israel's role as *mediator* of the light that had shone upon Israel. In these latter passages the specific idea of 'knowledge' does not occur, but it is used in the striking parallel passage where Cyrus is

hailed and commissioned as the Lord's 'messiah' 'that men may know
. . . that there is none besides me' (Isa. 45.1, 6).

All these parallels heighten the probability that *Jesus is being seen in
Matt. 11.27 more as the one who represents Israel in the last days*, or represents
the Israel of the last days, *than as Wisdom* – an emphasis which would
certainly accord with Matthew's own elsewhere (2.15; 4.3, 6 – see above
p. 49). Indeed it is quite probable that the *exclusivity* of the revelation
claim made in Matt. 11.27 should be traced back not to the Wisdom
parallels but to *the claims Jesus made concerning himself*: the claim that the
mutual knowing of Yahweh and Israel had come to fullest expression in
the eschatological immediacy of his knowledge of God's will ('Amen',
'But I say')[161] as God's son (see above pp. 28f.); the claim that he came
as the *climax* of the prophetic tradition (see above pp. 137f.);[162] and the
claim that through his ministry was already being realized the apocalyptic
hope for the coming of the kingdom (see above pp. 28, 137), the estab-
lishment of the new covenant (I Cor. 11.25; Luke 22.20),[163] wherein,
according to Jer. 31.31–4, all would 'know' Yahweh 'from the least to the
greatest'. It is not necessary for the present discussion to investigate
further whether Jesus actually said the words ascribed to him in Matt.
11.27;[164] what can be maintained with sufficient strength is that Matt.
11.27 expresses in summary (and rather formal) terms claims which were
implicit (and occasionally explicit) elsewhere in his ministry. In which
case the argument that Matt. 11.27 can only be made sense of against a
Wisdom background falls to the ground. Quite as coherent, indeed a
more coherent background is Jesus' own claim to a unique intimacy with
his Father and to an eschatological commissioning and authorization
from his Father.

In short, we may fairly conclude that the exclusivity of the mutual
knowledge of Father and Son in Matt. 11.27 is less likely to be that of
God and Wisdom, and more likely to be that of God and the one who
had been specially favoured with the knowledge of God and who had
been specially charged with the task of making God's purpose known and
of bringing God's purpose to completion among men. That is to say, in
Matt. 11.27 it is more likely that Q is merging apocalyptic and wisdom
motifs (as in Luke 7.35) to present Jesus as Wisdom's eschatological
envoy rather than as Wisdom, as the righteous man *par excellence* who
knows God as Father and has the task of bringing God's final wisdom to
men.

The situation is different however as soon as we move from Q to
Matthew, for it is quite clear that in the three verses added by Matthew
(Matt. 11.28–30) Jesus speaks *as Wisdom* and not merely as Wisdom's
envoy. In ben Sira 51.23–6, on which the Matthean passage seems to be
moulded, the teacher of wisdom invites pupils to draw near and put their

necks under the yoke of wisdom, and testifies to the rest he himself has
found in his labour (under Wisdom's yoke). In Matt. 11.28–30 Jesus calls
men to take *his* yoke upon them and promises them rest under *his* yoke
and burden. That is to say, *in Matt. 11.28–30 Jesus presents himself as the
Wisdom to whom ben Sira pointed his pupils.*[165] It would appear then that once
again Matthew has gone beyond Q and by his editorial insertion *has
transformed the christology of Q into a full-blown expression of Wisdom christology.*

  (c) *Luke 11.49–51/Matt. 23.34–6.*

  Luke 11.49 – Therefore also the Wisdom of God said,
               'I will send them prophets and apostles,
               some of whom they will kill and persecute',[166] . . .

  Matt. 23.34 – (Jesus' words) 'Therefore I send you prophets
               and wise men and scribes,
               some of whom you will kill and crucify,
               and some you will scourge in your synagogues
               and persecute from town to town . . .'

As the continuation of the passage makes clear, what we have here is
undoubtedly a Q saying. Luke's version is probably nearer the Q form.[167]
In particular, it is much more probable that Luke's attribution of the
saying to 'the Wisdom of God' is original than that he altered an I-saying
of Jesus in such a wholly exceptional way.[168] Thus in Q Jesus quotes a
saying of Wisdom in which divine Wisdom promises to send prophets
(and apostles) to Israel. Where Q derived the saying from is a matter of
debate. That it comes from a lost apocryphal book is possible;[169] but in
the absence of any other evidence for the existence of such a work this
must remain a hypothesis of last resort on which we may fall back if all
others prove unsatisfactory. It is also possible that the saying first
emerged as a prophetic utterance within the earliest Christian communities in Palestine;[170] but why it should then be attributed to Wisdom
rather than directly to the exalted Jesus becomes something of a puzzle.
It is rather more likely that in its original form the saying gave a bird's
eyeview of Israel's history ascribed to personified Wisdom, as particularly
in Wisd. 10–11[171] – not with any particular text in view, though perhaps
the saying should be regarded as a composite quotation of various pre-
Christian texts (note especially Wisd. 7.27 – 'prophets'; I Kings 14.6
LXX – 'apostle').[172] In this case the Q saying could very well go back to
Jesus himself, although we should not entirely dismiss the possibility that
it comes from a very early stage of the Palestinian Christian community's
self-understanding when prophetic inspiration was in some cases at least
attributed to divine Wisdom and not yet to the exalted Christ, or from
a particular community which greatly valued the Jewish Wisdom trad-

ition and saw Jesus as the climax of Wisdom's 'stret:hing out her hand' to Israel and rejection by Israel (cf. Prov. 1.20–31).

Be that as it may, the important point for us is that in Q Jesus clearly speaks as the ambassador or spokesman of Wisdom,[173] a presentation wholly consistent with the other Wisdom passages in Q examined above. To argue, alternatively, that Q intended an equation between the Wisdom that spoke in the past promising to send prophets and apostles, and Jesus who referred to Wisdom's saying but who now as the exalted one also sends prophets and apostles, is to force the obvious meaning of the passage.[174] To be sure Matthew interprets the saying that way, but as we shall see, he does so only by making significant alterations to the wording of the text.

When we turn to Matthew's version it becomes equally clear that he has transformed the saying of Wisdom into a saying of Jesus himself.[175] Whether his readers would have recognized here an equation of Jesus with Wisdom is uncertain; it would depend on whether the Q saying was already well known as a saying of Wisdom, Christian or pre-Christian in origin. But we today can certainly see that this was Matthew's own view: he has no difficulty in attributing a saying of Wisdom to Jesus, presumably because for him Jesus *is* Wisdom. Whether he thereby thought of Jesus as the incarnation of pre-existent Wisdom, or simply identified the exalted Christ as Wisdom somewhat as Paul did (see above §24) is less clear. The fact that he altered Q's future tense (ἀποστελῶ – I will send) to a present tense (ἀποστέλλω – I am sending) strongly suggests that he was thinking of his own present situation;[176] that is to say, the 'prophets, wise men and scribes' (cf. 13.52) probably denoted those commissioned by the exalted Christ for ministry, for evangelism and apologetic in face of an increasingly hostile rabbinic Judaism (hence the setting of the Q saying within the context of Matt. 23; cf. 5.10–12; 10.17,23).[177] So too if Matthew thought of Jesus being begotten (coming to be) as Son of God in his conception by the creative power of the Spirit (Matt. 1.18–20 – see above pp. 49f.) it would be less than likely that he also thought of him as pre-existent Wisdom. Once again then, whatever the precise character of Matthew's Wisdom christology we can say with confidence that Matthew has transformed a Q saying, in which Jesus was presented simply as the spokesman of Wisdom, into a vehicle of Wisdom christology, where Jesus is identified as Wisdom; *in Matt. 23.34–6 as elsewhere Jesus speaks not merely as the spokesman of Wisdom but as Wisdom herself.*

(d) *Matt. 23.37–9/Luke 13.34f.*

O Jerusalem, Jerusalem, killing the prophets and stoning those who are sent to you! How often would I have gathered your children together as a hen gathers her brood under her wings, and you would not! Behold your house is forsaken. And I tell you, you will not see me until you say, 'Blessed is he who comes in the name of the Lord' (Ps. 118.26).

This is one of the most difficult of the Q logia to assess in our present inquiry. There are fewer problems regarding the original form of the Q text.[178] But the meaning which it had for the Q community or collector is much less clear. The problem centres on the relation between the first two sections: is the one who speaks of gathering the children of Jerusalem ('I') the same as the one who sends the prophets? In favour of an affirmative answer is the fact that both statements are appropriate as applied to Wisdom: Wisdom sends prophets (as already in Q – Luke 11.49; cf. Prov. 9.3; Wisd. 6.16; Sir. 24.7–12; I Enoch 42.1f.), and the imagery of the mother hen is appropriate to maternal Wisdom (cf. Sir. 1.15).[179] Yet if the saying did follow Luke 11.49–51/Matt. 23.34–6 in Q,[180] then according to Q Jesus *distinguished* himself from Wisdom as one of those sent by Wisdom (the climax of the prophetic appeal to Jerusalem). The same is true if Luke is closer to the Q order[181] and if Luke 13.(31–)33 also belongs to Q, since in Luke 13.33f. Jesus clearly speaks as one who stands in the tradition of the prophets who must perish in Jerusalem. In either case it becomes much less likely that Q understood Jesus both as the one who sends prophets and the 'I' who would gather the children of Jerusalem. It is of course quite possible that the context of our saying in both Matthew and Luke is redactional[182] and that it was an independent saying preserved elsewhere in Q. But even so it is unlikely that Q would intend a meaning for this saying different from that in the sayings already examined. Only if the allusion to Wisdom was more specific and clear would it be necessary to postulate a Wisdom christology in our present logion different from that found elsewhere in Q.

The obvious alternative is that the one who laments over Jerusalem is *not* the one who sends the prophets, but he who has been sent as the climax of the prophetic appeal to Israel. It need not be assumed that the 'how often' requires a series of actual visits to Jerusalem as such, either by individual prophets in the past or by Jesus himself.[183] The saying could simply be an appropriately poignant expression of Jesus' frustration and disappointment at his rejection by the religious authorities centred in Jerusalem. The picture of a protective mother hen is wholly familiar from the OT and does not embody any specific allusion to Wisdom (cf. Deut. 32.11; Ruth 2.12; Ps. 17.8; 36.7; 57.1; 61.4; 63.7; 91.4; Isa. 31.5),[184] although it could be argued that, since the imagery usually describes God's protectiveness, he who used it for his own concern thereby claimed to have been divinely commissioned and to embody the 'steadfast love' of Yahweh for Israel. In other words Jesus could again be speaking here simply as the messenger of Wisdom, the one who brings God's final appeal to his people.[185] This would certainly accord with the christology of the other Q sayings examined above, especially if the position of our present saying was close to that of Luke 11.49 (as in Matthew) or that of Luke 13.33 (if Q).

The latter alternative therefore gives the more probable interpretation of the Q saying. In which case we may simply note that once again Q has combined terminology such as we find in the Wisdom literature with more apocalyptically coloured language (Luke 13.35 par.).[186] This combination (Jesus as the messenger of Wisdom, with Jesus as the agent of the apocalyptic climax) is clearly a characteristic of Q (see above (a) and (b) – p. 200).

When we move on to the Matthean level of meaning however it becomes clear that Matthew's redaction of the previous Q saying (c) has the effect of transforming our present logion into a further statement of Wisdom christology. For since in Matt. 23.34 Jesus himself is the one who sends prophets and wise men and scribes, in Matt. 23.37 he must again be the sender of the prophets rather than the sent. Again it is unclear whether the perspective in Matthew is that of pre-existent Wisdom (OT prophets) or that of the exalted Christ (early Christian prophets, Stephen, etc.). But the tie-in to the apocalyptic perspective of the second verse, which Matthew preserves, certainly suggests that he was thinking in terms of the exalted Christ (soon) to come again (cf. 10.23).[187] Be that as it may, anyone who recognized the Wisdom terminology used in Matt. 23.34–9 would readily recognize Matthew's intention to identify Jesus as Wisdom. In short, *whereas in Q Jesus seems to speak as the messenger of Q, once again in Matthew Jesus speaks as Wisdom herself.*

§25.2 *The significance of Matthew's Wisdom christology.* The synoptic traditions give us a unique opportunity to see into the developing thought of the first Christians. Because we can compare Matthew and Luke with their sources (Mark and Q), we can frequently detect where Matthew and Luke have modified or expanded the traditions about Jesus which they received; and where a consistent redaction becomes evident we are wholly justified in speaking of Matthew's or Luke's theology on that point. Not all the redactions are of great significance, but in the present case we can say with some confidence that we have detected a particular christological emphasis of Matthew which emerges specifically in his redaction of Q. Not only so but, more important, the difference between Q and Matthew is such that we can hardly avoid speaking of a *development* in earliest christology as we move from Q to Matthew.[188]

The facts are straightforward. The Q collector was clearly conscious of the Wisdom implications and overtones of his material: the form of his collection of sayings marks it out as belonging most closely to what J. M.

Robinson has appropriately dubbed *Logoi Sophōn* (Sayings of the Sages);[189] in Q much of the material is best classified as wisdom sayings;[190] and Jesus is specifically presented as one sent by divine Wisdom in at least two of the sayings examined above ((*a*) and (*c*)). The presentation of Jesus is clear, consistent and obviously deliberate, so that we can speak quite properly of a Q christology in which Jesus is understood as the *messenger* of Wisdom. Matthew however has taken over the Q material and edited it so that its meaning is different from that of Q, Jesus being *identified* as Wisdom. Here too the redaction and the presentation is clear, consistent and obviously deliberate. Consequently *it becomes impossible to deny a significant difference and a clear cut development between the christology of Q and the christology of Matthew.*

So far as the *significance* of this development is concerned it could of course be argued that the different christologies amount to the same thing – both seeing Jesus as bringing the same climactic appeal of God to Israel, as embodying the same apocalyptic revelation of God to Israel. But in terms of specific Wisdom christology the difference and the development cannot be denied. Nor can it be denied that the move from one to other opens up a whole range of new possibilities for assessing the significance and status of Christ – Jesus as messenger of Wisdom is one thing, Jesus as Wisdom is another. Such a development opens up in fact all the possibilities of moving from a christology which thinks of Jesus as (quantitatively) *different in degree* from earlier prophets to one which thinks of Jesus as (qualitatively) *different in kind* from earlier prophets, of moving from a christology which speaks of Jesus' divinely given *function* to one which speaks of Jesus' metaphysical *status*, of moving, in other words, beyond the impasse in which we found ourselves in discussing Jesus' sense of sonship (§4.5). Yet we must also note that *Matthew betrays no consciousness on his part that he is taking such a dramatic step* (neither did Paul), so that perhaps the difference was not so great for him after all; as we saw above, he seems to think of the *exalted* Jesus as Wisdom and to avoid the implication that Jesus spoke as pre-existent Wisdom (see (*c*) and (*d*)). Perhaps then it is after all the case that what appears to *us* to be significantly different statements in fact merged imperceptibly into each other in Matthew's thinking – Jesus as the final messenger of Wisdom, Jesus as the closest intimate with God, Jesus as the fullest embodiment of divine revelation and concern, Jesus as Wisdom. In other words, it may well be the case with Matthew as with Paul, that distinctions between degree and kind, between function and status, were not part of their christological thinking. They elaborated what to us is a Wisdom christology with clear implications about Christ's ontological status and preexistent being, but *to them was simply a more forceful way of saying what had already been said before* – Jesus as the one through whom God in his wisdom had made his final appeal to men and who, as the exalted one, still provides the medium and locus for the decisive encounter between God and man. We shall have to attempt a firmer conclusion about these matters in the final chapter when we have completed our survey of the relevant NT evidence. For the moment we must simply note the difference and development between the christologies of Q and Matthew and leave the significance of that development an open question.

Finally we should also note that *Matthew stands alone within the Synoptic tradition in maintaining a full Wisdom christology*, that is, in identifying Jesus as Wisdom.[191] This means: (1) that not only Q but also *Luke* does not entertain a Wisdom christology (in the sense we have been using the phrase);[192] (2) that so far as the evidence of the Synoptic tradition is concerned Wisdom christology may have been a specific development within the Hellenistic Jewish Christianity which Matthew represents; and (3) that when we press back behind Q, insofar as we reach back to the actual words of Jesus himself, the probability is that Jesus' own understanding of his relation to Wisdom is represented by Q rather than by Matthew.[193] In other words, *if Jesus thought of himself at all in relation to Wisdom it was as Wisdom's (eschatological) messenger*, and the earliest example of an actual equation of Jesus with Wisdom remains Paul's first letter to the Corinthians.

§25.3   Of the passages mentioned in the introduction to this chapter (§22) there remain those in Hebrews and John. It will be unnecessary to discuss the latter here: the main passage is John 1.1–18 which is more appropriately dealt with in ch. VII (§30.1; on Rev. 3.14 see p. 247); the other Wisdom motifs are few in number (see above p. 166) and of little additional significance within the context of a Son of God christology which totally dominates the rest of the Gospel (see above §6.5).

Hebrews 1.1–3 seems to incorporate (part of) an early Christian hymn,[194] set out below in five lines:

> In times past God spoke to the fathers through the prophets at many times and in diverse ways. ²But in these last days he spoke to us through a Son,
>   whom he appointed heir of all things,
>   through whom also he made the world (τοὺς αἰῶνας),
>   ³who is the radiance (ἀπαύγασμα) of God's glory
>   and the stamp (χαρακτὴρ) of his very being,
>   sustaining (φέρων) all things by his word of power.
> Having made purification for sins, he sat down at the right hand of the majesty on high . . .

The hymn is a striking expression of Wisdom christology. As we saw at the beginning of the chapter ἀπαύγασμα may well allude to Wisd. 7.26 – the only occurrence of the word in the LXX. In addition we can now see how closely the lines of the hymn (fragment) parallel those of Col. 1.15–17: If we may take the liberty of rearranging the lines in Col. 1 the parallel will become clearer –

Col. 1.16a   in him all things were created,
     15   who is the image of the invisible God,[195]
          the firstborn of all creation;
    17b   all things hold together in him.

Bearing in mind the extent to which Col. 1.15–17 echoes Wisdom language (above pp. 165f. and §24.5), it becomes clear that in Heb. 1.1–3 and Col. 1.15–17 we have a way of speaking about Christ in Wisdom terms in relation to the creation of the world which was fairly widespread at this time in Asia Minor and elsewhere (cf. also Rev. 3.14 – below p. 247).

    The echoes of Philo seem at first to be even stronger in the Hebrews hymn. (1) 'Whom he appointed heir of all things' may perhaps recall Philo's treatise on Gen. 15.2–18, *Quis Rerum Divinarum Heres* (Who is the heir of divine things), though of course the idea of an inheritance given by God (particularly the promised land) is typically Jewish and had already been taken up by Paul (Rom. 4.13f.; 8.17; I Cor. 6.9f.; 15.50; Gal. 3.18, 29; 4.1, 7, 30; 5.21; Eph. 1.14, 18; 5.5; Col. 3.24).[196] (2) 'Through whom he made the world' is very similar to what is said of the Logos in *Sac.* 8, *Immut.* 57, *Migr.* 6 and *Spec. Leg.* I.81. (3) Philo speaks of man's mind or soul as the ἀπαύγασμα of the divine Logos, of the divine nature (*Opif.* 146; *Spec. Leg.* IV.23). (4) More frequently he speaks of the human soul as receiving an impression (χαρακτήρ) of some virtue or of divine power (particularly *Leg. All.* I.61; *Sac.* 60; *Det.* 77; *Conf.* 102; *Heres* 38, 181, 294), or of being itself the impression either of divine power (*Det.* 83) or indeed specifically of the Logos (*Leg. All.* III.95–7). We may note again particularly *Plant.* 18 –

> our great Moses likened the fashion of the reasonable soul to no created thing, but averred it to be a genuine coinage of that dread Spirit, the divine and invisible one, signed and impressed by the seal of God, the stamp (χαρακτήρ) of which is the eternal Word.

(5) For parallels to 'sustaining all things by his word of power' see above p. 166.

    There are however significant differences between Philo and Heb. 1.2f.[197] Philo uses ἀπαύγασμα and χαρακτήρ more of the human soul than of the divine Logos (cf. IV Macc. 15.4), though as we shall see, the understanding of the Logos as the radiance of light streaming from the archetypal Light of God is typically Philonic (see below pp. 226f.), and thought easily slides over from the seal which produces the impression to the impression itself (see the discussion on Philo below §28.3). Moreover, in Philo the one who sustains all things is God, not the Logos – the Logos is more the *prop* by which he sustains the world (above p. 166). This latter observation highlights an oddity about the Hebrews passage:[198] viz. that Christ fulfilling the role of Wisdom or Word is said to sustain all things 'by his word of power' – the Word sustains by his word (cf. Heb. 11.3).[199]

All this indicates that the influence from Wisdom theology, as in Col. 1.15–17, is stronger at this point than that from the Logos of Philo. But it also suggests something of the ambivalence which is bound to be present in language which provides a way of speaking of God acting on the world and on the individual – are we in the end talking here about God himself as creator and sustainer, or about the man who is the perfect reproduction of the very being of God, or about the 'intermediate' Wisdom-Logos? Our study in this chapter indicates that the answer is probably something of *all three*; for the Wisdom of God is God himself reaching out in and through his creation to man, seeking to draw man to him and to impress the stamp of his image upon him.

It is probably this ambivalence which enabled the writer to the Hebrews to take over the hymn. In fact Hebrews has nothing else that can readily be labelled 'Wisdom christology'; so we can only recognize the significance of the hymn for the author of the letter when we set the hymn into its context in Hebrews. Here the first thing to become apparent is that the author uses the hymn (fragment) somewhat in the way that Paul used the Son of God confession in Rom. 1.3f., as part of his opening statement; and as there, so here – whatever the earlier formula/hymn meant, the present author has taken it over and made it his own.

Turning to the christology of the immediate context it becomes evident that *the author is thinking primarily of the exalted Christ*: Christ is the Son who is the eschatological climax ('in these last days') to all God's earlier and more fragmentary revelation (vv. 1–2a); that climactic revelation focuses on his sacrifice for sins, and exaltation to God's right hand (vv. 3d–e).[200] When we pursue this line of thought we find ourselves once again in the puzzle of Hebrews' understanding of Jesus' sonship – as a status which in some sense is pre-existent, but which in another is one to which he was appointed as one who suffered and was exalted (particularly 5.1–10; see above §6.4).[201] Probably significant then is the fact that the first line of the hymn ('whom he appointed heir of all things') shares the same ambivalence, since the verb used (ἔθηκεν) can mean either 'appointed' in eternity or 'designated' in advance.[202]

Moreover we recall how Hebrews presents a classic statement of Adam christology in Heb. 2.6–18 (above pp. 110f.) – Christ as the one in whom God's original plan for man finally (or eschatologically) came to fulfilment – that is in Christ the exalted-after-suffering one (the last Adam). Here we are back in the image/stamp (εἰκών/χαρακτήρ) ambivalence (1.3) – Christ as the one who is the perfect image of God, in the sense that he was the perfect man, the one who fulfilled God's master plan (2.6–9), the one through whom God spoke fully and finally (1.1f.).

The position therefore seems to be this: the Wisdom christology of the hymn could be merged with the Son of God christology of the author of Hebrews because both shared the ambivalence present in Wisdom language, and to some extent also in Adam christology. That is to say, in both cases we are confronted not with a particular pre-existent divine person (the Son, Christ), but *a way of speaking about God's interaction with men and things which could use the impersonal imagery of light and stamp/impression as well as the personification 'Wisdom'* – a way of speaking which stressed the direct continuity between God and that which may be seen of God ('the radiance of his glory'),[203] which stressed that the revelation of God bears the impress of God's own nature ('the stamp of his very being'),[204] which stressed the more personal character of God's relation with man ('Son'), as well as the continuity between God's creative, revelatory and redemptive action (1.1–3). The point of course for Hebrews (and presumably also the hymn) is that this language can appropriately be used of Christ, for it is Christ of whom all these things are pre-eminently true, especially when set beside all other claimants (prophets, angels, Moses, priesthood). *Christ alone so embodies God's Wisdom, that is, God's creative, revelatory and redemptive action, that what can be said of Wisdom can be said of Christ without remainder.*[205] The thought of pre-existence is present, but in terms of Wisdom christology it is the act and power of God which properly speaking is what pre-exists; Christ is not so much the pre-existent act and power of God as its eschatological embodiment.

In short, it would seem that our suggestions in ch. II (§6.4) have been borne out by our study of Heb. 1.1–3. We have a concept of pre-existent sonship in Hebrews, but it is the sonship which Philo ascribed to the Logos and which the Wisdom tradition in equivalent measure ascribed to Wisdom. That creative power of God, that revelation of God is now completely and exclusively identified as Christ.

§26. CONCLUSIONS

§26.1 *The earliest christology to embrace the idea of pre-existence in the NT is Wisdom christology.* By Wisdom christology at this earliest stage I mean a way of speaking about Christ, particularly in relation to the cosmos, which takes up language and phraseology widely used within pre-Christian Judaism when speaking of divine wisdom. This language would almost certainly have been understood by Paul and his readers as ascribing to Christ the role in relation to the cosmos which pre-Christian Judaism ascribed to Wisdom; that is, more briefly, they would understand Christ to be identified as God's wisdom. *So far as we can tell there was in the first instance no concept of 'the pre-existence of Christ' apart from this application of Wisdom categories to Jesus.*

§26.2   This kind of language was familiar in the ancient world, used quite widely in reference to divine beings and often understood as denoting one god among others. *Within Judaism, including Hellenistic Judaism however, there is no evidence that such talk of God's (pre-existent) wisdom ever transgressed Jewish monotheism.* The writers with whom we have to deal, including Philo, were able to retain their Wisdom talk within the bounds of their monotheism. They were evidently conscious of the way this language was used within the wider religiosity of the time, but they took it over precisely in order to challenge that wider polytheistic understanding by their own distinctive monotheism, and presumably also to attract those who found such language and categories meaningful to a recognition of the Torah as the sum and substance of God's wisdom. Of course they ran the risk that their message would be conformed to these categories as used in the wider Hellenistic religious philosophy. But so far as we can tell, the writers themselves were alive to that danger and did not succumb to it. *For them Wisdom never really became more than a convenient way of speaking about God acting in creation, revelation and salvation; Wisdom never became more than a personification of God's own activity.*

§26.3   *When* and *how* did earliest Christianity take up this language? Thanks to Matthew we can recognize that there was a 'when', that *there was a development in the course of which Wisdom categories were applied to Christ himself as a new step in Christian thinking about Christ.* The earliest large collection of Jesus' sayings (Q) spoke of Wisdom, and presented much of Jesus' teaching in the form of Jewish wisdom. But nowhere in Q can we say with any confidence that Jesus himself was identified as Wisdom. The implication is that the same was true also of Jesus' own teaching: *there is no evidence in the earliest traditions of Jesus' ministry that he understood himself as Wisdom, or as the incarnation of (pre-existent) Wisdom.* Throughout the earliest stages of the Synoptic tradition prior to Matthew, but including Luke, Jesus is presented *not as Wisdom, but as the messenger of Wisdom, as the eschatological envoy of (God in his) wisdom.* And the implication is that Jesus thought of himself (if at all) in the same terms. Only Matthew moves beyond this to embrace an explicit Wisdom christology (Jesus = Wisdom) – and he does this by careful but obviously deliberate redaction of his Q source. In short, the Synoptic tradition strongly suggests that there was a time when there was no Wisdom christology; but we also know of a later stage when Wisdom christology could be taken for granted (in the hymns of Colossians and Hebrews and in John). Matthew shows us one of the transition points.

§26.4 *How* did the transition from a christology of Jesus the eschatological teacher of wisdom to a Wisdom christology come about? Paul's first letter to the Corinthians may give us the answer. For in Corinth he was confronted by a group whose views were marked both by talk of wisdom and by a too casual attitude to creation. To respond to this situation Paul took up the language of wisdom and drawing on the wisdom tradition of Hellenistic Judaism and on Stoic terminology he framed a christology which met the needs of the Corinthian situation. In this he presented Christ as the one whose death and resurrection fulfilled God's original purpose for creation and for men and so served to characterize and define the wisdom of God in a normative way – Christ crucified is the wisdom of God (I Cor. 1.24, 30). He presented the Lordship of Christ within the context of Jewish monotheism and Christ as one whom Christians now see to embody and mediate that power of God which created and sustains the world (I Cor. 8.6). The Colossian hymn probably expresses and develops the same insight (written in one of the Pauline churches) and the christology involved spread quickly throughout the Hellenistic churches (as again Matthew, Heb. 1.2f. and John indicate).

In the early stages of this development at any rate it would be inaccurate to say that Christ was understood as a pre-existent being become incarnate, or that Christ himself was thought to have been present and active in creation. With the Fourth Gospel it may be another story, in part at least (see below §30.1); but with Matthew there seems to be no thought of pre-existence involved; and in the Pauline letters and probably the introduction to Hebrews also *the thought is primarily of Christ as the eschatological embodiment of the wisdom of God, as the one through whom the creator God in all his fullness had revealed himself most clearly and definitively for man's salvation and creation's renewal.*

The fact that Paul can speak of 'one Lord' in such close association with the 'one God' as he does in I Cor. 8.6 (just as elsewhere he speaks of God as 'God of our Lord Jesus Christ' – see above p. 182) can only mean that he sees Jesus not as a pre-existent divine being, but as a man, a Jew, whose God is the one God, and yet who so embodied God's creative power and saving wisdom (particularly in his death and resurrection) that he can be identified as 'the power of God and the wisdom of God'. In short, if the contemporary cosmologies of Hellenistic Judaism and Stoicism determined what *words* should be used in describing the cosmic significance of the Christ-event, the *meaning* of these words is determined by the Christ-event itself.

§26.5   At the same time, given the understanding of divine wisdom within Hellenistic Judaism at the time of Paul, we can see how it was that *his language should both retain Wisdom christology within the bounds of Jewish monotheism and yet at the same time drive the Christianity expressing it in a Trinitarian direction.* If I Cor. 8.6 and Col. 1.15–20 (also Heb. 1.2f.) should not be interpreted in a simplistic way as attributing personal pre-existence to Jesus Christ, *neither can these passages be reduced to a mere doctrine of Jesus as a man inspired by God.* Here we may observe is the difference between ch. V and ch. VI: in ch. V we saw that the understanding of the earthly Jesus in relation to the Spirit is essentially that of inspiration; but in ch. VI we have had to speak in terms of *identification. In this distinction we cross the boundary between 'inspiration' and 'incarnation':* Jesus = (the eschatological) prophet inspired by the Spirit; but Jesus = Wisdom. Again, we repeat, the thought is not of Jesus himself as there in the beginning, despite what to us seems the 'obvious' meaning of the language used in I Cor. 8.6, Col. 1.16 and Heb. 1.2, but of Jesus as the man Wisdom became – not merely inspired, but became. He who espouses a Wisdom christology does not assert that Christ was a pre-existent being, but neither does he assert that Christ was simply a man used by God, even in a climactic way. He asserts rather that *Christ fully embodies the creative and saving activity of God, that God in all his fullness was in him, that he represents and manifests all that God is in his outreach to men.*[206] We can express this as the *divinity* or even *deity* of Christ, so long as we understand what that means: the deity is the Wisdom of God, for the Wisdom of God is God reaching out to and active in his world. So the deity of Christ is the deity of Wisdom incarnate; that is, to recognize the deity of Christ is to recognize that in Christ God manifested himself, his power as Creator his love as Saviour, in a full and final way. But, to make the point one last time, we should use the language of *incarnation* at this point only if we use it properly. For while we can say that divine wisdom became incarnate in Christ, that does not mean that Wisdom was a divine being, or that Christ himself was pre-existent with God, but simply that Christ was (and is) the embodiment of divine Wisdom, that is, the climactic and definitive embodiment of God's own creative power and saving concern. Herein we see the origin of the doctrine of the incarnation.

VII

THE WORD OF GOD

§27. INTRODUCTION

In the beginning was the Word,
and the Word was with God,
and the Word was God.
He was in the beginning with God.
All things came into being through him,
and no created thing came into being without him.

. . .

And the Word became flesh
and dwelt among us . . . (John 1.1–3, 14).

Few if any passages have been so influential on subsequent theology. For it was the Logos (Word) concept, the explicit affirmation of the incarnation of the Logos, and the identification of Jesus as the incarnate Logos which dominated the christology of the second and third centuries. On the one hand Logos christology was central in early Christianity's attempts to explain itself to its cultured contemporaries. As we shall see, the simple opening phrases of the Johannine prologue expose us to a Christianity able and eager to speak in language familiar to the religious and philosophical discussions of the time, and the second-century apologists continued the same dialogue using the same key concepts.[1] At the same time the central Christian thrust of the prologue ('the Word became flesh' – v. 14) injected a new and unique element into that dialogue; by holding fast to the affirmation of the incarnation of the Logos in Jesus Christ patristic Christianity was able to maintain its distinctive testimony over against all other competing cults and systems.[2]

On the other hand, Logos christology served as a crucial phase in early Christianity's attempts to explain itself to *itself*, to come to a coherent understanding and statement of its faith concerning Christ. Logos christology, we may say, provided the bridge between the earliest Wisdom christology of Paul and the subsequent Son christology of the classic creeds. Of course there is a considerable overlap between all three formulations. The Logos prologue of John is considerably indebted to pre-Christian Wisdom speculation (see above pp. 164f.); and a somewhat similar overlap may be detected in the thought of the writer to the Hebrews (see above §25.3). The second-century apologists speak both of God's Word and of his Wisdom. Indeed there was some tendency to make a distinction between the two by equating Wisdom with the Spirit of God (Theophilus, *ad Autol.* 2.15; Irenaeus, *adv. haer.* IV.20.1).[3] But the dominant view was that of Justin and Tertullian (Justin, *Dial.* 129.3f.; Tertullian, *adv. Prax.* 6f.) which equates Wisdom with the Word,[4] and throughout this period it is clear enough that the Word was the principal category, with Wisdom providing little more than an occasional variant.[5]

Similarly talk of Jesus' divine sonship is widespread in the NT (much more so than either Word or Wisdom), and Son of God remained a popular christological title throughout the pre-Nicene period, particularly in the West. But in the East the Logos concept provided the main vehicle for developing christology at this stage, primarily because it afforded the better link with the philosophical speculation of the day and enabled Christians to contribute their own distinctive claims to the then dominant concern of wider religion and philosophy to understand and conceptualize the relation between God and the cosmos.[6] Only in the conflict with Arius did 'Logos' give way to 'Son', when particularly in Athanasius the emphasis swung from cosmology to soteriology[7] and a crucial distinction was drawn between 'uncreated' ($\dot{\alpha}\gamma\acute{\epsilon}\nu\eta\tau\sigma\varsigma$) and 'unbegotten' ($\dot{\alpha}\gamma\acute{\epsilon}\nu\nu\eta\tau\sigma\varsigma$).[8] From that time on one of the central affirmations of Nicene orthodoxy ('*begotten* not made') determined that the first christological title should be 'Son'. John 1.14 remained crucial in talk of the incarnation of course, and in the East we still find creeds in the fourth century whose second article confesses the Logos rather than the Son (Eusebius of Caesarea, St Macarius of Egypt),[9] but from Nicea onwards the confession of Jesus Christ as Son became the standard formulation of Christian faith in the East as well as the West.

Granted then the central importance of Logos christology in second- and third-century Christian thought and the significance of John 1.1–3, 14 in the debates of the patristic age,[10] it is obviously important for us to inquire into the original significance of John's words. Once again the (late) first century AD context of meaning is a crucial issue. What would the Fourth Evangelist have intended by the words with which he opened his Gospel? What meaning could he have expected his readers to draw from them? Moreover, since the Logos-prologue is such a distinctive and isolated element within the NT, even within the Fourth Gospel itself (the clearest parallels are in I John 1.1 and Rev. 19.13), where does it stand in relation to the rest of NT christology? – as the climax of a developing insight into the reality that was Christ, or as an idiosyncratic formulation which sets John closer to the wider religious-philosophical speculation of his time and somewhat apart from the other NT writers, or what? In attempting to answer these questions we must look at the understanding of the Word of God, the divine Logos both in pre-Christian thought and in pre-Johannine Christian thought.

§28. LOGOS IN PRE-CHRISTIAN THOUGHT

§28.1 The background to the Logos concept and its use in the prologue of John's Gospel has been discussed many times and we need not follow the familiar line of investigation which examines first the Hellenistic antecedents and then those in the pre-Christian Jewish literature.[11] The fact is that a considerable consensus has been achieved and the great majority of contemporary scholars would agree that the principal background against which the Logos prologue must be set is the OT itself and the thought of inter-testamental Hellenistic Judaism, particularly as expressed in the Wisdom literature.[12] Bultmann's attempt to argue for a more specific background in a pre-Christian Gnostic myth from which the Johannine prologue derived the concept of the Logos as an intermediary between God and the world who exercises both cosmological and soteriological functions,[13] falls to the ground before the same objections outlined above (p. 99): we simply have no evidence of the existence of such a pre-Christian myth; and the developed myth as hypothesized is best explained as a syncretistic attempt (which can be dated with any degree of probability no earlier than the first half of the second century AD) to incorporate Christian belief in Jesus into a wider framework of religious-philosophical world views.[14]

There have of course been restatements and modifications of Bultmann's thesis: in particular, S. Schulz has continued to maintain that 'the absolute personification' of the Logos cannot be explained from the Hellenistic Jewish Wisdom tradition and must 'go back to the speculation about intermediary beings in Hellenism influenced by Gnosis';[15] and J. T. Sanders thinks the evidence points not to an already developed myth but to 'an emerging mythical configuration' and a 'tendency to hypostatize divine qualities' which together provide the most meaningful background to the Johannine prologue, as well as to the other NT christological hymns.[16] In fact, however, the determinative evidence on which these theses have to depend is nothing more than the evidence we have in effect been reviewing throughout the earlier chapters of the present study, plus of course the material to be considered below – the divine Son, the Son of Man, the (Primal) Man, the 'intermediary' beings, and the divine 'hypostases' particularly Wisdom and Word. Thus far we have not found anything in pre-Christian sources which would warrant the description of 'an emerging mythical configuration', and the nearest we have come to it is the regular talk of Wisdom in the Wisdom of Solomon and Philo – but this is nothing other than the 'tendency to hypostatize divine qualities', so that Sanders' distinction between these two trends, as indeed his abstraction of 'an emerging mythical configuration' behind the NT documents should be sharply called in question. Similarly, Schulz's thesis depends on whether we can properly speak of 'the absolute personfication' of the Logos in the Johannine prologue, and on what assessment we make of 'the speculation about intermediary beings in Hellenism',[17] which again brings us back to the same difficult area of pre-Christian Hellenistic Judaism.

The problem of the background to the Johannine prologue thus largely boils down to the question: To what extent does the understanding of the Logos, the Word of God, in pre-Christian Hellenistic Judaism throw light on and explain the language and ideas of John 1.1–18? And so far as our wider inquiry is concerned the issue then becomes, To what extent would the original readers of the Johannine prologue, familiar with the literature of Hellenistic Judaism as many of them presumably would be, have identified the Logos of John 1.1–18 as a divine hypostasis or intermediary being between God and man? Whatever our findings in the case of Spirit and Wisdom we must realize that the same questions rise afresh in connection with the Word of God – above all because of Philo, where 'the divine Logos' is the dominant concept, and where the language suggestive of the Logos as a divine person distinct from God far outstrips anything said in the OT or LXX. In drawing Philo into the discussion at this point, it is not necessary to determine whether his writings directly influenced the Johannine prologue or not – there is in fact no clear evidence favouring an affirmative answer. It is sufficient for us however that Philo's writings were being published at least half a century before the Fourth Gospel, that they manifest to an unsurpassed degree how extensive and how sophisticated could be the interaction between Jewish faith and Hellenistic philosophy, and that they therefore provide as good a test case as we will find (in non-Christian writings) of the intellectual milieu out of which the Johannine prologue seems to have emerged and with a view to which it was probably written (see further below §30.1).

Our task then in this section must be first of all to review the OT and LXX conception of the Word of God, particularly with regard to whether it was at all conceived of as a divine hypostasis or intermediary being, and second to give particular attention to Philo with a view to discovering what someone familiar with his writings or way of thinking would have made of the opening words of the Johannine prologue.

§28.2   *The Word of God in OT and LXX.* Anyone familiar with the Jewish scriptures would be familiar too with the phrase 'the word of God', or its more usual form, 'the word of Yahweh'. The latter occurs more than 240 times, and the great bulk of these (over 90%) describe a word of prophecy. That is to say, the phrase is more or less a technical term for the prophetic claim that the prophet expresses the authoritative revelation and will of God in a particular situation.[18] Thus again and again we read, 'the word of Yahweh came . . .' – for example, Gen. 15.1, Deut. 5.5, Josh. 8.27, II Sam. 7.4, I Kings 13.20, and regularly in the prophets, most noticeably Jeremiah and Ezekiel; particularly striking is the prominence of the phrase 'the word of Yahweh' in the Elijah and Elisha cycle of stories in I and II Kings and again in Jeremiah.[19] Clearly then basic to the Hebraic concept of the word of God was the conviction that Yahweh revealed his will immediately and directly to his people through prophetic inspiration and vision. This belief was fundamental to the religion embodied in the OT writings.

The most significant references for us however are those where the 'word' is spoken of in a way that seems to give it an independent existence of its own. The passages which are most regularly cited when the discussion turns to the issue of hypostatization are Ps. 33.6, 107.20, 147.15, 18, Isa. 9.8, 55.10f. and Wisd. 18.14–16.[20]

Ps. 33.6   – By the word of Yahweh the heavens were made,
             and all their host by the breath of his mouth
             (τῷ πνεύματι τοῦ στόματος αὐτοῦ – LXX).

Ps. 107.20   – He sent forth (ἀπέστειλεν) his word, and healed them,
             and delivered them from destruction.

Ps. 147.15, 18 – He sends forth (ἀποστέλλων) his command to the earth;
             his word runs swiftly.
             He sends forth (ἀποστελεῖ) his word, and the ice is melted;
             he makes his wind (πνεῦμα) blow, and the waters flow.

Isa. 9.8   – Yahweh has sent a word against Jacob,
             and it shall fall upon Israel.

Isa. 55.10f. – For as the rain and the snow come down from heaven,
             and return not thither but water the earth,
             making it blossom and bear fruit,
             giving seed to the sower and bread to the eater,
             So shall it be with the word that goes forth from my mouth;
             it shall not return to me empty,
             but it shall accomplish that which I purpose,
             and prosper in the task for which I sent it.

Wisd. 18.14–16– (a description of the last of the ten plagues in Egypt)
> For while gentle silence enveloped all things,
>> and night in its swift course was now half gone,
> Your all powerful word leaped from heaven, from the royal throne,
>> into the midst of the land that was doomed,
> a stern warrior carrying the sharp sword of your authentic command,
>> and stood and filled all things with death,
>> and touched heaven while standing on the earth.[21]

Once again, however, I find myself asking whether these passages are rightly classified as hypostatizations of the word. We may consider, for example, Num. 22.38 – 'Balaam said to Balak, "... Have I now any power at all to speak anything? The word that God puts in my mouth, that must I speak" '; and Jer. 23.29 – ' "Is not my word like fire," says Yahweh, "and like a hammer which breaks the rock in pieces?" ' These passages clearly refer to the inspired utterance of the prophet and convey powerfully the prophet's sense both of the immediacy and compulsion of divine inspiration and of the certainty that what he says will be because it is God's will. In them Yahweh's word is spoken of as though it were independent of Yahweh, but that is more an accident of idiom than anything else. It is true of course that the word once uttered had as it were a life of its own, particularly as written down when it functioned as Torah or scripture and its continuing validity could be apostrophized, as already in Ps. 119.89, 160. But for the prophet the word he spoke under inspiration was no independent entity divorced from Yahweh. On the contrary, *it was precisely the word of Yahweh, the utterance of Yahweh, Yahweh himself speaking.* As Bultmann rightly perceived, '*God's Word is God* insofar as he calls men into being ... *God's Word is God's act* ... the manifestation of his power, the real manifestation of God. It is God present, the *praesens numen*'.[22]

The same I believe is true of the 'hypostatization' passages cited above (p. 217). For all their more grandiose imagery, the same concept comes to expression. Both Psalmist, prophet, and teacher of Wisdom are thinking of the word of Yahweh as Yahweh himself acting, acting decisively in creation, in judgment, in salvation. When a sovereign speaks his subjects obey; when he commands it is done. So the utterance and command of Yahweh are simply ways of saying that Yahweh brought his will to effect, that Yahweh achieved his purpose; when Yahweh speaks things happen. Even with Wisd. 18.14–16, one of the boldest 'hypostatizations' in the LXX, the same judgment holds good, especially when we recall that the passage is in fact a dramatic interpretation of Ex. 11–12: 'Thus says the Lord, "About midnight I will go forth in the

midst of Egypt; and all the firstborn in the land of Egypt shall die . . .
For I will pass through the land of Egypt that night, and I will smite all
the firstborn in the land of Egypt . . ." ' (11.4f.; 12.12). In short, I see no
reason to dissent from G. F. Moore's judgment on Wisd. 18.15f.: 'It is an
error to see in such personifications an approach to personalisation.
Nowhere either in the Bible or in the extra-canonical literature of the
Jews is the word of God a personal agent or on the way to become such'.[23]

Our conclusion here is borne out by what we learned above concerning
the Spirit of God and the Wisdom of God in pre-Christian Judaism (chs.
V and VI). As they were ways of speaking about Yahweh acting toward
and in his creation, so too with the Word of God. As they enabled the
Jewish writers to speak of the immanence of God without threatening his
transcendence, so with the Word. The advantage particularly of Wisdom
and the Word was that they gave scope for bolder images and extended
metaphors in a way that was less possible for the 'name' or the 'glory',
and impossible for the sacred name of Yahweh itself – not least because
Sophia (Wisdom) was a feminine noun and Logos (Word) a masculine
noun, thus affording such personifications as we have already noted, for
example, in Prov. 9.1–6 and Wisd. 18.14–16. But basically all three
phrases (Spirit, Wisdom, Word) are simply variant ways of speaking of
the creative, revelatory or redemptive act of God. This is borne out by
the parallelism between word and spirit in Ps. 33.6 and 147.18 (above p.
217), and the equivalence between Ps. 33.6 and Prov. 3.19 where the
same creative power is described as Yahweh's word, Yahweh's breath/
spirit, and Yahweh's wisdom.[24] The closeness of the equivalence is most
evident in Wisd. 9.1–2, 17:

> O God of my fathers and Lord of mercy,
>   who has made all things by your *word*,
>   and by your *wisdom* has formed man . . .
>
> Who has learned your counsel,
>   unless you have given *wisdom*
>   and sent your holy *Spirit* from on high?

In short, *all three expressions are simply alternative ways of speaking about the
effective power of God in his active relationship with his world and its inhabitants.*[25]

In all this I find it hard to avoid the conclusion that some exegetes
have allowed themselves to be too impressed by the linguistic parallels
between certain OT and LXX passages and the wider religious culture
of the time, and have paid too little attention to the life-setting of these
passages within the context of pre-Christian Judaism, particularly with
respect to the idioms and style used by Israel's spokesmen. Very often
their judgment seems to verge on a pedantic literalism which shows no
'feel' for the poetic imagination which gave rise to such vigorous meta-

phors and images as we have cited above (particularly pp. 172–5).[26] In other words *there does not seem to me to be any evidence in the literature of pre-Christian Judaism* (barring Philo for the moment) *of an 'emerging mythical configuration' centred on the Word (or Wisdom) of God.* If we argue thus for these concepts, consistency demands that we hypothesize not just an 'emerging mythical configuration' but already quite an elaborate myth where such concepts as 'wickedness' and 'righteousness' are also hypostatized. But if on the contrary, OT and LXX talk of the Word and Wisdom of God is of a piece with the much wider and more varied personifications of other divine functions and actions, as it is, then we must conclude that their treatment of the Word and Wisdom of God is simply another example of the vigorous metaphorical style of Israel's spokesmen. And the fact that Word and Wisdom were more regularly used in this way tells us no more than that Israel's spokesmen found these concepts the most congenial in their attempts to speak of God's immanent involvement with men and things. Whatever later writers made of these passages in a different context, where (on other grounds) we can speak of an emerging myth, pre-Christian Judaism itself gives us no real reason for supposing that they were understood as any more than personifications of the one God's activity towards and in his creation.

§28.3 What then of *Philo*? There can be no doubt of the importance of the word *logos* for Philo – he uses it more than 1400 times in his extant writings.[27] And on the face of it there would appear to be little room for dispute regarding our question: Philo quite often speaks of the Logos as though a real being distinct from God, who acts as intermediary between God and the world. We might note for example the passages cited by L. K. K. Dey.[28]

> *Heres* 2–5 – To his Word, his chief messenger, highest in age and honour, the Father of all has given the special prerogative, to stand on the border and separate the creature from the Creator. This same Word both pleads with the immortal as suppliant for afflicted mortality and acts as ambassador of the ruler to the subject.

> *Qu. Ex.* II.13 – (Therefore) of necessity was the Logos appointed as judge and mediator, who is called 'angel'.

> *Qu. Ex.* II.94 – The incorporeal world is set off and separated from the visible one by the mediating Logos as by a veil.

> *Immut.* 138 – . . . follow the guidance of that reason (λόγος) which is the interpreter and prophet of God.

Dey cites also *Som.* I.141f. and *Qu. Ex.* II.16, which do not refer to the Logos/logos; but in addition we might refer, for example to:

Cher. 36 – the divine reason (λόγος), the ruler and steersman of all;

Sac. 119 – It is reason (λόγος) which has taken refuge with God and become his suppliant . . .;

Agr. 51 – This hallowed flock (the heavenly bodies) he leads in accordance with right and law, setting over it his true Word (ὀρθὸν λόγον) and firstborn Son, who shall take upon him its government like some viceroy of a great king;

Conf. 146 – . . . God's firstborn, the Word, who holds the eldership among the angels, their ruler as it were . . .;

Qu. Gen. II.62 – Nothing mortal can be made in the likeness of the most high One and Father of the universe, but only in that of the second God, who is his Logos.

In all these texts the Logos seems to be envisaged as a wholly independent being who can act as intermediary between God and man. But to jump too quickly to any conclusion from such an excerption of texts would be unwise. With Philo more than any other ancient Jewish writer we have to pay special heed to a context of thought which is strange and difficult for those accustomed to twentieth-century thought. Only when we can understand these passages within the context of Philo's overall thought will we understand them properly.

If our interpretation of Philo had to depend on the broader context into which Philo himself should be placed we would be in some difficulty. Philo's place within the stream of ancient philosophy remains something of a puzzle. *The Cambridge History of Later Greek and Early Medieval Philosophy* only mentions him in passing in its section on 'Greek Philosophy from Plato to Plotinus',[29] even though at some points he seems to have anticipated syntheses and formulations which elsewhere, so far as we know, only emerged some decades later.[30] But since our knowledge of the philosophies current in the first century BC is very fragmentary it is best to restrict ourselves to Philo's own writings and see what overall view emerges from them. Fortunately we have enough of Philo's considerable literary output to enable us to build up a fairly full and clear picture, and questions of precise influence and broader contexts of thought are of less importance than they would be where the literary deposit is more limited.[31]

What is sufficiently clear is that Philo's thought, not least his concept of the Logos, is what can fairly be described as a unique synthesis of Platonic and Stoic world-views with Jewish monotheism. From *Plato* he derived the conviction that the world in which we live is not the only world or indeed the real world. There is also a world of eternal realities, 'forms' or 'ideas', which is entirely separate from the world we perceive by our senses and which can be known only by the mind. The relation between the two worlds is unclear in Plato, but the implication is that the contents of this world are but shadows and copies corresponding imperfectly to the ideal, or perfect form in the other world.[32] Thus in Philo we read, for example:

> *Opif.* 36 – The incorporeal world (ὁ ἀσώματος κόσμος) was now finished and firmly settled in the divine reason (ἐν τῷ θείῳ λόγῳ), and the world patent to sense (ὁ δ' αἰσθητός) was ripe for birth after the pattern of the incorporeal;

> *Ebr.* 132 – ... no actual tabernacle or altar is meant (Lev. 10.8–10), that is the visible objects fashioned from lifeless and perishable material, but those invisible conceptions perceived only by the mind, of which the others are copies (εἰκόνες) open to our senses;

> *Heres* 280 – ... the archetypal ideas which, invisible and intelligible there, are the patterns (παραδείγματα) of things visible and sensible here.[33]

In merging this Platonic cosmology with his Jewish faith Philo was of course greatly aided by Ex. 25.40 – 'See that you make them (the furniture of the tabernacle) after the pattern (τύπον) for them, which is being shown to you on the mountain'; so, for example, *Leg. All.* III.102, *Mos.* II.74 and *Qu. Ex.* II.52.[34]

From *Stoicism* comes talk of divine reason (λόγος) immanent in the world, permeating all things, and present also in man, the seminal logos (λόγος σπερματικός), so that man's highest good is to live in accordance with and by assent to this divine reason.[35] Thus we read:

> *Heres* 119 – He that opens the womb of each of these, of mind to mental apprehension, of speech to the activities of the voice, of the senses to receive the pictures presented to it by objects ... is the invisible, seminal artificer, the divine Word ...

And Philo regularly counsels his readers to live in accordance with 'right reason' (ὀρθὸς λόγος) – *Opif.* 143, *Leg. All.* I.46, 93, III.1, 80, 106, 148, 150, etc.[36]

The extent of Philo's *Jewish* inheritance is most clear in the fact that so much of his work consists of elaborate allegory and lengthy discussion of the Pentateuch, in which high place is given to the patriarchs, particularly Moses,[37] and in which the Jewish law is presented as the fullest revelation of God's will and divine truth.[38]

The Platonic and Stoic elements do not of course remain unchanged within the Philonic system. In Philo the Platonic ideas are understood as thoughts in the mind of *God*, the plan in the mind of the divine architect – though Plato's concept of 'the Good' in the *Republic* and of the divine architect in the *Timaeus* would have provided Philo with a convenient pointer towards his own synthesis.[39] The synthesis however demands a much more radical reshaping of the Stoic concepts, for the Stoic Logos is something material, in a system which tends towards pantheism, whereas in Philo the Logos is immaterial, the immanent Logos only an 'extension' of the incorporeal Logos; again in Stoicism the divine reason *is* God and beyond it there is nothing superior, whereas for Philo beyond the Logos there is always God, 'the apprehension of whom is removed to a very great distance from all human power of thought' (*Som.* I.66).[40] The question of course for us is whether or to what extent the same thing happened in the reverse direction, whether the strong monotheistic faith which was his birthright as a Jew was in its turn modified or diluted by the same synthesis.

How then are we to understand Philo's concept of the Logos within the context of his cosmology of an 'intermediate' world, the intelligible world (κόσμος νοητός), between God and this world, the world of the senses (κόσμος αἰσθητός)? A key which helps unlock his thought at this point is the meaning of *logos* itself; for the basic meaning of *logos* embraces both 'thought, reason' and 'speech, utterance', as even a cursory study of λόγος in Philo's writings reveals (above n. 27). The Stoics were accustomed to distinguishing two types of *logos* – *logos* = the unexpressed thought, the thought within the mind, and *logos* = the uttered thought, the thought expressed in speech (λόγος ἐνδιάθετος, and λόγος προφορικός). Philo was thoroughly familiar with this distinction and makes considerable use of it. We may refer particularly to:

> *Migr.* 70–85 – . . . 'logos' has two aspects, one resembling a spring, the other its outflow; 'logos' in the understanding resembles a spring, and is called 'reason', while utterance by mouth and tongue is like its outflow, and is called 'speech' . . .;

> *Abr.* 83 – he uses 'sound' as a figure for the spoken thought (προφορικὸν λόγον) and 'father' for the ruling mind, since the inward thought (ὁ ἐνδιάθετος) is by its nature father of the uttered, being senior to it, the secret begetter of what it has to say.

Hence also the typical Philonic allegorical distinction between Moses and Aaron, on the basis of Ex. 4.16 and 7.1, where Moses represents mind (λόγος ἐνδιάθετος) and Aaron speech (λόγος προφορικός) (*Det.* 39f., 126–32; *Migr.* 76–84; *Mut.* 208).[41] But what is of particular interest for us is the fact that the two meanings frequently merge into each other, so that it is not always clear whether *logos* means 'thought' or 'speech'. This is most noticeable in *Sac.* 80–3, *Ebr.* 157 and *Som.* I.102–14. And in *Gig.* 52 it is clear that the High Priest, Aaron, usually λόγος προφορικός, can only enter into the most holy place (Lev. 16.2, 34) as λόγος ἐνδιάθετος.[42] Thus we can see that the distinction between *logos* = unuttered thought and *logos* = uttered thought is in no way firm or fixed. It is the same word, and the two meanings run into each other, so that we have to define *logos* in Philo not as one or other, but basically as *thought coming to expression in speech*.[43]

This key begins to unlock our problem as soon as we realize that this relation between mind and speech in the individual is also for Philo the relation between on the one hand the divine Logos and the world of ideas and on the other the material world, the world of sense perception. The parallel is explicitly stated in

Mos. II.127–9 – ... the rational principle (λόγος) is twofold as well in the universe as in human nature. In the universe (τὸ πᾶν) we find it in one form dealing with the incorporeal and archetypal ideas from which the intelligible world was framed, and in another with the visible objects which are the copies and likenesses of these ideas and out of which this sensible world was produced. With man, in one form it resides within, in the other it passes out from him in utterance. The former is like a spring, and is the source from which the latter, the spoken, flows ...

The point to be noted here is that it is *one and the same logos* concerning which all this is said: not only do we have to say that as the logos in the mind is to the logos of speech, so the intelligible world is to the material world, but we also have to recognize that for Philo the logos which is reason in man is not to be distinguished from the divine Logos. As he says himself in so many words: '... the reasoning power (λογισμός) within us and the divine Word/Reason (λόγος) above us are indivisible' (*Heres* 233f.). This also explains why he can speak of 'right reason' (ὀρθὸς λόγος) as our 'father' (as in *Post.* 68, 91; *Ebr.* 68, 80f., 95; *Conf.* 43; *Spec. Leg.* II.29), for 'right reason' is not to be distinguished from the divine Logos (see also particularly *Agr.* 51f.).[44]

What this means for our understanding of Philo's talk of an intermediary world and intermediary beings between God and this world becomes clearer as soon as we realize the extent of the parallel between the logos in human mind and speech and the divine Logos, for *the divine Logos is for Philo in effect the thought of God coming to expression*, first in the world of ideas and then in the world of sense perception. The most explicit statement to this effect is in *Opif.* 16–44, where he likens God's creative action to that of the architect of a city who first plans the city in his mind and then constructs the city in accordance with the image, the blueprint in his mind.

[As the architect] begins to build the city of stones and timber, keeping his eye upon his pattern (i.e. in his mind) and making the visible and tangible objects correspond in each case to the incorporeal ideas. Just such must be our thoughts about God. We must suppose that, when he was minded to found the one great city, he conceived beforehand the model of its parts, and that out of these he constituted and brought to completion a world discernible only to the mind, and then, with that for a pattern, the world which our senses can perceive (18f.).

We should note that the plan or blueprint is not thought of as something separate from the architect; there is no intermediate state in which the plan in the mind is set down on paper before it is translated into stones and timber. The translation takes place direct from the mind of the architect to the building materials. So with the world of ideas which is the blueprint for the world of the senses, it has no other location than the mind of God (*Opif.* 20); indeed we can say it *is* the mind of God, the divine Logos coming to expression in creative act –

> the world discerned only by the intellect is nothing else than the Word of God when he (God) was already engaged in the act of creation. For (to revert to our illustration) the city discernible by the intellect alone is nothing else than the reasoning faculty of the architect in the act of planning to found the city (*Opif.* 24).

On this analogy then the Logos is 'the reasoning faculty of God in the act of planning to create the universe'. Alternatively expressed we can say that the Logos is the archetypal idea (*Opif.* 139; *Ebr.* 132f.; *Heres* 230f.; *Som.* II.45; *Qu. Gen.* I.4; *Qu. Ex.* II.122), particularly of course of the mind or soul or spirit of man (*Opif.* 146; *Plant.* 18, 20; *Decal.* 134; *Spec. Leg.* I.81, 171; III.207; *Praem.* 163). Or if we put the same point in terms of the world of ideas, we have to say that the divine Logos, the overall plan, can be spoken of in terms of its component parts, the mind of God can be spoken of in terms of its individual thoughts,[45] with the Logos understood, for example, as 'the idea of the ideas' (*Migr.* 103; *Qu. Ex.* II.124), or as the 'place' of the 'powers' (*Som.* I.62 – expounding Gen. 28.11), where 'ideas', 'forms', 'powers' (δυνάμεις) and 'thoughts/words' (λόγοι) are all synonymous (*Spec. Leg.* I.48, 323; *Qu. Gen.* III.15; *Qu. Ex.* II.42), and all to be understood as God putting forth his creative energy to create and sustain.[46] In one passage Philo can even express himself in these terms, 'When we reason about him we recognize in him partition and division into each of the divine powers and excellencies ... Each of these (attributes) calls for veneration and praise, both separately in itself and when ranked with its congeners' (*Spec. Leg.* I.209).[47]

Philo's concept of the Logos becomes still clearer when we look at the Logos's function from a different angle. Corresponding to the two worlds, the corporeal world of material entities, and the incorporeal world of ideas, there are two ways of knowing – perception by means of the senses, and perception by means of the mind. The invisible, intelligible world of ideas is not accessible to the senses but only to the mind (cf. e.g. *Opif.* 31; *Post.* 69; *Migr.* 52) – to know this intelligible world, the real world, the divine Logos, being the goal of philosophy (cf. e.g. *Gig.* 60f; *Cong.*

79). But beyond the intelligible world, beyond the Logos, is God himself, unknowable even to the purest intellect (cf. *Leg. All.* I.36f.; *Post.* 15, 168f.; *Immut.* 62; *Mut.* 9; *Praem.* 40, 44; *Legat.* 6; *Qu. Ex.* II.67). It is true that creation is as it were a 'shadow' cast by God and one can discern the artificer to some extent by means of his works (*Leg. All.* III.97–9), and since God is the archetype of the Logos (*Det.* 83; *Heres* 230f.; *Som.* I.75), to perceive the Logos is to perceive God in still fuller measure – the Logos is 'that by which God draws tne perfect man from things earthly to himself' (*Sac.* 8). The point is however, that the Logos is as close as one can attain to God (*Fuga* 101), to see the Logos or the powers is all that is attainable to man, even Abraham (*Conf.* 96f.; *Mut.* 15; *Spec. Leg.* I.32–50). Philo's thought here comes to clearest expression in *Som.* I.61–72, where he expounds Gen. 28.11 ('Abraham met a place') by means of Gen. 22.3f. – 'He came to the place of which God had told him: and lifting up his eyes he saw the place from afar':

> Tell me, pray, did he who had come to the place see it from afar? Nay, it would seem that one and the same word is used of two different things: one of these is a divine Word, the other God who was before the Word. One who has come from abroad under Wisdom's guidance arrives at the former place, thus attaining in the divine word the sum and consummation of service. But when he has his place in the divine Word he does not actually reach him who is in very essence God (τὸν κατὰ τὸ εἶναι θεόν), but sees him from afar: or rather, not even from a distance is he capable of contemplating him; all he sees is the bare fact that God is far away from all creation, and that the apprehension of him is removed to a very great distance from all human power of thought . . . The 'place' on which he 'lights' is . . . the Word of God . . . For God, not deeming it meet that sense should perceive him, sends forth his Words (λόγους) to succour the lovers of virtue . . .(*Som.* I.65f., 68f.; similarly *Post* 16–20).

What we may say then, indeed what we must say, is that *the Logos is what is knowable of God, the Logos is God insofar as he may be apprehended and experienced.* This does not mean that we should think of the Logos, and the powers, as gradations of the divine being, far less of the material world as the lowest gradation of divine being.[48] Philo is much too Jewish for that. We should think rather of gradations of *manifestations* of him who alone is God, gradations in the degree to which God has manifested himself through his creative power and by means of his creation, gradations in what may be known of God, experienced of God. It is only in and through the Logos and the powers that God even begins to enter within the range of man's perception (cf. *Abr.* 119–22; *Qu. Gen.* IV.2, 4).[49] Or to use Philo's favourite sun and light symbolism, the Logos is to God as the corona is to the sun, the sun's halo which man can look upon when he cannot look directly on the sun itself. That is not to say that the Logos is God as such, any more than the corona is the sun as such, but the

Logos is that alone which may be seen of God (cf. *Som.* I.239; also *Ebr.* 44; *Praem.* 45; *Qu. Ex.* II.67). Bearing in mind that Philo is as much, or more mystic than philosopher, one whose highest aim was to soar beyond the world of sense, beyond the world of ideas to see, were it possible, God, τὸ ὄν, as such (see *Opif.* 70f.; *Conf.* 95–7; *Spec. Leg.* I.345; *Legat.* 4f.; *Qu. Ex.* II.51),[50] the probability becomes very strong that this is the best way to express Philo's understanding of the Logos: God in himself, in his aloneness is unknowable; God is knowable in some small degree by means of his creation, more so through the world of intelligible reality, the ideas, and as fully as is possible to man in and as the Logos.

Thus it becomes clear how it is that Philo can speak of the Logos as an intermediary between God and creation, between God and man (above pp. 220f.) – simply because for Philo it is in and through the Logos that God reaches out to his creation, and it is by responding to the Logos that man comes as near as he can to God.[51] As Philo himself says:

Sac. 8 – . . . that same Word, by which he made the universe, is that by which he draws the perfect man from things earthly to himself;

Post. 14 – The cause of all is not . . . locally in any place at all, but high above both place and time. For he has placed all creation under his control, and is contained by nothing, but transcends all. But though transcending and being beyond what he has made, nonetheless has he filled the universe with himself; for he has caused his powers to extend themselves throughout the universe to its utmost bounds . . . (see the whole passage, 13–21; cf. *Som.* I.141f.).

That in using the metaphor of intermediaries Philo has no thought of the Logos as a real being with particular functions distinct from God becomes clear when we realize that for Philo God alone is creator (*Opif.* 170–2; *Som.* I.241); indeed, God alone *is* (*Det.* 160; cf. *Leg. All.* II.86). Philo can identify Plato's artificer (τεχνίτης) both as the Logos (*Heres* 119; *Qu. Ex.* II.53, 81) and, more regularly, as God himself (e.g. *Opif.* 20, 135; *Leg. All.* III.99; *Heres* 133; *Mut.* 31), because in each case he is saying the same thing (see also above p. 225). Similarly he can speak of God as charioteer or helmsman of creation (as in *Heres* 99, 228, 301; *Som.* I.157), but can readily use this metaphor for the Logos (*Migr.* 67; *Fuga* 101) for the same reason; or he can speak both of God and of the Logos as the supreme archetype (see above pp. 225 and 226). In such instances there is no conflict in Philo's thought and his monotheism is unchallenged. Similarly when he speaks of the Logos as the 'all-cutting Word' (*Heres* 140), or as 'the seal by which each thing that exists has received its shape' (*Fuga* 12f.), or as the instrument (ὄργανον) which God employed in fashioning the world (*Leg. All.* III.95f.; *Cher.* 127; *Migr.* 6), the thought is not of the Logos as an entity separable from God; rather Philo has evidently adapted the Aristotelian understanding of causality and form whereby the idea/form in the mind of the architect is as much an instrument in shaping the raw material as any tool.[52] God's Word is his act (*Sac.* 65; cf. *Fuga* 95). So too Philo can call the Logos the 'eldest' of created things (*Leg. All.* III.175; cf. *Ebr.* 132f.) and Wisdom the 'first' of all God's works (*Ebr.* 31, quoting Prov. 8.22), but also the world as 'the first and the greatest and the most perfect of God's works' (*Immut.* 106), because the Logos as creator and created, and Wisdom as 'mother of all' and created, simply denote God in his highest approach to his world. Thus we are not altogether surprised at the difficulty in distinguishing 'right reason' in man from the divine Logos (see above p. 224), since 'right reason' denotes God's will coming to expression in world and men, God as he may be perceived by the mind (cf. *Fuga* 5f., 117f.). Nor indeed are we altogether surprised when Philo's normal reserve slackens and he accepts the testimony of scripture that God appeared in the likeness of an angel (*Som.* I.232, 238), though his normal exegesis is to interpret the angel-theophanies (see above pp. 149f.) in terms of the Logos,[53] since the Logos is the visibility of God, the highest manifestation of God which is perceivable to man. So too when he completely blurs the distinction between God and his Word by defining the prophet as 'the interpreter of God who prompts from within what he should say' (*Praem.* 55; cf. *Migr.* 81), for the Logos is nothing other than God himself in his approach to men.[54]

We may conclude then that any approach to Philo which focuses attention simply on the 'intermediary' passages in his writings is liable to misunderstand Philo, unless the whole context of his thought is taken fully into consideration. When we do this it becomes evident that Philo was using the Platonic conception of a world of ideas to bridge the gulf between God and creation, between God and man. It is a gulf which Philo firmly maintains is ultimately unbridgeable: God is unknowable in himself. But his Jewish faith, and indeed his own experience of prophetic ecstasy (*Migr.* 35; *Spec. Leg.* III.1f.; cf. *Heres* 69f., 259–66; *Mos.* I.277, 283; II.188; *Spec. Leg.* I.65; IV.49) convinced him that God was in fact knowable in some degree, because God had chosen to make himself known. The language of philosophy, Stoicism in particular, agreed at this point with the language of Jewish prophecy in providing the most useful term for talk of this experience of revelation and 'right reason' – *logos* – and by means of allegorical interpretation this divine Logos could be shown to have a wide-ranging symbolical expression within the Torah. But in the end of the day *the Logos seems to be nothing more for Philo than God himself in his approach to man, God himself insofar as he may be known by man.*

§28.4 To sum up. Our task in this section has been to fill out the context of meaning within which many at least of the Fourth Gospel's readers would interpret the prologue to that Gospel, the context of meaning which the composer of the Johannine Logos poem would have drawn on in speaking of the Logos of God and which he would have to assume would inform his readers' understanding of what he wrote. Our task is not yet finished, of course, because in dealing with the context of the Fourth Gospel, written most probably towards the end of the first century (see above p. 31), we must also take account of about sixty years of *Christian* thinking. The pre-Johannine Christian context is what we turn to next. But our findings thus far are directly relevant, especially if the Fourth Gospel or the prologue itself was framed with a non-Christian audience in view.

In such a case our conclusion is fairly clear. If the background assumed in the Johannine prologue was principally that of the OT and LXX, the Word of God would be understood principally as *God's direct address to men*, through the inspiration of prophet and sage. Even when prophecy was thought to be silent, the Torah was thought of in an equivalent way, as the immediate utterance of God – hence the rabbinic formula 'the Holy Spirit *says*', rather than 'the Holy Spirit *said*' (see above p. 134), and also the (later) tendency to speak of the Torah as pre-existent in rabbinic Judaism (above VI n. 43). Whatever the arguments concerning Wisdom, there is no real evidence of a myth (Isis or otherwise – see above pp. 169f.) lying behind Jewish, including Hellenistic Jewish talk of the Word of God. In both cases indeed (Word and Wisdom), it is highly doubtful whether the thought ever goes beyond a literary personification of the immanent power and revelation of God.

Philo's work raises the same questions afresh. As we have noted above (p. 173), if it is arguable that his talk of Wisdom shows awareness of Isis mythology, it is equally probable, if not more than probable that Wisdom is for Philo simply the appropriate way to speak of God's approach to men when more feminine characteristics are to the fore or the particular imagery of birth is being used. But his Logos talk is in no way dependent on any particular myth (at least any extrabiblical myth), nor even expressive of an 'emerging mythical configuration', even though his allegorical interpretation at times may throw up similar sounding formulations. The importance of Philo at this point is rather that *he demonstrates the sort of cosmological speculation which must have been present* at least in certain sophisticated circles of his day, and also that *he shows how far a monotheistic Jew could go in using such speculation without, at least in his own eyes, compromising his monotheism*. If the metaphysical world view of 'middle Platonism' subsequently opened the way to the Gnostic understanding of an infinite series of emanations and beings between God and man, and also to some extent to the Christian understanding of the distinctions within the being of God, such developments are not yet present in Philo. His understanding is rather of the Jewish God, unknowable in himself, who has yet made himself known by means of his creation, and particularly to his people through his Word. Allegorical interpretation allows that basic assertion of faith to be elaborated in myriad biblical narratives using the language of Platonic and Stoic philosophy. But however strained and at times confusing or even contradictory particular allegories are (since each element in a passage has to be given some allegorical significance), the basic concept remains firmly Jewish: *the Logos of God is God in his self-revelation.*

§29. THE WORD OF GOD IN FIRST-CENTURY CHRISTIAN THOUGHT

Inquiry into the identification of Jesus as the Logos in John 1 has tended to concentrate too much on the Jewish and Hellenistic background and to give too little prominence to the earlier Christian talk of the word of God.[53] But if the Fourth Evangelist was writing near the end of the first century (see above p. 31) then it is *a priori* likely that the previous sixty years of Christian thought on the subject had exerted as strong an influence on him as any other line of thought. How then did the pre-Johannine Christian writers speak of the word? Are there any foreshadowings of the powerful statements of John 1.1 and 14 from earlier Christian writers?

§29.1 *The word of preaching.* From the earliest NT writings we can see that a clear manner of speech had already emerged, where 'the word' is thought of as the gospel, *the message about Christ.*[56] Paul thinks of the gospel without equivocation as 'the word of God': thus already in I Thess. 2.13 –

> We also thank God constantly for this, that when you received the word of God which you heard from us, you accepted it not as the word of men but as what it really is, the word of God which is at work in you believers;

(see also Rom. 9.6; I Cor. 14.36; II Cor. 2.17; 4.2; Phil. 1.14; Col. 1.25). But he can call the good news he preaches just as happily 'the word of the Lord' (I Thess. 1.8; II Thess. 3.1), 'the word of Christ' (Col. 3.16), 'the word of the cross' (I Cor. 1.18), 'the word of reconciliation' (II Cor. 5.19), 'the word of truth' (Eph. 1.13; Col. 1.5), 'the word of life' (Phil. 2.16), and even simply 'the word' (Gal. 6.6; Col. 4.3; I Thess. 1.6). In a manner with which we are now familiar from our study of Jewish imagery (above pp. 172–5) Paul can speak of this word in vigorous metaphors or near personifications. The word of God 'is at work' (I Thess. 2.13), he hopes that it will 'speed and triumph' (II Thess. 3.1), 'in the whole world it is bearing fruit and growing' (Col. 1.5f.), he prays that 'God might open for us a door for the word' (Col. 4.3). Most striking of all is his talk of Christ as the one preached, in a way which seems to identify Christ and the word of the gospel: it is *Christ* who is the good news (I Cor. 1.23; 15.12; II Cor. 1.19; 4.5; Phil. 1.15); the mystery of the gospel is the mystery of Christ (Eph. 1.9; 3.3f.; 6.19), 'Christ in you the hope of glory' (Col. 1.27; 2.2; 4.3; see further below pp. 235f.); where he urges the Colossians to 'let the word of Christ dwell in you richly' (Col. 3.16) Paul(?) prays for the Ephesians 'that Christ may dwell in your hearts by faith' (Eph. 3.17). It is clear from all this that Paul has no concept here of Christ as a pre-existent hypostasis (the Logos of God); it is simply that Christ is so much the centre and focus of the gospel that to speak of the word is to speak of Christ – the good news *is* Christ, particularly his crucifixion and resurrection. It is not that he identifies Christ with the divine Logos of Hellenistic Judaism or Stoicism and goes on from that to identify Christ (the Logos) with the word (logos) of preaching; it is rather that Christ is the heart and substance of the kerygma, not so much the Word as *the word preached*.[57]

From the Jesus-tradition preserved in the Synoptics it would appear doubtful that Jesus himself ever spoke of his proclamation or teaching as 'the word'.[58] But he may well have given his own words (plural) weighty significance (cf. Mark 8.38 par.; 13.31 pars.; Matt. 7.24, 26 par.; 10.14). Be that as it may, the Evangelists themselves certainly regarded their record of Jesus' preaching as gospel itself, as 'the word'; this is particularly evident in Mark (2.2; 4.14–20; 4.33; 8.32; 9.10 – the last two being references specifically to the cross and resurrection). Matthew adds nothing on this point. But it could be argued that Luke has added Luke 5.1 and modified Luke 8.11, 21 to bring out the continuity between the preaching of Jesus and the gospel of his disciples,[59] though the limited degree to which he has done so is surprising. Certainly there can be no doubt of the importance of 'the word' in Luke's account of earliest Christianity – the kerygma is regularly called 'the word of God' (Acts 4.31; 6.2, 7; 8.14; 11.1; 12.24; 13.5, 7, 44, 46, 48; 16.32; 17.13; 18.11), 'the word of the Lord' (8.25; 13.49; 15.35f.; 19.10, 20), and simply 'the word' (4.4; 6.4; 8.4; 10.36, 44; 11.19; 14.25; 16.6; 17.11; 18.5), as well as 'the word of salvation' (13.26), 'the word of the gospel' (15.7) and 'the word of grace' (20.32).[60] And just as with Paul, so with Luke, the gospel focuses so exclusively on Christ that he can equally say, The first evangelists preached Christ (8.5; 9.20; 19.13). We may note also here too the vivid imagery Luke can use, seeing the gospel as a living power that grows and multiplies (6.7; 12.24; 13.49; 19.20) – not as though the word was an inanimate tool which the first evangelists could use at will, but rather with the work of the evangelists, apostles included, seen as 'service of the word'.[61]

There are two verses in Luke-Acts of particular interest to us. In Luke 1.2 Luke speaks of 'those who from the beginning were eyewitnesses and ministers of the word', where it could be said that 'the word' has been personalized, almost hypostatized, and the distance between the conceptuality of John 1.1 and the Synoptics seems to grow perceptibly less.[62] Yet we should note that the thought does not really go beyond what is present elsewhere in Luke-Acts. There is certainly no thought of Jesus as a divine being called 'the Word' out of which arises the description of the gospel about Jesus as 'the Word'. Rather we are still confronted with the word of preaching personified which can be identified with Christ because Christ's life, death and resurrection are what the preaching is all about.

This comes out more clearly when we consider Acts 10.36–8.

> You know the word which he sent to Israel, preaching good news of peace by Jesus Christ (διὰ Ἰησοῦ Χριστοῦ) (he is Lord of all), the word which was proclaimed throughout all Judea . . .: how God anointed Jesus of Nazareth with the Holy Spirit and with power; how he went about doing good and healing all that were oppressed by the devil, for God was with him.

As we noted above, this speech probably makes use of Ps. 107.20 (p. 138) – 'He sent forth his word, and healed them and delivered them from destruction'.[63] As we also saw earlier in the present chapter (p. 217), that same verse, Ps. 107.20, is one of the passages most often cited as an example of hypostatization of the word in the OT. The point to be noted here is that the divine word which was sent forth is clearly identified with the word of preaching, the 'good news of peace' of which Jesus Christ was the spokesman ('by/through Jesus Christ'). Here, even where the OT text might seem to invite it, there is no attempt to identify Jesus as 'God's word sent forth'. Indeed the thought of such an identification does not seem to have occurred either to the original speaker or to Luke: 'the word' was so firmly established as a technical term for the gospel, for Luke both the message *of* Jesus and message *about* Jesus, that any thought of hypostatization of the word, let alone of Christ as pre-existent seems to have been far over the horizon (see also above p. 51).

In Hebrews the same firmly established understanding of 'the word (of God)' as the Christian gospel is clearly evident (Heb. 5.13; 6.1; 13.7). Most interesting is Heb. 4.12f.:

> The word of God is living and active, sharper than any two-edged sword, piercing to the division of soul and spirit, of joints and marrow, and discerning the thoughts and intentions of the heart.

The verse recalls both OT understanding of God's word as an effective, living power (see particularly Deut. 32.47 – ὅτι οὐχὶ λόγος κενὸς οὗτος ὑμῖν, ὅτι αὕτη ἡ ζωὴ ὑμῖν; Isa. 55.11; cf. Acts 7.38), and also Hellenistic Judaism's more vigorous objectification/personification (Wisd. 18.15f. – the 'all powerful word . . . carrying the sharp sword of your authentic command'; Philo, *Heres* 130–40 – 'God sharpened the edge of his all-cutting Word and divided universal being'; *Mut.* 108 – 'the sharp edged word, able to explore and probe each thing').[64] But even if this is another example of the influence of Alexandrian Judaism on the writer to the Hebrews we must note that once again there is no real hypostatization of the word, and certainly no thought of Christ as the Word. This is somewhat surprising in view of the indications commented on above (pp. 53–5, 207f.) that the writer was aware of and perhaps influenced by Philo's (or a Philonic-type) understanding of the Logos. But it may simply underscore the fact that the author of Hebrews understood the direct outreach of God in impersonal terms (see above p. 209). However, that may be reading too much into a too brief allusion which is hardly distinctively Hellenistic in character. What can be said with some greater confidence is that the identification of 'the word of God' as the gospel was so firmly established in the earliest decades of Christianity that the further equation of Christ as the Word does not seem to have occurred to the writer to the Hebrews, at this point at any rate.

Especially worthy of comment is the widespread recognition in earliest Christianity of the creative power of the word preached. Paul vividly recalled the experiences of his hearers being convicted and converted by his preaching (particularly I Cor. 2.4f.; I Thess. 1.5f.).[65] He reminds the Corinthians how he became their father in Christ Jesus through the gospel (I Cor. 4.15) and encourages the Philippians to 'hold fast the word of life' (Phil. 2.16). Similarly in John, Jesus' words are described as 'spirit and life'; 'you have the words of eternal life' (John 6.63, 68; cf. 5.24).[66] The same emphasis is evident in the verse discussed just above – 'the word of God is living . . .' (Heb. 4.12). In James we read, 'Of his own will he brought us forth by the word of truth' (James 1.18). And I Peter reminds its readers, 'You have been born anew, not of perishable seed but of imperishable, through the living and abiding word of God' (I Peter 1.23). All this vividly underscores the extent to which this established way of speaking of the gospel as 'the word' was rooted in the experience of so many of the first Christians – they experienced the kerygma as God addressing them, as a power which transformed their lives. There was no inherent logic either in their understanding of their experience or in the language they used to describe it which made it necessary for them to push the concept of the word beyond that of the (impersonal) power of God to that of a hypostatization or divine being. As I Peter continues:

'All flesh is grass

　　　and all its glory like the flower of the grass.
The grass withers, and the flower falls,
　　　but the word of the Lord abides for ever' (Isa. 40.6–8).
That word is the good news which was preached to you (I Peter 1.24f.).

The degree to which 'the word' had become fixed as a designation for the Christian message is indicated by the persistence of this usage into the later writings of the NT, with vigorous metaphors being regularly coined. Thus in the Catholic or Church Epistles of James and Peter – James 1.21 ('the implanted word'), 22f.; I Peter 2.8, 3.1. So too in the Pastorals – I Tim. 4.5 ('consecrated by the word of God'), 5.17, II Tim. 2.9 ('the word of God is not fettered'), 2.15, 4.2 – though already in the Pastorals the gospel is becoming a fixed and sacred word ('the true word' – I Tim. 1.15; 3.1; 4.9; II Tim. 2.11; Titus 1.9; 3.8; the 'sound words' – I Tim. 6.3; II Tim. 1.13; 'that the word of God might not be blasphemed' – Titus 2.5; cf. I Tim. 6.1).[67] The same is true of the Johannine writings – John 5.38, 8.31, 37, 43, 51f., 55, 12.48 ('the word that I have spoken will be his judge on the last day'), 14.23f., 15.3 ('made clean by the word which I have spoken to you'), 17.6, 14, 17, 20; I John 1.10, 2.5, 7, 14. In the Revelation of John the Seer, 'the word of God' is usually linked with 'the testimony of Jesus Christ', that is the Christian testimony to Christ (Rev. 1.2, 9; 6.9; 12.11; 20.4). In none of these instances is Jesus identified as the word, though the recognition of Jesus as the subject matter of the word is retained in some of the 'true words' quoted by the Pastorals (I Tim. 1.15; II Tim. 2.11; Titus 3.5–7) and in the double formula of Revelation. The one NT writing of any length which does not specifically preserve this talk of 'the word' as the word of preaching is II Peter, widely accepted as the latest of the NT writings.[68] What it does say about the word is somewhat surprisingly more reminiscent of pre-Christian usage than of the earlier NT teaching: 1.19 – 'the prophetic word' (cf. Philo, *Leg. All.* III.43; *Plant.* 117; *Sobr.* 68); 3.5 – 'by the word of God heavens existed long ago (συνεστῶσα τῷ τοῦ Θεοῦ λόγῳ)' (cf. Ps. 33.6 cited above p. 217; Heb. 11.3 – ῥήματι Θεοῦ). What is interesting in the latter verse is the straight reproduction of the OT talk of God's creative word, apparently without any awareness that elsewhere (already) in Christianity (John 1.1–18) that creative word had been identified with Christ (cf. I Clem. 27.4; Hermas, *Vis.* I.3.4).

§29.2 *The divine purpose revealed in Christ.* A halfway stage between the thought of Christ as the content of the word preached and the full identification of Christ as the word of God (incarnate) is the understanding of Christ as the one in whom God's pre-determined plan of salvation came to fulfilment. This is expressed most strongly in the speech attributed to Peter on the day of Pentecost – Acts 2.23:

this Jesus, delivered up according to the definite plan and foreknowledge of God (τῇ ὡρισμένῃ βουλῇ καὶ προγνώσει τοῦ Θεοῦ), you crucified and killed . . . (see also 4.28; cf. Luke 22.22; Acts 10.42; 17.31).

The same basic thought may be present in Rom. 1.3f. – 'appointed (ὁρισθέντος) Son of God in power' (see above p. 34); and it is certainly present in I Cor. 2.7 – 'we impart a secret and hidden wisdom of God, which God decreed (προώρισεν) before the ages . . .' (see above p. 178). In each case (perhaps including Rom. 1.3f.) what was determined long before in the will of God came to historical actuality in Christ – not, of course, in the sense that Jesus just happened to be the one who fitted the divine specifications, but in the sense that *Christ was the one who from the beginning had been pre-ordained for this role.* At the same time this may not be understood as an affirmation of Christ as himself pre-existent. It is the divine purpose for Christ which 'existed' from the beginning, not the one in whom it should be fulfilled; just as Paul can speak of the divine purpose similarly predetermined for those who believe in Christ (Rom. 8.28–30). No thought of the personal pre-existence of either Christ or believers is involved.[69] Similarly the hymnic opening to Ephesians (1.3–14):[70]

> [3]Blessed be the God and Father of our Lord Jesus Christ, who has blessed us in Christ with every spiritual blessing in the heavenly places, [4]even as he chose us in him before the foundation of the world, that we should be holy and blameless before him. [5]He destined (προορίσας) us in love to be his sons through Jesus Christ, according to the purpose of his will . . . [9]For he has made known to us in all wisdom and insight the mystery of his will, according to his purpose which he determined beforehand[71] in Christ [10]as a plan for the fullness of time, to unite all things in him, things in heaven and things on earth. [11]In him also we have been destined (προορισθέντες) and appointed according to the purpose of him who accomplishes all things according to the counsel of his will, [12]that we should live for the praise of his glory, we who first hoped in Christ.

Here too it is the divine choice or election which was made 'before the foundation of the world' – the predetermination of Christ as redeemer and of those who would be redeemed in and through Christ. We may speak of an ideal pre-existence at this point,[72] but of a real pre-existence of Christ or of believers once again there is no thought.[73] All this is simply the vigorous language of those who have no doubt that what has come to pass in and through Christ was part of God's plan from the beginning, indeed the climax of his original purpose in creating the world (1.9f.).[74]

Involved in this last passage is an alternative formulation, which comes to prominence particularly in Colossians and Ephesians, and which presents Jesus as the revelation and realization of God's hidden *mystery.*[75] We may note that Paul can identify the mystery both with the gospel (Col.

1.25f. – '. . . the word of God, the mystery hidden for ages . . .'; so Eph.
6.19 – 'the mystery of the gospel'; cf. Rom. 11.25f.) and with Christ (Col.
1.27 – 'this mystery, which is Christ in you . . .'; 2.2 – 'God's mystery,
Christ'; so Eph. 3.4 – 'the mystery of Christ').[76] What he means by this
language is fairly clear: God's master plan was hitherto hidden, unknown
to men, including the Jews; it was a mystery, 'kept secret for long ages'
(Rom. 16.25; also Eph. 3.9; Col. 1.26). But 'now it has been revealed to
the holy apostles and prophets by the Spirit' (Eph. 3.5) and through the
gospel to all the saints (Col. 1.26). What is this mystery? The mystery
was God's purpose, conceived before time began, to unite all things in
Christ (Eph. 1.10),[77] or more specifically, to bring the Gentiles into a
common salvation with the Jews, to unite Jew and Gentile as one body
in Christ (Rom. 11.25f.; 16.26; Eph. 3.6; Col. 1.27). Here again the
thought is not so much of pre-existence as of predetermination; it is the
mystery that was 'hidden for ages', not Christ.[78] Christ is the content of
this mystery as he is the content of the word of preaching. God having
previously kept secret his purpose has now realized (ἐποίησεν)[79] it in
Christ Jesus (Eph. 3.11) – Christ, in other words, seen not so much as
the mystery itself, but rather as the mystery revealed, the one who had
from the beginning been predetermined to bring the divine master plan
for men and world to its fulfilment.[80]

Rather more widespread is the related 'revelation-schema'[81] using φανεροῦσθαι (to be manifested, appear). The verb regularly has the connotation of a manifesting what was previously hidden (Mark 4.22; John
1.31; Rom. 16.26; Eph. 5.13; Col. 1.26; 3.4; I John 1.2), so that when
used of Christ particularly in I Peter 1.20, Heb. 9.26 and I Tim. 3.16, it
is a wholly logical step to conclude that the Christ who is thus described
as 'manifested' had previously been hidden – that is, had pre-existed
unknown to man.[82] However the verb can also be used simply in the
sense of 'appear' without any implication of a previous hiddenness (cf.
John 9.3; Rom. 3.21; II Cor. 3.3; 4.10f.; 5.10; I John 3.5, 8), so that the
context becomes of crucial importance in determining the intended meaning in any particular instance.

> I Peter 1.20 – He was predestined (προεγνωσμένου) before the foundation of
> the world but was made manifest (φανερωθέντος) at the end of the times for
> your sake.

J. N. D. Kelly argues plausibly that 'Christ's pre-existence, in some sense
at any rate, is assumed', rightly pointing out that this is not implied by
the word 'predestined, since God's foreknowledge extends to every being
destined at any time to come into existence', but maintaining that it is
implied by the word 'made manifest' 'which hints that he existed with
God, outside the process of history, prior to the incarnation'.[83] On the

other hand in I Peter 1.20 the key verb ('was made manifest') is set in antithesis with 'predestined'. That is to say, the contrast is not between pre-existence and incarnation, but between that which was predestined and that which was revealed. Christ was the one who was thus predestined and who was thus revealed or who appeared at the right time just as planned. In other words, Peter may well mean that what was 'made manifest' was not so much Christ as what was pre-destined for Christ, God's eternal plan of salvation for Christ, believers (cf. 1.2) and the world.[84]

In Hebrews however there is a clearer concept of the pre-existence of the Son (as we saw above pp. 55f., 209) and when we set πεφανέρωται in its context (Heb. 9.23–6) it presumably denotes the manifestation in this world of that which already existed in the heavenly world (see above pp. 52f.). At the same time we should recall that for Hebrews this pre-existence seems to be the existence of the platonic idea in the mind of God (see above p. 54), so that properly speaking what is revealed is the idea of Christ in the concrete historicity of Jesus of Nazareth, the appearance of the one who by his suffering and obedience showed himself to be (not merely to bear) the very stamp of divine sonship. This language of course alludes to Heb. 1.1–2[85] where, we may recall, the Son appears precisely as the historical actualization, the climactic articulation we might say, of the divine thought ('in these days he has spoken to us by a Son' – see above pp. 208f.). In which case we are again not so very far from the understanding of Christ as the content of the word preached, the revelation of the predetermined mystery of God's purpose of salvation.[86]

In the Pastorals the idea of the 'manifestation' or 'appearing' of Christ becomes very prominent (φανερόω – I Tim. 3.16; II Tim. 1.10; Titus 1.3; ἐπιφάνεια usually of his second appearing, I Tim. 6.14, II Tim. 4.1, 8, Titus 2.13, but in II Tim. 1.10 of his first appearing).[87] In I Tim. 3.16, 'manifested (ἐφανερώθη) in the flesh, vindicated in the Spirit', the contrast is between pre-Easter earthly existence and the Easter exaltation to heaven.[88] As in the parallel formulae in Rom. 1.3f. and II Tim. 2.8, there is no indication that the thought was intended to include a third stage of existence prior to appearance on earth. So φανεροῦσθαι may well be used here simply in the sense of 'appear', without any particular intention of implying a previous (pre-existent) hiddenness;[89] or since the hymn is presented as a statement of the Christian 'mystery', perhaps the thought is once again simply of the appearance of Christ as the unveiling of the divine mystery as in Colossians and Ephesians. Similarly reminiscent particularly of Eph. 1.3–14 is II Tim. 1.9f. –

God who saved us . . . in accordance with his own purpose and grace which was given us in Christ Jesus ages ago, but which has now been revealed (φανερωθεῖσαν) through the appearing (ἐπιφανείας) of our Saviour Jesus Christ.

We may note that it is the grace which was previously hidden and is now revealed; it 'was given us ages ago', given us 'in Christ Jesus' (as in Eph. 1), but that must mean that the gift was *purposed* 'ages ago', unless we are to take it that the actual giving and receiving, 'us' and 'Christ Jesus' were all alike pre-existent.[90] In other words, we still seem at this point to be in the circle of thought which understands Christ as the manifestation of.the pre-determined grace of God (rather than as the manifestation of the pre-existent Christ).[91] Finally we may note Titus 1.2f. –

in hope of eternal life which God ... promised ages ago and at the proper time manifested (in) his word (λόγον) through the kerygma ...

Here it is even clearer that what is thought of as happening 'ages ago' is God's promise; and it is that promise of eternal life which has been manifested. Indeed, the text says it is his word that he has manifested – that is, not Christ the Logos, but the word of promise, fulfilled in Christ and offered now in the kerygma.[92] In other words we are back where we started – Christ as the content of the word of preaching, the embodiment of the predetermined plan of salvation, the fulfilment of the divine purpose.

In short, the talk of purpose fulfilled, mystery revealed, that which was hidden manifested, goes beyond the talk of Christ as the content of the kerygma. Most important for us, it introduces the idea of pre-existence, of Christ as the one in whom the fore-ordained but hitherto hidden plan of God was brought to open display. The thought of course, it is perhaps worth repeating, is not of Christ as one who just happened to do all the right things and so fulfilled the divine purpose, but of Christ as the one who from the beginning was predestined to be the fulfiller, the revealer, the redeemer, so that the divine purpose could be said to have been determined beforehand 'in Christ' and those who came to be 'in Christ' by grace through faith could likewise think of themselves as chosen 'in Christ before the foundation of the world' (Eph. 1.4). At times the language seems to predicate pre-existence to Christ as such, and that may have been the intention, particularly in the φανεροῦσθαι formulation in I Peter 1.20, Heb. 9.26 and I Tim. 3.16; but whether such a meaning was actually intended in the first place remains unclear. It may indeed be the case that once again we find ourselves confronted with language which gathered to itself a developing christological significance as the formulations were detached from the context of the predetermined purpose and mystery and set more within the context of developing religious beliefs in pre-existent divine redeemers.[93] At any rate in these formulations we are somewhere between Christ understood as the word preached, and Christ understood as the word incarnate. The latter only comes to full expression in the writings of the Johannine circle.

§30. THE WORD INCARNATE

There remain those passages where Christ is identified specifically as the Word of God and where the identification seems in one case at least to imply a clear concept of Christ's pre-existence.[94] The passages in question are to be found, perhaps significantly, in what are probably the latest group of NT documents – viz. the Johannine writings, here including the Revelation of John the Seer. Their precise relation to each other is uncertain, but since I John is probably later than the Gospel of John,[95] and since anyway the Johannine prologue seems to make use of an earlier poem (see below), it is most appropriate if we start with the Gospel.

§30.1 *John 1.1–18*.[96] Without doubt John 1.1–18 expresses the most powerful Word-christology in the NT. Here, beyond dispute, the Word is pre-existent, and Christ is the pre-existent Word incarnate.

There is widespread agreement that the prologue uses poetic material which had probably been composed independently of the Gospel, though quite probably by the same Johannine circle (perhaps even by the same hand), and not necessarily much before the composition of the Gospel itself. Several scholars remain unhappy with this conclusion,[97] but it still seems to make the best sense of several features in the prologue. The short rhythmical clauses for the most part fall naturally into a poetic form; the lines exhibit a 'staircase parallelism' (particularly vv. 1–5), whereby a word prominent in one line is taken up in the next;[98] there are several important words in the prologue which do not recur again in the Gospel (particularly Logos, grace, fullness); and the references to John the Baptist do seem to disrupt both style and train of thought and so give the strong impression of being insertions into an already structured Logos poem (vv. 6–8, 15 – which reads as though it was a reference *back* to 1.30!).[99] The links with the Gospel, both verbal (particularly life, light and darkness, world, glory?) and structural (particularly vv. 11f.), are probably best explained as theological concepts and themes common to both authors (perhaps the same man), or by the hypothesis that the Logos poem itself actually influenced the composition of the Gospel in part at least. Whatever the precise facts of the matter, we most probably have to do with a Logos poem which originally had an existence independent of the Gospel.

This conclusion is important for us since we are endeavouring to trace what lay behind and what led up to the Logos christology of the Johannine prologue. For we cannot exclude the possibility that the christology of the Logos poem is in some respects, perhaps crucial respects, different from that of the Evangelist in his use of the poem. Fortunately the precise form of the Logos poem does not affect our discussion too much (though see n. 106 below), so that I may be permitted simply to suggest a plausible and not too controversial reconstruction as a basis on which to proceed further.[100]

> [1]In the beginning was the Word
> and the Word was with God
> and the Word was God.
> [2](He was in the beginning with God).
> [3]All things were made through him,
> and without him was made
> nothing that was made.[101]
>
> [4]In him was life
> and the life was the light of men;
> [5]the light shines in the darkness
> and the darkness has not overcome it.
> [9](This was the true light
> which enlightens everyman).
>
> [10]He was in the world
> (and the world was made through him)
> and the world knew him not.
> [11]He came to his own realm
> and his own people did not receive him.
> [12]But as many as received him
> to them he gave authority to become children of God.
>
> [14]And the Word became flesh
> and dwelt among us
> (and we looked upon his glory,
> glory as of the only Son from the Father)
> full of grace and truth;
> [16]for from his fullness
> we have all received,
> grace upon grace.

Two basic items are clear and almost beyond dispute.[102] First, in the Logos poem we are confronted with the *pre-existent* Logos: the Logos *was* (not 'came to be') in the beginning.[103] Here we have moved beyond any thought of the Logos as created, even the first created being (contrast Prov. 8.22; Sir. 24.8f.; Philo, *Leg. All.* III.175; *Ebr.* 31). Rather the point is made with emphasis that *everything* that came to be, came to be through the Logos (v.3). Second, the Logos *became* flesh – not merely entered into, clothed himself with (as the Spirit did Gideon – Judg. 6.34), not merely appeared as (as Yahweh appeared to Abraham – Gen. 18), but became flesh.[104] Here we have an explicit statement of *incarnation*, the first, and indeed only such statement in the NT.[105] And it was probably made already in the Logos poem, that is, prior to the writing of John's Gospel.[106]

At the same time we must recognize that *prior to v.14 nothing has been said which would be strange to a Hellenistic Jew* familiar with the Wisdom tradition or the sort of mystical philosophizing that we find in Philo. We have already outlined several parallels to John 1.1, 4, 11 and 14 in the Wisdom literature (above pp. 164f.). Although the Wisdom allusions provide the fuller backcloth to the Logos poem overall, at some points there are closer parallels with Philo's Logos.[107] As we have seen, Philo's Logos as the archetypal idea, was in the beginning before creation and was the instrument by which God created (above pp. 225, 227; cf. John 1.1a, 3). In *Immut*. 31f. we have the thought both of the intelligible world (κόσμος νοητός), the elder Son (i.e. = the Logos), at the side of God (παρ' ἑαυτῷ), and of the eternal timelessness of that relation (cf. John 1.1b). The dispute as to the significance of θεός (God/god) without the article in John 1.1c is clarified at least to some extent when we recall Philo's exposition of Gen. 31.13 in *Som*. I.227–30 –

> He that is truly God is One, but those that are improperly so called are more than one. Accordingly the holy word in the present instance has indicated him who is truly God by means of the articles saying 'I am the God', while it omits the article when mentioning him who is improperly so called, saying 'Who appeared to thee in the place' not 'of the God', but simply 'of God' (Gen. 31.13 LXX – ἐν τόπῳ θεοῦ). Here it gives the title of 'God' to his chief Word. . . .

The point does not depend on the author of the Logos poem being familiar with Philo. It is rather that Philo demonstrates that a distinction between ὁ θεός and θεός such as we find in John 1.1b–c, would be deliberate by the author and significant for the Greek reader.[108] Not only so, Philo shows that he could happily call the Logos 'God/god' without infringing his monotheism (or even 'the second God' – *Qu.Gen.* II.62).[109] Bearing in mind our findings with regard to the Logos in Philo, this cannot but be significant: the Logos for Philo is 'God' not as a being independent of 'the God' but as 'the God' in his knowability – the Logos standing for that *limited* apprehension of the one God which is all that the rational man, even the mystic may attain to.[110]

In vv.4–5 (second stanza) the thought of the Logos as light is equally familiar to the Wisdom tradition (particularly Wisd. 7.26) and to the Logos of Philo (*Opif.* 33; *Conf.* 60–3; *Som.* I.75).[111] Though the light/darkness contrast of v. 5 is less typical of the Wisdom-Logos tradition (though cf. Wisd. 7.29f.), we are by no means forced to the conclusion that we have here a Gnostic cosmological dualism, since a light/darkness antithesis is equally typical of Jewish apocalyptic thought (note particularly I Enoch 89.8; 104.8; 108.11; and the contrast between 'the sons of light' and 'the sons of darkness' in IQM).[112] So perhaps we should see here yet another example of the interweaving of Wisdom and apocalyptic thought which took place at a very early stage in Christian theologizing (see above pp. 200, 204). Of particular relevance for us is the linking of the Logos with life and light, though the precise linking is obscured by the uncertainty over punctuation (above n. 101). The thought is again very similar to what we find in Wisdom and Philo: according to Proverbs 'he who finds me (Wisdom) finds life' (Prov. 8.35; cf. Sir. 4.12); according to Philo, 'he who lives an irrational (ἀλόγως) life has been cut off from the life of God' (*Post.* 69) – that is, to live in accordance with right reason (ὀρθὸς λόγος) is to know the life of the Logos, of God (see above pp. 222, 224). In each case, as the metaphors of light and life also imply, the Logos-Wisdom is best understood less in personal terms and more in terms of the vivifying power and revelation of God, as God giving life and revealing how that life should be lived.[113]

In vv. 10–12b (third stanza) the antecedents are mainly to be found in the Wisdom tradition rather than in Philo – particularly the idea of Wisdom as hidden from men or rejected by men, but revealed to Israel ('his own') in the Torah (Sir. 24; Bar. 3.9–4.4; I Enoch 42). But the thought that lovers of Wisdom, the righteous, or those who live in harmony with the Logos, can properly be called 'sons of God' is familiar to both Wisdom and Philo (see above p. 15).[114] It is quite likely that v.11 alludes to the Jewish claim to a special revelation in the Torah: not only has the rest of the world rejected or ignored that wise power, that divine reason by which the world was created, but Israel too ('his own') has rejected the special focusing of the divine wisdom and reason which is the Torah (though some by living in accord with it thus showed themselves to be sons of God).[115] Thus would the Logos poem prepare for the dramatic disclosure about to be made in v.14 – the third and decisive stage of God's saving purpose – the Logos revealed previously in the world, and through the Torah, but now as the man Jesus of Nazareth. The point for us however would again be that in the earlier stages of the poem we are still dealing with the Wisdom and Logos figure of pre-Christian Judaism, that is, not as a personal being, but as the wise utterance of God personified.

It is only in v.14 (fourth stanza) that we go beyond anything pre-Christian. To be sure v.14b echoes the idea of Wisdom pitching her tent in Israel (Sir. 24.8 – above p. 165), and if v. 14c–d was originally part of the poem we would be back with the overlap between Wisdom and glory as near equivalent ways of speaking of the self-manifestation of Yahweh (cf. particularly Wisd. 7.25; see above p. 130). But the central and crucial affirmation is 'the Word became flesh', and that has no real parallel in pre-Christian Jewish thought. The nearest we come to it is probably in Philo's description of Moses as 'the law-giving Word' (*Migr.* 23f.; cf. 122). But here the thought is partly allegorical and partly that Moses is the wise man, the man of reason *par excellence*, the most holy of men,[116] the finest reproduction of the archetypal Logos. To speak of Moses as the 'incarnation of the Logos'[117] is to use the word 'incarnation' in a broader and looser way than is appropriate to John 1.14. That which belongs to the intelligible world is for Philo by definition incorporeal (ἀσώματος). Corporeal and incorporeal together make up man, but that does not reduce the sharp distinction between them; man is or has a mind (λόγος), but that does not mean that the mind has become flesh. For Philo it was inconceivable that the Logos should *become* flesh, as it is inconceivable for Greek thought generally, as indeed also for Jewish (cf. Isa. 31.3).[118] But this is precisely the claim that the Logos poem makes – 'the Word *became* flesh'.[119]

The conclusion which seems to emerge from our analysis thus far is that it is only with v.14 that we can begin to speak of the *personal* Logos. The poem uses rather impersonal language (became flesh), but no Christian would fail to recognize a reference here to Jesus Christ – the Word became not flesh in general but Jesus Christ. Prior to v.14 we are in the same realm as pre-Christian talk of Wisdom and Logos, the same language and ideas that we find in the Wisdom tradition and in Philo, where, as we have seen, we are dealing with personifications rather than persons, personified actions of God rather than an individual divine being as such. The point is obscured by the fact that we have to translate the masculine Logos as 'he' throughout the poem. But if we translated *logos* as 'God's utterance' instead, it would become clearer that the poem did not necessarily intend the Logos in vv.1–13 to be thought of as a personal divine being. In other words, the revolutionary significance of v.14 may well be that it marks *not only the transition in the thought of the poem from pre-existence to incarnation, but also the transition from impersonal personification to actual person.*[120]

This indeed is the astounding nature of the poem's claim. If it had asserted simply that an individual divine being had become man, that would have raised fewer eyebrows. It is the fact that the Logos poet has taken language which any thoughtful Jew would recognize to be the language of personification and has *identified* it with a particular person, *as* a particular person, that would be so astonishing: the manifestation of God become a man! God's utterance not merely come through a particular individual, but actually become that one person, Jesus of Nazareth! We now can see how logical was the step from the way of speaking of Christ examined above (§29), but it nevertheless was a huge leap from thinking of Jesus as the content of the word of preaching to identify him as the divine Logos become incarnate (see further below p. 245). So too Paul's use of Wisdom language in a free way when speaking of the cosmological significance of Christ, and Matthew's identification of Christ as Wisdom certainly prepared the way (above §§24–25), and implied that earthly as well as exalted Christ was to be identified as Wisdom, but neither actually was bold enough, or perhaps had occasion to sum up the christology implied in such a brief and devastating assertion as 'the Word became flesh'.[121]

Thus far our analysis has confined itself to discovering how the poem would have been understood at the pre-Johannine level. When the Fourth Evangelist takes it up he alters its sense in two ways: first by his insertions and additions to the poem; second by making the expanded poem the prologue to his Gospel. His addition of vv.6–8 make it clear that he interpreted vv.9–12 as referring already to the *incarnate* Logos, so that v.14 becomes more of a resumptive summary of a claim already made.[122] But more important, by affixing the expanded poem to his Gospel he conflates its Logos christology with his own Son of God christology, whereby it becomes clear that for John the pre-existent Logos was indeed a divine personal being (see above §6.5). 1.18 in fact serves as the connecting link, uniting the claim that Christ is both (the incarnation of) the Logos God and the only Son of the Father (μονογενὴς θεός).[123] It takes up the very Jewish thought,[124] that 'no one has ever seen God' (e.g. Ex. 33.20; Deut. 4.12; Sir. 43.31; Philo, *Post.* 168f.; Josephus, *Bell.* VII.346), and makes in effect the very Philonic assertion that the Logos is both as close to God as man can conceive or perceive, and reveals as much of God to man as is possible to be revealed (above pp. 226f.);[125] in the same way, as Son he makes God see-able as Father (12.45; 14.9).[126] The point, however, is that it is not the Philonic incorporeal Logos that provides this bridge to and from God, but the man Jesus Christ.

What John seems to have done therefore is to unite two rather different ways of understanding Christ within first-century Christianity. The one used Wisdom and Logos language of Christ, identifying Christ as Wisdom, as the man that the Logos became, but did not seem to think of pre-existent Wisdom-Logos as a personal being or of Christ as one who had been pre-existent as such. The other thought of Christ more as the Son of God 'sent' by the Father. Initially this latter had no overtones of pre-existence (above pp. 39f.), but in the earlier attempt to unite the two, in Hebrews, the combination of Platonic cosmology with Jewish salvation-history produced a kind of ideal (and impersonal) pre-existence (above pp. 54f., 209), and as the first century drew towards its close the concept of a pre-existent divine redeemer figure seems to have been coming into vogue (above pp. 21, 96). John either took these antecedents up and used them in his own way, or, just as, if not more probable, he himself took the step of speaking of Christ as the Son sent *from heaven*, as a personal being sent from his pre-existent glory into the world. This union of Logos christology and Son of God christology,[127] with its possibility of combining the metaphors and imagery appropriate to the personified Wisdom and the idea Logos of pre-Christian Judaism with the more intimate personal language appropriate to talk of Father and Son, became the matrix from which developed the christologies of subsequent centuries[128] – a dynamic combination, but one always in danger of slackening the tension of personal-impersonal and of falling back into either a less personal monotheism or a polytheism of two or more Gods.[129]

§30.2   To complete our picture of 'the word of God' in the NT there are two further passages within the Johannine writings to be considered – I John 1.1–3 and Rev. 19.13.

(*a*) *I John 1.1–3:*

> ¹That which was from the beginning, which we have heard, which we have seen with our eyes, which we have looked upon and our hands touched, concerning the word of life – ²and the life was manifested (ἐφανερώθη), and we have seen (it) and bear witness and proclaim to you the eternal life which was with the Father and was manifested to us – ³that which we have seen and heard, we proclaim also to you . . .[130]

At first glance the echo of John 1.1–18 is very strong: 'from the beginning' echoes 'in the beginning' (John 1.1); 'with the Father' (I John 1.2) perhaps echoes 'with God' (John 1.1); 'see', 'look upon', 'life' and 'bear witness' all occur at important points in the Johannine prologue (John 1.18; 1.14; 1.4; 1.7, 8, 15); and 'our hands touched' for us naturally evokes John 20.17, 27, even though the verbs and ideas are not the same (though cf. Luke 24.39). Yet the fact is, the subject of which I John 1.1–3 speaks is not Christ, not even Christ the incarnate Word, but '*that which concerns the word of life*' (the relative pronouns are neuter, not masculine); and what 'was manifested' is not Christ or the Word, but the *life*, 'the eternal life which was with the Father'. In other words, it is clearly the *content* of the message which is in view, not the person as such.[131] It is not so much Christ the incarnation of the pre-existent Word that the author speaks of, but Christ whose life, death and resurrection is the content of the proclamation and the means to eternal life. Indeed, were it not for John 1.1–18 we would naturally see I John 1.1–3 simply as a more ambitious statement along the lines of Luke 1.2 (cf. Phil. 2.16; John 6.68; Acts 5.20; and §29.1 above), stressing the historical facticity of the revelation which was (and is) Christ (cf. §29.2) over against those who would seek to reduce that historical facticity in a docetic direction (I John 4.2f.).

Even with the phrase 'from the beginning' it is by no means clear that pre-existence (whether of the word or of the life) is in mind. The formula (ἀπ᾽ ἀρχῆς) is different from that used in John 1.1 (ἐν ἀρχῇ) and is one which I John uses regularly. In two passages it does denote the beginning of time (I John 2.13f.; 3.8); but in three other passages it denotes the beginning of the *church* – the time when the readers first heard the proclamation of the word of life (2.7, 24; 3.11). The emphasis of 1.1–3 suggests that if anything it is the latter meaning which I John intends in 1.1[132] – the word they had heard was the very same word that those closest to Jesus, the first apostles and disciples had proclaimed 'from the beginning';[133] though a deliberate ambiguity should not be excluded.[134]

What we find then in I John 1.1–3 is a deliberate evocation of John 1.1–18, but one which equally recalls older and more established ideas of Christ as the content of the word of preaching. In other words, I John 1.1–3 serves as a bridge between the earliest Christian talk of the word of God and the prologue to John's Gospel,[135] and (assuming the two writings come from the same circle) shows that the Johannine prologue may not be so far removed from that earlier thought as at first appears: he who is so exclusively and completely the content of the word of preaching, the mystery revealed, is himself the Word made flesh.

At the same time, I John 1.1–3 may also give a clue to the christological developments following the Fourth Gospel. In particular, if R. E. Brown is correct, the secessionists from the Johannine community (2.19) based their understanding of Christ on the Fourth Gospel – a christology which devalued the earthly life and ministry of Jesus (4.2–3); hence by way of response the stronger emphasis in 1.1–3 on the tangible historicity of the beginning of the gospel in the life and ministry of Jesus.[136] In which case we can see how quickly the thought of Christ as the Son of God come down from heaven led in some minds to a devaluation of Jesus the man – how quickly the thought of a divine individual coming to earth as redeemer could be headed in a gnosticizing direction (Ignatius also makes us aware of the speed with which such speculation spread and developed – *Eph.* 7; *Trall.* 9–10; *Smyrn.* 1–3). In short, I John shows already the difficulty found in maintaining the Fourth Evangelist's tension between Jesus the Logos incarnate and Jesus the pre-existent Son of God.

(*b*) In *Rev. 19.11–13* the seer sees in a vision one sitting on a white horse to judge and make war, his eyes like a flame of fire, on his head many diadems. 'He is clad in a robe dipped in blood, and the name by which he is called is the Word of God' (v. 13). The writer can hardly be unmindful of his more frequent use of 'the word of God' as a description of the gospel (see above p. 234), and his vision at this point goes on to describe the 'sharp sword' coming out from the mouth of this majestic figure (v. 15; also 1.16; 2.16; cf. Heb. 4.12), probably using the imagery of Isa. 11.4 ('he shall smite the earth with the rod of his mouth' – LXX:

τῷ λόγῳ τοῦ στόματος αὐτοῦ), Isa. 49.2 ('he made my mouth like a sharp sword') and Ps. Sol. 17.27 ('He shall destroy the godless nations with the word of his mouth'). But the closer parallel is probably given by Wisd. 18.15f. – 'your all powerful word leaped down from heaven, from the royal throne ... a stern warrior carrying the sharp sword of your authentic command'.[137] There is no indication here that the author was thinking of Christ as the pre-existent Word or the incarnate Word as such – the thought is more of the apocalyptic mission of the exalted Christ.[138] On the other hand, if Revelation comes from the same circle as the other Johannine writings then an echo of the Johannine prologue (John 1.1–18) would not be out of place.[139] This suggestion is strengthened by the fact that elsewhere the seer calls the exalted Christ 'Alpha and Omega' (22.13; cf. 1.8; 21.6), 'the beginning and the end' (22.13; cf. 21.6) 'the beginning of the creation of God' (3.14). In the last named verse ἡ ἀρχὴ τῆς κτίσεως probably alludes to Prov. 8.22 – 'The Lord created me as (or in) the beginning of his way (LXX κύριος ἔκτισεν με ἀρχὴν ὁδῶν αὐτοῦ) ...' (see also Wisd. 6.22; Sir. 24.8f.). It cannot altogether be excluded that the phrase (ἡ ἀρχὴ τῆς κτίσεως) means 'the beginning of creation' = the first created being (cf. Gen. 49.3; Deut. 21.17; so still in Sir. 24.8f.; Philo, *Leg. All.* III.175; *Ebr.* 31; cf. above p. 189).[140] But most would take the phrase more in the sense that the developed Wisdom tradition took it, with ἀρχή understood more in the sense 'source', the one from or through whom creation took its beginning – as in John 1.3, Col. 1.16 and Heb. 1.2.[141] Perhaps we should simply accept that at this early stage, as in Philo (see above pp. 227f.; here cf. *Leg. All.* I.43), there was no clear distinction between the pre-existent Word as first created being and agent of creation. At all events, the exalted Christ of John's vision is called both 'the beginning' and 'the Word of God', so that the thought of Christ as the incarnation of the pre-existent Word is very close if not actually presupposed.

These two passages then do not add anything beyond the incarnation christology of the Johannine prologue. But they do perhaps take us a little behind the development which the Logos poem expressed, and may indeed show us that the thought of Christ as (the content of) the word of preaching played a bigger role in leading up to the formulation of the Logos poem than at first appears. Moreover, they remind us that the Johannine circle did not abandon the earlier understanding of the word of God as the word of preaching even after the identification of Christ as the Word incarnate in an exclusive sense. Perhaps then they also show us that the transition from thought of the word of God as the gospel to Christ as the Word incarnate was a quite natural step for them to take, or at least seemed so to them once it had first been made.

§31. CONCLUSIONS

§31.1 Our findings with regard to the pre-Christian Jewish understanding of the word of God are in all significant respects the same as those already arrived at in our study of the other so-called 'intermediary beings' or hypostases in pre-Christian Jewish thought. In the OT *'the word of God' is God's utterance, God himself making known his will to his people*, particularly through the agency of the prophet. Even when writers weave poetic imagery and metaphor round the concept the thought is still essentially of *God's effective power put forth to achieve his purpose*. In Philo the allegorical interpretation of the Jewish scriptures from a Platonic-Stoic world view results in a multifarious presentation of the Logos, not always consistent within itself, but always revolving round the basic understanding that the Logos is *God's rational energy reaching out into the world, God himself insofar as he may be known by man* whether through his own rationality or through prophetic ecstasy. It is possible to see how such language developed subsequently into what may properly be called the myth of a divine being distinct from God. But even with Philo we are still firmly in the realm of metaphor and allegorical illustration rather than of myth. Consequently, if we are rightly to characterize the stage at which Hellenistic Judaism had arrived prior to Christ, we should speak more carefully of imagery which was the precursor of myth, of language which could be adapted to the formulation of myth, rather than of 'an emerging mythical configuration', let alone of myth proper.

§31.2 When we turn to the NT writings themselves and compare early with late *it is difficult once again to avoid seeing some kind of development* – a development from the concept of the word as the word of preaching, where Christ is the sum and substance of the message proclaimed, to the concept of the word as Christ himself, Christ the *incarnation* of God's word uttered from the beginning of time in creative and redemptive power. Not that the latter assertion supersedes the former, for the conception of the word of God as the effective proclamation of the good news of Christ is consistent throughout almost the whole of the NT. But the identification of Christ with the word of God in a deliberately metaphysical way (John 1.14) must be regarded as marking a new stage in Christian thinking. We must as always beware of oversystematizing such expansions or deepening of thought. It is possible however that the understanding of the Christ-event as the *revelation* of God's supreme *mystery* served as something of a transition in this development. For in a series of documents which most probably span the two or three decades prior to the Fourth Gospel we find a popular way of speaking of the Christ-event whose ambiguity seems to hover hesitatingly between the idea of the divine predetermination of that which is proclaimed and a conception of the actual pre-existence of that which was predetermined. *Perhaps then we should recognize in that ambiguity a world view which was beginning to accommodate the conception of personal pre-existence* – the almost imperceptible transition in thought (hence the ambiguity), from what would have been taken for granted to be ideal pre-existence (as we now call it), to a conceptualization of Christ as himself having pre-existed (real pre-existence). Whether the thought of Christ himself as having pre-existed with God had actually become articulate in the minds of such writers as those who penned I Peter 1.20 and I Tim. 3.16 is far from clear; in each case it is rather more likely that the thought is still of Christ as the eschatological revelation of God's purpose pre-determined from the beginning. A similar ambiguity is evident in I John 1.1–3, presumably reflecting the same transition in thought. But by that time the idea of incarnation (the divine becoming human) had broken surface in the Logos poem behind the Johannine prologue. And however unclear were the thoughts of those who penned such language in transition, there can be no doubt that the Fourth Evangelist had a clear perception of the personal pre-existence of the Logos-Son. The importance of these steps taken by the Logos poet and the Fourth Evangelist should not be underestimated: so far as our evidence (Christian and non-Christian) is concerned, *the author of John 1.1–16 was the first to take that step which no Hellenistic-Jewish author had taken before him, the first to identify the word of God as a particular person;* and so far as our evidence is concerned *the Fourth Evangelist was the first Christian writer to conceive clearly of the personal pre-existence of the Logos-Son and to present it as a fundamental part of his message.* Certainly therefore the Fourth Gospel can properly be presented as the climax to the evolving thought of first-century Christian understanding of Christ: whether that climax is simply the outworking of the inherent logic of God's (final) revelation in and through Christ, or reflects something of wider developments of thought in the Hellenistic world of the late first century AD is an issue we will explore further in the final chapter.

§31.3   It is a lasting testimony to the inspired genius of the Fourth Evangelist that he brought together the Logos poem and the Father-Son christology in such a definitive way. Without the Fourth Gospel all the other assertions we have been looking at would have been resolvable into more modest assertions.[142] Of the canonical literature it is pre-eminently the Fourth Gospel which prevents Christian thought from settling for a more accommodating faith, more straightforwardly conceptualized, of Jesus simply the eschatological prophet, climax of God's revelation to man, or of Jesus simply God (or a god) appearing on earth in human guise. The Fourth Evangelist clarified the tension that had always been present in the Jewish conception of God – between God transcendent and God immanent, between the experience of the divine both as personal address and as impersonal numinous power. For he identified the impersonal Logos with the personal Son, and presented Jesus as the incarnate Logos who explains the unseeable God, the (immanent) Son who makes the (transcendent) Father visible (1.18; 12.45; 14.9). Yet in resolving the tension for Jewish faith he set up a fresh tension for Christian faith. For when the divine power that seizes upon conscience and will, heart and mind is identified with or as a particular person it is bound to have an effect on the resulting conception of God. However much the human encounter with God had been experienced as personal address, it had not been conceived in terms of a person distinct from God. But now in John the word of God is identified with a particular historical person, whose pre-existence as a person with God is asserted throughout. Now the Christian conception of God must make room for the person who was Christ, the Logos incarnate.

John it is then who sets the terms and provides the norm for the subsequent discussion on the Christian understanding of God and of Christ. For if Christ is the Logos, θεός and not ὁ θεός, the Son and not the Father, then the modalist option is ruled out (one God who manifested himself as the Son). And if the Logos *is* Christ, or became Christ, and not merely spoke through him, then the option of seeing Christ simply as an inspired prophet is also inadequate. But how can one speak finally of the Christ who is both one with the Father (10.30) and less than the Father (14.28), both Word become flesh (1.14) and 'only begotten god' (1.18)? That is the question which racked the church throughout the patristic period and continues to tease and test the minds of Christians still. In a real sense the history of christological controversy is the history of the church's attempt to come to terms with John's christology – first to accept it and then to understand and re-express it. The latter task will never end.

VIII

CONCLUSION

§32. SUMMARY

This book has been an inquiry into the beginnings of christology, the beginnings of the distinctive and striking (some would say peculiar and astonishing) claims made by Christians about Jesus whom they call Christ. More precisely, it has been an investigation of the origins of one of Christianity's central and foundational beliefs – the doctrine of the incarnation. How arose the claim that Jesus was Son of God 'begotten before all ages', sent from heaven to become flesh in or as the son of Mary? Our method of procedure has been to look at a series of 'vertical' cross-sections – Son of God, Son of Man, etc. In summarizing our findings the most helpful procedure will be to present them as a series of 'horizontal' sightings across the material at different stages (so far as they are distinguishable).

§32.1 *Pre-Christian antecedents.* At the end of §3.5 above we concluded that there was 'little or no good evidence from the period prior to Christianity's beginnings that the Ancient Near East seriously entertained the idea of a god or son of god descending from heaven to become a human being in order to bring men salvation, except perhaps at the level of popular pagan superstition'. But then the suggestion that Christianity had simply taken over fully fledged ideas of incarnation from more established cults never was particularly plausible, however impressive some of the individual 'parallels' discovered by History of Religions research at the turn of the century might be. There is of course always the possibility that 'popular pagan superstition' became popular *Christian* superstition, by a gradual assimilation and spread of belief at the level of popular piety (we must beware of assuming that all developments in Christian thought stem from the Pauls and the Johns of Christianity).

But the developments we are concerned with were already beginning to come to expression within thirty or forty years of Jesus' death and resurrection, and again and again in our inquiry we have been confronted with a level of sophistication which goes beyond the more simplistic categories of 'popular piety'.

That conclusion at the end of §3.5 was provisional and amounted simply to a clearing of the ground to open the way for a more detailed investigation of the most plausible candidates for the position of precursor of the Christian doctrine of the incarnation. We have now completed that examination and can draw more final conclusions. These are as follows. There is no evidence that there existed prior to Christianity a belief in a heavenly Son of Man who would appear from heaven as Israel's Messiah; so far as we can tell it was Christianity (Jesus or the first Christians) who made the first identification of the 'son of man' in Daniel's vision as a particular individual. Whether there was a belief current at the time of Jesus that Elijah or Enoch themselves would return from heaven at the end of the age is not clear, but in any case there is no real indication that Jesus was at any time identified as either, and the probability that Enoch's identification with Daniel's 'son of man' was provoked by Christianity's Son of Man christology is stronger than the vice-versa alternative. Again, there is no evidence of belief in a heavenly Man who would act as final redeemer in the period prior to Christianity; such speculation as there was concerning the first man or concept of a heavenly (Platonic) ideal of man did not regard him as a saviour descending to earth. Here too it is more probable that Christianity's own identification of Christ as last Adam provided the decisive impetus for the wider speculation towards the Primal Man Redeemer myth. Of the so-called intermediary figures in pre-Christian Judaism, only angels properly qualified for that description, and though there was a clear enough concept of angelic leadership of the faithful in the final climactic events of this age, there was certainly no thought of angels becoming men in order to redeem. Again, though there are indications that some of the earliest Christians (popular piety?) wanted to think of the exalted Christ as an angel, such speculation was strongly rejected by the leading voices in the communities in question and elsewhere the possibility of understanding Jesus as an angel was not even considered.

The other 'intermediary figures' most prominent in our inquiry, Spirit, Wisdom, Word, are *im*properly so called, since they never really reach the status of divine beings independent of God in Jewish thought. They all remain in the literature of our period (Philo included) ways of speaking of God's powerful interaction with his world and his people, God's experienced immanence through nature and revelation, in Torah, prophet and saving act, which yet did not infringe his transcendence. Their pre-existence is the pre-existence of God, of God's purpose to create and redeem. However much the language used of them may depict them as independent entities, it never rises above the vivid metaphors and poetic imagery of Hebrew thought. The attempt by those accustomed to more prosaic language to find a middle way between poetic personification and wholly independent entity by speaking of hypostases merely exhibits a failure to appreciate the vigour of Hebrew imagery as well as the importation of a category (hypostasis) whose technical meaning only developed later and which would have been meaningless to pre-Christian Judaism. And though parallels can be found in the wider religion of pagan polytheism, particularly for the way of speaking of divine Wisdom, they show only that Jewish writers knew how to present their faith in the one God and his law in a way that was attractive to their hearers, not that the writers concerned regarded Wisdom in the same way as worshippers of Isis regarded Isis. Once again it was most probably Christianity's identification of Jesus as God's Wisdom and God's Word which led to these concepts being drawn into subsequent Gnostic speculation as titles for emanations from the unknown God. In short, *we have found nothing in pre-Christian Judaism or the wider religious thought of the Hellenistic world which provides sufficient explanation of the origin of the doctrine of the incarnation, no way of speaking about God, the gods, or intermediary beings which so far as we can tell would have given birth to this doctrine apart from Christianity.* Where similar beliefs concerning heavenly redeemers did emerge it is more likely that the influence ran the other way, with Christian claims concerning Christ providing the catalyst for other systems and cults.

§32.2   *Jesus.* Did the doctrine of the incarnation begin with Jesus? If we accept the possibility of penetrating some way into Jesus' own self-consciousness, self-understanding, self-estimate, or whatever is the appropriate phrase, what do we find? We find one who was conscious of being God's son, a sense of intimate sonship, an implication that Jesus believed or experienced this sonship to be something distinctive and unique; but the evidence did not allow us to penetrate further or to be more explicit. We find one who may well have understood the vision of Dan. 7 to be a description or indication of his own role, as one who represented God's people at the climax of the present age, as the one who would be vindicated beyond his anticipated suffering and death and play the decisive role in the final judgment. We find one who claimed to be inspired by the Spirit of God, to be a prophet in the tradition of the prophets, but more than that, to be the eschatological prophet, the one anointed by God to announce and enact the good news of God's final rule and intervention. We find one who may well have claimed to speak as the final envoy of Wisdom, with an immediacy of revelatory authority that transcended anything that had gone before. But there is no indication that Jesus thought or spoke of himself as having pre-existed with God prior to his birth or appearance on earth. Such self-assertions appear only in the latest form of the canonical Gospel tradition and presuppose substantial developments in christological thinking which cannot be traced back to Jesus himself.

It may of course be the case that Jesus *was* more, much more than he himself explicitly claimed to be. But from the beginning Christianity's claims regarding Jesus have always been about the whole Christ-event, particularly his death and resurrection, and never simply his life as though that had independent value distinct from his passion and exaltation. Consequently Christianity's claims regarding Jesus have never depended solely on Jesus' own testimony regarding himself, let alone on its accessibility or otherwise. On the other hand, a complete discontinuity between Jesus' own self-assertions and the subsequent claims made about him would constitute a fatal flaw at the foundation of the whole superstructure of subsequent christology, not least the doctrine of the incarnation. It is of crucial importance therefore for Christianity that a sense of climactic finality, of immediacy of divine authority, of unique intimacy in his relationship with God can be detected in the earliest and probably authentic stratum of the Gospel tradition. *We cannot claim that Jesus believed himself to be the incarnate Son of God; but we can claim that the teaching to that effect as it came to expression in the later first-century Christian thought was, in the light of the whole Christ-event, an appropriate reflection on and elaboration of Jesus' own sense of sonship and eschatological mission.*

§32.3   *First generation Christianity. The single most striking feature of earliest christology is the impact of the resurrection of Jesus.* The language and proof texts used spoke of Jesus becoming or being appointed Son of God at or as from his resurrection. The influence of the Dan. 7 vision is consistently expressed in the Jesus-tradition as an expectation of Christ's coming again in the clouds of his exalted triumph. A quite widely spread Adam christology presented the risen Christ as the prototype of a new mankind, eldest brother in the eschatological family of God. More striking still was the degree to which the risen Christ was identified with the Spirit of God and Wisdom of God, the Christ-event being presented as the focus, indeed complete content of the word of God. This centrality of the resurrection as a 'becoming' in Jesus' relation with God, a new state in his role and status as Son of God, continues through the first-century writings and only fades in the Fourth Gospel.

In Paul in particular we find a most effective use of Adam christology to emphasize the earthly Jesus' complete oneness with fallen man and the dramatic consequence of Jesus' resurrection for mankind – his death understood as the end of the first Adam, his resurrection as the bursting through the cul-de-sac of death to begin a new humanity as last Adam. Paul's careful differentiation of the exalted Christ's approach to men through and as the life-giving Spirit from his role before God as eldest Son of the eschatological family of God in itself was enough to stretch Christian thought beyond a more comfortable binitarianism (God and Christ-Spirit) or modalism.

Most important of all, for our purposes, it seems to have been Paul who brought the Wisdom language of pre-Christian Judaism into service to express the cosmic significance of the Christ-event and the continuity between God's creative act and his redemptive purpose climaxed in Christ. In taking over the earlier Jewish talk of Wisdom the presumption is most persuasive that Paul understood divine Wisdom in the same way as his Jewish predecessors – that is, as the powerful and beneficent outreach of the transcendent God into his world in creative, providential and redemptive concern. In using Wisdom language of Christ then, the clear implication is that Paul understood Christ as the climactic embodiment of that outreach, understood the Christ-event, that is to say, as God's own action on behalf of men.

Did he then think of Christ as a man, a created being, chosen by God for this purpose, perhaps even appointed to this cosmic role as from his resurrection? or alternatively, as a heavenly being who had pre-existed with God from the beginning? Texts in Paul could be readily interpreted either way. The more plausible interpretation however is that such alternatives had not yet occurred to him: his overwhelming conviction was that God had himself acted in and through Christ, that what had happened in the whole Christ-event was God himself opening the way for man for righteousness and redemption, and that this had been the same power and purpose through which and for which God had created the world. In expressing this conviction in Wisdom language, as when he used the Adam language of the Philippian hymn, he introduced into christology phrases and terminology which when read apart from the original context of Wisdom and Adam christology would be understood as ascribing to Christ himself pre-existence and a role in creation. But there are insufficient indications that this was what Paul himself had in mind. What we may say with greater confidence is that in the Philippian and Colossian hymns we see language in transition, with a meaning that probably grew as the original context and thought culture changed. Similarly with the growth of 'mystery' language in the later Paulines (Colossians and Ephesians), where a language framed initially to express the conviction that Christ was the eschatological fulfilment of God's purpose from the beginning, the revelation and resolution of God's ultimate mystery, began to gather round it the implication that Christ himself was 'in the beginning'. *In the Wisdom christology (and mystery terminology) of the later Paulines we see the most immediate antecedent to the doctrine of the incarnation, the womb from which incarnational christology emerged,* the explicit assertion of an ideal pre-existence of Christ which was not far from an assertion of Christ's real pre-existence and which may have been understood in the latter sense quite soon after the letters were first written.

§32.4 *Second generation Christianity.* In the last decades (post-Pauline) of the first century there were at least two significant developments in the area of our inquiry and several significant attempts to express the growing understanding of Christ and the Christ-event. One development was *the backward extension of the Son of God language* – from resurrection, death and resurrection, to the beginning of Jesus' ministry (Jordan), to his conception and birth, to a timeless eternity. Whenever the writer wished to begin to speak of the Christ-event the language of divine sonship provided one of the most useful formulations. To speak of Christ at all was to speak of the Son of God. In so doing, language was often used which seemed to imply a becoming Son at each stage. In what sense Christ became something that he was not before is a question which apparently was not asked, even less whether the talk was of (divinely) elected office or ontological being. Only with the Fourth Evangelist is the implication of a sonship of degrees or stages left behind and we approach the concept of a divine sonship of unchanging timelessness.

The other development was *the emergence of full-blown Logos christology* in the Logos poem of John's prologue. Prior to that we can see how the writer to the Hebrews had been able to weave together the understanding of Christ as the climactic word of God's revelation with the cosmic christology of a Wisdom hymn. We can see how the thought of Christ as the eschatological manifestation of God's pre-ordained but hitherto hidden purpose begins to lend itself in one or two instances to the idea of Christ as the manifestation of one who himself had been hidden. And in the opening of I John (from the same Johannine circle) we see reflected the transition of thought, from Christ as the content of the word of preaching fore-ordained from the beginning, to Christ the word himself. But it is in the Logos poem of the Johannine prologue that the Wisdom and Logos speculation of Alexandrian Judaism reach their climax, with the explicit statement that the Logos, God's creative and revelatory utterance from the beginning of time, has become flesh, that Christ *is* and not merely speaks God's word to man.

The most significant attempts to express the growing understanding of Christ and to hold together what might otherwise have become divergent strands are Matthew, Hebrews and John. In *Matthew* we have a striking combination of emphases: Jesus was not only Son of David by his birth from Mary, but also Son of God by a divine act of creative power; Jesus fulfilled not only the messianic expectation, but also the role of eschatological Israel, not only the hope of a prophet like Moses, but also the universal mission of the Servant of Second Isaiah; Jesus spoke not only as an envoy of Wisdom, but also as Wisdom herself. There is no real indication that Matthew had attained a concept of incarnation, had come to think of Christ as a pre-existent being who became incarnate in Mary's womb or in Christ's ministry (as incarnate Wisdom). Nor is there any indication of course that he ignored or rejected such an understanding of Christ. Such indications as there are, in his presentation of the virginal conception of Jesus and in his editing of Q, point rather to the conclusion that the thought of Christ's pre-existence or a doctrine of incarnation had not yet occurred to him.

In many ways the epistle to the *Hebrews* is the most fascinating of the NT documents for our inquiry. The single most important way of confessing Christ is again as Son of God, but how precisely the author understood Christ's sonship remains something of a puzzle. First there is the strong opening which combines Wisdom christology with the understanding of Christ as the climax of God's revelatory utterance. This is followed immediately by an even stronger polemic against any sort of angel-christology, in the course of which we have the NT's most astonishing application to Christ of an (OT) address to Yahweh; but this is combined with adoptionist-like aorists which leave the reader wondering whether it is the exalted Christ who is in view throughout or the Son conceptualized in terms of pre-existent Wisdom. The puzzlement deepens when the anti-angel-christology polemic is rounded off with one of the most striking statements of Adam christology in the NT – again leaving the reader wondering whether Christ is higher than the angels simply because as the only man to fulfil God's plan for man it is he alone who has had all things (angels included) put in subjection under his feet. The tension thus set up in the opening chapters is never resolved. But as the epistle moves towards its climax it becomes increasingly clear that the author is attempting to maintain a dynamic synthesis between Jewish eschatology and a Platonic world view, with more than a hint that some sort of Logos christology (not dissimilar to Philo's Logos concept) lies in the background of his thought. And this recognition provides the most likely resolution of the tension. In other words, the author has in mind what is too clinically called 'an ideal Christ'; that is, he thinks of Christ as that divine pattern of revelation, of sonship, of mediation (Melchizedek), of man. Because Christ has broken through not only from the old age to the new (Jewish eschatology), but in the same act (his death and exaltation) has broken through also from the world of shadows to the real presence of God (Platonic world view), so he himself is to be regarded not merely as the copy of the ideal but *as the ideal itself*. He *is* the Wisdom of God to whom a hymn to Yahweh can be addressed; he is *the* Son; he is *the* Man; he is *the* Priest; he is *the* Sacrifice. He is not only the climax of God's revelatory and redemptive purpose but also he is more real, more really of heaven, more really divine, than anything on this imperfect earth. Whether this christology can have a life of its own outside of the dynamic synthesis in the mind of the author is a real question; and whether subsequent doctrines of the incarnation manage to maintain the tension set up by the author's synthesis, that is another. But certainly we can see that the synthesis implies some concept of pre-existence and is but a step away from a christology consistently incarnational through and through.

However ambitious was the synthesis offered by the author of Hebrews there can be no doubt that the synthesis achieved by the *Fourth Gospel* was the more successful and of greater influence on Christian thought. For John succeeded in welding together the Wisdom-Logos christology of the Logos poem in the prologue with his own dominant Son of God christology. Now at last we have the thought of Jesus as Son of God not merely from his resurrection or from the beginning of his ministry or from the beginning of his life but from eternity, and of the Logos-Son no longer as the impersonal (even if personified) utterance of God but as the Son of God conscious of his existence with the Father before the world was made. Here indeed in a clear and emphatic way we have a conception of personal pre-existence. Here indeed we have a doctrine of incarnation clearly formulated. In a very real sense all that follows hereafter is a dotting the 'i's and crossing the 't's of John's christology.

In short *as the first century of the Christian era drew to a close we find a concept of Christ's real pre-existence beginning to emerge, but only with the Fourth Gospel can we speak of a full blown conception of Christ's personal pre-existence and a clear doctrine of incarnation.*

§33. AND SO . . .

We can now attempt a more definitive answer to the questions posed in the opening chapter and offer some concluding reflections.

§33.1 How did the doctrine of the incarnation originate? How and when did it first come to expression? It did *not* emerge through the identification of Jesus with a divine individual or intermediary being whose presence in heaven was already assumed – the Hellenistic Judaism out of which the first Christians drew the christological categories which concern us had no room for such heavenly beings independent of God in their scheme of things – apart, that is, from angels, and it was precisely the option of identifying Christ with or as an angel which the first-century Christians either ignored completely or rejected so emphatically. It did *not* emerge from an identification of Jesus as Elijah or Enoch returned from heaven – there is no real evidence that Jesus was ever thought of as one of these two translated heroes, and when John the Baptist was identified as the expected Elijah (probably as early as Jesus himself) no overtone of pre-existence or incarnation is audible. It did *not* emerge as an inevitable corollary to the conviction that Jesus had been raised from the dead or as part of the logic of calling Jesus the Son of God – exaltation to heaven was not taken necessarily to presuppose or imply a previous existence in heaven, and the Son of God language as used of Jesus seems to have reflected more than provoked such developments as we have seen in first-century christology. It did *not* emerge as a corollary to the conviction that Jesus had been divinely inspired by the eschatological Spirit, a concept of inspiration giving way imperceptibly to one of incarnation – however much the *exalted* Christ merged with the Spirit in the thought of the NT writers their representation of the *earthly* Jesus's relation to the Spirit never went beyond that of inspiration. *The doctrine of the incarnation began to emerge when the exalted Christ was spoken of in terms drawn from the Wisdom imagery of pre-Christian Judaism*, when Christ came to be seen as the one who had filled and fulfilled in a complete and final way the role of Wisdom in effecting and sustaining the relation between God and his people, and the one who bodied forth the mystery of God's primordial purpose for cosmos and creature. The beginning of this process can be dated to the Wisdom passages in Paul's letters, but only in the post-Pauline period did a clear understanding of Christ as having pre-existed with God before his ministry on earth emerge, and *only in the Fourth Gospel can we speak of a doctrine of the incarnation*.

§33.2   What lies behind this emergence of a doctrine of the incarnation in the Fourth Gospel? Was it simply the result of identifying Wisdom with a particular historical person, crystallized by John's merging of his Son of God christology with the Logos poem of the prologue? Our inquiry has turned up a significant sequence of evidence which may help clarify what lay behind that final step. I am referring to the rather sudden appearance (or so it would seem) at the end of the first century and beginning of the second century on several fronts of ideas of divine redeemer figures who can be said to have pre-existed in heaven prior to their appearance on earth. Several Jewish writers took the step of identifying the Danielic 'son of man' as a pre-existent heavenly figure, seemingly in independence of each other. Speculation regarding the return of heroes of the faith from heaven (Elijah, Enoch, Moses, Ezra, Baruch) seems to have blossomed from about this time too. And the Enoch circle's use of the Dan. 7.9–14 vision was probably a factor in the emergence of the two-powers heresy condemned by the emerging orthodoxy of rabbinic Judaism. It was probably in this period also that we find the beginnings of the Gnostic redeemer myth proper – with Simon and Menander coming to be portrayed as heavenly redeemers, and the Adam and Wisdom speculation of Jew and Christian providing an important stimulus to- wards the Primal Man myth. In the wider spectrum of the late first- century and early second-century Judaism we find also indications of an escalating angelology, where the archangelic hierarchy seems to diminish the distance between God and his created messengers. Rabbinic specu- lation as to who or what pre-existed creation or was created on the eve of the first Sabbath may well have begun in this period too. In Christian writings as the century progresses towards its close we see an almost imperceptible transition from thought of Christ as the revelation of the hidden mystery, the original purpose of God, to the thought (perhaps) of Christ as himself the one who had been revealed and manifested. Not least in John's Gospel, best dated in the middle of this period (late first century), we find a christology of pre-existence suddenly blossoming into a vigorous and sustained exposition – Logos incarnate, Son of God sent, Son of Man descended.

The History of Religions school thought that this widespread variety of evidence could be explained only as a series of outgrowths from some earlier, simpler myth of a divine redeemer. But we have found no evidence of the existence of such a myth before the last decades of the first century AD outside of Christianity. And anyway the evidence does not read like variations on an original theme or disintegration of an earlier integrated speculation into its component parts. These different formulations are more like precursors than successors, the diverse elements which Gnostic speculation bonded together in the second century.

The more likely explanation I suggest is that in the last three decades of the first century the conceptualization of the *real* pre-existence of heavenly beings came to the surface of religious thought. It would not have been the first time, nor was it the last, that what we may loosely call 'cultural evolution' has thrown up a similar development in thought in different places at the same time. One might indeed claim it as a feature of the history of ideas that traditional ways of looking at reality can over even a short period be significantly challenged and revised from apparently independent standpoints which nevertheless show a striking similarity of approach (e.g. the beginning of the Enlightenment and the developments in art, music and poetry at the beginning of the present century) – where the interdependence of the suggested revisions is not at the surface level, but is expressive rather of a common dissatisfaction

with the current options and a mutual desire to forge more meaningful
and more expressive alternatives out of the available material. It is such
a process I believe which offers the best explanation for the emergence
of the concept of the real pre-existence of a heavenly redeemer in the last
decades of the first century AD. What had not previously been envisaged
emerged as a plausible way of thinking and understanding. What had
not previously been thought became *thinkable* – not in any abrupt way,
but partly as a natural progression of thought about divine Wisdom and
divine predestination, and partly as a response to the challenge to faith
which the events of AD 70 posed, which found renewed hope in speculation
focused on the earliest apocalyptic writing and on the possible intervention of Israel's translated heroes of the faith.

In this process, it has become increasingly clear, Christian faith in
Christ played a crucial role, and may indeed have to be credited with
much or most of the stimulus which resulted in this new break through
in religious thought. It was the Christian appropriation of the vision of
Daniel which quite probably drew it to the attention of wider Jewish
speculation in the aftermath of the first Jewish revolt. It was the Christian
use of the Wisdom imagery of pre-Christian Judaism which quite probably stretched the previous understanding of divine Wisdom so far that
it opened up new possibilities for both Jew and Christian to speak of
God's relation to man. Indeed if we were to focus attention on any
particular point within this evolutionary process as more crucial than
others, it would probably be Paul's use of Wisdom language to assess
Christ, and his description of Christ's significance in terms of Wisdom's
role in creation. Here we see conceptualization approaching the transition
point, the thought almost thinkable that John subsequently expressed so
clearly. And in Paul and John in particular we see Christian thought not
so much as a response to other and earlier clear conceptualizations, but
rather in the van of a wider and more inchoate movement of thought and
itself playing a decisive role and providing a decisive stimulus within that
movement of thought. In short, *it was probably Christian attempts to express
the reality of Christ, to encapsulate his significance in particular formulations, which
opened the way for the wider religious thought of the time to generate new ideas of
God's dealings with men and to formulate new expressions of their yearning for
salvation.*[1]

§33.3   We are now in a position to clarify the definition of 'incarnation'
which we left open at the beginning and to answer another of the questions posed in the Introduction: what precisely was it that was being
expressed in these initial statements which now speak to us so clearly of
incarnation? – bearing in mind what has just been said about the evolutionary transition in the religious thought of the period which concerns

us. Initially at least Christ was not thought of as a divine being who had pre-existed with God but as *the climactic embodiment of God's power and purpose* – his life, death and resurrection understood in terms of *God himself reaching out to men.* Christ was identified not with some heavenly redeemer figure but with *God's* creative wisdom, *God's* redemptive purpose, *God's* revelatory word expressed in a final way that made the Christ-event the normative definition of divine wisdom and revelation – *God's clearest self-expression, God's last word.*[2]

What lies behind this striking use of wisdom and word imagery? What would it have meant to those who first used it of Christ? Initially it would have meant not only that through the Christ-event and its proclamation the first Christians found themselves accepted by God, not only that Christ had revealed to them what God's purpose for man was; it would have meant also that *Christ showed them what God is like, the Christ-event defined God more clearly than anything else had ever done* – God as one concerned for man as for his neighbour, God as one thoroughly involved with his world, God as one reaching out to offer man salvation full and free. What these earliest formulations of Wisdom christology were expressing in their own distinctive way is that *Jesus had revealed God* – not the Son of God, not the 'divine intermediary' Wisdom, but God. *As the Son of God he revealed God as Father* who rejoices to hear believers call 'Abba' to him. *As the Wisdom of God he revealed God as Creator-Redeemer,* the character of God's creative power and of his creation, the character of his redemptive power and of his redemption. 'Incarnation' means initially that *God's* love and power had been experienced in fullest measure in, through and as this man Jesus, that Christ had been experienced as God's self-expression, the Christ-event as the effective, re-creative power of God.

Since thought was in transition at this stage there is more to be said, but we should perhaps pause at this point to draw out one corollary of relevance to the current debate. That is, that while it would be appropriate to speak of these early statements of Wisdom christology as *the initial formulations of a doctrine of God incarnate,* it would be inappropriate to label it as *'the myth* of God incarnate'.[3] In the beginnings of christology we are not yet dealing with the myth of a heavenly figure who comes down from heaven to redeem men. We are confronted to be sure with the Wisdom language of pre-Christian Judaism applied to Christ, but to describe that as myth is to *mis*understand the Jewish concept of divine Wisdom as a divine being in some significant sense independent of God rather than as personification of divine action. It is not the case that either pre-Christian Judaism or earliest Hellenistic Christianity simply appropriated current myths about the gods. Pre-Christian Judaism was evidently well enough aware of how their wisdom language was used elsewhere; but they appropriated it not as myth, rather as vigorous

imagery and metaphor to describe Yahweh's immanence, Yahweh's revelation in and through the Torah. And it was this imagery and metaphor
domesticated to the service of Jewish monotheism which early Hellenistic
Christianity took over as a way of confessing that in Christ they had
encountered God, the same divine power that had created and now
sustained the cosmos, the same redemptive concern that had chosen
Israel and shaped her history, the same revelatory utterance that had
spoken through prophet and Torah. The language lent itself to mythical
elaboration within the context of the more syncretistic religious speculation of the wider world, that is true; moreover, as we have already seen,
the Christian identification of Christ as the Wisdom of God probably
provided that wider speculation with a crucial stimulus and component
towards the full blown mythology of Gnosticism. But at the initial stage
of Wisdom christology it would be misleading to describe this as myth.
Indeed it would be unjust to the sophistication of these pre-Christian
Jewish and early Christian writers: in their own way they were as concerned with the over-simplifications of mythological thinking as any modern theologian, quite as alive to the dangers of a promiscuous imagery
begetting a threat to their monotheism. We do too little justice then to
the composers of these early Christian hymns and poems when we label
their efforts 'myth'.[4]

§33.4   What then of the Fourth Gospel? Even if there is no mythical
understanding of a divine being descending from heaven to help men
behind the earliest Wisdom christology, what of the Son of Man and Son
of God language used by John? The Logos becoming incarnate – that
could be said to move still within the thought world of the Wisdom
hymns in Colossians and Hebrews. But the Son of Man descending from
heaven, the Son of God being sent as one who pre-existed with the Father
from all eternity – is that not properly to be called mythological language,
in the sense that John conceived of Christ as a divine being from heaven?
Has not John left behind the earlier idea of God acting in and through
the Christ-event? Is not Christ here conceived as a heavenly being distinct
from God? This is certainly harder to deny. But perhaps something more
can be said following on from our conclusions above (§31.3).
   In one sense John's Logos-Son christology was only an elaboration of
the tension between transcendence and immanence, between personal
and impersonal which had always been present in the Jewish conception
of God. Just as the transcendent God was experienced in his immanence
through his wisdom and word, so the experience of God was not simply
of Spirit as a sort of fluid but of God revealing himself as Father: John
was not the first Jewish author to combine the concepts Logos and Son,
and Jesus was hardly the first Jew to speak of God as Father. In that

sense then we might even speak of a 'nascent binitarianism' in the Jewish conception of God – God far and God near, divine power experienced as both impersonal and personal. And in that sense Christian understanding of God as Father revealing himself in Jesus is only an extension of this 'nascent Jewish binitarianism'.[5]

The danger for a monotheistic faith, however, lies in an over-simplification or over-elaboration of the way in which the relation between God and Jesus illuminates the personal in God. The impersonal is no problem – the analogies beloved of Philo and the Fathers (the sun and the sun's rays, the fountainhead and the water flowing from it) provide an adequate conceptualization. But the personal relationship of Father and Son, particularly when the Son is the person Jesus, is much more of a problem. It may be of course that our modern conception of 'person' (a being self-consciously distinct from even though related to other beings) imposes a category on John which he never intended. But John does seem to present Jesus as 'a being self-consciously distinct' from his Father and to that extent is in danger of stretching the 'nascent binitarianism' of Jewish monotheism into some form of unacceptable ditheism (two gods). The relative popularity of the Fourth Gospel in second-century Gnosticism and relative disregard for it among more orthodox churchmen in the same period[6] highlights a certain unease which John's presentation caused early Christianity in this area.

It may be however that here too the suggestion outlined above (§33.2) throws a softer light on the issue. It could be said that the Fourth Evangelist was as much a prisoner of his language as its creator; or more precisely, that his formulation suffered from the 'cultural evolution' of thought in which it played such an important part. That is to say, perhaps we see in the Fourth Gospel what started as an elaboration of the Logos-Son imagery applied to Jesus, inevitably in the transition of conceptualizations coming to express a conception of Christ's personal pre-existence which early Gnosticism found more congenial than early orthodoxy. To put it another way: perhaps what we see in John is the clarification of the nature and character of God which Christ afforded brought to the point where the available categories of human language are in danger of simplifying the conception both of God and of Christ too much. It is a danger inherent in a writing which can speak so effectively to the simple believer and yet in the same words provide such resonant symbols and images as to exhaust the perception of the most sophisticated intelligence and religious imagination. Indeed, it is a danger inherent in any talk of God: in order to be understood one must run the risk of being misunderstood; in order to open windows of insight in the understanding and awareness of others one must often use language which causes the hearer to blink and question. It is a measure of John's inspired genius that he hazarded so much and yet pulled it off so successfully – shaping Christian thought about God and Christ for all time.

In short, we can sum up John's contribution to the beginnings of christology thus: *John is wrestling with the problem of how to think of God and how to think of Christ in relation to God in the light of the clarification of the nature and character of God which the Christ-event afforded.* If he runs the danger of over-simplifying, or overstretching the Jewish belief in God as one, that is more an accident of the conceptualization in transition which he used than of deliberate policy. What was more deliberate was the bold use of the language available, to challenge and convert those familiar with the current ways of speaking about God by focusing it in an exclusive way on Jesus Christ. We honour him most highly when we follow his example and mould the language and conceptualizations in transition today into a gospel which conveys the divine, revelatory and saving significance of Christ to our day as effectively as he did to his.[7]

§33.5   The subsequent dominance of the Johannine presentation should not blind us to *the diversity of christological formulation which is a feature of the first-century Christian writings.* In the NT Jesus is spoken of as being begotten or appointed Son of God at his resurrection and at Jordan, and again as being born Son of God through the creative power of the Spirit of God. He is identified as the human figure of Daniel's vision, the Son of Man in humility and suffering on earth, but now exalted and coming (again) on the clouds of heaven. He represents sinful man, Adam, in this life, and in his resurrection completes and fulfils God's plan for man, inaugurating a new (resurrected) humanity, master of all other creatures, last Adam, eldest brother in the eschatological family of God. He is the eschatological prophet in his ministry on earth, the prophet like Moses, inspired and anointed by the Spirit; but in his resurrection he is Lord of the Spirit, or at least known only in and through and as the life-giving Spirit, just as the Spirit is now for Christians known as the Spirit of Jesus. He is the Wisdom of God that created the world, the one whose life embodied in the fullest measure possible the creative power and redemptive concern of God, whose death defines in a final way the character of divine wisdom, whose risen Lordship is the eschatological fulfilment of God's interaction with the cosmos from the beginning. He is the Word of God, the climax of Yahweh's utterance through prophet and Torah, the end-time revelation of the divine mystery hidden from man since the first-time, the incarnation of God's self-expression.

Clearly here in this kaleidescope of imagery we see earliest Christianity searching around for the most suitable way of understanding and describing Christ, ransacking the available categories and concepts to find language which would do justice to the reality of Christ. In attempting to assess this diversity of christological formulations and to evaluate its significance for today we must avoid oversimplifying solutions. On the one hand a harmonizing synthesis will lose too much that is of distinctive value in the individual presentations. Certainly there is little evidence of such a harmonistic concern among the NT authors themselves: the several presentations of the Son of God's becoming at different stages exist alongside each other without embarrassment, and there is no sign of an attempt to merge the concept of virginal conception with that of incarnation; the talk of the Son of God being sent and the Son of Man's descending from heaven have not yet been run together in the Fourth Gospel; Adam christology and Wisdom christology are not in the end readily compatible without blurring the creator/creature distinction more than the Judaeo-Christian tradition would count acceptable; likewise the rationale of the firm distinction maintained between *inspiration by* the Spirit and *incarnation of* the Wisdom-Logos is not altogether easy to grasp, especially against the background of pre-Christian Jewish thought where Spirit, Wisdom and Logos were all more or less synonymous ways of speaking of God's outreach to man. The concern to harmonize soon became apparent in the second century but it is hardly evident in the first century.

On the other hand, an attempt to reduce the complexity of NT christology by focusing attention on only one of the formulations or by reducing the lot to some lowest common denominator would be equally misguided. To claim the precedent and authority of Paul, for example, for a christology of Jesus as the Man ('the man for others',[8] man 'filled with God',[9] or whatever), or for a christology of God as 'Christ-Spirit',[10], would ignore the fact that Paul found it equally necessary to speak of Christ in other categories and with other concepts. In other words, only a christology which embraces the diversity of Paul's and incorporates the checks and balances which his different formulations provided can really enlist Paul's support. Again, a lowest common denominator approach which contented itself with some deliberately vague assertion about God acting through Christ,[11] without committing itself on even the resurrection of Jesus let alone on any concept of incarnation, could only be advocated by deliberately ignoring the tensions and pressures within the earliest Christian assessment of the Christ-event which forced Christian thinking towards a modification of Jewish monotheism that would give adequate place to Christ, and could only be sustained by a somewhat arbitrary and blinkered resistance to the same tensions and pressures which are still there.

If all this has any normative significance for modern christology it is that *christology should not be narrowly confined to one particular assessment of Christ, nor should it play one off against another, nor should it insist on squeezing all the different NT conceptualizations into one particular 'shape', but it should recognize that from the first the significance of Christ could only be apprehended by a diversity of formulations which though not always strictly compatible with each other were not regarded as rendering each other invalid.* At the same time it would be unwise to attempt to hold all the diverse formulations in play at the same time, and impractical to insist on the equal validity of each in every circumstance. As Schillebeeckx rightly notes: 'A thoroughly scriptural orthodoxy does not entail conferring upon Jesus simultaneously all the images and titles available.'[12] If the NT does serve as a norm, the truth of Christ will be found in the individual emphasis of the different NT formulations as much as in that which unites them.

§33.6   Within this last more general consideration one point in particular should perhaps be singled out for special mention – that is the consistent emphasis in NT christology on the importance of the resurrection of Christ. For on the one hand all the NT writings give prominence to the resurrection/exaltation of Christ, and we noted above (§32.3) the centrality of the resurrection in the earliest Christian attempts to express the significance of the Christ-event – a key stage in Christ's becoming as Son of God, his exaltation to the heavenly role described in Dan. 7, the beginning of the new humanity as last Adam, his becoming life-giving Spirit, Lord of the Spirit, his entry into the cosmic role of divine Wisdom. On the other hand the diminution of the resurrection's role in Christ's becoming in the Fourth Gospel poses the danger that a subsequent orthodox christology, because it owns John's Gospel as its primary source and chief canonical influence, will give insufficient attention to the resurrection in its assessment of Christ.[13] The danger is that a lack of proper balance between incarnation and resurrection in christology will result in an unbalanced gospel and an unbalanced doctrine of the church, often signalled by a too casual use of the phrase, 'An incarnational theology requires or implies that. . . .'

For example, an overemphasis on the incarnation as God's taking humanity into the Godhead will readily produce a gospel which proclaims to man that he has already been redeemed, is already a Christian, whether he knows it or not, whether he likes it or not – a kind of gnostic gospel which consists in calling men to the self-realization that their humanity has already been divinized in the incarnation, that they are already in Christ in God. But where the resurrection is recognized to have christological significance, as a becoming in *Christ's* own relation with God, the gospel has to include much more of Jesus' own call for conversion, much more of the 'not yet' in Paul's concept of salvation, much more of the call to commitment to life 'according to the Spirit' and against a life 'according to the flesh' – where the slogan is not so much 'Become what you are', but 'Become what you are becoming', Allow yourself to be transformed more and more into the image of the last Adam by the life-giving Spirit.[14]

Again, an unbalanced emphasis on the incarnation could result in a doctrine of the church as simply the expression of man's natural religiosity, the humanity of man on earth in harmony with the humanity of the Man in heaven, or even in a belief that the state is actually the body of Christ on earth with the church (i.e. the national or established church) understood simply as the state at worship. Whereas when the resurrection of Christ is recognized as marking a not yet in Jesus' own becoming, the church will be seen not so much as representing the world but rather as representing the forces that seek to change the world, to transform it from what it has become to what God intended it to be and will make it again as he made again the last Adam; the church will be seen as the gathering of those whose citizenship is in heaven, to celebrate *that* citizenship, and who, while not denying their citizenship on earth, let neither the values nor the taboos of the present world with its fragmented nationalisms shape their present conduct but the values of Christ and of the world to come.

Perhaps we could sum up the whole in the following way. In Christmas we celebrate God become man – a shorthand phrase for all that Wisdom and Logos christology was seeking to express: that God has not abandoned his creation in all its self-centred fallenness, rather he has identified himself with it in Christ; that the creative power of God has its highest expression in the personal relationship of self-giving love which was the hallmark of Jesus' ministry; that the fullest expression of God's word is the Christ-event in all its historical relativity and consequent ambiguity. In Easter we celebrate man become God – again shorthand for all that the Adam and Spirit christologies were seeking to express: that in the death and resurrection of Christ God has broken the stranglehold of human selfishness, has proved the enduring and conquering strength of divine love, has overcome the bondage of historical relativities; that out of this poor human clay God has created afresh a man who is the crown of his creation and Lord of all. And, we might add, in Pentecost we celebrate the realization of faith that this Easter hope is not focused exclusively on one man in the past nor something we must simply await in total passivity, but a reality and process in which we can begin to share now – the God-become-man-become-God still 'the power and wisdom of God' today, still 'our righteousness and sanctification and redemption'. 'In substance the trinitarian confession means that God in Jesus Christ has proved himself to be self-communicating love and that as such he is permanently among us in the Holy Spirit.'[15]

NOTES

Chapter I   Introduction

1. C. Gore, *The Incarnation of the Son of God*, 1891, p. 17.

2. Translation as in R. W. Thomson, *Athanasius* Contra Gentes *and* De Incarnatione, Oxford University Press 1971.

3. Translation as in J. N. D. Kelly, *Early Christian Doctrines*, ²1960, p. 297.

4. See also the theses at the head of other paragraphs, particularly §§15, 40 and 58: §15 – 'The mystery of the revelation of God in Jesus Christ consists in the fact that the eternal Word of God chose, sanctified and assumed human nature and existence into oneness with himself, in order thus, as very God and very man, to become the Word of reconciliation spoken by God to man . . .'. Or we might refer to the provocative statement made in Barth's more popular lectures on the Apostles' Creed delivered in the summer of 1946: 'This Jesus of Nazareth, who passes through the cities and villages of Galilee and wanders to Jerusalem, who is there accused and condemned and crucified, this man is the Jehovah of the Old Testament, is the Creator, is God himself. A man like us in space and time, who has all the properties of God and yet does not cease to be a human being and a creature too. The Creator himself, without encroaching upon his deity, becomes, not a demi-god, not an angel, but very soberly, very really a man' (*Dogmatics in Outline*, ET SCM Press 1949, p. 84).

5. See Rahner's *Theological Investigations*, ET 1954ff., particularly, 'Current Problems in Christology', Vol. 1 (1954) pp. 149–200; 'On the Theology of the Incarnation' Vol. 4 (1958) pp. 105–20; 'Christology within an Evolutionary View of the World', and 'Dogmatic Reflections on the Knowledge and Selfconsciousness of Christ', Vol. 5 (ET 1966) pp. 157–92, 193–215; 'Christology in the Setting of Modern Man's Understanding of Himself and of his World', Vol. 11 (ET 1974) pp. 215–29; 'The Quest for Approaches Leading to an Understanding of the Mystery of the God-man Jesus' (1971) and 'The Two Basic Types of Christology', Vol. 13 (ET 1975) pp. 195–200, 213–23. See also Rahner, 'Incarnation' and 'Jesus Christ IV', *Sacramentum Mundi*, Vol. 3, Herder 1969, pp. 110–18, 192–209.

6. *Investigations*, Vol. 4, p. 105.

7. *Investigations*, Vol. 5, pp. 176f.

8. See H. R. Mackintosh, *The Doctrine of the Person of Jesus Christ*, 1912, pp. 247–84.

9. A. Harnack, *History of Dogma*, ³1894, ET 1897, Vol. I, p. 218.

10. J. M. Robinson (ed.), *The Nag Hammadi Library*, 1977. See further below pp. 99f.

11. See particularly J. T. Sanders, *The New Testament Christological Hymns*, 1971; K. Wengst, *Christologische Formeln und Lieder des Urchristentums*, 1972, Dritter Teil; C. H. Talbert, *What is a Gospel?*, 1977, ch. 3.

12. I am thinking particularly of course of O. Cullmann, *The Christology of the New Testament*, 1957, ET 1959; W. Kramer, *Christ, Lord, Son of God*, 1966; F. Hahn, *The Titles of Jesus in Christology*, 1963, ET 1969; and R. H. Fuller, *The Foundations of New Testament Christology*, 1965; cf. also G. Vermes, *Jesus the Jew*, 1973.

13. See the bibliographies below in the notes for §§15.1, 24.5 and 30.1. The debate about demythologizing sparked off by R. Bultmann's 'New Testament and Mythology' (1941), *Kerygma and Myth*, ed. H. W. Bartsch, 1953, pp. 1–44, did not focus particularly on the incarnation, more on the viability of God-talk in general, on the arbitrariness of Bultmann's existentialist interpretation of the kerygma, and also on the resurrection (see below n. 16).

14. Most recently see B. F. Meyer, *The Aims of Jesus*, 1979, with a review of the Quest in ch. II.

15. See particularly H. R. Balz, *Methodische Probleme der neutestamentlichen Christologie*, 1967, pp. 113–15. It is significant that four recent studies, all with the title 'The Beginnings or Origins of Christology', include very little (or no) account of the origin of incarnation christology within their purview – W. Marxsen, *The Beginnings of Christology*, 1960, ET 1969; J. Ernst, *Anfänge der Christologie*, SBS 57, 1972; I. H. Marshall, *The Origins of New Testament Christology*, 1976; C. F. D. Moule, *The Origin of Christology*, 1977.

16. It was not difficult to collect a list of 60 authors who had written on the resurrection of Jesus in the '50s and '60s – and this confined to books, excluding articles and (in all but one case) second or subsequent editions – W. Künneth (1951), H. A. Williams (1951), H. von Campenhausen (1952), K. H. Rengstorı (1952), P. de Haes (1953), R. Meyer (1953), H. Grass (1956), H. Lamparter (1956), J. Alfaro (1957), R. Niebuhr (1957), J. Comblin (1959), G. Koch (1959), C. M. Martini (1959), M. C. Perry (1959), G. D. Yarnold (1959), F. X. Durrwell (1960), E. Lohse (1961), D. M. Stanley (1961), E. Kamlah (1962), M. Hauş (1964), W. Kurtz (1964), H. W. Bartsch (1965), D. P. Fuller (1965), J. McLemar (1965), P. Benoit (1966), J. Kremer (1966), G. W. H. Lampe and D. M MacKinnon (1966), W. Anderson (1967), N. Clark (1967), S. H. Hooke (1967), G. W. Ittel (1967), B. Klappert (1967), H. H. Rex (1967), P. Seidensticker (1967), P. Klemm (1968), K. Lehmann (1968), W. Marxsen (1968), C. F. D. Moule (1968), E. Ruckstuhl (1968), L. Schenke (1968), H. Schlier (1968), E. Cold (1969), J. Danielou (1969), K. Gutbrod (1969), A. Kassing (1969), F. Mussner (1969), P. de Surgy (1969), E. L. Bode (1970), K. Burgener (1970), C. F. Evans (1970), G. Kegel (1970), H. Luduchowski (1970), F. Schnider (1970), U. Wilckens (1970), R. H. Fuller (1971), A. Geense (1971), L. Geering (1971), H. Haag (1971), X. Leon-Dufour (1971). It is significant that the major Protestant systematic christology of this period explicitly builds out from the resurrection of Jesus – W. Pannenberg, *Jesus – God and Man*, 1964, ET 1968; 'Only so long as the

perception of Jesus' resurrection remains precedent to the concept of incarnation is the biblical meaning of the idea of God preserved in christology . . .' (p. 158). Cf. also the way in which J. Moltmann's chief theological writings have focused first on Easter (*Theology of Hope*, 1965, ET 1967), then on Good Friday (*The Crucified God*, 1973, ET 1974) and then on Pentecost (*The Church in the Power of the Spirit*, 1975, ET SCM Press 1977).

17. We might instance also the comparative neglect of works more directly related to our subject in contemporary NT discussions – V. Taylor, *The Person of Christ in New Testament Teaching*, 1958, A. W. Wainwright, *The Trinity in the New Testament*, 1962, and A. T. Hanson, *Jesus Christ in the Old Testament*, 1965.

18. We might mention also R. E. Brown, *The Birth of the Messiah*, 1977, the first complete modern attempt to subject the birth narratives of Matthew and Luke to a thorough exegesis. In recent years there has also been a sequence of weighty contributions on christology from Roman Catholic scholars whose field is primarily dogmatic or systematic or philosophical theology, but who have displayed for the most part an impressive grasp of NT issues: in addition to Rahner (above n. 5; and note his discussion with W. Thüsing – K. Rahner and W. Thüsing, *Christologie – systematische und exegetisch*, Quaestiones Disputatae 55, 1972; ET with new material, *A New Christology*, 1980), Meyer (above n. 14) and Mackey (above p. 4) we should mention the impressive trio which first appeared in 1974 – W. Kasper, *Jesus the Christ*, ET 1976, H. Küng, *On Being a Christian*, ET 1976, particularly pp. 436–62, and E. Schillebeeckx, *Jesus. An Experiment in Christology*, ET 1979, followed by his *Christ. The Christian Experience in the Modern World*, 1977, ET 1980.

19. Knox, *Humanity*, pp. 12, 24, 53, 106.

20. M. Wiles in *Myth*, ed. Hick, p. 3; and Wiles, *Remaking*, p. 53, with reference to the earlier contributions of Caird and J. A. T. Robinson (listed on p. 3).

21. Lampe, *God as Spirit*, pp. 11, 12f., 23, 142.

22. Goulder in *Myth*, ed. Hick, ch. 3 and pp. 79, 85.

23. Young in *Incarnation*, ed. Goulder, pp. 174 (citing her earlier contribution in *Myth*, ed. Hick, p. 19) and 179.

24. Cupitt, *Debate*, p. 28.

25. Craddock, *Pre-existence*, p. 145.

26. Hamerton-Kelly, *Pre-existence*, p. 275, objecting to the view of Hahn that the christology of pre-existence first formulated in the Hellenistic church was a 'decisively new stage' in the history of doctrine (*Titles*, p. 304; cf. Fuller, *Foundations*, pp. 245f.).

27. Moule in *Incarnation*, ed. Goulder, p. 137.

28. Stanton in *Incarnation*, ed. Goulder, p. 152.

29. This last comment includes particularly the contributions of Craddock and Hamerton-Kelly (listed above p. 3).

30. Cf. Pannenberg, *Jesus*: 'How did Jesus, exalted through the resurrection from the dead, become the pre-existent divine being descended from heaven? This remains to the present a chief problem of the history of primitive Christian traditions' (p. 151).

31. J. D. G. Dunn, *Unity*, pp. 369, 376.

32. Dunn, *Unity*, §51.

33. We do not give separate treatment to the title 'Lord', since it is generally agreed that as the most common 'title of majesty' particularly in the Pauline

churches (Dunn, *Unity*, §12; also below p. 181 and n. 70) it denotes Christ's exalted (i.e. post-Easter) glory. On I Cor 2.8, 8.6 and II Cor. 8.9 as possible exceptions see below pp. 178, 179–82 and 121–3; also pp. 108f. It is perhaps significant that Luke, who after Paul in the NT shows the greatest fondness for the title 'Lord', has no christology of pre-existence (see below p. 51 and n. 202). The question of Jewish belief in the pre-existence of the *Messiah* is discussed in ch. III, since its principal support is the thesis that the 'one like a son of man' in the vision of Dan. 7 would have been identified as the Messiah. It is a tribute to the brilliance of J. Weiss that already in 1914 he had marked out so clearly the range of material which must be discussed – *Earliest Christianity*, 1914, ET 1937, 1959, Vol. II, pp. 475–91.

34. Cf. M. Hengel, *The Son of God*, 1975, ET 1976: 'the development of christology was from the beginning concerned with synthesis' (p. 75).

35. I have been conscious of the point made by J. Hick: 'there is nothing that can be called *the* Christian doctrine of the incarnation' (*Incarnation*, ed. Goulder, p. 48; similarly S. Sykes, *Incarnation*, pp. 115, 125). But I decided against using such alternative formulations as Knox's 'incarnationism' or overworking the vaguer 'incarnational christology', since it is the *origin* of that which may properly be called the 'Christian doctrine of the incarnation' (whatever diversity is contained within that phrase) with which we are concerned.

Chapter II The Son of God

1. The creed of Nicea (AD 325), following J. N. D. Kelly, *Early Christian Creeds*, ²1960, pp. 215f.

2. Kelly, *Creeds*, p. 142.

3. See particularly P. W. von Martitz, G. Fohrer, E. Schweizer and E. Lohse in *TDNT* VIII, pp. 335–62; P. Pokorný, *Der Gottessohn*, Theologische Studien 109, 1971, pp. 7–25; Vermes, *Jesus*, pp. 194–200, 206–13; Hengel, *Son*, pp. 21–56; also F. Young in *Myth*, ed. Hick, pp. 87–121. The older, undiscriminating study of G. P. Wetter, *Der Sohn Gottes*, 1916, is less helpful (see also n. 20 below). On the Gnostic redeemer myth see below pp. 98–100, 123–6.

4. T. Boslooper, *The Virgin Birth*, 1962, pp. 170–8; von Martitz, *TDNT* VIII, p. 336 – 'There are also many degrees and forms of deification' (p. 336 n.7); Pokorný, *Gottessohn*, pp. 11f.; Hengel, *Son*, p. 24; Talbert, *Gospel*, p. 46 n. 23.

5. von Martitz, *TDNT* VIII, p. 336.

6. A Deissmann, *Bible Studies*, 1895 and 1897, ET T. & T. Clark 1901, pp. 166f.; also *Light from the Ancient East*, ET ²1927, reissued Baker 1965, pp. 346f.; Liddell & Scott υἱός; Moulton & Milligan θεός, υἱός. The irrelevance of the mystery cults to our present discussion is stressed by Hengel, *Son*, pp. 25–30.

7. See H. Braun, 'Der Sinn der neutestamentliche Christologie' (1957), ET 'The Meaning of New Testament Christology', *JThC* 5, 1968, pp. 100f.

8. von Martitz, *TDNT* VIII, p. 337; Hengel, *Son*, p. 24; VI n.66 below.

9. See K. Lake, *Beginnings*, V, pp. 246f.; H. Conzelmann, *Apostelgeschichte*, HNT, 1963, pp. 101, 155.

10. G. Cooke, 'The Israelite King as Son of God', *ZAW* 32, 1961, pp. 202–25; also 'The Sons of (the) God(s)', *ZAW* 35, 1964, pp. 22–47; Fohrer, *TDNT* VIII, pp. 347–53; Pokorný, *Gottessohn*, pp. 9–11; W. Schlisske, *Gottessöhne und Gottessohn*

im Alten Testament, 1973; H. Haag, 'Sohn Gottes im Alten Testament', *ThQ* 154, 1974, pp. 222–31 (with further bibliography p. 223 n. 1).

11. See also V. Huonder, *Israel Sohn Gottes*, 1975.

12. See also the Qumran fragment cited in *Biblica*, 36, 1955, p. 265; and below n. 62. Patristic references in Lampe υἱός.

13. Further references in G. Schrenk, *TDNT* V, pp. 956f.; Schweizer, *TDNT* VIII, pp. 355f.; Hengel, *Son*, pp. 52f. See further below pp. 227f.

14. Vermes, *Jesus*, pp. 195–7; Hengel, *Son*, p. 43 and n. 87; K. Berger, 'Die königlichen Messiastraditionen des Neuen Testaments', *NTS* 20, 1973–74, pp. 28–37. In Justin Martyr, *Apol.* I.22, Jesus 'is worthy to be called the Son of God on account of his wisdom'.

15. The fact that Mark 3.11, 5.7 pars., Luke 4.41, represents Jesus as being addressed as 'Son of God' by demoniacs may be significant at this point (Vermes, *Jesus*, pp. 202f.).

16. D. Flusser, *Jesus*, 1968, ET 1969, pp. 93–5; Vermes, *Jesus*, pp. 69–78, 206f.; Hengel, *Son*, p. 42 n. 85.

17. For discussion on the restoration and meaning of the text see particularly M. Burrows, *More Light on the Dead Sea Scrolls*, Secker & Warburg 1958, pp. 300–3. Schillebeeckx draws on J. Starcky's interpretation of 4QMess.ar. as containing a reference to 'la génération divine du Messie' ('Les Quatre Étapes du Messianisme à Qumran', *RB* 70, 1963, pp. 502–4; but see J. A. Fitzmyer, 'The Aramaic "Elect of God" Text from Qumran Cave IV', *CBQ* 27, 1965, pp. 348–72), and goes on to the quite unwarranted speculation that 'when all is said and done, a virgin birth of a messiah descending out of heaven was perhaps already a pre-Christian, Jewish concept, associated with Davidic messianism' (*Jesus*, p. 454).

18. We might also note Mark 14.57–62: O. Betz, *What do we know about Jesus?*, 1965, ET 1968, has elucidated the rationale of the line of questioning at Jesus' trial in the light of the messianic interpretation of II Sam. 7.11–14 at Qumran (pp. 87–92).

19. Lohse, *TDNT* VIII, pp. 361f.; Vermes, *Jesus*, pp. 197–9; J. A. Fitzmyer, 'The Contribution of Qumran Aramaic to the Study of the New Testament', *NTS* 20, 1973–74, pp. 391–4; Hengel, *Son*, pp. 44f. Cf. IV Ezra 7.28f. (on which see S. Gero, ' "My Son the Messiah": A Note on IV Ezra 7.28f.', *ZNW* 66, 1975, pp. 264–7); 13.32,51f. (see below p. 79).

20. The most influential works were those of H. Windisch, *Paulus und Christus*, 1934, particularly pp. 24–114; L. Bieler, *ΘΕΙΟΣ ΑΝΗΡ*, 1935 and 1936, reissued 1967. They developed the earlier hypotheses of R. Reitzenstein, *Die hellenistischen Mysterienreligionen*, 1910, ³1927. The present discussion was stimulated principally by D. Georgi, *Die Gegner des Paulus im 2. Korintherbrief*, 1964.

21. See particularly von Martitz, *TDNT* VIII, pp. 338–40; O. Betz, 'The Concept of the So-called "Divine Man" in Mark's Christology', *Studies in New Testament and Early Christian Literature*, ed. D. E. Aune, SNT 33, 1972, pp. 229–34; D. L. Tiede, *The Charismatic Figure as a Miracle Worker*, SBL Dissertation Series 1, 1972; C. H. Holladay, *Theios Aner in Hellenistic Judaism*, SBL Dissertation Series 40, 1977. The value of the debate in illuminating the background to various NT writings (particularly II Cor., Mark and John) is by no means tied to or determined by the validity or otherwise of the 'divine man' concept (see e.g. Dunn, *Unity*, pp. 70f. and nn. 15, 16).

22. von Martitz, *TDNT*, VIII, p. 338.

23. Deissmann, *Light*, pp. 347f.

24. von Martitz, *TDNT* VIII, p. 338. Cf. Lampe θεῖος B.II.

25. 'It was natural and common to describe as "divine" any man who excelled in any desirable capacity – beauty, strength, wisdom, prestige, song, fame, skill in speaking, or success in love' (M. Smith, 'Prolegomena to a Discussion of Aretologies, Divine Men, the Gospels and Jesus', *JBL* 90, 1971, p. 184; cf. Talbert, *Gospel*, pp. 44f. n. 7).

26. Cf. the analyses of Plato's usage in J. van Camp and P. Canart, *Le sens du mot* θεῖος *chez Platon*, Louvain 1956, pp. 413f., cited by Holladay, *Theios Aner*, p. 90; and Holladay's own distinction of four meanings possible for the phrase 'divine man' in the writings of Hellenistic Judaism (*Theios Aner*, p. 237).

27. See particularly Talbert, *Gospel*, pp. 26–9.

28. Deissmann, *Light*, pp. 343–6; Liddell & Scott θεός, Moulton & Milligan θεός; H. Kleinknecht, *TDNT* III, pp. 68f.; Young, *Myth*, ed. Hick, 95–100. See also S. Weinstock, *Divus Julius*, Oxford University Press 1971, chs. XIV and XVIII.

29. See further J. A. Montgomery, *Daniel*, ICC 1927, p. 461; D. Cuss, *Imperial Cult and Honorary Terms in the New Testament*, Fribourg 1974, pp. 134–40; Schürer, *History*, I, p. 147 n. 23.

30. Arndt & Gingrich, θεός 4a; Smith, 'Prolegomena', p. 182 n. 54; Young, *Myth*, ed. Hick p. 94. See also Windisch, *Paulus*, pp. 59–78.

31. O. Weinrich, 'Antikes Gottmenschentum' (1926), *Ausgewählte Schriften* II, 1973, pp. 179ff.; Talbert, *Gospel*, p. 37.

32. Heb. 1.8 confirms that the text of Ps. 45 with which Hebrews' readers were familiar was understood to use 'god' in an address to the king; and John 10.34f. probably confirms (despite J. A. Emerton, 'Some New Testament Notes', *JTS* 11, 1960, pp. 329–32) that those addressed in Ps. 82.6 as 'gods' were thought of as men ('those to whom the word of God came') at least by the Fourth Evangelist. But see also C. H. Gordon, '*'lhym* in its Reputed Meaning of Rulers, Judges', *JBL* 54, 1935, pp. 139–44.

33. Most recently by Hengel, *Son*, pp. 46f. and Young, *Myth*, ed. Hick, pp. 109f.

34. See H. Odeberg, *III Enoch or the Hebrew Book of Enoch*, 1928, with Odeberg's introduction on Metatron (pp. 79–146, particularly pp. 79–90) and his note on III Enoch 12.5.

35. Cf. the less developed tradition of II Enoch 22.4–10. Odeberg dates the main body of III Enoch to the latter half of the third century AD (*III Enoch*, p. 41); but G. G. Scholem, *Major Trends in Jewish Mysticism*, 1955, dates it much later (pp. 45–7), and is followed by J. C. Greenfield in his Prolegomenon to the new edition of Odeberg's *III Enoch* (1973) – sixth or seventh centuries CE; see also P. S. Alexander, 'The Historical Setting of the Hebrew Book of Enoch', *JJS* 28, 1977, pp. 156–80 – III Enoch 3–15 between *c.* AD 450 and *c.* AD 850 (pp. 164f.).

36. Metatron/Enoch was so much like Yahweh that when Elisha ben Abuya 'came to behold the vision of the Merkabah' (the divine chariot of Ezek. 1) he said 'Indeed, there are two divine powers in heaven!', a heresy (denying the absolute unity of the Godhead) which was regarded as unforgivable by rabbinic Judaism (III Enoch 16.2–4). See Odeberg's note; and further below pp. 80f. and n. 93.

37. See also E. R. Goodenough, *By Light, Light*, 1935, pp. 223–9; J. Jeremias,

TDNT IV, p. 851; H. M. Teeple, *The Mosaic Eschatological Prophet, JBL* Monograph X, 1957, pp. 33–8; W. A. Meeks, *The Prophet-King*, SNT XIV, 1967, pp. 122–5.

38. Text and translation may conveniently be consulted in Tiede, *Charismatic Figure*, pp. 317–24.

39. See particularly Lucian, *Philopseudes, Lover of Lies;* also *Alexander the False Prophet*. A. D. Nock briefly discusses the story of Alexander in *Conversion*, Oxford University Press 1933, paper 1961, pp. 93–7.

40. There was a more or less sustained philosophical critique and scepticism concerning miracle claims, particularly of the grosser wonders, from the sixth century BC onwards; see further E. R. Dodds, *The Greeks and the Irrational*, California 1951, ch. 6; R. M. Grant, *Miracle and Natural Law in Graeco-Roman and Early Christian Thought*, Amsterdam 1952, chs. 4 and 5; G. Delling, 'Zur Beurteilung des Wunders durch die Antike', *Studien zum Neuen Testament und zum hellenistischen Judentum*, Göttingen 1970, pp. 53–71; Talbert, *Gospel*, pp. 31–5.

41. Cooke, 'Israelite King', pp. 206–18; Fohrer, *TDNT* VIII, pp. 349–51; Schlisske, *Gottessöhne*, 2. Teil; Haag, 'Sohn Gottes' p. 230; cf. Hengel, *Son*, pp. 22f.

42. Hengel, *Son*, pp. 53–6; Holladay, *Theios Aner*, p. 182.

43. See Holladay's careful analysis (*Theios Aner*, pp. 108–55); cf. Meeks, *Prophet-King*, pp. 104–6, 159, 211. W. R. Telford's review of Holladay's thesis rightly urges caution in evaluating the evidence, particularly Philo (*JTS* 30, 1979, pp. 246–52); but see the analysis of Philo below §28.3. Similarly Philo's talk of the Logos as 'the second god' (*Qu.Gen.* II.62) has to be set within the context of his overall understanding of the Logos (see below §28.3).

44. Holladay, *Theios Aner*, pp. 229–31; cf. Meeks, *Prophet-King*, pp. 138–42. On Philo, *Mos.* II.288 see Talbert, *Gospel*, pp. 29f. L. Ginzberg, *The Legends of the Jews*, Vol. VI, 1928, suggests a similar unwillingness in LXX and Targum of II Kings 2.1 and Josephus, *Ant.* IX. 28 to accept that Elijah had not died (pp. 322f.). In Ezekiel the Tragedian (second century BC) Moses' dream of being enthroned is interpreted of his leadership over Israel and significance as a prophet (Eusebius, *Praep. Evang.* IX.29.5–6 – text in A. M. Denis, *Fragmenta Pseudepigraphorum Quae Supersunt Graeca*, 1970, p. 210). See further below n. 63.

45. W. L. Knox, 'The "Divine Hero" Christology in the New Testament', *HTR* 41, 1948, pp. 229–49; Braun, *JThC* 5, pp. 104f.; Smith, 'Prolegomena', pp. 182–4; Cuss, *Imperial Cult*, pp. 116–30; Talbert, *Gospel*, pp. 28f.; J. H. W. G. Liebeschuetz, *Continuity and Change in Roman Religion*, Oxford University Press 1979, pp. 65f

46. For examples of visionary/ecstatic journeys to heaven see J. A. Bühner, *Der Gesandte und sein Weg im 4 Evangelium*, 1977, pp. 353–67; other references in J. D. G. Dunn, *Jesus and the Spirit*, 1975, p. 303 and X n. 8.

47. See Talbert, *Gospel*, pp. 49f. n. 80; and further above n. 44 and below §10.3.

48. J. Jeremias, *TDNT* III, pp. 218f.

49. See further Smith, 'Prolegomena', p. 181 n. 52; Talbert, *Gospel*, p. 55.

50. Cf. also S. Lösch, *Deitas Jesu und Antike Apotheose*, 1933, pp. 6–46.

51. See above p. 14; also Boslooper, *Virgin Birth*, pp. 179–81; C. Schneider, *Kulturgeschichte des Hellenismus*, München 1969, II, pp. 892f.; Weinstock, *Divus Julius*, p. 176; Young, *Myth*, ed. Hick pp. 95f. Further parallels may be found in Boslooper, pp. 162–7. For the idea of the *hieros gamos* see W. L. Knox, *St Paul and*

the Church of the Gentiles, 1939, pp. 200f.; H. Schlier, *Epheser*, Dusseldorf 1957, pp. 264–76; J. Gnilka, *Epheserbrief*, Herder 1971, ²1977, pp. 290–4.

52. The (Jewish–) Christian accounts of the virginal conception of Jesus are strikingly different (see below p. 50). The virginal conception of Melchizedek in the Melchizedek fragment (3.1–8, 17–21) of II Enoch (W. R. Morfill and R. H. Charles, *The Book of the Secrets of Enoch*, 1896, pp. 85–93) is most probably a sign of Christian influence in a later development of Melchizedek speculation. The material cited by W. L. Knox, *Some Hellenistic Elements in Primitive Christianity*, 1944, pp. 22–5, hardly provides close parallels. Nor is Philo's allegorical description of how virtues are generated in the human soul really relevant (see particularly *Cher.* 42–52; discussion in Boslooper, *Virgin Birth*, pp. 190–4; see also R. A. Baer, *Philo's Use of the Categories Male and Female*, Leiden 1970, pp. 55–64; cf. Vermes, *Jesus*, pp. 220f.; further bibliography in R. E. Brown, *The Virginal Conception and Bodily Resurrection of Jesus*, 1974, p. 64). Cf. C. H. Dodd, *The Interpretation of the Fourth Gospel*, 1953: 'The Hebrew-thinking Jew was never tempted to assimilate divinity and humanity in any way, nor did he confuse creation with procreation' (p. 252). A. D. Nock, ' "Son of God" in Pauline and Hellenistic Thought', *Essays on Religion and the Ancient World*, Vol. II, 1972, compares Philo's objection to the idea that the essence of God descended on Sinai (*Qu.Ex.* II.45, 47) (p. 934).

53. See Talbert, *Gospel*, pp. 40, 55.

54. See further Hengel, *Son*, pp. 40f.; Talbert, *Gospel*, pp. 77f.; 'The ruler-cult seems to have become a half-mocked convention performed solely for political reasons and probably not affecting the bulk of the populace' (Young, *Myth*, ed. Hick, p. 102); 'Romans were quite aware of the differences between a human emperor and a god. . . . The cults of loyalty at all times must have involved an appalling amount of hypocrisy' (Liebeschuetz, *Roman Religion*, p. 75).

55. Readers will not need reminding that both in Hebrew and in Greek the same word means both 'messenger' and 'angel' (*ml'k*, ἄγγελος).

56. Details are given in Talbert, *Gospel*, pp. 58–61; Bühner, *Gesandte*, pp. 335–41.

57. In the Melchizedek fragment of II Enoch (see n. 52 above) the infant Melchizedek is taken by the archangel Michael and placed in paradise (3.28f.; 4.1, 5, 9), where he exercises his priesthood (3.34–6), but apparently he does not return from there; the Melchizedek of Gen. 14 is 'another Melchizedek' (3.37; 4.5f.).

58. H. Windisch, *Hebräerbrief*, HNT 1913, p. 61; see also E. Käsemann, *Das wandernde Gottesvolk*, 1939, ⁴1961, pp. 129–40; cf. M. de Jonge and A. S. Van der Woude, '11Q Melchizedek and the New Testament', *NTS* 12, 1965–66, p. 321.

59. Strack-Billerbeck III, pp. 694f.; cf. Philo, *Det.* 178; *Ebr.* 61; *Fuga* 60.

60. On the inadvisability of interpreting Moses as an 'incarnation' of the Logos in Philo see below III n. 36 and p. 243.

61. Origen, *Comm. in John.* II.31. Text and commentary in J. Z. Smith, 'The Prayer of Joseph', *RAERG*, pp. 253–94.

62. Uriel is eighth in rank after Israel, and a puzzling phrase may refer to (another) 'angel that is before all' (M. R. James, *The Lost Apocrypha of the Old Testament*, SPCK 1920, p. 22; though see Smith, 'Prayer', p. 257). The name Uriel itself may be an indication of Christian influence since it seems to have replaced the earlier name Sariel (see J. T. Milik, *The Books of Enoch*, 1976, pp. 172–4); we

may note also that according to Targum Neofiti on Gen. 32.25–7 Sariel is 'the chief of those who praise', though in Pseudo-Jonathan the wrestling angel is only 'one of the praising angels'. Talbert says that in *The Prayer of Joseph* 'the angel is the firstborn son of God' (*Gospel*, p. 73); the phrase in question is 'the firstborn (πρωτόγονος) of every living thing to whom God gives life', and is probably based on Ex. 4.22 (Smith, 'Prayer', p. 268); we may note that the whole body of angels are also called 'the sons of God', echoing the old title for the heavenly court (see above p. 15).

63. In subsequent rabbinic legend the translated Elijah makes frequent interventions on earth (see Ginzberg, *Legends*, Vol. IV, 1913, pp. 202–35, Vol. VI, pp. 325–42). Since Moses' death was so clearly attested in scripture (Deut. 34.5) there was much less justification for ranking him with the immortals (see further G. Lohfink, *Die Himmelfahrt Jesu*, München 1971, pp. 61–9); but one Samaritan document looks for his coming (Memar Marqah 2.8; see Meeks, *Prophet-King*, pp. 248f.; and further below III n. 141). It is uncertain whether Matt. 16.14 can be taken as attacking a belief in Jeremiah's eschatological reappearance on earth (see Jeremias, *TDNT* III, pp. 220f.).

64. For details see W. Foerster, *Gnosis* I, 1969, ET 1972, pp. 27–33.

65. 'The most obvious explanation of the origin of the Gnostic redeemer is that he was modelled after the Christian conception of Jesus. It seems significant that we know no redeemer before Jesus, while we encounter other redeemers (Simon Magus, Menander) immediately after his time' (R. M. Grant, *Gnosticism: an Anthology*, 1961, p. 18). It is probably significant that in the first Hermetic tractate (which may go back as early as the beginning of the second century AD) Poimandres is neither a redeemer nor does he descend to earth.

66. See Lake and Cadbury, *Beginnings* IV, p. 91; H. Kippenberg, *Garizim und Synagoge*, 1971, who demonstrates a tradition in Samaritan documents where '*l* (God) is translated *hylh* (Power) (Kap. XIII); G. Lüdemann, *Untersuchungen zur simonianischen Gnosis*, 1975, who argues for a more syncretistic influence – the Great Power = Zeus (pp. 42–54). See also below VI n. 59.

67. Lüdemann, *Untersuchungen*, pp. 43f.; against M. Smith, 'The Account of Simon Magus in Acts 8', *Harry Austyn Wolfson, Jubilee Volume*, Jerusalem 1965, II, who is much too confident in his judgment: 'The notion that a particular historical human being was actually the appearance or incarnation of a particular supernatural power seems to have been common in Palestine during the first century AD' (p. 743); cf. the similar oversimplification of the evidence by Goulder: 'Simon Magus took himself to be an *incarnation* of one person of this (Samaritan) binity' (*Myth*, ed. Hick, pp. 70–3, here p. 72; see also Stanton's response to Goulder in *Incarnation*, ed. Goulder, pp. 243–6, and Goulder's reply, *Incarnation*. pp. 247–50 – 'straightforwardly binitarian'!); see also below VI n. 52. K. Beyschlag rightly warns against a too hasty use of later assertions of second-century Simonian Gnosis in evaluating Acts 8 ('Zur Simon-Magus-Frage', *ZTK* 68, 1971, pp. 395–426; also *Simon Magus und die christliche Gnosis*, 1974, ch. IV; against E. Haenchen, 'Gab es eine vorchristliche Gnosis?', *ZTK* 49, 1952, pp. 316–49, reprinted in *GMEH*, pp. 265–98). See also E. Yamauchi, *Pre-Christian Gnosticism*, 1973, pp. 57–62. The debate between Beyschlag and Haenchen is reviewed by K. Rudolph, 'Simon – Magus oder Gnosticus?', *TR* 42, 1977, pp. 314–28.

68. If second-century parallels are in order we could just as well quote Celsus: 'There are many who, although of no name, with the greatest facility and on the

slightest occasion, whether within or without temples, assume the motions and gestures of inspired persons . . . They are accustomed to say, each for himself, "I am God; I am the Son of God"; or, "I am the Divine Spirit" ' (Origen, *cont. Cels.* VII.9).

69. Cf. the conclusion of E. Schweizer, *Erniedrigung und Erhöhung bei Jesus und seinen Nachfolgern*, ²1962: 'There is no single Jewish example of the expectation that a heavenly being should descend from heaven at the end of time' (p. 40/§3f); similarly with regard to alleged parallels in Graeco-Roman religion (pp. 148–54/ §§12c–f). Contrast the too casual collection of parallels by Schillebeeckx, *Christ*, pp. 327f.: 'The heavenly redeemer was given different names: Wisdom, Logos, angel, Son, man, high priest' (p. 328).

70. F. D. E. Schleiermacher, *The Life of Jesus*, 1864, ET Fortress 1975, pp. 95–104.

71. H. P. Liddon, *The Divinity of our Lord and Saviour Jesus Christ*, Rivingtons 1867, ⁸1878 – Lecture IV is headed 'Our Lord's divinity as witnessed by his consciousness'.

72. Schleiermacher, *Jesus*: 'What John represents as the content of the discourses of Christ must have been what Christ really said and there is no reason to believe that John introduced any of his own ideas into Christ's discourses' (p. 262); Liddon, *Divinity*, pp. 169–92 and Lecture V.

73. E.g. H. M. Relton, *A Study in Christology*, 1934, pp. 236–74; J. R. W. Stott, *Basic Christianity*, Inter-Varsity Fellowship, 1958, pp. 22–7.

74. The crucial contributions here were made by D. F. Strauss, *The Life of Jesus Critically Examined*, 1835, ⁴1840, ET 1846, 1892, Fortress 1972, SCM Press 1973, ch. VII; also his critique of Schleiermacher's *Life*, *The Christ of Faith and the Jesus of History*, 1865, ET Fortress 1977, pp. 38–47; F. C. Baur, *Kritische Untersuchungen über die kanonische Evangelien*, Tübingen 1847, pp. 238–89.

75. See e.g. H. J. Holtzmann, *Die synoptischen Evangelien: ihr Ursprung und geschichtlicher Charakter*, Leipzig 1863, pp. 492–6; also *Das messianische Bewusstsein Jesu*, Tübingen 1907; W. Baldensperger, *Das Selbstbewusstsein Jesu im Lichte der messianischen Hoffnungen seiner Zeit*, Strassburg 1888; A. C. Headlam, *The Life and Teaching of Jesus the Christ*, John Murray 1923, ³1936; M. Goguel, *The Life of Jesus*, 1932, ET George Allen & Unwin 1933.

76. The significance of this feature of our sources was first emphasized in modern times by W. Wrede, 'The Task and Method of "New Testament Theology" ' (1897), ET in R. Morgan, *The Nature of New Testament Theology*, SCM Press 1973, especially pp. 98f.

77. Cf. the warnings of H. J. Cadbury, *The Peril of Modernizing Jesus*, Macmillan 1937, SPCK 1962.

78. Cautionary comments in this area have frequently been voiced in Britain by D. E. Nineham, most recently in his Epilogue to *Myth*, ed. Hick, pp. 186–204, and his review of my *Jesus*, *Religion* 7, 1977, pp. 232–4; see also *The Use and Abuse of the Bible*, Macmillan 1976, SPCK 1978.

79. See e.g. H. Conzelmann, 'Das Selbstbewusstsein Jesu', *Svensk Exegetisk Arsbok*, 28–29, 1963–64, pp. 39–53, reprinted in *Theologie als Schriftauslegung*, 1974, pp. 30–41; N. Brox, 'Das messianische Selbstverständnis des historischen Jesus', *Vom Messias zum Christus*, 1964, pp. 165–201, especially 185–93; see also Dunn, *Unity*, p. 208 and those cited in p. 403 n. 8.

80. See particularly J. M. Robinson, *A New Quest of the Historical Jesus*, SCM Press 1959, pp. 66–72; N. Perrin, *Rediscovering the Teaching of Jesus*, 1967, pp. 222f.

81. In a lecture at Tübingen, 'Die neue Gerechtigkeit in der Jesus-verkündigung' and private conversation (April-May 1979); also 'Existenzstellvertretung für die Vielen: Mark 10.45 (Matt. 20.28)', *Werden und Wirken des Alten Testaments, C. Westermann Festschrift*, hrsg. R. Albertz et al., Göttingen 1980, pp. 412–27; the earlier conclusion – *Das paulinische Evangelium I: Vorgeschichte*, Göttingen 1968, pp. 219f.

82. Jeremias, 'Abba', *TLZ* 79, 1954, col. 213f.; also *The Central Message of the New Testament*, 1965, pp. 9–30; also *The Prayers of Jesus*, 1966, ET 1967, pp. 11–65; also *New Testament Theology: Vol. I: The Proclamation of Jesus*, 1971, ET 1971, pp. 61–8.

83. E.g. Hahn, *Titles*, p. 307; Flusser, *Jesus*, p. 95; Perrin, *Teaching*, pp. 40f.

84. Taylor, *Person*, chs. 13 and 14. Cf. his earlier conclusion, 'It belongs to the self-consciousness of Jesus that he believed himself to be the Son of God in a pre-eminent sense' (*The Names of Jesus*, 1953, p. 65).

85. See particularly C. H. Dodd, *Historical Tradition in the Fourth Gospel*, Cambridge University Press 1963.

86. E. Stauffer, *Jesus and his Story*, 1957, ET SCM Press 1960, pp. 149–59; L. Morris, *Studies in the Fourth Gospel*, Eerdmans 1969, chs. 2 (especially pp. 128–37) and 3 (*passim*). Cf. the more careful assessments of H. Zimmermann, 'Das absolute "Ich bin" in der Redeweise Jesu', *TTZ* 69, 1960, pp. 1–20; A. Feuillet, 'Les *Ego Eimi* christologiques des quatrième Évangile', *RSR* 54, 1966, pp. 213–40; A. M. Hunter, *According to John*, SCM Press 1968, pp. 90–102; S. S. Smalley, *John – Evangelist and Interpreter*, 1978, pp. 184–90.

87. F. L. Cribbs, 'A Reassessment of the Date of Origin and the Destination of the Gospel of John', *CBQ* 89, 1970, pp. 38–55; J. A. T. Robinson, *Redating the New Testament*, SCM Press 1976, ch. IX.

88. Quoted by P. Erlanger in *Encyclopaedia Britannica* [15]1978, XI, p. 122.

89. W. Churchill, *The Second Word War*, Cassell 1948, reissued 1964, pp.238f.

90. R. Bultmann, *The History of the Synoptic Tradition*, 1921, [3]1958, ET Blackwell 1963, p. 126.

91. On the basis of these and other passages E. Käsemann comments: 'Jesus felt himself in a position to override, with an unparalleled and sovereign freedom, the words of the Torah and the authority of Moses . . . What is certain is that he regarded himself as being inspired . . . It signifies an extreme and immediate certainty, such as is conveyed by inspiration . . . this immediate assurance of knowing and proclaiming the will of God . . . he must have regarded himself as the instrument of the living Spirit of God, which Judaism expected to be the gift of the End' ('The Problem of the Historical Jesus', *ENTT*, pp. 40–2). See also J. Jeremias, 'Characteristics of the Ipsissima Vox Jesu' (1954), ET *Prayers*, pp. 112–15; also *Theology* I, pp. 315f.; also 'Zum nicht-responsorischen Amen', *ZNW* 64, 1973, pp. 122f.; H. Schürmann, 'Die Sprache des Christus', *BZ* 2, 1958, pp. 58–62; reprinted *Traditionsgeschichtliche Untersuchungen zu den synoptischen Evangelien*, Düsseldorf 1968, pp. 83–108.

92. *Jesus*, ch. II.

93. *Jesus*, pp. 21f.

94. So also Hengel, *Son*, p. 63 n. 116.

95. *Jesus*, pp. 22–4.

96. Jeremias, *Theology* I, pp. 64f., 66.

97. Vermes, *Jesus*, p. 210. P. M. Casey notes that the only examples of *abba* in Semitic material are bTaan. 23b, Targ.Ps. 89.27 and Targ.Mal. 2.10 ('The Development of New Testament Christology', forthcoming in *Aufstieg und Niedergang der römischen Welt*).

98. M. Smith, review of Dunn, *Jesus*, in *JAAR* 44, 1976, p. 726.

99. Most conveniently set out in P. Fiebig, *Jesu Bergpredigt*, Göttingen 1924, Teil I; pp. 106–11; Teil II, pp. 50f., and in English by P. B. Harner, *Understanding the Lord's Prayer*, Fortress 1975, pp. 123–7. See also J. J. Petuchowski and M. Brocke (eds.), *The Lord's Prayer and Jewish Liturgy*, 1974, ET Herder, and Burns & Oates 1978.

100. See also R. Bauckham, 'The Sonship of the Historical Jesus in Christology', *SJT* 31, 1978, pp. 246–8. How Smith can be so certain, with the evidence as it is, that '*abba* comes from lower class Palestinian piety' (above p. 27 and n. 98), is something of a puzzle. Vermes too builds a very broad conclusion on a very narrow foundation (above p. 27 and n. 97).

101. Jeremias, *Prayers*, pp. 57–62. This characterization holds good even when the popularization of Jeremias's earlier findings ('abba' = 'Daddy') is discounted.

102. Dunn, *Jesus*, pp. 24–6; also *Unity*, pp. 212f.

103. Dunn, *Jesus*, pp. 35f.

104. See also Bauckham, 'Sonship', pp. 249f.

105. Neither Luke 2.41–52 nor Mark 1.11 pars. add anything at this point. The story of Jesus' boyhood visit to the temple (Luke 2), if authentic (see e.g. the discussion in Brown, *Birth*, pp. 479–84), only tells us that Jesus enjoyed the sense of a close relation with God as Father from an early age. And the heavenly voice at Jordan (Mark 1), if we can deduce from the account an experience of Jesus (Dunn, *Jesus*, §10.1), tells us either of the dawning or of the confirming of Jesus' sense of sonship as one chosen to fulfil the role of eschatological anointed one (messiah). On the transfiguration (Mark 9.2–8 pars.) see below pp. 47f.

106. The suggestion that Mark 12.6 implies 'an undeveloped concept of an inactive pre-existence of the Son' (Talbert, *Gospel*, p. 39; cf. Fuller, *Foundations*, p. 194; W. G. Kümmel, *The Theology of the New Testament*, 1972, ET 1974, p. 120) has no foundation in the parable at the level either of Jesus or of Mark (were the 'servants' also pre-existent?); contrast R. Schnackenburg, *Johannes* II, Herder 1971, p. 158, ET Search Press 1980, p. 178; Stanton, *Incarnation*, ed. Goulder, p. 162.

107. Dunn, *Jesus*, pp. 27–35. Cf. the caution at precisely this point of Marshall, *Origins*, pp. 115f., and Bauckham, 'Sonship', p. 252.

108. So rightly Pokorný, *Gottessohn*, p. 29, against B. M. F. van Iersel, *Der 'Sohn' in den synoptischen Jesusworten*, SNT III, ²1964, p. 123. See further below p. 47.

109. Jeremias, *Prayers*, pp. 47f., 50f., and *Theology* I, pp. 58–60 (though see qualifications in Dunn, *Jesus*, p. 32, and Marshall, *Origins*, p. 115). Note also Dodd's comment: 'It is entirely in the manner of the Synoptic parables that typical figures from real life should be introduced as ὁ δοῦλος, ὁ υἱός. . . . In such cases an English speaker would naturally use the indefinite article' (*Historical Tradition*, p. 380). Cf. J. A. T. Robinson in n. 118 below.

110. Cf. Jeremias, *Prayers*, pp. 51f.; also *Theology* I, pp. 59–61; F. Mussner, 'Wege zum Selbstbewusstsein Jesu', *BZ* 12, 1968, pp. 167–9.

111. Quoted by Cullmann, *Christology*, p. 288; also by F. Christ, *Jesus Sophia*,

1970, p. 91; refuted by A. Vögtle, 'Exegetische Erwägungen über das Wissen und Selbstbewusstsein Jesu' (1964), *Das Evangelium und die Evangelien*, 1971, p. 335.

112. In the more extended Lukan parallel it is unlikely that Luke 10.18 was intended to refer to a pre-historical event and so to imply a consciousness of pre-existence on the part of Jesus; see e.g. J. Weiss, *Jesus' Proclamation of the Kingdom of God*, 1892, ET ed. R. H. Hiers and D. L. Holland, Fortress and SCM Press 1971, pp. 80f.; E. Barnikol, *Mensch und Messias*, 1932, pp. 17f.; I. H. Marshall, *Gospel of Luke*, Paternoster 1978, p. 428; against G. Kittel, *TDNT* IV, p. 130 and n. 220. Even if a heavenly event is alluded to (rather than the exorcistic successes of Jesus and his disciples) the event in question is almost certainly eschatological rather than pre-temporal; see U. B. Müller, 'Vision und Botschaft: Erwägungen zur prophetischen Struktur der Verkündigung Jesu', *ZTK* 74, 1977, pp. 416–48.

113. Cf. R. E. Brown, *Jesus God and Man*, 1968, pp. 91f. Cf. also V n. 44.

114. Dodd, *Historical Tradition*, Part II (here p. 388).

115. See further Dunn, *Unity*, pp. 75f.; Smalley, *John*, pp. 197–9, and those cited by him in n. 45.

116. Jeremias, *Prayers*, pp. 30, 36. For 'your Father' – Mark 1, Q 2, special Luke 1, special Matthew 12, John 2; for 'my Father' – Mark 1(?), Q 1, special Luke 3, special Matthew 13, John 25 (pp. 38, 44).

117. Such matters as the probability that John preserves otherwise unknown information about the Baptist, or the discovery of the pool of Bethesda (J. Jeremias, *Die Wiederentdeckung von Bethesda, John 5.2*, Göttingen 1949), do not influence the issues or evidence here at all. Morris's reading of the evidence (above n. 86) is regrettably too selective and of limited value.

118. Cf. W. Grundmann, 'Matt. 11.27 und die johanneischen "Der Vater-Der Sohn"-Stellen', *NTS* 12, 1965–66, pp. 42–9; Robinson, *Human Face*, pp. 185–90; Bauckham, 'Sonship', pp. 253–7.

119. See also Dunn, *Unity*, p. 27; R. E. Brown, *The Community of the Beloved Disciple*, 1979, pp. 26, 43–7; Bauckham, 'Sonship': 'The evidence does not demonstrate that he (Jesus) was conscious of his unique sonship as *divine* sonship, still less does it provide a proof of his divinity' (p. 258). Against Stauffer (as in n. 86 above). Contrast the reserve at this point of Taylor, *Person*; Marshall, *Origins*, and *I Believe in the Historical Jesus*, Hodder & Stoughton 1977; and Smalley, *John*, pp. 186f.

120. Robinson had earlier commented: 'In John we are dealing with a man who is . . . placing his stamp upon the oral tradition of his community with a sovereign freedom' ('The New Look on the Fourth Gospel' (1959), *Twelve New Testament Studies*, SCM Press 1962, pp. 97f.).

121. See further R. Scroggs, 'The Earliest Hellenistic Christianity', *RAERG*, pp. 176–206; Dunn, *Unity*, §60.

122. See particularly J. L. Martyn, *History and Theology in the Fourth Gospel*, 1968, ²1979. Against Robinson (as in n. 87 above). There had been earlier isolated incidents, as Robinson notes (p. 273), but nothing so authoritative, considered and systematic against *Jewish* Christians as the formulation of 9.22 implies.

123. See e.g. the discussion in D. Guthrie, *New Testament Introduction: Hebrews to Revelation*, Tyndale 1962, pp. 192f., 205f.

124. On the relation between John and I John cf. e.g. W. G. Kümmel, *Introduction to the New Testament*, ¹⁷1973, ET revised SCM Press 1975, pp. 442–5; Dunn, *Unity*, pp. 303f.; Brown, *Community*.

125. Cf e.g. the characterizations of John's purpose and method by Dodd, *Interpretation*, pp. 444f.; C. K. Barrett, *John*, SPCK 1955, ²1978, pp. 141f.; F. Mussner, *The Historical Jesus in the Gospel of John*, 1965, ET 1967; R. E. Brown, *John*, AB 1966, p. XLIX; B. Lindars, *John*, NCB 1972, pp. 51–6; J. A. T. Robinson, 'The Use of the Fourth Gospel for Christology Today', *CSNT*, pp. 61–78, who quotes J. A. Baker's argument that to take the pre-existence motif in John as historical is actually to deny rather than affirm the incarnation: 'It simply is not possible at one and the same time to share the common lot of humanity, and to be aware of oneself as one who has existed from everlasting with God. . . . You cannot have both the Jesus of John 8.58 as a piece of accurate reporting and the doctrine of the Incarnation' (*The Foolishness of God*, Darton, Longman & Todd 1970, p. 144; Fount 1975, p. 154).

126. See also Dunn, *Jesus*, pp. 38–40, 90–2. Cf. R. E. Brown, 'How Much did Jesus Know?', *CBQ* 29, 1967, pp. 337f. (quoted in Dunn, *Jesus*, pp. 370 n. 142); Schweizer: 'He stands in a special if not precisely defined relation to the Father' (*TDNT* VIII, p. 366).

127. J. D. G. Dunn, 'Jesus – Flesh and Spirit: an Exposition of Romans 1.3–4', *JTS* 24, 1973, particularly pp. 60f.

128. For further details and bibliography see Dunn, 'Rom. 1.3–4', pp. 40f.; to which add particularly C. Burger, *Jesus als Davidssohn*, 1970, pp. 25–33; Wengst, *Formeln*, pp. 112–14; H. Schlier, 'Zu Röm. 1.3f.', *NTGOC*, pp. 207–18.

129. So, surprisingly, Arndt & Gingrich, ὁρίζω 1b. But note the evidence quoted, together with Moulton & Milligan, ὁρίζω and H. Kleinknecht, *TDNT* V, p. 452 n. 1.

130. C. E. B. Cranfield, *Romans*, ICC Vol. I, 1975, p. 61. See also the strong assertions, e.g. of C. K. Barrett, *Romans*, Black 1957, pp. 19f.; J. Murray, *Romans*, Marshall, Morgan & Scott 1960, p. 9; O. Michel, *Römer*, KEK ¹²1963, p. 40; E. Käsemann, *Römer*, HNT 1973, pp. 9f.

131. L. C. Allen, 'The Old Testament Background of (*Pro*)*horizein* in the New Testament', *NTS* 17, 1970–71, pp. 104–8; cited with some approval by M. Black, *Romans*, NCB 1973, p. 36.

132. On the middle phrase, 'in terms of the Spirit of holiness', see below pp. 138f.

133. Cranfield, *Romans*, I p. 62.

134. See Dunn, 'Rom. 1.3–4', p. 56, and those cited there; also *Unity*, p. 323.

135. Cf. e.g. H. Conzelmann, *An Outline of the Theology of the New Testament*, ²1968, ET 1969, p. 77; H. Schlier, 'Die Anfänge des christologischen Credo', *Zur Frühgeschichte der Christologie*, hrsg. B. Welte, 1970, p. 44; Pokorný, *Gottessohn*, pp. 32f. – 'the title Son of God belongs originally to the presentation of the exaltation of Jesus as the resurrected one' (p. 35); Wengst, *Formeln*, pp. 114–16.

136. Cf. Kramer, *Christ*, pp. 108–11. See further below §29.2.

137. C. H. Dodd, *According to the Scriptures*, Nisbet 1952, pp. 31f.; B. Lindars, *New Testament Apologetic*, 1961, pp. 139–44.

138. See e.g. Lindars, *Apologetic*, pp. 140–3; E. Lövestam, *Son and Saviour*, 1961, pp. 23–48; van Iersel, *Sohn*, pp. 66–73, 83, 174f.; Schweizer, *TDNT* VIII, p. 367; Brown, *Birth*, pp. 29f., 136.

139. See particularly Kramer, *Christ*, pp. 19–26, 110f.; I. H. Marshall, 'The Resurrection in the Acts of the Apostles', *AHGFFB*, pp. 92–107; Hengel, *Son*: 'The statement "God has raised Jesus" could be described as the real primal

Christian confession which keeps recurring in the New Testament' (p. 62). See also below VI n. 94.

140. So a strong strand in German NT scholarship; see particularly H. Conzelmann, *The Theology of St Luke*, 1953, ET Faber & Faber 1960, pp. 173–6; U.Wilckens, *Die Missionsreden der Apostelgeschichte*, Neukirchen 1961, ²1963, pp. 191f.; E. Haenchen, *Acts*, KEK ¹⁴1965, ET Blackwell 1971, pp. 91f.

141. See e.g. M. Dibelius, *From Tradition to Gospel*, 1919, ET Nicholson & Watson 1934, pp. 17f.; S. S. Smalley, 'The Christology of Acts', *ExpT* 73, 1961–62, pp. 358–62; R. F. Zehnle, *Peter's Pentecost Discourse*, Abingdon 1971, pp. 66–70, 89–94; F. F. Bruce, 'The Speeches in Acts – Thirty Years After', *RHLLM*, pp. 53–68.

142. See further Schweizer, *TDNT* VIII, pp. 366–74; J. H. Hayes, 'The Resurrection as Enthronement and the Earliest Church Christology', *Interpretation* 22, 1968, pp. 333–45; Kümmel, *Theology*, pp. 110f.; cf. Ernst, *Anfänge*, p. 24; Hengel, *Son*, pp. 61–6.

143. The thesis that 'Son of God' in earliest Christianity was used initially to refer to Christ's role at the parousia and only subsequently in reference to his resurrection/exaltation (Hahn, *Titles*, pp. 284–8; followed by Fuller, *Foundations*, pp. 164–7) is at best flimsy and can only be maintained by a rather forced exegesis (see also Balz, *Probleme*, pp. 34–6; Marshall, *Origins*, pp. 118f.).

144. See Dunn, *Unity*, p. 46, with reference to E. Best, *I and II Thessalonians*, Black 1972, pp. 85–7, and those cited there; though see also T. Holtz, ' "Euer Glaube an Gott". Zu Form und Inhalt I Thess. 1.9f.', *KAHS*, pp. 459–88.

145. Schweizer, *TDNT* VIII, p. 384.

146. Kramer, *Christ*, p. 117/§26a.

147. See particularly K. H. Schelkle, *Die Passion in der Verkündigung des Neuen Testament*, Heidelberg 1949, pp. 70–2, 133–5.

148. E. D. Burton, *Galatians*, ICC 1921, p. 217; A. Oepke, *Galater*, THNT, ²1957, p. 96; H. Schlier, *Galater*, KEK ¹⁰1949, ¹³1965, p. 196; Taylor, *Person*, pp. 51, 56f.; Kramer, *Christ*, pp. 113f.; Hahn, *Titles*, pp. 304f.; Fuller, *Foundations*, p. 231; H. Ridderbos, *Paul: an Outline of his Theology*, 1966, ET 1975, pp. 68f.; Kümmel, *Theology*, pp. 160f.; F. Mussner, *Galater*, Herder 1974, p. 272; Hengel, *Son*, pp. 26, 31, 39; L. Goppelt, *Theologie des Neuen Testaments*, Vol. I, 1975, Vol. II, 1976, pp. 400f.; Talbert, *Gospel*, p. 72. An allusion to a virgin birth however is usually denied.

149. Further statistics in E. Schweizer, 'Zum religionsgeschichtlichen Hintergrund der "Sendungsformel" Gal. 4.4f., Röm. 8.3f., John 3.16f., I John 4.9', *ZNW* 57, 1966, pp. 199–210, reprinted in *Beiträge zur Theologie des Neuen Testaments*, 1970, p. 85.

150. Cf. K. H. Rengstorf, *TDNT* I, p. 406; P. Bonnard, *Galates*, CNT 1953, pp. 85f.; J. Blank, *Paulus und Jesus*, 1968, p. 267; Robinson, *Human Face*, pp. 161f.; H. D. Betz, *Galatians*, Hermeneia 1979, pp. 206f.

151. It is perhaps significant that Philo speaks of Moses as a prophet and as a wise man with similar frequency (references in Vol. X of Loeb edition of *Philo*, pp. 387f.).

152. See particularly Schweizer, 'Hintergrund', pp. 83–95; followed e.g. by Pokorný, *Gottessohn*, p. 36; Hamerton-Kelly, *Pre-existence*, pp. 111f.; Goppelt, *Theologie*, pp. 400f. I am surprised that Kümmel can find no background 'for the conceptions of the Son's being eternally with God, of his hiddenness in this

world . . .' in 'Jewish wisdom speculation' (*Theology*, p. 121; but see ch. VI below), and so should feel the need for continued recourse to the hypothesis of a pre-Christian Gnostic 'emissary' from heaven to explain the Hellenistic Christian conception of the Son of God (pp. 121f.). R. H. Fuller's vigorous rejection of a Wisdom background for Gal. 4.4f. ('The Conception/Birth of Jesus as a Christological Moment', *JSNT* 1, 1978, pp. 42f.) unfortunately ignores the Wisd. 9.10 parallel. But in addition to the evidence he cites for the view that 'in the Jewish wisdom speculation sophia was never "sent". She always comes on her own initiative' (p. 41), we can mention Luke 11.49 cited below in n. 155. Bühner, *Gesandte*, pp. 87–103, also rejects a Wisdom background for both Pauline and Johannine 'sending-christology' (see below III n. 128).

153. Philo does briefly debate a similar question: 'How can Wisdom, the daughter of God, be rightly spoken of as a father?' He concludes, 'Let us then pay no heed to the discrepancy in the gender of the words, and say that the daughter of God, even Wisdom, is not only masculine but father . . .' (*Fuga* 51f.; cf. *Abr.* 100–2). Here Philo shows that a masculine equation with feminine Wisdom would not go unremarked. But this is an issue which arises for Philo only from the complexity of his allegorizing.

154. It is possible that neither I Corinthian passage should be interpreted by reference to cosmic Wisdom: in I Cor. 1–2 wisdom has much less of a cosmic character, and I Cor. 8.6 could be explained totally by Stoic parallels; in which case there would be no clear Wisdom christology in Paul prior to Col. 1.15–20 (which many would regard as post-Pauline!); but see the discussion in ch. VI.

155. It may be significant that according to Luke 11.49 Jesus quotes *Wisdom* as saying, 'I will send prophets and apostles . . .' (see below pp. 203f.); cf. K. Berger, 'Zum traditionsgeschichtlichen Hintergrund christologischer Hoheitstitel', *NTS* 17, 1970–71, pp. 422–4.

156. Against Schweizer, 'Hintergrund', pp. 91f. Cf. L. Cerfaux, *Christ in the Theology of St Paul*, 1951, ET 1959: 'Paul was provided by Christian tradition with the theme of the sending of the Son of God. In the parable of the vineyard (Matt. 21.33–46 pars.), the owner sent his son last of all' (p. 447); Fuller, 'Christological Moment', p. 43.

157. Cf. Schlier, *Galater*, p. 196; Betz, *Galatians*, pp. 207f.

158. 'Only at John 8.58 (in the NT) is there any special distinction between γίνεσθαι and εἶναι' (F. Büchsel, *TDNT* I, p. 682).

159. Moulton & Milligan, γίνομαι.

160. M. D. Hooker, 'Interchange in Christ', *JTS* 22, 1971, pp. 349–61 (referring to Gal. 4.4 on p. 352).

161. As most recognize – e.g. E. Schweizer, *Jesus*, 1968, ET 1971, pp. 84f.; Hengel, *Son*, pp. 8f.; Stanton, *Incarnation*, ed. Goulder, pp. 154f.

162. Against Kramer, *Christ*, p. 114. Ἐξαγοράζειν obviously refers to Jesus' death as such (as in Gal. 3.13); cf. Schelkle, *Passion*, pp. 135–42; L. Morris, *The Apostolic Preaching of the Cross*, Tyndale 1955, pp. 52–6; G. Delling, *Der Kreuzestod Jesu in der urchristlichen Verkündigung*, Göttingen 1972, pp. 20f.

163. This can be expressed diagrammatically –
not an assertion about Jesus

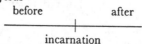

but an assertion about his redeeming action

previous state (slave)   present state (son)

act of redemption

164. Cf. Young, *Myth*, ed. Hick: 'There seems to be no exact parallel to the Christian doctrine of incarnation' (p. 87); similarly Brown, *Birth*, p. 523.

165. Cf. G. Dalman, *The Words of Jesus*, ET 1902: 'The statements as to pre-existence in the Similitudes of Enoch, of II Esdras, and in Pesikta Rabbati, do not presuppose any human birth of Messiah. He is to make his appearance upon earth as a fully developed personality . . . Judaism has never known anything of a pre-existence peculiar to the Messiah *antecedent to his birth as a human being*' (p. 131). On the lack of substantive Hellenistic parallels see particularly Nock, 'Son of God', pp. 933–9; Hengel, *Son*, pp. 35–41.

166. Brown, *Birth*, p. 141 and n. 27. See also Boslooper, *Virgin Birth*, pp. 28–33; H. von Campenhausen, *The Virgin Birth in the Theology of the Ancient Church*, 1962, ET 1964; Brown, *Virginal Conception*, pp. 47–52; and on Justin see especially D. C. Trakatellis, *The Pre-existence of Christ in Justin Martyr*, 1976, ch. 4.

167. The closest parallels (see above n. 52) would mislead rather than illuminate Paul's meaning. In particular, if the language had indeed suggested the idea of a 'miraculous' birth, anyone familiar with the Jewish scriptures would presumably have thought of births to women who were barren or past child-bearing age, like Sarah (Gen. 17.15f. – 'God said to Abraham . . . "I will give you a son by her" ') or Rachel (Gen. 30.22 – 'God opened her womb').

168. A. Seeberg, *Der Katechismus der Urchristenheit*, 1903, München 1966, pp. 59f.; Kramer, *Christ*, pp. 111–15; H. Paulsen, *Überlieferung und Auslegung in Römer 8*, Neukirchen 1974, pp. 40–3; Mussner, *Galater*, pp. 271f.; Hengel, *Son*, pp. 10–12.

169. See further Wengst, *Formeln*, p. 59 n. 22.

170. For notes on the translation see below pp. 111f.

171. That Paul is familiar with the book of Wisdom is suggested by several parallels particularly in Rom. 1 (see below IV n. 9);

172. See J. D. G. Dunn, 'Paul's Understanding of the Death of Jesus', *RHLLM*, pp. 125–41.

173. If a reference to incarnation cannot clearly be found in Gal. 4.4 and Rom. 8.3 it is even less likely to be implied in Paul's addition of 'concerning his Son' in Rom. 1.3. Hengel is much too confident in his assertion that Paul 'certainly understands' Rom. 1.3f. in terms of pre-existence (*Son*, p. 60); similarly P. Stuhlmacher, 'Theologische Probleme des Römerbriefspräskripts', *EvTh* 27, 1967, pp. 382f.; Burger, *Jesus*, p. 31; Schillebeeckx, *Jesus*, pp. 507f.; cf. E. Linnemann's protest on this point ('Tradition and Interpretation in Röm. 1.3f.', *EvTh* 31, 1971, pp. 270–2).

174. See particularly B. M. Metzger, 'The Punctuation of Rom. 9.5', *CSNT*, pp. 95–112; Cranfield, *Romans*, Vol. II, ICC 1979, pp. 464–70.

175. See e.g. RSV; NEB; Barrett, *Romans*, pp. 178f.; Taylor, *Person*, pp. 55f.; Kümmel, *Theology*, p. 164; Käsemann, *Römer*, pp. 247f.

176. Dunn, *Unity*, p. 53; cf. W. Bousset, *Kyrios Christos*, 1913, ²1921, ET 1970, p. 209.

177. As F. F. Bruce, *Romans*, Tyndale 1963, suggests (p. 187).

178. As Michel, *Römer*, suggests (p. 229).

179. Cf. Pokorný, *Gottessohn*: 'If we wish to see in Mark 1.11 the oldest piece of early Christian Son of God christology, then we must presuppose in Rom. 1.3f. a reduction of the divine sonship of Jesus, which is improbable' (p. 33).

180. Contrast the misleading title by H. Weinacht, *Die Menschwerdung des Sohnes Gottes im Markusevangelium*, 1972.

181. That a deliberate allusion to Ps. 2.7 is intended in the heavenly voice still seems to be the most obvious interpretation of Mark 1.11 (cf. Luke 3.22D) – see further Dunn, *Jesus*, p. 65 and n. 122, referring particularly to I. H. Marshall, 'Son of God or Servant of Yahweh – A Reconsideration of Mark 1.11', *NTS* 15, 1968–69, pp. 326–36.

182. Irenaeus tells us that some who separated Jesus from Christ, teaching that Christ remained impassible and only Jesus suffered, preferred the Gospel of Mark – presumably interpreting the scene at Jordan as the descent of the heavenly Christ on the man Jesus (*adv. haer.* III.11. 7). For the second-century Jewish Christian interpretation of the scene at Jordan see Dunn, *Unity*, p. 242.

183. Cf. e.g. Hahn, *Titles*, pp. 300-2.

184. Cf. H. C. Kee, *Community of the New Age*, SCM Press 1977, pp. 54f.

185. Further references in Strack-Billerbeck I, pp. 752f.; D. S. Russell, *The Method and Message of Jewish Apocalyptic*, 1964, pp. 377–9. See also e.g. W. Michaelis and J. Behm, *TDNT* IV, pp. 248f., 758; G. H. Boobyer, *St Mark and the Transfiguration Story*, 1942; H. Baltensweiler, *Die Verklärung Jesu*, 1959, pp. 118f.; M. E. Thrall, 'Elijah and Moses in Mark's Account of the Transfiguration', *NTS* 16, 1969–70, pp. 305–18; J. M. Nützel, *Die Verklärungserzählung im Markusevangelium*, 1973, particularly pp. 272f.; W. L. Liefeld, 'Theological Motifs in the Transfiguration Narrative', *NDNTS*, pp. 178f.; H. Anderson, *Mark*, NCB 1976, pp. 224f.

186. It has been suggested e.g. by Conzelmann, that this is 'an account of a first appointment of Jesus to the rank of Son of God (which) originally competed with the narrative of the baptism' (*Outline*, p. 128); but the narrative itself gives this hypothesis no real support.

187. Schweizer, *TDNT* VIII, p. 379. Cf. the similar comment by J. Weiss, cited by D. E. Nineham, *Mark*, Pelican 1963, p. 431.

188. E. Best, *The Temptation and the Passion: the Markan Soteriology*, Cambridge University Press 1965, p. 169.

189. See Dunn, *Unity*, pp. 49, 70f. and those cited on p. 394 n. 15. See also above nn. 20–22.

190. The evidence is cited by Best, *Temptation*, pp. 170–2, with reference to the contemporary discussion; but see now P. R. Davies and B. D. Chilton, 'The Aqedah: A Revised Tradition History', *CBQ* 40, 1978, pp. 514–46.

191. J. D. Kingsbury, *Matthew: Structure, Christology, Kingdom*, 1975, ch. II.

192. T. de Kruijf, *Der Sohn des lebendigen Gottes*, 1962, pp. 56–8, 109. The Matthean account of the temptations takes the form of a midrash on Deut. 6–8 (B. Gerhardsson, *The Testing of God's Son*, Lund 1966).

193. Schweizer, *TDNT* VIII, p. 380; Kingsbury, *Matthew*, p. 76.

194. Brown, *Birth*, §5; see also K. Stendahl, '*Quis et Unde?* An Analysis of Matt. 1–2', *Judentum, Urchristentum, Kirche*, 1964, pp. 94–105; R. Pesch, 'Der Gottessohn im matthäischen Evangelienprolog (Matt. 1–2)', *Biblica* 48, 1967, pp. 395–420 (particularly pp. 408–19); Kingsbury, *Matthew*, pp. 42–53.

195. Boslooper, *Virgin Birth*, pp. 185f.; Brown, *Birth*, p. 137. This step may

have been taken before Matthew, but the extent of the pre-Matthean material
and its date of origin is unclear. Brown discusses the extent of the pre-Matthean
material on pp. 104–21. See further below p. 51.

196. Brown, *Birth*, p. 141; Fuller, 'Christological Moment', p. 39. Matt. 1.23,
' "His name shall be called Emmanuel" (which means, God with us)', does not
affect this conclusion, since the child of whom Isaiah speaks would have been
understood to be simply a symbol of God's purpose for Judah. Matthew would
see it fulfilled in complete measure by Jesus, but not in a literal sense as though
he were identifying Jesus with God, only in the sense that Jesus is the full
(fulfilled) expression of God's presence with his people (Brown, *Birth*, p. 150 n.
52). See also below §§25.1–2.

197. The idea of the pre-existence of the soul, already present in Wisd. 8.19f.,
has no bearing on the issues here.

198. Cf. von Campenhausen, *Virgin Birth*: 'Mark and John stand over against
the infancy stories in Matthew and Luke; and almost all primitive Christian
literature confesses by its silence that the "doctrine" of the virgin birth was
foreign to it, or at least a matter of secondary importance or indifference' (p. 17).

199. See above pp. 35f. 'Son of God' occurs again in the confession of 8.37, but
by unanimous consent that is a later addition to Acts.

200. See particularly Brown, *Birth*, pp. 298–309, and Marshall, *Gospel*, pp. 69f.,
both with discussion of other views.

201. See further Brown, *Birth*, pp. 289–91, 314–16, 327; see also below V n.
68. Contrast the too casual assertion of P. Schoonenberg, *The Christ*, ET 1972,
that 'the virginal origin of Jesus can also be understood there (Luke 1.35) . . .
(as) a result of . . . his pre-existence as pneuma' (p. 54).

202. Conzelmann, *Theology of Luke*, p. 173; G. W. H. Lampe, 'The Lucan
Portrait of Christ', *NTS* 2, 1955–56, p. 171; C. F. D. Moule, 'The Christology of
Acts', *SLAPS*, pp. 178f.; I. H. Marshall, *Luke: Historian and Theologian*, Paternoster
1970, p. 169.

203. For supporters of the view that the Western reading is original see Dunn,
Jesus, p. 366 n. 73. For counter arguments and their proponents see Marshall,
Gospel, pp. 154f.

204. Brown, *Birth*, p. 90 n. 68.

205. See H. Zimmermann, *Das Bekenntnis der Hoffnung*, 1977, pp. 45–7 and
those cited there; also V. H. Neufeld, *The Earliest Christian Confessions*, 1963,
pp. 135f.; Dunn, *Unity*, p. 46.

206. E. F. Scott, *The Epistle to the Hebrews*, T. & T. Clark 1922, p. 152; cf.
Schweizer, *Erniedrigung*, p. 120/§10e; H. Braun, 'Die Gewinnung der Gewissheit
in dem Hebräerbrief', *TLZ* 96, 1971, cols. 323–5.

207. Knox, *Humanity*, p. 43.

208. G. B. Caird, 'Son by Appointment', in *B. Reicke Festschrift*, Leiden (forthcoming). Similarly Robinson, *Human Face*, pp. 155–61.

209. Further references in Dunn, *Unity*, pp. 259f.; also in those mentioned
above in n. 208; see also J. W. Thompson, 'The Structure and Purpose of the
Catena in Heb. 1.5–13', *CBQ* 38, 1976, pp. 352–63.

210. Cf. B. Klappert, *Die Eschatologie des Hebräerbriefs*, 1969; C. Carlston, 'The
Vocabulary of Perfection in Philo and Hebrews', *UDNTT*, pp. 133–60. The in-
fluence of Jewish apocalyptic on Hebrews is rightly emphasized by O. Michel,
Hebräer, KEK [7]1936, [12]1966, pp. 58–68, and C. K. Barrett, 'The Eschatology of

the Epistle to the Hebrews', *BNTE*, pp. 363–93. But the influence of Platonic philosophy is equally hard to deny – see those cited in n. 211 below. The synthesis is helpfully represented by diagram in G. Vos, *The Teaching of the Epistle to the Hebrews*, Eerdmans 1956, pp. 56f.

211. See J. Moffatt, *Hebrews*, ICC 1924, pp. xxxi–iv; C. Spicq, 'Le Philonisme de l'Epitre aux Hebreux', *RB* 56, 1949, pp. 542–72; 57, 1950, pp. 212–42; also *Hebreux*, EB Vol. I 1952, pp. 25–91; H. W. Montefiore, *Hebrews*, Black 1964, pp. 6–9; R. S. Eccles, 'The Purpose of the Hellenistic Patterns in the Epistle to the Hebrews', *RAERG*, pp. 207–26. Other references in F. F. Bruce, *Hebrews*, Eerdmans 1964, p. lvii n.135. R. Williamson, *Philo and the Epistle to the Hebrews*, 1970, disputes at length the narrow thesis that the author of Hebrews was directly dependent on and indebted to Philo (against particularly Spicq), but accepts that they belong to the same or similar intellectual religious circles (pp. 430, 493; though he rather plays this down – 'superficial similarities', pp. 433, 493). Certainly the attempt by Hebrews' author to develop a Christian apologetic on the backcloth of a Jewish eschatology combined with a Platonic world-view sets him apart from Philo. But it does not alter the fact that Hebrews works (at least in part) with a Platonic world-view such as comes to expression in a more thorough-going way in Philo (see further below §28.3), and that Philo can be used to illuminate one dimension of Hebrews' thought.

212. Cf. L. K. K. Dey, *The Intermediate World and Patterns of Perfection in Philo and Hebrews*, SBL Dissertation Series 25, 1975, p. 170.

213. Cf. G. Theissen, *Untersuchungen zum Hebräerbrief*, 1969, p. 27; Dey, *Intermediary World*, ch. 6; J. W. Thompson, 'The Conceptual Background and Purpose of the Midrash in Hebrews 7', *NovT* 19, 1977, pp. 209–23. It is quite probable that the author of Hebrews was acquainted with Philo's treatise *Legum Allegoriae*, particularly Book III. As we have noted above, the clearest parallels to his use of Platonic cosmology are found in *Leg. All.* III. In addition, only in *Leg. All.* II.67, III.103, 204, 228, does Philo make use of Num. 12.7, to which Hebrews refers in 3.2, 5, though Philo quotes it in order to honour Moses. The argument of Heb. 6.13–18 is closely paralleled in *Leg. All.* III.203 (the only other quotation of Gen. 22.16 is in the less close *Abr.* 273). And only in *Leg. All.* III.79–82 does he use the Melchizedek episode in Genesis in a way which approaches Heb. 7.

214. Cf. Scott: 'The Logos doctrine, although it seems to disappear after the opening chapter, is implicit in the argument throughout' (*Hebrews*, p. 166); Moffatt, *Hebrews*, pp. xlviif.

215. Though we should note the rabbinic phrase which regularly describes (all) men as 'those who come into the world' (Strack-Billerbeck II, p. 358; see also Michel, *Hebräer*, p. 336); cf. John 1.9 on which see T. F. Glasson, 'John 1.9 and a Rabbinic Tradition', *ZNW* 49, 1958, pp. 288–90. Despite Craddock, Heb. 11.26 is by no means a clear 'affirmation of Christ's pre-existence' (*Pre-existence*, pp. 15, 128). There is a general consensus among commentators that the wording of 11.26 frames an allusion to Ps. 89.50f. (LXX 88.51f.) – 'Remember O Lord the abuse suffered by your servant(s) (τοῦ ὀνειδισμοῦ τῶν δούλων σου) . . . how your enemies abused the succession of your anointed one (ὠνείδισαν τὸ ἀντάλλαγμα τοῦ χριστοῦ σου)'. Consequently we should translate Heb. 11.26, 'Moses considered the abuse suffered by the anointed one (τὸν ὀνειδισμὸν τοῦ χριστοῦ) greater wealth than the treasures of Egypt . . .', where the thought is of the sufferings of the elect people (and subsequently king) as a typological prefigure-

ment of Christ's sufferings. The thrust of the whole chapter is forward looking – the incompleteness of the heroes of faith without the completion brought by Christ and those following behind him (11.39–12.2). NEB thus quite properly translates 11.26 – 'He considered the stigma that rests on God's Anointed greater wealth than the treasures of Egypt, for his eyes were fixed on the coming day of recompense.'

216. This sense of Christ as embodying the very power of God that created the world probably explains 'the astonishing application to Christ in Heb. 1.10–12 of a Psalm (102) which seems manifestly to be addressed to God almighty as Creator, and which (one would think) could therefore have no cogency whatever as a scriptural proof about the status of Christ' (C. F. D. Moule, *The Birth of the New Testament*, A. & C. Black 1962, p. 77); see particularly Cullmann, *Christology*, pp. 310f.; Thompson, 'Catena in Heb. 1.5–13', pp. 359–62; cf. Philo, who names the two chief powers 'God' and 'Lord' (*Qu. Ex.* II. 68), and Philo and John who both call the Logos 'God' (see below p. 241). Similarly with Heb. 13.8 – 'Jesus Christ yesterday and today the same and for ever' – if 'the same' there carries an allusion to 'the same' of 1.12 (= Ps. 102.28) (cf. particularly Michel, *Hebräer*, pp. 490–3); but the 'yesterday' of 13.8 could simply refer to Jesus' earthly ministry in contrast to his present and continuing role as heavenly intercessor (cf. p. 246 below).

217. The significance of applying to the Son a psalm which addressed the king as 'god' should not be overrated, especially in view of our observations above (pp. 16f.).

218. F. L. Horton, *The Melchizedek Tradition*, 1976, rightly rejects the suggestion that Hebrews is dependent on 11Q Melch., since the whole point of Heb. 1–2 is to argue Christ's *superiority* to angels, whereas the Christ/Melchizedek parallel in Heb. 7 is quite different (pp. 167–70; so also Zimmermann, *Bekenntnis*, pp. 87–93); despite most recently R. N. Longenecker, 'The Melchizedek Argument of Hebrews', *UDNTT*, pp. 161–85, Christ is *not* presented in Hebrews as superior to Melchizedek (p. 176). But neither is it adequate to postulate a *merely* typological correspondence between Melchizedek and Christ. Melchizedek is *not* an earthly shadow of a heavenly priesthood; he is himself an embodiment of the *real* priesthood which Christ subsequently embodies 'after the order of Melchizedek' and beside which the *Levitical and Aaronic* priesthood is the inferior shadow.

219. Perhaps as a rejection of an Ebionite-like 'adoptionism' (see Dunn, *Unity*, pp. 260f.).

220. In 7.3 'without father or mother or genealogy' refers to priestly qualification not to a miraculous birth (Michel, *Hebräer*, pp. 261f.; Horton, *Melchizedek*, pp. 162f.). On 10.5 see above n. 214. O. Hofius, 'Inkarnation and Opfertod Jesu nach Hebr. 10.19f.', *RJAGJJ*, pp. 132–41, argues that 10.20b refers to the incarnation; but see J. Jeremias, 'Hebräer 10.20: τοῦτ' ἔστιν τῆς σαρκὸς αὐτοῦ', *ZNW* 62, 1971, p. 131.

221. 'The real heart of Johannine christology is found in a typically Johannine emphasis on the unique relationship between Father and Son' (M. de Jonge, *Jesus: Stranger from Heaven*, 1977, p. 141).

222. Cf. Bultmann, *Theology*, Vol. II, ET 1955, pp. 33–5.

223. E. L. Allen, 'Representative-Christology in the New Testament', *HTR* 46, 1953, pp. 166–9, Meeks, *Prophet-King*, pp. 301–5, P. Borgen, 'God's Agent in the Fourth Gospel', *RAERG*, pp. 137–48, and particularly Bühner, *Gesandte*, pp. 181–

267, have demonstrated how much of John's 'sending christology' can be explained against the background of the Jewish concept of the *šāliaḥ* (agent) acting in the place of the one who sent him; though Bühner's attempt to explain the Johannine understanding of the Son's pre-existence on the same basis (cf. pp. 234, 426) is hardly satisfactory. That apart, the merging of such a *šāliaḥ* christology with the idea of Jesus as the Son and leader/redeemer who brings many sons to glory (as in Heb. 2.10–15) would be sufficient explanation of those features of John's christology whose most obvious parallels have hitherto been found in the Gnostic redeemer myth (cf. Schnackenburg, *Johannes* II, pp. 162–6 ET, pp. 181–4).

224. See further Dodd, *Interpretation*, pp. 255–62; E. M. Sidebottom, *The Christ of the Fourth Gospel*, 1961, pp. 154–61; Kümmel, *Theology*, pp. 268–74; Schnackenburg, *Johannes* II, pp. 158f. ET, pp. 178f.; de Jonge, *Jesus*, pp. 141–9. But see also Barrett in VII n. 129 below.

225. Schweizer, *TDNT* VIII, p. 386; J. P. Miranda, *Der Vater, der mich gesandt hat*, 1972, pp. 132–47.

226. Outside the NT we might compare Justin Martyr (see Trakatellis, *Pre-existence*, pp. 177–9).

227. Dodd, *Interpretation*, p. 262.

228. See also de Jonge, *Jesus*, pp. 151–4.

229. Most commentators accept the reading 'the only god' (μονογενὴς θεός) as original rather than 'the only son' (μονογενὴς υἱός) in John 1.18, and also (though with less unanimity) that it is Jesus who is called 'the true God' in I John 5.20. In addition to commentators see Cullman, *Christology*, pp. 309f.; Brown, *Jesus*, pp. 12f., 18f.; B. A. Mastin, 'A Neglected Feature of the Christology of the Fourth Gospel', *NTS* 22, 1975–76, particularly pp. 37–41.

230. Cf. Sidebottom, *Christ*, p. 163; Schweizer, *TDNT* VIII, pp. 387f.; Brown, *John*, p. 408; though see also Mastin, 'Neglected Features', pp. 48–51; de Jonge, *Jesus*, p. 150.

231. Dodd, *Interpretation*, p. 260; Kümmel, *Theology*, p. 271; cf. Brown, *Virginal Conception*, p. 59. See also above p. 42.

232. Cf. Moffatt, *Hebrews*, p. 1.

233. Cf. Pannenberg, *Jesus*: 'In its content, the legend of Jesus' virgin birth stands in an irreconcilable contradiction to the christology of the incarnation of the pre-existent Son of God found in Paul and John' (p. 143); and Brown's rejoinder in *Virginal Conception*, pp. 43–5.

234. Cf. particularly G. Dix's remarks in *Jew and Greek: A Study in the Primitive Church*, A. & C. Black 1953, pp. 79f.

235. Cf. Bauckham, 'Sonship', p. 258.

236. Knox, *Humanity*, p. 11; cf. Pannenberg, *Jesus*, pp. 153f.; and the more carefully formulated arguments of Cullmann, *Christology*, p. 321, and Moule, *Origin*, pp. 138–40. A. E. J. Rawlinson, The *New Testament Doctrine of the Christ*, 1926, argued that Paul's doctrine of the pre-existence of Christ derived 'from the identification of Christ with the Son of Man' (pp. 111, 121–7); but see below ch. III and III n.133. A. Deissmann, *Paul: A Study in Social and Religious History*, 1912, ²1927, ET Harper Torchbook 1957, suggested that the idea of Christ's pre-existence arose from the identification of the exalted Christ with the Spirit (p. 195); but this is even less likely since there is *no* identification of Christ with

the Spirit prior to Jesus' resurrection-exaltation (see below §19). Cf. VII n. 93 below.

Chapter III The Son of Man

1. See further Lampe υἱός D.
2. See e.g. A. J. B. Higgins, 'Son of Man *Forschung* since "The Teaching of Jesus" ', *NTETWM*, pp. 119–35; the sequence of reviews by I. H. Marshall, 'The Synoptic Son of Man Sayings in Recent Discussion', *NTS* 12, 1965–66, pp. 327–51; also 'The Son of Man in Contemporary Debate', *EQ* 42, 1970, pp. 67–87; also *Origins*, ch. 4; and S. Legasse, 'Jesus historique et le Fils de l'Homme: Aperçu sur les opinions contemporaines', *ATE*, pp. 271–98.
3. The most recent contributions include G. Vermes, 'The Present State of the "Son of Man" Debate', *JJS* 29, 1978, pp. 123–34; also ' "The Son of Man" Debate', *JSNT* 1, 1978, pp. 19–32; M. Black, 'Jesus and the Son of Man', *JSNT* 1, 1978, pp. 4–18; J. A. Fitzmyer, 'The New Testament Title "Son of Man" Philologically Considered', *A Wandering Aramean: Collected Aramaic Essays*, 1979, pp. 143–60; also 'Another View of the "Son of Man" Debate', *JSNT* 4, 1979, pp. 58–68; M. D. Hooker, 'Is the Son of Man problem really insoluble?', *Text and Interpretation*, 1979, pp. 155–68; M. Casey, *The Son of Man: The Interpretation and Influence of Daniel 7*, 1980; A. J. B. Higgins, *The Son of Man in the Teaching of Jesus*, 1980; Stuhlmacher cited above II n. 81.
4. See particularly the continuing dispute between Vermes and Fitzmyer mentioned in n. 3 above.
5. The issue which particularly concerns us – see below §§9 and 10.3.
6. See e.g. Hahn, *Titles*, ch. I; H. Schürmann, 'Beobachtungen zum Menschensohn-Titel in der Redequelle', *JMAV*, 124–47; D. R. Catchpole, 'The Son of Man's Search for Faith', *NovT* 19, 1977, pp. 81–104.
7. Hamerton-Kelly, *Pre-existence*, p. 101.
8. Hamerton-Kelly, *Pre-existence*, pp. 37–47, 58–64.
9. See e.g. W. A. Meeks' review of Hamerton-Kelly in *JBL* 93, 1974, pp. 617–19; as well as those cited in n. 3 above.
10. Dan. 7.13 – ἐπὶ τῶν νεφελῶν τοῦ οὐρανοῦ ὡς υἱὸς ἀνθρώπου ἤρχετο.
Mark 13.26 – τὸν υἱὸν τοῦ ἀνθρώπου ἐρχόμενον ἐν νεφέλαις.
par. Matt. 24.30 – τὸν υἱὸν τοῦ ἀνθρώπου ἐρχόμενον ἐπὶ τῶν νεφελῶν τοῦ οὐρανοῦ.
Mark 14.62 – τὸν υἱὸν τοῦ ἀνθρώπου .. ἐρχόμενον μετὰ τῶν νεφελῶν τοῦ οὐρανοῦ.
Matt. 24.44/Luke 12.40 – ὁ υἱὸς τοῦ ἀνθρώπου ἔρχεται.
Matt. 10.23 – ἕως ἔλθῃ ὁ υἱὸς τοῦ ἀνθρώπου.
Matt. 16.28 – τὸν υἱὸν τοῦ ἀνθρώπου ἐρχόμενον ἐν τῇ βασιλείᾳ αὐτοῦ.
Matt. 25.31 – ὅταν ἔλθῃ ὁ υἱὸς τοῦ ἀνθρώπου ἐν τῇ δόξῃ αὐτοῦ.
Luke 18.8 – ὁ υἱὸς τοῦ ἀνθρώπου ἐλθών.
11. 'The fourth is so extraordinary, and so terrible, that the author can find no words or similies adequate to describe it' (M. D. Hooker, *The Son of Man in Mark*, 1967, pp. 19f.).
12. References may be found in L. F. Hartman and A. A. Di Lella, *Daniel*, AB 1978, pp. 85f.; see also C. Colpe, *TDNT* VIII, pp. 402–4. G. Vermes, in M.

Black, *An Aramaic Approach to the Gospels and Acts*, Oxford University Press, ³1967, pp. 316–19; Fitzmyer, *Wandering Aramean*, pp. 145–53. One of the most accurate translations of Dan. 7.13 is Good News Bible – 'I saw what looked like a human being'.

13. That 'son of man' in Dan. 7 is a pictorial symbol of 'the saints of the Most High' is widely recognized. See e.g. J. A. Montgomery, *Daniel*, pp. 303, 317–24; T. W. Manson, 'The Son of Man in Daniel, Enoch and the Gospels' (1949), *Studies in the Gospels and Epistles*, 1962, pp. 125–7; H. H. Rowley, *The Servant of the Lord*, Lutterworth 1952, p. 62; S. Mowinckel, *He that Cometh*, 1951, ET 1956, p. 350; Russell, *Method*, pp. 326f.; M. Delcor, *Le Livre de Daniel*, Paris 1971, pp. 155f.; O. Michel, 'Der Menschensohn', *TZ* 27, 1971, p. 95; A. Deissler, 'Der "Menschensohn" und "das Volk der Heiligen des Höchsten" in Dan. 7', *JMAV*, pp. 81–91; M. Casey, 'The Corporate Interpretation of "One like a Son of Man" (Dan. 7.13) at the Time of Jesus', *NovT* 18, 1976, pp. 176–80; also *Son of Man*, pp. 24–9; A. A. Di Lella, 'The One in Human Likeness and the Holy Ones of the Most High in Daniel 7', *CBQ* 39, 1977, pp. 1–19; Hartman and Di Lella, *Daniel*, pp. 85–102.

14. There is no real evidence of an older source behind the text of Dan. 7 containing a Son of Man figure who might have been interpreted differently (Casey, *Son of Man*, pp. 11–17, 22–24; see also J. J. Collins, *The Apocalyptic Vision of the Book of Daniel*, 1977, pp. 127–32; H. S. Kvanvig 'Struktur und Geschichte in Dan. 7.1–14', *StTh* 32, 1978, pp. 95–117); against, most recently, J. Theisohn, *Der auserwählte Richter*, 1975, pp. 5–9, who, however, adds nothing of substance to the earlier theses reviewed by Casey and who himself shows that the Similitudes of Enoch know only Dan. 7 and not some earlier form of (individual) Son of Man tradition (pp. 14–30; against particularly E. Sjöberg, *Der Menschensohn im äthiopischen Henochbuch*, 1946, p. 190) – a finding which makes any such hypothesis built on speculative redaction criticism of Dan. 7 still more precarious. T. F. Glasson has argued that Dan. 7.9–13 drew on the imagery of I Enoch 14.8–24 and that Enoch was the 'original' of Daniel's 'son of man' (cf. I Enoch 14.8 with Dan. 7.13); but he denies that Daniel intended to identify his human figure with Enoch – 'he merely drew upon the imagery of the earlier work in depicting this symbolic figure' (*The Second Advent*, 1945, pp. 14–17; also 'The Son of Man Imagery: Enoch 14 and Daniel 7', *NTS* 23, 1976–77, pp. 82–90). Others have argued for a deliberate association of ideas between the vision of Dan. 7 and that of Ezek. 1, with the implication that the son of man is 'a kind of visible manifestation of the invisible God' (Feuillet, n. 51 below p. 187; cf. M. Black 'Die Apotheose Israels: eine neue Interpretation des danielischen "Menschensohns" ', *JMAV*, pp. 92–9, and below n. 65). But in Ezekiel it is Ezekiel himself who is called 'Son of Man' (2.1 etc.); see also below p. 156.

15. See e.g. Hahn, *Titles*, pp. 17–19; Kümmel, *Theology*, (from whom the quotation in the text comes); Marshall, *Origins*, pp. 66f.

16. The different views on the origin of the Danielic son of man figure are laid out schematically by Theisohn, *Richter*, p. 4.

17. So e.g. W. F. Albright, *From Stone Age to Christianity*, 1940, ²1946, Anchor Book 1957, pp. 378f.; W. Manson, *Jesus the Messiah*, 1943, pp. 98–101, 173f.; W. D. Davies, *Paul and Rabbinic Judaism*, 1948, ²1955, p. 279; and more recently H. Gese, 'Der Messias', *Zur biblischen Theologie: alttestamentliche Vorträge*, 1977, pp. 140–

5; cf. W. Wifall, 'Son of Man – a Pre-Davidic Social Class?', *CBQ* 37, 1975, pp. 331–40; Schillebeeckx, *Christ*, pp. 172f.

18. Casey, *Son of Man*, pp. 30f.

19. Strack-Billerbeck I, pp. 485f.; on *Dial*. 32.1 see however A. J. B. Higgins, 'Jewish Messianic Beliefs in Justin Martyr's *Dialogue with Trypho*', *NovT* 9, 1967, pp. 301f.

20. A. Gelston, 'A Sidelight on the "Son of Man" ', *SJT* 22, 1969, pp. 189–96; D. Hill, ' "Son of Man" in Psalm 80.17', *NovT* 15, 1973, pp. 261–9. Why v. 15b crept in is now impossible to tell – presumably either as a deliberate attempt to exclude a messianic interpretation, or by dittography.

21. It is not cited in *Biblia Patristica: Index des Citations et Allusions Bibliques dans la littérature Patristique*, 2 Vols, Paris 1975, 1977. It is interpreted messianically in the Targum to the Psalms, but that is late (though see B. McNeil, 'The Son of Man and the Messiah: A Footnote', *NTS* 26, 1979–80, pp. 419–21).

22. Although the possibility that Ps. 80.17 was drawn in to supplement Dan. 7.13 in the framing of Mark 14.62 should not be entirely discounted (cf. Dodd, *Scriptures*, pp. 101f.; also *Interpretation*, p. 245 n. 1; O. F. J. Seitz, 'The Future Coming of the Son of Man: Three Midrashic Formulations in the Gospel of Mark', *SE* VI, 1973, pp. 478–88).

23. See H. Windisch, 'Die göttliche Weisheit der Juden und die paulinische Christologie', *Neutestamentliche Studien G. Heinrici*, hrsg. A. Deissmann and H. Windisch, 1914, pp. 228f.; Bousset-Gressmann, pp. 264f.; Strack-Billerbeck II, p. 334; F. H. Borsch, *The Son of Man in Myth and History*, 1967, pp. 108–12. See also VI n. 19 below.

24. J. Klausner, *The Messianic Idea in Israel*, ET 1956, p. 77; K. Rudolph, *Micha, Nahum, Habakuk, Zephanja*, Gütersloh 1975, points out that 'from ancient days' in Micah 5.2 will refer as in Amos 9.11, to the time of David (p. 96). With 'from of old' we should compare Ps. 74.2. Borsch in his discussion (pp. 108–16) tends to assume allusions in texts which are by no means obvious (e.g. his capitalizing of Son of Man). The evidence documented by Borsch and those he cites does not go beyond demonstrating that the king in Israel was thought to represent Yahweh in some sense – an association with Adam as such, let alone use of a Primal Man myth, has not been demonstrated (cf. Mowinckel, *He that Cometh*, pp. 81f.).

25. Davies, *Paul*, pp. 160–2.

26. D. M. Hay, *Glory at the Right Hand: Psalm 110 in Early Christianity*, SBL Monograph 18, 1973, p. 49. On the meaning of the Hebrew see Cooke, 'Israelite King', pp. 218–24.

27. E.g. Schlier, *Epheser*, p. 49.

28. See Strack-Billerbeck I, pp. 974f.; II, pp. 334f.

29. J. Macdonald, *The Theology of the Samaritans*, 1964, pp. 162f.

30. See further R. Bergmeier, 'Zur Frühdatierung samaritanischer Theologumena', *JSJ* 5, 1974, pp. 121–53.

31. Now probably better called The Testament of Moses (see J. H. Charlesworth, *The Pseudepigrapha and Modern Research*, 1976, pp. 160–6).

32. K. Haacker thinks Ass. Mos. is a Samaritan document, but from the second century AD ('Assumptio Mosis – eine samaritanische Schrift?', *TZ* 25, 1969, pp. 385–405). On the other hand J. Licht, 'Taxo, or the Apocalyptic Doctrine of Vengeance', *JJS* 12, 1961, pp. 95–103, and G. W. E. Nickelsburg, *Resurrection, Immortality and Eternal Life in Intertestamental Judaism*, Harvard Theo-

logical Studies 26, 1972, pp. 43–5, date the first version of Ass.Mos. to the early Maccabean period.

33. See the discussion in K. Haacker, *Die Stiftung des Heils*, 1972, pp. 122–5.

34. See D. L. Tiede, 'The Figure of Moses in The Testament of Moses', *Studies on the Testament of Moses*, ed. G. W. E. Nickelsburg, SBL Septuagint and Cognate Studies 4, 1973, pp. 90f.

35. 11.16 – '... sacrum spiritum dignum domino multiplicem et ....'; cf. Wisd. 7.22 – πνεῦμα ... ἅγιον ... πολυμερές. ...

36. Wisdom 7.22 speaks of Wisdom *possessing* such a spirit (against Haacker, *Stiftung*, p. 126). Philo, *Heres*, 205f. should not be taken as any more than a typically Philonic allegorical identification of the Logos with Moses (against Berger, 'Hintergrund', pp. 411f. n. 6, whose other evidence either presses a meaning upon the text with too little justification or else ignores the question of the text's/tradition's date). See further below p. 243.

37. 'That the Messiah himself existed before creation is nowhere stated in Tannaitic literature ... "the name of the Messiah" is the *idea* of the Messiah, or, more exactly, *the idea of redemption through the Messiah*. This idea did precede creation' (Klausner, *Messianic Idea*, p. 460); see also Strack-Billerbeck II, pp. 334f.; Mowinckel, *He that Cometh*, p. 334; R. Schnackenburg, *John*, Herder, Vol. I, 1965, ET 1968, pp. 495f.; Vermes, *Jesus*, pp. 138f. We may compare the rather entertaining rabbinic discussion concerning the ten things created on the eve of the Sabbath (e.g. Aboth 5.6; bPes. 54a(2); Targ. Ps. Jon. Num. 22.28) – including such candidates as 'the mouth of the ass', 'the manna' and 'the tongs made with the tongs' – all evidently mysterious and numinous manifestations of God's power (see W. S. Towner, *The Rabbinic Enumeration of Scriptural Examples*, Leiden 1973, pp. 66–71). On the pre-existence of the Torah see below VI n. 43.

38. See also J. Drummond, *The Jewish Messiah*, 1877, ch. XI.

39. For the range of Jewish exegesis at the time of Jesus see e.g. Dunn, *Unity*, §21, and those cited in the notes.

40. Rowley, *Servant*, pp. 61–88: 'There is no serious evidence of the bringing together of the concepts of the Suffering Servant and the Davidic Messiah before the Christian era' (p. 85). See also Nickelsburg, *Resurrection*, ch. II. The Isaiah Targum's manipulation of Isa. 52.13–53.12 is well known (see e.g. Manson, *Jesus*, pp. 168–70; W. Zimmerli and J. Jeremias, *The Servant of God*, ET revised SCM Press 1965, pp. 67–77; text in J. F. Stenning, *The Targum of Isaiah*, Oxford University Press 1949, pp. 78–81).

41. See further Mowinckel, *He that Cometh*, pp. 284–6; Hahn, *Titles*, pp. 136–48; U. B. Müller, *Messias und Meschensohn in jüdischen Apokalypsen und in der Offenbarung des Johannes*, 1972, pp. 72–81.

42. See particularly C. H. Kraeling, *Anthropos and the Son of Man*, 1927, particularly ch. VI. For examples of the influence of the Primal Man = Son of Man hypothesis see Manson, *Jesus*, pp. 174–90; Mowinckel, *He that Cometh*, pp. 420–37; Cullmann, *Christology*, pp. 139–52; all of these contain details of earlier bibliography.

43. See particularly Colpe, *TDNT* VIII, pp. 408–15; and further below ch. IV.

44. Hooker, *Son of Man*, pp. 20f.

45. See e.g. Strack-Billerbeck IV, p. 1214, Index 'Adam'.

46. See particularly R. Scroggs, *The Last Adam*, 1966, pp. ix–xv, 23–31, 54–8; Colpe, *TDNT* VIII, p. 410 and n. 67.

47. Scroggs, *Adam*, pp. 22f., 41–6.

48. Strack-Billerbeck III, pp. 248f.; IV, pp. 852f.

49. Cf. particularly J. A. Emerton, 'The Origin of the Son of Man Imagery', *JTS* 9, 1958, pp. 225–42; J. Morgenstern, 'The "Son of Man" of Daniel 7.13f.', *JBL* 80, 1961, pp. 65–77; Borsch, *Son of Man*, pp. 140–5; Colpe, *TDNT* VIII, pp. 415–19; Collins, *Apocalyptic Vision*, pp. 99–104. But see A. J. Ferch, 'Daniel 7 and Ugarit: A Reconsideration', *JBL* 99, 1980, pp. 75–86.

50. Cf. Colpe: 'What we have here is not the adoption of the term "man" from myth but the depiction of an appearance' (*TDNT* VIII, p. 419). See also the forceful discussion of Casey, *Son of Man*, pp. 34–8.

51. A. Feuillet, 'Le fils d'homme de Danièl et la tradition biblique', *RB* 60, 1953, pp. 170–202, 321–46; J. Muilenberg, 'The Son of Man in Daniel and the Ethiopic Apocalypse of Enoch', *JBL* 79, 1960, pp. 197–209; Balz, *Probleme*, pp. 87–9; Gese, *Theologie*, p. 143.

52. Wisdom's role in Israel's *history* is an expression of the immanence of divine counsel and divine aid in time of need (see below §23).

53. See also U. Wilckens, *TDNT* VII, p. 504; Berger, 'Hintergrund', p. 411 and n. 7; Schillebeeckx, *Jesus*, pp. 489, 546, who follows Berger too uncritically in all this and talks too glibly of 'the Jewish prophetic and sapiental concept of the messianic son of David' (p. 503) – a construct not to be found in pre-Christian Jewish sources.

54. Similarity in language between I Enoch 48.3 and Prov. 8.25f. is insufficient evidence of an equation or merging between the Son of Man and Wisdom in the thought of the Similitudes in view of the stronger and more direct influence of Isa. 11.2 (against Theisohn, *Richter*, pp. 126–39).

55. The equation of the son of man with Wisdom becomes plausible if the existence of a larger, all-embracing Primal Man myth can be established (Colpe, *TDNT* VIII, p. 412); but see below chs. IV and VI.

56. Within recent literature see particularly J. Coppens, 'La vision daniélique du Fils d'Homme', *VT* 19, 1969, pp. 171–82; Müller, *Messias*, pp. 27–30; J. J. Collins, 'The Son of Man and the Saints of the Most High in the Book of Daniel', *JBL* 93, 1974, pp. 50–66; also *Apocalyptic Vision*, ch. V; B. Lindars, 'Re-enter the Apocalyptic Son of Man', *NTS* 22, 1975–76, pp. 55f.

57. Against the view that 'the saints of the most High' are themselves angelic beings see particularly C. W. Brekelmans, 'The Saints of the Most High and their Kingdom', *OTS* 14, 1965, pp. 305–29; G. F. Hasel, 'The Identity of "the Saints of the Most High" in Daniel 7', *Biblica* 56, 1975, pp. 173–92; V. S. Poythress, 'The Holy Ones of the Most High in Daniel 7', *VT* 26, 1976, pp. 208–13; Casey, *Son of Man*, pp. 32, 40–5.

58. See also Gese, *Theologie*, pp. 138f.; Casey, *Son of Man*, pp. 31–3.

59. See further Hartman and Di Lella, *Daniel*, pp. 89–96.

60. Hamerton-Kelly, *Pre-existence*, pp. 38f.

61. The thought of Israel's pre-existence (deduced from Ps. 74.2) only appears in later rabbinic writings (see Strack-Billerbeck II, p. 335; III, pp. 579f.). Cf. VII n. 74 below.

62. See particularly Hooker, *Son of Man*, pp. 34–43 (with a helpful tabulation of the titles on p. 35).

63. All translations taken from M. A. Knibb, *The Ethiopic Book of Enoch*, 2 vols, 1978.

64. So particularly Sjöberg, *Henochbuch*, Kap. 4; Mowinckel, *He that Cometh*, pp. 370–3; Müller, *Messias*, pp. 47–9. This is disputed by e.g. R. Otto, *The Kingdom of God and the Son of Man*, ET 1938, pp. 214–17; M. Black, 'Unsolved New Testament Problems: The "Son of Man" in the old Biblical Literature', *ExpT* 60, 1948–49, pp. 13f.; Manson, *Studies*, pp. 132–42; Hooker, *Son of Man*, pp. 42f.; Lampe, *God as Spirit*, p. 122. It is certainly not beyond question whether the language was intended as a way of expressing the divine *purpose* 'before the world was created' for the Son of Man, rather than the Son of Man's personal pre-existence, since the Son of Man is finally identified as Enoch himself (71.14). It is unlikely that Enoch was thought to have pre-existed or to be the incarnation of the Son of Man since the Enoch speculation begins from the account of his translation (Gen. 5.24) and it is the exaltation (and apotheosis) of Enoch (subsequent to his translation) which dominates the whole Enoch cycle (see particularly Sjöberg, *Henochbuch*, pp. 168–87; also Borsch, *Son of Man*, p. 152; Vermes, *Jesus*, p. 175); likewise Enoch on earth is presented as the model of the man who pleased God by repentence and/or faith rather than as a messenger from on high – Sir. 44.16; Wisd. 4.10f.; Heb. 11.5 (see further D. Lührmann, 'Henoch und die Metanoia', *ZNW* 66, 1975, pp. 103–16). It is even less likely that I Enoch 70.4 was intended to denote the pre-existence of the righteous, since 'from the beginning' is the vaguer phrase and could mean simply 'from the beginning of man's living and dying on earth' (against M. Casey, 'The Use of the Term "Son of Man" in the Similitudes of Enoch', *JSJ* 7, 1976, p. 28).

65. 'I Enoch 46 . . . is virtually a midrash on Dan. 7.13' (Perrin, *Teaching*, p. 165). G. Quispel reads too much into the phrasing (46.1) when he finds an allusion to Ezek. 1.26 – 'the Son of Man described in this passage is identified by the author of I Enoch (*sic*) with the *kabod*, the glorious manifestation of God as Man' ('Ezekiel 1.26 in Jewish Mysticism and Gnosis', *VC* 34, 1980, p. 2). See above n. 14.

66. See particularly H. Lietzmann, *Der Menschensohn*, 1896, pp. 42–8; and most recently Casey, 'Similitudes', pp. 11–29; also *Son of Man*, pp. 100–6, who argues plausibly that in the four passages where the demonstrative is lacking (46.3; 62.7; 69.27; 71.14) the immediate context rendered it unnecessary, it being sufficiently clear that 'the Son of Man' was 'that Son of Man' introduced in 46.1f. (so earlier, e.g. Balz, *Probleme*, p. 66).

67. See also Theisohn, *Richter*, in n. 14 above; Nickelsburg, *Resurrection*, p. 76 and n. 114.

68. Balz, *Probleme*, pp. 75–8. We cannot speak of a title as such: the thought is always primarily of 'that man/human figure' in Daniel (Balz. pp. 66f.); and in 62.5 it becomes clear that 'that Son of a Woman' (if original) serves equally well as 'that Son of Man'. See further Colpe, *TDNT* VIII, pp. 423–6. The fact that three different phrases for 'Son of Man' are used in the Ethiopic need not imply different Greek phrases at each point; more likely they are simply stylistic variations by the Ethiopic translator (see e.g. Balz, p. 65), as perhaps also 62.5.

69. See Hooker, *Son of Man*, pp. 37–47, particularly pp. 44f., with its criticism of Sjöberg (who was followed by Mowinckel, *He that Cometh*, pp. 363f.): 'The Son of man is not introduced as a well-known recognizable figure, but as an enigmatic one which needs explanation' (p. 44). I am unconvinced by M. Black's suggestion that I Enoch 70–71 represent an older tradition than the rest of the Similitudes ('The Eschatology of the Similitudes of Enoch', *JTS* 3, 1952, pp. 1–10, which he

qualifies anyway in 'The Throne-Theophany Prophetic Commission and the "Son of Man": A Study in Tradition History', *JGCWDD*, p. 71), since *'that* Son of Man' of 70.1 refers back to 46.1f. just as clearly as the other Son of Man references, and since 70f. provide a surprising but not unfitting climax to the Similitudes (as Hooker shows; see also Balz, *Probleme*, pp. 98–101).

70. See the discussion in Theisohn, *Richter*, Kap. 3–4.

71. Cf. the older conclusion of R. H. Charles, *Daniel*, Oxford University Press 1929, on Dan. 7.14; 'There is no personal Messiah. The writer of the Parables of I Enoch 37–71 was the first student of our text, so far as our existing literature goes, to interpret "one like a son of man" in this passage as relating to an individual' (p. 187).

72. Colpe, *TDNT* VIII, pp. 426f.; and above n. 64; but see also A. Caquot, 'Remarques sur les chapitres 70 et 71 du livre éthiopièn d'Henoch', *ATE*, pp. 111–22.

73. See the brief introductions and bibliography in Charlesworth, *Pseudepigrapha*, pp. 98–107. The translation into Ethiopic would have been made some time in the fourth to sixth centuries AD (Knibb, *Enoch*, p. 22).

74. See particularly J. T. Milik, *Enoch*.

75. Eleven separate manuscripts have been identified. We may note that Greek manuscripts or fragments containing portions of I Enoch discovered earlier also lack the Similitudes; see C. Bonner, *The Last Chapters of Enoch in Greek*, 1937, reprinted Darmstadt 1968; Knibb, *Enoch*, pp. 15–21.

76. J. C. Greenfield and M. E. Stone, 'The Enochic Pentateuch and the Date of the Similitudes', *HTR* 70, 1977, pp. 51–65, attribute to D. Flusser the observation that the Similitudes 'would not have been acceptable to the sectaries of Qumran because of the manner in which the sun and moon are treated in ch. 41; their tasks and roles are equal – the sun does not receive the special place afforded to it in the various Qumran writings' (p. 56). But in 41.5 the superiority of the sun over the moon is clearly implied. C. L. Mearns suggests that the reason for Qumran rejection of the Similitudes was that they 'came from a small group of christianized Jews withi he Jewish circle which was cherishing and developing the Jewish Enoch traditions' ('The Parables of Enoch – Origin and Date', *ExpT* 89, 1977–78, pp. 118f.). See also n. 79 below.

77. See J. T. Milik, *Ten Years of Discovery in the Wilderness of Judaea*, 1957, ET SCM Press 1959, p. 28; F. F. Bruce, 'The Book of Daniel and the Qumran Community', *Neotestamentica et Semitica: Studies in Honour of M. Black*, ed. E. E. Ellis and M. Wilcox, T. & T. Clark 1969, pp. 221–35; A. Mertens, *Das Buch Daniel im Lichte der Texte vom Toten Meer*, Stuttgart 1971; Hartman and Di Lella, *Daniel*, p. 72. Seven manuscripts or portions have been found.

78. According to Milik, *Enoch*, p. 305; see also J. Strugnell, 'The Angelic Liturgy at Qumran – 4Q Serek Šîrôt 'ôlat Haššabbāt', *VT* Supp. 7, 1959, pp. 337, 340.

79. Milik, *Enoch*, pp. 89–98, argues for a third century AD date, but a late first century or early second century date is suggested by the fact that similar influence of the Dan. 7 vision (a pre-existent Man/Son of Man) is evident in three other documents from that period §§9.3 and 10.2). See further M. A. Knibb, 'The Date of the Parables of Enoch: A Critical Review', *NTS* 25, 1978–79, pp. 345–59; Black, 'Throne-Theophany', *JGCWDD*, p. 66; also 'The "Parables" of Enoch (I Enoch 37–71) and the "Son of Man" ', *ExpT* 88, 1976–77, pp. 5–8; Vermes, ' "Son of

Man" Debate', p. 132; also Schürer, *History*, Vol. II, pp. 520 n. 26 and 522. C. L. Mearns, 'Dating the Similitudes of Enoch', *NTS* 25, 1978–79, pp. 360–9, argues that the Testament of Abraham 11 (Recension B, in M. E. Stone, *The Testament of Abraham*, SBL 1972) is a polemic against I Enoch 71's attribution of the role of eschatological judge to Enoch (no judgmental role is actually ascribed to Enoch in I Enoch 70–71, but he is identified as the Son of Man who does exercise judgment earlier in the Similitudes – see above p. 76 and n. 70), so that I Enoch 70–71 must predate Test. Ab. which has been dated to the first half of the first century AD (Mearns, pp. 363f.). But the problem would have already been posed in Jub. 4.21f. and I Enoch 12–16, where Enoch has the specific task of announcing judgment to and reproving the Watchers. It is this role that Test. Ab. seems to be clarifying by insisting that Enoch is not the pronouncer of judgment, but simply the heavenly recorder, Enoch the 'scribe of righteousness' (Jub. 4.17–19; I Enoch 12.4): 'The one who demonstrates (the sins – ἀποδεικνύμενος) is . . . the scribe of righteousness, Enoch, for God sent them (Abel and Enoch) here that they might write down the sins and the righteous deeds of each man . . . It is not Enoch's business to declare judgement (ἀποφαίνεται), but the Lord is he who gives judgment, and this one's (i.e. Enoch's) task is only the writing' (Test. Ab. 11). Moreover, there is no allusion whatsoever in Test. Ab. 11 to the Son of Man or to Dan. 7, the lynch-pin of the Similitude's interpretation. In short, not only can the point of Test. Ab. be clarified adequately without reference to the Similitudes, but the Testament shows absolutely no knowledge of the Similitudes.

80. J. C. Hindley, 'Towards a Date for the Similitudes of Enoch: An Historical Approach', *NTS* 14, 1967–68, pp. 551–65; but see also Greenfield and Stone, 'Similitudes', particularly pp. 58–60; Knibb, 'Date', pp. 353–5.

81. Cf. R. N. Longenecker, *The Christology of Early Jewish Christianity*, 1970, pp. 82–5. The continued unwillingness of so much German speaking scholarship to take seriously these considerations is a surprising and regrettable feature of the whole discussion (Schweizer, *Erniedrigung*, pp. 36f./§3c, is something of an exception).

82. Theisohn, *Richter* Kap. 6, who also suggests influence from the Similitudes on Matt. 13.40–3; H. E. Tödt, *The Son of Man in the Synoptic Tradition*, ²1963, ET 1965, suggests also Matt. 16.27 (pp. 92, 223).

83. F. H. Borsch, 'Mark 14.62 and I Enoch 62.5', *NTS* 14, 1967–68, pp. 565–7, suggests a possible link between Mark 14.62 and Sim. En. 62.5 ('. . . see the Son of Man sitting . . .'). But the passages read more naturally as independent interpretations of the Dan. 7.13 vision – Sim. En. 62.5, that Son of Man/Woman as usual the judge in a judgment scene ('sitting on the throne of his glory'); Mark 14.62, the Son of Man ('sitting on the right hand of Power') as usual depicted in his 'coming with the clouds of heaven' – the verbal parallels more likely being the coincidence of two not dissimilar trains of thought drawn from Dan. 7.

84. Alternatively, both Sim. En. and Matt. could reflect a broader swell of speculation regarding Yahweh's throne in the late first century AD – evident also in the rabbinic speculation about the seven pre-existent entities (see above p. 71), including 'the throne of glory' (based on Ps. 93.2 and Jer. 17.12), and in Merkabah mysticism centred on the chariot vision of Ezek. 1 (Strack-Billerbeck I, pp. 974–9; Scholem, *Major Trends* p. 42).

85. Cf. Schnackenburg, *Johannes* II, p. 135, ET p. 107.

86. On E. Sjöberg's attempt to trace a link between the Messianic secret and

the hidden Son of Man of I Enoch (*Der verborgene Menschensohn in den Evangelien*, 1955) see Tödt, *Son of Man*, pp. 298–302.

87. For a review of Dan. 7's wider and subsequent influence see Casey, *Son of Man*, chs. 3–5.

88. Cf. particularly Müller, *Messias*, pp. 147–54.

89. Other clear references to Dan. 7 in IV Ezra are listed by Casey, *Son of Man*, p. 122.

90. 'In the interpretation, not only has the author of IV Ezra shorn this figure of all its special characteristics but he even treats it just as a symbol. This would be inconceivable if the Son of Man concept was readily recognizable to him and his readers' (M. Stone, 'The Concept of the Messiah in IV Ezra', *RAERG*, pp. 295–312, here p. 308).

91. See also Manson, *Studies*,: ' "heavenly man" is a question begging term' (p. 132); M. Black, 'The Son of Man Problem in Recent Research and Debate', *BJRL* 45, 1962–63, pp. 312–14; Perrin, *Teaching*: 'What we have, in fact, in Jewish apocalyptic is not a Son of man conception at all, as Tödt and others assume, but a use of Dan. 7.13 by subsequent seers' (p. 166); R. Leivestadt, 'Exit the Apocalyptic Son of Man', *NTS* 18, 1971–72, pp. 243–67; Vermes, *Jesus*, pp. 160–77; Fitzmyer, *Wandering Aramean*, pp. 153f. and n. 60; Casey, *Son of Man*, particularly ch. 5.

92. 'The "flying man" in IV Ezra 13 shows no reference back to the Son of Man concept of the Similitudes' (Theisohn, *Richter*, pp. 145f.; cf. Müller, *Messias*, pp. 121f.).

93. A. F. Segal, *Two Powers in Heaven*, 1977, especially pp. 33–57, 66f., 122f., 128f., 148f. See also Balz, *Probleme*, pp. 89–95, 102.

94. The Apocalypse of Abraham is generally held to have appeared about this time (end of first century AD) and seems to reflect a similar speculative use of Ex. 23.21 in its depiction of the angel Jaoel (Apoc.Ab. 10), who, significantly, is probably represented as worshipping God along with Abraham (Apoc.Ab. 17); see further below p. 153. Probably not unrelated is the rabbinic polemic against angelology which also seems to have begun in the first half of the second century AD (see P. S. Alexander, 'The Targumim and Early Exegesis of "Sons of God" in Genesis 6', *JJS* 23, 1972, pp. 60–71.

95. Akiba's alternative interpretation that the other throne mentioned in Dan. 7.9 is for David, the royal Messiah (i.e. the 'son of man' = the Messiah), was also seriously challenged, and even accused by one rabbi of 'profaning the Shekinah' (b Sanh.38b; see e.g. Vermes, *Jesus*, p. 171 and n. 34) – presumably an echo of the opposition aroused by Elisha ben Abuya's interpretation of the same passage.

96. See also N. A. Dahl and A. F. Segal, 'Philo and the Rabbis on the Names of God', *JSJ* 9, 1978, pp. 1–28.

97. Against those cited above in nn. 15, 42; also Fuller, *Foundations*, pp. 34–42. Hamerton-Kelly's more cautious conclusion that 'in early Judaism . . . the title (Son of Man) was the centre of a varying congeries of ideas, of which only the pre-existence and the humanity of the figure were constant' (*Pre-existence*, p. 58) is little improvement, since it envisages the phrase as a constant 'title' ('a recognized image' – p. 100), presupposes the idea of pre-existence in Dan. 7, and uses the Similitudes of Enoch and IV Ezra as a background for the interpretation of the earliest Synoptic tradition.

98. Influence of Dan. 7 has been detected also in Sib. Or. III. 397–400 and II Baruch 39–40, but it is not clear whether the Messiah in the latter is identified with the human figure of Daniel's vision. On the possibility that already in Jerusalem's final death throes (AD 70) Dan. 7.13f. proved the inspiration for a prophecy of a Jewish world ruler (Josephus, *Bell*, VI.312f.) cf. Strack-Billerbeck IV.2, pp. 1002f.

99. Bousset, *Kyrios Christos*, ET, pp. 35–49 (particularly p. 48, though note also p. 42); P. Vielhauer, particularly 'Gottesreich und Menschensohn in der Verkündigung Jesu', *Festchrift für G. Dehn*, 1957, pp. 51–79; also 'Jesus und der Menschensohn', *ZTK* 60, 1963, pp. 133–77; both reprinted in *Aufsätze zum Neuen Testament*, 1965, pp. 55–140; E. Käsemann, particularly 'The Beginnings of Christian Theology' (1960), ET *NTQT*, pp. 101f.; H. M. Teeple, 'The Origin of the Son of Man Christology', *JBL* 84, 1965, pp. 213–50; Perrin, *Teaching*, pp. 164–99; Conzelmann, *Outline*, pp. 132–7; W. O. Walker, 'The Origin of the Son of Man Concept as applied to Jesus', *JBL* 91, 1972, pp. 482–90.

100. See particularly Vermes in Black, *Aramaic Approach*, pp. 310–28; also *Jesus*, ch. 7 (and see above n. 3); M. Casey, 'The Son of Man Problem', *ZNW* 67, 1976, pp. 147–54; also *Son of Man*, ch. 9. Cf. the rather contrived thesis of J. P. Brown, 'The Son of Man: "This fellow" ', *Biblica* 58, 1977, pp. 361–87 (a self-deprecatory phrase originally used by Jesus' opponents in disparaging reference to Jesus).

101. R. Bultmann, *Theology of the New Testament*, Vol. I, 1948, ET 1952, pp. 29f.; G. Bornkamm, *Jesus of Nazareth*, 1956, ET Hodder & Stoughton 1960, pp. 175–8, 229; J. Knox, *The Death of Christ* (1958) 1967, pp. 77–80; Tödt, *Son of Man*, particularly pp. 42, 55–60; Hahn, *Titles*, pp. 22f., 28–34; Fuller, *Foundations*, pp. 122–5.

102. We may compare the influence of Hillel and the early Tannaim Eleazer ben Azariah, Eliezer ben Hyrkanus and also Akiba, who are all credited with developments in rabbinic hermeneutics (H. L. Strack, *Introduction to the Talmud and Midrash*, ET 1931, Harper Torchbook 1965, ch. 11), and particularly the Teacher of Righteousness who no doubt initiated the distinctive tradition of Essene exegesis evidenced in the Dead Sea Scrolls (see e.g. F. M. Cross, *The Ancient Library of Qumran and Modern Biblical Studies*, Duckworth 1958, p. 83).

103. Such polemic as there is in our period is against an over-exaltation of Enoch; but the earlier document (Test. Ab.) shows no knowledge of any interest in the son of man of Dan. 7.13 (see above n.79); and the later rabbinic condemnation of the two powers heresy has the burgeoning Enoch speculation of the (post AD 70) Enoch cycle wholly in view (see above pp. 19 and 80f.).

104. Cf. Tödt. 'There is no synoptic Son of Man saying which perceptibly reflects on the act of installation to Son of Man' (*Son of Man*, p. 286).

105. Passages whose authenticity was accepted by Bultmann (above p. 26). See also Jeremias, *Theology* I, pp. 275f.

106. See also Schweizer, *Erniedrigung*, pp. 38f./§3e; also 'The Son of Man Again', *NTS* 9, 1962–63, pp. 257f., reprinted in *Neotestamentica*, 1963, pp. 87f.; also *Jesus*, p. 19; W. G. Kümmel, 'Das Verhalten Jesus gegenüber und das Verhalten des Menschensohns', *JMAV*, pp. 219–24; Marshall, *Origins*, pp. 73f.; cf. R. Pesch, 'Über die Autorität Jesu: eine Rückfrage anhand des Bekenner- und Verleugnerspruche Luke 12.8f. par.', *KAHS*, pp. 25–55, particularly 39–41, 47f.

107. A. Schweitzer, *The Quest of the Historical Jesus*, 1906, ET A. & C. Black 1910, p. 360; Otto, *Kingdom*, pp. 225, 237 (modelled on Enoch's exaltation to

become Son of Man); R. H. Fuller, *The Mission and Achievement of Jesus*, SCM Press 1954, pp. 102–7; A. J. B. Higgins, *Jesus and the Son of Man*, 1964, pp. 200–3; Jeremias, *Theology* I, pp. 272–6.

108. Among recent contributions arguing variously, see Longenecker, *Christology*, pp. 88–91; Kümmel, *Theology*, pp. 76–90; Goppelt, *Theologie*, pp. 226–37; Moule, *Origin*, pp. 11–22; Lindars, 'Apocalyptic Son of Man', pp. 52–72; Marshall, *Origins*, ch. 4; J. Bowker, 'The Son of Man', *JTS* 28, 1977, pp. 19–48; Hooker (as above n. 3); Stuhlmacher, 'Mark. 10.45' (see above II n. 81).

109. Luke 24.7 and John 12.34 are no real exceptions.

110. C. F. D. Moule, 'Neglected Features in the Problem of "the Son of Man"', *NTKRS*, pp. 413–28, particularly p. 421.

111. Dunn, *Jesus*, §§9.2 and 9.3.

112. Cf. Bowker, 'Son of Man' particularly pp. 47f.; Hooker (as above n. 3).

113. See particularly Jeremias, *Theology* I, pp. 277–86; H. Schürmann, 'Wie hat Jesus seinen Tod bestanden und verstanden?', *Orientierung an Jesus: Für J. Schmid*, ed. P. Hoffmann, Herder 1973, pp. 325–63 – expanded in Schürmann, *Jesu ureigener Tod*, Freiburg und Göttingen 1973, pp. 133–47, 167–72, 258; Schillebeeckx, *Jesus*, pp. 294–312; Goppelt, *Theologie*, pp. 238–47; the essays by J. Gnilka, A. Vögtle and R. Pesch in K. Kertelge, hrsg., *Der Tod Jesu: Deutungen im Neuen Testament*, Herder 1976; J. D. G. Dunn, 'The Birth of a Metaphor – Baptized in Spirit', *ExpT* 89, 1977–78, pp. 134–8; V. Howard, 'Did Jesus Speak about his own Death?', *CBQ* 39, 1977, pp. 515–27.

114. Cf. particularly C. F. D. Moule, 'From Defendant to Judge – and Deliverer', *SNTS Bulletin* III, 1952, pp. 40–53, reprinted in *The Phenomenon of the New Testament*, 1967, pp. 82–99; Schweizer, *Erniedrigung*, §§2–3; L. Ruppert, *Jesus als der leidende Gerechte?*, SBS 59, 1972. For the background see also Nickelsburg, *Resurrection*, particularly ch. II.

115. Cf. the parallelism characteristic of Hebrew poetry – e.g. Ps. 114; see further G. B. Gray, *The Forms of Hebrew Poetry*, 1915, reissued Ktav 1972, ch. II.

116. Hamerton-Kelly, *Pre-existence*, p. 100.

117. Hamerton-Kelly, *Pre-existence*, pp. 45–7, 79f. – referring to Luke 12.40/ Matt. 24.44; Luke 17.23f./Matt. 24.26f.; Luke 17.26f./Matt. 24.37–9; Matt. 13.41f. Cf. the use of Mark 14.62 by W. Staerk, *Die Erlösererwartung in den östlichen Religionen*, 1938, p. 452.

118. Hamerton-Kelly, *Pre-existence*, pp. 60, 64f., 76f., 78f.

119. Hamerton-Kelly, *Pre-existence*, pp. 42–7.

120. Against Hamerton-Kelly, *Pre-existence*, pp. 61f.

121. Hamerton-Kelly, *Pre-existence*, pp. 53–6, 66f.

122. Hamerton-Kelly, *Pre-existence*, p. 64. Other sayings using ἦλθον (I came) or 'the Son of Man came' (ἦλθεν) are Mark 2.17 pars.; 10.45 par.; Matt. 10.34 par.; 5.17; Luke 12.49; 19.10.

123. Other examples in Bühner, *Gesandte*, pp. 140–2. See also E. Arens, *The HΛΘON-Sayings in the Synoptic Tradition*, 1976. Insofar as the ἦλθον sayings go back to Jesus, Arens thinks the meaning was 'my purpose is to . . . .' or 'my God-given mission is to. . . .'. On Luke 12.49, the only saying he traces back to Jesus with confidence: 'There is no question of his "having come from" (God) either. The weight of the logion lies on the purpose' (pp. 54f., 90). Mark 10.45 'presupposes an understanding of Jesus' pre-existence', but only on the basis of his conclusion that the saying is a church product and echoes the understanding of

the Son of Man in I Enoch (Similitudes) and IV Ezra (pp. 159–61); however see above particularly §§9.2 and 9.3.

124. Hamerton-Kelly, *Pre-existence*, pp. 81–3. On Matthew's possible dependence on the Similitudes see above pp. 77f. On the significance of Matthew's identification of Jesus with Wisdom see below §§25.1–2.

125. Tödt, *Son of Man*, p. 284 (my emphasis) – a conclusion all the more significant in view of Tödt's ready acceptance of a pre-Christian conception of a transcendent, pre-existent Son of Man in Jewish apocalyptic. Similarly Mowinckel, *He that Cometh*, p. 448; Braun, 'New Testament Christology', *JThC* 5, 1968, p. 96.

126. S. Schulz, *Untersuchungen zur Menschensohn-Christologie im Johannesevangelium*, 1957, pp. 109–14; Hamerton-Kelly, *Pre-existence*, pp. 221, 236; F. J. Moloney, *The Johannine Son of Man*, ²1978, pp. 81f; on 17.2 see particularly Dodd, *Historical Tradition*, pp. 362f. The anarthrous form 'Son of Man/son of man' (the only occasion in the Gospels when the phrase lacks the definite article) may put something of a question mark against an allusion to Dan. 7.14 in John 5.27 (Leivestad, 'Son of Man', p. 252; Casey, *Son of Man*, pp. 198f.).

127. Brown, *John*, p. 89; Hamerton-Kelly, *Pre-existence*, pp. 229f. Cf. Moloney who pushes the rather strained thesis that for John 'the Son of Man' is used only of Jesus in his human state, the Son of Man as such is not pre-existent ('It is a title which is entirely dependent upon the incarnation' – *Son of Man*, p. 213; strongly reaffirmed in the second edition, pp. 244–7; cf. B. Lindars, 'The Son of Man in the Johannine Christology', *CSNT*, p. 48 n. 16); but a writer who speaks of him 'who descended from heaven, the Son of Man' (3.13) and of 'the Son of Man ascending where he was before' (6.62) seems hardly concerned to make such a distinction.

128. Bühner, *Gesandte*, has argued the complicated thesis that John's christology developed from a merging of a concept of the Danielic son of man as an angel (= messenger from heaven) with the concept of a prophet as one with a heavenly commission (received in a visionary ascent to heaven); but his thesis fails completely to explain how the idea of the Son of Man's pre-existence and descent *prior* to his ascent first emerged (see further below V n. 67). On Rom. 10.6f. and Eph. 4.8–10 see below §24.4).

129. So e.g. Higgins, *Son of Man*, pp. 171–3, 176f.; Schnackenburg, *John* I, pp. 556f.; Brown, *John*, p. 133; S. S. Smalley, 'The Johannine Son of Man Sayings', *NTS* 15, 1968–69, p. 298; also *John*, pp. 212f. n. 125; Moule, *Origin*, p. 18; J. Schmitt, 'Apocalyptique et christologie johannique', *ATE*, pp. 345–7. For the function of the descending/ascending motif in the Fourth Gospel see W. A. Meeks, 'The Man from Heaven in Johannine Sectarianism', *JBL* 91, 1972, pp. 44–72.

130. Sidebottom, *Christ*: 'If John, then, was influenced in his use of the Christian term Son of Man by any speculation about Man it was most probably through that form of it which was entertained in the Wisdom circles of Judaism. The later Gnostic Saviour-Man is a product of various factors, one of which is the Johannine christology itself' (p. 111); Schnackenburg, *John*, I: John's ' "Son of Man" has nothing to do with the archetypal "primordial man" and the godhead "Man". It comes from the Christian tradition. It remains, of course, possible that for the descent and ascent of his Christ he drew on Gnostic notions. But it cannot be affirmed that such notions were inspired by the title of "Son of Man". . . . It is much more likely that the Johannine "Son of Man" is connected

with Wisdom speculation' (p. 541). See further below chs. IV and VI. On the implausible suggestion that a Son of Man christology lies behind John 19.5's 'Behold the man' (supported most recently by Moloney, *Son of Man*, pp. 202–7), see R. Schnackenburg, 'Die Ecce-Homo-Szene und der Menschensohn', *JMAV*, pp. 371–86; also *Johannes*, III, Herder 19/5, pp. 295f.

131. The arguments of G. D. Kilpatrick for an original 'Son of *God*' in Acts 7.56 ('Again Acts 7.56: Son of Man?', *TZ* 34, 1978, p. 232) are too slight to overthrow the established text.

132. So Weiss, *Earliest Christianity*, p. 485; Rawlinson, *Christ*, 1926, pp. 124f.; J. Jeremias, *TDNT* I, p. 143; Dodd, *Scriptures*, p. 121; Cullmann, *Christology*, p. 188, also pp. 166ff.; P. Giles, 'The Son of Man in the Epistle to the Hebrews', *ExpT* 86, 1974–75, pp. 328–32.

133. It is not clear why the 'Maranatha' invocation of I Cor. 16.22 should be linked specifically with a Son of Man christology as such (against Wengst, *Formeln*, p. 53); nor are parallels sufficient to demonstrate that I Thess. 1.10 was originally a Son of Man saying (against Schweizer, *TDNT* VIII, p. 370). On the possibility that an understanding of Jesus as the Son of Man lies behind Phil. 2.6–11 see below (IV n. 86). See also Casey, *Son of Man*, pp. 151–4.

134. See also e.g. A. Vögtle, 'Die Adam-Christustypologie und "der Menschensohn" ', *TTZ* 60, 1951, pp. 309–28; also ' "Der Menschensohn" und die paulinische Christologie', *SPCIC*, Vol. I, pp. 199–218; Fuller, *Foundations*, pp. 233f.; Scroggs, *Adam*, p. 102; Borsch, *Son of Man*, pp. 236–8; Schweizer, *TDNT* VIII, p. 371 n. 265; Hay, *Glory*, p. 109; E. Grässer, 'Beobachtungen zum Menschensohn in Heb. 2.6', *JMAV*, p. 409.

135. Note the parallel with Elisha ben Abuya's heresy (II n. 36 and p. 81) – a parallel to the source of the two powers heresy? See further C. Rowland, 'The Vision of the Risen Christ in Rev. 1.13ff: The Debt of an Early Christology to an Aspect of Jewish Angelology', *JTS* 31 1980, pp. 1–11.

136. Cf. E. Lohse, 'Der Menschensohn in der Johannesapokalypse', *JMAV*, pp. 415–20.

137. See particularly M. Black, 'The "Two Witnesses" of Rev. 11.3f. in Jewish and Christian Apocalyptic Tradition', *Donum Gentilicum*, 1978, pp. 227–37. Black does not refer to Luke 9 in this article but he does so in his 'Throne Theophany' (above n. 69) with explicit reference to the 'Rev. 11.3f.' article. In IV Ezra 6.26 (misquoted by Black as 8.18ff.) Enoch and Elijah presumably are again in view, though perhaps at that stage not only them (see below p. 93), and a descent from heaven is not necessarily envisaged (as again in the same references, below p. 93). Note also *Apoc. Pet.* 2. For further references from early Christian tradition and analysis see now particularly R. Bauckham, 'The Martyrdom of Enoch and Elijah: Jewish or Christian?', *JBL* 95, 1976, pp. 447–58 (supplemented by A. Zeron, 'The Martyrdom of Phineas-Elijah', *JBL* 98, 1979, pp. 99f.).

138. Cf. Lindars, 'Apocalyptic Son of Man': 'Although the Son of Man is not the designation of a particular figure in Judaism, apocalyptic thought embraces the concept of an agent of God in the coming judgment, who may be a character of the past reserved in heaven for this function at the end time . . . The identification of Jesus with this figure is fundamental to widely separated strands of the New Testament . . .' (p. 54).

139. Cf. J. A. T. Robinson, 'Elijah, John and Jesus: an Essay in Detection', *NTS* 4, 1957–58, pp. 263–81, reprinted in *Twelve New Testament Studies*, 1962,

pp. 28–52; R. E. Brown, 'Three Quotations from John the Baptist in the Gospel of John', *CBQ* 22, 1960, reprinted in *New Testament Essays*, 1965, pp. 138–40; see also J. L. Martyn in V n. 65. The suggestion that John the Baptist thought of the Coming One as the Son of Man (F. Lang, 'Erwägungen zur eschatologischen Verkündigung Johannes des Täufers', *JCHTHC*, pp. 470–3; see also J. Becker, *Johannes der Täufer und Jesus von Nazareth*, Neukirchen 1972, pp. 105f.; Schille-beeckx, *Jesus*, pp. 132, 471) depends on parallels with Sim. En. which are not sufficiently specific or close. The idea of baptism 'in . . . fire' need not depend on Dan. 7.10 ('stream of fire') as such; see e.g. IQH 3.29f. and the closer parallel in Isa. 30.27f. ('fire . . . breath . . . stream').

140. See further Strack-Billerbeck IV/2, pp. 764–98; J. Jeremias, *TDNT* II, pp. 928–41. The earliest attestation of the tradition of the translated Elijah inter-vening as helper in time of need (see above II n. 63) is in Mark 15.35f. par., where the possibility of Elijah's intervening from heaven is at least considered; but this is unrelated to the belief in Elijah's specifically eschatological role and somewhat at odds with it suggesting that no clear 'Elijahology' or conceptuality of Elijah's 'coming' had yet developed. The idea of successive appearances/incarnations of Christ as 'the true prophet' in the Kerygmata Petrou (Clem. *Hom.* III.20) is later (the Kerygmata are to be dated about AD 200 – G. Strecker in Hennecke, *Apocrypha*, pp. 110f.).

141. Jeremias draws attention to 'the much repeated principle' in rabbinic literature: 'As the first redeemer (Moses), so the final redeemer (the Messiah)' (*TDNT* IV, pp. 860f.). That Moses himself was expected to return in person is much less likely: his death was clearly reported in Deut. 34 (contrast Elijah) a fact which would certainly discourage such speculation (cf. above p. 19), espe-cially when the expectation of a 'prophet *like* Moses' was so firmly grounded in the Torah; the evidence of such an expectation in rabbinic circles is late (P. Volz, *Die Eschatologie der jüdischen Gemeinde*, Tübingen 1934, p. 195; Strack-Billerbeck I, pp. 753–6; Jeremias, *TDNT* IV, pp. 856f.); had such an expectation been current in the middle of the first century the name of Moses would almost certainly have appeared in such speculation as is recorded in Mark 6.15, alongside or in place of that of Elijah (cf. Teeple, *Prophet*, p. 47, who argues that two different hopes, a prophet like Moses and the return of Moses, were first combined in Samaritan messianic hope, p. 101; see also above II n. 63). The meaning and significance of the transfiguration scene and of the 'two witnesses' in Rev. 11.3 is not sufficient-ly clear to outweigh these considerations.

142. R. Hayward, 'Phinehas – the same is Elijah: The Origin of a Rabbinic Tradition', *JJS* 29, 1978, pp. 22–38; M. Wadsworth, 'A New Pseudo-Philo' (a review of D. J. Harrington and J. Cazeaux, *Pseudo-Philon: les Antiquités Bibliques*, Tome I, and M. Bogaert, Tome II, 1976), *JJS* 29, 1978, pp. 186–91; cf. M. Hengel, *Die Zeloten*, Leiden 1961, pp. 167–72. See also above II n. 44.

143. See Lohfink, *Himmelfahrt*, pp. 59–61.

144. I Enoch 83–90 is certainly pre-Christian, though unfortunately none of the four Qumran fragmentary manuscripts of this book (designated by Milik 'the Book of Dreams') contains the verses crucial to our discussion.

145. ET by H. P. Houghton, 'Akhmîmice: "The Apocalypse of Elias" ', *Ae-gyptus* 39, 1959, pp. 179–210.

146. See particularly J. M. Rosenstiehl, *L'Apocalypse d'Elie*, Paris 1972.

147. On the former, cf. Luke 24.39; Ignatius, *Smyrn.* 3; *Apoc. Pet.* 17; II Clement

9. On the latter, cf. II Thess. 2.3, 8 (a clearer echo of II Thess. 2.4 is in 14.10–12); Rev. 20.2–9; 21.1 (clearly echoed in the passage immediately following – 25.1–19).

148. See further Bauckham, 'Martyrdom', pp. 450f., 458.

149. Black suggests that 'the righteous man' in Wisd. 4.10–5.5 is intended as Enoch and therefore includes the thought of Enoch's death ('Two Witnesses', pp. 233f.). But there is no thought of Enoch as dying *prior* to his translation, not even in Pseudo-Philo, *Bib. Ant.* 48.1 – if Enoch is indeed in view there, which is itself questionable. Black's thesis here runs the risk of building supposition (Luke) upon supposition (Wisd.) upon supposition (Pseudo-Philo).

150. See e.g. W. Bousset, *Offenbarung*, KEK ⁶1906, pp. 318f.; R. H. Charles, *Revelation*, ICC 1920, Vol. I pp. 281f.; G. R. Beasley-Murray, *Revelation*, NCB 1974, p. 183; Black, 'Two Witnesses', p. 227.

151. The most obvious parallel was in Jesus' resurrection/ascension (understood as a translation to heaven like those of Enoch and Elijah) with his parousia (not his earlier life) seen as the return to earth of the one thus exalted – particularly Acts 1.9–11 (cf. II Kings 2.9–12); 3.19–21 (see particularly Schillebeeckx, *Jesus*, pp. 340–4 and those cited by him).

152. This conclusion applies also to Lindars' thesis (n. 138 above): when he argues that a fundamental element in NT christology was the 'identification of Jesus with this figure', we are obliged to ask, What figure? The only evidence cited is the Danielic 'son of man' (leader of the angels, and Messiah in IV Ezra – but see above pp. 73f., 79f.), Enoch in the Similitudes (pp. 58f. – but see above §9.2) and Melchizedek (pp. 57f. – but is it so 'apparent' that Melchizedek in 11Q Melch. was understood to be the Melchizedek of Gen. 14? – see below pp. 152f.; also above II n. 57). Has 'the apocalyptic Son of Man' of pre-Christian Judaism really 're-entered', or is he not rather still merely the construct of modern critical hypotheses?

Chapter IV   The Last Adam

1. Bultmann, *Theology*, Vol. I, pp. 166f.; see also his earlier 'Die Bedeutung der neuerschlossenen mandäischen und manichäischen Quellen für das Verständnis der Johannesevangelium', *ZNW* 24, 1925, pp. 100–46, reprinted *Exegetica*, 1967, pp. 55–104. Bultmann was building on and synthesizing the work of W. Bousset, R. Reitzenstein and M. Lidzbarski.

2. Bultmann, *Theology*, I, p. 175.

3. 'No one has yet brought forward such a reasonably proximate pre-Christian version where the emphasis is on a divinity who graciously descends from heaven to become a humble human being' (Borsch, *Son of Man*, p. 252). See also C. Colpe, *Die religionsgeschichtliche Schule*, 1961; Schweizer, *Erniedrigung*, (cited above II n. 69); Schnackenburg, *John* I, pp. 488–92, 543–57; Fuller, *Foundations*, pp. 93–7; E. Yamauchi, *Pre-Christian Gnosticism*, ch. 10 (who cites also E. Percy, Dodd, R. M. Grant, G. Quispel and R. McL. Wilson); Hengel's vigorous protest in *Son*, pp. 33–5; Talbert, *Gospel*, pp. 53f. The Gnostic Sophia myth probably developed out of the Jewish concept of personified Wisdom (see particularly G. W. Macrae, 'The Jewish Background of the Gnostic Sophia Myth', *NovT* 12, 1970, pp. 86–

101) and probably owes at least something to early Christian identification of Christ as Wisdom (see below ch. VI).

4. See e.g. J. M. Robinson, 'The Coptic Gnostic Library Today', *NTS* 14, 1967–68, pp. 377–80; other references in Yamauchi, *Pre-Christian Gnosticism*, pp. 107–16. Subsequent references to Nag Hammadi tractates are to the codices and page numbers as laid out in J. M. Robinson, *Nag Hammadi Library*. The references to Irenaeus, Epiphanius and Hippolytus can be conveniently consulted in W. Foerster, *Gnosis* I.

5. Against F. Wisse, 'The Redeemer Figure in the Paraphrase of Shem', *NovT* 12, 1970, pp. 130–40. See further Yamauchi, *Pre-Christian Gnosticism*, pp. 110–16; also 'Pre-Christian Gnosticism in the Nag Hammadi Texts?', *Church History* 48, 1979, pp. 129–41.

6. So e.g. H. Lietzmann, *Korinther*, HNT revised W. G. Kümmel 1949, pp. 85f.; J. Jervell, *Imago Dei*, 1960, pp. 258–63; Cullmann, *Christology*, pp. 167f.; C. K. Barrett, *I Corinthians*, Black 1968, pp. 374f.; Hamerton-Kelly, *Pre-existence*, pp. 132–44; R. A. Horsley, 'Pneumatikos vs. Psychikos: Distinction of Spiritual Status among the Corinthians', *HTR* 69, 1976, p. 277.

7. See particularly M. D. Hooker, 'Adam in Romans 1', *NTS* 6, 1959–60, pp. 297–306; Jervell, *Imago*, pp. 312–31; A. J. M. Wedderburn, 'Adam in Paul's Letter to the Romans', *Studia Biblica 1978*, Vol. III, *JSNT* Supp. 1980, pp. 413–30.

8. Sir. 14.17; 25.24; Wisd. 2.23f.; Jub. 3.28–32; note the importance of the theme in the sequence of documents all of which may well reflect Jewish speculation contemporary with Paul – IV Ezra 3.7, 21f.; 4.30; 7.118; II Bar. 17.3; 23.4; 48.42f.; 54.15, 19; 56.5f.; Apoc. Mos. and Vit. Adae. For rabbinic treatment see Strack-Billerbeck III, pp. 227f.

9. That Paul is indeed in touch with this understanding of sin and death, which first came to the fore in Wisdom literature (see above n. 8) is further suggested by the striking similarities between Rom. 1 and Wisd. 12–13 (see W. Sanday and A. C. Headlam, *Romans*, ICC ⁵1902, pp. 51f.). See further C. Romaniuk, 'Le Livre de la Sagesse dans le Nouveau Testament', *NTS* 14, 1967–68, pp. 503–13; C. Larcher, *Etudes sur le livre de la Sagesse*, EB 1969, pp. 14–20; U. Wilckens, *Römer* I, EKK 1978, pp. 96f., citing P. C. Keyser, *Sapientia Salomonis und Paulus*, Halle dissertation 1971.

10. Ps. 106.20 (= 105.20 LXX) – ἠλλάξαντο τὴν δόξαν αὐτῶν ἐν ὁμοιώματι μόσχου . . .; Jer. 2.11 LXX – ἠλλάξατο τὴν δόξαν αὐτοῦ. See also M. D. Hooker, 'A Further Note on Romans 1', *NTS* 13, 1966–67, pp. 181–3.

11. See Jervell, *Imago*, pp. 115f., 321f.; cf. W. A. Meeks, 'Moses as God and King', *RAERG*, pp. 363–5.

12. Cf. F. R. Tennant, *The Sources of the Doctrines of the Fall and Original Sin*, Cambridge University Press 1903, pp. 263ff.

13. Kühl, Lagrange, Moffatt, Lietzmann, Schlatter, Althaus, Nygren, Michel, Kuss, Gaugler, Bruce, Schmidt, Wilckens, *TDNT* VIII, p. 596.

14. Barrett, Murray, Scroggs, *Adam*, p. 73, Black, Käsemann, Cranfield, Schlier, Wilckens, *Römer*, p. 188 and n. 509.

15. On the one hand see Apoc. Mos. 20f. – Adam says, '. . . thou hast deprived me of the glory of God'; III Bar. 4.16; *Gen. Rab.* 11.2; 12.6; bSanh. 38b; cf. Rom. 1.23; see further Scroggs, *Adam*, pp. 48f. On the other side see IV Ezra 7.122–5; II Bar. 51.1, 3; 54.15, 21; and cf. Rom. 2.7, 10; 5.2; 8.18, 21; 9.23.

16. Cf. H. Müller, 'Der rabbinische Qal-Wachomer-Schluss in paulinischer Typologie: zur Adam-Christus-Typologie in Röm. 5', *ZNW* 58, 1967, pp. 73–92. The fullest treatment of the *religionsgeschichtlich* background to Rom. 5.12–19 is E. Brandenburger, *Adam und Christus: exegetischreligionsgeschichtliche Untersuchung zu Röm. 5.12–21 (I Kor. 15)*, 1962, Erster Teil – though his assessment of the Gnostic evidence is subject to the brief critique made above in §12; see also A. J. M. Wedderburn, 'The Body of Christ and Related Concepts in I Corinthians', *SJT* 24, 1971, pp. 90–5.

17. Käsemann, *Römer*, p. 186. See also those cited by Käsemann on pp. 185f. And since then see Cranfield, *Romans*, Vol. I, pp. 343, 350ff.; H. Schlier, *Römerbrief*, Herder 1977, pp. 222–6.

18. Cf. IV Ezra 7.11; Targ. Neofiti on Gen. 2.15. Further rabbinic references in Scroggs, *Adam*, p. 33 n. 3, pp. 42f. nn. 45 and 46; see also Jervell, *Imago*, pp. 29f., 43f., 78–84, 325. In Rom. 5.14 Paul thinks of Adam's disobedience as a transgression – that is, of law. In 7.8–12 'the command' and '(the) law' are manifestly synonymous – 8a/b, 9a/b, 12a/b (cf. Schlier, *Römer*, pp. 222f.).

19. Barrett, *Romans*, p. 143.

20. See again Käsemann, *Römer*, pp. 185f.; Cranfield, *Romans*, Vol. I, pp. 351f.; Schlier, *Römer*, p. 224.

21. Cf. II Cor. 11.3 – 'the serpent deceived (ἐξηπάτησεν) Eve'; I Tim. 2.14 – 'Adam was not deceived (ἠπατήθη), but the woman was deceived (ἐξαπατηθεῖσα)'.

22. I have argued elsewhere that a personal reference is included within the typical 'I'; see J. D. G. Dunn, 'Rom. 7.14–25 in the Theology of Paul', *TZ* 31, 1975, pp. 260f.

23. Cf. II Bar. 54.19 – 'Each of us has been the Adam of his own soul'. 'For Paul the sin of Adam is the sin of everyman' (Davies, *Paul*, p. 32).

24. Against, e.g., the view that Paul envisages a period of childhood innocence (as in C. H. Dodd, *Romans*, Moffatt 1932, pp. 110f.; Davies, *Paul*, pp. 24f.). For a review of alternative ways of interpreting vv. 9f. see O. Kuss, *Römerbrief*, Regensburg 1957, 1959, 1978, pp. 446–8; further literature in Käsemann, *Römer*, p. 183.

25. Cf. G. Bornkamm, 'Sünde, Gesetz und Tod' (1950), *Das Ende des Gesetzes*, München 1952, p. 59 (ET 'Sin, Law and Death (Romans 7)', *Early Christian Experience*, SCM Press 1969, pp. 93f.); F. J. Leenhardt, *Romans*, 1957, ET Lutterworth 1961, p. 185; Kuss, *Römer*, p. 448; U. Luz, *Das Geschichtsverständnis des Paulus*, 1968, pp. 166f.

26. See IV Ezra 7.11f.; and for rabbinic references Strack-Billerbeck III, pp. 247–55. We may note how this verse continues – God 'subjected (τὸν ὑποτάξαντα) in hope' – perhaps an allusion to Ps. 8 (see below pp. 108–11), as G. B. Caird has suggested (in private correspondence).

27. Sanday and Headlam, *Romans*, p. 208. Ματαιότης may denote spiritual powers (see C. K. Barrett, *From First Adam to Last*, 1962, pp. 9f.), and so the passage speak of Adam's subjection both to corruption and to the elemental spirits (Gal. 4.8f.).

28. For further Philo and rabbinic references see G. Kittel, *TDNT* II, pp. 392–4.

29. See Kittel, *TDNT* II, pp. 392f.; Jervell, *Imago*, pp. 39f., 91f., though Jervell argues against Kittel that the rabbis did think (at least by implication) of Adam

as having lost the divine image (pp. 112–14). The main disputes however were on the reference of the 'us' in Gen. 1.26, and on what the 'image' actually was (Kittel, pp. 392, 394; Jervell, pp. 74, 84f. and passim).

30. Scroggs, *Adam*, pp. 27–9.

31. The whole argument of I Cor. 11.2–16 is dominated by considerations drawn from 'the order of creation' with no thought apparently given to the possibility hinted at in Gal. 3.28 that God's saving purpose in Christ has brought about a new structure of social relationships. It reads rather as though Paul was confronted by an awkward and delicate situation in Corinth in which he reverted to arguments in which he had been trained as a rabbi, without attempting (here at any rate) to integrate them into the transformed theology which he developed from his conversion. Cf. Jervell, *Imago*, pp. 295ff.; U. Luz, 'The Image of God in Christ and Mankind: New Testament Perspectives,' *Concilium*, 5.10, 1969, p. 41; P. K. Jewett, *Man as Male and Female*, Eerdmans 1975, pp. 111–19.

32. See further Jervell, *Imago*, pp. 323f.

33. See also Jervell, *Imago*, pp. 100–3.

34. So e.g. Scroggs, *Adam*, pp. 26f., and those cited by him in n. 29; M. Black, *The Scrolls and Christian Origins*, Nelson 1961, p. 139; A. R. C. Leaney, *The Rule of Qumran and its Meaning*, SCM Press 1966, p. 160.

35. That we should read φορέσομεν (future) rather than φορέσωμεν ('let us bear') is the agreed opinion of most commentators.

36. See M. Black, 'The Pauline Doctrine of the Second Adam', *SJT* 7, 1954, pp. 174–6; Jervell, *Imago*, p. 174; M. E. Thrall, 'Christ Crucified or Second Adam? A christological debate between Paul and the Corinthians', *CSNT*, pp. 145f.

37. See also Jervell, *Imago*, pp. 189–94, 276–81; Scroggs, *Adam*, pp. 61–72, 95–9, 102–8.

38. Cf. Scroggs, *Adam*, pp. 91, 100f. Contrast the misleadingly entitled article by J. L. Sharpe, 'The Second Adam in the Apocalypse of Moses', *CBQ* 35, 1973, pp. 35–46.

39. Cf. Davies, *Paul*: 'Probably this conception (of Christ as the Second Adam) played a far more important part in Paul's thought than the scanty references to the Second Adam in I Corinthians and Romans would lead us to suppose' (p. 53). Davies goes on to argue that Paul's idea of the Church as the Body of Christ 'is largely influenced by Rabbinic ideas about Adam' (pp. 53–7). Similarly Black, 'Second Adam': 'The Second Adam doctrine provided St Paul with the scaffolding, if not the basic structure, for his redemption and resurrection christology' (p. 173).

40. For what follows see J. D. G. Dunn, 'I Cor. 15.45 – Last Adam, Life-giving Spirit', *CSNT*, pp. 127–41.

41. To interpret 'the man from heaven' as a reference to pre-existence mistakes the eschatological character of Christ's last-Adam-ness. Paul explicitly *denies* that Christ precedes Adam: 'the spiritual (= heavenly) is not first, but the psychical (= earthly), *then* the spiritual' (v. 46) – see A. Robertson and A. Plummer, *I Corinthians*, ICC 1911, p. 374; Jervell, *Imago*, pp. 258–71; Vögtle, 'Der Menschensohn', pp. 209–12 (with further references p. 209 n. 2); see further n. 35 above and n. 44 below; against J. Weiss, *I Korinther*, KEK 1910, pp. 374–6; Rawlinson, *Christ*, pp. 125–32; Cullmann, *Christology*, pp. 168f.; R. P. Martin, *Carmen Christi* 1967, pp. 116, 118.

42. See Jervell, *Imago*, pp. 276–81.

43. Similarly the other 'image' and 'glory of Christ' references (above p. 106) all refer to the exalted, glorified Christ (cf. Luz, 'Image of God', pp. 44f.; against Hamerton-Kelly, *Pre-existence*, pp. 144–8); though on Col. 1.15 see below pp. 188f.

44. So e.g. Kümmel's revision of Lietzmann, *Korinther*, p. 195; Black, 'Second Adam', pp. 171f.; Jervell, *Imago*, pp. 258–60; I. Hermann, *Kyrios und Pneuma*, 1961, pp. 61f.; D. M. Stanley, *Christ's Resurrection in Pauline Soteriology*, 1961, pp. 125f., 275; Scroggs, *Adam*, p. 92; Caird, 'Development', p. 72; H. Conzelmann, *I Korinther*, KEK 1969, pp. 341f. (ET Hermeneia, pp. 286f.).

45. See particularly Lindars, *Apologetic*, pp. 45–51; Hay, *Glory*; W. R. G. Loader, 'Christ at the Right Hand – Ps. 110.1 in the New Testament', *NTS* 24, 1977–78, pp. 199–217; M. Gourges, *A la Droite de Dieu: Résurrection de Jésus et actualisation du Psaume 110.1 dans le Nouveau Testament*, EB 1978.

46. Ps. 8.4–6 in English translations = Ps. 8.5–7 Hebrew and LXX. The LXX which the NT writers always cite differs slightly from the Massoretic text.

47. Cf. Luz, *Geschichtsverständnis*, pp. 344f.

48. But perhaps there is another allusion in Rom. 8.20f. (see above n. 26).

49. He omits LXX Ps. 8.7a, and probably takes βραχύ τι ('a little') in 8.6a in the alternative sense 'for a short time'.

50. Against Davies, *Paul*, pp. 41–4 – the conception of Christ as the Second Adam was probably introduced into the Church by Paul himself' (p. 44). Davies nowhere mentions Ps. 8.

51. Other echoes of Adam christology may be present in Mark 1.12f. and Luke 3.38 (Jeremias, *TDNT* I, p. 141; Schweizer, *Erniedrigung*, pp. 57f./§4d; cf. the rather contrived thesis of J. B. Cortes and F. M. Gatti, 'The Son of Man or The Son of Adam', *Biblica* 49, 1968, pp. 457–502); but neither Mark nor Luke make any attempt to develop a specific Adam christology (cf. Best, *Temptation*, pp. 6–8).

52. Cf. Barrett, *Adam*: 'Jesus the heavenly Man is he in whom man's rightful position in and over creation is restored' (p. 76).

53. On the possible implications of this phrase see above pp. 44f.

54. See e.g. W. D. Stacey, *The Pauline View of Man*, Macmillan 1956, pp. 154–73; Schweizer, *TDNT* VIII, pp. 125–35.

55. See Dunn, 'Paul's Understanding', p. 127.

56. See e.g. Barrett, *Romans*, p. 156; Kuss, *Römer*, p. 495; Blank, *Paulus*, p. 291; R. Jewett, *Paul's Anthropological Terms*, Leiden 1971, pp. 151f.

57. See e.g. NEB; NIV; H. Riesenfeld, *TDNT* VI, p. 55; Schweizer, *TDNT* VIII, p. 383 and n. 362; Dunn, 'Paul's Understanding', p. 132; N. T. Wright, 'The Meaning of περὶ ἁμαρτίας in Romans 8.3', *Studia Biblica 1978*, Vol. III, *JSNT* Supp. 1980, pp. 453–9.

58. Mussner notes the 'negative tone' in the use of the phrase 'born of woman' elsewhere (see above p. 40) in Jewish literature (*Galater*, p. 269 n. 117). I Corinthians 11.3–9 shows the extent to which Paul's theological understanding of women was determined by the creation (and fall) narratives of Gen. 2–3 (cf. I Tim. 2.11–15), so that a deliberate allusion to Eve may lurk behind the ἐκ γυναικός of Gal. 4.4

59. See also Dunn, 'Paul's Understanding', pp. 133, 136f.

60. Cf. Hooker, 'Interchange', pp. 349–61: 'It is because the Second Adam took the form of the first Adam that men can be conformed to *his* likeness in a new creation. . . . Christ became what we are – *adam* – in order that we might

share in what he is – namely the true image of God' (p. 355); also 'Interchange and Atonement', *BJRL* 60, 1977–78, pp. 462–81. L. Cerfaux however argues that ' "he who did not know sin" alludes to the pre-existence of Christ . . . . "he who was made sin" at one and the same time embraces the incarnation and the death of Christ' (*Christ*, p. 163); but see below n. 99. On Eph. 2.14f. cf. S. Hanson, *The Unity of the Church in the New Testament: Colossians and Ephesians*, Uppsala 1946, pp. 145f.

61. Bultmann, *Theology* I, p. 175; J. Gnilka, *Philipperbrief*, Herder 1968, pp. 146f.: 'Very probably we have here before us (Phil. 2.6–11) the oldest NT statement of the pre-existence of Christ.'

62. J. Murphy-O'Connor, 'Christological Anthropology in Phil. 2.6–11', *RB* 83, 1976, pp. 30f., 38, 43, 45, 46f. Barnikol in his intemperate *Mensch und Messias* also accepts that Phil. 2.1–11 is a pre-existence passage, but dismisses it from consideration of the Pauline texts, as being the only such passage in Paul (p. 52), and elsewhere suggests that vv. 6–7 are a Marcionite interpolation (*Der marcionitische Ursprung des Mythossatzes Phil. 2.6–7*, Kiel 1932)! For the difficulties which the pre-existence interpretation raises for interpretation of first-century Christian thought and for dogmatic theology see C. H. Talbert, 'The Problem of Pre-existence in Philippians 2.6–11', *JBL* 86, 1967, p. 141 n. 2. That Phil. 2.6–11 is a pre-Pauline hymn is widely accepted (see references in n. 63).

63. Martin, *Carmen Christi*, remains the most valuable guide to the debate up to 1963. More recent study is reviewed briefly in Martin, *Philippians*, NCB 1976, pp. 109–16; see also the bibliography in Murphy-O'Connor, 'Phil. 2.6–11', p. 25 n. 1. For older discussion see H. Schumacher, *Christus in seiner Präexistenz und Kenose nach Phil. 2.5–8*, 2 vols, 1914, 1921.

64. Cullmann, *Christology* – 'All the statements of Phil. 2.6ff. are to be understood from the standpoint of the Old Testament history of Adam' (p. 181); Barrett, *Adam* – 'At every point there is negative correspondence (between the story of Adam and Phil. 2.5–11)' (p. 16; see also pp. 69–72). See also e.g. Rawlinson, *Christ*, pp. 134f.; Davies, *Paul*, pp. 41f.; A. Feuillet, *Le Christ Sagesse de Dieu*, EB 1966, pp. 343–6; H. W. Bartsch, *Die konkrete Wahrheit und die Lüge der Spekulation*, 1974; M. D. Hooker, 'Philippians 2.6–11', *Jesus und Paulus*, 1975, pp. 160–4; F. Manns, 'Un hymne judéo-chrétien: Philippiens 2.6–11', *Euntes Docete: Commentaria Urbaniana* 29, 1976, pp. 259–90, condensed ET in *Theology Digest* 26, 1978, pp. 4–10; others cited by Martin, *Carmen Christi*, pp. 130ff., 142, 161–4.

65. Talbert, 'Phil. 2.6–11' argues that 'a proper delineation of *form* leads to a correct interpretation of *meaning*' (p. 141). I am much less certain both of the thesis and whether it can be sustained. Where form remains a matter of considerable dispute, speculative reconstruction is as likely to confuse as to clarify the meaning. Talbert's own analysis results in a very unbalanced set of four strophes. Where the basic movement of thought is sufficiently clear we should beware of making an exegesis dependent on a particular and controversial construction of form.

66. Cf. Hooker, 'Phil. 2.6–11', pp. 157–9.

67. It cannot be taken for granted that the participle ὑπάρχων has a connotation of timelessness and so an implication of pre-existence; it simply denotes the established state of the one in question at the time his ἡγήσασθαι was made (cf. Luke 7.25 and the frequent use of the present participle in the sense 'who is'

or 'since he is', etc. – Arndt & Gingrich ὑπάρχω 2; and see further Martin, *Carmen Christi*, pp. 65f. n. 2).

68. The contrast between God and man is usually framed in the form 'God' and 'men' (plural). Part of the contrast in Jewish thought is precisely between the holiness of the *one* God and the corruptibility and sin of *all* men. In Paul cf. Rom. 2.29; I Cor. 1.25; 14.2; Gal. 1.10; Eph. 6.7; I Thess. 2.4, 13; (cf. also I Cor. 3.4; 7.22f.; Col. 2.8; 3.23).

69. See particularly R. P. Martin, 'Μορφή in Philippians 2.6', *ExpT* 70, 1958–59, pp. 183f.; also *Carmen Christi*, pp. 102–19; also *Philippians*, p. 95.

70. Μορφή was preferred to εἰκών by the hymn's composer perhaps (1) be-cause there was no clear idea in either Jewish or earliest Christian thought that Adam had lost God's image (see above n. 29), and (2) because it made the second half of the contrast clearer: he actually became a slave, not just like a slave.

71. In Rom. 8.21 'the *slavery* of corruption' is contrasted with 'the freedom of glory . . .'; we have already seen that Rom. 8.21 belongs to Paul's Adam chris-tology (above p. 104 and nn. 26, 27).

72. Cf. Fuller, *Foundations*, p. 209; Martin, *Carmen Christi*, pp. 179f.; Schille-beeckx, *Christ*, pp. 168f.

73. T. F. Glasson, 'Two Notes on the Philippian Hymn (2.6–11)', *NTS* 21, 1974–75, p. 138, repeats M. R. Vincent's rather pedantic objection to the Adam interpretation of Phil. 2, that grasping at equality with God (Phil. 2.6) has nothing to do with the temptation to Adam that he would become as God/the gods 'knowing good and evil' (Gen. 3.5). Since Adam already enjoyed immortality by his free access to the tree of life, his sole ground for envying God was his dependence on God for his knowledge of good and evil. Consequently the temp-tation could be put to him that once he knew good and evil on his own account (the one thing lacking) he would be 'like God'. The Hebrew *kē'lōhîm* (Gen. 3.5) could be translated by ἴσα θεῷ equally as well as ὡς θεοί – the Hebrew *k* (like) is translated by ἴσα on a number of occasions in LXX (Job 5.14; 10.10; 13.28; 15.16; 24.20; 27.16; 29.14; 40.15; Isa. 51.23; cf. Deut. 13.6; Wisd. 7.3).

74. '. . . and become as men are' (JB). Cf. Hooker, 'Phil. 2.6–11', pp. 162f.

75. J. Reese, *Hellenistic Influence on the Book of Wisdom and its Consequences*, 1970, pp. 65f.

76. A reference to birth not necessarily implied by γενόμενος; cf. after all v.8b (J. F. Collange, *Phillipians*, CNT 1973, ET Epworth 1979, p. 103), and see above p. 40.

77. Notice how many of the key words in Adam theology are used by Wisd. 2.23f. – incorruption (ἀφθαρσία), cf. Rom. 1.23 (ἄφθαρτος θεός); 'image of his own eternity (εἰκόνα τῆς ἰδίας ἀϊδιότητος), cf. above p. 105 and Rom. 1.20 (ἀίδιος αὐτοῦ δύναμις); envy, cf. Rom. 7.7f.; 'death entered into the world' = Rom. 5.12. Murphy-O'Connor draws particular attention to Wisd. 2.23 without recognizing the full significance of the Adam motif as such and its *direct* influence on both Wisd. 2.23f. *and* Phil. 2.6–11.

78. Contrast NEB – 'he did not think to snatch at equality with God'; JB – 'he did not cling to his equality with God'. See e.g. the discussion in P. Grelot, 'Deux expressions difficiles de Philippiens 2.6–7', *Biblica* 53, 1972, pp. 495–507, and the review of the debate in Martin, *Carmen Christi*, pp. 134–53; also *Philippians*, pp. 96f. See also below n. 93.

79. Cf. Philo's treatment of the two accounts of the creation of man, discussed briefly below pp. 123f.

80. Cf. Hooker, 'Phil. 2.6–11', p. 161.

81. Hooker, 'Phil. 2.6–11', p. 162.

82. The phrases omitted are widely regarded as Pauline additions to the pre-Pauline hymn but on the former ('even death on a cross' – v. 8) see particularly M. Hengel, *Crucifixion*, 1976, ET enlarged SCM Press 1977, p. 62. However the issue of the hymn's Adam christology is not affected by this question.

83. Μορφή and ὁμοίωμα are both used to translate the same Hebrew words in LXX: *tō'ar* – Judg. 8.18 (A and B); *tabnît* – Isa. 44.13; Deut. 4.16–18; Josh. 22.28; etc.; *t'mûnāh* – Job 4.16; Ex. 20.4; Deut. 4.12, 15f., 23, 25; 5.8. On the large overlap between μορφή and σχῆμα see J. Behm, *TDNT* IV, pp. 743f.; and cf. Borsch, *Son of Man*, p. 255.

84. Cf. Hooker, 'Interchange', pp. 356f.

85. See Arndt & Gingrich, εὑρίσκω 2.

86. Cf. Martin, *Carmen Christi*, pp. 210f.; Talbert, 'Pre-existence', pp. 149f. That 'man' here is short for 'son of man' is unlikely (despite a fair amount of support for the suggestion – see e.g. Martin, *Carmen Christi*, p. 209 n.4.). Even less convincing is E. Larsson's attempt to trace a Son of Man theology behind v. 6 (*Christus als Vorbild*, 1962, pp. 237–42). There is no indication (apart from Acts 7.56) that a Son of Man christology flourished beyond the limits of the tradition of Jesus' sayings, and no evidence for an interaction between Son of Man imagery and the Adam christology we have traced out (see also above pp. 90–92, and especially Vögtle, 'Der Menschensohn', pp. 212–14). R. Deich-gräber, *Gotteshymnus und Christushymnus in der frühen Christenheit*, 1967, rejects the suggestion of a Semitic *Grundlage*: 'it was conceived and composed in Greek' (p. 130). Otherwise P. Grelot, 'Deux notes critiques sur Philippiens 2.6–11', *Biblica* 54, 1973, pp. 169–86.

87. See Martin, *Carmen Christi*, pp. 182–5 – though a more sustained allusion to the Servant of Isa. 53 is unlikely (Martin, pp. 211–13; Gnilka, *Philipper*, pp. 140f.; otherwise O. Hofius, *Der Christushymnus Philipper 2.6–11*, 1976, pp. 70–3). A more diffused influence from the motif of the suffering righteous man in the book of Wisdom is possible (see particularly Schweizer, *Erniedrigung*, pp. 98–102/ §§8h–n; D. Georgi, 'Der vorpaulinische Hymnus Phil. 2.6–11', *Zeit und Geschichte: Dankesgabe an R. Bultmann*, 1964, pp. 271–5; Murphy–O'Connor, 'Phil. 2.6–11'), but the clearest link comes where the Adam motif is strongest (Wisd. 2.23f. – see above n.77) and the more obvious and direct influence is from earliest Christianity's Adam christology. The attempt to argue that Phil. 2.6–11 is based on Christianized speculation about personified divine Wisdom (see ch. VI – so Schweizer, *Erniedrigung* §§8k–n; Georgi, 'Phil. 2.6–11' pp. 276–93) is even more tenuous: any broad similarities add nothing to the direct influence from and detailed points of contact with the Adam motif (cf. Feuillet, *Sagesse*, pp. 340–9; Gnilka, *Philipper*, pp. 141–3; Sanders, *Hymns*, pp. 70–3; Wengst, *Formeln*, pp. 151–3; Bartsch, *Wahrheit*).

88. See Hengel, *Crucifixion*, ch. 8.

89. The only other reference to Christ's sufferings in Heb. are 2.9f., 18 (clearly a passage built on Adam christology) and 9.26 (Christ would have to suffer 'from the foundation of the world' since sin came in at the very beginning with Adam).

90. 'Subjection and acclamation belong very closely together' (O. Michel, 'Zur

Exegese von Phil. 2.5–11' *Theologie als Glaubenswagnis: Festschrift Karl Heim*, Hamburg 1954, p. 95 – cited by Martin, *Carmen Christi*, p. 264). G. Howard, 'Phil. 2.6–11 and the Human Christ', *CBQ* 40, 1978, pp. 368–87, offers a rather strained argument that 'the entire hymn describes *only* the earthly Jesus', with vv. 9–11 referring to his post-resurrection but pre-ascension exaltation, thus postulating a distinction between resurrection and ascension unknown even to Luke (the only NT writer to make anything of a distinction between Jesus' resurrection and his ascension) and ignoring the weight of the NT parallels indicated in the text.

91. Jewish thinking about Adam was quite accustomed to using super-historical categories, as Scroggs, *Adam*, has shown; see also Jervell, *Imago*, pp. 66–8, 105f.

92. Cf. Murphy–O'Connor, 'Phil. 2.6–11', pp. 42, 43f., 49f.

93. Cf. C. F. D. Moule's interpretation of Phil. 2.6b – 'Jesus did not reckon equality with God in terms of snatching' ('Further Reflexions on Phil. 2.5–11', *AHGFFB*, pp. 264–76): 'Instead of imagining that equality with God meant *getting*, Jesus, on the contrary, *gave* . . . he thought of equality with God not as πλήρωσις but as κένωσις, not as ἁρπαγμός but as an open-handed spending – even to death' (p. 272). See also D. W. B. Robinson, 'ἁρπαγμός : The deliverance Jesus Refused', *ExpT* 80, 1968–69, pp. 253f.

94. See again Gerhardsson, *Testing*, (II n. 192 above).

95. 'Only II Cor. 8.9 (of the passages which involve the thought of pre-existence in Paul) lacks a directly demonstrable reference to Wisdom speculation' (E. Schweizer, 'Zur Herkunft der Präexistenzvorstellung bei Paulus', *EvTh* 19, 1959; reprinted *Neotestamentica*, p. 108) – an important observation if it was only through Wisdom speculation that the idea of pre-existence entered Paul's thought (see below p. 163).

96. In Gal. 4.4f. and Rom 8.3f. the 'redeeming' act *is* clearly Christ's death (cf. Gal. 4.5, ἐξαγοράσῃ, with 3.13, ἐξαγόρασεν). See further above pp. 41f.; on Heb. 2.14f. see above pp. 110f.

97. As by Craddock, 'The Poverty of Christ: an Investigation of II Corinthians 8.9', *Interpretation* 22, 1968, pp. 158–70; also *Pre-existence*, pp. 104–6.

98. Cf. Barnikol, *Mensch und Messias*, pp. 87–94.

99. It is of course possible to argue that the parallel between II Cor. 5.21 and 8.9 implies the thought of pre-existence in 5.21 as well (U. Mauser, *Gottesbild und Menschwerdung*, 1971, pp. 172f.; cf. Cerfaux in n. 60 above); but the thought of Jesus' sinlessness more obviously attaches to the earthly Jesus (seen in sacrificial terms as the unblemished lamb – cf. particularly Heb. 4.15).

100. *Anthologia Latina* 794.35 – 'Crimen opes redimunt, reus est crucis omnis egenus' (quoted by Hengel, *Crucifixion*, p. 60 n. 15).

101. H. Windisch, *II Korintherbrief*, KEK 1924, p. 252.

102. Scroggs, *Adam*, pp. 33–8.

103. Rom. 15.3 should not be taken as a reference to the pre-existent Christ (G. N. Stanton, *Jesus of Nazareth in New Testament Preaching*, Cambridge University Press 1974, pp. 107ff.; against H. D. Betz, *Nachfolge und Nachahmung Jesu Christi im Neuen Testament*, Tübingen 1967, p. 162).

104. See particularly E. Käsemann, 'A Critical Analysis of Phil. 2.5–11' (1950), *JThC* 5,˙1968, pp. 45–88; Wengst, *Formeln*, pp. 149–56; also H. M. Schenke, with his tendentious 'Die neutestamentliche Christologie und der gnostische Erlöser', *Gnosis und Neues Testament*, 1973, pp. 205–29 (here pp. 218–20); and Hamerton-

Kelly, *Pre-existence*, with his insufficiently critical acceptance of earlier hypotheses (pp. 156–68, summary p. 167).

105. The differences are listed by Georgi, 'Phil. 2.6–11', pp. 264–6. Wengst's reply to Georgi is too heavily dependent on the Hymn of the Pearl *(Acts of Thomas* 108–13) *(Formeln*, pp. 153–6), which is probably more than a century later than the Philippian hymn. The extent to which Poimandres has been influenced by Hellenistic Judaism's treatment of the Adam stories of Genesis (and therefore gives no support to the pre-Christian Gnostic redeemer myth hypothesis) has been clearly demonstrated by C. H. Dodd, *The Bible and the Greeks*, 1935, Part II.

106. Black, 'Second Adam', p. 171; Jervell, *Imago*, pp. 65, 259; Scroggs, *Adam*, pp. 116–19; Yamauchi, *Pre-Christian Gnosticism*, pp. 147f. (and those cited by him there); A. J. M. Wedderburn, 'Philo's "Heavenly Man" ', *NovT* 15, 1973, pp. 301–26; Horsley, 'Pneumatikos', pp. 275–80.

107. See also Conzelmann, *I Korinther*, pp. 341–3 (ET pp. 286–7). We cannot even argue with any confidence that a Corinthian faction had taken the step of identifying Christ with Philo's heavenly man. For the context indicates only that they assumed a priority of spiritual over psychical which reduced the Jewish Christian belief in resurrection of the body to absurdity: since spirit (= νοῦς, mind) was prior and superior to body, the gift of the Spirit had already secured all the redemption that was really necessary (or possible). Had the Corinthians been aware of Philo's distinction between heavenly and earthly man they could hardly have accepted Paul's addition of 'first' to Gen. 2.7 ('the first man Adam became living soul'), and Paul's whole argument would have been undermined. For the same reason Paul could hardly have been aware of or influenced by Philo's distinction, otherwise he would not have put so much weight on this particular argument.

108. Cf. Jervell, *Imago*, p. 241.

109. Cf. U. Wilckens, 'Christus, der "letzte Adam", und der Menschensohn', *JMAV*, pp. 388–93.

110. Fuller speaks of 'a complete myth in two parts' combining speculation about the first man and Wisdom *(Foundations*, p. 96). But there is no evidence that these were ever united prior to Christianity in any more than a casual way (the fact that both are called 'the image of God' – p. 78 – hardly amounts to proof to the contrary), or indeed that they were united within first-century Christianity (see above n. 87; against Fuller, pp. 211f.). What is more likely is that with the separate use of such language for Christ in first-century Christianity, Christ thereby became the uniting factor round whom previously diverse elements were gathered to form the Gnostic redeemer myth.

111. Adam christology thus offers no further illumination on the origin of the descent/ascent motif in the Johannine Son of Man sayings. Discussion of whether or what the Fourth Gospel's presentation of Christ contributes to an emerging primal Man myth is best reserved till ch. VII below.

112. Note particularly that the characteristic feature of Wisdom speculation, Wisdom's role as mediator in creation, is wholly lacking in Adam theology – and indeed in Heb. 2.10, a reference to mediation of creation in the heart of one of the most explicit statements of Adam christology, the διά formulation is referred *not* to Christ but to God himself. See also above n. 87; and on Wisdom below ch. VI.

113. Schweizer, 'Menschensohn und eschatologischer Mensch', *JMAV*, p. 113 n. 49.

114. For a fuller treatment see Dunn, *Jesus*, pp. 330–8.

115. He uses Jesus' teaching in his own ethical exhortation (Dunn, *Unity*, pp. 68, 224), but that is not the same thing.

116. Thus when Scroggs says, 'the Adamic christology speaks of the exalted Lord, not the historical activity of Jesus' (*Adam*, pp. 99f.), his emphasis is correct, but strictly speaking he is referring to the *last* Adam; the full sweep of Adam christology embraces Christ's death in the likeness of fallen Adam as well as his resurrection to become last Adam.

Chapter V Spirit or Angel

1. H. Ringgren, *The Faith of Qumran*, 1961, ET 1963, p. 81.

2. See further T. H. Gaster, 'Angel', *IDB* I, pp. 132–4; Russell, *Method*, ch. IX.

3. See I. Abrahams, *Studies in Pharisaism and the Gospels*, Second Series, 1924, reissued Ktav 1967, pp. 24–8; H. Bietenhard, *TDNT* V, pp. 268f.

4. Bousset-Gressmann, p. 349; W. Eichrodt, *Theology of the Old Testament*, Vol. II ⁵1964, ET 1967, pp. 44f.

5. Bousset-Gressmann, pp. 346f.

6. G. H. Box, 'The Idea of Intermediation in Jewish Theology: A Note on Memra and Shekinah', *JQR* 23, 1932–33, pp. 103–19. Examples in Strack-Billerbeck II, pp. 303f. Details of the usage in Targ. Neofiti and its possible significance may be found in R. Hayward, 'The Memra of YHWH and the Development of its Use in Targum Neofiti I', *JJS* 25, 1974, pp. 412–18.

7. See e.g. Davies, *Paul*, pp. 170f.; also *IDB* III, p. 94.

8. So P. Volz, *Der Geist Gottes*, 1910; Bousset-Gressmann, p. 348; see also H. Ringgren, *Word and Wisdom*, 1947, pp. 165–71; G. Pfeifer, *Ursprung und Wesen der Hypostasenvorstellungen im Judentum*, 1967, pp. 22, 39, 69f.

9. As e.g. by Bousset-Gressmann, p 319; R. Bultmann, *Primitive Christianity in its Contemporary Setting*, 1949, ET Thames & Hudson 1956, p. 61; Ringgren, *Qumran*, pp. 47, 81.

10. See particularly Dalman, *Words*, pp. 229–31; G. F. Moore, 'Intermediaries in Jewish Theology', *HTR* 15, 1922, pp. 41–85; also *Judaism* I, 1927, pp. 417–21, 423–38; Strack-Billerbeck, II pp. 302–33; V. Hamp, *Der Begriff "Wort" in den aramäischen Bibelübersetzungen*, 1938; and more recently, A. M. Goldberg, *Untersuchungen über die Vorstellung von der Schekhinah in der frühen rabbinischen Literatur*, 1969: 'the Shekinah is not and indeed cannot be an intermediary being (Mittelwesen), because the term Shekinah always designates the immediately present God. In contrast to the angels the Shekinah is the exact opposite of an intermediary being; it is no "power of God detached from God", no "personified abstraction" ' (pp. 535f., against Volz, *Geist*, p. 169); E. E. Urbach, *The Sages: their Concepts and Beliefs*, 1975, ch. III: 'The *Shekhina* – the Presence of God in the World'; E. P. Sanders, *Paul and Rabbinic Judaism*, SCM Press 1977, pp. 212–15.

11. Cited by Box, 'Intermediation', pp. 112f. Cf. the rabbinic attempt to play down the significance of Metatron in Jewish mystical speculation (especially

bSanh. 38b); see Odeberg, *III Enoch*, pp. 90f. (note on 16.2–4); and the contributions of Segal and Dahl above III nn. 93, 96.

12. Cf. H. F. Weiss, *Untersuchungen zur Kosmologie des hellenistischen und palästinischen Judentums*, 1966, p. 226.

13. Cf. Lampe, *God*, p. 217. Other references in M. E. Isaacs, *The Concept of Spirit*, 1976, p. 110.

14. R. N. Longenecker, 'Some Distinctive Early Christological Motifs', *NTS* 14, 1967–68, p. 532; also *Christology*, p. 31.

15. Cited by Lampe, *God*, pp. 211–13. See also Ignatius, *Eph.* 7.2; *Magn.* 15.2; II Clem. 9.5; Melito, *Peri Pascha* 66; and other references in Lampe, πνεῦμα E13b; A. Grillmeier, *Christ in Christian Tradition*, ET ²1975, pp. 198f.

16. See J. Danielou, *The Theology of Jewish Christianity*, 1958, ET 1964, ch. 4; Lampe, ἄγγελος K.

17. Danielou, *Jewish Christianity*, pp. 119–21; ' "angel" is one of the names given to Christ up to the fourth century' (p. 117).

18. See further J. Barbel, *Christos Angelos*, 1941; and on Justin, Trakatellis, *Pre-existence*, ch. 2.

19. Contrast the more materialistic concept of πνεῦμα in Greek thought – see H. Kleinknecht, *TDNT* VI, pp. 357–9; D. Hill, *Greek Words and Hebrew Meanings*, 1967, pp. 202–5; Isaacs, *Spirit*, pp. 15–19; Lampe, *God*, p. 133. For a critique of H. Leisegang, *Pneuma Hagion*, 1922, see Isaacs, *Spirit*, particularly pp. 141f.

20. Examples of the range of meaning of *rûaḥ*: (1) Wind – Gen. 8.1; Ex. 10.13, 19; Num. 11.31; I Kings 18.45; 19.11; etc.; (2) Breath – Gen. 6.17; 7.15, 22; Ps. 33.6; etc.; (3) the power that brings about ecstatic inspiration – Judg. 3.10; 6.34; 11.29; I Sam. 10.6, 10. For fuller references see J. D. G. Dunn, 'Spirit, Holy Spirit', *The Illustrated Bible Dictionary*, IVP 1980, pp. 1478–83.

21. H. Gunkel, *Die Wirkungen des heiligen Geistes*, 1888, particularly p. 47; see also e.g. H. Bertrams, *Das Wesen des Geistes nach der Anschauung des Apostels Paulus*, 1913, ch. II; H. W. Robinson, *The Christian Experience of the Holy Spirit*, 1928, p. 128; W. Grundmann, *Der Begriff der Kraft in der neutestamentlicher Gedankenwelt*, 1932, p. 47; W. Eichrodt, *Theology of the Old Testament*, II, ET 1967, pp. 46–57; F. Baumgärtel, *TDNT* VI, pp. 362f.; E. Käsemann, *RGG*³ II, 1272f.; Lampe, 'Holy Spirit', *IDB* II, p. 626.

22. Hence the title of Lampe's book, *God as Spirit*.

23. Ringgren, *Word*, pp. 165–7; followed by Eichrodt, *Theology* II, p. 60. Examples of rabbinic usage in Strack-Billerbeck II, pp. 135–8; IV, pp. 443–6.

24. 'The "Spirit" is to be separated from the person of God neither in this passage nor generally in the whole book of Wisdom' (Hamp, *'Wort'*, p. 118).

25. See particularly Pfeifer, *Ursprung*, pp. 52f.; Isaacs, *Spirit*, pp. 25, 54–8 – 'On no occasion does Philo speak of πνεῦμα as if it were separate from God' (p. 57).

26. See further R. Meyer, *TDNT* VI, pp. 821f.

27. Isaacs, *Spirit*, p. 25.

28. See particularly J. Abelson, *The Immanence of God in Rabbinical Literature*, 1912, pp. 224–37; Strack-Billerbeck II, pp. 134f.; P. Schäfer, *Die Vorstellung vom heiligen Geist in der rabbinischen Literatur*, 1972: 'er (ist) immer nur eine Offenbarungsweise *Gottes*' (p. 62); and above p. 130. Cf. e.g. the comment of T. W. Manson on Luke 11.49–51 – 'In the rabbinical literature the attributes (of God) of Justice and Mercy are constantly personified and represented as speaking.

When we read in these writings that "The attribute of Justice said", we realize that this is a picturesque way of saying, "God, in his justice, said" ' (*The Sayings of Jesus*, SCM Press 1949, p. 102). Cf. also the still current idiom – 'The Bible says'.

29. Cf. Weiss, *Untersuchungen*, pp. 212f.

30. Cf. H. A. Wolfson, *Philo*, 1947, Vol. II, pp. 24–36. See also below p. 228.

31. For the overlap between Logos and Spirit in Philo see *Plant.* 18; cf. *Leg. All.* I.42; *Det.* 83f.; *Plant.* 44; *Spec. Leg.* 1.171; see also below VII n. 25.

32. See Russell, *Method*, pp. 148–51; references on pp. 402–5; the bare statistics thus stated are rather misleading, however, since the latter ratio is considerably influenced by the frequency of the phrase 'the Lord of spirits' in I Enoch (over 100 times).

33. Moore, *Judaism* I, p. 421; Strack-Billerbeck II, pp. 127–34; Schäfer, *Vorstellung*, Erster Teil.

34. See particularly Schäfer, *Vorstellung*, pp. 89–134, 143–9.

35. See particularly Schäfer, *Vorstellung*, pp. 112–15.

36. See also Schäfer, *Vorstellung*, pp. 140–3.

37. Ringgren, *Qumran*, pp. 89f.; cf. W. Foerster, 'Der heilige Geist im Spätjudentum', *NTS* 8, 1961–62, pp. 129f.; A. A. Anderson, 'The Use of "Ruah" in IQS, IQH and IQM', *JSS* 7, 1962, pp. 301f.

38. See also Lampe, *God* especially ch. II: 'The Spirit of God is God disclosing himself as Spirit, that is to say, God creating and giving life to the spirit of man, inspiring him, renewing him, and making him whole. To speak of "the Spirit of God" or "Holy Spirit" is to speak of transcendent God becoming immanent in human personality . . .' (p. 61).

39. See Dunn, *Jesus*, §§8–9.

40. See further Dunn, *Jesus*, pp. 82f. – bibliography on p. 382 n. 80.

41. Jeremias: 'To possess the Spirit of God was to be a prophet' (*Theology* I, p. 78); Vermes, *Jesus*, pp. 88f.

42. On the historicity of this passage see Dunn, *Jesus*, §9.3. On the expectation of 'the eschatological prophet' in pre-Christian Judaism see particularly Hahn, *Titles*, pp. 352–65. That Jesus saw himself as fulfilling the hope of a 'prophet like Moses' (see below p. 138 and n. 46) may well also be implied (see J. Jeremias, *TDNT* IV, pp. 867f.).

43. Dunn, *Jesus*, pp. 44–9; F. Schnider, *Jesus der Prophet*, 1973, pp. 187–90, 258–60. Cullmann's denial that Jesus 'applied the concept of the Prophet to his person and work' (*Christology*, pp. 36f., 49) is based on too narrow a treatment of the evidence; in particular he does not consider the bearing of Isa. 61.1 on the issue (contrast Hahn, *Titles*, pp. 380f.; Fuller, *Foundations*, pp. 128f.; and cf. G. Friedrich, *TDNT* VI, p. 848; Teeple, *Prophet*, pp. 117f.).

44. Jesus' claim to an authority greater than that of Moses (often commented on since Käsemann focussed on it as a way of opening a 'new quest of the historical Jesus' – above p. 26 and n.91; see e.g. the discussion in Marshall, *Origins*, pp. 46–51) goes beyond that of prophet; but is it implied that his authority therein transcended the (presumably unique) authority of the eschatological prophet? The uncertainties that obscure the issue discussed by W. D. Davies, *Torah in the Messianic Age and/or the Age to Come*, SBL Monograph 7, 1952, leave our issue also obscure. Rawlinson compares Matt. 11.27 to the hope of the prophet

like Moses '*whom the Lord knew face to face*' – Deut. 34.10 (*Christ*, pp. 57f. – his emphasis).

45. See also Dunn, *Jesus*, pp. 46–9. Cf. B. D. Chilton, *God in Strength: Jesus' Announcement of the Kingdom*, Freistadt 1979.

46. See particularly Hahn, *Titles*, pp. 373–8; Fuller, *Foundations*, pp. 168f.; Zehnle, *Pentecost Discourse*, pp. 76–88, 91. On the Jewish expectation of a 'prophet like Moses' see Jeremias, *TDNT* IV, pp. 856–64; Teeple, *Prophet*, pp. 49–68; Vermes, *Jesus*, pp. 95f. On the possibility that Jesus was also identified as Elijah see above p. 92 and n. 139, and below n. 65.

47. See Stanton, *Jesus*, pp. 70–81.

48. O. H. Steck, *Israel und das gewaltsame Geschick der Propheten*, 1967, pp. 265–79, 284–9.

49. See further Dunn, 'Rom. 1.3–4', pp. 40–68; also *Jesus*, p. 447 n. 116; cf. Betz, *Jesus*, p. 96. I Tim. 3.16 and I Peter 3.18 may be interpreted similarly ('Rom. 1.3–4', pp. 62–5).

50. Cf. Dunn, *Unity*, p. 68.

51. See also R. Meyer, *Der Prophet aus Galiläa*, (1940) 1970, pp. 10–18; Dunn, *Jesus*, §14; D. Hill, *New Testament Prophecy*, Marshall, Morgan & Scott 1979, ch. 2.

52. Since the Q narrative of the temptations (Matt. 4.1–11/Luke 4.1–12) seems to presuppose the heavenly voice's hailing Jesus as Son, and since it also includes a version of John the Baptist's preaching (Matt. 3.7–10/Luke 3.7–9), Q probably also contained an account of Jesus' anointing at Jordan, an account which however largely (but not wholly) agreed with the Markan version, and so has been almost completely lost to view (cf. A. Polag, *Fragmenta Q: Textheft zur Logienquelle*, Neukirchen 1979, pp. 30f. – 'vermutlich').

53. See e.g. Jeremias, *TDNT* IV, p. 869; V. Taylor, *Mark*, Macmillan 1952, p. 392; Hahn, *Titles*, p. 382. Among recent commentators W. Grundmann, *Matthäus*, THNT 1968, p. 403; D. Hill, *Matthew*, NCB 1972, p. 268; Nützel, *Verklärungserzählung*, p. 248; Anderson, *Mark*, p. 226; Marshall, *Gospel*, p. 388.

54. Cf. Taylor, *Mark*, p. 163; Dunn, *Jesus*, p. 383 n. 105.

55. See particularly Schnider, *Jesus*, pp. 108–29; R. J. Dillon, *From Eye-Witness to Ministers of the Word: Tradition and Composition in Luke 24*, Rome 1978, pp. 114–27.

56. See further Friedrich, *TDNT* VI, pp. 846f.; Teeple, *Prophet*, pp. 74–83; Hahn, *Titles*, pp. 385f.; Dunn, *Unity*, p. 248, with other bibliography in the notes.

57. See e.g. G. B. Caird, *Luke*, Pelican 1963, p. 132; E. E. Ellis, *Luke*, NCB 1966, p. 142.

58. See C. F. Evans, 'The Central Section of St Luke's Gospel', *Studies in the Gospels: Essays in Memory of R. H. Lightfoot*, ed. D. E. Nineham, Blackwell 1955, pp. 37–53.

59. Schnider, *Jesus*, pp. 173–81.

60. Cf. Meyer, *Prophet*, pp. 18–23.

61. 'The divine passive'; see Jeremias, *Theology* I, pp. 9–14.

62. For discussion see Marshall, *Gospel*, pp. 768f.

63. Two manuscripts (P[66] and P[75]) read the definite article before prophet ('Look it up and see that the prophet does not come from Galilee'); see E. R. Smothers, 'Two Readings in Papyrus Bodmer II', *HTR* 51, 1958, pp. 109–11;

and the discussion e.g. in Brown, *John* p. 325; Schnackenburg, *Johannes* II, p. 223, ET p. 161; Lindars, *John*, p. 305.

64. See Brown, *John*, on these passages; and further Cullmann, *Christology*, pp. 28–30, 37; T. F. Glasson, *Moses in the Fourth Gospel*, 1963, pp. 27–32; Longenecker, *Christology*, pp. 36f.; Miranda, *Vater*, particularly pp. 314–20, 387f.; de Jonge, *Jesus*, ch. III; M. Boismard, 'Jésus, le Prophète par excellence, d'apres Jean 10.24–39', *NTKRS* pp. 160–71; Schillebeeckx, *Jesus*, pp. 478f.; also *Christ*, pp. 313–22.

65. Dodd, *Interpretation*, pp. 239f. – though note his later observation: 'It appears then that John has deliberately moulded the idea of the Son of God in the first instance upon the prophetic model. . . . The human mould, so to speak, into which the divine sonship is poured is a personality of the prophetic type' (p. 255); Schnider, *Jesus*, ch. V; cf. II n. 223 above; and note the thesis argued by J. L. Martyn and implied by his title, 'We have found Elijah', *JGCWDD*, pp. 181–219.

66. Brown, *John*, p. 931.

67. Bühner argues that behind John's christology lies the earlier ideas of a prophetic rapture to heaven (where Jesus was transformed into the Son of Man – cf. I Enoch 71.14) and a subsequent return to earth (*Gesandte*, particularly pp. 385–99). But clearly John 3.13, even if it is to be understood as a denial of such visionary rapture to others (see particularly H. Odeberg, *The Fourth Gospel*, Uppsala 1929, Amsterdam 1968, pp. 72–98; Meeks, *Prophet-King*, pp. 295–301; Moloney, *Son of Man*, pp. 54–7), roots the christological claim in something other than that – viz. the Son of Man's (prior) descent from heaven (cf. Moloney, pp. 233f.). Bühner's thesis leaves him unable to offer adequate explanation of the unique otherness of Christ's 'from above' in John's presentation (3.31f.; 8.23) (pp. 415–21).

68. The suggestion of Leisegang that behind the story of the dove's descent at Jordan lie pagan ideas of divine begetting (*Pneuma Hagion*, pp. 80–95) has little to commend it; and there is nothing whatever to commend the suggestion of J. C. Meagher, 'John 1.14 and the New Temple', *JBL* 88, 1969, pp. 57–68, that John 1.14 originally read πνεῦμα instead of σάρξ ('the Word became spirit . . .').

69. See further J. D. G. Dunn, *Baptism in the Holy Spirit*, SCM Press 1970, pp. 40–7.

70. See further Dunn, *Baptism*, pp. 20f.

71. Consider e.g. Zehnle's conclusion: 'In line with his theological plan for Acts, Luke has composed the discourse of chapter 2 by reworking traditions of the kerygma of the early community, which traditions can be found in more primitive form in the discourse of chapter 3' (*Pentecost Discourse*, p. 136). The nearest parallel to 2.33 in ch. 3 is 3.19f. – 'Repent . . . that times of refreshing may come from the presence of the Lord' – where 'the Lord' is clearly God.

72. Too casual statements to this effect are made e.g. by Rawlinson, *Christ*, p. 158, and H. Berkhof, *The Doctrine of the Holy Spirit*, 1964, p. 18.

73. Similarly he usually attributed power (δύναμις) and energy (ἐνέργεια) to God (Rom. 1.16, 20; 9.17; I Cor. 1.18, 24; 2.5; 6.14; II Cor. 4.7; 6.7; 13.4; Eph. 1.19; 3.7; Col. 2.12) and only occasionally to Christ (I Cor. 5.4; II Cor. 12.9; Phil. 3.21; Col. 1.29).

74. See e.g. A. Plummer, *II Corinthians*, ICC 1915, p. 102; F. Büchsel, *Der Geist Gottes im Neuen Testament*, 1926, p. 428; F. Prat, *The Theology of St Paul*, ET, Vol. II 1927, pp. 435–41; Bultmann, *Theology* I, p. 214; Davies, *Paul*, p. 196; Schweizer

TDNT VI, pp. 415f.; H. Ulonska, 'Die Doxa des Mose', *EvTh* 26, 1966, p. 387; Hill, *Greek Words*, pp. 278f.; and particularly Hermann, *Kyrios und Pneuma*.

75. See particularly J. D. G. Dunn, 'II Cor. 3.17 – "The Lord is the Spirit" ', *JTS* 21, 1970, pp. 309–20; C. F. D. Moule, 'II Cor. 3.18b, "καθάπερ ἀπὸ κυρίου πνεύματος" ', *NTGOC*, pp. 231–7.

76. Dunn, 'Rom. 1.3–4', p. 67. Outside Paul, I Peter 3.18 could be translated 'made alive by the Spirit', or 'in the sphere of the Spirit' (Schweizer, *TDNT* VI, p. 417). But it more probably either refers to Jesus' own spirit, with Jesus' life beyond death seen in more dualistic terms than is implied in I Cor. 15 (cf. RSV, NEB, JB – 'in the spirit'), or alludes to Jesus as raised by virtue of his life lived with reference to the Spirit (Dunn, 'Rom. 1.3–4', pp. 64f.). A reference to Jesus as a pre-existent spirit or spiritual being is hardly in view here; the focus is exclusively on Jesus' resurrection. Similarly with I Tim. 3.16 – 'vindicated in the sphere of the Spirit', or better 'in (his) spirit', or perhaps better still '(as one who had lived) in the power of the Spirit' (Dunn, 'Rom. 1.3–4', pp. 63f.; cf. JB – 'attested by the Spirit'). See also below pp. 237ff.

77. Perhaps here too we have the reason why only once in the NT is Jesus' death linked with the Spirit – Heb. 9.14, 'Christ who through the eternal Spirit (διὰ πνεύματος αἰωνίου) offered himself . . .'. This probably means simply that Christ's passion and self-sacrifice was in the inspiration and power of the Holy Spirit – hence its efficacy (cf. 5.8f.). So e.g. Michel, *Hebräer*, p. 314; Bruce, *Hebrews*, p. 205. There is no thought of identifying Christ *as* eternal Spirit.

78. This and the following paragraph are largely a summary of Dunn, *Jesus*, pp. 319–24. Cf. Lampe, *God*, ch. III and his definition of the 'Christ-Spirit' on p. 114.

79. Dunn, 'I Cor. 15.45', pp. 131f.

80. See particularly Hermann, *Kyrios*, pp. 65f., 71–6.

81. Cf. Hermann, *Kyrios*.

82. See also Kümmel, *Theology*, pp. 167f.

83. See Dunn, *Unity*, pp. 19 and 218, citing C. F. D. Moule's description of Acts' 'absentee christology' ('Christology of Acts', *SLAPS*, pp. 179f.).

84. R. E. Brown, 'The Paraclete in the Fourth Gospel', *NTS* 13, 1966–67, p. 128 (my emphasis); see further Dunn, *Jesus*, pp. 350f. If John 16.13 makes a deliberate use of Wisdom terminology (cf. Wisd. 9.10f.) (so Schnackenburg, *Johannes*, III pp. 152f.) the implication would be that the Paraclete continues the role of the Wisdom-Logos incarnate (see below pp. 156f. and n.112). Cf. the presentation of the Spirit(?) as the eyes of the Lamb in Rev. 3.1 and 5.6 – but what relationship between Spirit and exalted Christ is depicted by this imagery is impossible to ascertain (cf. Schweizer, *TDNT* VI, pp. 450f.; F. F. Bruce, 'The Spirit in the Apocalypse', *CSNT*, pp. 333–7; Isaacs, *Spirit*, p. 114). On I Peter 1.10f, see below pp. 159f. No other NT writings come to our aid on this particular question.

85. See above p. 15; also e.g. Gaster, *IDB* I, p. 130, also p. 129.

86. We may note that LXX translates *ʾlōhîm* in Ps. 8.5, 97.7 and 138.1 by ἄγγελοι.

87. G. von Rad, *TDNT* I, p. 78; C. J. Labuschagne, *The Incomparability of Yahweh in the Old Testament*, 1966.

88. See particularly von Rad, *TDNT* I, pp. 77f.; Eichrodt, *Theology* II, pp. 23–9. Von Rad suggests there may be a system in the seemingly haphazard way in

which the reference is sometimes to Yahweh and sometimes to the angel of Yahweh: 'When the reference is to God apart from men, Yahweh is used; when God enters the apperception of men then the angel of the Lord is introduced' (p. 77).

89. See further Eichrodt, *Theology* II, pp. 29–44. As Eichrodt points out, the value of formulating Yahweh's present involvement in men's affairs in terms of Spirit (as against the earlier angelic or man-like theophanies) was that both his immanence and his transcedence could be asserted without the one calling the other into question (p. 53).

90. See further Moore, *Judaism* I, pp. 403f.; H. B. Kuhn, 'The Angelology of the non-canonical Jewish Apocalypses', *JBL* 67, 1948, pp. 217–32; H. Bietenhard, *Die himmlische Welt im Urchristentum und Spätjudentum*, 1951, pp. 101–4, 108–13; Gaster, *IDB* I, p. 132; Russell, *Method*, p. 244; W. H. Brownlee, 'The Cosmic Role of Angels in the 11Q Targum of Job', *JSJ* 8, 1977, pp. 83f.

91. See Bietenhard, *Welt*, pp. 113–16; Gaster, *IDB* I, pp. 132f.; Russell, *Method*, pp. 249–57; Ringgren, *Qumran*, pp. 90–3.

92. An original 'Sariel' seems to have been replaced by 'Phanuel' in the Similitudes of Enoch (I Enoch 40.9; 54.6; 71.8; cf. 1QM 9.16) and by 'Uriel' in I Enoch 9.1, 10.1 and 20 (see G. Vermes, 'The Archangel Sariel: a Targumic Parallel to the Dead Sea Scrolls', *CJMS* III, pp. 159–66; and above II n. 62).

93. Moore, *Judaism* I, p. 410; Bietenhard, *Welt*, pp. 104–8; Gaster, *IDB* I, pp. 132f.; Russell, *Method*, pp. 241–3; Ringgren, *Qumran*, pp. 82f.; Strugnell, 'Angelic Liturgy', pp. 318–45. On the angelology of III Enoch see Odeberg, *III Enoch*, pp. 147–70.

94. Von Rad, *TDNT* I, p. 81; see also Moore, *Judaism* I, pp. 404f., 410f.; Kuhn, 'Angelology', pp. 228–30. On Philo it will suffice to quote Goodenough's observation: 'Philo knows nothing of such an angelology (that is, where angels had become such fixed personalities as, in many cases, to have names and distinct functions); his angels are only δυνάμεις (powers) of God, and not of a sort remotely to provoke or admit individual mythological elaboration. He could not possibly have made room for a literal Gabriel or Michael in his thinking, and allegorized away all resemblance of the Cherubim to that Palestinian tradition which seems to have been accepted and developed by the Pharisees' (*Light*, pp. 79f.; see also Pfeifer, *Ursprung*, pp. 58f., and further below §28.3).

95. See also Bietenhard, *Welt*, pp. 135–7; R. le Deaut, 'Aspects de l'Intercession dans le Judaïsme Ancien', *JSJ* 1, 1970, pp. 35–57.

96. Anderson, ' "Ruah" in 1QS, 1QH and 1QM' pp. 298f.; O. Betz, *Der Paraklet*, 1963, pp. 66–9, 156.

97. I have followed the text reproduced by de Jonge and van der Woude, '11Q Melchizedek', pp. 302f.

98. See e.g. de Jonge and van der Woude, pp. 304f.; J. A. Emerton, 'Melchizedek and the Gods: Fresh evidence for the Jewish Background of John 10.34–6', *JTS* 17, 1966, pp. 399–401; J. A. Fitzmyer, 'Further Light on Melchizedek from Qumran Cave 11', *JBL* 86, 1967, pp. 30–2, 36f.; M. P. Miller, 'The Function of Isa. 61.1–2 in 11Q Melchizedek', *JBL* 88, 1969, pp. 467–9. J. Carmignac, 'Le document de Qumran sur Melkisédeq', *RQ* 7, 1969–71, pp. 343–78, disputes the identification of Melchizedek as a celestial being (pp. 364–7). But see also M. Delcor, 'Melchizedek from Genesis to the Qumran Texts and the Epistle to the Hebrews', *JSJ* 2, 1971, pp. 133f.; Horton, *Melchizedek*, pp. 71, 74–7.

99. See de Jonge and van der Woude, pp. 305f.; F. du Toit Laubscher, 'God's Angel of Truth and Melchizedek: A Note on 11QMelch. 13b', *JSJ* 3, 1972, pp. 46–51; Horton, *Melchizedek*, p. 81; S. F. Noll, *Angelology in the Qumran Texts*, 1979, pp. 69–71 (I am grateful to Dr Noll for the loan of his thesis).

100. Cf. de Jonge and van der Woude, '11Q Melchizedek', p. 321. We should perhaps not emphasize the sense 'return' since 11QMelch. may have simply taken over the word from the Hebrew of Ps. 7.8 without intending to stress it (see Fitzmyer, 'Further Light', p. 37).

101. See J. T Milik, '*Milkî-ṣedeq* et *Milkî-reša*' dans les anciens écrits juifs et chrétiens', *JJS* 23, 1972, pp. 95–144 (particularly pp. 126–37); Noll, *Angelology*, pp. 66–9, 183f.

102. Referred to by Horton, *Melchizedek*, pp. 124–30. See further Strack-Billerbeck IV, pp. 463f.

103. For Apoc.Ab. see Charlesworth, *Pseudepigrapha* pp. 68f.; Rowland, 'Rev. 1.13ff.', p. 6, n. 1. Smith places 'The Prayer of Joseph' 'within the environment of first or second century Jewish mysticism' (*RAERG*, p. 291).

104. In one place Bühner speaks of 'the Spirit-possession of the prophet as katabatic incarnation of an angel' as the background to John's christology (*Gesandte*, p. 427); but see above III n. 128.

105. Whether there is any kind of anti-angel-christology polemic implied in Luke 24.13–43 is unclear. The pre-Lukan tradition can certainly be said to belong to the *Gattung* of 'OT anthropomorphic theophany stories' – cf. Gen. 18; Ex. 3–4; Judg. 6, 13; Tobit 5, 12; Test. Ab. (see J. E. Alsup, *The Post-Resurrection Appearance Stories of the Gospel Tradition*, 1975, pp. 214–65). It is also true that there was a strong tendency to interpret any account of the heavenly visitor's eating as mere appearance during our period (Tobit 12.19; Philo, *Abr*, 118; Josephus, *Ant.* I.197; Test. Ab. 4–5 – Recension A but not Recension B; see also Targum Pseudo-Jonathan and Targ. Neofiti (margin) on Gen. 19.3). Consequently it could be argued that the pre-Lukan account, which climaxes in the blessing, breaking and distribution of the bread and the consequent opening of the disciples' eyes, was amenable to an angel-christology interpretation (the risen Christ was an angel), and that Luke deliberately sought to exclude this possibility by emphasizing the materiality of Jesus' resurrection body and by having him actually eat something (Luke 24.39–43). But the *Gattung* as such is not specific as to the character of the heavenly visitor (it includes accounts both of appearances of Yahweh in the OT and of archangels in the intertestamental period), and the emphasis of Tobit, Philo, etc. on the eating of such a visitor as mere appearance is not a feature of the pre-Lukan tradition, which evidently focussed on the disciples' recognition of Jesus rather than on the meal (Alsup, pp. 196–9). Consequently a specific christology of the tradition (beyond that of assuming Christ's exaltation to heaven) is not evident in the pre-Lukan level; that is to say, we cannot deduce from it that a particular *status* within heaven, or in the heavenly hierarchy, was *thereby* being ascribed to the risen Christ. Moreover, the emphasis on the materiality of Jesus' resurrection body may simply be a consequence of Luke's own conceptuality of such phenomena, *including* visits of angels – note particularly Acts 12.9 (see Dunn, *Jesus*, pp. 121f.).

106. M. Werner attempts to demonstrate that earliest christology developed out of a concept of Christ as a high angel – *Die Entstehung des christlichen Dogmas*, 1941: 'Das Wesen des Christus nach der urchristlichen Lehre (Engelchristologie)'

(pp. 302–21). But the attempt founders from the first on a superficial and selective reading of the relevant data (see also W. Michaelis, *Zur Engelchristologie im Urchristentum*, 1942). More recently J. A. Sanders has suggested as background for Phil. 2.6–11 the belief in fallen angels – he who was in the form of God was one of the heavenly court, who however did not rebel ('Dissenting Deities and Phil. 2.6–11', *JBL* 88, 1969, pp. 279–90; cf. the somewhat confusing treatment of Schillebeeckx, *Christ*, pp. 172–6); but the Adam myth is much more deeply rooted and widespread in the pre-Christian and early Christian literature and provides the closer parallels to Phil. 2.6–11 (see above ch. IV). See also above II n. 218.

107. So rightly, e.g., G. S. Duncan, *Galatians*, Moffatt 1934, pp. 113–15; Oepke, *Galater*, p. 82; Bonnard, *Galates*, p. 73; Schlier, *Galater*, p. 158.

108. In I Cor. 4.9 and 13.1 angels are simply the citizens of heaven. I Corinthians 11.10 probably echoes the old myth of Gen. 6.1f., while II Cor. 11.14 and 12.7 also work with the belief in hostile angels (see above p. 151).

109. On 14.14–16 see particularly Müller, *Messias*, pp. 194–7. Cf. Rowland, 'Rev. 1.13ff.' (III n.135 above).

110. See also W. Bousset, *Offenbarung*, KEK 1906, pp. 307f.; I. T. Beckwith, *Apocalypse*, Macmillan 1919, p. 580; R. H. Charles, *Revelation*, ICC 1920, Vol. I, p. 259. In 14.14–16 the phrase 'another angel' (v. 15) need not refer back to the 'one like a son of man' (v. 14) as the first angel, since throughout the chapter the seer is referring to a sequence of angels using precisely this phrase each time (vv. 6(?), 8, 9, 15, 17, 18).

111. Elsewhere in pre-Christian(?) Judaism 'Spirit of truth' occurs only in Test. Jud. 20.1–5, a passage which appears to have at least been influenced by the Qumran dualism.

112. See particularly Betz, *Paraklet*, Teil B. But see also the qualifications made by Brown, 'Paraclete', pp. 121–6; G. Johnston, *The Spirit-Paraclete in the Gospel of John*, 1970, pp. 102–7. For criticism of Betz see also U. B. Müller, 'Die Parakletenvorstellung im Johannesevangelium', *ZTK* 71, 1974, pp. 33f.; Schnackenburg, *Johannes* III, pp. 165f. The evidence however does not particularly encourage the thesis of a specific dependence on Jewish wisdom tradition (as suggested by Isaacs, *Spirit*, p. 137), though see also above n. 84.

113. See N. Johansson, *Parakletoi*, 1940, pp. 24–31. A Targum of Job is attested for the period before the destruction of Jerusalem (M. McNamara, *Targum and Testament*, Irish University Press 1972, pp. 64f.; Schürer, *History* I, p. 102); and we now have 11QtgJob, though unfortunately the fragments do not contain either 16.19 or 33.23 (see J. P. M. van der Ploeg et A. S. van der Woude, *Le Targum de Job de la Grotte XI de Qumrân*, Leiden 1971). For other evidence of Jewish use of παράκλητος = advocate in transliteration, see Aboth 4.11 (R. Eliezer ben Jacob c. AD 135), and further J. Behm, *TDNT* V, p. 802.

114. Also of the Spirit as witness (Mark 13.11 pars.; Acts 5.32).

115. Hanson, *Jesus Christ*; the thesis is repeated in his *Studies in Paul's Technique and Theology*, SPCK 1974, particularly ch. 11, and in *Grace and Truth*, pp. 64–76, but has received little attention and apparently made little impact.

116. Against Hanson, *Jesus Christ*, pp. 12f. Similarly in exegesis of John 6.30–40 Hanson argues that John would have thought of Christ as the one who 'gave them (the wilderness generation) the bread from heaven' (John 6.32), ignoring the fact that John actually equates Christ with 'the bread from heaven' itself (6.35, 41f., 50f.) (Hanson, *Jesus Christ*, p. 120).

117. Hanson, *Jesus Christ*, pp. 36–8, 60; cf. M. Thrall, 'The Origin of Pauline Christology', *AHGFFB*, pp. 310–15. The one clear example is Heb. 10.5–7 where, however, the quotation from Ps. 40.6–8 is explicitly attributed to Christ 'at his coming into the world' (see above p. 54).

118. Hanson, *Jesus Christ*, pp. 40f., 130f.

119. Cf. W. Foerster, *TDNT* III, pp. 1086f.

120. Hanson, *Jesus Christ*, p. 177.

121. See further Dunn, *Unity*, ch. V.

122. See particularly E. G. Selwyn, *I Peter*, Macmillan ²1946, pp. 259–68.

123. Dunn, *Jesus*, pp. 172f.

124. Cf. II Cor. 1.21 – 'God who confirms us with you into Christ (εἰς Χριστόν)'.

125. See Dunn, *Jesus*, pp. 330–4.

126. Cf. F. W. Beare, *I Peter*, Blackwell 1947, pp. 65f. J. N. D. Kelly thinks the phrase 'presupposes a Spirit-Christology' (*Peter and Jude*, Black 1969, p. 60).

127. Lampe argues thus – *God*, particularly pp. 12f., 142–4.

128. The failure to appreciate this basic asymmetry of NT Spirit christology on either side (pre- and post-) of the Christ-event is a critical weakness of Lampe's thesis in *God as Spirit*. See further my review of Lampe's book in *Theological Renewal* 12, 1979, pp. 29–34. Cf. C. F. D. Moule's critique of a purely inspiration (as opposed to incarnation) model for christology (*The Holy Spirit*, pp. 52–60).

Chapter VI The Wisdom of God

1. Schweizer, 'Herkunft', p. 109.

2. Schweizer, 'Hintergrund', p. 92; see also *Jesus*, pp. 81–3.

3. Christ, *Jesus Sophia*, pp. 80, 99, 119, 135, 152, 153.

4. Cf. the comments of B. L. Mack, 'Wisdom Myth and Mythology', *Interpretation* 24, 1970, pp. 49f. See e.g. Bousset, *Kyrios Christos*, pp. 62 n. 89, 66f.; Bultmann, *Theology* I, particularly pp. 132, 176; also *John*, KEK 1964, ET Blackwell 1971, p. 23. But note Windisch, 'göttliche Weisheit', pp. 220–34; R. Harris in n. 6 below; and Bultmann's own earlier study 'Der religionsgeschichtliche Hintergrund des Prologs zum Johannes-Evangelium' (1923), *Exegetica* 1967, pp. 10–35, which was overshadowed in subsequent discussion by his more thoroughgoing 'Bedeutung' published two years later.

5. E. Norden, *Agnostos Theos*, 1913, reissued 1956, pp. 280–5.

6. See particularly R. Harris, *The Origin of the Prologue to St John's Gospel*, 1917, especially p. 43; Dodd, *Interpretation*, pp. 274f.; Brown, *John*, pp. 521–3; H. Gese, 'Der Johannesprolog', *Theologie*, pp. 173–81.

7. Windisch was one of the first to point out that the Jerusalem Targum inserted 'through Wisdom' into Gen. 1.1, obviously because of the echo of Prov. 8.22 ('göttliche Weisheit', p. 224).

8. On Aristobulus see M. Hengel, *Judaism and Hellenism*, ²1973, ET 1974, Vol. I, pp. 163–9; Charlesworth, *Pseudepigrapha*, pp. 81f.

9. See Weiss, *I Korinther*, pp. 226f.; Schweizer, 'Herkunft', p. 106; Feuillet, *Sagesse*, p. 75; R. A. Horsley, 'The Background of the Confessional Formula in I Kor. 8.6', *ZNW* 69, 1978, pp. 130–5.

10. See particularly Feuillet, *Sagesse*, pp. 185–91; N. Kehl, *Der Christushymnus*

im Kolosserbrief, 1967, pp. 61–76, 104–8; E. Lohse, *Kolosser und Philemon*, KEK 1968, pp. 85–90 (ET Hermeneia, pp. 47–50). For the background of Philonic thought see also the table in W. F. Eltester, *Eikon im Neuen Testament*, 1958, pp. 147f.; H. Hegermann, *Die Vorstellung vom Schöpfungsmittler im hellenistischen Judentum und Urchristentum*, 1961; S. Lyonnet, 'L'hymne christologique de l'Épître aux Colossiens et la fête juive du Nouvel An (Col. 1.20 et Philon, *Spec.Leg.*II.192)', *RSR* 48, 1960, pp. 93–100.

11. See also T. F. Glasson, 'Colossians 1.18, 25, and Sirach 24', *JBL* 86, 1967, pp. 214–16 = *NovT* 11, 1969, pp. 154–6.

12. For the meaning of the last difficult phrase see e.g. W. McKane, *Proverbs*, SCM Press 1970, pp. 356–8.

13. See particularly Moffatt, *Hebrews*, pp. 5–8; Michel, *Hebräer*, pp. 94–100; Dey, *Intermediary World*, ch. 4; cf. Williamson, *Philo and Hebrews*, pp. 36–41, 74–80, 95–103.

14. See particularly Christ, *Jesus Sophia*, II Teil, 1, 4 and 5 Kap.; D. W. Smith, *Wisdom Christology in the Synoptic Gospels*, 1970; and earlier A. Feuillet, 'Jesus et la Sagesse Divine d'apres Evangiles Synoptiques', *RB* 62, 1955, pp. 161–96.

15. See particularly Brown, *John*, pp. 178, 273, 318; for further suggested allusions see Brown's index, 'Wisdom'; see also G. Ziener, 'Weisheitsbuch und Johannesevangelium', *Biblica* 38, 1957, pp. 396–416; 39, 1958, pp. 37–60.

16. H. St. J. Thackeray, *The Septuagint and Jewish Worship*, British Academy 1923, pp. 95ff.; A. Feuillet, 'Les "Chefs de ce siecle" et la Sagesse divine d'apres I Cor. 2.6–8', *SPCIC* I, pp. 383–93; also *Sagesse*, pp. 325f. (see also his 'L'énigme de I Cor. 2.9', *RB* 70, 1963, pp. 52–74); A. W. Carr, 'The Rulers of this Age – I Corinthians 2.6–8', *NTS* 23, 1976–77, pp. 20–35.

17. The dominant view this century, especially since M. Dibelius, *Die Geisterwelt im Glauben des Paulus*, Göttingen 1909, pp. 89–98, and Lietzmann, *Korinther*, pp. 12f. In British scholarship see e.g. J. Moffatt, *I Corinthians*, Moffatt 1938, pp. 29f.; G. B. Caird, *Principalities and Powers*, 1956, pp. 16f.; Barrett, *I Corinthians*, p. 70; F. F. Bruce, *I & II Corinthians*, NCB 1971, pp. 38f. Further literature in Carr (above n. 16). The issue does not affect our discussion greatly; but see below §24.1.

18. Feuillet, *Sagesse*, pp. 150f.; C. K. Barrett, *II Corinthians*, Black 1973, p. 125; see also Hamerton-Kelly, *Pre-existence*, pp. 144–6. On ἀπαύγασμα (active 'radiance'; passive 'reflection') see Arndt & Gingrich.

19. A. van Roon, 'The Relation between Christ and the Wisdom of God according to Paul', *NovT* 16, 1974, pp. 207–39, denies that Paul embraced a Wisdom christology, but only by playing down or ignoring the most obvious parallels to the passages cited above; in contrast he accepts uncritically the far less plausible hypothesis that Paul 'based his idea of the pre-existence of the Messianic Son of God on Ps. 110.3 and Mic. 5.1' (p. 234; on Ps. 110.3 and Micah 5.1=5.2 ET see above pp. 70f.).

20. See particularly U. Wilckens, *Weisheit und Torheit*, 1959, pp. 190–7; also *TDNT* VII, pp. 508f.; H. Conzelmann, 'The Mother of Wisdom', *FRPRB*, pp. 232ff.

21. Ringgren, *Word*, p. 8 (quoting W. O. E. Oesterley and G. H. Box, *The Religion and Worship of the Synagogue*, ²1911, p. 195); see also W. Schencke, *Die Chokma (Sophia) in der jüdischen Hypostasenspekulation*, 1913; O. S. Rankin, *Israel's Wisdom Literature*, 1936, ch. IX, especially p. 224; Pfeifer, *Ursprung*, pp. 24, 26–8,

30f., 43f., 45f., 60f. (definition of 'hypostasis' on pp. 14f.); Hengel, *Judaism* I, pp. 153ff., 171.

22. E.g. R. Marcus, 'On Biblical Hypostases of Wisdom', *HUCA* 23, 1950–51, pp. 167ff.; R. B. Y. Scott, 'Wisdom in Creation: the *'āmôn* of Proverbs 8.30', *VT* 10, 1960, p. 223; R. N. Whybray, *Wisdom in Proverbs*, 1965, p. 103; Larcher, *Sagesse*, ch. V, particularly pp. 402–10.

23. G. von Rad, *Wisdom in Israel*, 1970, ET 1972, pp. 144–76.

24. Von Rad, *Wisdom*, p. 148.

25. Whybray, *Wisdom*, pp. 87–92.

26. See W. L. Knox, 'The Divine Wisdom', *JTS* 38, 1937, pp. 230–7; also *Gentiles*, ch. III; A. J. Festugiere, 'A propos des Arétalogies d'Isis', *HTR* 42, 1949, pp. 209–34; Conzelmann, 'Mother of Wisdom', pp. 230–43; C. Kayatz, *Studien zu Proverbien 1–9*, 1966, Kap. II; Hengel, *Judaism* I, pp. 157ff.; J. Marböck, *Weisheit im Wandel*, 1971, pp. 49–54; B. L. Mack, *Logos and Sophia*, 1973, pp. 38–42 – see further pp. 63–72, 90–5 for parallels between the Isis myth and the Wisdom of Solomon.

27. Cf. Nock, *Conversion*, pp. 150f.; J. G. Griffiths, *Plutarch's De Iside et Osiride*, University of Wales 1970, pp. 502f.; also *Apuleius of Madauros: the Isis-Book (Metamorphoses, Book XI)*, Leiden 1975, p. 145. See further Mack, *Logos*, pp. 118–20, 141–7, 154–71.

28. Cf. Goodenough, *Light*, pp. 119f.; 160–3; Weiss, *Untersuchungen*, pp. 206–9. Note particularly that to speak of a divine being as having 'many names' is a common phenomenon and by no means distinctive of Isis; e.g. the 105 names of Metatron in III Enoch 48D(1) (see Odeberg, *III Enoch*, note *ad. loc.*); see further Hengel, *Son*, p. 57 n. 109.

29. Cf. Pfeifer, *Ursprung*, p. 102; Mack, *Logos*, pp. 49–60.

30. Ringgren, *Word*, pp. 45–59.

31. Ringgren, *Word*, pp. 51f., 56f. For *Maat* as a source of Jewish Wisdom speculation see Mack, *Logos*, pp. 34–9.

32. Cf. Kayatz, *Studien*, pp. 138f. A similar contrast can be made with the hypostatizations of Graeco-Roman polytheism (cf. W. C. Greene, 'Personifications', *The Oxford Classical Dictionary*, 1949, pp. 669–71). See also H. A. Fischel, 'The Transformation of Wisdom in the World of Midrash', *AWJEC*, p. 74 and n. 45.

33. See also Wolfson, *Philo* I, pp. 20–6.

34. Cf. e.g. *Fuga* 97, 108f.; and *Som.* II.242, 245. In *Mut.* 259 manna is allegorized as 'heavenly Wisdom', though Philo usually sees manna as a picture of 'the word of God', 'the divine Word' (*Leg. All.* III. 169f.; *Sac.* 86; *Det.* 118; *Heres* 79; *Fuga* 137). See further Goodenough, *Light*, index Logos and Sophia; Wolfson, *Philo* I, pp. 258–61.

35. See further Goodenough, *Light*, pp. 56–8; and below p. 222.

36. 'As long as the unity of God and the supremacy of the Torah were preserved, Judaism was prepared to adopt any argument and any form of thought that seemed suited to the purpose' (Knox, *Gentiles*, p. 55).

37. 'It cannot be the aim of the self-praise to mark out a clearly outlined person or hypostasis, but to indicate through the presentation of the activity and attributes of Wisdom where and how *God's nearness*, his presence and his activity may be experienced ...' '... the Wisdom of God, the "Wisdom from above" ... is in ben Sira not to be conceived as an intermediary being between God and creation

or as a hypostasis. Wisdom in accordance with the kaleidoscope of metaphors is to be taken rather as a poetic personification for God's nearness and God's activity and for God's personal summons (Marböck, *Weisheit*, pp. 65f., 129f.).

38. 'Wisdom is in this book, like our word Providence, a reverential synonym for God, acting on the world and man . . . simply a periphrasis for God in action' (H. J. Wicks, *The Doctrine of God in the Jewish Apocryphal and Apocalyptic Literature*, 1915, p. 85).

39. Cf. Knox, *Gentiles*, pp. 81–9.

40. See further Hegermann, *Schöpfungsmittler*, pp. 71ff.; Mack, *Logos*, pp. 115–17, 173; Weiss, *Untersuchungen*: 'Wisdom, Torah and Logos are in Philo as also in rabbinic Judaism only the side of God turned towards the world and man, that is, they describe his revelatory activity as it comes to expression in the creation (and in the redemption) of the world and of man' (p. 330).

41. See e.g. Staerk, *Erlösererwartung*, pp. 75ff.; Knox, *Gentiles*, pp. 68, 80, 112f.; and those cited above in nn. 22, 37–40, and V n. 10. Caird tells an illuminating and cautionary tale of the NEB Apocrypha translation panel's difficulty in deciding when to translate σοφία as 'Wisdom' and when as 'wisdom' in Sir. and Wisd.: 'We were thus compelled to recognize that there is all the difference in the world between personification and a person. . . . The personified Wisdom of Jewish literature remains from start to finish an activity or attribute of God' ('Development', p. 76).

42. Cf. Moore, 'Intermediaries': 'For the modern reader "hypostasis" has no use or meaning except that which it acquired in the controversies of the third and fourth centuries over the ontological relation of the Logos-Son to the Father; and to employ this term, with its denotation and all its trinitarian connotations, of the supposed personal, or quasi-personal, "Memra" of the Targums, is by implication to attribute to the rabbis corresponding metaphysical speculation on the nature of the Godhead. But of speculation on that subject there is no trace either in the exoteric teaching of Judaism or in anything we know of its esoteric, theosophic, adventures into the divine mysteries' (p. 55).

43. In these early texts there is no thought of the Torah having a real pre-existence, simply that the Torah is where divine wisdom is to be found. The concept of a real pre-existence only emerges in the later rabbinic tradition, as Pfeifer, *Ursprung*, p. 67, and Craddock, *Pre-existence*, pp. 46–53 recognize; see Strack-Billerbeck II, pp. 353–5 and above III n. 37.

44. Pfeifer in fact does not hesitate to classify such passages as hypostatizations (*Ursprung*, pp. 32f., 73f.).

45. Ringgren, *Word*, pp. 38–44.

46. See also G. Gerlemann, 'Bemerkungen zum alttestamentlichen Sprachstil', *Studia Biblica et Semitica: T. C. Vriezen Festschrift*, Wageningen 1966, pp. 108–14; also 'Dabar', *Theologisches Handwörterbuch zum Alten Testament*, hrsg. E. Jenni and C. Westermann, München 1971, Vol. I col. 442.

47. As will become apparent in ch. VII, Philo's allegorizing techique is in effect simply an elaboration of the vivid imagery of the Hebrew idiom.

48. As we shall see below there is no real evidence of a Wisdom christology in the Synoptic traditions prior to Matthew (below pp. 206). James is possibly as early as the Pauline letters or preserves teaching characteristic of the first generation Jerusalem/Palestinian churches, and can be called a wisdom document

somewhat in the style of Proverbs (see e.g. Kümmel, *Introduction*, pp. 408f.); but it does not contain anything approaching a Wisdom christology.

49. The other Pauline passages cited above (pp. 166f.) do not add significantly to the discussion. On Gal. 4.4 and Rom. 8.3 see above §§5.4–4.

50. So e.g. Wilckens, *TDNT* VII, pp. 519, 522; Barrett, *I Corinthians*, p. 60; B. A. Pearson, *The Pneumatikos-Psychikos Terminology in I Corinthians*, 1973, p. 31; H. W. Kuhn, 'Jesus als Gekreuzigter in der frühchristlichen Verkündigung bis zur Mitte des 2. Jahrhunderts', *ZTK* 72, 1975, pp. 30f.

51. The near synonymity of 'wisdom' and 'knowledge' in the context of I Cor. (cf. 12.8) strongly supports the broad consensus that the 'know-alls' confronted in ch. 8 are precisely the 'wiseacres' confronted in ch. 1–2. In particular R. A. Horsley, ' "How can some of you say that there is no resurrection of the dead?" Spiritual Elitism in Corinth', *NovT* 20, 1978, pp. 203–31, has shown how much light can be shed on the Corinthian teaching confronted in I Cor. by setting it against the background of Jewish wisdom tradition, particularly in the Wisdom of Solomon and Philo.

52. For the prominence of Wisdom in later Gnostic thought, particularly Valentinianism, see Foerster, *Gnosis*, index 'Sophia'; G. C. Stead 'The Valentinian Myth of Sophia', *JTS* 20, 1969, pp. 75–104. Goulder's suggestion that 'wisdom and knowledge' were 'two *Samaritan* categories . . . introduced into the church by his (Paul's) opponents' (*Myth*, ed. Hick, pp. 76f. – my emphasis) completely ignores the much wider currency of such language (see also above II n. 67).

53. See also W. Schmithals, *Gnosticism in Corinth*, ³1969, ET Abingdon 1972, pp. 138–40; H. Conzelmann, 'Paulus und die Weisheit', *NTS* 12, 1965–66, p. 237; also *I Korinther*, p. 81 (ET, p. 63); R. Scroggs, 'Paul: Σοφός and Πνευματικός ', *NTS* 14, 1967–68, pp. 33–55; B. A. Pearson, 'Hellenistic-Jewish Wisdom Speculation and Paul', *AWJEC*, pp. 43–66. Against Wilckens, *Weisheit*, pp. 70–80, 205–13; also *TDNT* VII, p. 519.

54. See further Dunn, *Jesus*, p. 219.

55. See e.g. J. M. Robinson, 'Kerygma and History in the New Testament' (1965), reprinted in *Trajectories through Early Christianity*, 1971, pp. 30–40; Barrett, *I Corinthians*, pp. 347f.; J. H. Wilson, 'The Corinthians who say there is no resurrection of the dead', *ZNW* 59, 1968, pp. 90–107. Other references in Dunn, 'I Cor. 15.45' p. 128 n. 2; also *Jesus*, p. 387 n. 43.

56. See e. g. K. Maly, *Mündige Gemeinde*, Stuttgart 1967, pp. 35f.; Dunn, *Jesus*, p. 220. Cf. I Cor. 1.21, on which see A. J. M. Wedderburn, 'ἐν τῇ σοφίᾳ τοῦ θεοῦ – I Kor. 1.21', *ZNW* 64, 1973, pp. 132–4.

57. Against Wilckens, *Weisheit*, pp. 71–4; Hamerton-Kelly, *Pre-existence*, pp. 114–17, who forces the parallels between I Cor. 2.6–16 and the Similitudes of Enoch to support his thesis. 'The Lord of glory', as elsewhere in Paul, is what Jesus became by virtue of his resurrection/exaltation, not a description of pre-existent status. The 'rulers of this age' were ignorant not concerning Christ's identity, but concerning God's plan of salvation (Pearson, *Pneumatikos*, pp. 33f.). See also above n. 53.

58. Conzelmann, 'Weisheit', pp. 236f.; also *I Korinther*, pp. 55f., 64; (ET, pp. 41f., 48); Dunn, *Jesus*, p. 220.

59. See Arndt & Gingrich, δύναμις 6; Moulton & Milligan, δύναμις; M. P. Nilsson, *Geschichte der griechischen Religion*, Vol. II, München ²1961, pp. 535f.; in OT and LXX cf. particularly Job 12.13; Wisd. 7.25; on Philo see below pp. 225f.;

in the NT note Mark 14.62 – '. . . on the right hand of the power'; Acts 8.10 – 'the Great Power' (see above p. 21); rabbinic parallels in Dalman, *Words*, p. 201; Strack-Billerbeck I, pp. 1006f.; for Jewish mysticism see G. G. Scholem, *Jewish Gnosticism, Merkabah Mysticism, and Talmudic Tradition*, Jewish Theological Seminary of America 1960, pp. 67–9. Cf. 'righteousness' in I Cor. 1.30 with Ps. 85.10f. cited above p. 174;

60. Cf. Mauser, *Gottesbild*, pp. 126f.

61. See e.g. the most recent discussions: R. Kerst, 'I Kor. 8.6 – ein vorpaulinisches Taufbekenntnis?', *ZNW* 66, 1975, pp. 130–9; Horsley, 'I Kor. 8.6', p. 130; J. Murphy-O'Connor, 'I Cor. 8.6: Cosmology or Soteriology', *RB* 85, 1978, pp. 253–9; and those cited by them.

62. See also E. Peterson, *ΕΙΣ ΘΕΟΣ*, 1926, pp. 276–99; Wengst, *Formeln*, p. 137; Kerst, 'I Kor. 8.6', pp. 132f.

63. See e.g. Neufeld, *Confessions*, ch. IV (with earlier bibliography on p. 43 n. 4); Kramer, *Christ*, §15; Dunn, *Unity*, §12.

64. See e.g. Pseudo-Aristotle, *De Mundo* 6 – ὅτι ἐκ θεοῦ πάντα καὶ διὰ θεοῦ συνέστηκε (see Nilsson, *Religion*, p. 297 n. 1); Seneca, *Ep.* 65.8 – Quinque ergo causae sunt, ut Plato dicit: id ex quo, id a quo, id in quo, id ad quod, id propter quod; Marcus Aurelius, *Medit.* 4.23 – ἐκ σοῦ πάντα, ἐν σοὶ πάντα, εἰς σὲ πάντα; the Hermetic *Asclepius* 34 – omnia enim ab eo et in ipso et per ipsum. We may note also Rom. 11.36 – ὅτι ἐξ αὐτοῦ καὶ δι' αὐτοῦ καὶ εἰς αὐτὸν τὰ πάντα. See further Norden, *Agnostos Theos*, pp. 240–50; J. Dupont, *Gnosis: la connaissance religieuse dans les épitres de saint Paul*, 1949, pp. 335–45; with summary treatments in Conzelmann, *I Korinther*, pp. 171ff. (ET, p. 144) and nn. 44, 46, 48; Lohse, *Kolosser*, pp. 88f. and notes (ET pp. 49f. nn. 119–24); Kerst, 'I Kor. 8.6', pp. 131f.

65. That Paul here quotes from the Corinthians themselves is widely accepted; see e.g. RSV and NEB, and especially J. C. Hurd, *The Origin of I Corinthians*, SPCK 1965, pp. 120–3.

66. Gentiles would have been as familiar with the belief that Zeus is the 'Father of men and gods' as Jews with the belief that Yahweh is Father of Israel (see Schrenk, *TDNT* V, pp. 952f); see also II n. 8 above.

67. Deut. 6.4 – κύριος ὁ Θεὸς ἡμῶν κύριος εἷς ἐστιν;

I Cor. 8.6 – ἡμῖν εἷς Θεὸς ὁ πατήρ . . . καὶ εἷς κύριος Ἰησοῦς Χριστός.

68. Cf. Neufeld, *Confessions*, pp. 57, 65; and contrast the parallels adduced by Peterson, *ΕΙΣ ΘΕΟΣ*, pp. 254–6.

69. Cf. Craddock, *Pre-existence*, pp. 88–94. I cannot follow Murphy-O'Connor, 'I Cor. 8.6', pp. 253–67, who argues that 'the verse has an exclusively soteriological meaning' and that 'the all' should be interpreted accordingly and not as a reference to creation (so already Barnikol, *Mensch und Messias*, pp. 76–9). The issue at Corinth however was precisely that of the correct attitude to and use of created things; the parallels he quoted (I Cor. 2.10–13; 12.4–6; II Cor. 4.14f.; 5.18; Rom. 8.28, 31f.) are hardly as close as the Stoic formulations cited in n. 64 above; and the difference from the Stoic parallels is the result of Paul's deliberate adaptation of the Stoic formulae. How could a first-century reader have failed to understand 'the all' when described as 'from' the 'one God' and 'through' the 'one Lord' as other than a reference to creation (see further n. 115 below). Cf. H. Langkammer, 'Literarische und theologische Einzelstücke in I Kor. 8.6', *NTS* 17, 1970–71, pp. 193–7; and the sounder treatment of Thüsing (below n. 71).

70. Cf. e.g. Cullmann, *Christology*, pp. 203–34; Longenecker, *Christology*,

pp. 129, 131; Moule, *Origin*, pp. 43f.; Dunn, *Unity*, pp. 51f. Cf. also W. Thüsing, *Erhöhungsvorstellung und Parusieerwartung in der ältesten nachösterlichen Christologie*, SBS 42, 1970. II Cor. 8.9 could possibly be a statement about the pre-existent Christ as Lord; but see above §15.2.

71. See also W. Thüsing, *Per Christum in Deum*, 1965, pp. 225–30; G. Schneider, 'Präexistenz Christi: der Ursprung einer neutestamentlichen Vorstellung und das Problem ihrer Auslegung', *NTKRS*, pp. 403–5. Cf. Wainwright, *Trinity*: I Cor. 8.6 'refers to Christ's present activity in maintaining or sustaining the created universe' (p. 144).

72. See also G. Schneider, 'Urchristliche Gottesverkündigung in hellenistischer Umwelt', *BZ* 13, 1969, pp. 59–75, especially pp. 74f.

73. Cf. Kümmel, *Theology*, pp. 170–2. If the familiar εἰς Ζεὺς Σέραπις formula (Peterson, *ΕΙΣ ΘΕΟΣ*, pp. 227–40) was a close enough parallel we could say that the Lord Christ was being *identified* with the one God, the Father of all ('gods' and 'lords' in v. 5 could be readily understood by Paul's readers as synonymous); that is, the one Lord Jesus Christ is being presented as a manifestation of the one God, the Father. But the Zeus Serapis formula reflects rather the syncretism of polytheistic paganism *assimilating* gods of different countries to each other; and the parallel is not close enough – Paul does *not* speak of 'one God, the Father, the Lord, Jesus Christ'. In I Cor. 8.6 we see rather reflected monotheistic Judaism's attempt to hold the one God in active relation to his creation through the personification of divine wisdom.

74. Paul also shows familiarity ('the rock was *following*') with other contemporary elaborations of the wilderness wanderings tradition reflected in Pseudo-Philo, *Bib. Ant.* 10.7, 11.15, and Tosefta, Sukkah 3.11f. See further E. E. Ellis, 'A Note on I Cor. 10.4', *JBL* 76, 1957, pp. 53–6, reprinted in *Prophecy and Hermeneutic in Early Christianity*, Tübingen 1978, ch. 14.

75. Hamerton-Kelly, *Pre-existence*, p. 132.

76. Barrett, *I Corinthians*, p. 223. See also Weiss, *I Korinther*, p. 251; Knox, *Gentiles*, ch. 5, particularly p. 123; Schweizer, 'Herkunft', pp. 106f.; Craddock, *Pre-existence*, pp. 115f.; Hanson, *Jesus Christ*, pp. 12f.

77. See those cited in Dunn, *Baptism*, p. 126 n. 32; among more recent commentators see J. Ruef, *I Corinthians*, Pelican 1971, p. 90; Bruce, *Corinthians*, p. 90.

78. The imperfect tense, 'the rock *was* Christ', is usually taken to rule out this interpretation, since elsewhere the interpretative key is given in the present tense (cf. CD 6.4; Gal. 4.24f.; II Cor. 3.17) – Robertson and Plummer, *I Corinthians*, pp. 201f.; Conzelmann, *I Korinther*, p. 196 (ET, p. 167) n. 26; Hamerton-Kelly, *Pre-existence*, pp. 131f. But in each of the cases cited that which is interpreted allegorically is something which was present to the interpreter there and then (the well, Hagar/Sinai, the veil – the *same* veil, II Cor. 3.14); whereas the rock belonged exclusively to the past; 'was', therefore, not because Christ was there in the past, but because the rock is *not* in the present (cf. Lampe, *God*, pp. 123f.).

79. Cf. particularly M. M. Bourke, 'The Eucharist and Wisdom in First Corinthians', *SPCIC* I, pp. 372–7.

80. The variation from the Hebrew and LXX text may be explained either as an adaptation of the biblical tradition in the light of the kerygmatic tradition (Christ did not go beyond the sea, he went down into the abyss; a pesher citation – see Dunn, *Unity*, §23); or by Paul making use of an already established in-

terpretation of Deut. 30.13 also attested in Targ. Neofiti (see below n. 83); cf. Ps. 107.26; Sir. 24.5.

81. As by A. Nygren, *Romans*, 1944, ET SCM Press 1952, p. 381; Barrett, *Romans*, p. 6; Cranfield, *Romans*, Vol. II, p. 525. Though Hamerton-Kelly, *Preexistence*, surprisingly makes nothing of the passage.

82. Schweizer, 'Herkunft', p. 107; Feuillet, *Sagesse*, pp. 325f.; M. J. Suggs, "The Word is near you": Romans 10.6–10 within the Purpose of the Letter', *CHIJK*, pp. 304–11.

83. Targ. Neofiti: ' "It is not in heaven": The Law is not in heaven, saying Oh that we had one like Moses the Prophet who would ascend to heaven and receive it for us . . . "And it is not beyond (the sea)": And the Law is not beyond the great sea, saying, Oh that we had one like Jonah the Prophet who descended into the depths of the great sea to bring it up for us . . .' (See M. Black, 'The Christological Use of the Old Testament in the New Testament', *NTS*, 18, 1971–72, p. 9). For discussion of Targum Neofiti's date see A. Diez Macho, *Neophiti I, Tomo I Genesis*, 1968, pp. 57–95; J. Bowker, *The Targums and Rabbinic Literature*, Cambridge University Press 1969, pp. 16–20. H. Chadwick, 'St Paul and Philo of Alexandria', *BJRL* 48, 1965–66, pp. 286–307, notes that Philo refers to Deut. 30.14 no less than four times – *Post.* 84f., *Mut.* 236f., *Virt.* 183, *Praem.* 80 (p. 295).

84. Cf. the observation of Sanday and Headlam: 'It seems probable that here the Apostle does not intend to base any argument on the quotation from the OT, but only selects the language as being familiar, suitable, and proverbial, in order to express what he wishes to say' (*Romans*, p. 289).

85. So e.g. Bruce: 'Do not say to yourself, "Who will go up to heaven?" – that is, to bring Christ down (as though he had never become incarnate and lived on earth). Do not say, "Who will go down to the nethermost deep?" – that is, to bring him back from the abode of the dead (as though he had not already been raised up to newness of life)' (*Romans*, p. 204).

86. When the contrast (heaven/abyss) is posed as a question it would naturally be understood as a rhetorical assertion of human impotence – that which is impossible to man (cf. Prov. 30.4; IV Ezra 4.8; bBM94a) (Strack-Billerbeck III, p. 281; H. Lietzmann, *Römer*, HNT ⁴1933, p. 96; Michel, *Römer*, pp. 256f.).

87. See particularly Käsemann, *Römer*, p. 276.

88. M. McNamara, *The New Testament and the Palestinian Targum to the Pentateuch*, Rome 1966, pp. 78–81.

89. Among recent commentators see particularly Gnilka, *Epheser*, pp. 208–10; M. Barth, *Ephesians*, AB 1974, pp. 433f. Some dependence on the 'Gnostic redeemer myth' (cf. Schlier, *Epheser*, p. 194) is both an unlikely (see above p. 99f.) and an unnecessary explanation (a typically Palestinian midrash or pesher – see n. 88). A reference to Pentecost in Eph. 4.9 is almost as unconvincing (against G. B. Caird, 'The Descent of Christ in Eph. 4.7–11', *SE* II, 1964, pp. 535–45; also *Paul's Letters from Prison*, Clarendon 1976, pp. 73–5) – in 'he gave gifts to men' (4.8), that is, from heaven, yes; but that Paul thought of the Pentecostal gift of the Spirit as the *descent* of Christ to earth is most unlikely (R. Schnackenburg, 'Christus, Geist und Gemeinde (Eph. 4.1–16)', *CSNT*, p. 287).

90. No distinction between comparative (κατώτερος) and superlative (κατώτατος) is involved; see J. H. Moulton-N. Turner, *A Grammer of New Testament Greek*, Vol. III, T. & T. Clark 1963, p. 29.

91. B. F. Westcott, *Ephesians*, Macmillan 1906, p. 61; F. Büchsel, *TDNT* III,

p. 641; J. Schneider, *TDNT* IV, pp. 597f.; Blass-Debrunner-Funk, §167. Text critical considerations hardly support the omission of μέρη from the original text, despite the weight of P⁴⁶.

92. Büchsel, *TDNT* III, p. 641. So already J. A. Robinson, *Ephesians*, Macmillan 1903, p. 180. See further Büchsel, pp. 641f. As Büchsel notes, there is no thought of the descent to Hades as a victorious invasion to liberate the dead. It is Christ's ascension which Ephesians depicts as Christ's triumph (1.20f.), in contrast to Col. 2.14f.; against Barth, *Ephesians*, pp. 433f.

93. Kramer, *Christ*, §5.

94. Kramer argues convincingly that 'the statements about the resurrection may be regarded as the oldest piece in the pistis-formula' (*Christ* §§6, 7b). See also above pp. 35f. and n. 139.

95. See also McNamara, *Palestinian Targum*, p. 81 and n. 28. It is not of course necessary to postulate a developed myth of Christ's descent into hell: Rom. 10.7 and Eph. 4.9 are only the beginning of the elaboration of the confession of Christ's death, though the next stage has already been reached in I Peter 3.19, 4.6.

96. 'Κατάβασις is a technical term for descent into the underworld' (J. Schneider, *TDNT* I, p. 523 and n. 11).

97. Though by no means all accept that a pre-Pauline hymn can be discerned (see Kümmel, *Introduction*, pp. 342f.; Caird, *Letters*, pp. 174f.).

98. P. Benoit, 'L'hymne christologique de Col. 1.15–20. Jugement critique sur l'état des recherches', *CJMS* I, pp. 226–63, gives a useful tabulation of disagreements on p. 238. Likewise C. Burger, *Schöpfung und Versöhnung*, 1975, on pp. 9–11, 15f. Burger's own suggested reconstruction of the original hymn is very brief, consisting only of vv.15a, c, 16a, c, 18b, c, 19, 20c. At the other end of the spectrum comes Wengst who would be prepared to ascribe only τῆς ἐκκλησίας (v. 18) to the redaction (*Formeln*, pp. 172–5). See also R. P. Martin, *Colossians*, NCB 1974, pp. 61–6. The earlier debate is reviewed in H. J. Gabathuler, *Jesus Christus: Haupt der Kirche – Haupt der Welt*, 1965.

99. I have bracketed the most likely insertions and underlined the parallel phrases. As always there is a danger of making a reconstruction dependent on what *we* now consider to be the most appropriate style and form. For example, no Christian congregation would have difficulty in reconciling the apparent contradiction that 'all things' though created 'in him' (v. 16a) yet need to be reconciled 'through him' (v. 20a): God's creative power and purpose had been thwarted by man's sin (against Burger, *Schöpfung*, pp. 23f., 50f.). As R. Schnackenburg notes on the same issue: 'We should not forget that a Christian community sings the Christ-hymn of Col. 1 and therein thinks of its redemption in Jesus Christ' ('Die Aufnahme des Christushymnus durch den Verfasser des Kolosserbriefes', EKK *Vorarbeiten*, Heft 1, 1969, p. 69).

100. See e.g. M. Dibelius, *Kolosser*, revised by H. Greeven, HNT 1953, p. 10; Hegermann, *Schöpfungsmittler*, p. 116; Gabathuler, *Jesus Christus*, p. 130; Schnackenburg, 'Aufnahme', p. 33.

101. Similarly with the Logos in Philo – see below n. 104 and pp. 226f.

102. Kehl, *Christushymnus*, pp. 76–81; Caird, 'Development', pp. 73f.

103. Cf. Lohse, *Kolosser*, p. 87 (ET, p. 48).

104. J. B. Lightfoot, *Colossians*, Macmillan 1875, p. 143; Eltester, *Eikon*, pp. 37f., 148f.; Jervell, *Imago*, pp. 218–26; Martin, *Colossians*, p. 57; Schweizer, *Kolosser*, p. 58. For the Logos as the 'knowability of God' see below pp. 226f.

105. 'Christ = the eschatological interpretation (Auslegung) of God' (F. J. Steinmetz, *Protologische Heils-Zuversicht*, 1969, p. 70.

106. See particularly Lightfoot, *Colossians*, pp. 146–8; Feuillet, *Sagesse*, pp. 178–85; A. Hockel, *Christus der Erstgeborene*, 1965.

107. Cf. Hockel, *Erstgeborene*, pp. 128f.; Schillebeeckx, *Christ*, p. 185.

108. See e.g. W. Michaelis, *TDNT* VI, pp. 878–80; Hockel, *Erstgeborene*, pp. 129f.; Lohse, *Kolosser*, p. 88 (ET, pp. 48f.); K. H. Schelkle, *Theology of the New Testament*, Vol. I 1968, ET 1971, p. 26; Martin, *Colossians*, pp. 57f.; cf. N. Turner, *Grammatical Insights into the New Testament*, T. & T. Clark 1965, pp. 122–4.

109. Schweizer, *Kolosser*, p. 60.

110. See particularly C. F. Burney, 'Christ as the APXH of Creation', *JTS* 27, 1926, pp. 160–77. Similarly with Philo's Logos thought (see below p. 228f.); Philo speaks of the Logos as πρωτόγονος (*Agr.*51; *Conf.* 146; *Som.* I. 215).

111. Cf. Burger, *Schöpfung*, pp. 42–5.

112. Cf. W. L. Knox, *St Paul and the Church of Jerusalem*, Cambridge University Press, 1925, pp. 127–9; also *Gentiles*, p. 159.

113. F. Zeilinger, *Der Erstgeborene der Schöpfung*, 1974, IV. Teil (here particularly pp. 195–200).

114. Cf. those cited by J. G. Gibbs, 'Pauline Cosmic Christology and Ecological Crisis', *JBL* 90, 1971, p. 471 n. 16; though Gibbs himself wishes to qualify this. See further his *Creation and Redemption: a Study in Pauline Theology*, 1971; also 'The Cosmic Scope of Redemption according to Paul', *Biblica* 56, 1975, pp. 13–29.

115. See particularly the parallels cited by W. Pöhlmann, 'Die hymnischen All-Prädikationen in Kol. 1.15–20', *ZNW* 64, 1973, pp. 53–74. We may note that in v.16e the εἰς of the Stoic formula is also used in reference to Christ (contrast Rom. 11.36; I Cor. 8.6 – see above p. 180), with only the ἐκ (by implication) being reserved for God.

116. See Kehl, *Christushymnus*, p. 108; Caird, *Letters*, p. 178; Schillebeeckx, *Christ*, pp. 185f., 191; cf. also E. Percy, *Die Probleme der Kolosser- und Epheserbriefe*, Lund 1946, pp. 69ff., who cites the ἐν αὐτῷ of Eph. 1.4 as a parallel (on which see below pp. 235, 238).

117. Kehl, *Christushymnus*, p. 106.

118. The parallel line in the original hymn (v. 16e) and the parallel with Ps. 104.24 (see also those cited above p. 165) lead me to understand the ἐν in an instrumental rather than local sense (see particularly Lohse, *Kolosser*, p. 90 n. 4 – ET, p. 50, n. 129). But even if we understood ἐν in a local sense (see particularly Schweizer, *Kolosser*, pp. 60f.) we are still in the realm of Hellenistic-Jewish thought concerning divine Wisdom and the divine Logos, since it is precisely part of the ambivalence of the Logos in Philo that it is both instrument (e.g. *Leg. All.* III.95f.) and 'place' of God's creative activity (*Opif.* 20). See also A. Feuillet, 'La Creation de l'Univers "dans le Christ" d'après l'Epitre aux Colossiens (1.16a)', *NTS* 12, 1965–66, pp. 1–9; also *Sagesse*, pp. 202–10. There is no need to hypothesize a pre-Christian Primal Man myth to explain the language here (against F. B. Craddock, ' "All Things in Him": A Critical Note on Col. 1.15–20', *NTS* 12, 1965–66, pp. 78–80; and the broader thesis of H. M. Schenke, 'Der Widerstreit gnostischer und kirchlicher Christologie im Spiegel des Kolosserbriefes', *ZTK* 61, 1964, pp. 391–403, that in Col. one gnostic christology opposes another); see further below n. 119 and above p. 99.

119. That the hymn originated in Christian circles is clearly indicated by the

first line of the second strophe – as most now recognize (against E. Käsemann, 'A Primitive Christian Baptismal Liturgy' (1949), *ENTT*, pp. 154–9).

120. The perfect tense of v. 16e (ἔκτισται) may also perhaps be taken as indicating that the thought is on the continuing relation between Christ and the cosmos in the present rather than on the act of creation in the past.

121. In a somewhat similar way it could be said of one of Britain's Prime Ministers: Prime Minister Wilson studied economics at Oxford. No one misunderstands the phrase to mean that Harold Wilson was already Prime Minister when he was at Oxford (though that is the most 'natural' meaning of the sentence). Each one who reads it, consciously or unconsciously, interprets it as saying (in more precise language): Harold Wilson, who later became Prime Minister, studied economics at Oxford. Paul's readers could obviously make the same paraphrase without difficulty: By wisdom, that later 'became' Christ Jesus, all things were created.

122. Cf. Kehl, *Christushymnus*, p. 106.

123. So C. F. D. Moule, *Colossians and Philemon*, Cambridge University Press, 1957, pp. 66f.; Schweizer, *Kolosser*, pp. 61f.

124. So Lohse, *Kolosser*, p. 92 (ET, pp. 52); Caird, *Letters*: 'not a statement about remote antiquity, but about the absolute and universal priority of Christ' (p. 179).

125. See Dupont, *Gnosis*, pp. 431–5; Schweizer, *TDNT* VII, pp. 1029f., 1037f.; Lohse, *Kolosser*, pp. 93f. (ET, pp. 53f.).

126. See further Hegermann, *Schöpfungsmittler*, pp. 58–67; and note Lohse, *Kolosser*, p. 94 n. 8 (ET, p.54n.160).

127. Schweizer, *Kolosser*, p. 62.

128. On πρωτεύων see Arndt & Gingrich, πρωτεύω ; Michaelis, *TDNT* VI, p. 882.

129. The fullest listing is in Burger, *Schöpfung*, pp. 15f.

130. See J. Ernst, *Pleroma und Pleroma Christi*, 1970, Kap. 6.

131. Cf. Ps. 68.17 (LXX 67.17); 132.13f. (LXX 131.13f.); Targum on I Kings 8.27 and on Ps. 68.17 (see further Ernst, *Pleroma*, p. 85; Lohse, *Kolosser*, pp. 99f. (ET, p. 58).

132. See particularly Moule, *Colossians*, pp. 70f., 164–9; Ernst, *Pleroma*, particularly pp. 83–7; 'If the original hymn speaks of the Pleroma, then it means thereby God himself . . .' (pp. 86f.).

133. P. Benoit, 'Body, Head and *Pleroma* in the Epistles of the Captivity', *RB* 63, 1956, ET *Jesus and the Gospel*, Vol. 2, 1974, p. 81.

134. Benoit, '*Pleroma*', pp. 82f.; see also Dupont, *Gnosis*, pp. 454–68; Ernst, *Pleroma*, Kap. 2.

135. Benoit, '*Pleroma*', p. 85; cf. H. Langkammer, 'Die Einwohnung der "absoluten Seinsfülle" in Christus: Bemerkungen zu Kol. 1.19', *BZ* 12, 1968, pp. 258–63.

136. See furtner Ernst, *Pleroma*, Kap. 3. G. Münderlein, 'Die Erwählung durch des Pleroma: Bemerkungen zu Kol. 1.19', *NTS* 8, 1961–62, pp. 264–76, suggests a reference to Jesus' baptism and finds in πλήρωμα here 'a remarkable paraphrase of the Holy Spirit' (p. 272; cf. Kehl, *Christushymnus*, pp. 120–5); but while understanding of the Spirit as the power of God manifested in the world is certainly part of this whole way of thinking (see above pp. 133f.), it is less likely that a specific allusion to the Spirit is intended here.

137. For the wisdom associations of πλήρωμα see further Feuillet, *Sagesse*, pp. 236–8.

138. That Col. 2.9 should not be interpreted solely in reference to the earthly Jesus (the incarnation) is indicated by the present tense ('dwells' – κατοικεῖ) and the context (cf. Ernst, *Pleroma*, particularly pp. 169–72).

139. Cf. Philo, *Cher.* 125 – πρὸς γὰρ τήν τινος γένεσιν πολλὰ δεῖ συνελθεῖν, τὸ ὑφ' οὗ, τὸ ἐξ οὗ, τὸ δι' οὗ, τὸ δι' ὅ.

140. Schweizer: 'Col. 1.15–18a knows that one can understand the creative activity of God only by reference to Christ. A God who does not have the face of Christ would not actually be God' (*Kolosser*, p. 63).

141. Cf. Davies, *Paul*, pp. 147–55, 168–75.

142. On the differences between Matthew and Luke see H. Schürmann, *Lukas*, Herder 1969, I, pp. 423–8; S. Schulz, *Q: die Spruchquelle der Evangelisten*, 1972, pp. 379f.; Marshall, *Gospel*, pp. 299–304. For a possibly illuminating rabbinic parallel see D. Zeller, 'Die Bildlogik des Gleichnisses Matt. 11.16f./Luke 7.31f.', *ZNW* 68, 1977, pp. 252–7.

143. See e.g. Christ, *Jesus Sophia*, pp. 75f.; M. J. Suggs, *Wisdom, Christology and Law in Matthew's Gospel*, 1970, pp. 35 n.9, 37, 56f.; Schulz, *Q*, p. 380 and n. 18; G. N. Stanton, 'On the Christology of Q', *CSNT*, p. 36.

144. Suggs, *Wisdom*, pp. 57f.; Stanton, *CSNT*, p. 36; E. Schweizer, *Matthäus*, NTD 1973, pp. 172, 292; H. Conzelmann, *IDBS*, p. 958. M. D. Johnson, 'Reflections on a wisdom approach to Matthew's Christology', *CBQ* 36, 1974, pp. 44–64, in his critique of Suggs does not give enough weight to the double redaction of 11.2 and 11.19 (pp. 57f.).

145. A. Harnack, *The Sayings of Jesus*, 1970, ET Williams & Norgate 1908, p. 19; Christ, *Jesus Sophia*, p. 79; Schürmann, *Lukas*, pp. 427f.; P. Hoffmann, *Studien zur Theologie der Logienquelle*, 1972, p. 197; Schulz, *Q*, p. 380; O. Linton, 'The Parable of the Children's Game', *NTS* 22, 1975–76, p. 165.

146. Suggs, *Wisdom*, pp. 35, 44; Hamerton-Kelly, *Pre-existence*, pp. 30f.; R. A. Edwards, *A Theology of Q*, 1976, p. 99.

147. For Wisdom's children, cf. particularly Prov. 8.32; Sir. 4.11 – a Wisdom motif (Feuillet, 'Jesus et Sagesse', p. 166).

148. D. Lührmann, *Die Redaktion der Logienquelle*, Neukirchen 1969, pp. 29f.

149. Wilckens, *Weisheit*, pp. 197f.; also *TDNT* VII, p. 516; Schweizer, *Matthäus*, p. 292; Schulz, *Q*, p. 386; J. M. Robinson, 'Jesus as Sophos and Sophia: Wisdom Tradition and the Gospels', *AWJEC*, pp. 5f.; Marshall, *Gospel*, p. 304.

150. Smith, *Wisdom Christology*, p. 55; Stanton, *CSNT*, pp. 36f.; against Christ, *Jesus Sophia*, who argues implausibly that Jesus appears in the Q version 'simultaneously as bearer of wisdom and as Wisdom herself' (pp. 73–5).

151. See e.g. G. Barth, in G. Barth, G. Bornkamm and H. J. Held, *Tradition and Interpretation in Matthew*, 1960, ET SCM Press 1963, p. 103 n. 1; van Iersel, *Sohn*, pp. 148f.; H. D. Betz, 'The Logion of the Easy Yoke and of Rest (Matt. 11.28–30)', *JBL* 86, 1967, pp. 19f.; Suggs, *Wisdom*, pp. 79f.; Hill, *Matthew*, p. 204. Most recent studies of Q (Hoffmann, Schulz, Stanton, Edwards, A. Polag, *Die Christologie der Logienquelle*, Neukirchen 1977; also *Fragmenta Q*) reject or ignore the possibility of Matt. 11.28–30 being part of Q.

152. For discussion of the text of Q see those cited in Schulz, *Q*, pp. 213f. and Dunn, *Jesus*, p. 367 n. 78.

153. See particularly the parallels cited by Christ, *Jesus Sophia*, pp. 82–91.

154. Lührmann, *Redaktion*, p. 99; Suggs, *Wisdom*, p. 96; Stanton, *CSNT*, p. 37; Schweizer, *Matthäus*, p. 292; against Wilckens, *TDNT* VII, pp. 515–17, 519.

155. Christ, *Jesus Sophia*, pp. 88f. (the passages in the text are those cited by him); Schulz, *Q*, pp. 224f.; Robinson, 'Jesus as Sophos', pp. 9f.; cf. Conzelmann, *IDBS*, p. 958.

156. Schweizer, *TDNT* VIII, pp. 372f.; Schulz, *Q*, pp. 222f. On the apocalyptic character of 11.25f. see Schulz, *Q*, pp. 216–20 with those cited there.

157. Christ, *Jesus Sophia*, p. 90.

158. Cf. Schweizer, *TDNT* VIII, p. 373.

159. Cf. Bultmann, *TDNT* I, p. 698; Dodd, *Interpretation*, p. 90. For broader parallels in the Dead Sea Scrolls see W. D. Davies, ' "Knowledge" in the Dead Sea Scrolls and Matt. 11.25–30', *HTR* 46, 1953, reprinted in *Christian Origins and Judaism*, Darton, Longman and Todd 1962, pp. 119–44.

160. Suggs, *Wisdom*, pp. 91f.

161. See particularly Jeremias, *Theology* I, pp. 35f., 250–5. See also above p. 26.

162. See also Jeremias, *Theology*, on Matt. 5.17 (pp. 82–5).

163. See Dunn, *Unity*, pp. 166f.

164. See Dunn, *Jesus*, pp. 26–34. Cf. Hill, *Matthew*, who regards Matt. 11.27/ Luke 10.22 as 'the intermediate stage' in the development from the *abba* of Jesus' own words to the Johannine theology of the Son (p. 207); and above pp. 28f.

165. Smith, *Wisdom Christology*, pp. 40f.; Suggs, *Wisdom*: 'No *sophos* invites men to take his yoke; rather he counsels men to accept the yoke of Sophia. The *sophos* promises that men will find rest; only Sophia can promise to give rest' (pp. 99f.); and see further pp. 99–108. Johnson's response on this point is inadequate ('Reflections', p. 60f.). See also above n. 154.

166. RSV, NEB and NIV end the quotation from 'the Wisdom of God' at this point. JB continues it to the middle of v. 51.

167. See Schulz, *Q*, pp. 336–9 and those cited by him.

168. Schulz, *Q*, p. 336 and those cited by him in n. 96; also E. E. Ellis, *Luke*, p. 171; Suggs, *Wisdom*, p. 14; Hill, *Matthew*, p. 314; Stanton, *CSNT*, p. 37; Robinson, 'Jesus as Sophos', p. 11; Marshall, *Gospel*, p. 502.

169. Bultmann, *Tradition*, p. 114; Suggs, *Wisdom*, pp. 18–20; see also those cited by Schulz, *Q*, p. 341 n. 145.

170. Cf. E. E. Ellis, 'Luke 11.49–51: an Oracle of a Christian Prophet?', *ExpT* 74, 1962–63, pp. 157f.; also *Luke*, pp. 170–3; Hoffmann, *Studien*, pp. 166–71; Schulz, *Q*, p. 341.

171. Cf. Steck, *Israel*, pp. 99–105, 222–7.

172. Within a Wisdom tradition passages like Jer. 7.25f. and 25.4–7 might readily be ascribed to Wisdom (cf. Wisd. 10–11). On whether 'apostles' is an addition to the original saying, see the discussion in Suggs, *Wisdom*, pp. 22–4. Marshall follows G. Klein, 'Die Verfolgung der Apostel: Lukas 11.49', *NTGOC*, pp. 113–24, in arguing that Matthew's text is original at this point (*Gospel*, pp. 504f.). But see also Schulz, *Q*, pp. 336f. For other composite quotations see Matt. 2.23, John 7.38, I Cor. 2.9 and James 4.5 (Dunn, *Unity*, p. 93).

173. Suggs, *Wisdom*, pp. 27f.; Hamerton-Kelly, *Pre-existence*, pp. 31f.

174. Against Christ, *Jesus Sophia*, p. 130.

175. Suggs, *Wisdom*, pp. 58–61; Smith, *Wisdom Christology*, p. 75; Stanton, *CSNT*, p. 37.

176. Cf. e.g. Smith, *Wisdom Christology*, p. 100; Schulz, *Q*, p. 336; Marshall, *Gospel*, p. 504; otherwise Hamerton-Kelly, *Pre-existence*, pp. 68–70. We may compare Matt. 18.20, where Jesus' (risen) presence in the community of his disciples can be closely paralleled to Aboth 3.2: 'If two sit together and words of the Law (are spoken) between them, then the Shekinah rests between them.'

177. That Matthew was written in the period following AD 70, when rabbinic Judaism and Jewish Christianity became more hostile, is implied by Matt. 23 in particular, and widely agreed among commentators; see e.g. Kümmel, *Introduction*, pp. 119f.

178. For details see Schulz, *Q*, pp. 346f.

179. So Bultmann, *Tradition*, pp. 114f.; Steck, *Israel*, pp. 230–3; Christ, *Jesus Sophia*, pp. 138–48; Suggs, *Wisdom*, pp. 66–70; Schulz, *Q*, pp. 349 n. 194, 351–6; Conzelmann, *IDBS*, p. 958. Suggs (p. 67) and Schulz (p. 352) argue that Q would not have identified Jesus with Wisdom in this passage – in Suggs' case presumably because it would clash with his thesis that Matthew was the first (within the Synoptic tradition) to identify Jesus with Wisdom. But if the speaker here was so obviously divine *Wisdom*, then Q could hardly include the logion within a collection of the sayings of *Jesus* without making the identification (as Wilckens, *TDNT* VII, p. 515, and Johnson, 'Reflections', pp. 58f., have noted).

180. So e.g. Bultmann, *Tradition*, pp. 114f.; Suggs, *Wisdom*, pp. 64–6; Robinson, 'Jesus as Sophos', p. 13.

181. Cf. Manson, *Sayings*, p. 102; E. Haenchen, 'Matthäus 23', *ZTK* 48, 1951, p. 47, reprinted *GMEH*, p. 47; W. G. Kümmel, *Promise and Fulfilment*, ³1956, ET SCM Press ²1961, pp. 80f.

182. See the discussion in Schulz, *Q*, p. 347 n. 184.

183. Cf. Manson, *Sayings*: 'This text cannot be pressed. It says, "How often have I longed", not "how often have I tried". And we cannot be certain that "Jerusalem" is to be taken literally' (p. 127).

184. See also II Bar. 41.4; II Ezra/Esdras (or V Ezra) 1.30; *Lev. Rab.* 25; see further Strack-Billerbeck I, pp. 927, 943.

185. Kümmel, *Promise*, pp. 79–82; Stanton, *CSNT*, pp. 37f.; Marshall, *Gospel*, p. 574; cf. Hoffmann, *Studien*, pp. 174f.

186. See particularly Hoffmann, *Studien*, pp. 174–8; also Schulz, *Q*, pp.357–60; cf. N. Perrin, 'Wisdom and Apocalyptic in the Message of Jesus', *SBL Seminar Papers 1972*, Vol. 2 pp. 543–72; W. Grundmann, 'Weisheit im Horizont des Reiches Gottes: Eine Studie zur Verkündigung Jesu nach der Spruchüberlieferung Q', *KAHS*, pp. 175–99.

187. This suggestion is strengthened by Matthew's addition ἀπ' ἄρτι ('you will not see me *any more/again*') – see Schulz, *Q*, pp. 346f. See also the consideration stemming from Matthew's understanding of the virginal conception of Jesus (above pp. 49f.).

188. Cf. Matthew's redaction of Mark as instanced by G. M. Styler, 'Stages in Christology in the Synoptic Gospels', *NTS* 10, 1963–64, pp. 404–6.

189. J. M. Robinson, '*Logoi Sophōn*: on the *Gattung* of Q', *FRPRB*, pp. 84–130. Though see also Dunn, *Unity*, §62.

190. See Bultmann, *Tradition*, pp. 69–108; Edwards, *Q*, ch. V.

191. Here we agree with those cited above in n. 154; also Smith, *Wisdom Christology*. The account of Jesus' rejection in Nazareth (Mark 6.1–6), even with the mention of his wisdom in 6.2, hardly counts as evidence enough to indicate

the presence of 'the Wisdom myth' in Mark (against Hamerton-Kelly, *Pre-existence*, p. 52).

192. Contrast the implication of the possible parallel between Luke 2.41-52 and Sir. 51.13-17 (cf. H. J. de Jonge, 'Sonship, Wisdom, Infancy: Luke 2.41-51a', *NTS* 24, 1977-78, p. 348).

193. Cf. Conzelmann, *IDBS*: 'It is certain that Jesus was himself a teacher of wisdom. Were this not the case, the volume of wisdom in the Christian tradition would be inexplicable' (p. 958).

194. See particularly Deichgräber, *Gotteshymnus*, pp. 137-40; Wengst, *Formeln*, pp. 166-70; Zimmermann, *Bekenntnis*, pp. 53-60. The hymn is usually confined to v. 3 – but the content of v. 2b is wholly of a piece with v. 3a and matches closely the hymnic content of Col. 1.15-17 (see p. 207); the relative clauses of v. 2b fit as well to v. 3a as the aorist participle of v. 3b which introduces a significant shift in thought that runs on with much less of a break into v. 4 (Deichgräber p. 137 n. 3, suggests that something, a statement regarding incarnation perhaps, has been omitted between vv. 3 and 4; but Col. 1.15-20 provides a closer parallel than Phil. 2.6-11); and v. 3b introduces the distinctive high priestly christology of Hebrews (cf. Hofius, 'Phil. 2.6-11', p. 84). For the whole section see also E. Grässer, 'Hebräer 1.1-4: Ein exegetisch Versuch', EKK *Vorarbeiten*, Heft 3, 1971, pp. 55-91.

195. Image and stamp (εἰκών and χαρακτήρ) are quite close in meaning (Michel, *Hebräer*, p. 98; Bruce, *Hebrews*, p. 6).

196. See particularly J. D. Hester, *Paul's Concept of Inheritance*, *SJT* Occasional Papers 14, 1968.

197. See particularly Williamson, *Philo and Hebrews*, pp. 36-41, 74-80, 95-103.

198. Cf. also Hofius, 'Phil. 2.6-11', pp. 81-3.

199. 'One may not distinguish between ῥῆμα as the word of creation and λόγος as the word of revelation in Hebrews' (Michel, *Hebräer*, p. 100 n. 2).

200. Cf. F. Büchsel, *TDNT* IV: 'He is the reflection of God's glory and image of his nature (1.3) only in personal fellowship with God. This is not stated in 1.3, but it can hardly be contested, since in 1.5 he is the Son of God in virtue of the Word of God addressed to him. If his divine sonship were a natural or substantial relation to God, it would hardly be possible to refer a saying like Ps. 2.7 to him' (p. 339 n. 5).

201. Hofius seeks to explain the tension on the parallel of Israel's talk of Yahweh as both king already and becoming king (cf. Ps. 47.7 with Zech. 14.9; Isa. 6.3 with Ps. 72.19) ('Phil. 2.6-11'; pp. 93f.); but while the parallel illuminates something of the eschatological dimension in Hebrews, the pre-existence language in 1.2f. belongs more to the Wisdom and Platonic side of Hebrews thought.

202. J. Hering, *Hebrews*, CNT 1954, ET Epworth 1970, p. 3; cf. Michel, *Hebräer*, p. 94 n. 1. H. Langkammer draws attention to the salvation-history connection between this phrase and Gen. 17.5 (' "Den er zum Erben von allem *eingesetzt* hat" (Heb. 1.2)', *BZ* 10, 1966, pp. 273-80).

203. This glory is 'God's mode of appearance (Ex. 24.16; 33.18ff.; 40.34)' (Michel, *Hebräer*, p. 98 n. 3).

204. On ὑπόστασις ('very being') see H. Köster, *TDNT* VIII, p. 585.

205. Cf. U. Wilckens, *TDNT* IX, p. 422; Michel, *Hebräer*, p. 99. See also above II n. 215.

206. Cf. Knox, *Gentiles*, p. 178; Robinson, *Human Face*, p. 179.

Chapter VII   The Word of God

1. Kelly, *Doctrines*, pp. 95–101.
2. Cf. the famous comment of Augustine: 'In them (some of the books of the Platonists) I read – not, of course, word for word, though the sense was the same and it was supported by all kinds of different arguments – that "at the beginning of time the Word already was; and God had the Word abiding with him, and the Word was God. . . . And the light shines in darkness, a darkness which was not able to master it". I read too that the soul of man, although it "bears witness of the light, is not the Light". But the Word, who is himself God, "is the true Light, which enlightens every soul born into the world. He, through whom the world was made, was in the world, and the world treated him as a stranger". But I did not find it written in those books that "he came to what was his own, and they who were his own gave him no welcome. But all those who did welcome him he empowered to become the children of God, all those who believe in his name". In the same books I also read of the Word, God, that his "birth came not from human stock, not from nature's will or man's, but from God". But I did not read in them that "the Word was made flesh and came to dwell among us" ' (*Confessions* VII.9 – following the translation by R. S. Pine-Coffin in Penguin Classics 1961).
3. Kelly, *Doctrines*, pp. 102, 106; other references in T. E. Pollard, *Johannine Christology and the Early Church*, 1970, pp. 40, 48; see further G. Kretschmar, *Studien zur frühchristlichen Trinitätstheologie*, 1956, pp. 27–61.
4. Kelly, *Doctrines*, pp. 97, 111.
5. On the Patristic use of Wisdom see also H. Jaeger, 'The Patristic Conception of Wisdom in the Light of Biblical and Rabbinical Research', *SP* IV, 1961, pp. 90–106, who rightly warns against a too casual and uncritical use of the slogan 'wisdom speculation' over our whole period (p. 91).
6. Cf. e.g. Grillmeier, *Christ*, pp. 108–13, 135, 173; A. Heron, ' "Logos, Image, Son": Some Models and Paradigms in early Christology', *Creation Christ and Culture*, 1976, pp. 43–62.
7. Cf. Harnack, *History of Dogma*, Vol. III, pp. 140–4, 290–5.
8. Grillmeier, *Christ*, pp. 230, 267.
9. Kelly, *Creeds*, pp. 182, 190f.
10. See Pollard, *Johannine Christology*.
11. Still one of the fullest and most useful treatments is by J. Drummond, *Philo Judaeus*, 2 vols., 1888. On the Greek and Hellenistic background see also H. Kleinknecht, *TDNT* IV, pp. 77–91. Parallels between John 1.1–18 and Heraclitus are listed most recently by B. Jendorff, *Der Logosbegriff*, 1976, pp. 75–84. The Targum's *Memra* (see above p. 130 and n.6) has been re-introduced into the discussion of possible backgrounds to the Logos poem of John 1 in the light of Targ. Neofiti's use of *Memra* in Gen. 1; see most recently C. T. R. Hayward, 'The Holy Name of the God of Moses and the Prologue of St John's Gospel', *NTS* 25, 1978–79, pp. 16–32. But J. A. Fitzmyer continues to urge caution in view of the evidence of 11Q tg Job ('The Aramaic Language and the Study of the New Testament', *JBL* 99, 1980, pp. 19f.).
12. See e.g. Cullmann, *Christology*, pp. 251–8; Sidebottom, *Christ*, chs. 3–4; J. N. Sanders, 'Word', *IDB* IV, p. 870; J. Jeremias, 'Zum Logos-Problem', *ZNW* 59, 1968, pp. 82–5; R. Kysar, *The Fourth Evangelist and his Gospel*, 1975, pp. 107–11; and see above pp. 164f.

13. Bultmann, *John*, pp. 20–31.

14. According to R. H. Fuller, Bultmann himself readily admitted that his chief 'evidence' for his theory of a pre-Christian Gnostic redeemer myth lies in the Johannine discourses themselves (R. H. Fuller, *The New Testament in Current Study*, SCM Press 1963, p. 136 and n.1). But Bultmann's hypothesis of a Gnostic discourse source lying behind the Fourth Gospel has met with little acceptance (see e.g. D. M. Smith, *The Composition and Order of the Fourth Gospel*, Yale 1965, ch. 2; B. Lindars, *Behind the Fourth Gospel*, SPCK 1971, pp. 20–6).

15. S. Schulz, *Johannes*, NTD 1972, p. 28. See also his earlier *Komposition und Herkunft der johanneischen Reden*, 1960, pp. 7–69.

16. Sanders, *Hymns*, pp. 29–57, 96f. Cf. E. S. Fiorenza's thesis of 'a trajectory of "reflective mythology" in Hellenistic Judaism and Gnosticism' ('Wisdom Mythology and the Christological Hymns of the New Testament', *AWJEC*, pp. 17–41).

17. Schulz's addition 'influenced by Gnosis' begs the question of whether and in what sense we can speak of a pre-Christian Gnosis. See also M. Rissi, 'Die Logoslieder im Prolog des vierten Evangeliums', *TZ* 31, 1975, pp. 324f., with further bibliography in n. 21. I observe here the distinctions recommended by U. Bianchi (ed.), *Le Origini dello Gnosticismo*, Leiden 1967, pp. xxviff. The recent suggestion that the Nag Hammadi codex, *Trimorphic Protennoia* (XII.35.1 – 50.24, particularly 46–50), provides evidence of a (Gnostic) *Vorlage* for the Johannine prologue (referred to by Yamauchi, *Church History* 48, 1979, p. 141 n.71) is difficult either to substantiate or to disprove; on the evidence of the text alone it is as likely that the Johannine prologue provides the *Vorlage* for the (subsequent) Gnostic document.

18. O. Grether, *Name und Wort Gottes im Alten Testament*, 1934, p. 77; B. Klappert, 'Word', *NIDNTT* III, p. 1087.

19. See further W. H. Schmidt, *TDOT* III, pp. 111–14.

20. See particularly L. Dürr, *Die Wertung des göttlichen Wortes im Alten Testament und im Antiken Orient*, 1938, pp. 122–8; Ringgren, *Word*, pp. 157–64; Pfeifer, *Ursprung*, pp. 34f., 44, 72f.; the most recent discussion is in Schmidt, *TDOT* III, pp. 120–5.

21. The LXX renders Hab. 3.5, 'before him went pestilence (*deber* = plague)', as 'Before him will go logos (*dābār* = word)'; see Jeremias, 'Logos-Problem', pp. 83f.

22. R. Bultmann, 'The Concept of the Word of God in the New Testament' (1933), ET *Faith and Understanding*, 1969, pp. 286–90; also *John*, pp. 21f.

23. Moore, *Judaism* I, p. 415. See further Hamp, '*Wort*', pp. 129–36; Weiss, *Untersuchungen*, pp. 219–34.

24. Sidebottom, *Christ*: 'In Sir. 24.3, Prov. 2.6, Wisdom comes from God's mouth and is presumably therefore regarded as his Word' (p. 31).

25. For Logos = Wisdom in Philo see above VI n. 34; and for the overlap between Logos and Spirit see above V n. 31 (Wilckens, *Weisheit*, pp. 158f. refers also to *Gig.* 47, 53–6; *Heres* 264f.).

26. Cf. Isaac's insightful comment: 'Logical contradictions are often a feature of writing which employs the literary device of personification, because, as a technique, it is not primarily intended as a vehicle for philosophical logic and authors are not averse to sacrificing such logic in the interests of dramatic effect' (*Spirit*, p. 53). Cf. also L. R. Farnell's protest against regarding epithets applied

to deities in Greek religion as evidence of belief in 'Sonder-Götter' (*Greek Hero Cults and Ideas of Immortality*, 1921, ch. IV).

27. See G. Mayer, *Index Philoneus*, 1974, λόγος, plus index of R. Marcus, *Philo Supplement*, Loeb 1953, 'Logos' and 'Speech' (Vol. II, pp. 293f., 303).

28. Dey, *Intermediary World*, p. 15. In the passages quoted I follow the translation of the Loeb edition for convenience.

29. Cambridge University Press 1967, ed. A. H. Armstrong, Part I by P. Merlan – presumably in part at least an editorial decision since a chapter is devoted to Philo in Part II, 'Philo and the Beginnings of Christian Thought', by H. Chadwick.

30. Particularly the synthesis whereby the (Platonic) 'ideas' are understood as thought/plans in the mind of the maker (see below pp. 224f.); see A. H. Armstrong and R. A. Markus, *Christian Faith and Greek Philosophy*, Darton, Longman & Todd 1960, pp. 16f.; Chadwick, 'Philo', p. 142 and n. 13, who cites Seneca, *Ep.* 58.18f.; 65.7.

31. Cf. Goodenough, 'Wolfson's *Philo*', *JBL* 67, 1948: '. . . the religious point of view of the author of each document which survives from the period must be reconstructed out of that document itself, and its relation to any other document or tradition is the end, not the beginning of our search' (p. 98f.).

32. See e.g. A. H Armstrong, *An Introduction to Ancient Philosophy*, Methuen 1947, pp. 36–40.

33. See further Mayer, *Index*, ἀρχέτυπος, ἰδέα.

34. See further Wolfson, *Philo* I, pp. 181f., 204–17.

35. See e.g. Kleinknecht, *TDNT* IV, pp. 84f.; Armstrong, *Introduction*, pp. 119–29.

36. See also Drummond, *Philo* II, pp. 165–70; M. Pohlenz, *Die Stoa*, 1948, Vol. I, pp. 369–78; E. Bréhier, *Les idées philosophiques et religieuses de Philon d'Alexandrie*, ³1950, pp. 83–111; F. H. Colson speaks of 'a vast amount of Stoicism in Philo' (*Philo*, Loeb edition, I, p. xviii).

37. See Vol. X of *Philo* (Loeb edition) pp. 379–90; and *Philo Supplement* Vol. II, p. 295; Goodenough, *Light*, chs. VII and VIII.

38. See Goodenough, *Light*, chs. II and III, particularly pp. 72–85; Weiss, *Untersuchungen*, pp. 275–82; and especially the discussion by V. Nikiprowetzky, *Le Commentaire de l'Écriture chez Philon d'Alexandrie*, Leiden 1977, ch. V. For the influence of Jewish wisdom literature on Philo see also J. Laporte, 'Philo in the Tradition of Biblical Wisdom Literature', *AWJEC*, pp. 103–41.

39. Cf. the discussion in Wolfson, *Philo* I, 200–17.

40. See also Wolfson, *Philo* I, pp. 327f.; Goodenough, *Light*, pp. 93f., 108f.

41. See also *Det.* 66; *Migr.* 12; *Fuga* 90–2; *Mut.* 69; *Mos.* II. 127–9; *Qu.Gen.* IV.90; *Qu.Ex.* II.111; also Mayer, *Index*, ἐνδιάθετος, προφορά, προφορικός. For examples of Stoic usage see Liddell & Scott, προφορικός.

42. F. H. Colson, *Philo* II, p. 503.

43. Cf. E. R. Goodenough, *An Introduction to Philo Judaeus*, Blackwell 1940, ²1962: 'Logos means primarily the formulation and expression of thought in speech' (p. 103); Wolfson, *Philo* – Logos 'is not only a mind capable of thinking; it is also a mind always in the act of thinking' (I, p. 233); C. H. Dodd, *Johannine Epistles*, Moffatt 1946 – '*Logos* as "word" is not mere speech, but rational speech; not mere utterance, but the utterance of a meaning; and *logos* as "reason" is not the reasoning faculty, but a rational content of thought, articulate and fit for

utterance; the meaning which a word expresses' (p. 4; see also *Interpretation*, p. 263).

44. See further Drummond, *Philo* II, pp. 171–82; Goodenough, *Light*, pp. 100–5, 116f.

45. Cf. Drummond, *Philo* II, pp. 161–4; L. Cohn, 'Zur Lehre vom Logos bei Philo', *Judaica: Festschrift für H. Cohen*, 1912, pp. 321f.; Wolfson, *Philo*: Logos = the ideas and the powers 'as a totality' (I, pp. 184, 226f.); D. E. Gershenson, 'Logos', *Enc. Jud.*: 'it is the most inclusive expression of the thoughts and ideas of God' (Vol. II, col. 462).

46. Weiss, *Untersuchungen*, pp. 272–5; cf. Drummond, who defines the Logos as 'the rational energy of God acting within the realms of time and space' (*Philo* II, p. 200).

47. See further Drummond, *Philo* II, pp. 88–132, 217–22; Goodenough, *Light*, pp. 23–37, 108, and the summary statement on p. 243: 'These powers have not distinct existence, but are only aspects of the single nature and activity of God' (p. 26; cf. pp. 45, 64, 135); Knox, *Gentiles*, pp. 50–3; against Pfeifer, *Ursprung*, pp. 53–7.

48. Wolfson's analysis of Philo's Logos as having 'two stages of existence prior to the creation of the sensible world' (*Philo* I, p. 239, also pp. 287–9) is too clinical, and does not take sufficient account of the fluidity and flexibility of Philo's thought at this point (see further above p. 225 and below pp. 227f.). Note the difficulty he has with *Opif.* on this count (I, p. 245).

49. Cf. Drummond, *Philo* II, pp. 90–6; Hegermann, *Schöpfungsmittler*: 'der Logos als Theophanieträger' (pp. 67–87); E. Mühlenberg, 'Das Problem der Offenbarung in Philo von Alexandrien', *ZNW* 64, 1973, pp. 1–18.

50. Goodenough, *Light*; Y. Amir, 'Philo Judaeus', *Enc.Jud.* Vol. 13, cols. 411–15; Carlston, 'Vocabulary of Perfection', *UDNTT*, p. 145; cf. Hegermann, *Schöpfungsmittler*, pp. 21–6.

51. Note particularly the comment of Drummond on *Heres* 205 (*Philo* II, pp. 236f.), cited also by Williamson, *Philo and Hebrews*, pp. 425f.

52. See the discussion in Wolfson, *Philo* I, pp. 261–82.

53. *Leg. All.* III. 177; *Cher.* 3,35; *Agr.* 51f.; *Fuga* 5; *Qu.Gen.* IV. 91; *Qu.Ex.* II.13, cf. *Immut.* 182; *Som.* I.115, 147f.

54. See also Drummond's lengthy demonstration that Philo did not regard the Logos as a distinct divine person (*Philo* II, pp. 222–73).

55. A notable exception is E. C. Hoskyns, *The Fourth Gospel*, ed. F. N. Davey, Faber & Faber 1940, ²1947, pp. 159–62.

56. See also G. Kittel, *TDNT* IV, pp. 114–18; Klappert, *NIDNTT* III, pp. 1110–14. On Rom. 10.6–10 see above §24.4.

57. 'It is to be noted – and this of absolutely decisive importance – that these statements do not rest on a concept of the "Word". If they are understood conceptually, they are wholly and hopelessly distorted. They arise, and derive their life, only from the event which is given in the person of Jesus. At the head of the train of thought sketched by the term λόγος there stands, not a concept, but the event which has taken place, and in which God declares himself, causing his word to be enacted' (Kittel, *TDNT* IV, p. 125).

58. G. Frost, 'The Word of God in the Synoptic Gospels', *SJT* 16, 1963, pp. 188–90. 'The word of God' = scripture in Mark 7.13 par.; so too probably in Luke 11.28 if authentic (if the phrase here = Jesus' preaching it would probably

have to be reckoned a mark of Lukan redaction) – see Marshall, *Gospel*, p. 481. It is widely accepted that Mark 4.14–20 pars. is a church interpretation attached to the parable of Jesus – and the absolute use of 'the word' would support that view (see particularly J. Jeremias, *The Parables of Jesus*, ⁶1962, revised ET SCM Press 1963, pp. 77–9).

59. Marshall, *Luke*, p. 160; cf. Haenchen, *Acts*, p. 98.

60. See also Dunn, *Unity*, p. 357.

61. Cf. the formal rabbinic parallel, 'service of the Torah', (Strack-Billerbeck I, pp. 527–9; II, p. 647).

62. So Hoskyns, *Fourth Gospel*, p. 160; Frost, 'Word of God', pp. 193f.; A. Feuillet, ' "Temoins oculaires et serviteurs de la parole" (Luke 1.2b)', *NovT* 15, 1973, pp. 241–59.

63. According to J. Carmignac's documentation ('Les citations de l'Ancien Testament, et spécialement des Poèmes du Serviteur, dans les Hymnes de Qumran', *RQ* 2, 1960, pp. 357–94), Ps. 107 was often alluded to – but he lists no allusion to v. 20.

64. See also Moffatt, *Hebrews*, pp. 54f.; Spicq, *Hébreux* II, pp. 88f.; Michel, *Hebräer*, pp. 200f.; Bruce, *Hebrews*, pp. 80f.; G. W. Trompf, 'The Conception of God in Hebrews 4.12–3', *StTh* 25, 1971, pp. 123–32.

65. See Dunn, *Jesus*, pp. 226f.

66. For I John see Dunn, *Baptism*, ch. XVI.

67. See further Dunn, *Unity*, p. 69.

68. See particularly Kümmel, *Introduction*, pp. 429–34.

69. See above, pp. 35, 178n.57. Cf. the somewhat ambiguous comment of K. L. Schmidt: 'in the christological passages adduced, Acts 10.42 and 17.31 as well as Rom. 1.4, the appointment of Jesus (Christ) as what he is to be must be equated with what he already is from the very beginning of the world, from all eternity in God's decree' (*TDNT* V, p. 453).

70. Whether we have here too a pre-Pauline hymn is greatly disputed; see e.g K. M. Fischer, *Tendenz und Absicht der Epheserbriefes*, Göttingen 1973, pp. 112–14; Barth, *Ephesians*, pp. 97–101.

71. The προέθετο of 1.9 could be taken either as 'set forth' (RSV; cf. Rom. 3.25); but NEB ('determined beforehand') is probably better (see C. Maurer, *TDNT* VIII, pp. 165–7).

72. Schlier, *Epheser*, p. 49; Hamerton-Kelly, *Pre-existence*, p. 180; cf. Gnilka, *Epheser*, pp. 70f.

73. Cf. the closing paragraph of Barth's discussion of pre-existence in *Ephesians*, p. 112; Caird, *Letters*, pp. 34f. To cite 'the Jewish theologoumen of the pre-existence not only of the Messiah, but also of the people and blessings of salvation' (Schlier, *Epheser*, p. 49) is to beg the question of when this became a 'Jewish theologoumen'. On the passages cited by Schlier see above pp. 70f.,§9.2. The closer parallel to our present passage is I Enoch 106.19 – 'for I know the mysteries of the holy ones; for he, the Lord, has showed me and informed me, and I have read (them) in the heavenly tablets'. Moreover, since there is no thought here of the act of creation, Col. 1.15ff. and John 1.1ff. do not present real parallels (against Steinmetz, *Protologische Heils-Zuversicht*, p. 76). Ephesians 1.20–3 speaks of the resurrection and exaltation of Christ, and however much 1.23 (cf. 2.16) may be indebted to the Greek thought of the cosmos as a gigantic body (Macroanthropos – see Schlier, *Epheser*, p. 91; and above VI nn.125f.), there is no

suggestion in the text that already a developed Primal Man myth was in view (cf. ch.IV above; see the brief review of the discussion in Barth, *Ephesians*, pp. 185f., 194f.). Similarly 2.13–18 clearly refers to Christ's atonement and not to incarnation (so most commentators – against e.g. J. L. Houlden, *Paul's Letters from Prison*, 1970, SCM Press 1977, p. 291; see particularly Barth, *Eph.*, pp. 302–4; other references to Schlier, *Eph.*, p. 135 n.1; the most recent review of the larger exegetical debate is W. Rader, *The Church and Racial Hostility: A History of Interpretation of Ephesians 2.11–22*, Tübingen 1978, particularly pp. 177–96).

74. Cf. Caird, *Letters*, pp. 34f., 38, 40f.; Schillebeeckx, *Christ*, pp. 212f. For Israel's·premundane election by God as a Jewish theologoumen see O. Hofius, ' "Erwählt vor Grundlegung der Welt" (Eph. 1.4)', *ZNW* 62, 1971, pp. 123–8; cf. III n. 61 above.

75. On Paul's use of 'mystery' see G. Bornkamm, *TDNT* IV, pp. 819–22 ('it always has an eschatological sense' in the NT – p. 822); R. E. Brown, *The Semitic Background of the Term "Mystery" in the New Testament*, from *CBQ* 20, 1958, and *Biblica* 39, 1958, and 40, 1959, reproduced as Fortress Facet Book 1968; J. Coppens, ' "Mystery" in the Theology of St Paul and its Parallels at Qumran', *Paul and Qumran*, 1968, pp. 132–58; C. C. Caragounis, *The Ephesian Mysterion: Meaning and Content*, 1977. Colossians and Ephesians are both cited here (despite the well-known doubts about the Pauline authorship particularly of the latter) since their ideas at this point are all of a piece.

76. D. Lührmann, *Das Offenbarungs-Verständnis bei Paulus und in paulinischen Gemeinden*, 1965, insists that the μυστήριον is not Christ himself, but the revelation of the mystery consists in the proclamation of the significance for salvation of the Christ-event (particularly p. 132).

77. Cf. also A. Lindemann, *Die Aufhebung der Zeit: Geschichtsverständnis und Eschatologie im Epheserbrief*, Gütersloh 1975, pp. 94–9.

78. Against Wilckens, *Weisheit*, pp. 202f.; Hamerton-Kelly, *Pre-existence*, p. 177.

79. So RSV; NEB; Barth, *Ephesians*, pp. 346f.; against Schlier, *Epheser*, p. 157; Gnilka, *Epheser*, p. 177.

80. In the Dead Sea Scrolls the Teacher of Righteousness may have regarded himself in a similar way as the embodiment of the divine mystery (IQH 5.11f., 25f.; 8.10f. – Brown, *Mystery*, pp. 26f., 56; Coppens, 'Mystery', p. 151). The parallel with the hidden Son of Man (I Enoch 48.6; 62.7 – Brown, p. 55) is less close, and the passages in question are confined to the (post-Christian) Similitudes (see above pp. §9.2).

81. Cf. N. A. Dahl, 'Formgeschichtliche Beobachtungen zur Christusverkündigung in der Gemeindepredigt', *Neutestamentliche Studien für R. Bultmann*, Berlin 1954, ET in *Jesus in the Memory of the Early Church*, 1976, pp. 32f.; Lührmann, *Offenbarung*, pp. 124f.

82. So e.g. Fuller, *Foundations*, pp. 217–9; Deichgräber, *Gotteshymnus*, p. 133; Schweizer, *Jesus*, pp. 88f.; Wengst, *Formeln*, pp. 156–64 cites I Tim. 3.16 and I Peter 1.20, 3.18, 22 as examples (together with Phil. 2.6–11) of *Weglieder* using 'the Gnostic scheme of the way of the redeemer', as one 'who appears in the earthly sphere out of divine pre-existence and then returns again into the heavenly sphere' (p. 164).

83. Kelly, *Peter and Jude*, p. 76; cf. E. Best, *I Peter*, NCB 1971, p. 71; Hamerton-Kelly, *Pre-existence*, pp. 260f.

84. See L. Goppelt, *I Petrusbrief*, KEK 1978, pp. 125f. Cf. R. Le Déaut, 'Le Targum de Gen. 22.8 et I Pet. 1.20', *RSR* 49, 1961, pp. 103–6.

85. And behind Heb. 1.2f. the broader sweep of Philonic-type thought (see above pp. 207f.).

86. Cf. Cullmann, *Christology*, p. 261.

87. Even with the second coming 'epiphany' language we should not necessarily think of God and Christ as distinct divine beings. V. Hasler, 'Epiphanie und Christologie in den Pastoralbriefen', *TZ* 33, 1977, pp. 193–209, points out the extent to which the thought is still of the manifestation of the (one) transcendent God: not least on Titus 2.13 – 'The appearance of "our Saviour Jesus Christ" as righteous judge on "that day" is not to be understood as triumphal return of the Lord, but as appearance of "the glory of the great God" ... He appears neither as identical with God, nor as a second Godhead, but is divine manifestation' (p. 201). Cf. Schillebeeckx, *Christ*, p. 296.

88. Cf. J. Jeremias, *Timotheus und Titus*, NTD 1936, pp. 23f.; R. H. Gundry, 'The Form, Meaning and Background of the Hymn Quoted in I Timothy 3.16', *AHGFFB*, pp. 209f.; Schillebeeckx, *Christ*, p. 299. It is improbable that 'manifested in the flesh' denotes 'the glorious appearances of the risen Christ' (suggested by B. Schneider, 'Κατὰ Πνεῦμα Ἁγιωσύνης (Romans 1.4)', *Biblica* 48, 1967, pp. 384f.; other references in Gundry, p. 210 n.1), despite the parallels in Luke 24.39 and Ignatius, *Smyrn.* 3.1f. Gundry also dismisses the suggestion of Stanley (*Resurrection*, p. 237) that the clause alludes 'to Christ's death in its redemptive character'.

89. Cf. M. Dibelius, *Pastoralbriefe*, HNT revised H. Conzelmann 1955, p. 51 (ET, Hermeneia, p. 63); McNamara, *Palestinian Targum*, pp. 249f. The same is true of the phrase 'came into the world' in I Tim. 1.15; see above II n.215; H. Windisch, 'Zur Christologie der Pastoralbriefe', *ZNW* 34, 1935, p. 222; cf. N. Brox, *Pastoralbriefe*, Regensburg 1969; 'The exaltation statements describe a "first time" exaltation, in the style of I Tim. 2.5, 6.13–16, II Tim. 2.8, not a return to the glory already possessed earlier (cf. John 17.5)' (p. 164).

90. Cf. R. St J. Parry, *Pastoral Epistles*, Cambridge University Press 1920, p. 51; Windisch, 'Christologie der Past.', pp. 224f.

91. Brox, *Pastoralbriefe*, p. 164; Schillebeeckx, *Christ*, pp. 296f. Many commentators however assume that both I Tim. 3.16 and Titus 1.2f. are straight assertions of Christ's pre-existence (e.g. W. Lock, *Pastorals*, ICC 1924, pp. 45, 87; E. F. Scott, *Pastorals*, Moffatt 1936, pp. 41, 93f.; C. K. Barrett, *Pastorals*, Clarendon 1963, pp. 65, 95; Hamerton-Kelly, *Pre-existence*, pp. 187–90).

92. Windisch, 'Christologie der Past.', p. 225 n. 23; cf. J. N. D. Kelly, *Pastorals*, Black 1963: 'By "his word" Paul does not in the first instance mean the pre-existent Logos, as some have assumed; this seems ruled out by the defining phrase which follows. The expression stands rather for God's purpose (that is to give eternal life to the elect) as declared in the gospel' (p. 228).

93. Knox's statement, 'The affirmation of Jesus' pre-existence was all but implicit in the affirmation of God's foreknowledge of him and was bound to have become explicit eventually, whether in a Jewish or a Greek environment' (*Humanity*, p. 10), is too much of an oversimplification. Cf. II n.236 above.

94. We need say no more here on the implicit Logos christology of Hebrews. Our study of Philo has confirmed the picture already sketched out in ch. II (§6.4), and our findings in ch. VI (§25.3) and above (p. 237) have filled out that

picture without significant modification. The parallel between Heb. 1.3 (the Son/ Wisdom upholds the universe by the word of his power – τῷ ῥήματι τῆς δυνάμεως αὐτοῦ) and 11.3 (the world was created by the word of God – ῥήματι Θεοῦ) shows how firmly the thought is still rooted in the OT concept of the creative utterance of Yahweh.

95. On the relation of I John to John see above II n. 124 and below p. 246.

96. Bibliography up to 1965 in E. Malatesta, *St John's Gospel 1920–65*, Rome 1967, pp. 49, 69–78; from 1966 to 1974 see H. Thyen, 'Aus der Literatur zum Johannesevangelium', *TR* 39, 1974, pp. 53–69, 222–52; Kysar, *Fourth Evangelist*, pp. 107–11.

97. See e.g. W. Eltester, 'Der Logos und sein Prophec', *Apophoreta: Festschrift für E. Haenchen*, 1964, pp. 109–34; M. D. Hooker, 'John the Baptist and the Johannine Prologue', *NTS* 16, 1969–70, pp. 354–8; C. K. Barrett, *The Prologue of St John's Gospel*, (1971) reprinted 1972, pp. 27–48.

98. Brown, *John*, p. 19. Gese is able to reconstruct a poetic *Vorlage* in Hebrew from which he excludes only vv. 6–8, 15 ('Johannesprolog', pp. 154–73).

99. Barrett, *Essays*: 'In 1.15 later material is actually quoted in an awkward manner which evidently presupposes that the reader of the Prologue must be familiar with the narrative that follows' (p. 44). See further particularly R. Schnackenburg, 'Logos-Hymnus und johanneischer Prolog', *BZ* 1, 1957, pp. 72–82; also *John* I, pp. 225f. The polemical thrust against those who held too high a view of the Baptist in vv. 6–8, 15 is too abrupt, too clear and yet too close to what follows the prologue (particularly 1.20, 30) to be easily explained as belonging to the original form of 1.1–18. Hooker's explanation (above n. 97) serves only to illuminate the use of the poem by the Evangelist not its original form; similarly P. von der Osten-Sacken, 'Der erste Christ. Johannes der Täufer als Schlüssel zum Prolog des vierten Evangeliums', *Theologica Viatorum* XIII, 1975–76, pp. 155–73.

100. See Brown, *John*, p. 22, for the various divisions suggested by different commentators. For subsequent bibliography see Rissi, 'Logoslieder', particularly pp. 321f. I accept that vv. 12c–13, 17–18 are probably interpretative additions by the Evangelist, as well as vv. 6–8, 15. The bracketed lines are also regarded by several as additions by the Evangelist. A set of four regular six-line stanzas is attractive, but there is the danger as always that the regularity is in the eye of the commentator rather than that of the poet. Most recently W. Schmithals, 'Der Prolog des Johannesevangeliums', *ZNW* 70, 1979, pp. 16–43, has suggested a *Vorlage* consisting of two strophes – vv. 1–5 with 12a, b, and v. 14 with v. 17a, b.

101. The punctuation in vv. 3–4 is a notorious crux. I have given both alternatives – in the quotation of John 1 at the beginning of this chapter and here. I find myself unable to decide finally between the two. For the punctuation as at the beginning of the chapter see Brown, *John*, p. 6, who refers to I. de la Potterie, 'De interpunctione et interpretatione versum Joh. 1.3–4', *Verbum Domini* 33, 1955, pp. 193–208; K. Aland, 'Eine Untersuchung zu John 1.3–4: über die Bedeutung eines Punktes', *ZNW* 59, 1968, pp. 174–209. For the punctuation as in the text at p. 240 see Barrett, *John*, pp. 156f.; Schnackenburg, *John* I, pp. 239f.

102. I say 'almost' since H. Zimmermann reconstructs a hymn which omits both vv. 1a, c and 1.14a, but only by forcing the Logos poem unnaturally to conform to the hymns in Phil. 2, Col. 1 and Heb. 1 ('Christushymnus und johanneischer Prolog', *NTKRS*, pp. 249–65; also *Jesus Christus: Geschichte und Ver-*

kündigung, 1973, ²1975, pp. 279–84). For those who separate v. 14 from the poem in vv. 1–12 see below n. 106.

103. The imperfect in all three clauses of 1.1 expresses 'continuous timeless existence' (J. H. Bernard, *John*, ICC 1928, Vol. I p. 2). Cf. Philo '. . . time there was not before there was a world. Time began either simultaneously with the world or after it . . .' (*Opif*. 26). See also Bultmann, *John*, pp. 31f.

104. The force of 'became' (ἐγένετο) cannot be weakened either by putting the emphasis on the third clause (against E. Käsemann, *The Testament of Jesus*, 1966, ET 1968, ch. II), or by attempting to deny the most obvious meaning of σάρξ ἐγένετο (against K. Berger, 'Zu "das Wort ward Fleisch" John 1.14a', *NovT* 16, 1974, pp. 161–6 – in the only real counter-parallel Berger adduces, Justin, *Dial*. 127.4, it is likely that Justin uses γίνομαι in its usual sense, 'become, be', rather than in the elsewhere unwarranted sense 'appear'; the other passages in Justin cited by Berger demonstrate the semantic range of φαίνομαι, not that of γίνομαι). I do not understand Barrett's reasoning when he argues that ἐγένετο 'cannot mean "became", since the Word continues to be the subject of further statements. . . . Perhaps ἐγένετο is used in the same sense as in v.6: the Word came on the (human) scene – as flesh, man' (*John*, p. 165; contrast Arndt & Gingrich, γίνομαι 4a). U. B. Müller, *Die Geschichte der Christologie in der johanneischen Gemeinde*, SBS 77, 1975, argues that 1.14, 16 was originally the expression of a wonder-worker christology (as in the Signs Source), pressing the possibility (cf. Berger) of understanding σάρξ ἐγένετο along the lines of Rom. 8.3 and I Tim. 3.16 (particularly pp. 22–6). But ὁ λόγος σάρξ ἐγένετο was inevitably a much more provocative phrase for a Hellenistic readership than the parallels adduced, as the Evangelist's own use of σάρξ underscores (1.13; 3.6; 6.51–6, 63; 8.15; see also below n. 118). It remains more probable that the Evangelist has taken the full point of 1.14 (the whole verse – 'became flesh' and 'we beheld his glory' – both elements being part of the *Vorlage* on Müller's reconstruction), rather than that 1.14a was an unexceptional antecedent to the affirmation of the (incarnate) Logos's manifest glory. See also G. Richter, 'Die Fleischwerdung des Logos im Johannesevangelium', *NovT* 13, 1971, pp. 87–9; Dunn, *Unity*, pp. 300f.; see also K. M. Fischer, 'Der johanneische Christus und der gnostische Erlöser', *Gnosis und Neues Testament*, 1973, pp. 262–5. H. M. Teeple, *The Literary Origin of the Gospel of John*, Evanston 1974, argues that the Logos poem is both gnostic *and* anti-docetic (p. 140)!

105. So Wiles is inaccurate when he affirms that 'incarnation, in its full and proper sense, is not something directly presented in scripture' (*Myth*, ed. Hick, p. 3).

106. That the poem originally ended at v. 11 (Sanders, *Hymns*, pp. 20–4) is most improbable: within the Wisdom tradition, which provides the nearest parallels, the hiddenness or rejection of Wisdom is usually resolved or balanced by the assertion of Wisdom's revelation or embodiment in the law (Sir. 24.23; Bar. 3.36–4.4; Wisd. 6.18). An ending after v. 12 is certainly more likely (E. Käsemann, 'The Structure and Purpose of the Prologue to John's Gospel' (1957), *NTQT*, pp. 138–67, particularly pp. 150–2; M. E. Boismard, 'Saint Luc et la rédaction du quatrième évangile (John 4.46–54)', *RB* 69, 1962, pp. 206–10; G. Richter, 'Ist ἐν ein strukturbildendes Element im Logoshymnus John 1.1ff?', *Biblica* 51, 1970, pp. 539–44, reprinted in *Studien zum Johannesevangelium*, 1977, pp. 143–8). But despite some differences between vv. 1–5, 9–12 and vv. 14, 16,

there are as many indications in vv. 14–16 of a *Vorlage* as in vv. 1–13 – particularly
the awkward insertion of v. 15, and the distinctive vocabulary (word, dwell,
grace, fullness). One could hypothesize a previous redaction in which vv. 14, 16
were added to the poem (cf. C. Demke, 'Der sogenannte Logos-Hymnus im
johanneischen Prolog', *ZNW* 58, 1967, pp. 45–68, who suggests that vv. 1, 3–5,
10–12b form a hymn used in Christian worship to 'the heavenly one', and vv. 14,
16 the community's responsive confession of the 'earthly one'; Rissi, 'Logoslieder',
pp. 321–6, who argues that vv. 1–5, 10–12b and vv. 14, 16–17 formed two separate
hymns; similarly Müller, as in n. 104 above); but that seems unnecessarily complicated and makes too much of such tensions as there are between the two parts.
Much less plausible is Richter's attempt to argue that 1.14(–18) comes from the
hand of a *later* redactor (subsequent to the writing of the main body of the
Gospel), but only at the cost of eliminating other important sections from the
Gospel as the work of the same redactor – e.g. 5.28f.; 6.51–8; 13.12–17; 15–16;
19.34f., 39f. ('Die Fleischwerdung des Logos im Johannesevangelium', *NovT* 13,
1971, pp. 81–126 and 14, 1972, pp. 257–76, reprinted in *Studien*, pp. 149–98;
similarly Thyen, *TR* 39, 1974, pp. 222–41). The hypothesis of a substantial *Vorlage*
with a christology significantly different from that imposed on it by the final
redactor involves a circularity of argument and assumptions regarding the consistency and inconsistency of the author and final editor which I find unconvincing
(cf. de Jonge, *Jesus*, pp. 198f.; also earlier pp. 117f., 186 n. 9). Cf. the implausible
reconstruction P. Hofrichter, ' "Egeneto anthropos." Text und Zusätze im
Johannesprolog', *ZNW* 70, 1979, pp. 214–37.

107. The parallels are laid out most concisely by Dodd, *Interpretation*, pp. 276f.:
'it seems certain that any reader influenced by the thought of Hellenistic Judaism,
directly or at a remove, would inevitably find suggested here a conception of the
creative and revealing λόγος in many respects similar to that of Philo; and it is
difficult not to think that the author intended this' (p. 277). In addition, we may
note something of a parallel between John 1.16 and *Post.* 145 (J. Danielou, *Philon
d'Alexandrie*, Paris 1958, p. 207). See also A. W. Argyle, 'Philo and the Fourth
Gospel', *ExpT* 63, 1951–52, pp. 385f., with response to R. McL. Wilson, 'Philo
and the Fourth Gospel', *ExpT* 65, 1953–54, pp. 47–9. Barrett plays down the
influence of Philo, on the grounds that Philo 'equates the Logos with an archetypal
Man in whose image the whole human race was made' (*John*, p. 73) – an over-
simplification of Philo's understanding of the Logos (above pp. 123f. and §28.3).

108. Contrast Wainwright, *Trinity*: 'There is no reason to suppose that a
deliberate contrast is intended' (p. 60).

109. 'For nothing mortal can be made in the likeness of the most high One
and Father of the universe but (only) in that of the second God, who is his Logos.'
Cf. Philo's naming of the two chief powers as 'God' and 'Lord' in *Qu.Ex.* II.68;
on the powers see above pp. 225f.

110. See also Bultmann, *John*, pp. 33–6; and below n. 125.

111. So too the connection between light-life, already given in the creation
story of Gen. 1 (Dodd, *Bible and Greeks*, p. 135). Cf. P. Borgen, 'Observations on
the Targumic Character of the Prologue of John', *NTS* 16, 1969–70, pp. 288–95:
'The use of the term Logos in John 1.1, 18 presupposes an exposition of Gen. 1.3
like the one evidenced in Philo, *Som.* I.75' (p. 290); also 'Logos was the True
Light', *NovT* 14, 1972, pp. 115–30; M. McNamara, 'Logos of the Fourth gospel
and Memra of the Palestinian Targum', *ExpT* 79, 1967–68, pp. 115–17.

112. See also Rissi, 'Logoslieder', p. 327f.; Gese, 'Johannesprolog', pp. 190–2. Schnackenburg draws attention particularly to IQM 13.15 – God wills 'to bring darkness low and to raise up light' (*John* I, p. 246; see also pp. 248f.).

113. Cf. Dodd, *Interpretation*, p. 277.

114. Schnackenburg excludes both vv. 5 and 12 from the Logos poem because they contain characteristic Johannine themes. But since a pre-Johannine background can be exemplified it is just as possible to argue that the Fourth Evangelist derived these themes from the same source as the Logos poem, or even through the Logos poem, in part at least. Most analyses accept v.5 as part of the pre-Johannine poem; opinion is more divided on v. 12 (see Brown, *John*, p. 22); we may note again that a pre-Johannine hymn which ended before v. 14 would almost certainly have included v. 12 (see above n. 106).

115. Cf. Gese, 'Johannesprolog', pp. 183–5; and see also Glasson on 1.9 (above II n. 215). Perhaps I Enoch 42.1f. constitutes a similar protest against the wisdom literature's identification of Wisdom with the Torah, and if so probably at about the same time (cf. U. Luck, 'Das Weltverständnis in der jüdischen Apokalyptik', *ZTK* 73, 1976, pp. 292–4). For an alternative view and the diversity of opinion on this point, see Schnackenburg, *John* I, pp. 259f. If the Logos poem did originally end with v. 12 (above n. 106), then vv. 11f. would more naturally be referred to the coming of Jesus (as by Rissi, 'Logoslieder', p. 329).

116. See references in index to *Philo*, Loeb Vol. X, pp. 387f.

117. Goodenough, *Light*, p. 8. See also above III n. 36.

118. Lindars, *John*, p. 79; cf. the 'scandalous' suggestion of John 6.53–6 (Dodd, *Interpretation*, p. 341).

119. A closer parallel is given in Od.Sol. 7.4, 12, but the Odes are Christian, of uncertain date though quite probably from the same religious environment as John, and the statement is less explicitly incarnational. On the relation between the Odes and the Fourth Gospel see particularly J. H. Charlesworth and R. A. Culpepper, 'The Odes of Solomon and the Gospel of John', *CBQ* 35, 1973, pp. 298–322. The imagery used of the 'word' in the Odes does not go beyond the scope that we find in the OT and hardly warrants talk of 'the hypostatization of the Word' (as by Sanders, *Hymns*, pp. 114–20).

120. Cf. H. Langkammer, 'Zur Herkunft des Logostitels im Johannesprolog', *BZ* 9, 1965, pp. 91–4; Goppelt, *Theologie* II: 'The *logos* of the prologue *becomes* Jesus; Jesus is the incarnate *Logos*, not the *logos* as such' (p. 634). Against Schnackenburg, *John* I, who insists on 'the personal character' of the Johannine Logos throughout, since 'the prologue (or the Logos-hymn) is orientated from the start to the incarnate Logos' (p. 233; cf. Kittel, *TDNT* IV, pp. 129, 131f., Cullmann, *Christology* – 'this pre-temporal existence of Jesus' (p. 249); H. Ridderbos, 'The Structure and Scope of the Prologue to the Gospel of John', *NovT* 8, 1966, pp. 180–201). But it by no means necessarily follows that at the pre-Johannine stage the Logos poem envisaged a *personal* Logos prior to v. 14. The parallels with the Wisdom-Logos traditions in pre-Christian Judaism tell strongly against Schnackenburg here (cf. the oddly expressed comment on p. 243 – 'Hence the Logos of Philo also takes over the same task fundamentally as the personal Logos who is God in our hymn' – almost as though the hymn preceded Philo in time). And Schnackenburg's methodological failure to keep his discussion of the pre-Johannine poem distinct from his discussion of John's use of it in relation to his Gospel is also a critical weakness.

121. Kittel rightly comments: 'The Evangelist's acquaintance with the ὁ λόγος σὰρξ ἐγένετο, is not the result of reflection on the λόγος and its personification. ... It derives from the fulfilment of ἐθεασάμεθα in this σάρξ, that is, the historical figure of Jesus.' 'This apparently speculative statement arises out of and gains its only light from, the historical process of seeing and hearing Christ in faith' (*TDNT* IV, pp. 130f.; similarly Cullmann, *Christology*, pp. 263f.).

122. That the Logos poem envisages the incarnation first at v. 14 (and not at v. 9) is widely recognized (Brown, *John*, p. 29 cites Westcott, Bernard, Boismard and Schnackenburg; see also Bultmann, *John*, pp. 17, 60f.; Dodd, *Interpretation*, pp. 270f., 272, 279–83; E. Schweizer, 'Aufnahme und Korrektur jüdischer Sophiatheologie im Neuen Testament', *Neotestamentica*, p. 114; E. Haenchen, 'Probleme des johanneischen "Prologs"', *ZTK* 60, 1963, reprinted *GMEH*, pp. 131, 138; Wengst, *Formeln*, pp. 201, 207f.; Lindars, *John*, pp. 78, 82, 90; Hamerton-Kelly, *Pre-existence*, pp. 205f., 213–15; Klappert, *NIDNTT* III, pp. 1114f.; Gese, 'Johannesprolog', pp. 167, 171; Schmithals, 'Prolog', p. 32). Brown himself thinks v. 12 points conclusively towards a reference to Jesus' ministry; but see above p. 242. He cites Phil. 2.6–11 as a parallel (p. 30), but as we have seen above (§15.1), that uses a different conceptuality (Adam christology).

123. Schnackenburg, *John* I, p. 280. On the textual problem of 1.18 at this point see above II n. 229.

124. Despite Bultmann, 'Untersuchungen zum Johannesevangelium', *ZNW* 29, 1930, pp. 169–92, reprinted *Exegetica*, pp. 174–97.

125. Philo makes little or no use of ἐξηγέομαι but it is often used in Greek literature in the sense of 'revealing divine secrets' both about and by the gods (Arndt & Gingrich). Cf. H. Schlier, 'Zur Christologie des Johannesevangelium', *Das Ende der Zeit*, 1971: The Word 'is not a divine emanation and also not a divine function. ... The Word is God as Logos, or God as revealer, God revealing himself' (p. 91); similarly Cullmann, *Christology*, pp. 265–7; Schweizer, 'Aufnahme', p. 115; Conzelmann, *Outline*, p. 340.

126. Cf. Haenchen, 'Vater', p. 71; Bühner, *Gesandte*, pp. 215–21; Schillebeeckx, *Christ*, pp. 431f. See also H. Zimmermann, 'Das absolute ἐγώ εἰμι als die neutestamentliche Offenbarungsformel', *BZ* 4, 1960, pp. 54–69, 266–76; also *Jesus Christus*, pp. 276f.; Schillebeeckx, *Christ*, pp. 384–97.

127. The union is not entirely complete: the Son of Man language, which combines talk of *ascent* with descent (lacking in the Wisdom tradition prior to I Enoch 42.1f.), is not yet integrated with the united Logos-Son of God christology (see above p. 56.).

128. Cf. R. S. Barbour, 'Creation, Wisdom and Christ', *Creation Christ and Culture*, 1976, pp. 36f.

129. Cf. also C. K. Barrett, ' "The Father is greater than I" (John 14.28): Subordinationist Christology in the New Testament', *NTKRS*, pp. 144–59.

130. For the form of the statement cf. Philo, *Decal.* 88.

131. So most commentators – see e.g. B. F. Westcott, *Epistles of John*, Macmillan 1883, p. 4; Dodd, *Epistles*, pp. 2–5; J. L. Houlden, *Johannine Epistles*, Black 1973, pp. 47f., 51f.; cf. I. H. Marshall, *Epistles of John*, Eerdmans 1978, pp. 101–3. Against Kittel: 'It is beyond question that the λόγος is meant to be the historical figure of Jesus Christ' (*TDNT* IV, p. 127).

132. H. H. Wendt, 'Der "Anfang" am Beginn des I Johannesbriefes', *ZNW* 21, 1922, pp. 38–42; R. Bultmann, *Johannesbriefe*, KEK 1967, p. 15 (ET, Herme-

neia p. 9); F. F. Bruce, *Epistles of John*, Pickering & Inglis 1970, p. 35; Houlden, *Epistles*, p. 49; I. de la Potterie, 'La notion de "commencement" dans les écrits johanniques', *KAHS*, pp. 396–402; Brown, *Community*, pp. 120f. Otherwise, R. Schnackenburg, *Johannesbriefe*, Herder 1952, ⁵1975, p. 59.

133. Even if the 'we' cannot be confidently taken as an assertion that the author and his circle knew Jesus during his life, it certainly affirms the continuity of the Johannine circle with the first witnesses. For discussion and bibliography see K. Wengst, *Häresie und Orthodoxie im Spiegel des ersten Johannesbriefes*, Gütersloh 1976, pp. 65f. n. 149.

134. Cf. H. Conzelmann, ' "Was von Anfang War" ', *Neutestamentliche Studien für R. Bultmann*, pp. 194–210, reprinted in *Theologie als Schriftauslegung*, 1974, pp. 207–14: 'The church orients itself in relation to its origin and understands that as an absolute datum' (p. 213).

135. J. A. T. Robinson suggests that 'the opening of the first Epistle represents the first sketch for the Prologue' ('The Relation of the Prologue to the Gospel of St John', *NTS* 9, 1961–62, p. 124).

136. Brown, *Community*, pp. 103–23.

137. So most commentators – see e.g. Charles, *Revelation*, II, p. 134; G. B. Caird, *Revelation*, Black 1966, p. 244; G. R. Beasley-Murray, *Revelation*, NCB 1974, p. 280. The Wisd. 18 passage is closer than that of the charioteer Logos in Philo, *Som.* I.157–9 (suggested by J. M. Ford, *Revelation*, AB 1975, p. 314).

138. Cf. Caird, *Revelation*, p. 244.

139. So Bousset, *Offenbarung*, p. 431; Beckwith, *Apocalypse*, p. 732; M. Kiddle, *Revelation*, Moffatt 1940, p. 386; E. Lohmeyer, *Offenbarung*, HNT ²1953, p. 159; Beasley-Murray, *Revelation*, p. 280.

140. Cf. Bousset, *Offenbarung*, p. 231.

141. NEB – 'the prime source of all God's creation'. See particularly Beckwith, *Apocalypse*, pp. 488f. The closeness of the parallel with Col. 1.15, 18 (see above p. 189) and the strong plausibility that Col. and Rev. share the same circle of thought is emphasized particularly by Charles, *Revelation* I, pp. 94f.

142. Cf. J. Jocz, 'The Invisibility of God and the Incarnation', *Judaica* 17, 1961: 'The christology of the Church is essentially Johannine. Without the Fourth Gospel even the Pauline Epistles would not have sufficed as a basis for the Trinitarian doctrine we have today . . .' (p. 196).

Chapter VIII   Conclusion

1. Cf. Hengel, *Son*, pp. 66f., although a too cursory analysis of such texts as Gal. 4.4 (see also his 'Christologie und neutestamentliche Chronologie', *NTGOC*, p. 58), and the assumption that Wisdom was an 'intermediary figure' in pre-Christian Judaism, result in a foreshortening of the period of christological development in the first generation of Christianity more than the evidence actually indicates.

2. Cf. Cullmann, *Christology*, pp. 324–7.

3. The title of the collection of essays edited by Hick – see above p. 3. The broader sense of 'myth' to embrace all ways of talking about God, including analogy, metaphor and symbol, is not in question here; see further J. D. G. Dunn,

'Demythologizing – The Problem of Myth in the New Testament', *New Testament Interpretation*, ed. I. H. Marshall, Paternoster 1977, pp. 285–307.

4. Cf. E. Jüngel, *Paulus und Jesus*, 1962, ³1967, p. 283.

5. 'The Logos doctrine (of Philo) entails a kind of binitarian view of God, an acknowledged distinction between God transcendent and God immanent' (Young, *Myth*, ed. Hick, p. 114). The influence of Alexandria on developing christology has often been noted – e.g. Nock, 'The Christian hope has its roots in Palestine; Christian theology and above all christology have theirs in Alexandria' (*Essays*, Vol. II, p. 574, cited by Young, p. 113); W. Völker, 'Die Wertung der Weisheitsliteratur bei den christlichen Alexandrinern', *ZKG* 64, 1952, pp. 1–33; Kretschmar, *Trinitätstheologie*, pp. 62–94.

6. See Dunn, *Unity*, pp. 296f.

7. A striking contemporary attempt to use information theory in analysing the role and significance of Jesus within the beginnings of Christianity has recently been offered by J. Bowker, *The Religious Imagination and the Sense of God*, 1978: 'It is credibly and conceptually possible to regard Jesus as a wholly God-informed person, who retrieved the theistic inputs coded in the chemistry and electricity of brain-process for the scan of every situation and for every utterance, verbal and non-verbal. We cannot, of course, say with absolute certainty that that *is* what happened historically. But we can say – with absolute certainty – that it could have happened, and that the result would have been the incarnating (the embodying) of God in the only way in which it could possibly have occurred. No matter what God may be in himself, the realization of that potential resource of effect would have to be mediated into the process and continuity of life-construction through brian-process interpreted through the codes available at any particular moment of acculturation. There is no other way of being human, or indeed of being alive, because otherwise consciousness ceases. . . . That is as true of Jesus *de humanitate* as of anyone else. But what seems to have shifted Jesus into a different degree of significance in making manifest, and in recreating in others the desire to realize, the possibility of God as an available resource of effect (and thus shifted him also into being regarded as a different kind of signifying of that possibility in relation to the lives of men) was the stability and the consistency with which his own life-construction was God-informed. . . . It is possible on this basis to talk about a wholly human figure, without loss or compromise, and to talk also, at exactly the same moment, of a wholly real presence of God so far as that nature (whatever it is in itself) can be mediated to and through the process of life-construction in the human case, through the process of brain behaviour by which any human being becomes an informed subject – but in this case, perhaps even uniquely, a wholly God-informed subject. Whatever the godness of God may be, it could only be established and mediated through a *human* life by some such process as this' (pp. 187f.). One of the strengths of Bowker's approach is that he is able thereby to bring out the continuity between Jesus' own perception of his role and subsequent christological affirmations about him – 'It is because, according to the surviving evidence, Jesus gave the impression of solving the problem of God's effect in and through his own person, and because others also discerned the extension and continuity of that effect in their own experience and in their observation of others, that Christological and Trinitarian reflection was inevitable . . .' (p. 179).

8. A christological slogan gives wide currency by J. A. T. Robinson, *Honest to God*, SCM Press 1963, ch. 4.

9. Cupitt, quoted above p. 5; 'In his theology the main thing that Paul wants to say about Christ is *not* that Christ is God but that Christ is the perfect heavenly Man . . .' (p. 104); similarly *Incarnation*, ed. Goulder, p. 168.

10. In effect Lampe's thesis in *God as Spirit* – note p. 114.

11. Cf. e.g. the formulae produced by Goulder and Nineham in *Myth*, ed. Hick, pp. 60, 202.

12. *Jesus*, p. 53.

13. Cf. Knox, ' "Divine Hero" Christology', pp. 248f.; Kasper: 'If the divine-human person Jesus is constituted through the incarnation once and for all, the history and activity of Jesus, and above all the cross and the resurrection, no longer have any constitutive meaning whatsoever. Then the death of Jesus would be only the completion of the incarnation. The resurrection would be no more than the confirmation of his divine nature. That would mean a diminution of the whole biblical testimony. According to Scripture, christology has its centre in the cross and the resurrection. From that mid-point it extends forward to the parousia and back to the pre-existence and the incarnation' (*Jesus*, p. 37).

14. Cf. Cerfaux's objection against the tendency in the Greek Fathers to see in the incarnation itself the cause of our divinization (*Christ*, pp. 168–72) – 'St Paul's position never varies: the starting point of his soteriology, which is the death and resurrection, and his concept of Christ according to the flesh, always prevent him from attributing to the incarnation a positive and efficacious action in the order of salvation' (p. 171).

15. Kasper, *Jesus*, p. 172.

BIBLIOGRAPHY

PRIMARY TEXTS AND PRINCIPAL SOURCES

Aland, K., Black, M., Metzger, B. M., and Wikgren, A. (eds.), *The Greek New Testament*, Bible Societies, Stuttgart 1966

Allenbach, J., *et al.*, *Biblia Patristica: Index des citations et allusions bibliques dans la littérature patristique*, 2 vols., Paris 1975, 1977

Box, G. H., *The Apocalypse of Abraham*, SPCK 1918

Charles, R. H., *The Assumption of Moses* (Latin text and ET), A. & C. Black 1897

— *The Apocrypha and Pseudepigrapha of the Old Testament*, 2 vols., Oxford University Press 1913

Colson, F. H., Whitaker, G. H., *et al.*, *Philo*, Loeb Classical Library, 12 vols., 1929–53

Danby, H., *The Mishnah*, Oxford University Press 1933

Denis, A. M. (ed.), *Fragmenta Pseudepigraphorum Quae Supersunt Graeca*, Leiden 1970

Diez Macho, A., *Neophiti I*, Madrid 1968–

Dupont-Sommer, A., *The Essene Writings from Qumran*, 1959, ET Blackwell 1961

Epstein, I. (ed.), *The Babylonian Talmud*, Soncino Press 1935–52

Etheridge, J. W., *The Targums of Onkelos and Jonathan ben Uzziel on the Pentateuch*, 2 vols., Longmans Green 1862, 1865

Foerster, W., *Gnosis: A Selection of Gnostic Texts*, 2 vols. 1969 and 1971, ET ed. R. McL. Wilson, Oxford University Press 1972 and 1974

Freedman, H. and Simon, M. (eds.), *Midrash Rabbah*, 10 vols., Soncino Press, 1939

Gifford, E. H., *Eusebii Pamphili: Evangelicae Praeparationis Libri XV*, 5 vols. Oxford University Press 1903

Ginzberg, L., *The Legends of the Jews*, Jewish Publication Society, 7 vols.

1909–38, abbreviated in one vol., *Legends of the Bible*, Jewish Publication Society 1972

Grant, R. M., *Gnosticism: An Anthology*, Collins 1961

Harrington, D. J., Cazeaux, J., Perrot, C., and Bogaert, P. M., *Pseudo-Philon, Les Antiquites Bibliques*, 2 vols., Paris 1976

Hennecke, E., *New Testament Apocrypha*, ed. W. Schneemelcher, 2 vols., 1959 and 1964, ET ed. R. McL. Wilson, Lutterworth 1963 and 1965

Herford, R. T., *Pirke Aboth: The Ethics of the Talmud: Sayings of the Fathers*, 1945, Schocken 1962

Houghton, H. P., 'Akhmîmice: "The Apocalypse of Elias" ', *Aegyptus* 39, 1959, pp. 179–210

James, M. R., *The Apocryphal New Testament*, Oxford University Press 1924
— *The Biblical Antiquities of Philo*, Macmillan 1917, reprinted Ktav 1971

Kittel, R. (ed.), *Biblia Hebraica*, Stuttgart ⁷1951

Knibb, M. A., *The Ethiopic Book of Enoch*, 2 vols., Oxford University Press 1978

Lake, K. (ed.), *The Apostolic Fathers*, Loeb Classical Library, 2 vols., 1912–13

Lightfoot, J. B., *The Apostolic Fathers*, Macmillan 1891

Lohse, E., *Die Texte aus Qumran: Hebräisch und Deutsch*, Darmstadt ²1971

Mayer, G., *Index Philoneus*, Berlin 1974

Milik, J. T., *The Books of Enoch: Aramaic Fragments of Qumran Cave 4*, Oxford University Press 1976

Morfill, W. R., and Charles, R. H., *The Book of the Secrets of Enoch*, Oxford University Press 1896

Nestle, E., *Novum Testamentum Graece*, Stuttgart ²⁵1963

Odeberg, H., *III Enoch or the Hebrew Book of Enoch*, Cambridge 1928, reissued with Prolegomenon by J. C. Greenfield, Ktav 1973

Rahlfs, A. (ed.), *Septuaginta*, 2 vols., Stuttgart 1959

Richardson, C. C. (ed.), *Early Christian Fathers*, Library of Christian Classics Vol. I, SCM Press 1953

Roberts, A. and Donaldson, J., *The Ante-Nicene Fathers*, reprinted 10 vols., Eerdmans 1977f.

Robinson, J. M. (ed.), *The Nag Hammadi Library in English*, Harper and Row 1977

Smith, J. Z., 'The Prayer of Joseph', *RAERG*, pp. 253–94

Stone, M. E., *The Testament of Abraham: the Greek Recensions*, SBL Texts and Translations 2, Pseudepigrapha Series 2, 1972

Strugnell, J., 'The Angelic Liturgy at Qumran: 4Q Serek Šîrôt 'Olat Haššabāt', *VT* Supp. VII 1960, pp. 318–45

Thackeray, H. St. J., Marcus, R., *et al.*, *Josephus*, Loeb Classical Library, 9 vols. 1926–65

Vermes, G., *The Dead Sea Scrolls in English*, Pelican 1962, ²1975 van der Woude, A. S., 'Melchizedek als himmlische Erlösergestalt in den neugefundenen eschatologischen Midraschim aus Qumran Höhle XI', *OTS* 14, 1965, pp. 354–73

For a more comprehensive listing of source material see particularly the bibliographies in Schürer, *History* §3 (up to Spring 1972) and J. H. Charlesworth, *The Pseudepigrapha and Modern Research*, SBL Septuagint and Cognate Studies 7, Scholars Press, 1976.

GENERAL BIBLIOGRAPHY

I have endeavoured to give a comprehensive list of the works consulted which have most direct bearing on the above study, though omitting commentaries and dictionary articles. On complementary and tangential issues I have been merely selective.

Aalen, S., *Die Begriffe 'Licht' und 'Finsternis' im Alten Testament, im Spätjudentum und im Rabbinismus*, Oslo 1951

Aall, A., *Geschichte der Logosidee in der griechischen Philosophie: Der Logos*, 2 Bde, Leipzig 1896/99

Abelson, J., *The Immanence of God in Rabbinical Literature*, Macmillan 1912

Achtemeier, P. J., 'Gospel Miracle Tradition and the Divine Man', *Interpretation* 26, 1972, pp. 174–97

Ackerman, J. S., 'The Rabbinic Interpretation of Psalm 82 and the Gospel of John', *HTR* 59, 1966, pp. 186–91

Adam, K., *Der Christus des Glaubens: Vorlesungen über die kirchliche Christologie*, Düsseldorf 1954

Alexander, P. S., 'The Targumim and Early Exegesis of "Sons of God" in Genesis 6', *JJS* 23, 1972, pp. 60–71

— 'The Historical Setting of the Hebrew Book of Enoch', *JJS* 28, 1977, pp. 156–80

Allen, E. L. 'Representative-Christology in the New Testament', *HTR* 46, 1953, pp. 161–9

— 'Jesus and Moses in the New Testament', *ExpT* 67, 1955–56, pp. 104–6

Allen L. C., 'The Old Testament Background of (προ)ὁρίζειν in the New Testament', *NTS* 17, 1970–71, pp. 104–8

Alsup, J. E., *The Post-Resurrection Appearance Stories of the Gospel Tradition*, Stuttgart and SPCK 1975

Altermath, F., 'The Purpose of the Incarnation according to Irenaeus', *SP* 13, 1975, pp. 63–8

Amberg, E. H., 'Bemerkungen zur Christologie', *TLZ* 99, 1974, cols. 1–10

Anderson, A. A., 'The Use of "Ruah" in IQS, IQH and IQM', *JSS* 7, 1962, pp. 293–303

Anderson, J. N. D., *The Mystery of the Incarnation*, Hodder and Stoughton 1978

Andresen, C., 'Zur Entstehung und Geschichte des trinitarischen Personbegriffes', *ZNW* 52, 1961, pp. 1–38

Arens, E. *The HΛΘON-Sayings in the Synoptic Tradition*, Freiburg and Göttingen 1976

Argyle, A. W., 'Philo and the Fourth Gospel', *ExpT* 63, 1951–52, pp. 385f.

— *The Christ of the New Testament*, Carey Kingsgate 1952

— 'The Logos of Philo: Personal or Impersonal', *ExpT* 66, 1954–55, pp. 13f.

— 'πρωτότοκος πάσες κτίσεως (Colossians 1.15)', *ExpT*, 66, 1954–55, pp. 61f.

Asting, R., *Die Verkündigung des Wortes im Urchristentum*, Stuttgart 1939

Bacon, B. W., *Jesus the Son of God or Primitive Christology*, Yale and Oxford University Press 1911

Baillie, D. M., *God was in Christ: An Essay on Incarnation and Atonement*, 1948, Faber and Faber 1961

Bakker, A., 'Christ an Angel? A Study of Early Christian Docetism', *ZNW* 32, 1933, pp. 255–65

Baltensweiler, H., *Die Verklärung Jesu*, Zürich 1959

Balz, H. R., *Methodische Probleme der neutestamentlichen Christologie*, Neukirchen 1967

Bammel, E., 'Versuch zu Kol. 1.15–20', *ZNW* 52, 1961, pp. 88–95

— 'Jesus und der Paraklet in Johannes 16', *CSNT*, pp. 199–217

Bandstra, A., 'Did the Colossian Errorists need a Mediator?', *NDNTS*, pp. 329–43

Barbel, J., *Christos Angelos: die Anschauung von Christos als Bote und Engel in der gelehrten und volkstümlichen Literatur des christlichen Altertums*, Bonn 1941, reprinted with Anhang, 'Christos Angelos: Die frühchristliche und patristische Engelchristologie im Lichte der neueren Forschung', 1964

Barbour, R. S., 'Creation, Wisdom and Christ', *Creation, Christ and Culture: Studies in Honour of T. F. Torrance*, ed. R. W. A. McKinney, T. & T. Clark 1976, pp. 22–42

Barnard, L. W., 'God, the Logos, the Spirit and the Trinity in the Theology of Athenagoras', *StTh* 24, 1970, pp. 70–92

Barnikol, E., *Mensch und Messias: der nichtpaulinische Ursprung der Präexistenz-Christologie*, Kiel 1932

Barr, J., 'Christ in Gospel and Creed', *SJT* 8, 1955, pp. 225–37

— 'The Word Became Flesh: The Incarnation in the New Testament', *Interpretation* 10, 1956, pp. 16–23

Barrett, C. K., *The Holy Spirit and the Gospel Tradition*, SPCK 1947

— 'The Eschatology of the Epistle to the Hebrews', *BNTE*, pp. 363–93

— *From First Adam to Last*, A. & C. Black 1962

— *Jesus and the Gospel Tradition*, SPCK 1967

— *The Prologue of St John's Gospel*, Athlone Press 1971, reprinted in *New Testament Essays*, SPCK 1972, pp. 27–48

Bartsch, H. W., 'Zur vorpaulinischen Bekenntnisformel im Eingang des Römerbriefes', *TZ* 23, 1967, pp. 329–39

— *Die Konkrete Wahrheit und die Lüge der Spekulation: Untersuchung über den vorpaulinischen Christushymnus und seine gnostische Mythisierung*, Bern/Frankfurt 1974

— (ed.), *Kerygma and Myth*, ET SPCK Vol. I 1953, Vol. II 1962, reprinted as single volume 1972

Bauckham, R., 'The Martyrdom of Enoch and Elijah: Jewish or Christian?', *JBL* 95, 1976, pp. 447–58

— 'The Sonship of the Historical Jesus in Christology', *SJT* 31, 1978, pp. 245–60

Beasley-Murray, G. R., 'Jesus and the Spirit', *Mélanges Bibliques en hommage R. P. Béda Rigaux*, ed. A. Descamps and A. de Halleux, Gembloux 1970, pp. 463–78

Becker, J., 'Wunder und Christologie', *NTS* 16, 1969–70, pp. 130–48

Bell, G. K. A. and Deissmann, A. (eds.), *Mysterium Christi*, Longmans 1930

Benoit, P., 'Body, Head and *Pleroma* in the Epistles of the Captivity', *RB* 63, 1956, pp. 5–44, ET *Jesus and the Gospel*, Vol. II, Darton, Longman and Todd 1974, pp. 51–92

— 'Paulinisme et Johannisme', *NTS* 9, 1962–63, pp. 193–207

— 'Préexistence et incarnation', *RB* 77, 1970, pp. 5–29

— 'L'hymne christologique de Col. 1.15–20: Jugement critique sur l'état des recherches', *CJMS* Vol. I, pp. 226–63

Bentzen, A., *King and Messiah*, 1948, ET Lutterworth 1955

Berger, K., 'Zum traditionsgeschichtlichen Hintergrund christologischer Hoheitstitel', *NTS* 17, 1970–71, pp. 391–425

— 'Die königlichen Messiastraditionen des Neuen Testaments', *NTS* 20, 1973–74, pp. 1–44

— 'Zu "das Wort ward Fleisch" John 1.14a', *NovT* 16, 1974, pp. 161–6

Berkhof, H., *The Doctrine of the Holy Spirit*, Epworth 1965

Bertram, G., 'Der religionsgeschichtliche Hintergrund des Begriffs "Erhohung" in der LXX', *ZAW* 68, 1956, pp. 57–71

Bertrams, H., *Das Wesen des Geistes nach der Anschauung des Apostels Paulus*, Münster 1913

Beskow, P., *Rex Gloriae: the Kingship of Christ in the Early Church*, Uppsala 1962

Best, E., *One Body in Christ: a Study of the Relationship of the Church to Christ in the Epistles of the Apostle Paul*, SPCK 1955

Betz, H. D., 'The Logion of the Easy Yoke and of Rest (Matt. 11.28–30)', *JBL* 86, 1967, pp. 10–24

Betz, O., *Der Paraklet: Fürsprecher im haretischen Spätjudentum, im Johannes-Evangelium and in neu gefundenen gnostischen Schriften*, Leiden 1963

— 'Die Frage nach dem messianischen Bewusstsein Jesu', *NovT* 6, 1963, pp. 20–48

— *What do we know about Jesus?*, 1965, ET SCM Press 1967

— 'The Concept of the So-called "Divine Man" in Mark's Christology', *Studies in New Testament and Early Christian Literature: Essays in Honour of A. P. Wikgren*, ed. D. E. Aune, SNT 33, 1972, pp. 229–40

Beyschlag, K., *Simon Magus und die christliche Gnosis*, Tübingen 1974

Bieler, L., *ΘΕΙΟΣ ANHP: Das Bild des "gottlichen Menschen" in Spätantike und Frühchristentum*, Wien 1935 and 1936, reissued Darmstadt 1967

Bieneck, J., *Sohn Gottes als Christusbezeichnung der Synoptiker*, Zürich 1951

Bietenhard, H., *Die himmlische Welt im Urchristentum und Spätjudentum*, Tübingen 1951

Black, M., 'The "Son of Man" in the old Biblical Literature', *ExpT* 60, 1948–49, pp. 11–15

— 'The "Son of Man" in the Teaching of Jesus', *ExpT* 60, 1948–49, pp. 32–6

— 'The Eschatology of the Similitudes of Enoch', *JTS* 3, 1952, pp. 1–10

— 'Servant of the Lord and Son of Man', *SJT* 6, 1953, pp. 1–11

— 'The Pauline Doctrine of the Second Adam', *SJT* 7, 1954, pp. 170–9

— 'The Son of Man Problem in Recent Research and Debate', *BJRL* 45, 1962–63, pp. 305–18

— 'The "Son of Man" Passion Sayings in the Gospel Tradition', *ZNW* 60, 1969, pp. 1–8

— 'The Christological Use of the Old Testament in the New Testament', *NTS* 18, 1971–72, pp. 1–14

— 'Die Apotheose Israels: eine neue Interpretation des danielischen "Menschensohns" ', *JMAV*, pp. 92–9

— 'The Throne-Theophany Prophetic Commission and the "Son of Man": A Study in Tradition History', *JGCWDD*, pp. 57–73

— 'The "Parables" of Enoch (I Enoch 37–71) and the "Son of Man" ', *ExpT* 88, 1976–77, pp. 5–8

— 'The "Two Witnesses" of Rev. 11.3f. in Jewish and Christian Apocalyptic Tradition', *Donum Gentilicum: New Testament Studies in Honour of D. Daube*, ed. E. Bammel, C. K. Barrett and W. D. Davies, Oxford University Press 1978, pp. 227–37

— 'Jesus and the Son of Man', *JSNT* 1, 1978, pp. 4–18

Blank, J., *Paulus und Jesus: Eine theologische Grundlegung*, München 1968

Bloch, J., 'Some Christological Interpolations in the Ezra-Apocalypse', *HTR* 51, 1958, pp. 89–94

Boers, H., 'Jesus and the Christian Faith: New Testament Christology since Bousset's *Kyrios Christos*', *JBL* 89, 1970, pp. 450–6

— 'Where Christology is Real: A Survey of Recent Research on New Testament Christology', *Interpretation* 26, 1972, pp. 300–27

Boice, J. M., *Witness and Revelation in the Gospel of John*, Paternoster 1970

Boismard, M. E., 'Constitué Fils de Dieu Rom. 1.4', *RB* 60, 1953, pp. 5–17

— *Le Prologue de Saint Jean*, Paris 1953

— 'Jésus, le Prophète par excellence, d'après Jean 10.24–39', *NTKRS*, pp. 160–71

Bonnard, P. E., *La Sagesse en Personne annoncée et venue: Jésus Christ*, Lectio divina 44, Paris 1966

Boobyer, G. H., *St Mark and the Transfiguration Story*, Edinburgh 1942

— 'Jesus as "Theos" in the New Testament', *BJRL* 50, 1967–68, pp. 247–61

Borgen, P., 'God's Agent in the Fourth Gospel', *RAERG*, pp. 137–48

— 'Observations on the Targumic Character of the Prologue of John', *NTS* 16, 1969–70, pp. 288–95

— 'Logos was the True Light', *NovT* 14, 1972, pp. 115–30

Bornkamm, G., 'Das Bekenntnis im Hebräerbrief' (1942), *Studien zu Antike und Urchristentum*, Gesammelte Aufsätze II, München 1959, ²1963, pp. 188–203

— 'Der Paraklet im Johannes-Evangelium' (1949), *Geschichte und Glaube* I, Gesammelte Aufsätze III, München 1968, pp. 68–89

— 'Zur Interpretation des Johannes-Evangeliums: Eine Auseinandersetzung mit E. Käsemanns Schrift "Jesu letzter Wille nach Johannes 17" ' (1967), *Geschichte und Glaube* I, pp. 104–21

— 'Christ and the World in the Early Christian Message' (1950), 'On Understanding the Christ-hymn (Philippians 2.6–11)' (1959), ET *Early Christian Experience*, SCM Press 1969, pp. 14–28, 112–22

Borsch, F. H., *The Son of Man in Myth and History*, SCM Press 1967

— 'Mark 14.62 and I Enoch 62.5', *NTS* 14, 1967–68, pp. 565–7

— *The Christian and Gnostic Son of Man*, SCM Press 1970

Boslooper, T., *The Virgin Birth*, SCM Press 1962

Bourke, M. M., 'The Eucharist and Wisdom in First Corinthians', *SPCIC* I, pp. 372–7

Bousset, W., *Hauptprobleme der Gnosis*, Göttingen 1907, reprinted 1973

— *Kyrios Christos: A History of the Belief in Christ from the Beginnings of Christianity to Irenaeus*, 1913 ²1921, ET Abingdon 1970

Bouyer, L., 'La notion christologique du Fils de l'homme a-t-elle disparu dans la patristique grecque?', *Mélanges bibliques rédigés en l'honneur de André Robert*, Paris 1957, pp. 519–30

— *Le Fils éternal: Theologie de la parole de Dieu et Christologie*, Paris 1974

Bowker, J., 'The Son of Man', *JTS* 28, 1977, pp. 19–48

— *The Religious Imagination and the Sense of God*, Oxford University Press 1978

Bowman, J., 'The Background of the term "Son of Man" ', *ExpT* 59, 1947–48, pp. 283–8

Box, G. H., 'The Idea of Intermediation in Jewish Theology: A Note on Memra and Shekinah', *JQR* 23, 1932–33, pp. 103–19

Brandenburger, E., *Adam und Christus: exegetisch-religionsgeschichtliche Untersuchung zu Röm. 5.12–21 (I Kor. 15)*, Neukirchen 1962

— 'Text und Vorlagen von Heb. 5.7–10: Ein Beitrag zur Christologie des Hebräerbriefs', *NovT* 11, 1969, pp. 190–224

Braaten, C. E., and Harrisville, R. A. (eds.), *Kergyma and Myth*, Abingdon 1962

Braun, F. M., 'Saint Jean, la Sagesse et l'Histoire', *Neotestamentica et Patristica*, O. Cullmann Festschrift, SNT VI, 1962, pp. 123–33

— *Jean le Théologien: Sa Théologie*, 2 vols., EB 1966, 1972

Braun, H., 'Der Sinn der neutestamentliche Christologie', *ZTK* 54, 1957, pp. 341–77, ET 'The Meaning of New Testament Christology', *JThC* 5, 1968, pp. 89–127

— 'Die Gewinnung der Gewissheit in dem Hebräerbrief', *TLZ* 96, 1971, pp. 321–30

Bréhier, E., *Les idées philosophiques et religieuses de Philon d'Alexandrie*, Paris 1908, ³1950

Brekelmans, C. W., 'The Saints of the Most High and their Kingdom', *OTS* 14, 1965, pp. 305–29

Brown, J. P., 'The Son of Man: "This fellow" ', *Biblica* 58, 1977, pp. 361–87

Brown, R. E., 'The Semitic Background of the Term "Mystery" in the New Testament', *CBQ* 20, 1958 and *Biblica* 39, 1958, and 40, 1959, reproduced as Fortress Facet Book 1968

— 'The Theology of the Incarnation in John', *New Testament Essays*, Chapman 1965, pp. 96–101

— 'Does the New Testament call Jesus God?', *TS* 26, 1965, pp. 545–73, and 'How Much did Jesus Know?', *CBQ* 29, 1967, pp. 315–45, reprinted together as *Jesus God and Man*, Chapman 1968

— 'The Paraclete in the Fourth Gospel', *NTS* 13, 1966–67, pp. 113–32

— *The Virginal Conception and Bodily Resurrection of Jesus*, Chapman 1974

— *The Birth of the Messiah: a Commentary on the Infancy Narratives in Matthew and Luke*, Chapman 1977

— *The Community of the Beloved Disciple*, Chapman 1979

Brownlee, W. H., 'The Cosmic Role of Angels in the 11Q Targum of Job', *JSJ* 8, 1977, pp. 83f.

Brox, N., 'Das messianische Selbstverständnis des historischen Jesus', in *Vom Messias zum Christus*, Wien 1964, pp. 165–201

Bruce, F. F., 'The Spirit in the Apocalypse', *CSNT*, pp. 333–44

— 'Christ and Spirit in Paul', *BJRL* 59, 1976–77, pp. 259–85

Brückner, M., *Die Entstehung der paulinische Christologie*, Strassburg 1903

Büchsel, F., *Die Christologie des Hebräerbriefes*, Gütersloh 1923

— *Der Geist Gottes im Neuen Testament*, Gütersloh 1926

Bühner, J. A., *Der Gesandte und sein Weg im 4. Evangelium*, Tübingen 1977

Bultmann, R., 'Der religionsgeschichtliche Hintergrund des Prologs zum Johannes-Evangelium', *EYXAPIΣTHPION: Festschrift für H. Gunkel*, Göttingen 1923, 2. Teil, pp. 3–26, reprinted *Exegetica: Aufsätze zur Erforschung des Neuen Testaments*, Tübingen 1967, pp. 10–35

— 'Die Bedeutung der neuerschlossenen mandäischen und manichäischen Quellen für das Verständnis des Johannesevangeliums', *ZNW* 24, 1925, pp. 100–46, reprinted *Exegetica*, pp. 55–104

— 'Untersuchungen zum Johannesevangelium', *ZNW* 29, 1930, pp. 169–92, reprinted *Exegetica*, pp. 174–97

— 'The Christology of the New Testament', and 'The Concept of the Word of God in the New Testament', *Faith and Understanding: Collected Essays*, 1933, ET SCM Press 1969, pp. 262–85 and 286–312

— 'Johanneische Schriften und Gnosis', *Orientalische Literaturzeitung* 43, 1940, pp. 150–75, reprinted *Exegetica*, pp. 230–54

— *Theology of the New Testament*, 1948–53, ET 2 vols., SCM Press 1952, 1955

— 'The Christological Confession of the World Council of Churches' (1951), *Essays Philosophical and Theological*, ET SCM Press 1955, pp. 273–90

— 'Adam and Christ according to Romans 5' (*ZNW* 50, 1969, pp. 145–65; *Exegetica*, pp. 424–44), ET *CINTI*, pp. 143–65

Burger, C., *Jesus als Davidssohn: Eine Traditionsgeschichtliche Untersuchung*, Göttingen 1970

— *Schöpfung und Versöhnung: Studien zum liturgischer Gut im Kolosser- und Epheserbrief*, Neukirchen 1975

Burkill, T. A., 'The Hidden Son of Man in St Mark's Gospel', *ZNW* 52, 1961, pp. 189–213

Burney, C. F., 'Christ as the ἀρχή of Creation', *JTS* 27, 1926, pp. 160–77

Cadman, W. H., *The Open Heaven: the Revelation of God in the Johannine Sayings of Jesus*, Blackwell 1969

Cahill, P. J., 'The Johannine Logos as Center', *CBQ* 38, 1976, pp. 54–72

Caird, G. B., *Principalities and Powers: A Study in Pauline Theology*, Oxford University Press 1956

— 'The Descent of Christ in Ephesians 4.7–11', *SE* II, 1964, pp. 535–45

— 'The Development of the Doctrine of Christ in the New Testament', *Christ for Us Today*, ed. N. Pittenger, SCM Press 1968, pp. 66–81

— 'Son by Appointment', *B. Reicke Festschrift*, Leiden (forthcoming)

Cambier, J., 'La Signification Christologique d'Eph. 4.7–10', *NTS* 9, 1962–63, pp. 262–75

— 'La Bénédiction d'Eph. 1.3–14', *ZNW* 54, 1963, pp. 58–104

Campbell, J. C., 'In a Son: The Doctrine of the Incarnation in the Epistle to the Hebrews', *Interpretation* 10, 1956, pp. 24–38

Campbell, J. Y., 'The Origin and Meaning of the Term Son of Man', *JTS* 48, 1947, pp. 145–55, reprinted in *Three New Testament Studies*, Leiden 1965, pp. 29–40

Campenhausen, H. von, *The Virgin Birth in the Theology of the Ancient Church*, 1962, ET SCM Press 1964

Caquot, A., 'Remarques sur les chapitres 70 et 71 du livre éthiopien d'Hénoch', *ATE*, pp. 111–22

Caragounis, C. C., *The Ephesian Mysterion: Meaning and Content*, Lund 1977

Carlston, C. E., 'Transfiguration and Resurrection', *JBL* 80, 1961, pp. 233–40

— 'The Vocabulary of Perfection in Philo and Hebrews', *UDNTT*, pp. 133–60

Carmignac, J., 'L'Importance de la place d'une négation (Philippiens 2.6)', *NTS* 18, 1971–72, pp. 131–66

— 'Le document de Qumran sur Melkisédeq', *RQ* 7, 1969–71, pp. 343–78

Carr, A. W., 'The Rulers of this Age – I Corinthians 2.6–8', *NTS* 23, 1976–77, pp. 20–35

Casey, P. M., 'The Use of the Term "Son of Man" in the Similitudes of Enoch', *JSJ* 7, 1976, pp. 11–29

— 'The Corporate Interpretation of "One like a Son of Man" (Dan. 7.13) at the Time of Jesus', *Nov T* 18, 1976, pp. 167–80

— 'The Son of Man Problem', *ZNW* 67, 1976, pp. 147–54.

— *The Son of Man: the Interpretation and Influence of Daniel 7*, SPCK 1980

Casey, R. P., 'The Earliest Christologies', *JTS* 9, 1958, pp. 253–77

Casper, B., *Jesus, Ort der Erfahrung Gottes*, Freiburg 1976

Cerfaux, L., 'L'Hymne au Christ – Serviteur de Dieu (Phil. 2.6–11 = Isa. 52.13–53.12)', *Miscellanea historica Alberti de Meyer*, Vol. I, Louvain 1946, pp. 117–30

— *Christ in the Theology of St Paul*, 1951, ET Herder 1959

— 'Les sources scripturaires de Matt. 11.25–30', *ETL* 30, 1954, pp. 740–6

Ceroke, C. P., 'The Divinity of Christ in the Gospels', *CBQ* 24, 1962, pp. 125–39

Chadwick, H., 'St Paul and Philo of Alexandria', *BJRL* 48, 1965–66, pp. 286–307

— 'Philo and the Beginnings of Christian Thought', *The Cambridge History of Later Greek and Early Medieval Philosophy*, ed. A. H. Armstrong, Cambridge University Press 1967, pp. 137–57

Chamberlain, J. V., 'The Functions of God as Messianic Titles in the Complete Qumran Isaiah Scroll', *VT* 5, 1955, pp. 366–72

Charlesworth, J. H. and Culpepper, R. A., 'The Odes of Solomon and the Gospel of John', *CBQ* 35, 1973, pp. 298–322

Chevallier, M. A., *L'Esprit et le Messie dans le bas-judaisme et le Nouveau Testament*, Paris 1958

Christ, F., *Jesus Sophia: die Sophia-Christologie bei den Synoptikern*, Zürich 1970

Clavier, H., 'Mediation in the Fourth Gospel', *SNTS Bulletin*, 1950, pp. 11–25

— 'ὁ λόγος τοῦ Θεοῦ dans l'épitre aux Hébreux', *NTETWM*, pp. 81–93

Clines, D. J. A., 'The Image of God in Man', *Tyndale Bulletin* 19, 1968, pp. 53–103.

Cohn, L., 'Zur Lehre vom Logos bei Philo', *Judaica: Festschrift für H. Cohen*, Berlin 1912, pp. 303–31

Cohon, S. S., 'The Unity of God: A Study in Hellenistic and Rabbinic Theology', *HUCA* 26, 1955, pp. 425–79

Collins, J. J., 'The Son of Man and the Saints of the Most High in the Book of Daniel', *JBL* 93, 1974, pp. 50–66

— *The Apocalyptic Vision of the Book of Daniel*, Scholars Press 1977

Colpe, C., *Die religionsgeschichtliche Schule: Darstellung und Kritik ihres Bildes vom gnostischen Erlösermythus*, Göttingen 1961

— 'Zur Leib-Christi-Vorstellung im Epheserbrief', *Judentum, Urchristentum, Kirche*, J. Jeremias Festschrift, hrsg. W. Eltester, Berlin 1964, pp. 172–87

— 'New Testament and Gnostic Christology', *RAERG*, pp. 227–43

Congar, Y., 'Christ in the Economy of Salvation and in our Dogmatic Tracts', *Concilium* 2.1, 1966, pp. 4–15

Conzelmann, H., ' "Was von Anfang War" ', *Neutestamentliche Studien für R. Bultmann*, Berlin 1954, reprinted in *Theologie als Schriftauslegung*, München 1974, pp. 207–14

— 'Das Selbstbewusstsein Jesu', *Svensk Exegetisk Årsbok* 28–29, 1963–64, pp. 39–53, reprinted *Schriftauslegung*, pp. 30–41

— 'The Mother of Wisdom', ET *FRPRB*, pp. 230–43

— 'Paulus und die Weisheit', *NTS* 12, 1965–66, pp. 231–44, reprinted *Schriftauslegung*, pp. 177–90

— *An Outline of the Theology of the New Testament*, ²1968, ET SCM Press 1969

Cooke, G., 'The Israelite King as Son of God', *ZAW* 32, 1961, pp. 202–25

— 'The Sons of (the) Gods', *ZAW* 35, 1964, pp. 22–47

Copeland, E. L., '*Nomos* as a Medium of Revelation – Paralleling *Logos* – in Ante-Nicene Christianity', *StTh* 27, 1973, pp. 51–61

Coppens, J., 'La Portée Messianique du Psaume 110', *ETL* 32, 1956, pp. 5–23

— 'Le messianisme sapiental et les origines littéraires du Fils de l'homme daniélique', *Wisdom in Israel and the Ancient Near East*, H. H. Rowley Festschrift, ed. M. Noth and D. W. Thomas, *VT* Supp. III, 1960, pp. 33–41

— ' "Mystery" in the Theology of St Paul and its Parallels at Qumran', *Paul and Qumran*, ed. J. Murphy-O'Connor, Chapman 1968, pp. 132–58

— 'La vision daniélique du Fils d'Homme', *VT* 19, 1969, pp. 171–82

— 'Le Fils de l'Homme dans l'Évangile johannique', *ETL* 52, 1976, pp. 28–81

Coppens, J., and Dequeker, L., 'Le fils de l'homme et les Saints du Très-Haut en Daniel 7, dans les Apocryphes et dans le Nouveau Testament', *Analecta Lovaniensia Biblica et Orientalia* III.23, 1961

Cortes, J. B. and Gatti, F. M., 'The Son of Man or the Son of Adam', *Biblica* 49, 1968, pp. 457–502

Craddock, F. B., ' "All things in him": A critical note on Col. 1.15–20', *NTS* 12, 1965–66, pp. 78–80

— *The Pre-existence of Christ in the New Testament*, Abingdon 1968

— 'The Poverty of Christ: An Investigation of II Corinthians 8.9', *Interpretation* 22, 1968, pp. 158–70

Crawford, R. G., 'Is the Doctrine of the Trinity Scriptural?', *SJT* 20, 1967, pp. 282–94

Creed, J. M., 'The Heavenly Man', *JTS* 26, 1925, pp. 113–36

— *The Divinity of Jesus Christ: A Study in the History of Christian Doctrine since Kant*, Cambridge University Press 1938, Fontana 1964

Cullmann, O., *The Christology of the New Testament*, 1957, ET SCM Press 1959

Cupitt, D., *The Debate about Christ*, SCM Press 1979

Dahl, N. A., 'Christ, Creation and the Church', *BNTE*, pp. 422–43, reprinted in *Jesus in the Memory of the Early Church: Essays by N. A. Dahl*, Augsburg 1976, pp. 120–40

Dahl, N. A. and Segal, A. F., "Philo and the Rabbis on the Names of God', *JSJ* 9, 1978, pp. 1–28

Dalman, G., *The Words of Jesus*, ET T. & T. Clark 1902

Danielou, J., 'Trinité et Angelologie dans la Théologie judéo-chrétienne', *RSR* 45, 1957, pp. 5–41

— *The Theology of Jewish Christianity*, 1958, ET Darton, Longman and Todd 1964

Davenport, S. F., *Immanence and Incarnation*, Cambridge University Press 1925

Davey, J. E., *The Jesus of St John: Historical and Christological Studies in the Fourth Gospel*, Lutterworth 1958

Davies, P. E., 'Jesus in Relation to Believing Men', *Interpretation* 12, 1958, pp. 3–15

— 'The Projection of Pre-existence', *BR* 12, 1967, pp. 28–36

Davies, W. D., *Paul and Rabbinic Judaism: Some Rabbinic Elements in Pauline Theology*, SPCK 1948, ²1955

Davis, G. M., 'The Humanity of Jesus', *JBL* 70, 1951, pp. 105–12

Dawe, D. G., 'A Fresh Look at the Kenotic Christologies', *SJT* 15, 1962, pp. 337–49

Deaut, R. le, 'Aspects de l'Intercession dans le Judaïsme Ancien', *JSJ* 1, 1970, pp. 35–57

Deichgräber, R., *Gotteshymnus und Christushymnus in der frühen Christenheit: Untersuchungen zu Form, Sprache und Stil der frühchristlichen Hymnen*, Göttingen 1967

Deissler, A., 'Der "Menschensohn" und "das Volk der Heiligen des Höchsten" in Dan. 7', *JMAV*, pp. 81–91

Delcor, M., 'Melchizedek from Genesis to the Qumran Texts and the Epistle to the Hebrews', *JSJ* 2, 1971, pp. 115–35

Demke, C., 'Der sogennante Logos-Hymnus im johanneischen Prolog', *ZNW* 58, 1967, pp. 45–68

Dembowski, H., *Einführung in die Christologie*, Darmstadt 1976

Dey, L. K. K., *The Intermediary World and Patterns of Perfection in Philo and Hebrews*, SBL Dissertation 25, Scholars Press 1975

Dibelius, M., 'Jungfrauensohn und Krippenkind: Untersuchungen zur Geburtsgeschichte Jesu im Lukas-Evangelium' (1932), *Botschaft und Geschichte: Gesammelte Aufsätze*, Vol. I, Tübingen 1953, pp. 1–78

— 'Die Christianisierung einer hellenistischer Formel' (1915), 'Der Herr und der Geist bei Paulus' (1939), and 'Der himmlische Kultus nach dem Hebräerbrief' (1942), *Botschaft und Geschichte*, Vol. II, Tübingen 1956, pp. 14–29, 128–33, 160–76

Dillistone, F. W., 'Wisdom, Word and Spirit: Revelation in the Wisdom Literature', *Interpretation* 2, 1948, pp. 275–87

Dodd, C. H., *The Bible and the Greeks*, Hodder and Stoughton 1935

— *The Interpretation of the Fourth Gospel*, Cambridge University Press 1953

Drummond J., *The Jewish Messiah: A Critical History of the Messianic Ideas of the Jews from the Rise of the Maccabees to the Closing of the Talmud*, Longmans 1877

— *Philo Judaeus, or The Jewish-Alexandrian Philosophy in its Development and Completion*, Williams and Norgate, 2 vols., 1888

Duling, D. C., 'The Promises to David and their Entrance into Christianity: Nailing down a Likely Hypothesis', *NTS* 20, 1973–74, pp. 55–77

Duncan, G. S., *Jesus, Son of Man*, Nisbet 1947

Dunn, J. D. G., 'II Corinthians 3.17 – "The Lord is the Spirit" ', *JTS* 21, 1970, pp. 309–20

— 'Jesus – Flesh and Spirit: an Exposition of Romans 1.3–4', *JTS* 24, 1973, pp. 40–68

— 'Paul's Understanding of the Death of Jesus', *RHLLM*, pp. 125–41

— 'I Corinthians 15.45 – Last Adam, Life-giving Spirit', *CSNT*, pp. 127–41

— *Jesus and the Spirit: A Study of the Religious and Charismatic Experience of Jesus and the First Christians as Reflected in the New Testament*, SCM Press 1975

— *Unity and Diversity in the New Testament: an Inquiry into the Character of Earliest Christianity*, SCM Press 1977

Dupont, J., '*Filius meus et tu*, l'interpretation de Ps. 2.7 dans le Nouveau Testament', *RSR* 35, 1948, pp. 522–43

— *Gnosis: la connaissance religieuse dans les épitres de saint Paul*, Paris 1949

— 'Jesus Christ dans son abaissement et son exaltation, d'apres Phil. 2.6–11', *RSR* 37, 1950, pp. 500–14

— *Essais sur le Christologie de Saint Jean: Le Christ, Parole, Lumière et Vie, La Gloire du Christ*, Bruges 1951

— 'Ascension du Christ et don de l'Esprit d'après Actes 2.33', *CSNT*, pp. 219–28

Dürr, L., *Die Wertung des göttlichen Wortes im Alten Testament und im Antiken Orient: Zugleich ein Beitrag zur Vorgeschichte des neutestamentlichen Logosbegriffes*, Leipzig 1938

Dusen, H. P. Van, *Spirit, Son and Father*, A. & C. Black 1960

Eccles, R. S., 'The Purpose of the Hellenistic Patterns in the Epistle to the Hebrews', *RAERG*, pp. 207–26

Edwards, R. A., *A Theology of Q*, Fortress 1976

Eichholz, G., *Die Theologie des Paulus im Umriss*, Neukirchen 1972

Eichrodt, W., *Theology of the Old Testament*, Vol. I, [6]1959, ET SCM Press 1961, Vol. II, [5]1964, ET SCM Press 1967

Ellis, E. E., 'Christ and Spirit in I Corinthians', *CSNT*, pp. 269–77

Eltester, W. F., *Eikon im Neuen Testament*, Berlin 1958
— 'Der Logos und sein Prophet', *Apophoreta: Festschrift für E. Haenchen*, Berlin 1964, pp. 109–34
Elwell, W., 'The Deity of Christ in the Writings of Paul', *CIMCT*, pp. 297–308
Emerton, J. A., 'The Origin of the Son of Man Imagery', *JTS* 9, 1958, pp. 225–42
— 'Some New Testament Notes', *JTS* 11, 1960, pp. 329–36
— 'Melchizedek and the Gods: Fresh Evidence for the Jewish Background of John 10.34–6', *JTS* 17, 1966, pp. 399–401
Epp, E. J., 'Wisdom, Torah, Word: the Johannine Prologue and the Purpose of the Fourth Gospel', *CIMCT*, pp. 128–46
Ernst, J., *Pleroma und Pleroma Christi: Geschichte und Deutung eines Begriffs der paulinischen Antilegomena*, Regensburg 1970
— *Anfänge der Christologie*, SBS 57, 1972

Farnell, L. R., *Greek Hero Cults and Ideas of Immortality*, Oxford University Press 1921
Festugière, A. J., 'A propos des arétalogies d'Isis', *HTR* 42, 1949, pp. 209–34
Feuillet, A., 'Le fils d'homme de Danièl et la tradition biblique', *RB* 60, 1953, pp. 170–202, 321–46
— 'Jésus et la Sagesse divine d'après les évangiles synoptiques', *RB* 62, 1955, pp. 161–96
— 'Les perspectives propres à chaque évangeliste dans le récit de la Transfiguration', *Biblica* 39, 1958, pp. 281–301
— 'Les "Chefs de ce siecle" et la Sagesse divine d'après I Cor. 2.6–8', *SPCIC* I, pp. 383–93
— 'L'énigme de I Cor. 2.9: Contribution a l'étude des sources de la christologique paulinienne', *RB* 70, 1963, pp. 52–74
— 'L'hymne christologique de l'épître aux Philippiens (2.6–11)', *RB* 72, 1965, pp. 352–80, 481–507
— 'La Création de l'Univers "dans le Christ" d'après L'Épître aux Colossiens (1.16a)', *NTS* 12, 1965–66, pp. 1–9
— 'Les *Ego Eimi* christologiques du quatrième Évangile', *RSR* 54, 1966, pp. 5–22, 213–40
— *Le Christ Sagesse de Dieu d'après les Épîtres Pauliniennes*, EB 1966
— *Le prologue du quatrième évangile: Étude de théologie johannique*, Bruges 1968
— ' "Témoins oculaires et serviteurs de la parole" (Luke 1.2b)', *NovT* 15, 1973, pp. 241–59
Findlay, J. A., *Jesus, Divine and Human*, Epworth 1938
Fiorenza, E. S., 'Wisdom Mythology and the Christological Hymns of the New Testament', *AWJEC*, pp. 17–41

Fischer, K. M., 'Der johanneische Christus und der gnostische Erlöser', *Gnosis und Neues Testament*, hrsg. K. W. Tröger, Gütersloh 1973, pp. 245–66

Fitzmyer, J. A., 'Further Light on Melchizedek from Qumran Cave 11', *JBL* 86, 1967, pp. 25–41, reprinted in *Essays on the Semitic Background of the New Testament*, Chapman 1971, pp. 245–67

— 'The Virginal Conception of Jesus in the New Testament', *TS* 34, 1973, pp. 541–75

— 'The Contribution of Qumran Aramaic to the Study of the New Testament', *NTS* 20, 1973–74, pp. 382–407, reprinted in *A Wandering Aramean: Collected Aramaic Essays*, Scholars Press 1979, pp. 85–113 (with 'Addendum: Implications of the 4Q "Son of God" Text' – pp. 102–7)

— 'The New Testament Title "Son of Man" Philologically Considered', *Wandering Aramean*, pp. 143–60

— 'Another View of the "Son of Man" Debate', *JSNT* 4, 1979, pp. 58–68

Flusser, D., *Jesus*, 1968, ET Herder 1969

Foakes-Jackson, F. J. and Lake, K., 'Christology', *Beginnings* Vol. I, pp. 345–418

Foerster, W., 'Der heilige Geist im Spätjudentum', *NTS* 8, 1961–62, pp. 117–34

Ford, J. M., ' "The Son of Man – a Euphemism?', *JBL* 87, 1968, pp. 257–66

Formesyn, R. E. C., 'Was there a Pronomial Connection for the Bar Nasha Self designation?', *NovT* 8, 1966, pp. 1–35

Fortna, R. T., 'Christology in the Fourth Gospel: Redaction-Critical Perspectives', *NTS* 21, 1974–75, pp. 489–504

Francis, F. O., and Meeks, W. A., (eds.), *Conflict at Colossae: A Problem in the Interpretation of Early Christianity Illustrated by Selected Modern Studies*, Scholars Press 1973

Freed, E. D., 'The Son of Man in the Fourth Gospel', *JBL* 86, 1967, pp. 402–9

— 'Theology Prelude to the Prologue of John's Gospel', *SJT* 32, 1979, pp. 257–69

Frost, G., 'The Word of God in the Synoptic Gospels', *SJT* 16, 1963, pp. 186–94

Frövig, D. A., *Das Sendungsbewusstsein Jesu und der Geist*, Gütersloh 1924

Fuchs, E., *Christus und der Geist bei Paulus*, Leipzig 1932

— 'Muss man an Jesus glauben, wenn man an Gott glauben will?', *ZTK* 58, 1961, pp. 45–67

Fuller, R. H. 'The Virgin Birth: Historical Fact or Kerygmatic Truth?', *BR* 1, 1956, pp. 1–8

— *The Foundations of New Testament Christology*, Lutterworth 1965

— 'The Conception/Birth of Jesus as a Christological Moment', *JSNT* 1, 1978, pp. 37–52

Furness, J. M. 'Behind the Philippian Hymn', *ExpT* 79, 1967–68, pp. 178–82

Gabathuler, H. J., *Jesus Christus: Haupt der Kirche – Haupt der Welt: Der Christushymnus Kolosser 1.15–20 in der theologischen Forschung der letzten 130 Jahre*, Zürich 1965

Gager, J. G., *Moses in Greco-Roman Paganism*, SBL Monograph 16, 1972

Galloway, A. D., *The Cosmic Christ*, Nisbet 1951

Galot, J., *La Personne du Christ: Recherche ontologique*, Gembloux and Paris 1969

— *La Conscience de Jésus*, Gembloux and Paris 1971

— *Vers une nouvelle christologie*, Gembloux and Paris 1971

Gärtner, B. E., 'The Pauline and Johannine Idea of "to know God" against the Hellenistic Background', *NTS* 14, 1967–68, pp. 209–31

Gelston, A., 'A Sidelight on the "Son of Man" ', *SJT* 22, 1969, pp. 189–96

Georgi, D., 'Der vorpaulinische Hymnus Phil. 2.6–11', *Zeit und Geschichte: Dankesgabe an R. Bultmann*, hrsg. E. Dinkler, Tübingen 1964, pp. 263–93

— *Die Gegner des Paulus im 2. Korintherbrief*, Neukirchen 1964

Gerber W., 'Die Metamorphose Jesu, Mark 9.2f., par.', *TZ* 23, 1967, pp. 385–95

Gero, S., ' "My Son the Messiah": A Note on IV Ezra 7.28f.', *ZNW* 66, 1975, pp. 264–7

Gese, H., 'Der Messias' and 'Der Johannesprolog', *Zur biblische Theologie: Alttestamentliche Vorträge*, München 1977, pp. 128–51, 152–201

Gewiess, J., 'Zum altkirchlichen Verständnis der Kenosisstelle (Phil. 2.5–11)', *ThQ* 120, 1948, pp. 463–87

— 'Die Philipperstelle 2.6b', *Neutestamentliche Aufsätze: Festschrift für J. Schmid*, hrsg. J. Blinzler, O. Kuss and F. Mussner, Regensburg 1963, pp. 69–85

Gibbs. J. G., 'The Relation between Creation and Redemption according to Phil. 2.5–11', *NovT* 12, 1970, pp. 270–83

— *Creation and Redemption: A Study in Pauline Theology*, SNT XXVI, Leiden 1971

— 'Pauline Cosmic Christology and Ecological Crisis', *JBL* 90, 1971, pp. 466–79

— 'The Cosmic Scope of Redemption according to Paul', *Biblica* 56, 1975, pp. 13–29

Giblin, C. H., 'The Monotheistic Texts in Paul', *CBQ* 37, 1975, pp. 527–47

Giles, P., 'The Son of Man in the Epistle to the Hebrews', *ExpT* 86, 1974–75, pp. 328–32

Glasson, T. F., *The Second Advent: The Origin of the New Testament Doctrine*, Epworth 1945, ³1963

— 'Heraclitus' Alleged Logos Doctrine', *JTS* 3, 1952, pp. 231–8

— 'John 1.9 and a Rabbinic Tradition', *ZNW* 49, 1958, pp. 288–90

— *Moses in the Fourth Gospel*, SCM Press 1963

— ' "Plurality of Divine Persons" and the Quotations in Hebrews 1.6ff.', *NTS* 12, 1965–66, pp. 270–2

— 'Colossians 1.18, 25 and Sirach 24', *JBL* 86, 1967, pp. 214–16 = *NovT* 11, 1969, pp. 154–6

— 'The Uniqueness of Christ: the New Testament Witness', *EQ* 43, 1971, pp. 25–35

— 'Two Notes on the Philippians Hymn (2.6–11)', *NTS* 21, 1974–75, pp. 133–9

— 'The Son of Man Imagery: Enoch 14 and Daniel 7', *NTS* 23, 1976–77, pp. 82–90

Gnilka, J., *Jesus Christus nach frühen Zeugnisses des Glaubens*, München 1970

Gogarten, F., *Christ the Crisis*, 1967, ET SCM Press 1970

Goldberg, A. M., *Untersuchungen über die Vorstellung von der Schekhinah in der frühen rabbinischen Literatur*, Berlin 1969

Goldin, J., ' "Not by Means of an Angel and not by Means of a Messenger" ', *RAERG*, pp. 412–24

Goodenough, E. R., *By Light, Light*, New Haven 1935

Goppelt, L., 'Zum Problem des Menschensohns: Das Verhältnis von Leidens– und Parusieankündigung' (1963), *Christologie und Ethik: Aufsätze zum Neuen Testament*, Göttingen 1968, pp. 66–78

— *Theologie des Neuen Testaments*, Göttingen Vol. I, 1975, Vol. II, 1976

Gore, C., *The Incarnation of the Son of God*, John Murray 1891

Göttsberger, J., *Die göttliche Weisheit als Persönlichkeit im Alten Testament*, Münster 1919

Goulder, M., (ed.), *Incarnation and Myth: The Debate Continued*, SCM Press 1979

Gourges, M., *A la Droite de Dieu: Résurrection de Jésus et actualisation du Psaume 110.1 dans le Nouveau Testament*, EB 1978

Grant, R. M., *Gnosticism and Early Christianity*, 1959, Harper Torchbook ²1966

Grässer, E., 'Hebräer 1.1–4: Ein exegetisch Versuch', *EKK Vorarbeiten*, Heft 3, 1971, pp. 55–91, reprinted in *Text und Situation: Gesammelte Aufsätze zum Neuen Testament*, Gütersloh 1973, pp. 182–228

— 'Zur Christologie des Hebräerbriefes: Eine Auseinandersetzung mit Herbert Braun', *NTCEHB*, pp. 195–206

— 'Beobachtungen zum Menschensohn in Heb. 2.6', *JMAV*, pp. 404–14

Green, M. (ed.), *The Truth of God Incarnate*, Hodder and Stoughton 1977

Grelot, P., 'La Legende d'Hénoch dans les Apocryphes et dans la Bible: Origine et signification', *RSR* 46, 1958, pp. 5–26, 181–210

— 'Deux expressions difficiles de Philippiens 2.6–7', *Biblica* 53, 1972, pp. 495–507

— 'La valeur de οὐκ . . . ἀλλά dans Philippiens 2.6–7', and 'Deux notes critiques sur Philippiens 2.6–11', *Biblica* 54, 1973, pp. 25–42, 169–86

Grensted, L. W., *The Person of Christ*, Nisbet 1933

Grether, O., *Name und Wort Gottes im Alten Testament*, Giessen 1934

Grillmeier, A., *Christ in Christian Tradition*, ET Mowbray ²1975

Grundmann, H., *Der Begriff der Kraft in der neutestamentlicher Gedankenwelt*, Stuttgart 1932

— 'Sohn Gottes', *ZNW* 47, 1956, pp. 113–33

— 'Matt. 11.27 und die Johanneischen "Der Vater-Der Sohn"–Stellen', *NTS* 12, 1965–66, pp. 42–9

— 'Weisheit im Horizont des Reiches Gottes: Eine Studie zur Verkündigung Jesu nach der Spruchüberlieferung Q', *KAHS*, pp. 175–99

Gundry, R. H., 'The Form, Meaning and Background of the Hymn Quoted in I Timothy 3.16', *AHGFFB*, pp. 203–22

Gunkel, H., *Die Wirkungen des heiligen Geistes nach der populären Anschauung der apostolischen Zeit und nach der Lehre des Apostels Paulus*, Göttingen 1888

Gutwenger, E., 'The Problem of Christ's Knowledge', *Concilium* 2.1, 1966, pp. 48–55

Haacker, K., *Die Stiftung des Heils: Untersuchungen zur Struktur der johanneischen Theologie*, Stuttgart 1972

Haacker, K. and Schäfer, P., 'Nachbiblische Traditionen vom Tod des Mose', *Josephus Studien: Untersuchungen zu Josephus, dem antiken Judentum und dem Neuen Testament*, O. Michel Festschrift, hrsg. O. Betz, K. Haacker and M. Hengel, Göttingen 1974, pp. 147–74

Haag, H., 'Sohn Gottes im Alten Testament', *ThQ* 154, 1974, pp. 223–31

Haenchen, E., 'Gab es eine vorchristliche Gnosis?', *ZTK* 49, 1952, pp. 316–49, reprinted *GMEH*, pp. 265–98

— 'Der Vater, der mich gesandt hat', *NTS* 9, 1962–63, pp. 208–16, reprinted *GMEH*, pp. 68–77

— 'Probleme des johanneischen "Prologs" ', *ZTK* 60, 1963, pp. 305–34, reprinted *GMEH*, pp. 114–43

— 'Die frühe Christologie', *ZTK* 63, 1966, pp. 145–59

— 'Vom Wandel des Jesusbildes in der frühen Gemeinde', *Verborum Veritatis: Festschrift für G. Stählin*, hrsg. O. Böcher and K. Haacker, Wuppertal 1970, pp. 3–14

Hahn, F., *The Titles of Jesus in Christology: Their History in Early Christianity*, 1963, ET Lutterworth 1969

— 'Methodenprobleme einer Christologie des Neuen Testaments', *VuF* 15, 1970/2, pp. 3–41

Hagner, D. A., 'The Vision of God in Philo and John: A Comparative Study', *Journal of the Evangelical Theological Society* 14, 1971, pp. 81–93

Hamerton-Kelly, R. G., *Pre-existence, Wisdom and the Son of Man: A Study of the Idea of Pre-existence in the New Testament*, Cambridge University Press 1973

Hamilton, N. Q., *The Holy Spirit and Eschatology in Paul*, *SJT* Occasional Paper 6, 1957

— *Jesus for a No-God World*, Westminster 1969

Hamp, V., *Der Begriff 'Wort' in den aramäischen Bibelübersetzungen: Ein exegetischer Beitrag zur Hypostasen-Frage und zur Geschichte der Logos-Spekulation*, München 1938

Hanson, A. T., 'John's Citation of Ps. 82', *NTS* 11, 1964–65, pp. 158–62

— 'John's Citation of Ps. 82 Reconsidered', *NTS* 13, 1966–67, pp. 363–7

— *Jesus Christ in the Old Testament*, SPCK 1965

— *Grace and Truth: a Study in the Doctrine of the Incarnation*, SPCK 1975

— 'John 1.14–18 and Exodus 34', *NTS* 23, 1976–77, pp. 90–101, reprinted in *The New Testament Interpretation of Scripture*, SPCK 1980, pp. 97–109

Harnack, A., *History of Dogma*, ³1894, ET Williams and Norgate 1897

Harner, P. B., *The 'I Am' of the Fourth Gospel: A Study in Johannine Usage and Thought*, Fortress Facet Book 1970

Harris, R., *The Origin of the Prologue of St John's Gospel*, Cambridge University Press 1917

— 'Athena, Sophia and the Logos', *BJRL* 7, 1922–23, pp. 56–72

Harrison, E. F., 'A Study of John 1.14', *UDNTT*, pp. 23–36

Harvey, J., 'A New Look at the Christ Hymn in Philippians 2.6–11', *ExpT* 76, 1964–65, pp. 337–9

Hasel, G. F., 'The Identity of "The Saints of the Most High" in Daniel 7', *Biblica* 56, 1975, pp. 173–92

Hasler, V., 'Epiphanie und Christologie in den Pastoralbriefen', *TZ* 33, 1977, pp. 193–209

Haufe, G., 'Entrückung und eschatologische Funktion im Spätjudentum', *Zeitschrift für Religions- und Geistesgeschichte* 13, 1961, pp. 105–13

— 'Das Menschensohn-Problem in der gegenwärtigen wissen-schaftlichen Diskussion', *EvTh* 26, 1966, pp. 130–41

Hay, D. M., *Glory at the Right Hand: Psalm 110 in Early Christianity*, SBL Monograph 18, Abingdon 1973

Hayes, J. H., 'The Resurrection as Enthronement and the Earliest Church Christology', *Interpretation* 22, 1968, pp. 333–45

Hayward, C. T. R., 'The Memra of YHWH and the Development of its Use in Targum Neofiti I', *JJS* 25, 1974, pp. 412–18

— 'Phinehas – the same is Elijah: the Origins of a Rabbinic Tradition', *JJS* 29, 1978, pp. 22–38

— 'The Holy Name of the God of Moses and the Prologue of St John's Gospel', *NTS* 25, 1978–79, pp. 16–32

Hebblethwaite, B., 'The Propriety of the Doctrine of the Incarnation as a Way of Interpreting Christ', *SJT* 33, 1980, pp. 201–22

Hegermann, H., *Die Vorstellung vom Schöpfungsmittler im hellenistischen Judentum und Urchristentum*, Berlin 1961

— 'Er kam in sein Eigentum', *RJAGJJ*, pp. 112–31

Helmbold, A. K., 'Redeemer Hymns – Gnostic and Christian', *NDNTS*, pp. 71–8

Hendry, G. S., *The Holy Spirit in Christian Theology*, 1956, SCM Press ²1965

— *The Gospel of the Incarnation*, Westminster 1958, SCM Press 1959

Hengel, M., 'Christologie und neutestamentliche Chronologie', *NTGOC*, pp. 43–67

— *Judaism and Hellenism: Studies in their Encounter in Palestine during the Early Hellenistic Period*, ²1973, ET SCM Press 1974

— *The Son of God: The Origin of Christology and the History of Jewish-Hellenistic Religion*, 1975, ET SCM Press 1976

Héring, J., 'Kyrios Anthropos', *RHPR* 16, 1936, pp. 196–209

— *Le Royaume de Dieu et sa Venue*, Paris/Neuchatel 1937, ²1959

Hermann, I., *Kyrios und Pneuma: Studien zur Christologie der paulinischen Hauptbriefe*, München 1961

Heron, A., ' "Logos, Image, Son": Some Models and Paradigms in Early Christology', *Creation, Christ and Culture: Studies in Honour of T. F. Torrance*, ed. R. W. A. McKinney, T. & T. Clark 1976, pp. 43–62

— 'Article Review: Doing without the Incarnation?', *SJT* 31, 1978, pp. 51–71

Hick, J., (ed.), *The Myth of God Incarnate*, SCM Press 1977

Higgins, A. J. B., 'Son of Man *Forschung* since "The Teaching of Jesus" ', *NTETWM*, pp. 119–35

— *Jesus and the Son of Man*, Lutterworth 1964

— 'Jewish Messianic Belief in Justin Martyr's *Dialogue with Trypho*', *NovT* 9, 1967, pp. 298–305

— 'Is the Son of Man Problem Insoluble?', *Neotestamentica et Semitica: Studies in Honour of Matthew Black*, ed. E. E. Ellis and M. Wilcox, T. & T. Clark 1969, pp. 70–87

— ' "Menschensohn" oder "ich", in Q: Luke 12.8–9/Matt. 10.32–3?', *JMAV*, pp. 117–23

— *The Son of Man in the Teaching of Jesus*, Cambridge University Press 1980

Hill, D., 'The Relevance of the Logos Christology', *ExpT* 78, 1966–67, pp. 136–9

— *Greek Words and Hebrew Meanings*, Cambridge University Press 1967

— ' "Son of Man" in Psalm 80.17', *NovT* 15, 1973, pp. 261–9

Hockel, A., *Christus der Erstgeborene: zur Geschichte der Exegese von Kol. 1.15*, Düsseldorf 1965

Hodgson, L., *The Doctrine of the Trinity*, Nisbet 1943

Hodgson, P. C., *Jesus – Word and Presence: An Essay in Christology*, Fortress 1971

Hoffmann, P., *Studien zur Theologie der Logienquelle*, Münster 1972

Hofius, O., 'Inkarnation und Opfertod Jesu nach Heb. 10.19f.', *RJAGJJ*, pp. 132–41

— ' "Erwählt vor Grundlegung der Welt" (Eph. 1.4)', *ZNW* 62, 1971, pp. 123–8

— *Der Christushymnus Philipper 2.6–11*, Tübingen 1976

Holladay, C. H., *Theios Aner in Hellenistic Judaism*, SBL Dissertation 40, 1977

Holtz, T., *Die Christologie der Apokalypse des Johannes*, Berlin 1962

Hooke, S. H., 'The Translation of Romans 1.4', *NTS* 9, 1962–63, pp. 370f.

Hooker, M. D., 'Adam in Romans 1', *NTS* 6, 1959–60, pp. 297–306

— 'A Further Note on Romans 1', *NTS* 13, 1966–67, pp. 181–3

— *The Son of Man in Mark*, SPCK 1967

— 'John the Baptist and the Johannine Prologue', *NTS* 16, 1969–70, pp. 354–8

— 'Interchange in Christ', *JTS* 22, 1971, pp. 349–61

— 'Philippians 2.6–11', *Jesus und Paulus: Festschrift für W. G. Kümmel*, hrsg. E. E. Ellis and E. Grässer, Göttingen 1975, pp. 151–64

— 'Interchange and Atonement', *BJRL* 60, 1977–78, pp. 462–81

— 'Is the Son of Man problem really insoluble?', *Text and Interpretation: Studies in the New Testament presented to Matthew Black*, ed. E. Best and R. McL. Wilson, Cambridge University Press 1979, pp. 155–68

Horsley, R. A., 'Pneumatikos vs. Psychikos: Distinction of Spiritual Status among the Corinthians', *HTR* 69, 1976, pp. 269–88

— 'The Background of the Confessional Formula in I Kor. 8.6', *ZNW* 69, 1978, pp. 130–5

— ' "How can some of you say that there is no resurrection of the dead?" Spiritual Elitism in Corinth', *NovT* 20, 1978, pp. 203–31

Horstmann, M., *Studien zur markinischen Christologie: Mark 8.27–9.13 als Zugang zum Christusbild des Zweiten Evangeliums*, Münster 1969

Horton, F. L., *The Melchizedek Tradition: a critical examination of the sources to the fifth century AD and in the Epistle to the Hebrews*, Cambridge University Press 1976

Houlden, J. L., 'The Doctrine of the Trinity and the Person of Christ', *Church Quarterly Review* 169, 1968, pp. 4–18; reprinted in *Explorations in Theology 3*, SCM Press 1978, pp. 25–39

Howard, G., 'The Tetragram and the New Testament', *JBL* 96, 1977, pp. 63–83

— 'Phil. 2.6–11 and the Human Christ', *CBQ* 40, 1978, pp. 368–87

Howton, J., ' "Son of God" in the Fourth Gospel', *NTS* 10, 1963–64, pp. 227–37

— 'The Theology of the Incarnation in Justin Martyr', *SP* 9, 1966, pp. 231–9

Hruby, K., 'La Torah identifiée à la Sagesse et l'activité du "Sage" dans la tradition rabbinique', *Bible et Vie Chrétienne* 76, 1967, pp. 65–78

Hudson, D. F., 'A Further Note on Philippians 2.6–11', *ExpT* 77, 1965–66, p. 29

Hughes, J. H., 'John the Baptist: the Forerunner of God Himself', *NovT* 14, 1972, pp. 191–218

Hunter, A. M., 'Crux Criticorum – Matt. 11.25–30: A Re-appraisal', *NTS* 8, 1961–62, pp. 241–9

Huntress, E., ' "Son of God" in Jewish Writings prior to the Christian Era', *JBL* 54, 1935, pp. 117–23

Hunzinger, C. H., 'Zur Struktur des Christus-Hymnen in Phil. 2 und I Pet. 3', *RJAGJJ*, pp. 142–56

Huonder, V., *Israel Sohn Gottes: Zur Deutung eines alttestamentlichen Themas in der jüdischen Exegese des Mittelalters*, Freiburg and Göttingen 1975

Hurtado, L. W., 'New Testament Christology: A Critique of Bousset's Influence', *TS* 40, 1979, pp. 306–17

Iersel, B. M. F. van, *'Der Sohn' in den synoptischen Jesusworten* , SNT III ²1964

Imschoot, P. van, 'Sagesse et Esprit dans l'Ancien Testament', *RB* 47, 1938, pp. 23–49

Irwin, W. A., 'Where shall Wisdom be Found?', *JBL* 80, 1961, pp. 133–42

Isaacs, M. E., *The Concept of Spirit: A Study of Pneuma in Hellenistic Judaism and its Bearing on the New Testament*, Heythrop Monograph 1, 1976

Jaeger, H., 'The Patristic Conception of Wisdom in the Light of Biblical and Rabbinical Research', *SP* IV, 1961, pp. 90–106

Jay, E. G., *Son of Man, Son of God*, SPCK 1965

Jendorff, B., *Der Logosbegriff: seine philosophische Grundlegung bei Heraklit von Ephesos und seine theologische Indienstnahme durch Johannes den Evangelisten*, Frankfurt and Bern 1976

Jeremias, J., 'Zu Phil. 2.7: Ἑαυτὸν ἐκένωσεν', *NovT* 6, 1963, pp. 182–8

— *The Central Message of the New Testament*, SCM Press 1965

— 'Die älteste Schicht der Menschensohn-Logien', *ZNW* 58, 1967, pp. 159–72

— *The Prayers of Jesus*, 1966, ET SCM Press 1967

— *New Testament Theology: Vol. I – The Proclamation of Jesus*, 1971, ET SCM Press 1971

— 'Zum Logos-Problem', *ZNW* 59, 1968, pp. 82–5

— 'Hebräer 10.20: τουτ' ἔστιν τῆς σαρκὸς αὐτοῦ', *ZNW* 62, 1971, p. 131

Jervell, J., ' "Er kam in sein Eigentum": Zum John 1.11', *St Th* 10, 1956, pp. 14–27

— *Imago Dei: Gen. 1.26f. im Spätjudentum, in der Gnosis und in den paulinischen Briefen*, Göttingen 1960

Jocz, J., 'The Invisibility of God and the Incarnation', *Judaica* 17, 1961, pp. 195–206

Johansson, N., *Parakletoi: Vorstellungen von Fürsprechern für die Menschen vor Gott in der alttestamentlichen Religion, im Spätjudentum und Urchristentum*, Lund 1940

Johnson, A. R., *The One and the Many in the Israelite Conception of God*, University of Wales 1942

Johnson, M. D., 'Reflections on a Wisdom Approach to Matthew's Christology', *CBQ* 36, 1974, pp. 44–64

Johnston, G., *The Spirit-Paraclete in the Gospel of John*, Cambridge University Press 1970

Jones, G. V., *Christology and Myth in the New Testament*, Allen and Unwin 1956

Jonge, M. de and Woude, A. S. van der, '11Q Melchizedek and the New Testament', *NTS* 12, 1965–66, pp. 301–26

Jonge, M. de, 'The Role of Intermediaries in God's Final Intervention in the Future according to the Qumran Scrolls', *Studies on the Jewish Background of the New Testament*, O. Michel *et al.*, Assen, 1969, pp. 44–63

— 'Jewish Expectations about the "Messiah" according to the Fourth Gospel', *NTS* 19, 1972–73, pp. 246–70

— *Jesus: Stranger from Heaven*, Scholars Press 1977

Jüngel, E., *Paulus und Jesus: eine Untersuchung zur Präzisierung der Frage nach dem Ursprung der Christologie*, Tübingen 1962 ³1967

— 'Das Verhältnis von "ökonomischer" und "immanenter" Trinität', *ZTK* 72, 1975, pp. 353–64

Käsemann, E., *Das wandernde Gottesvolk: Eine Untersuchung zum Hebräerbrief*, Göttingen 1939, ⁴1961

— 'The Problem of the Historical Jesus' (1954) and 'A Primitive Christian Baptismal Liturgy' (1949), *ENTT*, pp. 15–47, 149–68

— 'A Critical Analysis of Philippians 2.5–11' (*ZTK* 47, 1950, pp. 313–60), ET *JThC* 5, 1968, pp. 45–88

— 'The Structure and Purpose of the Prologue to John's Gospel' (1957), ET *NTQT*, pp. 138–67

— *The Testament of Jesus*, 1966, ET SCM Press 1968

Kasper, W., *Jesus the Christ*, 1974, ET Search Press 1976

— 'Wer ist Jesus Christus für uns heute?', *ThQ* 154, 1974, pp. 203–22

Katz, S., 'Christology – A Jewish View', *SJT* 24, 1971, pp. 184–200

Kayatz, C., *Studien zu Proverbien 1–9*, Neukirchen 1966

Kee, H. C., 'The Transfiguration in Mark: Epiphany or Apocalyptic Vision?', *Understanding the Sacred Text*, M. S. Enslin Festschrift, ed. J. Reumann, Valley Forge 1972, pp. 135–52

Kehl, N., *Der Christushymnus im Kolosserbrief: Eine motiv-geschichtliche Untersuchung zu Kol. 1.12–20*, Stuttgart 1967

Keller, W., *Die Logoslehre von Heraklit bis Origenes*, Stuttgart 1958

Kelly, B., 'Current Problems in Christology', *Irish Theological Quarterly* 37, 1970, pp. 280–91

Kelly, J. N. D., *Early Christian Creeds*, Longmans 1950, ²1960

— *Early Christian Doctrines*, A. & C. Black 1958, ²1960

Kennedy, H. A. A., *Philo's Contribution to Religion*, Hodder & Stoughton 1919

Kerst, R., 'I Kor. 8.6 – ein vorpaulinisches Taufbekenntnis', *ZNW* 66, 1975, pp. 130–9

Kingsbury, J. D., *Matthew: Structure, Christology, Kingdom*, Fortress 1975

Kippenberg, H. G., *Garizim und Synagoge: Traditionsgeschichtliche Untersuchungen zur samaritanischen Religion der aramäischen Period*, Berlin 1971

Kittel, H., *Die Herrlichkeit Gottes: Studien zu Geschichte und Wesen eines neutestamentlichen Begriffs*, Giessen 1934

Klappert, B., *Die Eschatologie des Hebräerbriefes*, München 1969

Klausner, J., *The Messianic Idea in Israel*, ET Allen and Unwin 1956

— 'The Messianic Idea in the Apocryphal Literature', *The World History of the Jewish People*: I.8 – *Society and Religion in the Second Temple Period*, ed. M. Avi-Yonah and Z. Baras, Jerusalem 1977, pp. 153–86

Knight, G. A. F., *A Biblical Approach to the Doctrine of the Trinity*, *SJT* Occasional Paper 1, 1953

Knox, J., *The Death of Christ: the Cross in New Testament History and Faith*, Abingdon 1958, Fontana 1967

— *The Church and the Reality of Christ*, Collins 1962

— *The Humanity and Divinity of Christ*, Cambridge University Press 1967

Knox, W. L., 'The Divine Wisdom', *JTS* 38, 1937, pp. 230–7

— *St Paul and the Church of the Gentiles*, Cambridge University Press 1939

— *Some Hellenistic Elements in Primitive Christianity*, Oxford University Press for the British Academy 1944

— 'The "Divine Hero" Christology in the New Testament', *HTR* 41, 1948, pp. 229–49

Koch, G., 'Jesus Christus – Schöpfer der Welt', *ZTK* 56, 1959, pp. 83–109

Kodell, J., ' "The Word of God Grew": the Ecclesial Tendency of Λόγος in Acts 1.7, 12.24, 19.20', *Biblica* 55, 1974, pp. 505–19

Kraeling, C. H., *Anthropos and the Son of Man: A Study in the Religious Syncretism of the Hellenistic Orient*, New York 1927

Krämer, M., 'Die Menschwerdung Jesu Christi nach Matthäus (Matt. 1): Sein Anliegen und sein literarisches Verfahren', *Biblica* 45, 1964, pp. 1–50

Kramer, W., *Christ, Lord, Son of God*, 1963, ET SCM Press 1966

Kretschmar, G., *Studien zur frühchristlichen Trinitätstheologie*, Tübingen 1956

Kruijf, T. de, *Der Sohn des lebendigen Gottes: ein Beitrag zur Christologie des Matthäusevangeliums*, Analecta Biblica 16, Rome 1962

— 'The Glory of the Only Son (John 1.14)', *Studies in John: Presented to J. N. Sevenster*, SNT XXIV, 1970, pp. 111–23

Kuhn, H. B., 'The Angelology of the non-canonical Jewish Apocalypse', *JBL* 67, 1948, pp. 217–32

Kümmel, W. G., 'Mythische Rede und Heilsgeschehen im Neuen Testament' (1947), and 'Mythos im Neuen Testament' (1950), *Heilsgeschehen und Geschichte: Gesammelte Aufsätze 1933–64*, Marburg 1965, pp. 153–68, 218–29

— *The Theology of the New Testament According to its Major Witnesses, Jesus – Paul – John*, 1972, ET SCM Press 1974

— 'Das Verhalten Jesu gegenüber und das Verhalten des Menschensohns', *JMAV*, pp. 210–24

Küng, H., *On Being a Christian*, ET Collins 1976

Kvanvig, H. S., 'Struktur und Geschichte in Dan. 7.1–14', *StTh* 32, 1978, pp. 95–117

Kysar, R., 'Rudolf Bultmann's Interpretation of the Concept of Creation in John 1.3–4', *CBQ* 32, 1970, pp. 77–85

— 'The Background of the Prologue of the Fourth Gospel: A Critique of Historical Methods', *Canadian Journal of Theology* 16, 1970, pp. 250–5

— *The Fourth Evangelist and his Gospel*, Augsburg 1975

Labuschagne, C. J., *The Incomparability of Yahweh in the Old Testament*, Leiden 1966

Lacan, M. F., 'L'oeuvre du verbe incarné: le don de la vie (John 1.4)', *RSR* 45, 1957, pp. 61–78

Lacey, D. R. de, 'Image and Incarnation in Pauline Christology: A Search for Origins', *Tyndale Bulletin* 30, 1979, pp. 3–28

Ladd, G. E., *A Theology of the New Testament*, Eerdmans 1974, Lutterworth 1975

Laflamme, R. and Gervais, M. (eds.), *Le Christ hier, aujourd'hui et demain: Colloque de christologie tenu à l'Université Laval (1975)*, Quebec 1976

Lagrange, M. J., 'Vers le Logos de Saint Jean', *RB* 32, 1923, pp. 161–84, 321–71

— 'Les origines du dogme paulinien de la divinité du Christ', *RB* 45, 1936, pp. 5–33

Lamarche, P., 'Le Prologue de Jean', *RSR* 52, 1964, pp. 497–537

Lampe, G. W. H., 'The Lucan Portrait of Christ', *NTS* 2, 1955–56, pp. 160–75

— 'The New Testament Doctrine of *Ktisis*', *SJT* 17, 1964, pp. 449–62

— 'The Essence of Christianity', *ExpT* 87, 1975–76, pp. 132–7

— *God as Spirit: the Bampton Lectures 1976*, Oxford University Press 1977

Langevin, P. E., 'Une confession prépaulinienne de la "Seigneurie" du Christ: Exégèse de Romains 1.3–4', *Le Christ hier, aujourd'hui et demain*, ed. R. Laflamme et M. Gervais, Quebec 1976, pp. 277–327

Langkammer, H., 'Zur Herkunft des Logostitels im Johannesprolog', *BZ* 9, 1965, pp. 91–4

— ' "Den er zum Erben von allem eingesetzt hat" (Heb. 1.2)', *BZ* 10, 1966, pp. 273–80

— 'Die Einwohnung der "absoluten Seinsfülle" in Christus: Bemerkungen zu Kol. 1.19', *BZ* 12, 1968, pp. 258–63

— 'Literarische und theologische Einzelstücke in I Kor. 8.6', *NTS* 17, 1970–71, pp. 193–7

Larcher, C., 'Divine Transcendence: Another Reason for God's Absence', *Concilium* 5.10, 1969, pp. 26–33

— *Études sur le livre de la Sagesse*, Paris 1969

Larsson, E., *Christus als Vorbild: Eine Untersuchung zu den paulinischen Tauf- und Eikontexten*, Uppsala 1962

Laubscher, F. du Toit, 'God's Angel of Truth and Melchizedek: A Note on 11QMelch. 13b', *JSJ* 3, 1972, pp. 46–51

Laurentin, A, 'Le pneuma dans la doctrine de Philon', *ETL* 27, 1951, pp. 390–437

Leaney, A. R. C., ' "Conformed to the Image of his Son" (Rom. 8.29)', *NTS* 10, 1963–64, pp. 470–9

Lebram, J. C. H., 'Die Theologie der späten Chokma und häretisches Judentum', *ZAW* 77, 1965, pp. 202–11

Lebreton, J., *History of the Dogma of the Trinity: From its Origins to the Council of Nicaea*, ET Burns, Oates and Washbourne 1939

Legasse, S., 'Jésus historique et le Fils de l'Homme: Aperçu sur les opinions contemporaines', *ATE*, pp. 271–98

Leisegang, H., *Pneuma-Hagion: Der Ursprung des Geistesbegriffes der synoptischen Evangelien aus der griechischen Mystik*, Leipzig 1922

Leivestad, R., 'An Interpretation of Matt. 11.19', *JBL* 72, 1953, pp. 179–81

— 'Der apokalyptische Menschensohn ein theologische Phantom', *Annual of the Swedish Theological Institute* VI, 1968, pp. 49–105

— 'Exit the Apocalyptic Son of Man', *NTS* 18, 1971–72, pp. 243–67

Lella, A. A. Di, 'The One in Human Likeness and the Holy Ones of the Most High in Daniel 7', *CBQ* 39, 1977, pp. 1–19

Lentzen-Deis, F., 'Ps. 2.7, ein Motiv früher "hellenistischer" Christologie?', *Theologie und Philosophie* 44, 1969, pp. 342–62

Liefeld, W. L., 'Theological Motifs in the Transfiguration Narrative', *NDNTS*, pp. 162–79

Lienhard, J. T., 'The Christology of the Epistle to Diognetus', *VC* 24, 1970, pp. 280–9

Lietzmann, H., *Der Menschensohn*, Freiburg and Leipzig 1896

Lindars B., *New Testament Apologetic: The Doctrinal Significance of the Old Testament Quotations*, SCM Press 1961

— 'The Son of Man in the Johannine Christology', *CSNT*, pp. 43–60

— 'The Apocalyptic Myth and the Death of Christ', *BJRL* 57, 1974–75, pp. 366–87

— 'Re-Enter the Apocalyptic Son of Man', *NTS* 22, 1975–76, pp. 52–72

— 'Jesus as Advocate: a Contribution to the Christology Debate', *BJRL* 62, 1979–80, pp. 476–97

Lindars, B. and Smalley, S. S., *Christ and Spirit in the New Testament: Studies in Honour of C. F. D. Moule*, Cambridge University Press, 1973

Lindeskog, G., 'Das Rätsel des Menschensohnes', *StTh* 22, 1968, pp. 149–76

Linnemann, E., 'Tradition und Interpretation in Röm. 1.3f.', *EvTh* 31, 1971, pp. 264–75

Linton, O., 'The Trial of Jesus and the Interpretation of Psalm 110', *NTS* 7, 1960–61, pp. 258–62

Loader, W. R. G., 'Christ at the right hand – Ps. 110.1 in the New Testament', *NTS* 24, 1977–78, pp. 199–217

— 'The Apocalyptic Model of Sonship: Its Origin and Development in New Testament Tradition', *JBL* 97, 1978, pp. 525–54

Lohfink, G., *Die Himmelfahrt Jesu: Untersuchungen zu den Himmelfahrts- und Erhöhungstexten bei Lukas*, München 1971

— 'Gab es im Gottesdienst der neutestamentlichen Gemeinde eine Anbetung Christi?', *BZ* 18, 1974, pp. 161–79.

Lohmeyer, E., *Kyrios Jesus: Eine Untersuchung zu Phil. 2.5–11*, Heidelberg 1928, reprinted Darmstadt 1961

Lohse, E., 'Imago Dei bei Paulus', *Libertas Christiana: Festschrift F. Delekat*, München 1957, pp. 122–35

— 'Christusherrschaft und Kirche im Kolosserbrief', *NTS* 11, 1964–65, pp. 203–16, reprinted in *Die Einheit des Neuen Testaments: Exegetische Studien zur Theologie des Neuen Testaments*, Göttingen 1973, pp. 262–75

382 BIBLIOGRAPHY

— 'Der Menschensohn in der Johannesapokalypse', *JMAV*, pp. 415–20
Lonergan, B., *The Way to Nicea*, 1964, ET Darton, Longman and Todd 1976
Longenecker, R. N., 'Some Distinctive Early Christological Motifs', *NTS* 14, 1967–68, pp. 529–45
— *The Christology of Early Jewish Christianity*, SCM Press 1970
— 'The Melchizedek Argument of Hebrews: A Study in the Development and Circumstantial Expression of New Testament Thought', *UDNTT*, pp. 161–85
Loofs, F., *Leitfaden zum Studium der Dogmengeschichte*, Halle [4]1906
Lorenzmeier, T., 'Zum Logion Matt. 12.28 Luke 11.20', *NTCEHB*, pp. 289–304
Lösch, S., *Deitas Jesu und Antike Apotheose: Ein Beitrag zur Exegese und Religionsgeschichte*, Rottenburg 1933
Lövestam, E., *Son and Saviour: A Study of Acts 13.32–37*, Coniectanea Neotestamentica XVIII, Lund 1961
Luck, U., 'Himmlische und irdisches Geschehen im Hebräerbrief', *NovT* 6, 1963, pp. 192–215
Lüdemann, G., *Untersuchungen zur simonianischen Gnosis*, Göttingen 1975
Lueken, W., *Michael: Eine Darstellung und Vergleichung der jüdischen und der morgenländisch-christlichen Tradition vom Erzengel Michael*, Göttingen 1898
Lührmann, D., *Das Offenbarungs-Verständnis bei Paulus und in paulinischen Gemeinden*, Neukirchen 1965
— 'Henoch und die Metanoia', *ZNW* 66, 1975, pp. 103–16
Lust, J., 'Daniel 7.13 and the Septuagint', *ETL* 54, 1978, pp. 62–9
Luz, U., *Das Geschichtsverständnis des Paulus*, München 1968
— 'The Image of God in Christ and Mankind: New Testament Perspectives', *Concilium* 5.10, 1969, pp. 41–6.
Lyonnet, S., 'L'hymne christologique de l'Épître aux Colossiens et la fête juive du Nouvel An (Col. 1.20 et Philon *Spec.Leg.*II.192)', *RSR* 48, 1960, pp. 93–100

McCasland, S. V., ' "The Image of God" according to Paul', *JBL* 69, 1950, pp. 85–100.
McCaughey, J. D., *Diversity and Unity in the New Testament Picture of Christ*, University of Western Australia 1969
McCown, C. C., 'Jesus, Son of Man: A Survey of Recent Discussion', *Journal of Religion* 28, 1948, pp. 1–12
Macdonald, J., 'The Samaritan Doctrine of Moses', *SJT* 13, 1960, pp. 149–62
— *The Theology of the Samaritans*, SCM Press 1964
MacDonald, W. G., 'Christology and "the Angel of the Lord" ', *CIMCT*, pp. 324–35

Machen, J. G., *The Virgin Birth of Christ*, 1930, reissued James Clarke 1958

McIntyre, J., *The Shape of Christology*, SCM Press 1966

Mack, B. L., 'Wisdom Myth and Mytho-logy', *Interpretation* 24, 1970, pp. 46–60

— *Logos und Sophia: Untersuchungen zur Weisheitstheologie im hellenistischen Judentum*, Göttingen 1973

Mackey, J. P., *Jesus: the Man and the Myth*, SCM Press 1979

Mackintosh, H. R., *The Doctrine of the Person of Christ*, T. & T. Clark 1912

McNamara, M., 'Logos of the Fourth Gospel and Memra of the Palestinian Targum', *ExpT* 79, 1967–68, pp. 115–17

McNeil, B., 'The Son of Man and the Messiah: A Footnote', *NTS* 26, 1979–80, pp. 419–21

Macquarrie, J., 'A Dilemma in Christology', *ExpT* 76, 1964–65, pp. 207–10

— 'The Pre-existence of Christ', *ExpT* 77, 1965–66, pp. 199–202

— *Principles of Christian Theology*, SCM Press 1966

— 'Christology', *ExpT* 88, 1976–77, pp. 36–9

MacRae, G. W., 'The Coptic Gnostic Apocalypse of Adam', *Heythrop Journal* 6, 1965, pp. 27–35

— 'The Jewish Background of the Gnostic Sophia Myth', *NovT* 12, 1970, pp. 86–101

— ' "Whom Heaven Must Receive Until the Time": Reflections on the Christology of Acts', *Interpretation* 27, 1973, pp. 151–65

Maddox, R., 'The Function of the Son of Man according to the Synoptic Gospels', *NTS* 15, 1968–69, pp. 45–74

— 'The Quest for Valid Methods in "Son of Man" Research', *Australian Biblical Review* 19, 1971, in German as 'Methodenfragen in der Menschensohnforschung', *EvTh* 32, 1972, pp. 143–60

— 'The Function of the Son of Man in the Gospel of John', *RHLLM*, pp. 186–204

Maher, M., 'Some Aspects of Torah in Judaism', *Irish Theological Quarterly* 38, 1971, pp. 310–25

Malatesta, E., 'The Spirit/Paraclete in the Fourth Gospel', *Biblica* 54, 1973, pp. 539–50

Manson, T. W., *The Teaching of Jesus*, Cambridge University Press 1931

— 'The Son of Man in Daniel, Enoch and the Gospels' (1949), *Studies in the Gospels and Epistles*, Manchester University Press 1962, pp. 123–45

Manson, W., *Jesus the Messiah: The Synoptic Tradition of the Revelation of God in Christ*, Hodder and Stoughton 1943

Marböck, J., *Weisheit im Wandel: Untersuchungen zur Weisheitstheologie bei ben Sira*, Bonn 1971

Marcus, R., 'Divine Names and Attributes in Hellenistic Jewish

Literature', *Proceedings of American Academy for Jewish Research*, 1931–32, pp. 43–120

— 'On biblical hypostases of wisdom', *HUCA* 23, 1950–51, pp. 157–71

Margerie, B. de, *La Trinité Chrétienne dans l'Histoire*, Theologique Historique 31, Paris 1975

Marlow, R., 'The "Son of Man" in recent journal literature', *CBQ* 28, 1966, pp. 20–30

Marshall, I. H., 'The Synoptic Son of Man Sayings in Recent Discussion', *NTS* 12, 1965–66, pp. 327–51

— 'The Divine Sonship of Jesus', *Interpretation* 21, 1967, pp. 87–103

— 'The Development of Christology in the Early Church', *Tyndale Bulletin* 18, 1967, pp. 77–93

— 'The Christ-hymn in Philippians 2.5–11', *Tyndale Bulletin* 19, 1968, pp. 104–27

— 'The Resurrection in the Acts of the Apostles', *AHGFFB*, pp. 92–107

— *The Origins of New Testament Christology*, IVP 1976

Martin, F., 'Pauline Trinitarian Formulas and Christian Unity', *CBQ* 30, 1968, pp. 199–219

Martin, R. P., 'Μορφή in Philippians 2.6', *ExpT* 70, 1958–59, pp. 183f.

— 'An Early Christian Hymn (Col. 1.15–20)', *EQ* 36, 1964, pp. 195–205

— *Carmen Christi: Philippians 2.5–11 in Recent Interpretation and in the Setting of Early Christian Worship*, Cambridge University Press 1967

Martyn, J. L., *History and Theology in the Fourth Gospel*, Harper 1968

— 'We have found Elijah', *JGCWDD*, pp. 181–219

Marxsen, W., *The Beginnings of Christology: a Study in its Problems*, 1960, ET Fortress Facet Book 1969; reprinted with *The Lord's Supper as a Christological Problem*, Fortress 1979

Mascall, E. L., *Theology and the Gospel of Christ: An Essay in Reorientation*, SPCK 1977

Mastin, B. A., 'The Imperial Cult and the Ascription of the Title Θεός to Jesus (John 20.28)', *SE* VI, 1973, pp. 352–65

— 'A Neglected Feature of the Christology of the Fourth Gospel', *NTS* 22, 1975–76, pp. 32–51

Mauser, U., 'Image of God and Incarnation', *Interpretation* 24, 1970, pp. 336–56

— *Gottesbild und Menschwerdung: eine Untersuchung zur Einheit des Alten und Neuen Testaments*, Tübingen 1971

May, H. G., 'Cosmological Reference in the Qumran Doctrine of the Two Spirits and in Old Testament Imagery', *JBL* 82, 1963, pp. 1–14

Meagher, J. C., 'John 1.14 and the New Temple', *JBL* 88, 1969, pp. 57–68

Mealand, D. L., 'The Christology of the Fourth Gospel', *SJT* 31, 1978, pp. 449–67

Meeks, W. A., *The Prophet-King: Moses Traditions and the Johannine Chris-tology*, SNT XIV, 1967
— 'Moses as God and King', *RAERG*, pp. 354–71
— 'The Man from Heaven in Johannine Sectarianism', *JBL* 91, 1972, pp. 44–72
— 'The Divine Agent and his Counterfeit in Philo and the Fourth Gospel', *Aspects of Religious Propaganda in Judaism and Early Christianity*, ed. E. S. Fiorenza, Notre Dame 1976, pp. 43–67
Meinhold, P., 'Der Ursprung des Dogmas in der Verkündigung Jesu', *ZKT* 89, 1967, pp. 121–38
Messel, M., *Der Menschensohn in den Bilderreden des Henoch*, Giessen 1922
Metzger, B. M., 'Consideration of Methodology in the Study of the Mystery Religions and Early Christianity', *HTR* 48, 1955, pp. 1–20
— 'The Punctuation of Rom. 9.5', *CSNT*, pp. 95–112
Meyer, B. F., *The Aims of Jesus*, SCM Press 1979
Meyer, P. W., 'The Problem of the messianic self-consciousness of Jesus', *NovT* 4, 1961, pp. 122–38
Meyer, R., *Der Prophet aus Galiläa: Studie zur Jesusbild der drei ersten Evan-gelien*, Leipzig 1940, Darmstadt 1970
Michaelis, W., *Zur Engelchristologie im Urchristentum*, Basel 1942
Michel, O., 'Die Entstehung der paulinischen Christologie', *ZNW* 28, 1929, pp. 324–33
— 'Der Menschensohn: die eschatologische Hinweisung; die apokalyp-tische Aussage; Bemerkungen zum Menschensohn-Verständnis des Neuen Testaments', *TZ* 27, 1971, pp. 81–104
— 'Das Licht des Messias', *Donum Gentilicum: New Testament Studies in Honour of D. Daube*, ed. E. Bammel, C. K. Barrett and W. D. Davies, Oxford 1978, pp. 40–50
Michel, O. and Betz, O., 'Von Gottgezeugt', *Judentum, Urchristenum, Kirche*, J. Jeremias Festschrift, hrsg. W. Eltester, Berlin 1960, pp. 3–23
Middleton, R. D., 'Logos and Shekinah in the Fourth Gospel', *JQR* 29, 1938–39, pp. 101–33
Milik, J. T., *Milkî-ṣedeq et Milkî-rěsaʿ* dans les anciens ecrits juifs et chretiens', *JJS* 23, 1972, pp. 95–144
Minear, P. S., 'The Idea of Incarnation in First John', *Interpretation* 24, 1970, pp. 291–302
Miranda, J. P., *Der Vater, der mich gesandt hat: Religionsgeschichtliche Unter-suchungen zu den johanneische Sendungsformeln*, Bern/Frankfurt 1972
Moe, O., 'Der Menschensohn und der Urmensch', *StTh* 14, 1960, pp. 119–29
Moingt, J., *et al.*, *Visages du Christ: Les tâches presentes de la christologie*, *RSR* 65, 1977

Molin, G., 'Elijahu: Der Prophet und sein Weiterleben in den Hoffnungen des Judentums und der Christenheit', *Judaica* 8, 1952, pp. 65–94

Moloney, F. J., *The Johannine Son of Man*, Rome 1976 ²1978

Moltmann, J., *Theology of Hope*, 1965, ET SCM Press 1967

— *The Crucified God*, 1973, ET SCM Press 1974

Montefiore, H. W., 'Towards a Christology for Today', *Soundings: Essays Concerning Christian Understanding*, ed. A. R. Vidler, Cambridge University Press 1962, pp. 147–72

Moore, G. F., 'Intermediaries in Jewish Theology: Memra, Shekinah, Metatron', *HTR* 15, 1922, pp. 41–85

— *Judaism in the First Centuries of the Christian Era: The Age of the Tannaim*, 3 vols., Harvard 1927–30

Morgenstern, J., 'The Mythological Background of Psalm 82', *HUCA* 14, 1939, pp. 29–126

— 'The "Son of Man" of Daniel 7.13f.', *JBL* 80, 1961, pp. 65–77

Moule, C. F. D., 'From Defendant to Judge – and Deliverer: an inquiry into the use and limitations of the theme of vindication in the New Testament', *SNTS Bulletin* III, 1952, pp. 40–53, reprinted in *Phenomenon* (see below) pp. 82–99

— 'The Influence of Circumstances on the Use of Christological Terms', *JTS* 10, 1959, pp. 247–63

— 'The Christology of Acts', *SLAPS*, pp. 159–85

— *The Phenomenon of the New Testament*, SCM Press 1967

— 'Further Reflection on Philippians 2.5–11', *AHGFFB*, pp. 264–76

— 'II Cor. 3.18b "καθάπερ ἀπὸ κυρίου πνεύματος" ', *NTGOC*, pp. 231–7

— 'The New Testament and the Doctrine of the Trinity', *ExpT* 88, 1976–77, pp. 16–20

— *The Origin of Christology*, Cambridge University Press 1977

— *The Holy Spirit*, Mowbray 1978

Mowinckel, S., 'Die Vorstellungen des Spätjudentums von Heilige Geist als Fürsprecher und der johanneische Paraklet', *ZNW* 32, 1933, pp. 97–130

— *He that Cometh*, 1951, ET Blackwell 1956

Moxnes, H., 'God and his Angel in the Shepherd of Hermas', *StTh* 28, 1974, pp. 49–56

Mühlen, H., *Der Heilige Geist als Person: In der Trinität bei der Inkarnation und im Gnadenbund: Ich-Du-Wir*, Münster 1963, ³1969

Mühlenberg, E., 'Das Problem der Offenbarung in Philo von Alexandria', *ZNW* 64, 1973, pp. 1–18

Muilenburg, J., 'The Son of Man in Daniel and the Ethiopic Apocalypse of Enoch', *JBL* 79, 1960, pp. 197–209

Müller, H., 'Der rabbinische Qal-Wachomer-Schluss in paulinischer Typologie: zur Adam-Christus-Typologie in Röm. 5', *ZNW* 58, 1967, pp. 73–92

Müller, H. P., 'Die Verklärung Jesu', *ZNW* 51, 1960, pp. 56–64

Müller, K., 'Menschensohn und Messias', *BZ* 16, 1972, pp. 161–87; 17, 1973, pp. 52–66

— 'Der "Menschensohn" im Danielzyklus', *JMAV*, pp. 37–80

Müller, M., 'Uber den Ausdruck "Menschensohn" in den Evangelien', *StTh* 31, 1977, pp. 65–82

Müller, P. G., *ΧΡΙΣΤΟΣ ΑΡΧΗΓΟΣ: Der religionsgeschichtliche und theologische Hintergrund einer neutestamentlichen Christusprädikation*, Bern/Frankfurt 1973

Müller, U. B., *Messias und Menschensohn in jüdischen Apokalypsen und in der Offenbarung des Johannes*, Gütersloh 1972

— 'Die Parakletenvorstellung im Johannesevangelium', *ZTK* 71, 1974, pp. 31–77

— *Die Geschichte der Christologie in der johanneischen Gemeinde*, SBS 77, 1975

Münderlein, G., 'Die Erwählung durch das Pleroma: Bemerkungen zu Kol. 1.19', *NTS* 8, 1961–62, pp. 264–76

Muraoka, T., 'Sirach 51.13–30: an Erotic Hymn to Wisdom?', *JSJ* 10, 1979, pp. 166–78

Murphy-O'Connor, J., 'Christological Anthropology in Phil. 2.6–11', *RB* 83, 1976, pp. 25–50

— 'I Cor. 8.6: Cosmology or Soteriology', *RB* 85, 1978, pp. 253–67

Muschalek, G., 'Gott in Jesus: Dogmatische Überlegungen zur heutigen Fremdheit des menschgewordenen Sohnes Gottes', *ZKT* 94, 1972, pp. 145–57

Mussner, F., 'Der nicht erkannte Kairos (Matt. 11.16–9 = Luke 7.31–5)', *Biblica* 40, 1959, pp. 599–612

— *The Historical Jesus in the Gospel of John*, 1965, ET Herder 1967

— 'Wege zum Selbstbewusstsein Jesu', *BZ* 12, 1968, pp. 161–72

Myre, A., 'Développement d'un instanté christologique le prophète eschatologique', *Le Christ hier, aujourd'hui et demain*, ed. R. Laflamme et M. Gervais, Quebec 1976, pp. 277–327

Nagel, W., ' "Die Finsternis hat's nicht begriffen" (John 1.5)', *ZNW* 50, 1959, pp. 132–8

Neufeld, V. H., *The Earliest Christian Confessions*, Leiden 1963

Neugebauer, F., 'Die Davidssohnfrage (Mark 12.35–7 parr.) und der Menschensohn', *NTS* 21, 1974–75, pp. 81–108

Nock, A. D., ' "Son of God" in Pauline and Hellenistic Thought' (Review of Schoeps, *Paul, Gnomon* 33, 1961, pp. 581–90), *Essays on Religion and the Ancient World*, 2 vols., Oxford University Press 1972, pp. 928–39

Noll, S. F., *Angelology in the Qumran Texts*, Manchester PhD thesis 1979

Norden, E., *Agnostos Theos: Untersuchungen zur Formengeschichte religiöser Rede*, 1913, reissued Stuttgart 1956
— *Die Geburt des Kindes: Geschichte einer religiösen Idee*, 1924, Darmstadt 1958
Nötscher, F., 'Geist und Geister in den Texten von Qumran', *Mélanges bibliques réligés en l'honneur de André Robert*, Paris 1957; reprinted *Vom Alten zum Neuen Testament*, Bonn 1962, pp. 175–87
Nützel, J. M., *Die Verklärungserzählung im Markusevangelium*, Bamberg 1973

Oesterley, W. O. E. and Box, G. H., 'Intermediate Agencies between God and Man', *The Religion and Worship of the Synagogue*, Pitman 1907, ²1911, ch. IX
Oeyen, C., 'Die Lehre der göttlichen Kräfte bei Justin', *SP* 11, 1972, pp. 215–21
O'Neill, J. C., 'The Prologue to St John's Gospel', *JTS* 20, 1969, pp. 41–52
— 'The Source of Christology in Colossians', *NTS* 26, 1979–80, pp. 87–100
Osten-Sacken, P. von, 'Der erste Christ: Johannes der Täufer als Schlüssel zum Prolog des vierten Evangeliums', *Theologica Viatorum* XIII, 1975–76, pp. 155–73
Ottley, R. L., *The Doctrine of the Incarnation*, Methuen 1896, ⁴1908
Otto, R., *The Kingdom of God and the Son of Man*, ET Lutterworth 1938

Pannenberg, W., 'Der philosophische Gottesbegriff in frühchristlicher Theologie', *ZKG* 70, 1959, pp. 1–45
— *Jesus – God and Man*, 1964, ET SCM Press 1968
Parker, P., 'The Meaning of "Son of Man" ', *JBL* 60, 1941, pp. 151–7
Parzen, H., 'The Ruach Hakodesh in Tannaitic Literature', *JQR* 20, 1929–30, pp. 51–76
Pax, E., *ΕΠΙΦΑΝΕΙΑ: Ein religionsgeschichtlicher Beitrag zur biblischen Theologie*, München 1955
Pearson, B. A., *The Pneumatikos-Psychikos Terminology in I Corinthians*, SBL Dissertation 12, Scholars Press 1973
— 'Hellenistic-Jewish Wisdom Speculation and Paul', *AWJEC*, pp. 43–66
Percy, E., *Untersuchungen über den Ursprung der johanneischen Theologie: Zugleich ein Beitrag zur Frage nach der Entstehung des Gnostizismus*, Lund 1939
Perrin, N., 'Mark 14.62: the End Product of a Christian Pesher Tradition?', *NTS* 12, 1965–66, pp. 150–5, reprinted in *Modern Pilgrimage* (see below), pp. 10–22 (with Postscript)
— 'The Son of Man in Ancient Judaism and Primitive Christianity: A Suggestion', *BR* 11, 1966, pp. 17–28, reprinted in *Modern Pilgrimage* (see

below), pp. 23–40 (with Postscript)

— *Rediscovering the Teaching of Jesus*, SCM Press 1967

— 'The Son of Man in the Synoptic Tradition', *BR* 13, 1968, pp. 3–25, reprinted in *Modern Pilgrimage* (see below) pp. 57–83

— *A Modern Pilgrimage in New Testament Christology*, Fortress 1974

Pesch, R., 'Der Gottessohn im matthäischen Evangelienprolog (Matt. 1–2)', *Biblica* 48, 1967, pp. 395–420

— 'Über die Autorität Jesu: Eine Ruckfrage anhand des Bekenner- und Verleugnerspruche Luke 12.8f. par.', *KAHS*, pp. 25–55

Pesch, R. and Schnackenburg, R. (eds.), *Jesus und der Menschensohn: Für Anton Vögtle*, Freiburg 1975

Peterson, E., *ΕΙΣ ΘΕΟΣ: Epigraphische, formgeschichtliche und religions-geschichtliche Untersuchungen*, Göttingen 1926

Pfeifer, G., *Ursprung und Wesen der Hypostasenvorstellungen im Judentum*, Stuttgart 1967

Pittenger, N., *The Word Incarnate*, Nisbet 1959

— (ed.), *Christ for Us Today* (Papers from the Conference of Modern Churchmen, 1967), SCM Press 1968

— *Christology Reconsidered*, SCM Press 1970

Places, E. des, 'Épithètes et attributs de la "Sagesse" (Sg. 7.22–23 et *SVF* I.557 Arnim)', *Biblica* 57, 1976, pp. 414–19

Pohlenz, M., *Die Stoa: Geschichte einer geistigen Bewegung*, 2 vols., Göttingen 1948–49

Pöhlmann, W., 'Die hymnischen All-Prädikationen in Kol. 1.15–20', *ZNW* 64, 1973, pp. 53–74

Pokorný, P., 'Epheserbrief und gnostische Mysterien', *ZNW* 53, 1962, pp. 160–94

— *Der Gottessohn*, Theologische Studien 109, Zürich 1971

Polag, A., *Die Christologie der Logienquelle*, Neukirchen 1977

Pollard, T. E., 'The Exegesis of John 10.30 in the Early Trinitarian Controversies', *NTS* 3, 1956–57, pp. 334–49

— 'Cosmology and the Prologue of the Fourth Gospel', *VC* 12, 1958, pp. 147–53

— *Johannine Christology and the Early Church*, Cambridge University Press 1970

Porsch, F., *Pneuma und Wort: Ein exegetischer Beitrag zur Pneumatologie des Johannesevangeliums*, Frankfurt 1974

Porteus, N. W., 'Royal Wisdom', *Wisdom in Israel and in the Ancient Near East*, H. H. Rowley Festschrift, ed. M. Noth and D. W. Thomas, *VT* Supp. III, 1960, pp. 33–41

Potterie, I. de la, 'Le Christ, Plérôme de l'Église (Eph. 1.22–3)', *Biblica* 58, 1977, pp. 500–24

— 'La notion de "commencement" dans les ecrits johanniques', *KAHS*, pp. 396–402

Poythress, V. S., 'Is Romans 1.3–4 a *Pauline* Confession After All?', *ExpT* 87, 1975–76, pp. 180–3

— 'The Holy Ones of the Most High in Daniel 7', *VT* 26, 1976, pp. 208–13

Prat, F., *The Theology of St Paul*, 2 vols, ET Burns, Oates and Washbourne 1927

Prestige, G. L., *God in Patristic Thought*, SPCK 1936, ²1952

Prümm, K., 'Joh. Weiss als Darsteller und religionsgeschichtlicher Erklärer der paulinischen Botschaft', *Biblica* 40, 1959, pp. 815–36

— 'Zur Früh- und Spätform der religionsgeschichtlichen Christusdeutung von H. Windisch', *Biblica* 42, 1961, pp. 391–422, and 43, 1962, pp. 22–56

Quispel, G., 'Der gnostische Anthropos und die jüdische Tradition' (1954), 'Gnosticism and the New Testament' (1965), *Gnostic Studies*, Istanbul, Vol. I, 1974, pp. 173–95, 196–212

— 'Ezekiel 1.26 in Jewish Mysticism and Gnosis', *VC* 34, 1980, pp. 1–13

Rad, G. von, *Wisdom in Israel*, 1970, ET SCM Press 1972

Rahner, K., 'Current Problems in Christology', *Theological Investigations*, ET Darton, Longman and Todd, Vol. I 1954, pp. 149–200

— 'On the Theology of the Incarnation', *Theological Investigations*, Vol. 4, 1958, pp. 105–20

— 'Christology within an Evolutionary View of the World', 'Dogmatic Reflections on the Knowledge and Selfconsciousness of Christ', *Theological Investigations*, Vol. 5 1966, pp. 157–92, 193–215

— 'Christology in the Setting of Modern Man's Understanding of Himself and of his World', *Theological Investigations*, Vol. 11 1974, pp. 215–29

— 'The Quest for Approaches Leading to an Understanding of the Mystery of the God-man Jesus', 'The Two Basic Types of Christology', *Theological Investigations*, Vol. 13 1975, pp. 195–200, 213–23

Rahner, K. and Thüsing, W., *Christologie – systematische und exegetisch*, Quaestiones Disputatae 55, Herder 1972; ET with new material, *A New Christology*, Search Press 1980

Ramsey, A. M., *The Glory of God and the Transfiguration of Christ*, Longmans 1949

— 'What was the Ascension?', *SNTS Bulletin* II, 1951, pp. 43–50, reprinted in D. E. Nineham, *et al.*, *Historicity and Chronology in the New Testament*, SPCK Theological Collection 6, 1965, pp. 135–44

Rankin, O. S., *Israel's Wisdom Literature: its Bearing on Theology and the History of Religion*, T. & T. Clark 1936

Rawlinson, A. E. J., *The New Testament Doctrine of the Christ*, Longmans, Green & Co., 1926

— (ed.), *Essays on the Trinity and the Incarnation*, Longmans 1928

Reese, J. M., *Hellenistic Influence on the Book of Wisdom and its Consequences*, Rome 1970

Refoulé, F., *Le Christ, visage de Dieu*, Paris 1975

Reitzenstein, R., *Die hellenistischen Mysterienreligionen*, Leipzig 1910, ³1927

— *Das iranische Erlösungsmysterium*, Bonn 1921

Relton, H. M., *A Study in Christology: the Problem of the Relation of the Two Natures in the Person of Christ*, SPCK 1934

Richard, J., ' "Fils de Dieu": Reconsidération de l'inteprétation adoptioniste', *Le Christ hier, aujourd'hui et demain*, ed. R. Laflamme et M. Gervais, Quebec 1976, pp. 431–65

Richardson, A., *An Introduction to the Theology of the New Testament*, SCM Press 1958

Richter, G., 'Die Fleischwerdung des Logos im Johannesevangelium', *Nov T* 13, 1971, pp. 81–126; and 14, 1972, pp. 257–76, reprinted *Studien zum Johannesevangelium*, hrsg. J. Hainz, Regensburg 1977, pp. 149–98

— 'Ist ἐν ein strukturbildendes Element im Logoshymnus John 1.1ff?', *Biblica* 51, 1970, pp. 539–44, reprinted *Studien*, pp. 143–8

Ridderbos, H., 'The Structure and Scope of the Prologue to the Gospel of John', *NovT* 8, 1966, pp. 180–201

— *Paul: an Outline of his Theology*, 1966, ET Eerdmans 1975, SPCK 1977

Riesenfeld, H., *Jésus Transfiguré: L'arrière-plan du récit évangélique de la transfiguration de Notre-Seigneur*, Copenhagen 1947

— 'The Mythological Background of New Testament Christology', *BNTE*, pp. 81–95, reprinted *The Gospel Tradition: Essays by H. Riesenfeld*, Fortress and Blackwell 1970, pp. 31–49

Rigaux, B., 'Révélation des Mystères et Perfection à Qumrân et dans le Nouveau Testament', *NTS* 4, 1957–58, pp. 237–62

Ringgren, H., *Word and Wisdom: Studies in the Hypostatization of Divine Qualities and Functions in the Ancient Near East*, Lund 1947

— *The Faith of Qumran*, Fortress 1963

Rissi, M., 'Die Menschlichkeit Jesu nach Heb. 5.7–8', *TZ* 11, 1955, pp. 28–45

— 'Die Logoslieder im Prolog des vierten Evangeliums', *TZ* 31, 1975, pp. 321–36

Robbins, C. J., 'Rhetorical Structure of Phil. 2.6–11', *CBQ* 42, 1980, pp. 73–82

Robinson, D. W. B., 'ἁρπαγμός: the Deliverance Jesus Refused', *ExpT* 80, 1968–69, pp. 253f.

Robinson, H. W., *The Christian Experience of the Holy Spirit*, Nisbet 1928.

Robinson, J. A. T., 'The Most Primitive Christology of All?', *JTS* 7, 1956, pp. 177–89, reprinted in *Twelve New Testament Studies*, SCM Press 1962, pp. 139–53

— *Jesus and his Coming: The Emergence of a Doctrine*, SCM Press 1957; revised edition 1979

— 'Elijah, John and Jesus: an Essay in Detection', *NTS* 4, 1957–58, pp. 263–81, reprinted *Studies*, pp. 28–52

— 'The Relation of the Prologue to the Gospel of St John', *NTS* 9, 1962–63, pp. 120–9

— *The Human Face of God*, SCM Press 1973

— 'The Use of the Fourth Gospel for Christology Today', *CSNT*, pp. 61–78

Robinson, J. M., 'A Formal Analysis of Colossians 1.15–20', *JBL* 76, 1959, pp. 270–87

— 'Jesus as Sophos and Sophia: Wisdom Tradition and The Gospels', *AWJEC*, pp. 1–16

Robinson, J. M. and Koester, H., *Trajectories through Early Christianity*, Fortress 1971

Romaniuk, C., 'Le Livre de la Sagesse dans le Nouveau Testament', *NTS* 14, 1967–68, pp. 503–13

Roon, A. van, 'The Relation between Christ and the Wisdom of God according to Paul', *Nov T* 16, 1974, pp. 207–39

Rosato, P. J., 'Spirit Christology: Ambiguity and Promise', *TS* 38, 1977, pp. 423–49

Rosenberg, R. A., 'The God Ṣedeq', *HUCA* 36, 1965, pp. 161–77

Rost, L., 'Zur Deutung des Menschensohnes in Daniel 7', *Gott und die Götter: Festgabe E. Fascher*, Berlin 1958, pp. 41–3

Rowland, C., 'The Visions of God in Apocalyptic Literature', *JSJ* 10, 1979, pp. 137–54

— 'The Vision of the Risen Christ in Rev. 1.13ff.: The Debt of an Early Christology to an Aspect of Jewish Angelology', *JTS* 31, 1980, pp. 1–11

Ruckstuhl, E., 'Abstieg und Erhöhung des johanneischen Menschensohns', *JMAV* pp. 314–41

Russell, D. S., *The Method and Message of Jewish Apocalyptic*, SCM Press 1964

Rylaarsdam, J. C., *Revelation in Jewish Wisdom Literature*, University of Chicago 1946

Sanders, J. A., 'Dissenting Deities and Philippians 2.1–11', *JBL* 88, 1969, pp. 279–90

Sanders, J. T., *The New Testament Christological Hymns: their Historical Religious Background*, Cambridge University Press 1971

Sandmel, S., 'Parallelomania', *JBL* 81, 1962, pp. 1–13

Schäfer, P., *Die Vorstellung vom heiligen Geist in der rabbinischen Literatur*, München 1972

Schäfer, R., *Jesus und der Gottesglaube: Ein christologischer Entwurf*, Tübingen 1970

Scheidweiler, F., 'Paradoxie in der neutestamentlichen Christologie?', *ZNW* 49, 1958, pp. 258–64

Schelkle, K. H., *Theology of the New Testament*, 4 vols. 1968–76, ET Collegeville 1971–78

Schenke, H. M., *Der Gott 'Mensch' in der Gnosis: Ein religionsgeschichtlicher Beitrag zur Diskussion über die paulinische Anschauung von der Kirche als Leib Christi*, Göttingen 1962

— 'Der Widerstreit gnostischer und kirchlicher Christologie im Spiegel des Kolosserbriefes', *ZTK* 61, 1964, pp. 391–403

— 'Die neutestamentliche Christologie und der gnostische Erlöser', *Gnosis und Neues Testament*, hrsg. K. W. Tröger, Gütersloh 1973, pp. 205–29

— 'Erwägungen zum Rätsel des Hebräerbriefes', *NTCEHB*, pp. 421–37

Schenke, W., *Die Chokma (Sophia) in der jüdischen Hypostasenspekulation*, Kristiana 1913

Schille, G., 'Erwägungen zur Hohepriesterlehre des Hebräerbriefes', *ZNW* 46, 1955, pp. 81–109

— *Frühchristliche Hymnen*, Berlin 1965

Schillebeeckx, E., *Jesus. An Experiment in Christology*, ET Collins 1979

— *Christ. The Christian Experience in the Modern World*, 1977, ET SCM Press 1980

Schlatter, F. W., 'The Problem of John 1.3b–4a', *CBQ* 34, 1972, pp. 54–8

Schlier, H., *Christus und die Kirche im Epheserbrief*, Tübingen 1930

— 'Im Anfang war das Wort: Zum Prolog des Johannesevangeliums', *Die Zeit der Kirche: Exegetische Aufsätze und Vorträge* I, Freiburg 1956, pp. 274–87

— 'The New Testament and Myth', *The Relevance of the New Testament*, 1964, ET Herder 1967, pp. 76–93

— 'Der Offenbarer und sein Werk nach dem Johannesevangelium', *Besinnung auf das Neue Testament: Exegetische Aufsätze* II, Freiburg 1964, pp. 254–63

— 'Die Anfänge des christologischen Credo', *Zur Frühgeschichte der Christologie*, hrsg. B. Welte, Freiburg 1970, pp. 13–58

— 'Zur Christologie des Johannesevangelium', *Das Ende der Zeit: Exegetische Aufsätze* III, Freiburg 1971, pp. 85–101

— 'Zu Röm. 1.3f.', *NTGOC*, pp. 207–18

Schlisske, W., *Gottessöhne und Gottessohn im Alten Testament*, Stuttgart 1973

Schmid, H. H., 'Schöpfung, Gerechtigkeit und Heil: "Schöpfungstheologie" als Gesamthorizont biblischer Theologie', *ZTK* 70, 1973, pp. 1–19

Schmidt, K. L., 'Das Pneuma Hagion als Person und als Charisma', *Eranos Jahrbuch* 13, 1945, pp. 187–235

Schmithals, W., 'Gnosis und Neues Testament', *VuF* 21, 1976/2, pp. 22–46

— 'Der Prolog des Johannesevangeliums', *ZNW* 70, 1979, pp. 16–43

Schnackenburg, R., 'Logos-Hymnus und johanneischer Prolog', *BZ* 1, 1957, pp. 69–109

— *New Testament Theology Today*, 1961, ET Chapman 1963

— 'Der Menschensohn im Johannesevangelium', *NTS* 11, 1964–65, pp. 123–37

— 'The "New Man" According to Paul', 'Johannine Christology and the Gnostic Myth of the Saviour', *Present and Future: Modern Aspects of New Testament Theology*, Notre Dame 1966, pp. 81–100, 163–84

— 'Die Aufnahme des Christushymnus durch den Verfasser des Kolosserbriefes', *EKK Vorarbeiten*, Heft 1, Neukirchen 1969, pp. 33–50

— 'Christologie des Neuen Testaments', *Mysterium Salutis* 3.1, Einsiedeln 1970, pp. 227–388

Schneider, B., 'Κατὰ Πνεῦμα Ἁγιωσύνης (Romans 1.4)', *Biblica* 48, 1967, pp. 359–87

Schneider, G., 'Urchristliche Gottesverkündigung in hellenistischer Umwelt', *BZ* 13, 1969, pp. 59–75

— 'Präexistenz Christi: der Ursprung einer neutestamentlichen Vorstellung und das Problem ihrer Auslegung', *NTKRS*, pp. 399–412

Schneider, H., ' "The Word was made Flesh": An Analysis of the Theology of Revelation in the Fourth Gospel', *CBQ* 31, 1969, pp. 344–56

Schnider, F., *Jesus der Prophet*, Freiburg and Göttingen 1973

Schniewind, J., *Das Selbstzeugnis Jesu nach den drei ersten Evangelien*, Berlin 1922

Schoeps, H. J., *Paul: The Theology of the Apostle in the Light of Jewish Religious History*, 1959, ET Lutterworth 1961

Scholem, G. G., *Major Trends in Jewish Mysticism*, Thames and Hudson 1955

— *Jewish Gnosticism, Merkabah Mysticism and Talmudic Tradition*, Jewish Theological Seminary of America 1960, ²1965

— *The Messianic Idea in Judaism and Other Essays on Jewish Spirituality*, Allen and Unwin 1971

Schoonenberg, P., 'The Kenosis or Self-Emptying of Christ', *Concilium* 2.1, 1966, pp. 27–36

— *The Christ*, ET Sheed and Ward 1972

Schrage, W., 'Theologie und Christologie bei Paulus und Jesus auf dem Hintergrund der modernen Gottesfrage', *EvTh* 36, 1976, pp. 121–54

Schubert, K., 'Einige Beobachtungen zum Verständnis des Logosbegriffes im frührabbinischen Schrifttum', *Judaica* 9, 1953, pp. 65–80

Schulz, S., *Untersuchungen zur Menschensohn-Christologie im Johannesevangelium*, Göttingen 1957

— 'Die Komposition des Johannesprologs und die Zusammensetzung des 4. Evangeliums', *SE* I, 1959, pp. 351–62

— *Komposition und Herkunft der johanneischen Reden*, Stuttgart 1960

— *Q: die Spruchquelle der Evangelisten*, Zürich 1972

Schumacher, H., *Christus in seiner Präexistenz und Kenose nach Phil. 2.5–8*, 2 vols., Rome 1914, 1921

Schürmann, H., 'Beobachtungen zum Menschensohn-Titel in der Redequelle', *JMAV*, pp. 124–47

Schweizer, E., *Ego Eimi: Die religionsgeschichtliche Herkunft und theologische Bedeutung der johanneischen Bildreden*, Göttingen 1939, [2]1965

— 'Die sieben Geister in der Apokalypse', *EvTh* 11, 1952, pp. 502–12, reprinted *Neotestamentica*, Zürich 1963, pp. 190–202

— 'Röm. 1.3f. und der Gegensatz von Fleisch und Geist vor und bei Paulus', *Ev Th* 15, 1955, pp. 563–71, reprinted *Neotestamentica*, pp. 180–9

— *Erniedrigung und Erhöhung bei Jesus und seinen Nachfolgern*, Zürich 1955, [2]1962. (ET of first German edition, *Lordship and Discipleship*, SCM Press 1960)

— 'Zur Herkunft der Präexistenzvorstellung bei Paulus', *Ev Th* 19, 1959, pp. 65–70, reprinted *Neotestamentica*, pp. 105–9

— 'Der Menschensohn', *ZNW* 50, 1959, pp. 185–209, reprinted *Neotestamentica*, pp. 56–84

— 'The Son of Man', *JBL* 79, 1960, pp. 119–29

— 'Die Kirche als Leib Christi in den paulinischen Homologumena', 'Die Kirche als Leib Christi in den paulinischen Antilegomena', *TLZ* 86, 1961, pp. 161–74, 241–56, reprinted *Neotestamentica*, pp. 272–92, 293–316

— 'Two New Testament Creeds Compared: I Corinthians 15.3–5 and I Timothy 3.16', *CINTI*, pp. 166–77, reprinted *Neotestamentica*, pp. 122–35

— 'Aufnahme und Korrektur jüdischer Sophiatheologie im Neuen Testament', *Hören und Handeln: Festschrift für E. Wolf*, München 1962, pp. 330–40, reprinted *Neotestamentica*, pp. 110–21

— 'The Son of Man Again', *NTS* 9, 1962–63, pp. 256–61, reprinted *Neotestamentica*, pp. 85–92

— 'Zum religionsgeschichtlichen Hintergrund der "Sendungsformel" Gal. 4.4f., Röm. 8.3f., John 3.16f., I John 4.9', *ZNW* 57, 1966, pp. 199–210, reprinted *Beiträge zur Theologie des Neuen Testaments*, Zürich 1970, pp. 83–95

— 'The Concept of the Davidic "Son of God" in Acts and its Old Testament Background', *SLAPS*, pp. 186–93

— *Jesus*, 1968, ET SCM Press 1971

— 'Kolosser 1.15–20', *EKK Vorarbeiten*, Heft 1, Neukirchen 1969, pp. 7–31, reprinted *Beiträge*, pp. 113–45

— 'Jesus der Zeuge Gottes: zum Problem des Doketismus im Johannesevangelium', *Studies in John: Presented to J. N. Sevenster*, SNT XXIV, 1970, pp. 161–8

— 'Menschensohn und eschatologischer Mensch im Frühjudentum', *JMAV*, pp. 100–16

Scott, E. F., *The Spirit in the New Testament*, Hodder and Stoughton 1923

Scott, R. B. Y., 'Behold, He Cometh with Clouds', *NTS* 5, 1958–59, pp. 127–32

— 'Wisdom in Creation: the *'āmôn* of Proverbs 8.30', *VT* 10, 1960, pp. 213–23

Scroggs, R., *The Last Adam: A Study in Pauline Anthropology*, Blackwell 1966

— 'Paul: Σοφός and Πνευματικός', *NTS* 14, 1967–68, pp. 33–55

Segal, A. F., *Two Powers in Heaven: Early Rabbinic Reports about Christianity and Gnosticism*, Leiden 1977

Seitz, O. J. F., 'Two Spirits in Man: an Essay in Biblical Exegesis', *NTS* 6, 1959–60, pp. 82–95

— 'The Future Coming of the Son of Man: Three Midrashic Formulations in the Gospel of Mark', *SE* VI, 1973, pp. 478–94.

Sevenster, G., 'Remarks on the Humanity of Jesus in the Gospel and Letters of John', *Studies in John: Presented to J. N. Sevenster*, SNT XXIV, 1970, pp. 185–93

Sharpe, J. L., 'The Second Adam in the Apocalypse of Moses', *CBQ* 35, 1973, pp. 35–46

Sidebottom, E. M., 'The Son of Man as Man in the Fourth Gospel', *ExpT* 68, 1956–57, pp. 231–5, 280–3

— *The Christ of the Fourth Gospel*, SPCK 1961

Sjöberg, E., *Der Menschensohn im äthiopischen Henochbuch*, Lund 1946

— *Der verborgene Menschensohn in den Evangelien*, Lund 1955

Smail, T. A., *Reflected Glory: The Spirit in Christ and Christians*, Hodder and Stoughton 1975

Smalley, S. S., 'The Christology of Acts', *ExpT* 73, 1961–62, pp. 358–62

— 'The Johannine Son of Man Sayings', *NTS* 15, 1968–69, pp. 278–301

— *John – Evangelist and Interpreter*, Paternoster 1978

Smith, D. M., 'The Presentation of Jesus in the Fourth Gospel', *Interpretation* 31, 1977, pp. 367–78

Smith, D. W., *Wisdom Christology in the Synoptic Gospels*, Rome 1970

Smith, M., 'The Image of God', *BJRL* 40, 1958, pp. 473–512

— ' "God's Begetting the Messiah" in 1QSa', *NTS* 5, 1958–59, pp. 218–24

— 'Prolegomena to a Discussion of Aretalogies, Divine Men, the Gospels and Jesus', *JBL* 90, 1971, pp. 174–99

Sobrino, J., *Christology at the Crossroads: a Latin American Approach*, SCM Press 1978

Spicq, C,, 'Le Philonisme de l'Épitre aux Hébreux', *RB* 56, 1949, pp. 542–72 and 57, 1950, pp. 212–42

Staerk, W., *Soter: die biblische Erlösererwartung als religionsgeschichtliches Problem, I. Teil: Der biblische Christus*, Gütersloh 1933

— *Die Erlösererwartung in den östlichen Religionen: Untersuchungen zu den Ausdrucksformen der biblischen Christologie (Soter II)*, Stuttgart 1938

Stählin, G., 'Τὸ Πνεῦμα 'Ιησοῦ (Apostelgeschichte 16.7)', *CSNT*, pp. 229–52

Stamm, J. J., *Die Gottebildlichkeit des Menschen im Alten Testament*, Theologische Studien 54, Zollikon 1959

Stanley, D. M., *Christ's Resurrection in Pauline Soteriology*, Analecta Biblica 13, Rome 1961

Stanton, G. N., 'On the Christology of Q', *CSNT*, pp. 27–42

Stauffer, E., *New Testament Theology*, 1941, ET SCM Press 1955

Stead, C., 'The Concept of Divine Substance', *VC* 29, 1975, pp. 1–14

— *Divine Substance*, Oxford University Press 1977

Stecher, R., 'Die persönliche Weisheit in den Proverbien Kap. 8', *ZKT* 75, 1953, pp. 411–51

Steck, O. H., *Israel und das gewaltsame Geschick der Propheten*, Neukirchen 1967

Steinmetz, F. J., *Protologische Heils-Zuversicht: die Strukturen des soteriologischen und christologischen Denkens im Kolosser- und Epheserbrief*, Frankfurt 1969

Stendahl, K., '*Quis et Unde*? An Analysis of Matt. 1–2', *Judentum, Urchristentum, Kirche*, J. Jeremias Festschrift, hrsg. W. Eltester, Berlin [2]1964, pp. 94–105

Stenger, W., 'Der Christushymnus in I Tim. 3.16; Aufbau-Christologie–Sitz im Leben', *TTZ* 78, 1969, pp. 33–48

Stier, F., *Gott und sein Engel im Alten Testament*, Münster 1934

Stone, M., 'The Concept of the Messiah in IV Ezra', *RAERG*, pp. 295–312

Strecker, G., 'Redaktion und Tradition in Christushymnus Phil. 2.6–11', *ZNW* 55, 1964, pp. 63–78

— (ed.), *Jesus Christus in Historie und Theologie: Neutestamentliche Festschrift für H. Conzelmann*, Tübingen 1975

Strobel, A., *Kerygma und Apokalyptik: Ein religionsgeschichtlicher und theologischer Beitrag zur Christusfrage*, Göttingen 1967

Strong, E. L., *The Incarnation of God*, Longmans 1920

Stuhlmacher, P., 'Theologische Probleme des Römerbriefspräskripts', *EvTh* 27, 1967, pp. 374–89

— 'Zur paulinische Christologie', *ZTK* 74, 1977, pp. 449–63

Styler, G. M., 'Stages in Christology in the Synoptic Gospels', *NTS* 10, 1963–64, pp. 398–409

Suggs, M. J., ' "The Word is near you": Romans 10.6–10 within the purpose of the letter', *CHIJK*, pp. 289–312

— *Wisdom, Christology and Law in Matthew's Gospel*, Harvard 1970

Sundberg, A. C., 'Christology in the Fourth Gospel', *BR* 21, 1976, pp. 29–37

Swete, H. B., *The Holy Spirit in the New Testament*, Macmillan 1909

Sykes, S. W. and Clayton, J. P. (eds.), *Christ, Faith and History: Cambridge Studies in Christology*, Cambridge University Press 1972

Takahashi, M., 'An Oriental's Approach to the Problems of Angelology', *ZAW* 37, 1966, pp. 343–50

Talbert, C. H., 'The Problem of Pre-existence in Philippians 2.6–11', *JBL* 86, 1967, pp. 141–53

— 'The Concept of Immortals in Mediterranean Antiquity', *JBL* 94, 1975, pp. 419–36

— 'The Myth of a Descending-Ascending Redeemer in Mediterranean Antiquity', *NTS* 22, 1975–76, pp. 418–40

— *What is a Gospel? The Genre of the Canonical Gospels*, Fortress 1977, SPCK 1978

Taylor, V., *The Names of Jesus*, Macmillan 1953

— *The Person of Christ in New Testament Teaching*, Macmillan 1958

— 'Does the New Testament Call Jesus "God"?' *ExpT* 73, 1961–62, pp. 116–18, reprinted *New Testament Essays*, Epworth 1970, pp. 83–9

Teeple, H. M., 'The Origin of the Son of Man Christology', *JBL* 84, 1955, pp. 213–50

— *The Mosaic Eschatological Prophet*, SBL Monograph 10, 1957

TeSelle, E., *Christ in Context: Divine Purpose and Human Possibility*, Fortress 1975

Theisohn, J., *Der auserwählte Richter: Untersuchungen zum traditionsgeschichtlichen Ort der Menschensohngestalt der Bilderreden des äthiopischen Henoch*, Göttingen 1975

Theissen, G., *Untersuchungen zum Hebräerbrief*, Gütersloh 1969

Thompson, J. W., 'The Structure and Purpose of the Catena in Heb. 1.5–13', *CBQ* 38, 1976, pp. 352–63

— 'The Conceptual Background and Purpose of the Midrash in Hebrews 7', *NovT* 19, 1977, pp. 209–23

Thornton, L. S., *The Incarnate Lord: an Essay concerning the Doctrine of the Incarnation in its Relation to Organic Conceptions*, Longmans 1928

Thrall, M. E., 'Elijah and Moses in Mark's Account of the Transfiguration', *NTS* 16, 1969–70, pp. 305–17

— 'The Origin of Pauline Christology', *AHGFFB*, pp. 304–16

— 'Christ Crucified or Second Adam? A christological debate between Paul and the Corinthians', *CSNT*, pp. 143–56

Thuren, J., 'Gebet und Gehorsam des Erniedrigten', *NovT* 13, 1971, pp. 136–46

Thüsing, W., *Per Christum in Deum: Studien zum Verhältnis von Christozentrik und Theozentrik in den paulinischen Hauptbriefen*, Münster 1965

— *Erhöhungsvorstellung und Parusieerwartung in der ältesten nachösterlichen Christologie*, SBS 42, 1970

Tiede, D. L., *The Charismatic Figure as a Miracle Worker*, SBL Dissertation 1, 1972

— 'The Figure of Moses in *The Testament of Moses*', *Studies on the Testament of Moses*, ed. G. W. E. Nickelsburg, SBL Septuagint and Cognate Studies, Scholars Press 1973, pp. 86–92

Tödt, H. E., *The Son of Man in the Synoptic Tradition*, ²1963, ET SCM Press 1965

Torrance, T. F., *Space, Time and Incarnation*, Oxford 1969

Tournay, R., 'Le Psaume 8 et la doctrine biblique du nom', *RB* 78, 1971, pp. 18–30

Trakatellis, D. C., *The Pre-existence of Christ in Justin Martyr*, Harvard Dissertations in Religion 6, Scholars Press 1976

Treitel, L., 'Die alexandrinische Lehre von den Mittelwesen oder göttlichen Kräften, insbesondere bei Philo, geprüft auf die Frage, ob und welchen Einfluss sie auf das Mutterland Palästina gehabt', *Judaica: Festschrift zu H. Cohen*, Berlin 1912, pp. 177–84

Trinidad, J. T., 'The Mystery Hidden in God: A Study of Eph. 1.3–14', *Biblica* 31, 1950, pp. 1–26

Turner, H. E. W., *Jesus the Christ*, Mowbray 1976

Unnik, W. C. van, 'Jesus the Christ', *NTS* 8, 1961–62, pp. 101–16

Urbach, E. E., *The Sages: their Concepts and Beliefs*, Jerusalem 1975

Vanhoye, A., 'Un médiateur des anges en Gal. 3.19–20', *Biblica* 59, 1978, pp. 403–11

Vawter, B. F., 'What came to be in him was life, John 1.3b–4a', *CBQ* 25, 1963, pp. 401–6

— 'The Colossian Hymn and the Principle of Redaction', *CBQ* 33, 1971, pp. 62–81

— *This Man Jesus: An Essay towards a New Testament Christology*, Chapman 1975

Vermes, G., 'The Use of *br ns/br ns'* in Jewish Aramaic', Appendix to M. Black, *An Aramaic Approach to the Gospels and Acts*, Oxford University

Press, [3]1967, pp. 310–28, reprinted in *Post-Biblical Jewish Studies*, Leiden 1975, pp. 147–65

— *Jesus the Jew*, Collins 1973

— 'The Archangel Sariel: a Targumic Parallel to the Dead Sea Scrolls', *CJMS* III, pp. 159–66

— 'The Present State of the "Son of Man" Debate', *JJS* 29, 1978, pp. 123–34

— ' "The Son of Man" Debate', *JSNT* 1, 1978, pp. 19–32

Vielhauer, P., 'Gottesreich und Menschensohn in der Verkündigung Jesu', *Festschrift für G. Dehn*, Neukirchen 1957, pp. 51–79, reprinted *Aufsätze zum Neuen Testament*, München 1965, pp. 55–91

— 'Jesus und der Menschensohn: Zur Diskussion mit H. E. Tödt und E. Schweizer', *ZTK* 60, 1963, pp.133–77, reprinted *Aufsätze*, pp. 92–140

— 'Erwägungen zur Christologie des Markusvangeliums', *Zeit und Geschichte: Dankesgabe an R. Bultmann*, hrsg. E. Dinkler, Tübingen 1964, pp. 155–69, reprinted *Aufsätze*, pp. 199–214

— 'Ein Weg zur neutestamentlichen Christologie? Prüfung der These F. Hahns', *EvTh* 25, 1965, pp. 24–72, reprinted *Aufsätze*, pp. 141–98

Vischer, W., 'Der Hymnus der Weisheit in den Sprüchen Salomos 8.22–31', *EvTh* 22, 1962, pp. 309–26

Vögtle, A., 'Die Adam-Christustypologie und "der Menschensohn" ', *TTZ* 60, 1951, pp. 308–28

— ' "Der Menschensohn" und die paulinische Christologie', *SPCIC* Vol. I, pp. 199–218

— 'Exegetische Erwägungen über das Wissen und Selbstbewusstsein Jesu' (1964), *Das Evangelium und die Evangelien: Beiträge zur Evangelienforschung*, Düsseldorf 1971, pp. 296–344

Völker, W., 'Die Wertung der Weisheits–Literatur bei den christlichen Alexandrinern', *ZKG* 64, 1952, pp. 1–33

Volz, P., *Der Geist Gottes und die verwandten Erscheinungen im Alten Testament und im anschliessenden Judentum*, Tübingen 1910

Vorländer, H., ' "Mein Herr und mein Gott": Christus als "persönlicher Gott" im Neuen Testament', *KuD* 21, 1975, pp. 120–46

Vos, G., *The Self-Disclosure of Jesus: the Modern Debate about the Messianic Consciousness*, 1926, Eerdmans 1954

Wainwright, A. W., 'The Confession "Jesus is God" in the New Testament', *SJT* 10, 1957, pp. 274–99

— *The Trinity in the New Testament*, SPCK 1962

Walker, W. L., *The Spirit and the Incarnation*, T. & T. Clark 1899

Walker, W. O., 'The Origin of the Son of Man Concept as applied to Jesus', *JBL* 91, 1972, pp. 482–90

Wedderburn, A. J. M., 'The Body of Christ and Related Concepts in I Corinthians', *SJT* 24, 1971, pp. 74–96

— 'ἐν τῇ σοφίᾳ τοῦ Θεοῦ – I Kor. 1.21', *ZNW* 64, 1973, pp. 132–4

— 'Philo's "Heavenly Man" ', *NovT* 15, 1973, pp. 301–26

— 'Adam in Paul's Letter to the Romans', *Studia Biblica 1978*, Vol. III, *JSNT* Supp. 1980, pp. 413–30

Weinacht, H., *Die Menschwerdung des Sohnes Gottes im Markusevangelium*, Tübingen 1972

Weinreich, O., 'Antikes Gottmenschentum', *Jahrbuch für Wissenschaft und Jugendbildung* 2, 1926, pp. 633–51, reprinted *Ausgewählte Schriften* II, Amsterdam 1973, pp. 171–97

Weiss, H. F., *Untersuchungen zur Kosmologie des hellenistischen und palästinischen Judentums*, Berlin 1966

Weiss, J., *Christus: Die Anfänge des Dogmas*, Tübingen 1909; ET, *Christ: The Beginnings of Dogma*, Philip Green 1911

— *Earliest Christianity*, 1914, ET 1937, Harper Torchbook 1959

Wendt, H. H., 'Der "Anfang" am Beginn des I Johannesbriefes', *ZNW* 21, 1922, pp. 38–42

Wengst, K., *Christologische Formeln und Lieder des Urchristentums*, Gütersloh 1972

Wernberg-Møller, P., 'A Reconsideration of the Two Spirits in the Rule of the Community (IQSerek 3.13–4.26)', *RQ* 3, 1961, pp. 413–41

Werner, M., *Die Entstehung des christlichen Dogmas*, Bern and Tübingen 1941, abbreviated ET *The Formation of Christian Dogma: An Historical Study of its Problems*, A. & C. Black 1957

Wetter, G. P., *Der Sohn Gottes: Eine Untersuchung über den Charakter und die Tendenz des Johannes-Evangeliums*, Göttingen 1916

Whiteley, D. E. H., *The Theology of St Paul*, Blackwell 1964

Whybray, R. N., *Wisdom in Proverbs*, SCM Press 1965

— 'Proverbs 8.22–31 and its supposed prototypes', *VT* 15, 1965, pp. 504–14

Wickings, H. F., 'The Nativity Stories and Docetism', *NTS* 23, 1976–77, pp. 457–60

Wicks, H. J., *The Doctrine of God in Jewish Apocryphal and Apocalyptic Literature*, Hunter and Longhurst 1915, reissued Ktav 1971

Widengreen, G., 'Early Hebrew Myths and their Interpretation', *Myth, Ritual and Kingship*, ed. S. H. Hooke, Oxford 1958, pp. 149–203

Wifall, W., 'Son of Man – a Pre-Davidic Social Class?', *CBQ* 37, 1975, pp. 331–40

Wilckens, U., *Weisheit und Torheit: Eine exegetisch-religionsgeschichtliche Untersuchung zu I Kor 1 und 2*, Tübingen 1959

— 'Christus, der "letzte Adam" und der Menschensohn: Theologische

Überlegungen zum überlieferungsgeschichtlichen Problem der paulinischen Adam-Christus-Antithese', *JMAV*, pp. 387–403

Wiles, M., 'Some Reflections on the Origins of the Doctrine of the Trinity', *JTS* 8, 1957, pp. 92–106; reprinted in *Working Papers in Doctrine*, SCM Press 1976, pp. 1–17

— *The Making of Christian Doctrine: A Study in the Principles of Early Doctrinal Development*, Cambridge University Press 1967

— *The Remaking of Christian Doctrine*, SCM Press 1974

— ' "Myth" in Theology', *BJRL* 59, 1976–77, pp. 226–46

Wilkinson, J., 'Apologetic Aspects of the Virgin Birth of Jesus Christ', *SJT* 17, 1964, pp. 159–81

Williamson, R., *Philo and the Epistle to the Hebrews*, Leiden 1970

— 'Hebrews 4.15 and the Sinlessness of Jesus', *ExpT* 86, 1974–75, pp. 4–8

— 'The Background of the Epistle to the Hebrews', *ExpT* 87, 1975–76, pp. 232–7

— 'Philo and New Testament Christology', *ExpT* 90, 1978–79, pp. 361–5

Wilson, R. McL., 'Philo and the Fourth Gospel', *ExpT* 65, 1953–54, pp. 47–9

— 'Gnosis, Gnosticism and the New Testament', *Le Origini dello Gnosticismo: Colloquio di Messina 1966*, Studies in the History of Religions (Supp. to *Numen*) 12, Leiden 1967, pp. 511–27

— *Gnosis and the New Testament*, Blackwell 1968

Wilson, S. G., 'Image of God', *ExpT* 85, 1973–74, pp. 356–61.

Winandy, J., 'Le logion de l'ignorance (Mark 13.32 Matt. 24.36)', *RB* 75, 1968, pp. 63–79

Windisch, H., 'Die göttliche Weisheit der Juden und die paulinische Christologie', *Neutestamentliche Studien Georg Heinrici*, hrsg. A. Deissmann and H. Windisch, Leipzig 1914, pp. 220–34

— 'Jesus und der Geist im Johannesevangelium', *Amicitiae Corolla*, Festschrift J. R. Harris, ed. H. G. Wood, University of London 1933, pp. 303–18; ET, *The Spirit-Paraclete in the Fourth Gospel*, Fortress Facet Book 1968, pp. 27–38

— *Paulus und Christus: Ein biblisch-religionsgeschichtlicher Vergleich*, Leipzig 1934

— 'Zur Christologie der Pastoralbriefe', *ZNW* 34, 1935, pp. 213–38

Winter, P., 'Some Observations on the Language in the Birth and Infancy Stories of the Third Gospel', *NTS* 1, 1954–55, pp. 111–21

Wisse, F., 'The Redeemer Figure in the Paraphrase of Shem', *NovT* 12, 1970, pp. 130–40

Witt, R. E., ' ΥΠΟΣΤΑΣΙΣ (Hypostasis)', *Amicitiae Corolla*, Festschrift, J. R. Harris, ed. H. G. Wood, University of London 1933, pp. 319–43

Wolfson, H. A., *Philo: Foundation of Religious Philosophy in Judaism, Christianity and Islam*, 2 vols., Harvard 1947

Wood, J., *Wisdom Literature: An Introduction*, Duckworth 1967

Yamauchi, E., *Pre-Christian Gnosticism*, Tyndale 1973
— 'The Descent of Ishtar, the Fall of Sophia, and the Jewish Roots of Gnosticism', *Tyndale Bulletin* 29, 1978, pp. 143–75
— 'Pre-Christian Gnosticism in the Nag Hammadi Texts?' *Church History* 48, 1979, pp. 129–41

Yarnold, E., 'The Trinitarian Implications of Luke and Acts', *Heythrop Journal* 7, 1966, pp. 18–32

Young, F. W., 'Jesus the Prophet: A re-examination', *JBL* 68, 1949, pp. 285–99

Zeilinger, F., *Der Erstgeborene der Schöpfung: Untersuchungen zur Formalstruktur und Theologie des Kolosserbriefes*, Wien 1974

Ziener, G., 'Weisheitsbuch und Johannesevangelium', *Biblica* 38, 1957, pp. 396–416, and 39, 1958, pp. 37–60

Ziesler, J., *The Jesus Question*, Lutterworth 1980

Zimmermann, H., 'Das absolute ἐγώ εἰμι als die neutestamentliche Offenbarungsformel', *BZ* 4, 1960, pp. 54–69, 266–76
— 'Christushymnus und johanneischer Prolog', *NTKRS*, pp. 249–65
— *Das Bekenntnis der Hoffnung: Tradition und Redaktion im Hebräerbrief*, Köln 1977
— *Jesus Christus: Geschichte und Verkündigung*, Stuttgart 1973, [2]1975

INDEXES

Throughout the indexes references to the text are cited by page number and are given first. References to notes are cited by chapter and note number.

INDEX OF BIBLICAL AND ANCIENT WRITINGS

I *OLD TESTAMENT*

Genesis					
		6.2,4	15	*Exodus*	
		6.17	V.20	1.22	140
1–3	101f., 115–	7.15,22	V.20	3–4	V.105
	16, 121	8.1	V.20	3.2–6	150
1–2	100, 123f.	9.6	105	3.2	149
1	116	14	20, 55, 153,	3.12	39
1.1	VI.7		II.57,	4.16	17, 19, 223
1.3	VII.111		III.152	4.22	15, 199,
1.26f.	72, 100, 105,	15.1	217		II.62
	116, 123	15.2–18	207	7.1	17, 19, 223
1.26	105, IV.29	16.7–12	149	9.14	38
2–3	103–5, IV.58	16.13	150	10.13, 19	V.20
2	101,116	17.5	VI.202	11–12	218
2.7	100, 107,	17.15f.	II.165	11.4f.	219
	123, 134,	18	150, 241,	12.12	219
	IV.107		V.105	14.19f.	150
2.17	103f.	18.19	199	14.19	150, 157
2.19f.	72	21.17f	149f.	14.24	150
3	101–3	22.2	48	15.8	133
3.4f.	101	22.3f.	226	20.4	IV.83
3.5	115, 116,	22.11	152	21.6	17
	118, IV.73	22.12	48	22.8	17
3.13	104	22.16	48, II.213	23.20f.	152
3.17f.	104	24.40	39	23.20	150
3.22–4	103	28.11	225, 226	23.21	17, III.94
3.22	116	28.12	149	23.23	150
5.1–3	105	30.22	II.165	24.10	130
5.1	105	31.11–13	150	24.16	VI.203
5.24	III.64	31.13	241	25.40	53, 222
6.1–4	102	32.24–30	150	32.34	150
6.1f.	V.108	49.3	247	33.2f.	150

33.12, 13   199
33.18ff.   VI.203
33.20   244
33.21   153
34.29–35   143f.
34.29   47
34.34   143f.
40.34   VI.203
40.35   47, 51

Leviticus
10.8–10   222
16.2, 34   223

Numbers
11.31   V.20
12.7   II.213
16.5   199
20.16   150
22.38   218
25   93

Deuteronomy
4.12   244, IV.83
4.15–18   102
4.15f.   IV.83
4.15   102
4.16–18   IV.83
4.23, 25   IV.83
5.5   217
5.8   IV.83
6–8   121, II.192
6.4   179–80, 182,
         VI.67
13.6   IV.73
14.1   15
18.15   138f.
18.18f.   141
18.18   138
21.17   247
30.11–14   185
30.11   185
30.12–14   184
30.12f.   167, 185
30.13   VI.80
32.8   15
32.11   203
32.47   232f.
34.5   II.63,
         III.141
34.10   V.44

Joshua
5.13–15   150
8.27   217

22.28   IV.83

Judges
2.1   150
3.10   V.20
6   V.105
6.8, 14   39
6.34   241, V.20
8.18   IV.83
9.23   39, 133
11.29   V.20
13   V.105

Ruth
2.12   203

I Samuel
10.6, 10   V.20
16.14–16   133
16.14   133
18.12   133

II Samuel
7.11–14   15, II.18
7.14   15, 54, 55
22.16   133

I Kings
13.20   217
14.6   201
18.45   V.20
19.11   V.20
22.19–23   133
22.19   149

II Kings
2.9–12   III.151

I Chronicles
17.13   15
22.10   15
28.6   15

II Chronicles
36.15   39

Nehemiah
9.6   150

Job
1–2   174
1.6–12   15
2.1–6   15
4.9   133
4.16   IV.83

5.14   IV.73
9.8, 13   72
10.10   IV.73
11.14   175
12.13   VI.59
13.28   IV.73
14.1   40
15.14   40
15.16   IV.73
16.19   84, 151, 157,
         V.113
19.25   151
24.20   IV.73
25.2   174
25.4   40
26.12   72
27.16   IV.73
28   168, 171,
         198–9
28.20, 23   199
29.14   IV.73
33.4   133
33.23   84, 151, 157,
         V.113
34.14   133
38.7   15
40.15   IV.73

Psalms
2.2, 6   35
2.7   15, 33, 34,
         35–6, 46,
         47, 51, 55,
         59f., 62,
         II.181,
         VI.200
7.8   152, V.100
8   90, 108–9,
         111, 113,
         127,
         IV.26, 50
8.4–6   54, 108–111,
         IV.46
8.4f.   110
8.4   69, 70, 90f.
8.5f.   109f.
8.5   110f., V.86
8.6f.   190
8.6   90, 108–11,
         115, 117–
         18, 155,
         IV.49
8.7   IV.49
9.10   199
17.8   203

18.5 133
24.1 180
29.1 15
33.6 133, 217, 219, 234, V.20
36.7 203
36.10 199
40.6–8 54, V.117
43.3 174
45.2 45
45.4 175
45.6f. 55, II.32
45.6 17, 45
47.7 VI.201
57.1 203
57.3 174
61.4 203
63.7 203
63.9 187
68.17 VI.131
68.18 186f.
72.19 VI.201
74.2 III.24, 61
74.9 135
74.12–14 72
80.15–17 70
80.15 III.20
80.17 70, III.22
82.1 152
82.6 17, 58, II.32
85.10f. 174, VI.59
89.5–8 150
89.6 15
89.9f. 72
89.21 70
89.26f. 15
89.27 189
89.50f. II.215
91.4 203
93.2 III.84
96.6 174
97.7 V.86
102 II.216
102.28 II.216
104.24 190, VI.118
105.26 39
105.28 38
106.19f. 102
106.20 IV.10
107.20 138, 217, 232, VII.63
107.26 VI.80
107.42 175

110 108–9
110.1 70f., 91, 108f., 109f., 115, 118, 155
110.2f. 70
110.3 70f., VI.19
110.4 71, 153
114 III.115
118.26 203
119.89, 160 218
132.13f. VI.131
138.1 V.86
139.7 133f., 193
143.10 134
147.15 217
147.18 217, 219
148.2 150
151.4 39

Proverbs
1.20–33 169
1.20–31 202
1.28 166
2 169
2.6 171, VII.24
3.19 165, 171, 189, 219
5, 6, 7 169
8.1–35 169, 171
8.12 198
8.22–31 73, 168–9
8.22 165, 166, 189, 191, 228, 240, 247, VI.7
8.25f. III.54
8.25 165
8.27–30 165f.
8.30 VI.22
8.32 VI.147
8.35 242
9.1–6 169, 219
9.3 203
9.5 166
30.4 VI.86

Isaiah
6.3 193, VI.201
9.6f. 17
9.8 217
11.2 73, III.54
11.4 247
11.9 199

19.21 199
27.1 72
30.1 133
30.27f. 133, III.139
31.3 133, 243
31.5 203
35.10 175
40.6–8 234
40.7, 13 133
42.6 199
43.6 15
43.10 31, 199
44.13 IV.83
45.1, 6 200
45.23 118, 158
49.2 247
49.6 199
51.9 72, 175
51.23 IV.73
53 72, IV.87
53.12 118
55.10f. 217
55.11 233
61.1f. 86, 137
61.1 137f., V.43
63.9–14 134
63.10 134

Jeremiah
1.5 71, 199
1.7 39
2.11 102, IV.10
7.25f. VI.172
7.25 39
9.24 199
17.12 III.84
23.24 193
23.29 218
25.4–7 VI.172
31.9 15, 199
31.31–4 28, 200
49.14 89
51.34–7 72

Ezekiel
1 II.36, III.14, 84
1.26 III.65
2.1 III.14
2.3 39
3.5f. 39
3.12–15 93
3.14 133
8.1–3 133
8.2 156

29.3f.	72		83, 91,	*Amos*	
32.18	187		103	1.4, 7, 10	38
37.1	133	7.14	68, 199,	3.2	199
			III.71,	3.7	29, 47
Daniel			126	9.11	III.24
2	79	7.17f.	68f.		
2.31–45	74	7.17	69	*Obadiah*	
2.44	69	7.21–7	88	1	39, 89
3.25	15, 39	7.21f.	68f.		
7	66f., 68–76,	7.26f.	68	*Jonah*	
	79f., 82–4,	8.15f.	74	4.2	157
	91, 96,	8.16	151		
	253f., 267,	8.21f.	69	*Micah*	
	I.33,	9.21	151	5.2	70f., III.24,
	III.13, 14,	10.13	74, 151f.		VI.19
	79, 87, 89,	10.18	74	6.4	39
	97, 98	10.20f.	74, 152		
7.2, 3	80	10.20	151	*Habakkuk*	
9.9–14	76, 260,	10.21	69	2.14	199
	III.14	11.32	199	3.5	VII.21
7.9f.	77, 80	11.36	20		
7.9	48, 76, 91,	12.1	69, 74, 153	*Haggai*	
	III.95	12.3	48	1.12	39
7.10	III.139				
7.13f.	66, 68–75,	*Hosea*		*Zechariah*	
	76, 77, 95,	1.10f.	28	1.12	151
	199,	1.10	15	7.12	39
	III.98	11.1	15, 49, 199	13.2–6	135
7.13	7, 76, 80f.,	13.5	199	14.9	VI.201
	82–4, 86–				
	9, 91, 95f.,	*Joel*		*Malachi*	
	III.10, 12,	2.32	158	3.1–3	92
	14, 22, 65,			3.1	39
				4.5	92

II *OLD TESTAMENT APOCRYPHA AND PSEUDEPIGRAPHA*

Abraham, Apocalypse of		*Aristobulus*	164, VI.8	*II Baruch*	81
	81, III.94,			13.3	93
	V.103	*Artapanus*		17.3	IV.8
10	153, III.94	Frag. 3.6	17, 19	21.4	130
11	156			23.4	IV.8
17	III.94	*Baruch*		25.1	93
		3.9–4.4	166, 168,	39–40	III.98
Abraham, Testament of			171, 242	41.4	VI.184
	III.79, 103,	3.15–32	198–9	43.2	93
	V.105	3.16	166	46.7	93
4–5	V.105	3.27	199	48.30	93
7.3–17	20	3.29–32	186	48.42f.	IV.8
11	III.79	3.29–31	199	51.1	IV.15
		3.29f.	185	51.3	48, IV.15
Adam and Eve, Life of		3.29	167	51.5	48
	IV.8	3.36–4.4	186, VII.106	51.10	48,105
14.1f.	105	3.36	199	51.12	105
37.3	105	3.37–41	199	54.15	IV.8, 15

54.19	IV.8, 23	43.4	129	85–90	105
54.21	IV.15	45.2f.	129	85.3	105
56.5f.	IV.8	45.3–4	74	86	102
56.10	102	45.3	78	89.8	242
76.3	93	46	III.65	89.52	93
85.1–3	135	46.1–2	76, 86,	89.76	129
			III.66, 69	90.22, 25	93
		46.1	155, III.65	90.31	21, 92, 93,
III Baruch		46.2	73		94
4.16	IV.15	46.3f.	75	90.37f.	105
		46.3	III.66	90.38	48
		46.6–8	129	90.39	93
Elijah, Apocalypse of		47.2	129	99.3	129, 152
	92, 94	48.2–6	75	104	105
3.90–9	21	48.3	III.54	104.1	152
14.10–12	III.147	48.6	VII.80	104.8	242
24.11–15	93f.	48.7	73, 129	106.5	15
25.1–19	III.147	48.10	73, 75, 129	106.19	VII.73
		49.1–3	73	108.11f.	48
		49.2–4	75	108.11	242
		51.3	73		
I Enoch		52.4	73, 75	*II Enoch*	77
	7, 77, 135	52.6–9	75	1.5	156
6–11	102	54.6	74, V.92	4.1f.	151
9.1f.	151	55.4	75, 78	18.4f.	102
9.1	V.92	56.5, 7	77	22.4–10	II.35
9.3	129, 152	61.8f.	75	22.8	19
10.1	V.92	61.8	78	30.11	105
12–16	84, III.79	61.10	21, 155	65.2	105
12.4	III.79	62.2	73	Melchizedek fragment
13.8	15	62.5	78, III.68,		II.52, 57
14.8–24	III.14		83		
14.8	III.14	62.6–7	75	*III Enoch*	19, 77, II.35,
15.2	129	62.7	III.66,		V.93
15.4, 7	131		VII.80	3–16	17, 153
17–36	93	64–5	102	3–15	II.35
20	21, V.92	68.2–4	74	12.5	17, II.34
20.1–8	151	69.4–5	15	16.2–4	II.56, V.11
37–71 (*the*	69, 73, 75–8,	69.11	105	48D	VI.28
Similitudes	81, 84, 91,	69.27	78, III.66		
of	95, III.14,	70–71	III.69, 79	*II Esdras*	see *II Ezra*
Enoch)	71, 79, 80,	70.1	III.69		
	139	70.4	III.64	*Ezekiel the Tragedian*
39.7, 9, 13	129	71	74, III.79		II.44
40	74, 151	71.1	15		
40.9	V.92	71.8	V.92	*II Ezra/Esdras*	
41	III.76	71.11	19	1.30	VI.184
41.2	129	71.14	19, 76, 85,		
41.5	III.76		153,	*IV Ezra*	79f., 81, 84,
41.6	129		III.64, 66,		91, 95
42	73, 168, 242		V.67	3.7, 21f.	IV.8
42.1f.	203,	75.3	151	4.8	VI.86
	VII.115,	80.6	151	4.30	IV.8
	127	82.10–20	151	5.20	151
42.2	164f.	83–90	74, III.144	6.26	79, III.137

7.11f.	IV.26
7.11	IV.18
7.28f.	79, II.19
7.118	IV.8
7.122–5	IV.15
8.44	105
11–12	74
12.32	79
13	79f., III.92
13.1–3	79
13.1f.	86
13.2	80
13.3	74, 80
13.5	80
13.6	79
13.12	80
13.25f.	79
13.25	80
13.32	79, 80
13.51f.	79, 80
14.9	79, 93

V Ezra   see *II Ezra*

Isaiah, Ascension of
9.9	19
9.36, 39f.	131
10.4	131
11.33	131

Job, Testament of
2–5	20

Joseph and Asenath
6.2–6	15
13.10	15
14–17	20
21.3	15

Joseph, Prayer of
21, 153, 155, V.103

Jubilees
1.24f.	15
1.25	131
1.27, 29	151
2.2f.	151
2.2	21, 131, 151
3.28–32	IV.8
4.17–19	III.79
4.21f.	III.79
4.22f.	84
4.23	19
5.1–10	102

13.25	153
15.31f.	151
15.32	131
18.9–12	152
48.9–19	152

Judith
16.14	130, 134

I Maccabees
4.46	135
9.27	135

II Maccabees
7.34	15
15.13f.	19

III Maccabees
6.3, 8	27

IV Maccabees
15.4	207

Melchizedek
see *II Enoch*

Moses, Apocalypse of
	IV.8
10.3	105
12.1	105
19.3	103
20f.	IV.15
33.5	105
35.2	105

Moses, Assumption of (Testament of)
71, 77, III.32

1.14	71
10.2	152f.
11.15f.	71

Philo, Pseudo- (Liber Antiquitatum Biblicarum)
10.7	VI.74
11.15	VI.74
48.1	93, III.149

Sibylline Oracles
II.187–9	92
III.397–400	III.98
IV	81

Sira, Jesus ben (Ecclesiasticus)
1.1	171
1.4	166, 189
1.6, 8	198–9
4.10	15, 199
4.11	VI.147
4.12	242
14.17	IV.8
14.26–15.2	172
15.3	183
16.26	172
18.1, 2, 4	172
23.1, 4	27
24	168–9, 242, VI.11
24.3	VII.24
24.5	186, VI.80
24.7–12	203
24.8f.	240, 247
24.8	164f., 242
24.9	71, 73, 165, 189
24.19–21	166
24.21	166
24.23	170, 199, VII.106
24.25	170
24.33	135
25.24	IV.8
39.1	172
42.21	172
43.26	166
43.27	172
43.31	244
44.16	III.64
48.10f.	92
51	164
51.10	15, 27, 199
51.13–17	VI.192
51.23–7	164
51.23–6	200

Solomon, Odes of
	VII.119
7.4, 12	VII.119
36.3	65

Solomon, Psalms of
13.8	15
17	72
17.27	247
17.30	15
17.37	73

Solomon, Wisdom of
168
1.4f. 130
1.6f. 135
1.6 134, 172
1.7 130, 134,
193
2.13, 16 15, 27, 199
2.18 15
2.23f. IV.8, 77, 87
2.23 105, 116,
IV.77
2.24 116
4.10–5.5 III.149
4.10f. III.64
5.1–5 87, 88
5.5 15
6.9, 12–16 172
6.12–11.1 168
6.16 203
6.17 172
6.18 171, 174,
VII.106
6.22 247
7.3 IV.73
7.8–10, 11f. 172
7.15f. 173
7.17–21 172
7.22–5 135, 169,
172
7.22 71, 73, 134,
169,
III.35, 36
7.24 194
7.25ff. 198
7.25 242, VI.59

7.26 165f, 167,
206, 241
7.27 135, 201
7.28 199
7.29f. 241
7.29 172
8.1 169, 172
8.2 172
8.3f. 172f., 198
8.4–6 129, 165,
189
8.5f. 169
8.5 174
8.8f. 198
8.8 173
8.19f. 54, II,197
8.21–9.6 173
9.1–2 219
9.4 169, 198
9.7 15
9.9 164, 198
9.10f. V.84
9.10 39, 44, 166,
II.152
9.11 198
9.17 39, 44, 130,
134f., 166,
219
10–11 VI.172
10.15 174
11.17 175
11.20 133
12–13 IV.9
12.25 44
14.3 27
16.20 44

18.13 15
18.14–16 217–19,
VII.137
18.15f. 219, 233,
247

*Twelve Patriarchs,
Testaments of*
135

Reuben
5 102

Levi
3.5 129, 151f.
4.2 16
5.6f. 129, 152

Judah
20.1–5 V.111
25.2 151

Dan
6.2 129, 152

Naphtali
2.5 105

Tobit
3.16f. 20
4.21 121
5, 12 V.105
12.15 129, 151f.
12.19 V.105
13.2 187

Wisdom of see *Solomon,
Solomon Wisdom of*

III *DEAD SEA SCROLLS, PHILO, JOSEPHUS, AND RABBINIC TEXTS*

DEAD SEA SCROLLS

CD
3.20 106
5.18 152
6.4 VI.78

IQapGen
22.14–17 153

IQH
1.10f. 151
1.11 131

1.21 136
3.22 105
3.29f. III.139
5.11f. VII.80
5.25f. VII.80
6.13 129, 151
8.10f. VII.80
11.12f. 105
12.11f. 136
13.8 131
13.14 40

17.15 106
18.12f,16 40

IQM 242
9.15f. 19
9.15 151
9.16 V.92
10.12 131
13.5f. 153
13.10–16 153
13.10–12 153

13.10	131, 152	IQSa		4QTeharot^d	
13.15	VII.112	2.11f.	15	2.2	153
17.5–8	153				
17.6	19, 152	4Q 'Amram^b		11QMelchizedek	19, 20, 55,
		2.3	153		152f., 155,
					II.218,
IQS		4QFlor.			III.152,
2.3	136	1.10ff.	15, 72		V.100
3.13–4.26	135				
3.20f.	153	4QMess.ar.II.17		9–11	152
3.20, 24	152, 156			11	153
4.2–4	136	4QpsDanA^a		13f.	152f
4.23f.	152, 156		16		
4.23	106			11QtgJob	
11.7f.	105	4QS1		29	151, V.113,
11.20f.	40	37–40	151		VII.10

PHILO

(The number in brackets following each title refers to the relevant volume of the Loeb edition of Philo.)

De Abrahamo (VI)		*De Congressu quaerendae*			VI.34
83	223	*Eruditionis gratiae* (IV)		109	165, 169
100–2	II.153	12f.	173	112	166
118	V.105	79	225f.	117f.	228
119–22	226			137	VI.34
273	II.213	*De Decalogo* (VII)		186	135
		88	VII.130		
De Agricultura (III)		134	225	*De Gigantibus* (II)	
51f.	224, VII.53	142	103	27	194
51	129, 221,	150, 153	103	47	194, VII.25
	VI.110			52	54, 223
		De Ebrietate (III)		53–6	VII.25
De Cherubim (II)		30f.	165	60f.	225
3, 35	VII.53	31	169, 228,		
36	221		240, 247	*Legum Allegoriae* (I)	
42–52	II.52	44	227	I.31	100
44–7, 49	173	61	II.59	I.32f.	134
125	VI.139	68, 80f., 95	224	I.36f.	226
127	227	132f.	225, 228	I.37	134
		132	222	I.40	19
De Confusione Linguarum		157	223	I.42	V.31
(IV)				I.43	165, 169,
41	100	*De Fuga et Inventione* (V)			191, 247
43	224	5f.	228	I.44	194
49	169	5	VII.53	I.46	222
60–3	241	12f.	227	I.53f.	100
62f.	100	51f.	II.153	I.61	207
95–7	227	52	199	I.64f.	173
96f.	226	60	II.59	I.93	222
102	207	90–2	VII.41	II.49	169
145–7	15	95	228	II.67	II.213
146f.	100	97	173, VI.34	II.82	173
146	15, 221,	101	226–7	II.86f.	173
	VI.110	108–9	54, 173,	II.86	129, 167,

	183, 227
III	II.213
III.1	222
III.3	173
III.4	194
III.43	234
III.46, 52	173
III.79–82	II.213
III.80	222
III.82	54, 55
III.95–7	207
III.95f.	227, VI.118
III.97–9	226
III.99	174, 227
III.100–3	53
III.102	222
III.103	II.213
III.106	222
III.148,	222
150	
III.161	134
III.169f.	VI.34
III.175	228, 240, 247
III.177	VII.53
III.203, 204	II.213
III.228	II.213

De Legatione ad Gaium (X)

| 4f. | 227 |
| 6 | 226 |

De Migratione Abrahami (IV)

6	207, 227
12	VII.41
23f.	243
35	228
52	225
67	227
70–85	223
76–84	223
81	228
84	19
102	54
103	225
122	243
130	171

De Mutatione Nominum (V)

| 9, 15 | 226 |
| 31 | 227 |

69	VII.41
108	233
128	19
208	223
236f.	VI.83
256	166
259	VI.34

De Opificio Mundi (I)

	VII.48
16–44	224
17–19	124
18f.	224f.
20	225, 227, VI.118
24	225
26	VII.103
31	225
33	241
36	222
70f.	227
84	15
134	100, 124
135	227
139	225
143	222
146	207, 225
152	103
170–2	227

De Plantatione (III)

8f.	166
18	134, 166, 207, 225, V.31
20	225
44	V.31
117	234

De Posteritate Caini (II)

13–21	227
14	227
15, 16–20	226
68	224
69	225, 242
84f.	VI.83
91	224
136–8	173
145	VII.107
168f.	226, 244

De Praemiis et Poenis (VIII)

| 40, 44 | 226 |
| 45 | 227 |

55	228
80	VI.83
163	225

Quaestiones in Exodum (Supp. II)

I.4	100
II.13	220, VII.53
II.16	220
II.29	17
II.42	225
II.45, 47	II.52
II.51	227
II.52	222
II.53	227
II.67	226–7
II.68	II.216, VII.109
II.81	227
II.94	220
II.111	VII.41
II.117	191
II.118	166
II.122, 124	225

Quaestiones in Genesin (Supp. I)

I.4	225
II.59	134
II.62	221, 241, II.43
III.15	225
IV.2, 4	226
IV.47	169
IV.90	VII.41
IV.91	VII.53
IV.97	165, 199
IV.130	194

Quis Rerum Divinarum Heres (IV)

	207
2–5	220
36	166
38	207
53	169
55–7	134
69f.	228
79	VI.34
99	227
119	222, 227
127	173
130–140	233
133, 140	227
181	207

188, 199	166
201	54
205f.	III.36
205	VII.51
228	227
230f.	225–6
233f.	224
236	15
249, 258	134
259–66	228
264f.	VII.25
264	134
280	222
294	207
301	227

Quod Deterius Potiori Insidiari Soleat (II)

39f.	223
54	165, 169, 189
66	VII.41
77	207
83f.	V.31
83	207, 226
115–17	169
117	173
118	VI.34
124	173f.
126–32	223
160	227
161f.	19
178	II.59

Quod Deus Immutabilis (III)

31f.	15, 241
57	207
62	225
106	228
138	220

182	VII.53

Quod Omnis Probus Liber (IX)

13	173
43	17
117	173

De Sacrificiis Abelis et Caini (II)

8	207, 226–7
9	17
60	207
64	174
65	228
67	194
80–3	223
86	VI.34
119	221

De Sobrietate (III)

68	234

De Somniis (V)

I.61–72	226
I.62	225
I.65f.	226
I.66	223
I.68f.	226
I.75	226, 241, VII.111
I.102–14	223
I.115	VII.53
I.141f.	220, 227
I.147f.	VII.53
I.157–9	VII.137
I.157	227
I.215	15, VI.110
I.227–30	241
I.232, 238	228
I.239	227
I.241	166, 227

II.45	225
II.189	17
II.242	173, VI.34
II.245	VI.34

De Specialibus Legibus I–II (VII), IV (VIII)

I.32–50	226
I.48	225
I.65	134, 228
I.81	207, 225
I.96	15
I.171	225, V.31
I.209	225
I.318	15
I.323	225
I.345	227
II.29	224
II.165	15
II.192	VI.10
III.1f.	228
III.189	15
III.207	225
IV.23	207
IV.49	228
IV.75	173
IV.123	134

De Virtutibus (VIII)

62–5	171
183	186, VI.83
217	134

De Vita Mosis (VI)

I.158	17
I.277	135, 228
I.283	228
II.74	222
II.127–9	224, VII.41
II.188	228
II.246	134
II.288	17, II.44

JOSEPHUS

Antiquities

I.197	V.105
II.232	16
III.96f.	17
III.180	16
IV.326	17, 19
VIII.34	16
VIII.102, 106	134
VIII.114	134

VIII.187	16
VIII.234, 243	16
IX.28	II.44
X.35	16
X.241	16
XIV.24	27
XVIII.64	16
XIX.343–50	20

Bellum Judaicum

III.400	89
IV.625	16
VI.312f.	III.98
VII.346	244

Contra Apionem

I.41	135

RABBINIC TEXTS

Mishnah
Taanith
3.8   15, 27
Yoma
3.8, 4.2,   129
  6.2
Sanhedrin
6.5   129
Aboth
3.2   129, VI.176
4.11   V.113
5.6   III.37

Tosefta
Sukkah
  3.11f.   VI.74
Sotah 13.2 135

Babylonian Talmud
Pesahim
54a   71, III.37
Sukkah
52b   153
Taanith
23b   II.97
24b   15
Nedarim
39b   71

Baba Mezia
94a   VI.86
Sanhedrin
38b   III.95,
                    IV.15,
                    V.11

Midrash Rabbah
Gen.   106, IV.15
  11.2   106, IV.15
  12.6   106, IV.15
Lev.
  25   VI.184
Num.
  13.12   106
Deut.
  11.3   106

Targums
Neofiti   185, V.6
Gen. 1   VII.10
Gen. 2.15   IV.18
Gen. 19.3   V.105
Gen.
  32.25–7   II.62
Deut.
30.12f.   VI.80, 83

Onkelos
Ex. 33.14f. 129
Ex. 34.6, 9 129

Pseudo-Jonathan
  (Jerusalem Targum)
Gen. 1.1   VI.7
Gen. 19.3   V.105
Gen.
  32.25–7   II.62
Num.
  22.28   III.37
Zech. 4.7   71
on I Kings
  8.27   VI.131
on II Kings
  2.1   II.44
on Job   157
on Psalms   186, III.21
Psalm
  68.17   VI.131
Psalm
  89.27   II.97
on Isa.
  52.13–   III.40
  53.12
on Mal.
  2.10   II.97

IV *NEW TESTAMENT*

Bold type indicates that some exegesis of the text is offered in these pages/notes.

Matthew
1–2   49
1.1–17   49
1.1   49
1.2–17   88
1.16   40, 50
1.18–25   49
1.18–20   49, 202
1.18   140
1.20   49, 50, 140,
                    154
1.23   II **196**
1.24   154
2.13   154
2.15   **49**, 200
2.16–18   140
2.19   154
2.23   VI.172

3.7–12   92
3.7–10   V.52
3.11   142
3.15   49
3.16   139
3.17   49
4.1–11   121, V.52
4.1   139, 140
4.3   49, 200
4.6   49, 154, 200
4.11   154
5–7   140
5.3–6   85,137
5.10–12   202
5.11   66
5.17   III.122
5.48   28
6.25–33   122

7.7–11   28
7.24, 26   231
8.20   88, 122
8.38   154
9.27   49
9.36–10.42 140
10.14   231
10.17   202
10.19   141
10.23f.   29
10.23   67, 202, 204,
                    III.10
10.32f.   29
10.32   66
10.34   III.122
10.40   137
11.2–19   197
11.2–6   24, 86

11.2	197, VI.144	19.12	40	2.17	III.122
11.3–6	137	19.28	67, 77, 85	3.11	**47**, II.15
11.3	85	20.30f.	49	3.29	139
11.5f.	26, 85	21.9, 15	49	3.34	28
11.5	137	21.33–46	II.156	4.14–20	231, VIII.58
11.10	86, 93	21.39	49	4.22	236
11.11	40	22.44	109	4.33	231
11.14	93	22.45	49	5.7	**47**, II.15
11.16–19	166, 197	23–25	140	6.1–6	VI.191
11.16f.	VI.142	23	202, VI.177	6.2	VI.191
11.19	88, **197–8**,	23.34–9	204	6.4	137
	VI.144	23.34–6	166, **201–2**,	6.15	85, 92, 94,
11.25–30	164		203		III.141
11.25–7	49, 166,	23.34	204	6.50	31
	198–201	23.37–9	166, **202–4**	7.6f.	86
11.25f.	VI.156	23.37	204	7.13	VII.58
11.25	27	24.5	31	8.12	141
11.27–30	164	24.26f.	III.117	8.27	66
11.27	28, **29**, 30,	24.27	67	8.28f.	140
	35, 37,	24.30	67, III.10	8.28	85, 92, 94
	198–200,	24.37–9	III.117	8.29	47, 85
	V.44,	24.37, 39	67	8.31	66
	VI.164	24.44	67, III.10,	8.32	231
11.28–30	**49**, 164, 166,		117	8.38	46, 67, 78,
	198, **200–**	25.31f.	78		89, 231
	1, VI.151	25.31	67, 154,	9	93
12.18	140		III.10	9.1	83
12.23	49	26.53	154	9.2–8	**47f.**, **89**,
12.28	26, **137f.**,	26.63	48		II.105
	139	26.64	31	9.7	47, 48, 139
12.31f.	139	27.40, 43	49	9.9	47
12.32	88	27.50	141	9.10	231
12.41f.	26, 85, 140	28.2	154	9.11–13	93
12.41	137	28.3	48	9.11f.	92
13.1–52	140	28.5	154	9.37	40, 44
13.16f.	26, 85, 140	28.18	49	10.28–30	122
13.40–3	III.82	28.19	**49**	10.45	24, **89**,
13.41f.	III.117	28.28	49		III.122, 123
13.41	67, 154			12.1–9	138
13.52	202	*Mark*		12.2–6	**28**, 55
14.33	48	1.1	47	12.6f.	40
15.22	49	1.2	93	12.6	28, 35, **40**,
15.24	40, 137	1.8	142		47, II.106
16.13	66	1.10f.	47, 60	12.7–9	44
16.14	II.63	1.10	139	12.24f.	105
16.16	48	1.11	35, **46–8**,	12.25	154
16.27f.	89		59f.,	12.26f.	86
16.27	III.82		II.**105**,	12.35–7	88
16.28	67, 83,		179, **181**	12.36f.	86
	III.10	1.12f.	IV.51	12.36	108
17.10–13	93	1.12	139, **140**	13.6	31
17.22–	140	1.13	154	13.11	141, V.114
18.35		2.2	231	13.26f.	78, 79
17.25f.	28	2.8	141	13.26	67, 83,
18.20	49, VI.176	2.10	**88f.**		III.10

13.27 154
13.31 231
13.32 **28f.**, 35, **47**, 154, 156
14.24 28
14.33–6 48
14.36 28
14.57–62 II.18
14.61f. **47, 48**
14.61 47, 48
14.62 21, 24, 31, 67, 78, 83, 89, 108, III.10, 22, **83**, 117, VI.59
15.34 122
15.35f. III.40
15.39 **46–8**

Luke
1 51
1.2 **232**, 245
1.11 154
1.16f. 93
1.17 92
1.19 154
1.26–38 154
1.32f. 51, 72
1.32, 34 50
1.35 **50–1**, 140, **141**, 142, II.201
1.69 72
1.76 93
2.9f. 154
2.41–52 II.**105**, VI.192
2.49 50
3.7–9 92, V.52
3.16f. 92
3.16 142
3.22 35, **51**, 139, 142, II.181
3.23–38 51
3.38 112, IV.51
4.1–12 121, V.52
4.1 139, 140
4.10 154
4.14 140
4.18 40, 140, 142
4.26 44
4.41 II.15
5.1 231

6.20f. 137
6.20 86
6.22 66
7.16 140
7.18–35 197
7.18–23 24, 86
7.20–23 137
7.22f. 26, 85
7.22 137
7.25 IV.67
7.27 86, 93
7.29 198
7.31–5 166, 197
7.31f. VI.142
7.34f. 88
7.35 **197–8**, 200
7.39 140
8.11, 21 231
9.8, 19 92, **94**, III.137
9.31 50, 140
9.58 88, 122
10.16 40, 44, 137
10.18 II.**112**
10.21f. 49, 166, **198–201**
10.21 27, 140
10.22 28, 35, 37, 50, VI.164
10.23f. 26, 85
11.2 **27**, 28
11.20 26, **137f.**, 139
11.28 VIII.58
11.31f. 26, 85
11.32 137
11.49–51 166, **201–2**, 203, V.28, VI.170
11.49 203f., II.152, 155
11.51 VI.166
12.8f. 29, **84–5**, **87**, 90, 95, 154
12.8 66, 67
12.10 88, 139
12.40 67, III.10, 117
12.49 III.122, 123
12.54–6 26, 85
13.31–3 203
13.33f. 203
13.33 137f., 140, 204

13.34f. 166, **202–4**
13.35 204
16.16 140
17.22 67
17.23f. III.117
17.24 67
17.26f. III.117
17.26, 30 67
18.8 67, III.10
19.10 III.122
20.13 44
20.36 28, 154
21.15 141
21.36 67
22.20 200
22.22 34, 235
22.29f. 28
22.29 37, 85
22.30 67
22.43 154
22.48 66
23.46 141
24.7 III.109
24.13–43 V.105
24.19 140
24.23 154
24.39–43 V.105
24.39 245, III.147, VII.88
24.49 39, 142

John
1.1–18 164, 196, 206, 216, 230, 234, **239–45**, 245f., 247, VII.10, 73, 99
1.1–16 249
1.1–13 243
1.1–12 VII.102
1.1–5 239, VII.100, 106
1.1–3 213, VII.106
1.1 58, 164, 230, 232, **241**, 245, 246, VII.102, **103**, 106, 111
1.3–5 VII.106
1.3f. VII.101

1.3	240, 247	1.32f.	139, **141**	6.51–8	VII.106
1.4–5	**241f.**	1.33	142	6.51–6	VII.104
1.4	164, 241, 245	1.34	56	6.53–6	VII.118
1.5	241, VII.114	1.49	56	6.58	29, 90
1.6–8	239, 244, VII.98, 99, 100	1.51	**89f.**, 154	6.62	29, 56, **89f.**, III.127
1.6	VII.104	2.22f.	56	6.63	145, 233, VII.104
1.7, 8	245	2.22	32	6.68	233, 245
1.9–12	244, VII.106	3.5–8	40	7.34	166
1.9	II.215, VII.115, 122	3.6	VII.104	7.38	VI.172
		3.13	29, 56, 63, **89f.**, 186, III.127, V.**67**	7.39	141, 142
1.10–12	242, VII.106			7.40	141
1.11f.	239, VII.115	3.16f.	57	7.52	141, V.**63**
1.11	164f., 241, 242, VII.106	3.16	29, 58	8.15	VII.104
		3.17	42, 56	8.16	57
1.12f.	VII.100	3.18	29, 56, 68	8.23	57, V.67
1.12	58, VII.100, 106, 114, 115, 122	3.19	29	8.24, 28	31
		3.23	56	8.31, 37	234
1.13	VII.100	3.31f.	V.67	8.38, 42	29, 57
1.14–16	VII.106	3.31	29	8.43, 51f.	234
1.14	8, 29, 31, 57–8, 141, 164f., 213–14, 230, **241**, **242f.**, 244–5, 248, 250, V.68, VII.100, 102, **104**, 106, 114, 120, 122	3.34	**141**	8.52f.	141
		3.35	58	8.55	234
		3.36	56	8.58	23, 29, 31, 57, II.158
		4.10	142		
		4.14	142, 166	9.3	236
		4.15	56	9.17	141
		4.19	141	9.22	31, II.122
		4.34	56	9.35	56
		5.5, 10, 13	56	9.39	29
		5.18	58	10.17	58
		5.19	57	10.30	57, 250
		5.20	58	10.31–8	**58**
		5.21f., 23	57	10.34f.	17, II.32
		5.24	56, 233	10.36	29, 56, 57
		5.25f.	57	11.27	56
1.15	239, 245, VII.98, 99, 100, 106	5.27	78, 89, III.126	11.33	141
		5.28f.	VII.106	11.52	58
		5.30, 37	56	12.16	32
1.16f.	VII.106	5.38	234	12.34	81, III.109
1.16	VII.104, 106, 107	6	166	12.42	31
		6.14	141	12.45	244, 250
1.17f.	VII.100	6.30–40	V.116	12.46	29
1.17	VII.100	6.32	V.116	12.47f.	141
1.18	29, 58, **244**, 245, 250, II.**229**, VII.111, 123, 125	6.33	29, 56, 90	12.48	234
		6.35	V.116	13.3	29
		6.38f.	56	13.12–17	VII.106
		6.38	29, 56, 57, 90	13.19	31
		6.40	57	13.20	44
		6.41f.	29, 90, V.116	13.21	141
1.20	VII.99			14.1–3	148
1.21	92	6.44	56	14.3	58
1.30	239, VII.99	6.50f.	29, 90, V.116	14.7	57
1.31	236			14.9	244, 250
				14.10	57, 141

14.15–26	148	3	138, V.71	12.24	231
14.16f.	156f.	3.19–21	III.151	13.5, 7, 26	231
14.17	142, 156	3.19f.	V.71	13.30–7	35
14.23f.	234	3.22f.	85	13.33	**35–6**, 50, 51
14.23	57	3.22	44, **138**, 158	13.44, 46	231
14.26	142	4.1f.	35	13.48, 49	231
14.28	250, VII.129	4.4	231	14.8–18	20
15–16	VII.106	4.26	158	14.11–13	18
15.3	234	4.28	235	14.14–18	18
15.26	142, 156f.	4.31	231	14.25	231
16.13	**V.84**	4.33	35	15.7	231
16.27f.	29	5.19	154	15.8	142
16.28	29, 57	5.20	245	15.35f.	231
17.1	57	5.32	V.114	16.6	147, 231
17.2	89, III.126	6–7	31	16.7	147, 154
17.5	29, 57, VII.89	6.2, 4, 7	231	16.32	231
		7	138	17.11, 13	231
17.6	234	7.37	94, **138**	17.18, 28	15
17.8	29, 141	7.38	233	17.28f.	18
17.14, 17	234	7.52	138	17.30f.	35
17.18	43, 56, 57	7.56	87, 90, 95, III.131, IV.86	17.31	34, 235, VII.69
17.20	234			18.5	231
17.21	57	8	II.67	18.9f.	147
17.23–6	58	8.4, 5	231	18.11	231
17.24	57	8.10	**21**, VI.59	19.10, 13, 20	231
18.37	29, 141	8.11	21		
19.5	III.130	8.14, 25	231	20.32	231
19.7	56	8.26	131, 147, 154	22.17–21	147
19.30	141, 142			22.21	39
19.34f.	VII.106	8.29	131, 147	23.9	131
19.34	31	8.37	II.199	27.23	154
19.39f.	VII.106	8.39	131	28.6	18
20.9	32	9.10–16	147		
20.12	154	9.20	50, 85, 231		
20.17	90, 245	10.3–6	147	*Romans*	
20.21	57	10.3, 7	154	1	102, 104, II.171, IV.9
20.22	141, 142	10.19	147		
20.27	245	10.22	154		
20.28	58	10.36–8	**232**	1.3f.	**33–5**, 36, 38, 45, 51, 62, **138f.**, **144**, 208, 235, 237, II.**173**, 179
20.31	56	10.36	45, 231		
		10.38	**138**, 142		
		10.40f.	35		
Acts		10.42	235, VII.69		
1.2	142	10.44	231		
1.5, 8	142f.	11.1	231	1.4	145, VII.69
1.9–11	III.151	11.13	154	1.9	37
1.10	48	11.16	142f.	1.16	V.73
2	V.71	11.19	231	1.18–25	**101f.**
2.23	34, 234, V.71	12.7–11	154	1.18, 19ff.	101
		12.9	V.105	1.20	101, 189, IV.77, V.73
2.24–32	35	12.11	39, 154		
2.33	**142**, 148	12.20–3	20		
2.34f.	108	12.22	21		
2.36	36, 181	12.23	154	1.21–3	116
2.39	158				

1.21	101f., 104		II.173, VI.49, VII.104	11.12	122
1.22	102, 118			11.25f.	236
1.23	102, 104, 116, IV.15, 77	8.4f.	139	11.33f.	158
		8.4	112	11.36	180, VI.64, 115
1.24–8	102	8.6	139	14.9	187
1.25	101f.	8.9–11	**145**	14.15	38
1.28	101	8.9	143	15.3	121, IV.103
2.7, 10	IV.15	8.10f.	110	15.5	145
2.28	139	8.11	139, 143, **144**	15.6	182
2.29	IV.68	8.13	139	15.9–11	158
3.21–5	196	8.14–17	44, 58, **145**	16.25, 26	236
3.21	236	8.14	143		
3.23	**102f.**, 106, 109	8.15–17	37	*I Corinthians*	
3.25	VII.71	8.15f.	**26, 27,** 145	1–4	43
4.6–8	158	8.15	35	1–2	**176–9,** 182, II.154, VI.51
4.13f.	207	8.16	146	1	182
4.24f.	35	8.17f.	159	1.5	121–2
4.25	38, 121, 187	8.17	106, 207	1.9	37
5	118, 127	8.18–21	115	1.13	38
5.2	106, IV.15	8.18	106, IV.15	1.18–2.9	177
5.5	143	8.19–22	**104**	1.18–25	177, 195
5.6–8, 10	38	8.20f.	IV.48	1.18	178, 230, V.73
5.12–19	**103, 111,** IV.16	8.20	104	1.20–5	178
5.12	121, IV.77	8.21	104, 106, 116, IV.15, 71	1.21	VI.56
5.14	**111,** 119, 127, IV.18	8.23	139	1.22–4	**177f.**
5.15–19	126, **127**	8.28	VI.69	1.23	231
5.15	121	8.29	37, 41, 58, 103, 106, **108,** 145, 189	1.24	39, 167, 176, 178, 182, 194, 196, 211, V.73
5.19	118	8.31f.	VI.69		
5.21	121	8.32	38	1.25	IV.68
6.3	183	8.34	35, 108, 157, 187	1.30	39, 167, 177f., **178f.,** 194, 196, 211, VI.59
6.4	**144**	9.5	**45**		
6.5–11	112	9.6	230		
6.6	112	9.17	V.73	2.1–5	177
7.5	112	9.23	IV.15	2.4f.	178, 233
7.7–11	**103f.,** 116, **120**	10.5f.	185	2.5	V.73
7.7f.	IV.77	10.6–10	**184–7,** VII.56	2.6–16	VI.57
7.7	103	10.6–8	157, 176	2.6ff.	181, VI.16
7.8–12	IV.18	10.6f.	167, 187, III.128	2.6f.	**178**
7.8	103			2.6	166, 177
7.9–11	116	10.6	185–6	2.7f.	178
7.9f.	104, IV.24	10.7	185–6, VI.95	2.7	178, 235
7.11	104	10.9f.	181	2.8	166, 177, I.33
7.14	112	10.9	35, 179, 187		
8.3f.	45, 121, IV.96	10.13	158	2.9	VI.16, 172
		10.15	157	2.10–3.4	177
8.3	38, 42f., **44–5,** 46, 56, 64, **111–12,** 117f., 126f., 166,	11.2–4	158	2.10–13	VI.69
				2.11,12,14	143

3.4	IV.68	12	**145**	2.20	37, 38
3.16	143	12.3	143, **145**, 179	3.3	143, 236
3.19f.	158			3.6	145
4.8	121–2, 177	12.4–6	**145**,VI.69	3.7–18	**143f.**
4.9	V.108	12.7–13	181	3.7–11	143
4.15	233	12.8	181, VI.51	3.12–15	143
5.4	V.73	12.13	143, 183	3.14	VI.78
6.3	156	13.1	V.108	3.16–18	143
6.9f.	207	14.2	IV.68	3.16f.	143
6.11	143	14.36	230	3.17f.	**143f.**
6.12–20	182	15	43, 91, 111, 119, 127, V.76	3.17	143, VI.78
6.14	144, V.73			3.18	105, 106, 143, **145**, 167, 196
6.17	**145f.**				
7.22f.	IV.68	15.3–11	35		
7.40	143	15.3–5	187	4.2	230
8	177, VI.51	15.3	38	4.4	106, 145, 189, 196
8.4–7	179	15.12	177, 231		
8.4	177, 180, 181	15.20–3	139	4.5	231
8.5f.	164, 180, 181	15.20	**111**, 144	4.6	106, 145, 196
		15.21f.	107, 127		
8.5	VI.73	15.22	126	4.7	V.73
8.6	39, 165, 176, **179–83**, 194–5, 211f., I.33, II.154, VI.61, 67, 71, 73, 115	15.24–8	37, 109, 146, 148, 182	4.10f.	159, 236
		15.24–6	45	4.11	38
		15.25–7	108	4.14f.	VI.69
		15.25	108	4.16f.	159
		15.27	90, **109**, **111**	4.17	106
		15.42–50	104	5.5	143
		15.44–9	144	5.10	156, 236
8.7–13	180f.	15.44f.	124	5.15	187
8.7	180	15.44	144	5.18	VI.69
8.8	181	15.45–9	109-11, 119	5.19	45, 196, 230
8.28–30	235	15.45–7	100, 113f., **123f.**		
10.1–12	177			5.21	111, **112**, 121–2, IV.60, **99**
10.1–4	**183f.**	15.45	**107f.**, 111, **127**, 132, **145**, 148, 196		
10.1–2	183			6.7	V.73
10.2	**157**			6.10	121–2
10.3–4	183	15.46–9	127	6.16f.	158
10.4	167, 176, **184**, 185, 187, VI.74, 78	15.46	144	8–9	122
		15.47–9	108, 111, 124	8	122
				8.2	122
		15.49	105, 106, 145	8.9	99, 113f., **121–3**, 123–6, I.33, IV.95, 99, VI.70
10.5	184	15.50	207		
10.6	183f.	15.51–3	48		
10.9f.	184	16.22	181, III.133		
10.11	183f.			9.11	121–2
10.26	180			10.13	43
11.2–16	IV.31	*II Corinthians*		11.3	IV.21
11.3–9	IV.58	1.3	182	11.14	V.108
11.3	191	1.19	37, 231	11.31	182
11.7	105	1.21f.	143	12.7	V.108
11.10	V.108	1.21	V.124	12.9	V.73
11.24	38	2.17	230	13.4	144, V.73
11.25	28, 200				

Galatians
1.8 132, **155–6**
1.10 IV.68
1.15 71
1.16 37
2.20f. 121
3–4 41
3 42
3.3 139
3.5 143
3.13f. 121
3.13 II.162, IV.96
3.18 207
3.19f. 132
3.19 43, **155–6**
3.27 183
3.28 IV.31
3.29 207
4.1 41, 112, 207
4.3 115
4.4–7 40
4.4f. 41f., 45, II.152, IV.96
4.4 **38–44**, 46, 56, 64, 111, **112**, 121, 126f., 166, II.160, 173, IV.58, VI.49, VIII.1
4.5 IV.96
4.6f. **27**, 37, 112
4.6 **26**, 35, 39, 41, 143
4.7 41, 207
4.8f. IV.27
4.9 155
4.14 132, **155–6**
4.23 40
4.24f. VI.78
4.29 139
4.30 207
5.16f. 139
5.21 207
6.1f. 145
6.6 230
6.8 139

Ephesians
1.3–14 **235**, 237–8

1.3 182
1.4 71, 238, VI.116
1.6f. 121
1.9f. 235
1.9 231, VII.71
1.10 192, 236
1.17 143, 182
1.18 207
1.19 V.73
1.20–2 108
1.20f. VI.92
1.20 108, 187
1.22 **109**
2.14f. 111, 127, IV.60
3.3f. 231
3.4, 5, 6 236
3.7 V.73
3.9, 11 236
3.16 143
4.1–16 **145**
4.5 179
4.8–10 **186f.**, III.128
4.8 VI.89
4.9f. 186
4.9 187, VI.89, 95
4.13 37
4.24 105
4.30 143
5.2 38
5.5 207
5.13 236
5.25 38
6:7 IV.68
6.19 231, 236

Philippians
1.14 230
1.15 231
1.19 143
2 124, 126
2.1–11 IV.62
2.6–11 99, 113, **114–21**, 123, 125–8, III.133, IV.61, 62, 64, 77, 87, V.106, VI.194, VII.82, 102, 122

2.6–8 121
2.6f. 115–17, IV.62
2.6 114, 126, 188, IV.73, 86, 93
2.7f. 117
2.7 114, 117, 118
2.8 118, IV.82
2.9–11 45, 117–18, 154f., 158, 181, IV.90
2.10f. 158
2.10 118
2.11 179, 182
2.16 230, 233, 245
3.3f. 139
3.3 143
3.7f. 123
3.10f. 159
3.10 127
3.21 48, 106, **108**, **109f.**, 117, 159, V.73

Colossians
1.3 182
1.5f. 231
1.5 230
1.13 37
1.15–20 165, 176, **187–94**, 212, II.154, VI.194, VII.73, 102
1.15–18 188–91, VI.140
1.15–17 39, 164, 207–8, VI.194
1.15 106, 165, 188–9, 191–2, 195, VI.98, VII.141
1.16f. 154, 195
1.16 188–90, 212, 247,

	VI.98, 99,
	115, 118,
	120
1.17	165, 191–2
1.18–20	191
1.18	37, 108, 189,
	191,
	VI.11, 98,
	VII.141
1.19	192, 195–6,
	VI.98, 136
1.20	192, VI.10,
	98, 99
1.25f.	235f.
1.25	230, VI.11
1.26	236
1.27	231, 236
1.29	V.73
2.2	231, 236
2.8–10	155
2.8	IV.68
2.9	**192f.,**
	VI.**138**
2.12	V.73
2.14f.	VI.92
2.17	53
2.18f.	**156**
3.1	108
3.4	106, 236
3.10	105, 106
3.16	230–1
3.17	231
3.23	IV.68
3.24	207
4.3	230f.

I Thessalonians	
1.5f.	233
1.6, 8	230
1.9f.	37
1.10	35, **37,**
	III.133
2.4	IV.68
2.12	106
2.13	230, IV.68
2.15f.	138
4.8	143
4.14	187

II Thessalonians	
1.7	156
2.3–12	20
2.3, 4, 8	III.147
2.14	106
3.1	230

I Timothy	
1.15	234, VII.89
2.5	179, VII.89
2.11–15	IV.58
2.14	IV.21
3.1	234
3.16	156, 236,
	237, 238,
	249, V.49,
	76,
	VII.82,
	88, 91,
	104
4.5, 9	234
5.17	234
5.21	156
6.1, 3	234
6.13–16	VII.89
6.14	237

II Timothy	
1.7	143
1.9f.	**237f.**
1.10	237
1.13	234
2.8	34, 35, 237,
	VII.89
2.9, 11, 15	234
4.1	237
4.2	234
4.8	237

Titus	
1.2f.	**238**, VII.91
1.3	237
1.9	234
2.5	234
2.13	237, VII.**87**
3.5–7	234
3.5f.	143
3.8	234

Hebrews	
1–2	II.218
1	155
1.1–3	164, **206–9,**
	VII.102
1.1f.	55, 209, 237
1.2–5	62
1.2–4	**53,** 54
1.2f.	55, 207,
	211f.,
	VI.194,
	201,
	VII.85

1.2	52, 54, 55,
	212, 247,
	VI.202
1.3–5	36
1.3f.	155, 166
1.3	108, 166,
	209,
	VI.200,
	VII.94
1.4f.	55
1.4	52, VI.194
1.5	35, 52, 54,
	55, 155,
	VI.200
1.6	54
1.7	131
1.8	17, 55, II.32
1.9	55
1.10–12	II.**216**
1.12	II.216
1.13–2.8	108f.
1.13	108
1.14	131
2	91, 119
2.6–18	208
2.6–9	54, **110f.,**
	117, 127,
	190, 209
2.6–8	90, 117
2.6	**91**
2.8f.	**109**
2.8	110
2.9–18	118
2.9f.	IV.89
2.9	110
2.10–18	110
2.10–15	II.223
2.10–12	58
2.10	53, IV.112
2.14f.	IV.96
2.14	121
2.18	IV.89
3.2–6	**53**
3.2	II.213
3.3–4	53
3.5	55, II.213
3.6	55
3.7–11	157
4.12f.	**232f.**
4.12	233, 246
4.14–16	53
4.14	52, 53
4.15	IV.99
5.1–10	208
5.1	53

5.5–10	36, 52	12.5–9	54	2.13f.	246
5.5–9	55	12.5–7	158	2.14	234
5.5	35, 55	13.7	232	2.19	246
5.6	53	13.8	II.**216**	2.24	57, 246
5.8–10	55			3.1f.	58
5.8f.	V.77	*James*	46, VI.48	3.5	236
5.8	55, 118	1.15	103	3.8	236, 246
5.9	53	1.18	233	3.10	58
5.13	232	1.21, 22f.	234	3.11	246
6.1	232	2.5	121	4.2f.	31, 245
6.6	55	3.9,	105	4.2	31
6.13–18	II.213	4.5	VI.172	4.9	42, 56, 58
7	53, II.213,	5.4	158	4.10	42, 57
	218	5.11	157	4.14	42
7.2f.	55			4.15	57
7.3	**20f.**, 52, 53,	*I Peter*	46	5.2	58
	55, II.**220**	1.2	237	5.6	31
7.15–17	53	1.10f.	**159f.**	5.11f.	57
7.16	54	1.11	161	5.20	57, 58,
7.21	158	1.12	155		II.229
7.24–6	53	1.20	**236f.**, 238,		
7.28	36, 55		249,	*Revelation*	21
8.1–10.18	52		VII.82	1.1	156
8.1	108	1.23–5	158	1.2	234
8.5	53	1.23	233	1.5	37
8.6–13	53	1.24f.	234	1.7	91
8.8–11	158	2.8	234	1.8	91, 247
9.1	53	2.19f.	159	1.9	234
9.8–12	53	2.19	179	1.13	**91**, 94
9.11–14	53	2.24	121	1.15f.	156
9.14	V.77	3.1	234	1.16	91, 246
9.15	53	3.14, 17	159	1.17	91
9.23–6	237	3.18	121, V.49,	2–3	91
9.23f.	53		**76**, VII.82	2.9	121
9.24–6	53	3.19	VI.95	2.16	246
9.26	53, 236, **237**,	3.22	108, 109,	3.1	V.84
	238, IV.89		155,	3.4f.	48
10.1	53		VII.82	3.5	156
10.5–10	**54**	4.6	VI.95	3.14	166, 206f.,
10.5–7	V.117	4.13, 15,	159		**247**
10.5	52, 54, 55,	19		5.6	V.84
	II.220	5.9f.	159	5.11–14	155
10.9	53			6.9	234
10.12f.	108	*II Peter*		10.1	**156**
10.16, 19–	53	1.19	234	11.3f.	93, **94**
22		3.5	234	11.3	92, III.141
10.20	II.220			11.5f.	94
10.29	55	*I John*		12.5	93
10.30f.	158	1.1–3	**245f.**, 249	12.7–9	153
11.3	208, 234,	1.1	215, 246	12.11	234
	VII.94	1.2	236, 245	14.6, 8, 9	V.110
11.5	III.64	1.7	57	14.10	156
11.26	II.**215**	1.10	234	14.14–20	91
11.39–12.2	II.215	2.1	157	14.14–16	156, V.109,
12.2	108, 121	2.5	234		110
		2.7	234, 246		

14.14	**91**, 94,	19.11–13	**246f.**	21.1	III.14
	V.110	19.13	215, 245,	21.6	247
14.15, 17,	V.110		246	22.8f.	156
18		19.15	246	22.13	91, 247
15.11–14	156	20.2–9	III.147	22.16	156
19.10	156	20.4	234		

V *EARLY CHRISTIAN, GNOSTIC AND OTHER ANCIENT WRITINGS*

Adam, Apocalypse of
see Nag Hammadi

Anthologia Latina
794.35   IV.100

Anselm, *Cur Deus Homo*
II.6   1

Apuleius, *Metamorphoses*
11.5   169

Aristides, *Apology*
15.1   42

(Pseudo-) Aristotle, *De Mundo*
6   VI.64

Asclepius,
34   VI.64

Athanasius, *De Incarnatione*
    214
54   1

Augustine, *Confessions*
VII.9   VII.2

Barnabas, Epistle of
12.10   65

Clement of Alexandria,
Excerpta Theodoti
35.1   123
43.4   123

I Clement
27.4   234

II Clement
9   III.147
9.5   V.15

(Pseudo-) Clementines
Homilies
III.20   III.140
XVIII.4   132

Recognitions
II.42   132
Cyprian, *De idolorum vanitate*
11   132

Epiphanius, *Panarion seu adversus lxxx haereses*
30.16.4   132
39.1–3   99

Epistula Apostolorum
14   154

Eugnostos see Nag Hammadi

Eusebius, *Praeparatio evangelica*
VII.14.1   166
IX.27   17, 19
IX.29.5–6   II.44
XIII.12.10   164
Gregory of Nazianzus, *Epistles*
101.7   1

Heraclitus VII.10

Hermas,
Similitudes
V.6.5   132
VII.5   132
IX.1.1   132
IX.6.1   132
Visions
I.3.4   234
V.1   132

Hilary, *de Trinitate*
2.26   132

Hippolytus, *Refutatio omnium haeresium*
V.6.4–7   100
V.7.11   123
V.8.22   123
V.10   99
V.19.1–   99
22.1
V.19.21   123

Horace, *Odes*
I.2.41–52   20

Ignatius,
Ephesians
7   246
7.2   42, V.15
20.2   65
Magnesians
1.2   31
15.2   V.15
Smyrneans
1–3   31, 246
3   III.147
3.1f.   VII.88
Trallians
9–10   246

Irenaeus, *Adversus haereses*
I.29.3   100
I.30.1f.   100
III.11.7   II.182
III.16.7   65
III.17.1   65
III.21.10   99
III.22.4   99
IV.20.1   214
V.1.1   128

John, Apocryphon of
see Nag Hammadi

Justin,
Apology I
21.1   42
22   II.14
32.10–14   42
33   50
63.15f.   42
Dialogue with Trypho
16   31
32.1   70, III.19
45.4   42
47   31
49   92
49.1   72
56.4, 10   132
58.3   132
59.1   132
61.1   132
63.3   71
76.1   65
76.7   71
84.2   42
85.2   42
88.3   99
100   65
127.4   42, VII.104
128.1   132
129.3f.   214

Lucian, of Samosata,
*Alexander the False
  Prophet*
           II.39
*Philopseudes, Lover of
  Lies*
           II.39
de morte Peregrini
39–40   18
Marcus Aurelius,
  Meditations
4.23   VI.64

Melito, *Peri Pascha*
66   V.15

Nag Hammadi Library
Adam, Apocalypse of
V.77–9   99
Eugnostos
III.8.27–   100
  30

John, Apocryphon of
II.15.9–13   100
Origin of the World
II.108.19–   100
  22
II.117.28–   100
  31
Philip, Gospel of
II.58.
  17–22   100
(logion 28)
II.71.
  16–21   99
(logion 83)
Pistis Sophia
III.100.16   100
  –101.15
III.104.6–   100
  9
Shem, Paraphrase of
VII.31–2   99
Thomas, Gospel of
logion 2   122
logion 30   122
Trimorphic Protennoia
XII.35.1–   VII.17
  50.24

Origen,
Commentarii in John
II.31   II.61
Contra Celsum
V.2   20
VII.9   II.68

Origin of the World
  see Nag Hammadi

Ovid, *Metamorphoses*
VIII.626–   20
  721

Peter, Apocalypse of
2   III.137
17   III.147

Philip, Gospel of
  see Nag Hammadi

Philostratus, *Apollonius
  of Tyana*
VIII.4   17

Plutarch,
De Iside et Osiride
53   169
Lives: Romulus
28.2   20

Poimandres II.65,
           IV.105

Seneca,
Epistles
58.18f.   VII.30
65.7   VII.30
65.8   VI.64
*Pumpkinification of
  Claudius*
           18

Shem, Paraphrase of
  see Nag Hammadi

Sophia, see Nag
  Hammadi

Suetonius, *Twelve
  Caesars*
IV.22   21

Tertullian,
adversus Praxean
6f.   214
26   132
de carne Christi
14.5   132

Theophilus, *ad
  Autolycum*
2.15   214

Thomas, Acts of
27   123
108–13   IV.105

Thomas, Gospel of
  see Nag Hammadi

Virgil, *Eclogues*
IV.6–10   20

INDEX OF MODERN AUTHORS

(*Italics* indicate that a new title appears for the first time.)

Abelson, J., V.*28*
Abrahams, I., V.*3*
Aland, K., VII.*101*
Albertz, R., II.*81*
Albright, W. F., III.*17*
Alexander, P. S., II.*35*, III.*94*
Alfaro, J., I.16
Allen, E. L. II.*223*
Allen, L. C. II.*131*
Alsup, J. E. V.*105*
Althaus, P., IV.13
Amir, Y., VII.*50*
Anderson, A. A., V.*37*, 96
Anderson, H., II.*185*, V.53
Anderson, W., I.16
Arens, E., III.*123*
Argyle, A. W., VII.*107*
Armstrong, A. H., VII.*29, 30, 32*, 35
Arndt, W. F., II.30, 129, IV.67, 85,
  VI.18, 59, 128, VII.104, 125
Aune, D. E., II.*21*

Baer, R. A., II.*52*
Baker, J. A., II.*126*
Baldensperger, W., II.*75*
Baltensweiler, H., II.*185*
Balz, H. R., I.*15*, II.143, III.51, 66,
  68, 69, 93
Barbel, J., V.*18*
Barbour, R. S., VII.*128*
Barnikol, E., II.*112*, IV.*62*, 98,
  VI.69
Barrett, C. K., II.*125, 130*, 175, *210*,

224, IV.*6*, 14, 19, *27*, 52, 56, 64,
  VI.17, *18*, 50, 55, 76, 81, VII.*91, 97*,
  99, 101, 107, *129*
Barth, G., VI.*151*
Barth, K., 2, I.*4*
Barth, M., VI.*89*, 92, VII.70, 73, 79
Bartsch, H. W., I.*13*, 16, IV.*64*, 87
Bauckham, R., II.*100*, 104, 107, 118,
  119, 235, III.*137*, 148
Baumgärtel, F., V.*21*
Baur, F. C., II.*74*
Beare, F. W., V.*126*
Beasley-Murray, G. R., III.*150*,
  VII.*137*, 139
Becker, J., III.*139*
Beckwith, I. T., V.*110*, VII.139, 141
Behm, J., II.*185*, IV.*83*, V.*113*
Benoit, P., 192, I.16, VI.*98, 133*,
  134, 135
Berger, K., II.*14, 155*, III.36, 53,
  VII.*104*
Bergmeier, R., III.*30*
Berkhof, H., V.*72*
Bernard, J. H., VII.*103*, 122
Bertrams, H., V.*21*
Best, E., II.*144, 188*, 190, IV.51,
  VII.*83*
Betz, H. D., II.*150*, 157, IV.*103*,
  VI.*151*
Betz, O., II.*18, 21*, V.49, *96*, 112
Beyschlag, K., II.*67*
Bianchi, U., VII.*17*
Bieler, L., II.*20*

Bietenhard, H., V.*3*, *90*, 91, 93, 95
Billerbeck, P., II.59, 185, 215,
III.19, 23, 28, 37, 45, 48, 61, 84,
98, 140, 141, IV.8, 26, V.6, 10, 23,
28, 33, 102, VI.43, 59, 86, 184,
VII.61
Black, M., II.*131*, III.*3*, *12*, *14*, *64*,
69, *79*, *91*, 100, *137*, 149, 150 IV.14,
34, *36*, 39, 44, 106, VI.*83*
Blank, J., II.*150*, IV.56
Blass, F., VI.91
Bode, E. L., I.16
Bogaert, M., III.*142*
Boismard, M., V.*64*, VII.*106*, 122
Bonnard, P., II.*150*, V.107
Bonner, C., III.*75*
Boobyer, G. H., II.*185*
Borgen, P., II.*223*, VII.*111*
Bornkamm, G., III.*101*, IV.*25*,
VI.*151*, VII.*75*
Borsch, F. H., III.*23*, 24, 49, 64, *83*,
134, IV.3, 83
Boslooper, T., II.*4*, 51, 52, 166, 195
Bourke, M. M., VI.*79*
Bousset, W., II.*176*, III.23, 99, *150*,
IV.1. V.5, 8, 9, *110*, VI.4, VII.139,
140
Bowker, J., III.*108*, 112, VI.*83*,
VIII.7
Box, G. H., V.*6*, 11, VI.*21*
Brandenburger, E., IV.*16*
Braun, H., II.7, 45, *206*, III.125
Bréhier, E., VII.*36*
Brekelmans, C. W., III.*57*
Brocke, M., II.*99*
Brown, J. P. III.*100*
Brown, R. E., 49f., 164, 246, I.*18*,
II.*52*, 105, *113*, *119*, 124, *125*, *126*,
138, 164, 166, 194, 195, 196, 200,
201, 204, 229, 230, 231, 233,
III.127, 129, *139*, V.63, 64, 66, *84*,
112, VI.6, 15, VII.*75*, 80, 98, 100,
101, 114, 122, 132, 136
Brownlee, W. H., V.*90*
Brox, N., II.*79*, VII.*89*, 91
Bruce, F. F., II.*141*, *177*, *211*, III.*77*,
IV.13, V.77, *84*, VI.*17*, 77, 85, 195,
VII.64, *132*

Büchsel, F., II.*158*, V.*74*, VI.*91*, 92,
200
Bühner, J. A., II.*46*, 56, 152, 223,
III.123, 128, V.67, 104, VII.126
Bultmann, R., 24, 26, 98f., 113, 215,
218, I.*13*, II.*90*, *222*, III.*101*, IV.*1*,
2, 61, V.*9*, 74, VI.*4*, *159*, 169, 179,
180, 190, VII.13, 14, *22*, 103, 110,
122, *124*, *132*
Burgener, K., I.16
Burger, C., II.*128*, 173, VI.*98*, 99,
111, 129
Burney, C. F., VI.*110*
Burrows, M., II.*17*
Burton, E. D., II.*148*

Cadbury, H. J., II.66, *77*
Caird, G. B., *3*, I.20, II.*208*, IV.26,
44, V.*57*, VI.*17*, 41, *89*, 97, 102,
116, 124, VII.73, 74, *137*, 138
Camp, J. van, II.*26*
Campenhausen, H. von, I.16, II.*166*,
198
Canart, P., II.*26*
Caquot, A., III.*72*
Caragounis, C. C., VII.*75*
Carlston, C., II.*210*, VII.50
Carmignac, J., V.*98*, VII.*63*
Carr, A. W., VI.*16*, 17
Casey, P. M., II.*97*, III.*3*, *13*, 14, 18,
50, 57, 58, *64*, 66, 87, 89, 91, *100*,
126, 133
Catchpole, D. R., III.*6*
Cazeaux, J., III.*142*
Cerfaux, L., II.*156*, IV.60, 99,
VIII.14
Chadwick, H., VI.*83*, VII.*29*, 30
Charles, R. H., II.*52*, III.*71*, *150*,
V.*110*, VII.137, 141
Charlesworth, J. H., III.*31*, 73,
V.103, VI.8, VII.*119*
Chilton, B. D., II.*190*, V.*45*
Christ, F., 163, 199, II.*111*, VI.3, 14,
143, 145, 150, 153, 155, 157, 174,
179
Churchill, W., II.*89*
Clark, N., I.16
Clayton, J. P., *3*
Cohn, L., VII.*45*

Cold, E., I.16
Collins, J. J., III.*14*, 49, *56*
Colpe, C., III.*12*, 43, 46, 49, 50, 55, 68, 72, IV.*3*
Colson, F. H., VII.*36*, 42
Comblin, J., I.16
Conzelmann, H., II.*9*, *79*, *135*, *140*, 186, 202, III.99, IV.*44*, 107, VI.*20*, 26, *53*, 58, 64, 78, *144*, 155, 179, 193, VII.*89*, 125, *134*
Cooke, G., II.*10*, 41, III.26
Cöppens, J., III.*56*, VII.*75*, 80
Cortes, J. B., IV.*51*
Craddock, F. B., *3*, I.25, 29, II.215, IV.*97*, VI.43, 69, 76, *118*
Cranfield, C. E. B., 34, II.*130*, 133, 174, IV.14, 17, 20, VI.81
Cribbs, F. L., II.*87*
Cross, F. M., III.*102*
Cullmann, O., I.*12*, II.111, 216, 229, 236, III.42, 132, IV.6, 41, 64, V.43, 64, VI.70, VII.12, 86, 120, 121, 125, VIII.2
Culpepper, R. A., VII.*119*
Cupitt, D., *4*, I.24, VIII.9
Cuss, D., II.*29*, 45

Dahl, N. A., III.*96*, V.11, VII.*81*
Dalman, G., II.*165*, V.10, VI.59
Danielou, J., 149, I.16, V.*16*, 17, VII.*107*
Davey, F. N., VII.*55*
Davies, P. R., II.*190*
Davies, W. D., III.*17*, 25, IV.23, 24, 39, 50, 64, V.*7*, *44*, 74, VI.141, *159*
Deaut, R. le, V.*95*, VII.*84*
Debrunner, A., VI.91
Deichgräber, R., IV.*86*, VI.194, VII.82
Deissler, A., III.*13*
Deissmann, A., II.*6*, 23, 28, *236*, III.*23*
Delcor, M., III.*13*, V.*98*
Delling, G., II.*40*, *162*
Demke, C., VII.*106*
Denis, A. M., II.*44*
Dey, L. K. K., II.*212*, 213, VI.13, VII.28

Dibelius, M., II.*141*, VI.*17*, *100*, VII.*89*
Diez Macho, A., VI.*83*
Dillon, R. J. V.*55*
Dix, G., II.*234*
Dodd, C. H., 30, 57, II.*52*, *85*, 109, 114, 125, 137, 224, 227, 231, III.22, 126, 132, IV.3, *24*, *105*, V.65, VI.6, 159 VII.*43*, 107, 111, 113, 118, 122, 131
Dodds, E. R., II.*40*
Drummond, J., III.*38*, VII.*11*, 36, 44, 45, 46, 47, 49, 51, 54
Duncan, G. S., V.*107*
Dunn, J. D. G., *6*, I.31, 32, 33, II.21, *46*, 79, 92, 93, 95, 102, 103, 105, 107, 109, 115, 119, 121, 124, 126, *127*, 128, 134, 144, *172*, 176, 181, 189, 203, 205, 209, 219, III.39, 111, *113*, IV.*22*, *40*, 55, 57, 59, 114, 115, V.*20*, 39, 40, 42, 43, 45, 49, 50, 51, 54, 56, *69*, 70, *75*, 76, 78, 79, 83, 84, 105, 121, 123, 125, 128, VI.54, 55, 56, 58, 63, 70, 77, 80, 152, 163, 164, 172, 189, VII.60, 65, 66, 67, 104, VIII.*3*, 6
Dupont, J., VI.*64*, 125, 134
Dürr, L., VII.*20*
Durrwell, F. X., I.16

Eccles, R. S., II.*211*
Edwards, R. A., VI.*146*, 151, 190
Eichrodt, W., V.*21*, 23, 88, 89
Ellis, E. E., III.*77*, V.*57*, VI.*74*, 168, *170*
Eltester, W. F., VI.*10*, 104, VII.*97*
Emerton, J. A., II.*32*, III.*49*, V.*98*
Erlanger, P., II.*88*
Ernst, J., I.*15*, II.142, VI.*130*, 131, 132, 134, 136, 138
Evans, C. F., I.16, V.*58*

Farnell, L. R., VII.*26*
Ferch, A. J., III.*49*
Festugiere, A. J., VI.*26*
Feuillet, A., II.*86*, III.14, *51*, IV.*64*, 87, VI.9, 10, *14*, *16*, 18, 82, 106, *118*, 137, 147, VII.*62*
Fiebig, P II.*99*

Fiorenza, E. S., VII.*16*
Fischel, H. A., VI.*32*
Fischer, K. M., VII.*70, 104*
Fitzmyer, J. A., II.*17, 19*, III.*3*, 4, 12, 91, V.*98*, 100, VII.*10*
Flusser, D., II.*16*, 83, III.76
Foerster, W., II.*64*, IV.4, V.*37, 119*, VI.52
Fohrer, G., II.*3*, 10, 41
Ford, J. M., VII.*137*
Friedrich, G., V.*43*, 56
Frost, G., VII.*58*, 62
Fuller, D. P., I.16
Fuller, R. H., I.*12*, 16, 26, II.106, 143, 148, *152*, 156, 196, III.97, 101, *107*, 134, IV.3, 72, 110, V.43, 46, VII.*14*, 82
Funk, R. W., VI.91

Gabathuler, H. J., VI.*98*, 100
Gaster, T. H., V.*2*, 85, 90, 91, 93
Gatti, F. M., IV.*51*
Gaugler, E., IV.13
Geense, A., I.16
Geering, L., I.16
Gelston, A., III.*20*
Georgi, D., II.*20*, IV.*87*, 105
Gerhardsson, B., II.*192*, IV.94
Gerlemann, G., VI.*46*
Gero, S., II.*19*
Gershenson, D. E., VII.*45*
Gese, H., III.*17*, 51, 58, VI.*6*, VII.98, 112, 115, 122
Gibbs, J. G., VI.*114*
Giles, P., III.*132*
Gingrich, F. W., II.30, 129, IV.67, 85, VI.18, 59, 128, VII.104, 125
Ginzberg, L., II.*44*, 63
Glasson, T. F., II.*215*, III.*14*, IV.*73*, V.*64*, VI.*11*, VII.115
Gnilka, J., II.*51*, III.*113*, IV.*61*, 87, VI.89, VII.72, 79
Goguel, M., II.*75*
Goldberg, A. M., V.*10*
Goodenough, E. R., II.*37*, V.94, VI.28, 34, 35, VII.*31*, 37, 38, 40, 43, 44, 47, 50, 117
Goppelt, L., II.*148*, 152, III.108, 113, VII.*84*, 120

Gordon, C. H., II.*32*
Gore, C., 1, I.*1*
Goulder, M. D., 3, *4*, I.22, II.67, VI.52, VIII.11
Gourges, M., IV.*45*
Grant, R. M., II.*40, 65*, IV.3
Grässer, E., III.*134*, VI.*194*
Grass, H., I.16
Gray, G. B., III.*115*
Greene, W. C., VI.*32*
Greenfield, J. C., II.*35*, III.*76*, 80
Greeven, H., VI.*100*
Grelot, P., IV.*78, 86*
Gressmann, H., III.23, V.5, 8, 9
Grether, O., VII.*18*
Griffiths, J. G., VI.27
Grillmeier, A., V.*15*, VII.6, 8
Grundmann, W., II.*118*, V.*21, 53*, VI.*186*
Gundry, R. H., VII.*88*
Gunkel, H., 133, V.*21*
Gutbrod, K., I.16
Guthrie, D., II.*123*

Haacker, K., III.*32, 33*, 36
Haag, H., I.16, II.*10*, 41
Haenchen, E., II.*67, 140*, VI.*181*, VII.59, *122*, 126
Haes, P.de, I.16
Hahn, F., I.*12*, 26, II.83, 143, 148, 183, III.6, 15, 41, 101, V.42, 43, 46, 53, 56
Hamerton-Kelly, R. G., 3, 7, 65f., 88f., I.26, 29, 152, III.7, 8, 9, 60, 97, 116–22, 124, 126, 127, IV.6, 43, 104, VI.18, 57, 75, 78, 81, 146, 173, 176, 191, VII.72, 78, 83, 91, 122
Hamp, V., V.*10*, 24, VII.23
Hanson, A. T., 3, I.*17*, V.*115*, 116–18, 120, VI.76
Hanson, S., IV.*60*
Harnack, A., 2f., I.*9*, VI.*145*, VII.7
Harner, P. B., II.99
Harrington, D. J., III.*142*
Harris, R., VI.4, *6*
Hartman, L. F., III.*12*, 13, 59, 77
Hasel, G. F., III.*57*
Hasler, V., VII.*87*
Haug, M., I.16

Hay, D. M., III.*26*, 134, IV.45
Hayes, J. H., II.*142*
Hayward, C. T. R., III.*142*, V.*6*, VII.*11*
Headlam, A. C., II.*75*, IV.*9*, 27, VI.84
Hegermann, H., VI.*10*, 40, 100, 126, VII.49, 50
Held, H. J., VI.*151*
Hengel, M., I.*34*, II.3, 4, 6, 8, 13, 14, 16, 19, 33, 41, 42, 54, 94, 139, 142, 148, 161, 165, 168, 173, III.*142*, IV.3, *82*, 88, 100, VI.*8*, 21, 26, 28, VIII.*1*
Hennecke, E., III.140
Héring, J., VI.*202*
Hermann, I., IV.*44*, V.74, 80, 81
Heron, A., VII.*6*
Hester, J. D., VI.*196*
Hick, J., *3*, 6, I.35, VIII.3
Hiers, R. H., II.*112*
Higgins, A. J. B., III.*2*, *3*, *19*, *107*, 129
Hill, D., III.*20*, V.*19*, *51*, *53*, 74, VI.151, 164, 168
Hindley, J. C., III.*80*
Hockel, A., VI.*106*, 107, 108
Hoffmann, P., VI.*145*, 151, 170, 185, 186
Hofius, O., II.*220*, IV.*87*, VI.194, 198, 201, VII.*74*
Hofrichter, P., VII.*106*
Holladay, C. H., II.*21*, 26, 42, 43, 44
Holland, D. L., II.*112*
Holtz, T., II.*144*
Holtzmann, H. J., II.*75*
Hooke, S. H., I.16
Hooker, M. D., 41, II.*160*, III.*3*, *11*, 44, 62, 64, 69, 108, 112, IV.*7*, *10*, *60*, *64*, 66, 74, 80, 81, 84, VII.*97*, 99
Horsley, R. A., IV.*6*, 106, VI.*9*, *51*, 61
Horton, F. L., II.*218*, 220, V.98, 99, 102
Hoskyns, E. C., VII.*55*, 62
Houghton, H. P., III.*145*
Houlden, J. L., VII.*73*, *131*, 132
Howard, G., IV.*90*

Howard, V., III.*113*
Hunter, A. M., II.*86*
Huonder, V., II.*11*
Hurd, J. C., VI.*65*

Iersel, B. M. F. van, II.*108*, 138, VI.151
Isaacs, M. E., V.*13*, 19, 25, 27, 84, 112, VII.26
Ittel, G. W., I.16

Jaeger, H., VII.*5*
James, M. R., II.*62*
Jendorff, B., VII.*11*
Jenni, E., VI.*46*
Jeremias, J., 24, 26f., 30, II.*37*, *48*, 63, *82*, *91*, 96, 101, 109, 110, 116, *117*, *220*, III.*40*, 105, 107, 113, *132*, *140*, 141, IV.51, V.41, 42, 46, 53, 61, 161, 162, VII.*12*, 21, *58*, *88*
Jervell, J., IV.*6*, 7, 11, 18, 29, 31–33, 36, 37, 41, 42, 44, 91, 106, 108, VI.104
Jewett, P. K., IV.*31*
Jewett, R., IV.*56*
Jocz, J., VII.*142*
Johansson, N., V.*113*
Johnson, M. D., VI.*144*, 165, 179
Johnston, G., V.*112*
Jonge, H. J. de, VI.*192*
Jonge, M. de, II.*58*, *221*, 224, 228, 230, V.64, 97–100, VII.106
Jüngel, E., VIII.*4*

Käsemann, E., 24, 103, II.*58*, *91*, *130*, 175, III.*99*, IV.14, 17, 20, 24, *104*, V.*21*, 44, VI.87, *119*, VII.*104*, 106
Kamlah, E., I.16
Kasper, W., I.*18*, VIII.13, 15
Kassing, A., I.16
Kayatz, C., VI.*26*, 32
Kee, H. C., II.*184*
Kegel, G., I.16
Kehl, N., VI.*10*, 102, 116, 117, 122, 136
Kelly, J. N. D., 236, I.*3*, II.*1*, 2, V.*126*, VII.1, 3, 4, 9, 83, *92*
Kerst, R., VI.*61*, 62, 64

Kertelge, K., III.*113*
Keyser, P. C., IV.*9*
Kiddle, M., VII.*139*
Kilpatrick, G. D., III.*131*
Kippenberg, H., II.*66*
Kittel, G., II.*112*, IV.*28*, 29, VII.*56*, 57, 120, 121, 131
Klappert, B., I.16, II.*210*, VII.*18*, 56, 122
Klausner, J., III.*24*, 37
Klein, G., VI.*172*
Kleinknecht, H., II.*28*, *129*, V.*19*, VII.*11*, 35
Klemm, P., I.16
Knibb, M. A., III.*63*, 73, 75, *79*, 80
Knox, J., *3*, 52, 63, I.19, 35, II.207, 236, III.101, VII.93
Knox, W. L., II.*45*, *51*, *52*, VI.*26*, 36, 39, 41, 76, *112*, 206, VII.47, VIII.13
Koch, G., I.16
Köster, H., VI.*204*
Kraeling, C. H., III.*42*
Kramer, W., I.*12*, II.136, 139, 146, 148, 162, 168, VI.63, 93, 94
Kremer, J., I.16
Kretschmar, G., VII.*3*, VIII.5
Kruijf, T. de, II.*192*
Kühl, E., IV.13
Kümmel, W. G., II.*106*, *124*, 142, 148, 152, 175, 224, 231, III.15, *106*, 108, IV.*6*, 44, V.82, VI.48, 73, 97, 177, *181*, 185, VII.68
Küng, H., I.*18*
Künneth, W., I.16
Kuhn, H. B., V.*90*, 94
Kuhn, H. W., VI.*50*
Kurtz, W., I.16
Kuss, O., IV.13, *24*, 25, 26
Kvanvig, H. S., III.*14*
Kysar, R., VII.*12*, 96

Labuschagne, C. J., V.*87*
Lagrange, M. J., IV.13
Lake, K., II.9, 66
Lamparter, H., I.16
Lampe, G. W. H., *3*, 7, I.16, 21, II.12, 24, *202*, III.1, 64, V.13, 15,

16, 19, *21*, 22, 38, 78, 127, 128, VI.78, VIII.10
Lang, F., III.*139*
Langkammer, H., VI.*69*, *135*, *202*, VII.*120*
Laporte, J., VII.*38*
Larcher, C., IV.*9*, VI.22
Larsson, E., IV.*86*
Laubscher, F. du Toit, V.*99*
Leaney, A. R. C., IV.*34*
Leenhardt, F. J., IV.*25*
Legasse, S., III.*2*
Lehmann, K., I.16
Leisegang, H., V.*19*, 68
Leivestadt, R., III.*91*, 126
Lella, A. A. Di, III.*12*, *13*, 59, 77
Leon-Dufour, X., I.16
Licht, J., III.*32*
Liddell, H. G., II.6, 28, VII.41
Liddon, H. P., 23, II.*71*, 72
Lidzbarski, M., IV.1
Liebeschuetz, J. H. W. G., II.*45*, 54
Liefeld, W. L., II.*185*
Lietzmann, H., III.*66*, IV.*6*, 13, 44, VI.17, *86*
Lightfoot, J. B., VI.*104*, 106
Lindars, B., II.*125*, *137*, 138, III.*56*, 108, *127*, 138, 152, IV.45, V.63, VII.*14*, 118, 122
Lindemann, A., VII.77
Linnemann, E., II.*173*
Linton, O., VI.*145*
Loader, W. R. G., IV.*45*
Lock, W., VII.*91*
Lösch, S., II.*50*
Lövestam, E., II.*138*
Lohfink, G., II.*63*, III.143
Lohmeyer, E., VII.*139*
Lohse, E., I.16, II.*3*, 19, III.*136*, VI.*10*, 64, 103, 108, 118, 124, 125, 126, 131
Longenecker, R. N., II.*218*, III.*81*, 108, V.*14*, 64, VI.70
Luck, U., VII.*115*
Luduchowski, H., I.16
Lüdemann, G., II.*66*, 67
Lührmann, D., III.*64*, VI.*148*, 154, VII.*76*, 81
Luz, U., IV.*25*, *31*, 43, 47

Lyonnet, S., VI.*10*

Macdonald, J., III.*29*
Mack, B. L., VI.*4, 26*, 27, 29, 31, 40
McKane, W., VI.*12*
Mackey, J. P., *4*, I.18
MacKinnon, D. M., I.16
Mackintosh, H. R., I.*8*
McLeman, J., I.16
McNamara, M., V.*113*, VI.*88*, 95, VII.89, *111*
McNeil, B., III.*21*
Macrae, G. W., IV.*3*
Malatesta, E., VII.*96*
Maly, K., VI.*56*
Manns, F., IV.*64*
Manson, T. W., III.*13*, 64, 91, V.*28*, VI.181, 183
Manson, W., III.*17*, 40, 42
Marböck, J., VI.*26*, 37
Marcus, R., VI.*22*, VII.27
Markus, R. A., VII.*30*
Marshall, I. H., I.*15*, II.107, 109, *112, 119, 139*, 143, *181*, 200, *202*, 203, III.2, 15, 106, 108, V.44, 53, 62, VI.142, 149, 168, 172, 176, 185, VII.58, 59, *131*, VIII.3
Martin, R. P., IV.*41, 63*, 64, 67, *69*, 72, 78, 86, 87, 90, VI.*98*, 104, 108
Martini, C. M., I.16
Martitz, P. W. von, II.*3*, 4, 5, 8, 21, 22, 24
Martyn, J. L., II.*122*, III.139, V.*65*
Marxsen, W., I.*15*, 16
Mastin, B. A., II.*229*, 230
Maurer, C., VII.*71*
Mauser, U., IV.*99*, VI.60
Mayer, G., VII.*27*, 33, 41
Meagher, J. C., V.*68*
Mearns, C. L., III.*76, 79*
Meeks, W. A., II.*37*, 43, 44, 63, 223, III.*9, 129*, IV.*11*, V.67
Merlan, P., VII.29
Mertens, A., III.77
Metzger, B. M., II.*174*
Meyer, B. F., I.*14*, 18
Meyer, R., I.16, V.*26, 51*, 60
Michaelis, W., II.*185*, V.*106*, VI.*108*, *128*

Michel, O., II.*130*, 178, *210*, 215, 216, 220, III.*13*, IV.13, *90*, V.77, VI.13, 86, 195, 199, 202, 203, 205, VII.64
Milik, J. T., II.*62*, III.74, *77*, 78, 79, 144, V.*101*
Miller, M. P., V.*98*
Milligan, G., II.6, 28, 129, 159, VI.59
Miranda, J. P., II.*225*, V.64
Moffatt, J., II.*211*, 214, 232, IV.13, VI.13, *17*, VII.64
Moloney, F. J., III.*126*, 127, 130, V.67
Moltmann, J., I.*16*
Montefiore, H. W., II.*211*
Montgomery, J. A., II.*29*, III.13
Moore, G. F., 219, V.*10*, 33, 90, 93, 94, VI.42, VII.23
Morfill, W. R., II.*52*
Morgan, R., II.*76*
Morgenstern, J., III.*49*
Morris, L., II.*86*, 117, *162*
Moule, C. F. D., *4*, I.*15*, 16, 27, *202*, *216*, 236, III.108, *110, 114*, 129, IV.*93*, V.*75, 83, 128*, VI.70, *123*, 132
Moulton, J. H., II.6, 28, 129, 159, VI.59, *90*
Mowinckel, S., III.*13*, 24, 37, 41, 42, 64, 69, 125
Mühlenberg, E., VII.*49*
Müller, H., IV.*16*
Müller, U. B., II.*112*, III.*41*, 56, 64, 88, 92, V.109, *112*, VII.*104*, 106
Münderlein, G., VI.*136*
Muilenberg, J., III.*51*
Murphy-O'Connor, J., 114, 120, IV.*62*, 63, 77, 87, 92, VI.*61*, 69
Murray, J., II.*130*, IV.14
Mussner, F., I.16, II.*110, 125, 148*, 168, IV.58

Neufeld, V. H., II.*205*, VI.63, 68
Nickelsburg, G. W. E., III.*32, 34*, 40, 67, 114
Niebuhr, R., I.16
Nikiprowetzky, V., VII.*38*
Nilsson, M. P., VI.*59*, 64

Nineham, D. E., II.*78*, *187*, V.*58*, VIII.11
Nock, A. D., II.*39*, *52*, 165, VI.27, VIII.5
Noll, S. F., V.*99*, 101
Norden, E., VI.*5*, 64
Nützel, J. M., II.*185*, V.53
Nygren, A., IV.13, VI.*81*

Odeberg, H., II.*34*, 35, 36, V.11, *67*, 93, VI.28
Oepke, A., II.*148*, V.107
Oesterley, W. O. E., VI.*21*
Osten-Sacken, P. von der, VII.*99*
Otto, R., III.*64*, 107

Pannenberg, W., I.*16*, 30, II.233, 236
Parry, R. St. J., VII.*90*
Paulsen, H., II.*168*
Pearson, B. A., VI.*50*, *53*, 57
Percy, E., IV.3, VI.*116*
Perrin, N., II.*80*, 83, III.65, 91, 99, VI.*186*
Perry, M. C., I.16
Pesch, R., II.*194*, III.*106*, *113*
Peterson, E., VI.*62*, 68, 73
Petuchowski, J. J., II.*99*
Pfeifer, G., V.*8*, 25, 94, VI.21, 29, 43, 44, VII.20, 47
Pine-Coffin, R. S., VII.*2*
Pittenger, N., *3*
Ploeg, J. P. M. van der, V.*113*
Plummer, A., IV.*41*, V.*74*, VI.78
Pöhlmann, W., VI.*115*
Pohlenz, M., VII.*36*
Pokorný, P., II.*3*, 4, 10, 108, 135, 152, 179
Polag, A., V.*52*, VI.*151*
Pollard, T. E., VII.*3*, 10
Potterie, I. de la, VII.*101*, *132*
Poythress, V. S., III.57
Prat, F., V.*74*

Quispel, G., III.*65*, IV.3

Rad, G. von, V.*87*, 88, 94, VI.*23*, 24
Rader, W., VII.*73*
Rahner, K., 2, I.*5*, 6, 7, *18*

Rankin, O. S., VI.*21*
Rawlinson, A. E. J., II.*236*, III.132, IV.41, 64, V.44, 72
Reese, J., IV.*75*
Reicke, B., II.208
Reitzenstein, R., II.*20*, IV.1
Relton, H. M., II.*73*
Rengstorf, K. H., I.16, II.*150*
Rex, H. H., I.16
Richter, G., VII.*104*, *106*
Ridderbos, H., II.*148*, VII.*120*
Riesenfeld, H., IV.*57*
Ringgren, H., 129, 135f., 170, V.*1*, *8*, 9, 23, 37, 91, 93, VI.21, 30, 31, 45, VII.20
Rissi, M., VII.*17*, 100, 106, 112, 115
Robertson, A., IV.*41*, VI.78
Robinson, D. W. B., IV.*93*
Robinson, H. W., V.*21*
Robinson, J. A., VI.*92*
Robinson, J. A. T., *3*, I.20, II.*87*, 109, 118, *120*, 122, *125*, 150, 208, III.*139*, VI.206, VII.*135*, VIII.*8*
Robinson, J. M., 204f., I.*10*, II.*80*, IV.*4*, VI.*55*, *149*, 155, 168, 180, 189
Romaniuk, C., IV.*9*
Roon, A. van, VI.*19*
Rosenstiehl, J. M., III.*146*
Rowland, C., III.*135*, V.103
Rowley, H. H., III.*13*, 40
Ruckstuhl, E., I.16
Rudolph, K., II.*67*, III.*24*
Ruef, J., VI.*77*
Ruppert, L., III.*114*
Russell, D. S., II.*185*, III.13, IV.2, V.32, 90, 91, 93

Sanday, W., IV.*9*, 27, VI.84
Sanders, E. P., V.*10*
Sanders, J. A., V.*106*
Sanders, J. N., VII.*12*
Sanders, J. T., 215f., I.*11*, IV.87, VII.16, 106, 119
Schäfer, P., V.*28*, 33–36
Schelkle, K. H., II.*147*, 162, VI.*108*
Schenke, H. M., IV.*104*, VI.*118*
Schenke, L., I.16
Schenke, W., VI.*21*
Schillebeeckx, E., I.*18*, II.17, 69,

173, III.17, 53, 113, 139, 151,
IV.72, V.64, 106, VI.107, 116,
VII.74, 87, 88, 91, 126
Schlatter, A., IV.13
Schleiermacher, F. D. E., 2, 23,
II.70, 72, 74
Schlier, H., I.16, II.51, 128, 135, 148,
157, III.49, IV.14, 17, 18, 20,
V.107, VI.89, VII.72, 73, 79, 125
Schlisske, W., II.10, 41
Schmidt, H. W., IV.13
Schmidt, K. L., VII.69
Schmidt, W. H., VII.19, 20
Schmithals, W., VI.53, VII.100, 122
Schmitt, J., III.129
Schnackenburg, R., II.106, 223, 224,
III.37, 85, 129, 130, IV.3, V.63, 84,
112, VI.89, 99, 100, VII.99, 101,
112, 114, 115, 120, 122, 123, 132
Schneider, B., VII.88
Schneider, C., II.51
Schneider, G., VI.71, 72
Schneider, J., VI.91, 96
Schnider, F., I.16, V.43, 55, 59, 65
Scholem, G. G., II.35, III.84, VI.59
Schoonenberg, P., II.201
Schrenk, G., II.13, VI.66
Schürer, E., II.29, III.79, V.113
Schürmann, H., II.91, III.6, 113,
VI.142, 145
Schulz, S., 215f., III.126, VI.142,
143, 145, 149, 151, 152, 155, 156,
167–70, 172, 176, 178, 179, 182,
186, 187, VII.15, 17
Schumacher, H., IV.63
Schweitzer, A., III.107
Schweizer, E., 126, 163, 166, II.3,
13, 69, 126, 138, 142, 145, 149, 152,
156, 161, 187, 193, 206, 225, 230,
III.81, 106, 114, 133, 134, IV.3, 51,
54, 57, 87, 95, 113, V.74, 76, 84,
VI.1, 2, 9, 76, 82, 104, 109, 118,
123, 125, 127, 140, 144, 149, 154,
156, 158, VII.82, 122, 125
Scott, E. F., II.206, 214, VII.91
Scott, R., II.6, 28, VII.41
Scott, R. B. Y., VI.22
Scroggs, R., II.121, III.46, 47, 134,

IV.14, 15, 18, 30, 34, 37, 38, 44, 91,
102, 106, 116, VI.53
Seeberg, A., II.168
Segal, A. F., 80, III.93, 96, V.11
Seidensticker, P., I.16
Seitz, O. F. J., III.22
Selwyn, E. G., V.122
Sharpe, J. L., IV.38
Sidebottom, E. M., II.224, 230,
III.130, VII.12, 24
Sjöberg, E., III.14, 64, 69, 86
Smalley, S. S., II.86, 115, 119, 141,
III.129
Smith, D. M., VII.14
Smith, D. W., VI.14, 150, 165, 175,
176, 191
Smith, J. Z., II.61, 62, V.103
Smith, M., 27, II.25, 30, 45, 49, 67,
98, 100
Smothers, E. R., V.63
Spicq, C., II.211, VII.64
Stacey, W. D., IV.54
Staerk, W., III.117, VI.41
Stanley, D. M., I.16, IV.44, VII.88
Stanton, G. M., 4, I.28, II.67, 106,
161, IV.103, V.47, VI.143, 144, 150,
151, 154, 168, 175, 185
Starcky, J., II.17
Stauffer, E., II.86, 119
Stead, G. C., VI.52
Steck, O. H., V.48, VI.171, 179
Steinmetz, F. J., VI.105, VII.73
Stendahl, K., II.194
Stenning, J. F., III.40
Stone, M. E., III.76, 79, 80, 90
Stott, J. R. W., II.73
Strack, H. L., II.59, 185, 215,
III.19, 23, 28, 37, 45, 48, 61, 84,
98, 102, 140, 141, IV.8, 26, V.6, 10,
23, 28, 33, 102, VI.43, 59, 86, 184,
VII.61
Strauss, D. F., II.74
Strecker, G., III.140
Strugnell, J., III.78, V.93
Stuhlmacher, P., 24, II.81, 173,
III.3, 108
Styler, G. M., VI.188
Suggs, M. J., VI.82, 143, 144, 146,

151, 154, 160, 165, 168, 169, 172, 173, 175, 179, 180
Surgy, P. de, I.16
Sykes, S., *3*, I.35

Talbert, C. H., I.*11*, II.4, 25, 27, 31, 40, 44, 45, 47, 49, 53, 54, 56, 62, 106, 148, IV.3, *62*, 65, 86
Taylor, V., 24, I.*17*, II.*84*, 119, 148, 175, V.*53*, 54
Teeple, H. M., II.*37*, III.*99*, 141, V.*43*, 46, 56, VII.*104*
Telford, W. R., II.*43*
Tennant, F. R., IV.*12*
Thackeray, H. St. J., VI.*16*
Theisohn, J., III.*14*, 16, 54, 67, 70, 82, 92
Theissen, G., II.*213*
Thompson, J. W., II.*209*, *213*, 216
Thomson, R. W., I.2
Thrall, M. E., II.*185*, IV.*36*, V.*117*
Thüsing, W., I.*18*, VI.69, *70*, *71*
Thyen, H., VII.*96*, 106
Tiede, D. L., II.*21*, 38, III.*34*
Tödt, H. E., 89, III.*82*, 86, 91, 101, 104, 125
Towner, W. S., III.*37*
Trakatellis, D. C., II.*166*, 226, V.18
Trompf, G. W., VII.*64*
Turner, N., VI.*90*, *108*

Ulonska, H., V.*74*
Urbach, E. E., V.*10*

Vermes, G., 27, I.*12*, II.3, 14–16, 19, 52, 97, 100, III.*3*, 4, *12*, 37, 64, 79, 91, 95, 100, V.41, 46, *92*
Vielhauer, P., III.*99*
Vincent, M. R., IV.*73*
Vögtle, A., II.*111*, III.*113*, *134*, IV.41, 86
Völker, W., VIII.*5*
Volz, P., III.*141*, V.*8*, 10
Vos, G., II.*210*

Wadsworth, M., III.*142*
Wainwright, A. W., I.*17*, VI.71, VII.108
Walker, W. O., III.*99*

Wedderburn, A. J. M., IV.*7*, *16*, *106*, VI.*56*
Weinacht, H., II.*180*
Weinrich, O., II.*31*
Weinstock, S., II.*28*, 51
Weiss, H. F., V.*12*, 29, VI.28, 40, VII.23, 38, 46
Weiss, J., I.*33*, II.*112*, 187, III.132, IV.*41*, VI.9, 76
Welte, B., II.*135*
Wendt, H. H., VII.*132*
Wengst, K., I.*11*, II.128, 135, 169, III.133, IV.87, 104, 105, VI.62, 98, 194, VII.82, 122, *133*
Werner, M., V.*106*
Westcott, B. F., VI.*91*, VII.122, *131*
Westermann, C., VI.*46*
Wetter, G. P., II.*3*
Whybray, R. N., VI.*22*, 25
Wicks, H. J., VI.*38*
Wifall, W., III.*17*
Wilckens, U., I.16, II.*140*, III.*53*, IV.*9*, *13*, 14, *109*, VI.*20*, 50, 53, 57, 149, 154, 179, *205*, VII.25, 78
Wilcox, M., III.*77*
Wiles, M., *3*, I.20, VII.105
Williams, H. A., I.16
Williamson, R., II.*211*, VI.13, 197, VII.51
Wilson, J. H., VI.*55*
Wilson, R. McL., IV.3, VII.*107*
Windisch, H., II.*20*, 30, *58*, III.*23*, IV.*101*, VI.4, 7, VII.*89*, 90, 92
Wisse, F., IV.*5*
Wolfson, H. A., V.*30*, VI.33, 34, VII.34, 39, 40, 43, 45, 48, 52
Woude, A. S. van der, II.*58*, V 97-100, *113*
Wrede, W., 24, II.*76*
Wright, N. T., IV.*57*

Yamauchi, E., II.*67*, IV.3, 4, *5*, 106, VII.17
Yarnold, G. D., I.16
Young, F., *3*, I.23, II.*3*, 28, 30, 33, 51, 54, 164, VIII.5

Zehnle, R. F., II.*141*, V.46, 71
Zeilinger, F., VI.*113*

Zeller, D., VI.*142*

Zeron, A., III.*137*

Ziener, G., VI.*15*

Zimmerli, W., III.*40*

Zimmermann, H., II.*86, 205,* 218, VI.194, VII.*102, 126*

INDEX OF SUBJECTS

Abba, 24, 26–8, 32, 35–7, 122, 145,
  262, II.100, 101, VI.164
Abel, III.79
Adam, 6, 7, 99–107, 188, III.24
  -christology, 7, 41, 45, 91, ch.IV,
    139, 160f., 188, 208f., 254f., 257f.,
    265f., 268, IV.39, 51, 60, 64, 116,
    VII.122
  fall of, 101–7, 111f., 115–17, 122,
    IV.58, V.106
  glory of, 102f., 106, 119
  heavenly man, 99f., 107, 121, 123f.,
    127, 252, 268, IV.107
  image of God, see Image of God
  last Adam, 4, 7, 107f., 110f., 112f.,
    117–19, 124–7, 132, 149, 208,
    252, 255, 265, 267f., IV.41
  = Logos, see Word
  = man, 7, 101, 104
  and pre-existence, 113–25
  and Son of Man, see Son of Man
  and Wisdom, IV.87, 110, 112
Adoptionist, 9, 52, 62, 193, 257,
  II.219
  see also Christ, 'becoming of'
Angel, 7, 43, 47, 84, 89, 99f., 105,
  110, 127, 129, 131, 149–59, 209,
  260, II.55
  archangel, 19–21, 74, 81, 151–4,
    159, II.62, III.94
  -christology, 7, 38, 132, 149, 155,
    161f., 252, 257, 259, V.17, 105,
    106
  and earthly Jesus, 154
  fall of, V.106, 108
  host of heaven, 149f., 174
  intermediaries, 151f., 155–8, 161f.,
    252
  of the Lord, 132, 149f., 152, 154,
    157f., V.88
  in Philo, V.94
  polemic against, III.94, V.105
  of presence, 134, 151f.,
  and Son of Man, 73f., 154
  sons of God, 15, 149f., 153, II.62
  subject to Christ, 109, 154–6, 257,
    II.218
  worship of, 156, 158
Apotheosis, 19–21, 63, 76, 153, 155,
  158, 268, II.4, III.64
Arian controversy, 12, 189, 214

Baruch, 93, 259
'Binitarian', 80, 255, 264, II.67,
  VIII.5

Christ,
  'becoming of', 34–6, 46f., 50–2, 55,
    59, 60–2, 83f., 107f., 113, 116f.,
    126–8, 142, 159f., 161, 191f., 202,
    254–6, 265–8, II.186, VI.57
  = creature, 189, 247, 255
  descent to hell, 186–7, VI.92, 95, 96
  divinity of, 1, 4, 192, 212, 246, see
    also Christ = God
  exaltation of, 107–10, 114f., 118f.,
    155, 158, 186, 202, 204–5, 208,
    III.151,
  see also Jesus, resurrection of

= God, 182, 187f., 190–6, 209, 255, 262–5, VI.140, VII.87, *see also* God, title of Christ; Image of God
humanity of, 1, 4, 246, *see also* Son of Man
obedience of, 111, 113, 118
post-existence of, 3, 161, 163
pre-existence of, 3–9, 30f., 42, 46–7, 49f., 51f., 55–62, 72, 99, 113–14, 119–21, 128, 132, 157f., 160f., 163–4, 177–8, 179, 182f., 183f., 185, 189–91, 193–6, 205, 209–12, 231, 235, 236–9, 243–6, 249f., 255–8, 260, 264, II.215, 236, III.123, IV.61, 103, VII.91, 93, 120
second coming/parousia, 37, 47, 88, 89, 96, 265, II.143, III.151, VII.87
see also Christology; Jesus
Christology,
cosmic, 108f., 167, 181f., 187–96, 207–11, 255, 261, IV.52, VI.115, 118, 120, 140
development in, 51, 60f., 204–6, 210f., 214f., 238f., 248f., 254–9, 261, 264, I.26, 34, VI.164, VIII.1, 3
diversity in, 59–63, 365–7
high, 5, 32, 63
implicit, 6, 24, see also Jesus, self-consciousness
two-stage, 33–6, 107–13, 115, 160f.
see also Adam-christology; Divine man christology; Prophet christology; Son of God; Son of Man; Spirit christology; Wisdom christology; Word christology
Context of meaning, 10, 13–22, 33, 114, 125f., 170–6, 183, 189, 195f., ?14f., 219f., 221, 228f.

Deification, *see* Apotheosis
Divine man, 16, II.21, 25, 26
christology, 48

Elijah, 19, 21, 63, 79, 93–7, 126, 217, 252, 259, 261, II.44, 63, III.137, 140, 141, 151

= Jesus, 92–4, 97, 252, 259, V.46
Enoch, 17, 19, 21, 63, 78, 79, 92–7, 126, 153, 252, 259, 261, II.36, III.14, 64, 76, 79, 103, 137, 149, 151
= Son of Man, 19, 76, 78, 252, III.64, 107, 152
Ezra, 93, 259

Fourth Gospel,
christology, of, 56–9, 61f., 63, 77f., 89f., 95, 96, 99, 141–2, 147f., 239–45, 246, 249f., 256, 258–60, 263–5, II.221, 223, V.65, 67
date of, 24, 31, 78, 239, 260, II.87
historicity, 23, 29–32, II.72, 120, 125
'I am's, 29, 30f.
importance in christology, 23, 249f., 256, 258–9, 264f., VII.142
and I John, 31, 246, II.124, VII.133, 135
redaction, VII.106, 114

Gabriel, 74, 151, 154, V.94
Glory, 47f., 53, 57, 102f., 105f., 115–17, 119, 144, VI.203
of Adam, *see* Adam
of Christ, 106, 108f., 127
of God, 129, 151, 219, 242f., VII.87, *see also* Shekinah
Gnostic redeemer myth, 2f., 7, 20f., 72f., 98–100, 113, 123–6, 128, 163, 215f., 220, 229f., 248, 252f., 260, 263, II.65, 152, 223, III.24, 42, 55, 130, IV.3, 105, 110, VI.89, 118, VII.14, 16, 17, 82
God
= angel, 150f., 152f.
appearing as man, 20
face of, 151
as Father, 15, 30, 49, 262, 263f., II.116, VI.66
finger of, 137f., 151
immanence of, 130, 176, 219f., 229, 250, 252, 263, V.89
invisible, 226f., 244, 250
name of, 129f., 151, 153f., 176, 219
power of, 6, 21, 99f., 144, 147f.,

178f., 190, 193f., 196, 225–6,
VII.47
range of usage, 16f.
righteousness of, 179, 196, 220,
V.28, VI.59
as Spirit, 7, 133, 134–6, 143f., 146,
148, 150f., 160f., 219, 252, 263,
266, V.24, 25, 28, 38, 89
throne of, *see* Merkabah
title of Christ, 45, 58, *see also* Christ
= God
transcendence of, 129f., 176, 219,
250, 252, 263, V.89
as Trinity, *see* Trinitarian tendency
unity of, *see* Monotheism

Heavenly beings, 6f., 15, 17f., 38, 47,
100, 151, 154, 161f., 195f., 258f.,
263
as redeemer, 19, 21f., 81, 92f., 98,
100, 123, 126, 128, 250, 252f.,
259f., 262, II.69, *see also* Angels;
Gnostic redeemer myth;
Intermediary figures; Wisdom;
Word
Hebrews,
christology of, 51–6, 61f., 91, 109–
11, 206–9, 211, 237, 256, 257–8,
VII.94
History of Religions school, 2f., 20,
170, 251, 260
Hymns (NT), 3, 114–21, 125, 187–93,
206–9, 215, 237, 255, 263, IV.62,
VI.97, 98, 99, 119, 194, VII.70,
106
Hypostasis, 9, 129–31, 133, 136, 168,
170, 174–6, 178, 194, 215f., 217–
20, 231–3, 248, 253, VI.21, 32,
37, 42, 44, 204, VII.26, 119

Image of God, 98, 100, 105f., 115f.,
196, IV.110, VI.195
= Adam, 102, 115f., 119, 124,
IV.29, 70, *see also* Adam
= Christ, 106, 108, 110, 149, 165,
188f., 209, 268, VI.200, *see also*
Christ
Incarnation,
of angel, 21, 149, 153f., 158f., V.104

centrality of, 1f., 128
definition, 9, 261f., I.35
of heavenly beings, 6, II.67
and inspiration, 4, 8, 141, 148,
160f., 212, 250, 259, 266, V.104,
128
origin of, 2–11, 42–4, 55f., 59, 63f.,
96–9, 128–32, 183, 187, 211f.,
247f., 248f., 251–3, 255–61, I.15,
II.164, 236, VII.93
and predestination, 236f.,
and resurrection, 267f., VIII.13
and soteriology, 41f., 267f., VIII.14
of Spirit, 132, 136, 141, 148, 158f.,
161f., II.201, V.76
Intermediary,
angelic, 150–2, 155, 157, 161f., 252
Christ as, 142, 147, 149, 151, 157
figures, 7f., 21, 129–31, 133, 151f.,
155–6, 161f., 176, 195–6, 208,
215f., 220, 224, 228, 248, 252,
262, VIII.1
Isis, 169–71, 173, 229, 253, VI.26, 28
Israel,
angel, 21, 153
= Christ, *see* Jesus = Israel
son of God, 15
pre-existence of, *see* Pre-existence

Jacob, *see* Israel
Jaoel, 153, III.94
Jesus,
continuity between Jesus and
Christ, 3, 6, 32f., VIII.7
death of, 38, 42, 45f., 48f., 52, 55,
57, 59, 61, 110–15, 118, 121–3,
127, 138, 187, 254, 256
divine purpose fulfilled in, 4, 28f.,
34, 109, 110–12, 117, 127f., 178,
190, 194, 208f., 211f., 234–8, 249,
255–6, 257, 262, 268
inspiration of, 4, 8, 137–41, 148,
160f., 212, 253, 259, 265, II.91,
V.42, 43, 44
= Israel, 49f., 199f., 257
at Jordan, 46f., 59, 62, 99, 120, 139,
141, 256, II.182, V.52, 67,
VI.136
poverty of, 121f.

resurrection of, 3, 6, 34–6, 47, 57, 59, 60, 62–3, 83f., 86, 89, 107f., 111–13, 121, 124, 126f., 139, 142, 144, 148, 155, 159f., 186–7, 190, 254, 256, 266
importance of, 159, 254, 267–8, II.139, VI.94, VIII.13
self-consciousness,
  of divinity, 23f., 28, 60, II.119
  eschatological, 28f., 32, 253f.
  messianic, 23f.
  of pre-existence, 29, 32, 254, II.112
  of sonship, 22–33, 60, 63, 199f., 253, II.84, 105, 119
self-understanding, 7, 22–33, 65f., 137f., 253f.
sinlessness of, 120f., 122
Spirit of, see Spirit
teacher of Wisdom, 198, 205, 210, VI.193
transfiguration of, 47f., 89, 93, 140, III.141
virginal conception and birth, 40–2, 49f., 50f., 58, 147–8, 256, 266, II.52, 148, 198, 233, VI.187
Jeremiah, 19, II.63
John, see Fourth Gospel
John the Baptist, 92–4, 197, 239, III.139
Joseph, son of God, 15

King,
  = god, 17, 20, 45, II.217
  son of God, 14–15, 18, 20
  ruler cult, 16

Logos, see Word
Lord, title of Christ, 6, 45, 109, 115, 117f., 125, 149, 157f., 179–81, 194, 211, I.33, VI.57
Luke,
  christology of, 50f., 61f., 140, 142, 147f., 206, 232, V.83
  redaction by, 197f., 203, VII.58

Man, see Adam
Mark, christology of, 46–8, 61–2
Matthew,
  christology of, 48–50, 61, 77f., 89, 140, 197f., 200f., 202, 204–6, 210f., 244, 256f., III.124, VI.187
  date of, 78, VI.177
  redaction by, 48f., 197f., 200f., 202–4, 210, 257, VI.188
Melchizedek, 19–21, 52–5, 152f., 257, II.52, 57, 213, 218, III.152, V.98
Memra, 130
Menander, 21, II.65
Merkabah, 81, 92, 94, 96, II.36, III.84
Messiah,
  name of, 71, III.37
  pre-existence of, 21, 70–2, 79, 81, 88, I.33, II.17, 165, III.37, VI.19, VII.73
  son of God, 15f., 79
  son of Man, see Son of Man
Metatron, 17, 19, 153, II.34, 36, V.11, VI.28, see also Two powers heresy
Michael, 19, 69, 132, 151–3, II.57, V.94, see also Angel
Monotheism, 81f., 92, 96, 118, 130f., 133, 151, 170–4, 179–80, 182, 195, 210–12, 221, 223, 227, 229f., 241, 245, 250, 255, 263–6, II.36, VI.36, 73
Moses, 17, 19, 39, 47, 52, 53, 63, 79, 143f., 149f., 155, 157, 183f., 186, 209, 222f., 243, 259, 265, II.44, 63, 151, 213, 215, V.44, 46, VI.83
  ascension/exaltation of, 17, 19, 79, II.44
  incarnation of Wisdom/Logos, 71, 243, II.60, III.36
  pre-existence of, 71
  prophet like, 85, 93f., 138–41, 160, 257, III.141, V.42
  return of, III.141
Mystery, 236, 237, VII.75, 76, 80
Myth, 2, 6, 9, 215–16, 220, 229, 248, 262f., I.13, III.50, VIII.3
  creation myths, 72f., see also Adam
  Primal Man myth, see Gnostic redeemer myth

Nestorian controversy, 192–3

Paraclete, 132, 147f., 156f., 158, V.84
Paul, christology of, 36–46, 61, 64,
    90f., ch.IV, 143–9, 176–96, 211,
    244, 254f., 261, II.154, IV.39, 50,
    VI.19, VIII.9
Philo, influence of, 21, 53–5, 165–7,
    183f., 207f., 216, 233, 241–4, 257,
    II.211, 213, IV.107, VI.10, 51,
    VII.107
Phineas, 93
Plato, influence of, 52–4, 55, 59, 61,
    123–6, 169, 171, 221f., 225–6,
    230, 252, 257, II.211, VI.201
Poimandres, II.65
Powers, see God, power of
Predestination, 234–8, 249, 261,
    VII.69, 71, 74, 92, see also Jesus,
    divine purpose fulfilled in
Pre-existence,
    of believers, 235, 238, VII.73
    of God's throne, III.84
    ideal, 54–6, 61, 82, 88, 124f., 235,
        237, 249, 256f., III.37, 64
    of Israel, III.61, 64, VII.74
    of Jesus, see Christ, pre-existence of
    personal, 4, 56f., 58f., 61, 212, 243–
        5, 249, 256, 258, 260f., 264,
        VII.120
    seven pre-existent things, 71, 260,
        III.84
    of Torah, 4, 229, III.37, VI.43
Primal Man, see Gnostic redeemer
    myth
Prophet,
    commissioning, 39f., 89, 137–8, 218,
        III.128, V.67
    christology, 53, 55, 137–41, 161,
        203, III.140, V.65, 67
    eschatological, 92–4, 137, 140, 148,
        212, 250, 253, 265, V.42, 44
    like Moses, see Moses

Q, christology of, 197–205, 210,
    VI.150, 179

Revelation (Book of),
    christology of, 91f., 94f., 96, 246f.
    date of, 91

Righteous man, 15, 17, 49, 87, 88,
    IV.87

Samaritans, 4, 21, 71, II.63, 66, 67,
    III.32, 141, VI.52
Satan, 151–3
Shekinah, 47, 51, 129–31, 135, 162,
    176, III.14, 65, 95, V.10, VI.176
Simon Magus, 4, 21, 260, II.65, 67
Son of David, 34f., 49, 51, 72, 79,
    256f., III.53
Son of God, ch.II
    Christian's sonship dependent on
        Christ's, 28, 32, 37, 57f.
    and death, 38, 42, 45f., 48f., 55, 57,
        59, 61, 112
    first-born, 37, 146f., 149, 165, 189,
        191, 221, II.62
    eschatological sonship, 28f., 32,
        34f., 36f., 46, 53, 55, 60, 63, 208
    in Hebrews, 51–6, 208f., 257
    in John, 30, 56–9, 244–5, 263,
        II.221
    in Luke-Acts, 50f.
    in Mark, 46–8
    in Matthew, 48–50, 256f.,
    only-begotten, 12, 29, 57f., 244
    pre-existence of, 4, 7, 32, 42, 46, 47,
        55–9, 90, 98, 208f., 246, 263,
        II.106, 223, 233
    range of usage, 14–16, 59
    as from resurrection, 34–6, 46, 254,
        265, II.135, see also Christ,
        'becoming of'
    sending of, 38–40, 42–5, 56, 244,
        260, 263, 266, II.152, 223
    the Son, 28, 198–200, 264, II.109
    title of Christ, 6–8, 85, 95, 112,
        160f., 206, 214, 246, 255f., VI.200
Son of Man, ch.III,
    absence in Paul, 90f.,
    = angel, 73–4, III.128, 152
    apocalyptic symbol, 67, 69, 72–4,
        III.14
    = Coming One, III.139
    descent of, 56, 66, 89f., 95, 260,
        266, III.127–9, V.67
    = Enoch, see Enoch

442   INDEX OF SUBJECTS

= First Man, 72–3, 90, 216, III.42,
    IV.111
= God, III.14, 65
= heavenly individual, 67, 69, 74,
    75f., 78, 79–82, 84f., 95–7, 252,
    259, III.71, 91, 152
= humanity of Jesus, 12, 65
humility of, 88, 95, 265
= I, 66, 83, 86
influence of Dan.7, 66f., 76, 79f.,
    83–9, 91, 95
= Israel/saints of Most High, 68f.,
    71, 73f., 86, III.13
Jesus' use of, 65, 83–7, 253
= man, 7, 79f., 83, 86, 90, III.68,
    IV.86
= Messiah, 69–72, 75f., 79–82, 95–
    7, 252, III.86, 95, 98
pre-existence of, 7, 21, 65–7, 74f.,
    75f., 78f., 81f., 88–90, 95–7,
    II.236, III.64, 127, 128
title of Jesus, 5, 7f., 12, 66, 77f., 82,
    83–5, 96, 113, 125f., 154, 160,
    265
= Wisdom, 73, 76, 90, III.54, 55,
    VII.127
Spirit, 38f., 162, 192, 196, 207, 252
= Christ, 132, 136, 145–7, 161, 254,
    259, II.236, V.77, 78, VI.89
of Christ, 26f., 37, 141–9, 159f., 265
-christology, 160f., 268, V.126, 128
and creation, 130
demonic, 135
of God, 4, 7f., 21, 44, 47f., 112,
    130–49, 176, 219, VI.136, see also
    God as Spirit and Jesus, 59, 62,
    137–41, 259, V.68, 84, see also
    Jesus, inspiration of; Prophet,
    eschatological
in Jesus' birth, 49f., 51, 59, 61,
    II.201
life-giving, 6, 107f., 110f., 127, 132,
    145–7, 149, 159–61, 196, 255,
    265, 267
= power, 133, 147, 148
of prophecy, 135f., 137–9, V.41, see
    also Prophet
at Qumran, 135f.
Stoic philosophy, influence of, 14f.,

169, 171, 173, 179–80, 190–3,
    211, 221–3, 230, VI.64, 69,
    VII.36
Syncretism, 2, 5, 72f., 131, VI.73, see
    also Wisdom, pagan influence

Torah, 130, 155, 185f., 194, 222, 252,
    263, VI.40
pre-existence of, see Pre-existence
and Wisdom, see Wisdom
Two powers heresy, 17, 19, 80f., 87,
    92, 153, 260, II.36, III.95, 103,
    135
Trinitarian tendency, 149, 212, 229f.,
    245, 250, 255, 264f., 266, VIII.7

Uriel, 151, 153, II.62, V.92

Wisdom, 6, 8, 39, 44, 125, 129, 131,
    162, ch.VI
and Adam, see Adam
and apocalyptic, 200, 204, 209–11,
    242, VI.186
christology, 5–8, 39, 49, 64, 163–7,
    176–212, 214, 244, 247, 253f.,
    257f., 261–3, 265–8, VI.19, 150,
    179, 192
creator, 165f., 189
created, 228
envoy of, 88, 198, 200, 202, 203–6,
    210, 253f., 257
of God, 8, 21, 53, 219f., 261
= God, 172–4, 176, 188–9, 208f.,
    219, 252, 255, 266, III.52, VI.37,
    38, 40
incarnation of, 71, 202, 210, 212
in Jewish thought, 164–76, 185f.,
    194f., 255, 262f., VI.51
= the law, 170–2, 174, 186, 188,
    195, 210, VII.115
= Logos, see Word
pagan influence, 168–71, 175
personification, 168, 174–6, 189,
    194, 201, 209–10, 219f., 229, 243,
    253, 262, VI.37, 41, 73
in Philo, 165–7, 169, 171, 173f.,
    226, 228, 229, II.153, VI.110
= plan of God, 178f.

pre-existence of, 8, 49, 163, 167–8, 177f., 195, 202, 204f., 209f., 252f.

rejection of, 242

= Son of God, 39, 257, II.152

and Son of Man, 71, 73, III.130

-speculation, 8, 90, 125, 163, II.152, VII.5

and Spirit, 130, 134f., 214, 219, 266, V.84, 112

teacher of, *see* Jesus

Word (Logos), 8, 129, 131, 162, 163, 191f., 196, 208, ch.VII

= angel, 220f., 228

-christology, 6f., 8, 12, 213–15, 230–50, 253, 254, 256, 262, 263, 265, 268, VII.120, 131

created, 228, 247

creator, 228, 234, 240f.

definition, 223f., VII.43, 45, 46

divine reason, 15, 169, 171, 222f.

= God, 218–19, 226–30, 241–2 248, 250, 252, 266, VI.40, VII.54, 125

second God, 221, 241

of God, 8, 21, 151

= gospel, 230–4, 237–9, 244, 245–7, 248f., 256

= heavenly man, 100, VII.107

incarnation of, 213, 239, 241, 243–7, 248–50, 256, 260, 263, II.60, VII.122

intermediary, 220f., 228

in Jewish thought, 215–30, 248

and life, 230–3, 238, 242, 245

as light, 207, 226f., 241f., VII.111

= Melchizedek, 21

personification, 219f., 232, 242f., 253

in Philo, 15, 53f., 166, 171, 191, 207f., 216, 220–30, 241–4, V.31

pre-existence of, 239f., 243–5, 247, 252f., VII.92

= prophecy, 217–18, 229

son of God, 15, 54, 241, 244f., 249f., 258, 263f.

and Spirit, 135, 219, 266, V.31, 84, VII.25

= Torah, 171, 218, 229, 242

and Wisdom, 39, 171, 173, 207f., 214, 219, 241–5, 258, 266, VI.34, VII.24, 25

Zeus, father 14f., VI.66, 73